KNOW YOUR ENEMY

KNOW YOUR ENEMY

The Rise and Fall of America's Soviet Experts

DAVID C. ENGERMAN

OXFORD
UNIVERSITY PRESS

2009

OXFORD
UNIVERSITY PRESS

Oxford University Press, Inc., publishes works that further
Oxford University's objective of excellence
in research, scholarship, and education.

OXFORD NEW YORK
Auckland Cape Town Dar es Salaam Hong Kong Karachi
Kuala Lumpur Madrid Melbourne Mexico City Nairobi
New Delhi Shanghai Taipei Toronto

WITH OFFICES IN
Argentina Austria Brazil Chile Czech Republic France Greece
Guatemala Hungary Italy Japan Poland Portugal Singapore
South Korea Switzerland Thailand Turkey Ukraine Vietnam

Library of Congress Cataloging-in-Publication Data
Engerman, David C., 1966–
Know your enemy : the rise and fall of America's Soviet experts / David C. Engerman.
   p.   cm.
Includes bibliographical references and index.
ISBN 978-0-19-532486-0
1. Soviet Union—Study and teaching (Higher)—United States.   2. Cold War—Study and
teaching (Higher)—United States.   3. Soviet Union—Research—United States—History—
20th century.   4. Sovietologists—United States—History—20th century.   5. Scholars—
United States—History—20th century.   6. Social scientists—United States—History—20th
century.   7. Political scientists—United States—History—20th century.   8. Intellectuals—
United States—History—20th century.   9. United States—Intellectual life—20th
century.   I. Title.

DK38.8.E54 2009
947.084072—dc22   2009010880

9 8 7 6 5 4 3 2 1

Printed in the United States of America
on acid-free paper

To Nina and Simon

CONTENTS

ABBREVIATIONS

AAASS	American Association for the Advancement of Slavic Studies
ABM	Antiballistic missile
ACLS	American Council of Learned Societies
AFCS	Adjusted factor cost system
AHA	American Historical Association
APSA	American Political Science Association
ASTP	Army Specialized Training Program
ASU	American Student Union
AVC	American Veterans Committee
CATP	Civil Affairs Training Program (U.S. Army)
CCNY	Carnegie Corporation of New York
CCP	Committee on Comparative Politics (SSRC)
CDSP	*Current Digest of the Soviet Press*
CENIS	Center for International Studies (MIT)
CIA	Central Intelligence Agency
CPD	Committee on the Present Danger
CPSU	Communist Party of the Soviet Union
CU	Bureau of Educational and Cultural Affairs (U.S. State Department)
DP	Displaced person
FAFP	Foreign Area Fellowship Program (Ford Foundation)
FF	Ford Foundation
HRRI	Human Resources Research Institute (U.S. Air Force)
IEA	International Education Act (1966)
IPR	Institute of Pacific Relations
IREX	International Research and Exchange Board
IUCTG	Inter-University Committee on Travel Grants
JCSS	Joint Committee on Slavic Studies (ACLS/SSRC)
NBER	National Bureau of Economic Research
NCSEER	National Council for Soviet and East European Research

NDEA   National Defense Education Act (1958)
NEH   National Endowment for the Humanities
NIE   National Intelligence Estimate
NSC   National Security Council
NSMGA Naval School of Military Government and Administration
OLS   Oriental Languages School (U.S. Navy)
ORR   Office of Research and Reports (CIA)
OSD   Office of the Secretary of Defense
OSS   Office of Strategic Services
PFIAB President's Foreign Intelligence Advisory Board
R&A   Research and Analysis Branch (OSS)
RADIR Revolution and the Development of International Relations (Hoover
       Institution)
RAPP   Russian Association of Proletarian Writers
RF   Rockefeller Foundation
RI   Russian Institute (Columbia University)
RIP   Refugee Interview Project (Harvard University)
RRC   Russian Research Center (Harvard University)
SALT   Strategic Arms Limitation Talks/Treaty
SIP   Soviet Interview Project
SNIP   Soviet National Income and Product
SRC   Survey Research Center (University of Michigan)
SSRC   Social Science Research Council

KNOW YOUR ENEMY

KNOWING THE COLD WAR ENEMY

When Winston Churchill ominously announced in March 1946 that an "Iron Curtain had descended over Europe," the U.S. government was grossly unprepared for a world divided between East and West; it employed around two dozen Soviet experts and even fewer on Central and Eastern Europe. Two years later, after a steady drumbeat of Cold War crises, the young Central Intelligence Agency employed thirty-eight Soviet analysts, a number less impressive than it seems. Only twelve spoke any Russian, only one had a Ph.D., and their college majors ranged from civil engineering to library science. The government could not draw on scholars knowledgeable about its enemy, as it had done in World War II; there were only a few dozen academic Soviet experts, many of whom had never been to the USSR. How could American officials chart a foreign policy without knowing what was going on inside the Kremlin—without even knowing exactly who was inside the Kremlin—and without any idea of the people in that vast and diverse country, let alone their views? Never before, one professor-cum-intelligence analyst warned, "did so many know so little about so much."[1]

Know Your Enemy tells the story of the U.S. intellectual mobilization against Soviet Communism from the World War II–era crises to the collapse of the USSR. Government officials worked together with scholars and foundation officers to establish a new enterprise, unprecedented in academic life. Variously known as Russian Studies, Soviet Studies, or—often with a hint of derision—Sovietology, it aimed to serve both Mars and Minerva, both the national security state and academic life.[2] It sat at the heart of Cold War thought and not too far from the center of foreign policy making. Sovietology brought together iconoclasts, geniuses, lone wolves, and careerists to analyze an entire nation: its people and its past, its economy and its politics, its rulers and its ruling ideas. The group included some of America's best minds from the left, the right, and, especially, from the center of the political spectrum. It included intelligence analysts and scholars—though this distinction sometimes was blurred because World War

II had brought so much traffic between intelligence agencies and the academy. Rumpled sociologists became regulars at classified Pentagon briefings. Political scientists began not just studying power but holding it (or advising those who did) as they worked in or with expanding government agencies.

The professor-consultant was a new role for university faculty, at least in the realm of foreign policy. Before World War II, the idea that academic experts should help to shape diplomacy, let alone warfare, found few takers. A scientist who wanted to contribute to the American effort in World War I, for instance, applied to the War Department but was rebuffed with the explanation that it already had the one chemist that it needed.[3] After the Great War, a White House advisor created a group of scholars, the Inquiry, to prepare for the Versailles Peace Conference, but there is little indication that its work was read by anyone but later historians.[4] The State Department's Foreign Service was an insular and proud place, with little interest in academic theorizing. Gentlemen-scholars might rub shoulders with gentlemen-diplomats at the oak-paneled Council on Foreign Relations, but those contacts were based on personal relations, not scholarly expertise. This skepticism survived the war. As late as 1950, diplomat George Kennan exemplified the State Department attitude in his reply to an inquiry about bringing social science into diplomacy: "the judgment and instinct of a single wise and experienced man, whose knowledge of the world rests on the experience of personal, emotional, and intellectual participation in a wide cross-section of human effort, are something we hold to be more valuable than the most elaborate synthetic structure of demonstrable fact and logical deduction."[5] By the time Kennan wrote those lines, however, the rest of Washington sought demonstrable facts and logical deduction, not just wise and experienced people.

Even if government agencies had sought out Soviet expertise in the United States before World War II, they would have found precious little. There was no field of Russian Studies, just a handful of scholars, varying widely in interest, energy, training, and talents, spread thinly across American universities. Russian-language teachers were scattered among departments of French, German, or Oriental studies; the few social scientists and historians in the field languished on the margins of their departments. The most enterprising joined the amateurish Institute of Pacific Relations or tried to start a caucus at annual meetings, but there was no unifying body or esprit de corps.[6]

World War II brought about a fundamental change in the use of academic expertise and in the academic institutions themselves. Many leading universities' faculties faced depletion as a legion of Professor Smiths went to Washington. They joined classified research teams—not just the laboratories that developed radar and the atomic bomb but also the groups that studied American soldiers' loyalty, Japanese culture, the destruction of German cities, and the odds that the USSR could withstand Nazi invasion. The scholars were spread all over wartime Washington. The Office of War Information hired anthropologists (including Ruth Benedict and Margaret Mead) to analyze Japanese culture. The largest group of scholars gathered at the Research and Analysis Branch—also known as the "chairborne division"—of the Office of Strategic Services (OSS), precursor to the CIA.[7] Even the State Department hired a handful of historians as political advisors or, occasionally, as diplomats.

In the wake of the war, academic study of the USSR went from laughingstock to juggernaut, from a dispersed group of isolated scholars to a vibrant enterprise making headlines, advising presidents, and shaping foreign policy, all the while fulfilling the traditional academic roles of research and teaching. These changes took place quickly. In the decade after the start of World War II, a network of educators—some with degrees, others with connections, some with money, others with ideas—came together to plot a new way of studying the world, one especially amenable to informing foreign policy. The new Soviet experts consulted with the foreign policy apparatus from bottom to top, advising everyone from military researchers to cabinet secretaries and presidents. These arrangements had little room for older experts like Kennan, solo practitioners who preferred elegant prose to elaborate social science models. While early Sovietologists sought Kennan's endorsement for their work, they did not quite consider him one of their own: he had no graduate training in the United States, knew much about Russia but little about social science, and explained Soviet policy through the vagaries of Russian character, not the structure of Soviet society. A man of his stature could not be ignored—but Kennan represented Sovietology's past, not its future.

These new scholars made their institutional homes in burgeoning area-studies programs, which brought experts on a single region together irrespective of discipline. Russian Studies, the first such area program, was a wartime innovation in teaching and research that set the pattern for postwar universities. Interdisciplinary programs were ideally suited to conducting research oriented around practical problems rather than disciplinary expectations and to training practical experts to work in government agencies. As Harvard-dean-turned-national-security-advisor McGeorge Bundy noted, it was a "curious fact" that "the first great center of area studies" was the OSS.[8]

The Soviet launch of the Sputnik satellite in 1957 kept Russian Studies in the spotlight. The National Defense Education Act (NDEA) of 1958 supported language and science education in secondary schools and universities, aiming to close the language gap, which posed a threat to American interests much as the bomber gap had a few years earlier. Administered by the Office of Education (not the military), the NDEA brought some funds—and even more attention—to Russian Studies. It did the same for foreign language and area studies in general, with all major languages seeing rapid jumps in enrollment after 1958. Russian Studies leaders worried about how to put the attention to good use. They took pride in having outgrown the know-the-enemy approach of the field's first years;

they hoped to encourage study of the Russian language as a key to understanding an important world culture, as a part of liberal arts education.

In describing the informal network of professors, soldiers, foundation officials, and spies as well as the field—Russian Studies—that they built, this book calls into question some of the standard interpretations of the era. Contrary to familiar depictions of postwar America as deeply conservative and conformist, the field of Russian Studies brought together scholars from a wide—though certainly not infinite—spectrum of political views. European Social Democrats joined Eisenhower Republicans in Russian Studies, united around their common hatred of Stalin. Members of Communist parties received different treatment, but a handful of Communists did receive fellowships and grants from the major institutions of Russian Studies. Prior scholars have emphasized the way that the academy removed scholars on the left. H. Stuart Hughes was turned out of his job at Harvard's Russian Research Center, apparently because he supported Henry Wallace in 1948, but at the very same time questions arose about Harvard's employment of Barrington Moore Jr. on the grounds that he was too anti-Soviet to be an objective scholar.[9] Neither the field nor its founders were dominated by the fervent anti-Communists who appear in familiar depictions of postwar reaction; it was instead a wide-ranging group determined to build expertise and to make itself useful in intellectual life, public debate, and foreign policy.[10]

This network took shape when the USSR was a difficult wartime ally, not an entrenched enemy, and dramatically changed the relationship between government and university. Their brief wartime fling became a long-term relationship during the Cold War. The marriage barely weathered the 1960s before descending into mutual recrimination and sullen silence. Early conflicts were over how the universities might serve national security, but later ones were over whether they should do so at all. Policy makers and academics were each sustained and scarred by these interactions, and the fallout is still with us in the twenty-first century.[11]

Sovietology was often a moderating impulse, its exemplars clashing with ideologically driven experts; they saw to it that the Cold War stayed cold. Research projects funded by the military services and the CIA undermined public assumptions that the Soviet Union was an all-powerful state ruling over an atomized population that was waiting for an outside power to unshackle it. An air force project, for instance, concluded that the Soviet system was stable and stressed how the United States would not be greeted as liberators in an attack. Individual scholars participated in the Operation Solarium policy exercises that rolled back U.S. efforts to supplant Soviet power in Eastern Europe. And a joint army-CIA project underscored the limits of the Kremlin's reach even within the USSR. These results were the product of systematic government-university cooperation bolstered by informal ties dating back to World

War II. Many of these connections went through Philip Mosely, the best-connected Sovietologist of his generation; he published little but was directly responsible for the most significant projects, policy-oriented as well as academic, in early Soviet Studies.

When a new generation of policy entrepreneurs came to the fore in the 1970s, they were more likely to promote a hard line toward the USSR. Richard Pipes in the Reagan White House continued what Zbigniew Brzezinski had started under Carter: policies to increase the stresses on the Soviet system. Sovietologists did not just influence policy but helped to change the way policy was made in the postwar world; specialized expertise within and beyond the government became central to policy, though in ways that changed over the course of the Cold War.

Soviet Studies was the quintessential Cold War intellectual endeavor, as the field's many critics claim. It existed during the Cold War and received the attention and resources that it did in large part because its subject—the USSR—opposed the United States. Yet what does it mean to describe Soviet Studies as a Cold War field? There was no single Cold War party line. Experts on the Soviet economy, for instance, were criticized by the Right in the 1950s for overestimating Soviet economic capacity—and then criticized by the Left in the 1970s and 1980s for doing precisely the same thing. In the 1980s, the right lambasted the whole field of Soviet Studies for being soft on Communism, while the left attacked it for being rigidly anti-Communist.[12] Which is the Cold War stance: overestimating strength or underestimating it? arguing that the enemy is stable or that it is about to collapse? These questions call into doubt a general scholarly tendency to Cold War determinism, in which every event between 1947 and 1991 is attributed to that conflict. American-Soviet tensions had a profound impact on American life, most certainly including Russian Studies, but such impacts need to be investigated, not assumed.

Know Your Enemy undertakes such an investigation, seeking to understand in concrete terms how intellectual life took place in an era of government support or government interference, depending on one's perspective. It shows how government funds, and larger amounts from foundations, supported and promoted some of the most productive ideas in the late twentieth century. Working in concert, officials from federal agencies joined with program officers at the Carnegie Corporation and the Ford and Rockefeller foundations to build an academic field, not just a policy consultancy. They did so because knowing the Communist enemy meant learning other things as well: how to measure economic growth, how power is diffused (even in totalitarian societies), how languages share universal structures, how cultures interact, and how much modern societies have in common. Scholars in Russian Studies participated, with varying degrees of influence, in debates over the meanings of industrial society and the nature of nondemocratic governance. They remade American studies of language and of comparative literature and laid the groundwork for new strands of literary criticism. The success in the humanities was no accident. The founders of Russian Studies considered wartime area studies research and training programs to be successful because of their emphasis on linguistic competence and cultural knowledge. By the 1960s, the Ford Foundation and the State Department were each contributing upward of $300,000 per year to support American-Soviet scholarly exchange programs, knowing full well that as many as 75% of the participants were historians and humanists. While the government agencies and foundations that supported Russian Studies had created the field to learn more about the Politburo, they also created experts on Pushkin. Though they sought insights into Brezhnev, they also boosted the study of Bulgakov and, eventually, Bakhtin.

What the Sovietologists studied, of course, was shaped by that funding, but not necessarily in predictable ways. Some of the most significant scholarly projects of the 1950s—some of which gave rise to bold new reinterpretations of the USSR—were supported out of the Pentagon budget. Each of the armed services, plus the CIA, had its favorite projects and approaches, The U.S. Air Force, the newest service, led the way in social science research, sponsoring projects from the banks of the Charles River to the beaches of Santa Monica to learn about Soviet society, economics, and politics. In the dozen or so years after World War II, the military sponsors had a capacious idea of what they sought, desiring not operational intelligence but good social science. This would change in the 1960s, as ideas of relevance narrowed.

Scholars' ideas about the USSR were, not surprisingly, shaped by outside events, including those in the Soviet Union. American fears heightened in the 1940s, with the Sovietization of Eastern Europe, news of a Soviet atomic bomb, and the rise of the People's Republic of China (widely credited to Stalin). Scholars rethought their ideas after Stalin's death in 1953 and the slow and sporadic thaw that followed, and again after Nikita Khrushchev was unceremoniously dumped in a 1964 palace coup that brought Leonid Brezhnev to power. The violent suppression of the Prague Spring in 1968 followed by Richard Nixon's efforts to reduce American-Soviet tensions (détente) helped to politicize the field. And the emergence of the young Mikhail Gorbachev from the gerontocracy of the 1980s Politburo prompted new hopes as well as new fears.

Events and ideas closer to home mattered, too. Postwar social scientists, especially in the United States, sought all-encompassing theories through which all nations and all peoples could be understood. This aspiration shaped ideas about the USSR, as scholars tried to fit the country into frameworks whose claims to universality were often undercut by their implicit reliance on Western societies. The tension between universalist aims and national particularity would dominate, in different ways, the study of Soviet economics, politics, and society. History also happened outside faculty offices, of course; the campus turmoil of the 1960s raised tensions within the university and turned academic disputes into political and, ultimately, personal ones. Soviet Studies was hardly impervious to this trend.

Know Your Enemy analyzes the ideas, institutions, and individuals of American Sovietology. Part I describes the origins of the field, showing how the Cold War missions of training and research drew on World War II antecedents. The war's total mobilization of intellectual resources put academics in government service as analysts, advisors, consultants, and teachers of soldiers and sailors. Buoyed by their wartime successes, scholars and government sponsors alike wanted to maintain strong government-academic ties. If the war against Germany and Japan was the physicists' war (though economists claimed it as their own too), many academics saw the brewing conflict with the USSR as the social scientists' war.[13] When Columbia's Russian Institute, the subject of chapter 1, opened its doors in 1946, it built on the wartime experiments in area studies training on campuses across the country. Harvard's Russian Research Center, discussed in chapter 2, was also inspired by wartime academic-government collaboration, but of a very different sort. From its start in 1948, the Russian Research Center built on the growing interest in behavioral science, a new approach to studies of society that, its proponents declared, would unite the social sciences with its combination of anthropology, psychology, and sociology. Both training and research at Columbia and Harvard would be organized along interdisciplinary lines to advance pedagogical as well as policy aims. And both institutions established fundamentally new relationships with foundations and government agencies as the wartime networks worked together to shape Cold War Russian Studies. Columbia, supported by the Rockefeller Foundation, built on army and navy training programs; Harvard, funded by the Carnegie Corporation, established closer ties to the air force and the CIA.

These overlapping networks created Russian Studies at these two institutions, but they soon aspired to build a national enterprise, as chapter 3 recounts. By the mid-1960s, they had succeeded. Russian Studies was no longer an Ivy League affair; centers in Berkeley, Bloomington, and Seattle expanded, and new ones opened in Ann Arbor, Urbana-Champaign, and Los Angeles. The National Defense Education Act supported these new programs, which soon were joined together by a new national organization and a revitalized scholarly journal. As the field grew, it also moved into new areas. Sparked by the slow and uneven liberalization in the Soviet Union, the first scholarly grants program began in 1956 and expanded into a full-fledged scholarly exchange in 1958. The exchange alleviated one of the many anomalies of Soviet Studies: students and scholars had no opportunity to visit the object of their studies, let alone conduct meaningful research there.

Soviet Studies grew impressively in the 1950s and 1960s, the era that one historian rightly termed "the bonanza years."[14] The expansion amounted, in more critical eyes, to "growth by dispersion": more scholars at a larger number of institutions were looking at more world regions and more countries within each region.[15] With dispersion came divergence, and in many ways the costs of growth balanced or even exceeded the benefits. Intellectual trends and different opportunities put an end to the field's hopes of being a united enterprise. Part II, which examines the field's intellectual history from the 1940s through the 1960s, is divided by discipline, with separate chapters detailing the trajectories of economics, literary studies, history, sociology, and political science. These five fields defy easy generalization, as scholars in them navigated their disciplines in markedly different ways. While the founders built Russian Studies to encompass all disciplines and to encourage interdisciplinary work, these aims became increasingly unrealistic in the 1960s. For example, the study of the Soviet economy was slotted into what was becoming a backwater called "comparative economics," which covered those places where universal theories of markets did not apply. Other economists rarely explored comparative economics, while the highly technical nature of the work intimidated many Russian Studies scholars. So the excellent work of Sovietological economists was appreciated by an audience that, by default, was primarily in the policy world. The study of Russian and Soviet literature and language boomed, but it too was out of sync with the discipline; the valuable work of recovery and the problems of access (though reduced thanks to the exchange programs) set the field apart from studies of other literatures. Historians were perhaps the main beneficiaries of the decade's transformations; the exchange programs put them in libraries and archives and allowed them to reduce the gap between their work and that of their fellow historians. Sociologists of the Soviet Union were so few in number by the late 1960s that they barely constituted a "field." Political scientists felt the area-versus-discipline tension most acutely; their efforts to join disciplinary conversations did not put them in a position to generate broad theories—and at the same time made their work less relevant in policy debates. The very fact that the disciplines moved along such different trajectories illustrated the growing divisions within the field.

The growth and dispersion of Russian Studies mirrored broader trends in American universities. And, similarly, the increasingly tumultuous campus life of the 1960s affected Russian Studies. The field, along with other area studies programs, led the rest of the universities in the abrupt decline of external support. Part III traces the impact of campus conflicts and fiscal stringency, which transformed the field. Chapter 9 describes how generational differences about sex and politics combined with general financial retrenchment to bring an end to some of the key institutions of Soviet Studies. New organizations arose to fill the gap, but these were neither as comprehensive nor as well funded as their predecessors. Not all of the problems were financial, however, as the 1960s also increased the politicization of the field. A field that once hosted a range of viewpoints about the nature of Soviet politics and society divided into "totalitarian" and "revisionist" schools, the subjects of chapters 10 and 11, respectively. These labels came from the schools' critics and misrepresented both the aims and the arguments of the other. The increasingly energetic debates produced useful contrasts and discussions at first, but ultimately ended up like trench warfare, generating heavy casualties but little progress. The price of this politicization was visible as Soviet Studies entered what should have been its most exciting moment, the Soviet reforms (and ultimate collapse) of the late 1980s and early 1990s. Yet, as chapter 12 shows, scholars used Soviet events to score points in internal debates rather than using them to shape theories or deepen understanding of the USSR. By the time their subject disappeared in 1991, Sovietologists were deeply divided among themselves—a fact evident in the divergent, even bellicose, histories of the field that began appearing in the late 1980s. History became present politics.

Know Your Enemy shows how the history of Soviet Studies confounds standard notions of American thought and politics in the Cold War. Scholars have emphasized the distortions of anti-Communist inquests and government funding, stressed ideological and political conformism, and highlighted an overarching intellectual orthodoxy. This book in no way denies the influence of external funding or investigations, but seeks to understand the specific impacts and mechanisms of that influence. As an intellectual and institutional history, it relies on the varied and overlapping sources available to historians of the recent past, primarily archival documents, scholarly publications, and newspaper and magazine accounts. Taken together, these sources depict the rapid growth and slow decline of Sovietology.

The sources shape this story, for better and for worse. The quantity and breadth of the Harvard Russian Research Center's holdings, especially compared with the relative paucity of records of Columbia's Russian Institute, is reflected in the footnotes and, unfortunately, in the text. At least one of Sovietology's major supporters and customers is underrepresented: the CIA, which has taken full advantage of the loopholes in the Freedom of Information Act to minimize the release of its documents. For similar reasons, Soviet sources about the exchange program are also very limited. Thus, looming questions about the involvement of Soviet and American security services in the exchanges cannot be answered with documentary evidence, at least not yet. While I heard many participants describe their encounters or near-encounters with CIA and/or KGB officers, I could not adequately reflect these in the text without more documentation. Similarly, many scholars recount fears—their own or their friends'—of the anti-Communist inquisitions of the early 1950s, which, they compellingly suggest, resulted in books not written, degrees not completed, and careers not started. While the FBI was far more forthcoming with its documents than was the CIA, even the file drawers of its reports cataloging hearsay and innuendo do not contain references to works not written or careers not started. This is not to deny the inquests nor the fears themselves.

The availability of sources was not, of course, the only factor that shaped the book that follows. The breadth and unwieldiness of the topic required choices at every step: which institutions mattered most in a given moment, which scholars best represented trends in their fields, which works of scholarship had the greatest impact. I have made these choices as carefully as possible but am all too aware that other historians, plus the Soviet Studies scholars themselves, would make different ones. One of the great benefits of writing a history of the recent past has been the opportunity to speak with so many of my historical subjects, all of whom provided helpful perspectives on what I found (and did not find) in the written sources. They too, I fear, will disagree with some of the choices I have made. Among those choices was a decision to focus primarily on U.S. academic life, looking abroad only rarely and then only to shed light on American trends. This decision was not a matter of patriotism but an effort to understand one national variant of Russian Studies in the twentieth century—debatably, the most important one.[16] Similarly, I focus especially on studies of Russia and the Soviet Union, noting only occasionally studies of other nationalities within the USSR and other nations in the so-called Soviet bloc. One topic missing from the bulk of the book—though this was not solely my choice—is the role of women in Slavic Studies. This reflects an educational system that was dominated by men, especially at the most influential universities in the field; through the mid-1960s, women accounted for only about 10% of Ph.D. recipients.[17] One measure of the slow change is that the Association for Women in Slavic Studies did not come into being until 1986, well after women scholars and feminist scholarly approaches were well established elsewhere in the American academy. Finally, I give short shrift to pre–World War II studies of Russia and the USSR because the field in that era was small, disorganized, and on the margins of academe.[18]

In detailing the growth of Russian Studies from these humble origins, *Know Your Enemy* tells the story of a new kind of intellectual enterprise, one that promised to serve both Mars and Minerva. The commitment to serving both gods accounted for the rapid rise of Soviet Studies. It explained the field's successes, whether measured in terms of scholarship or scholars, policies or policy makers. Over time, that commitment introduced tensions—intellectual, political, and occasionally personal—that would divide the field. The worship of two gods, despite whatever successes it produced for Russian Studies, ultimately accounted for the field's fall.

PART I

A FIELD IN FORMATION

CHAPTER I

THE WARTIME ROOTS OF RUSSIAN STUDIES TRAINING

For a field that would sit at the center of a vast Cold War enterprise, Soviet studies in the early twentieth century was remarkably modest, indeed a little pathetic. Samuel Harper, the one-man Russian program at the University of Chicago for some four decades after 1903, dissuaded one student from entering the field, saying it was the exclusive province of "freaks and nuts," himself included.[1] Harper had a point. Columbia University's Slavonic Department was by far the largest in the country, but it was a collection of academic oddities, founded by a gentleman-scholar who devoted most of his energies to translating American Indian languages.[2] Berkeley's group lacked the color of Columbia's, and also lacked the ambition and administrative backing. Harvard, meanwhile, had only one Slavicist, Samuel Hazzard Cross, who published as much in five years as a commercial attaché in the early 1920s as he did in the next twenty years as a scholar. Yale had no scholars of Slavic literature, and its language teacher after World War I was an émigré chiropractor who taught his native tongue between medical appointments.[3] Students were a similarly motley bunch. Of the 140 or so students who wrote their doctoral dissertations on Russian topics before 1940, no more than a half dozen had successful academic careers; this small group included the movers and shakers of postwar Sovietology. The best known of the whole group was probably a Berkeley graduate turned Soviet spy, Nathan Gregory Silvermaster.[4]

The keenest observers of the Soviet Union were typically radicals who had returned disenchanted from pilgrimages to the Communist holy land or diplomats, like George Frost Kennan, who had received specialized training in European universities. There were few Russia experts in the U.S. federal government—around twenty in the early 1940s, according to one estimate.[5] The boundaries among ivory tower, press room, and embassy were sufficiently high that academics had few chances to meet and learn from their counterparts in other pursuits.

By the end of the 1940s, Soviet studies would be an entirely different enterprise, rippling with energy and rich with financial support. Surviving a number of false steps, the Rockefeller Foundation settled on an area studies model oriented toward language and the humanities; it focused on instruction and infrastructure. With the rise of area studies programs modeled on Sovietology, expertise about the world migrated from journalists' watering holes to faculty clubs and government briefing rooms. The reason had more to do with World War II than with the tentative efforts of the prewar years or the desire to know the Cold War enemy. The wartime programs, quickly overshadowing the efforts of the 1930s, provided the basis for Cold War Sovietology.

The first small steps toward creating a field of Slavic studies came in the 1930s. At Harvard, Cross began working with Ph.D. students in Russian and in comparative literature while Michael Karpovich trained a handful of doctoral students in Russian history. Among them was historian Philip Mosely, the most important Sovietologist of his generation. Raised in rural Massachusetts, Mosely first grew interested in Russian after a chance meeting with a Russian immigrant. He continued language study as an undergraduate and graduate student at Harvard. Thanks to a traveling fellowship, Mosely lived in the USSR in 1931 and 1932, thoroughly immersing himself in research on Russian diplomacy in the 1830s; he was one of a very few Western scholars to use Russian archives. He quickly picked up the language, no doubt helped by his marriage to a Russian woman, Tatiana Terentiev.[6] His letters home offered fulsome praise of Soviet policy. This was hardly a surprise, given the political tendencies of his teenage years, when he and friends went to greet perennial Socialist Party candidate Eugene Victor Debs upon his release from prison in 1921.[7] He maintained a fairly sanguine view of the sanguinary 1930s. He celebrated collectivization—a brutal process that led to the dispossession of millions of villagers and the death of many thousands—as a means to "tremendous economic improvement" that stood to benefit "the whole mass of the people."[8] Mosely noted the strong hand of the Soviet government, but insisted that the people wanted it that way.[9] As late as 1938, he described the show trials and purges that wracked the USSR, but concluded that the "Soviet government is among the defenders of peace to-day." Domestically, the Soviet Union had set up a "system of social welfare which may eventually create real social security," and its planning had prepared the country to make use of its "best human resources."[10] Mosely returned to the United States for a while and survived four years of itinerancy, including a year-long fellowship in the Balkans. He landed a tenure-track job at Cornell in 1939 and soon won a $15,000 grant from the Rockefeller Foundation (RF) to build a Russian program at Cornell; his first priorities were library materials and part-time language instructors.

At the same time, he convinced the university to hire Ernest Simmons as its first faculty appointment in Russian language and literature. Like Mosely, Simmons was born in small-town Massachusetts and studied at Harvard. He did graduate work in German literature before switching to Russian. He stayed at Harvard after graduating, teaching introductory English courses on annual contracts. Frustrated by his position, Simmons joined and was soon elected president of the Cambridge Union of University Teachers, which worked with the American Civil Liberties Union (ACLU) to bring attention to an ever-broader set of workplace concerns, including the "democratic" restructuring of the modern university.[11] Simmons published a well-received biography of Alexander Pushkin in time for the centenary of the author's death in 1937. On the strength of this book, he was offered a job at Cornell in 1940.[12]

Since there was no national organization of Russia experts, Mosely, Simmons, and their few fellow Russia experts typically joined the Institute of Pacific Relations (IPR), whose membership tended toward missionaries and merchants. The group's interest in the USSR was ostensibly related to that nation's small Pacific coastline, but was really an indication of the leadership's leftward leanings. In 1934, IPR began sponsoring summer instruction in Russian language, which it saw as "increasingly necessary for students of Far Eastern affairs."[13] The Berkeley director, a Russian émigré with the unlikely name of George Z. Patrick, designed a program of intensive study that emphasized oral communication over grammar and translation. This technique emerged out of the revolution of modern linguistics, which replaced its obsession with grammar and word formation with spoken language. The most important American linguistics text of the era, Leonard Bloomfield's *Language* (1933), emphasized that a language was what people spoke, not what linguists theorized; it was the "bearer of a culture."[14] Fortunately, the Bay Area was home to plenty of Russian speakers who could provide oral communication drills to complement lectures on grammar by credentialed scholars. By the admittedly modest criteria of the day, the program was a success, training a few dozen students as it floated from Berkeley to Harvard to Columbia in the mid-1930s.[15] This small project soon set its sponsors, the Rockefeller Foundation and the American Council of Learned Societies (ACLS), on a path that would culminate in their predominant role in World War II area studies.

The next step for the ACLS was the establishment of a Committee on Slavic Studies in 1939. Harvard's Cross served as chair; Mosely was the secretary and (the records suggest) the only active member of the group. The committee aimed only to produce a list of relevant books for college libraries and to agitate for an American journal for Slavic studies.[16] Even these modest goals, however, proved beyond the reach of its desultory and disorganized efforts in the 1930s.

The war changed everything. As U.S.–Japanese tensions rose in early 1941, IPR leaders invited some members (including Mosely and Cross) to discuss how to contribute to the "emergency" but found few experts on its new enemy, Japan, or its new ally, the USSR.[17] The IPR was not up to the task of providing significant expertise on the crucial Pacific region. In October 1941, four months after Hitler invaded the USSR, Mosely worked out a plan for an "intensive emergency" course in Russian at Cornell that winter. The course would be a first step in the longer-term problem of increasing the number of Slavic specialists in universities, and in the short-term it would "enable the Government to meet its rapidly expanding need for men able to use Russian." The language effort was led by Jack Posin, who managed to bridge the native speaker/scholar gap; he was born in Ashkhabad but had a Ph.D. in Slavic languages from Berkeley, where he had been a drill instructor in the IPR intensive language program. Thanks to Rockefeller support, the Cornell program was a great success on its small scale. The ACLS quickly planned an expansion. Its new Intensive Language Program brought together scholars and language teachers (including Mosely) from around the country. Within six months of Pearl Harbor, the program had done more than the IPR could have imagined; it had located dozens of language experts at American universities and had trained some 700 students in twenty-six different languages, from Melanesian Pidgin English to Kurdish. Russian quickly overtook all of the others in popularity, in large part, the organizers noted, because of the "wide-spread feeling of cultural affinity" between Americans and Russians, with both countries by then allied against Hitler. Among the program's students were several future Sovietologists: economists Herb Dinerstein and Donald Hodgman, sociologist Alex Inkeles, and political scientist Robert Tucker.[18]

The methods of the 1930s proved exceptionally useful in wartime programs that needed to work quickly and on a large scale. It was easier to find (and cheaper to pay) untrained native speakers as drill instructors, allowing the few trained scholars to teach more students and teach them more intensively. Proponents of the method cited "better instruction at a lower unit cost," while critics complained that it reduced language instruction to "industrial mass production." Military officials likely took both comments as endorsements of their programs.[19] This system relied heavily on native speakers, who were not always easy to locate but were nevertheless poorly treated; Bloomfield made abundantly clear that the drill instructor's job was merely to speak: "the informant is not a teacher and must not be treated as such," he expounded in his wartime how-to manual. Or, as one teacher put it, the drill instructor "is not a teacher, but an animated phonograph record."[20]

The ACLS program was quickly dwarfed by the arrival of the military services, which incorporated the intensive approach as the keystone of their work.[21] The U.S. Navy started first, organizing intensive instruction in Japanese at the University of California in October 1941, just as Mosely launched Cornell's program. The original hope was to use Bay Area residents of Japanese origin as native informants, but shortly after Pearl Harbor, the authorities began planning for the internment, not the employment, of first- and second-generation Japanese living in the United States. By late 1942, the navy's program, the Oriental Languages School (OLS), had relocated to the University of Colorado at Boulder, in large part so it could employ Japanese native speakers without running afoul of their exclusion from the West Coast.[22] When adding Russian in 1944—along with Malay, Korean, and what one local newspaper called "Thai-ese"—it had in mind only a small program, patterned on the intensive curriculum used for Japanese, which was, in turn, patterned on the IPR Russian-language experiments. The original order called for twenty students chosen, as the chief of naval operations put it, "in response to a specific request for Russian language officers to ful-fill liaison functions." One such trainee, Martin Malia, recalled that his liaison work required knowledge not just of Russian language but of Russian drink-ing customs; the few Russian naval officers whom he met in Alaska seemed anxious to describe the failings of the Soviet system, providing the future his-torian with all the evidence he needed to be wary of the USSR.[23] The program quickly grew; between May and September 1942, the Russian group employed more than two dozen native speakers, including one-time socialist revolution-ary Mark Vishniak.[24] The grueling schedule (four hours in class plus nine hours of homework each day) put the program, by one report, at "the extreme limit of intensive learning of languages."[25] Posin, who led the Russian program, clearly had imbibed the spirit of interservice rivalry; he later boasted that the navy program was "better rounded and more ambitious" than army efforts because it emphasized writing as well as aural and oral skills.[26] Among its 250 or so gradu-ates were Malia, behavioral scientist Raymond Bauer, literature specialist Hugh McLean, and William Remington, a friend of Bauer's who was later accused of being a Soviet spy.[27]

The navy also set up an East Coast operation to prepare its personnel for military occupation in the Pacific: the Naval School of Military Government and Administration (NSMGA) at Columbia University. If the scale was small, the academic scope was broad: lessons included "native customs," indigenous and especially colonial systems of rule, and intensive language instruction. Like the other area studies endeavors, the navy's was "frankly experimental," seek-ing to serve the national interest and pedagogical innovation simultaneously. One novelty of the navy program was to combine teaching with publication; NSMGA staff produced a series of "Civil Affairs Handbooks" designed for use by officers during the occupation.[28]

Posin may have been correct about the strengths of the navy language pro-gram, but he was wrong to accuse the army of a lack of breadth and ambition. While the OLS trained officers who could interact at a professional level with Soviet officials, the army sought to prepare soldiers to work in a long-term military occupation. The Army Specialized Training Program (ASTP) would produce trainees who would be fluent in a language, would "know the area in which the languages are used, and [would] have insight into the elements which favor or endanger relations between the Army of the United States and the people in that area." Language training occupied 60% of the instructional time. Early oral drills covered prisoner interrogation: "Who is your commander? ... How many divisions?" One oral exam included the following exercise: "Explain to native officials that there is no food for immediate distribution because the occupying forces have not come from a productive area and have had trans-portation space for only military material."[29] Drill instructors included future scholars René Wellek (who taught Czech at the University of Iowa) and Adam Ulam (who taught Polish at the University of Wisconsin), among others. The army also ran a similar program for officers, the Civil Affairs Training Program (CATP). Harvard's CATP was run by political scientist Carl Friedrich, whose program included interdisciplinary courses on the people, culture, economy, and history of a given country. The ASTP earned encomiums from scholars and soldiers alike, with the head of Yale's program calling it "a revelation to us and to the country."[30] Others saw a blueprint for a new form of education, not just a short-term army program to meet immediate military needs.[31]

The campus directors of the military training programs must have felt that there were as many surveyors as there were students. Both the Smithsonian Institution and the American Council on Education dispatched researchers to study the military programs; the Social Science Research Council (SSRC) and various language-teacher groups also investigated, ready to lobby for their members' needs.[32] But the groups that had set down the prewar groundwork were hardly ready to yield control of the area studies work that they rightfully claimed as their own. Both the Rockefeller Foundation and the ACLS (spend-ing, for the most part, Rockefeller funds) wanted to be sure that the wartime programs would not interfere with their grand plans for the postwar expansion of area studies.

The Rockefeller Foundation began planning its major area studies initia-tive not long after the United States entered the war. Even as its program officers scurried to contribute to the war effort, the foundation focused on long-term goals, not wartime emergencies. It wanted to promote area stud-ies not as a means for knowing enemies, friends, or subjects, but as a means of spurring more cosmopolitan general education, promoting interdisciplin-ary research, and reducing the "provincialism" of the social sciences. Working together with two of their major academic beneficiaries, the ACLS and the SSRC, RF officers drafted a National Plan of Work on Foreign Languages, Institutions, and Customs. This document recognized what the army and navy programs had done, but called them "wasteful" for using so many experts for such a short period of time. Future developments must be "orderly," coordinated by universities together with government agencies and business representatives; only central planning would ensure adequate representation by region and institution. After a few rounds of discussion, the officers agreed that the Humanities Division would "chair" the foundation's efforts, but would work closely with the Social Science Division.[33] This seemingly minor turf battle had major implications; it ensured that language and culture would remain at the core of area studies programs. Advanced training, whether for undergraduate or graduate students, required intensive language work along the lines of the army and navy programs. The only exception would be a "general orientation" to another culture, using English-language sources, which would be ideal for the "junior college" level.[34] General education was an important element in the plans; as the ACLS put it, a college without courses on various world areas—it noted especially Russia and the Far East—"is simply not equipped to educate students for life in the late nineteen hundreds [i.e., the late twentieth century]."[35] The Rockefeller Foundation saw work on Russia as a great test case for area studies; a handful of American universities had gathered enough experts—thanks in part to the military work—to make the "Russian complex" a natural place to start.[36]

By this point, Mosely had already begun working with RF officials to displace what he saw as "showmanship" with scholarship in Russian Studies.[37] In March 1943, Mosely—who had left Cornell for a succession of foreign policy posts—convened a Rockefeller conference on Slavic studies. The conference brought together his old and new colleagues; academics and Washington officials attended in equal numbers. Harvard's Cross and Cornell's Simmons were there, as was historian George Vernadsky from Yale.[38] Decrying the wartime programs as "ridiculously modest in quantity," participants vowed not to "let the war situation interfere too much with our planning of a long-term program." As Simmons put it, ASTP had convinced many that "instead of having a man majoring in German literature and language,... he [should] major in Germany." (Simmons also noted that the government's need for people with Russian skills was so severe that the Cornell program was now allowing women to enroll.) Mosely identified the criteria for future Russia experts: they should have training in a "solid discipline" but also experience with interdisciplinary work. Language skills were essential, as was "direct experience in the country or culture of his study."[39] These criteria would become the bedrock of postwar Soviet studies.

The RF's curricular aims were very broad. Slavic Studies needed to reach beyond history and language/literature—the principal fields represented at the conference—to all of the disciplines. Even economists, already proclaiming the universal validity of their techniques, had to be persuaded that the study of so-called regional economics was advantageous. Finally, the group emphasized the need to build infrastructure from the ground up: it had to find ways to train future teachers, create pedagogical materials, and build up holdings at the Library of Congress as well as at campus facilities. Educators with the army and navy, with their focus on immediate goals, gave little thought to these matters. But the Rockefeller Foundation was already looking far beyond the war.[40]

At a conference in the spring of 1944, the foundation worked out a justification for area studies programs that would outlast the wartime emergency. Such an approach, declared conference chair Mortimer Graves of ACLS, had a bright future: "people are pretty well decided that something called area studies is going to be part of the postwar educational experience." Area studies, most participants agreed, served a variety of important educational purposes. Programs could serve both liberal arts and vocational objectives, simultaneously providing a mental "disciplining effect" and laying the groundwork for future employment in government or business overseas. Area studies would simultaneously give students wider perspectives on their own country and teach them how to live "in the crowded world of the second half of the twentieth century." Only through intensive exposure to another culture could young citizens "acquire the tolerance for foreign thought and ways that will make life possible in a spherical world."[41] The conference also considered the role of area studies in academic research, but primarily as an afterthought; the main focus was on bringing area studies into the general college curriculum and into specialized training programs.

Cornell continued its trailblazing role in wartime Russian Studies, even with Mosely based in Washington. With the arrival of Ernest Simmons, it established a Department of Slavic Languages and Literatures in which he was the sole member.[42] Within months of coming to Ithaca, Simmons began inundating the dean with proposals, including one for a summer workshop on the USSR.[43] Simmons envisioned this Intensive Study of Contemporary Russian Civilization Program, inaugurated in 1943, as a means to help students obtain a basic understanding of the Soviet Union. While the ASTP—taking place at the same institution with many of the same faculty—put language learning at the center of its program, the summer workshop sought an integrated understanding of modern Russia through English sources. The nucleus of the instructors came from Cornell's faculty, with additional teachers from outside. Simmons and the Rockefeller staff hoped to bring at least one instructor from the Soviet Union, but were not able to do so.[44] Simmons devoted almost half of the initial proposal to establishing the need to work out a "future curriculum in international education"; his summer workshop would be an experiment, successful so long as it could "provide valuable data" on curricula.[45]

The roster of workshop faculty revealed the dearth of Russia experts on college campuses. Simmons taught the core course on literature, and Sir Bernard

Pares, the founder of Russian Studies in Britain, helped to run the course on government. But the rest of the core group was light on academic credentials and, in some cases, good judgment. Corliss Lamont, scion of the New York banking family, had a Ph.D. in philosophy but was better known for lightweight works such as *You Might Like Socialism* (1940), which extolled the virtues of Soviet life. Most controversial was Vladimir Kazakevich, a Soviet sympathizer who taught Soviet economics in the summer program as well as at ASTP. He came to Cornell from a prior job at the National Association of Manufacturers, where he helped to identify pro-Soviet propaganda—but he might well have reported himself. For instance, he gave a speech in 1942 called "What the Revolution Accomplished," praising not just Soviet educational and economic achievements but also dubious political ones like the absence of a "fifth column" of opposition. Some reporters singled out Cornell's "red professor" and called for him to be fired if not deported. The Cornell administration insisted that it had hired the best person available, in spite of Kazakevich's lack of academic credentials. Privately, though, Cornell's president conceded that Kazakevich was "fully convinced of the virtues of the Soviet system." Cornell's ASTP director, meanwhile, reminded his instructors of their "obligation of protecting members of the armed forces in their essential loyalty to their army and their country." One student, Richard Pipes, later called the courses "propaganda," but his view was not universally shared.[46] After the head of ASTP told a congressional committee that Kazakevich's appointment had been a "silly stupid blunder," Cornell removed him from the ASTP staff while expanding his role in Simmons's summer program. After all, those students had "uniformly approved" of Kazakevich's teaching and found no signs of bias.[47] The outcome was full of ironies. Kazakevich's job in the army program was filled by a former *New Masses* editor. The Kazakevich controversy, as it played out in the New York City press, had little impact on either ASTP or Simmons's program; indeed, enrollment in the summer workshop doubled between 1943 and 1944.[48]

The Cornell summer experiment would be hard to judge a success in academic terms, though both Simmons and the Rockefeller staff saw it as one. Compared to the ASTP program meeting on the same campus, and with many of the same faculty, the summer workshop was less serious. The workshop did not require Russian instruction, even though fewer than half of the students had ever been exposed to the language. Many of the instructors had no scholarly credentials, and the collected publications of the group amounted to a series of encyclopedia articles with a distinct pro-Soviet tilt. It was the last gasp for an amateur approach to Soviet studies—one, as Harvard's president noted tartly, "with the savor of women's clubs."[49]

Meanwhile, the Rockefeller Foundation's other wartime efforts fared little better. By the end of 1944, it had convened representatives from Western institutions (including Berkeley, the Claremont colleges, Stanford, and Washington) to explore strengthening the work in Asian studies on the Pacific coast. Like the RF-supported Institute of Pacific Relations, this initiative saw three linguistic pillars as essential: Chinese, Japanese, and Russian. Building up West Coast institutions would serve another RF priority, ensuring the presence of area studies programs across the United States. But the Rockefeller efforts to plant the seeds for Slavic studies on the West Coast—the grant program was advertised as "The Far West Looks to the Far East"—fell on barren ground even at the region's premier institutions. The RF started a grant program in 1944 for "the development of Far Eastern and Slavic Studies" on the West Coast. Totaling $1 million by the end of the 1940s, the grants helped to coordinate library purchases and curricular offerings, provided for national and international travel, and supported graduate training.[50] In pursuing these goals, foundation officers let optimism overrule their own knowledge of the weakness of the institutions and personnel involved.

Take, for instance, Slavic studies at the University of California. Berkeley was among the first American universities to offer Russian language courses, starting in 1901. If the administration had based its decisions on popularity, instructor George Noyes (split between English and Russian) would have left quickly; enrollment in Russian courses started at five students and did not exceed twenty for a decade. By the mid-1920s, however, the program was booming. Noyes was joined by Russian émigrés Patrick (originally hired in French) and Alexander Kaun. Until World War II, these three scholars sought, with some success, to convince their students and administrators alike that scholarly interest in Russia was not "something freakish, the mark of an eccentric, almost unbalanced mind."[51] Yet, after a 1941 visit, one RF staffer called the situation "anything but promising." In 1943, another foundation official agreed: Berkeley "was not ready to rebuild" in Slavic studies. Postwar efforts at Berkeley could not come from the Slavic Department: Noyes was "feeble" and approaching retirement, Patrick "hopelessly ill." The department's youngest member, fifty-five-year-old Alexander Kaun, then died.[52] Historian Robert Kerner tried to take up the slack. Trained at Harvard in Hapsburg history, Kerner recast himself as a Soviet expert despite the fact that he never really learned Russian. Placing a great stake on policy relevance, Kerner felt keenly the distance between Berkeley and Washington, D.C.; George Kennan described him as one of those who had "an understandable yearning to be closer to the actual operations of diplomacy and a sneaking suspicion that if they were in on it, they could do it much better." Kerner resented East Coast Slavicists because he thought they looked down on him; he in turn looked down on other West Coast Slavicists as inferior. Rockefeller personnel agreed with Berkeley's president that Kerner's "rough edges" left him "temperamentally unfit" for administrative work. Kerner's resentments shaped the Berkeley program. He felt that Slavs were unable to remain objective about their own history, so wanted to hire only Americans. The initial announcement for the Institute of Slavic Studies (founded 1948) limited graduate student funding to American citizens. He preferred to hire his own students, though only a few exceeded his own slim scholarly record.[53] Kerner boasted—rightfully—about the dozen or so doctorates granted by 1955. What Berkeley had in quantity, however, it lacked in quality; of these graduates, only a handful—Basil Dmytryshijn, Charles Jelavich, Oleg Maslenikov, and Wayne Vucinich—had noteworthy academic careers.

Across the bay, Stanford's efforts in Slavic studies were just as troubled—and here too the RF staff were well aware of the problems. David Stevens, RF humanities director, saw Stanford as the core of its West Coast efforts in Slavic studies. Yet Stanford had no historians of Russia; the head of the Slavic program, Henry Lanz, was a Russian émigré with a doctorate in philosophy. Two members of the history department taught on Russia: Merrill Spalding, with a Harvard Ph.D. and no significant publications, and H. H. Fisher, who never earned a doctorate but had found his way to Stanford through the Hoover War Library after World War I. Fisher headed Stanford's army training programs during the war, but these focused on the Asian, not the Slavic, world. After the war, Fisher received a major grant from the RF for an undergraduate program in Pacific, Asiatic, and Russian Studies—the Russian added only at the foundation's request. The program aimed to promote general education on other regions of the world and emphasized the humanities' obligation "to furnish the foundation for a sympathetic appreciation of Asiatic culture."[54] Here and elsewhere, the proposal's references to Russia appear as afterthoughts; key courses would be in "Oriental" civilizations. Stanford's attempts to upgrade its Russian offerings were hindered by Lanz's death in 1945; RF still supported this goal because it wanted to provide advanced training for the graduates of the navy's OLS program.[55]

Stanford's main attraction was not personnel but the sources held at the Hoover Institution on War, Revolution, and Peace.[56] Herbert Hoover had created it in the aftermath of World War I to gather information about the Great War, to maintain documents about its namesake, and to provide employment for a number of his old pals. Its original holdings covered the theater of operations for Hoover's relief organizations, which included most of Europe and the USSR. Additional materials about revolutionary Russia arrived in the 1920s.[57] It had an anomalous place at Stanford, under the control of its own board (in turn controlled by its namesake), but with a director appointed by the Stanford president. Its holdings on the modern political history of Eastern Europe and Russia, however, were unmatched, with both archival and published materials unavailable outside the USSR (and, for other reasons, unavailable within it). Contrary to its later reputation and its namesake's own wishes, the Hoover Institution in the 1940s was an extraordinarily liberal institution. Fisher's work in the Institute of Pacific Relations was one indicator of his politics. Another was his proposal to Rockefeller for an academic program to build on the wartime efforts. The proposal bore all the marks of wartime "one-worldism"; Fisher emphasized the need to "build up a consciousness of our common humanity" by teaching about universals in the arts, music, science, and technology. This attitude carried into the postwar world, when Fisher lectured about and wrote a book called *America and Russia in the World Community*. He acknowledged Russia's differences—for instance, an "interpretation of freedom of the press [that] does not correspond with our[s]"—but optimistically declared that divergences would soon give way to unity. The closing chapter: "One World or None."[58]

Fisher also devoted himself to fundraising. He won a grant to promote access to Hoover's Russian collections, providing fellowships mostly for graduate students but also for Communist William Mandel.[59] He also beefed up the institution's own research capacities, hiring an assistant director who came directly from Alger Hiss's office at the State Department—employment that hardly endeared him to Hoover and his conservative friends.[60] The Hoover Institution soon won a major grant for a project on Revolution and the Development of International Relations (RADIR). The project, led by a gaggle of wartime psychological warriors and supported by the Carnegie and RAND corporations, sought to provide a quantitative account of the evolution of a "world community."[61] The RADIR project had some similarities to Fisher's own writings. As Rothwell put it, the purpose of RADIR was to determine "on what basis the people of Magnitogorsk, Detroit, and Batavia can get along."[62] Among the RADIR staff was graduate student Alexander Vucinich, who also worked for a classified offshoot, MELITE; some fruits of these labors were published in his "Soviet Factory" and "Soviet Academy of Science."[63]

Herbert Hoover, according to one friend, soon grew tired of "'value-free' scholasticism and of social science 'interpretative' studies that somehow always managed to display a left-wing bias." He waged a decade-long battle to reorient his institution's politics. A detailed report commissioned by Hoover charged institution staff with writing "radical" and "anti-American" works. The fact that the red-baited "China hand" Owen Lattimore had worked in the library was considered proof that Fisher had renounced his stewardship of the documents. Professor Lattimore, after all, was a "conscious articulate instrument of the Soviet conspiracy," and Communists believe that "it is ethical to purloin books and papers from a library." (No documents in the collections Lattimore used were ever reported as missing.)[64]

The institution found itself under pressure from every side. While Herbert Hoover attacked its academic mission, Rockefeller personnel grew increasingly frustrated with Stanford's academic failings. Both Stanford and the Hoover Institution were already stretched thin, with the university's Russian resources folded into a Department of Asiatic and Slavic Studies and the institution pursuing contract research. The RF staff grew increasingly skeptical of Stanford's intellectual promiscuity and lack of qualified personnel in Slavic affairs. They were joined by Carnegie officers, who felt that the hundreds of thousands of dollars they had given to RADIR were wasted. When Carnegie and Rockefeller representatives met in 1947, they collectively pulled the plug on Stanford's aspirations in Slavic studies. Both foundations would continue to help make Hoover's Slavic collections more accessible to scholars, but they wrote off the possibility of a major West Coast center in Slavic studies. The far West might look to the Far East, but Russia was no longer in its line of vision.[65] Meanwhile, the Rockefeller Foundation set its sights on the near North: Columbia University.

Columbia had not been at the center of the foundation's initial moves toward area studies. Yet the development of Russian Studies there paralleled the agenda set out by Rockefeller and its penumbra of recipients. The establishment of the NSMGA prompted a general assessment of international studies at the university. A faculty committee reached conclusions very much along the lines of those of the Rockefeller Foundation. Area studies, the group reported, are "important, necessary, even indispensable" for Columbia; "no American in the future can be called educated who is ignorant about his world neighbors." It also hoped that area studies would help to integrate academic disciplines. Citing the success of the military programs, the committee believed that languages should be at the center of area studies; since Columbia's own language departments were not all suited to the task, the committee proposed outsourcing some language classes to other universities. The committee chair privately noted another advantage: "we should be able to offer eloquent petitions to the great Foundations."[66] And, indeed, they did.

The NSMGA became the basis for Columbia's new School of International Affairs. Graduates of the school would be qualified for "technical and managerial posts" in government, international agencies, or the corporate world. The school would be "federal in character," organized around six regional institutes, including three on Western Europe and one each for Russia, Latin America, and the Far East. For much the same reason as Rockefeller, Columbia opted to enter the area studies arena with its Russian Institute (RI); other centers would follow.[67] Rockefeller offered substantial support for RI, with an initial grant of $250,000—slightly less than the "Far West" program—in 1946.

The RI's founding director was Geroid Tanquary Robinson, a historian who had been at Columbia for some two decades. His interest in Communism dated back at least to 1913, when he wrote a high-school paper demonstrating Karl

Marx's impact on contemporary American socialism.[68] Diving into Greenwich Village's café-and-small-magazine culture in the early 1920s, Robinson's interest in Russia and Communism deepened. Echoing the comments of fellow *Dial* writers John Dewey and Thorstein Veblen, Robinson praised Bolshevik Russia for organizing an entire country for economic production, and insisted that it provided a valuable experiment of a society "based on general developed intelligence."[69] Robinson continually stressed the need for a deeper historical understanding of Bolshevism; the "Communist experiment," he insisted in one early article, must be understood as "a Russian problem of the past." And understanding the Russian past, Robinson believed, meant understanding the Russian peasantry, the driving force of Russian history. He spent two years in Moscow archives trying to prove this point; his *Rural Russia under the Old Regime* (1932) showed how the problems of agricultural production and rural organization had driven Russian history for centuries. The book ended on the eve of 1917, with the country on the verge of a "peasant revolt."[70] Robinson planned a sequel on 1917 itself, but made little progress on it.[71] Even without its sequel, *Rural Russia* earned its author kudos as the best Russian historian in an American university. But neither his longevity nor his scholarly credentials explained Robinson's selection to run the RI; his primary qualification was his wartime work, as chief of the USSR Division at the Office of Strategic Services (OSS), America's wartime intelligence agency.

Robinson had received a summons to Washington in September 1941 to head Russian research for a new organization, which soon became OSS. The research branch of this new organization—nicknamed the "chairborne division"—was stocked with Ivy League professors. Robinson got the USSR job after Philip Mosely turned it down in favor of diplomatic work. Once on board, Robinson put his administrative strengths to immediate use; he began ransacking universities, Ivy League and otherwise, for students and scholars with any form of Russia expertise (preferably firsthand) without regard to seniority or discipline. This would be the great innovation of the OSS; as one analyst put it, the military was "not interested in the production of principles of social sciences, neatly departmentalized" but in analyses that "involved all the disciplines" to answer strategic questions. After a series of conflicts in 1942, this regional approach won out, leaving Robinson in charge of a USSR Division that included economists, geographers, historians, sociologists, and political scientists.[72]

There were many advantages to what one historian aptly called "social science in one country." Army officers and diplomats did not care whether academics considered an issue to be political science or economics; they wanted answers to concrete questions. Answers to the most important policy questions—Would the USSR survive the Nazi onslaught? Would the Soviet war

Figure 1.1. A U.S. Army general awarding Geroid Robinson the Medal of Freedom for his work with the Office of Strategic Services, 1947. The citation praised the work of his USSR Division for among other things, contributing to "mutual understanding and harmonious relations" among the Allies.

effort benefit from Lend-Lease aid? What would Soviet priorities be after the war?—did not reside in one discipline alone. From Washington's perspective, the interdisciplinary research model, what came to be called area studies, was oriented from the start toward serving policy needs.[73] This perspective meshed nicely with RF's interest in using area studies, and knowledge of the world more generally, to expand the horizons of American higher education.

Freed of their usual hierarchies, the professors struggled to create new ones. Associate professors demanded the rank of major—and then insisted on the perquisites of military brass. "Vanity," one cloak-and-dagger type at the OSS concluded, "seemed to rule the whole [research] setup." Robinson replaced academic discipline with the iron-fisted sort. He drove the staff hard—plenty of mandatory overtime (including all-nighters)—and maintained tight control over every aspect of his group. He would not let so much as a routine telegram go out without completely rewriting it. A number of his staff—including

Barrington Moore Jr., a former student well acquainted with Robinson's style—fled the USSR Division.[74] But those who could tolerate Robinson's perfectionism took part in a remarkable enterprise: the group produced thorough and detailed intelligence reports, ranging from narrow technical questions (transportation and communications in southeastern Siberia, the status of civilian health care) to a civil affairs handbook—similar to the ones produced at Columbia for NSMGA—written for troops in Germany who would deal with the Red Army. This handbook, whose authors included sociologist Alex Inkeles (fresh from Cornell's intensive language training) and émigré literary scholar Vera Dunham, was a how-to guide to getting along with the Russians, primarily political in content, but leavened (in the words of one OSS-er) with "Emily Post and Dale Carnegie."[75]

These reports relied on painstaking work in piecing together only the narrowest scraps of information. Even mainstays like *Pravda* arrived six to eight weeks after publication, if they arrived at all; major Soviet quarterlies were even less reliable. Robinson believed that the solution was to place in Moscow an OSS researcher, who would be tasked with gathering and shipping as many sources as possible. Straining mightily against opposition from the State Department, Robinson managed to redeploy a young political philosopher on his staff, Robert C. Tucker (who learned Russian at Cornell), to the Moscow embassy. Tucker was later joined by another OSS veteran, Melville Ruggles, who served as "publications procurement officer" in Moscow—this lofty title meant mostly wandering from kiosk to kiosk in search of newspapers, then bundling up and mailing them.[76]

At the same time that Robinson was riding herd over OSS staff, he was also laying the groundwork for the Russian Institute. Throughout his Washington stint, he had been lobbying Columbia to let him build its Russian program. His mission was imperial: to "bring together" under his control "*all* the work on Russia that is done anywhere at Columbia." Robinson wanted his Russian Institute to follow the OSS model. "The *uniqueness* and *close integration* of the Russian pattern," he wrote, called for the "integration of Russian Studies."[77]

The RI borrowed not just its structure but its sense of purpose from its direct predecessor, the naval school. Robinson's wartime proposal for the RI emphasized the need to do "all that it can do" to train Russia experts, who would be "indispensable" for the foreseeable future. It would offer a two-year program for "regional majors," which would soon be replicated in the other area institutes. As in the military programs, the RI curriculum had a heavy dose of language training, more than half of the workload in the first year. In the second year, students would continue gaining interdisciplinary area expertise at the same time that they developed a disciplinary specialization. A secondary goal of the institute was to expand course offerings on Russia for nonmajors.[78]

Robinson frequently invoked OSS achievements in justifying interdisciplinary area studies. The atomic bomb showed what scientists could accomplish through group research on a single problem; Robinson wanted his humanist and social scientist colleagues to take the same approach. The main problem was that there were not enough of them. As a result, Robinson directed his primary attention to training. Rockefeller officials, too, recognized that research "may well be subordinate to training" in the RI's early years.[79] The RI teaching approach was interdisciplinary for the same reason that the OSS research model had been: to serve policy. Broad training in a given region would be important for analysts-in-training. The RI also touted other benefits of interdisciplinarity: the opportunities to deprovincialize American scholarship and teaching and to encourage intellectual innovation.

Robinson rehearsed all of the arguments for the Russian Institute in an article published in the uncertain months after the war's end. He considered knowledge of the USSR to be a top national priority; never before, he worried, had "so many know[n] so little about so much." But reversing this dangerous position did not mean simply expanding existing inquiries. Because the "separate phases of Russian life" were so "deliberately and thoroughly united," they could not "be studied in isolation." Russian émigrés, he argued, were ill suited for objective analysis of their home country; the task must be taken up by Americans—but only those who had "spent time in Russia." Robinson also envisioned plenty of traffic between the United States and the Soviet Union. He hoped to send Americans to conduct research in Soviet archives and libraries and to bring Soviet scholars to the United States for temporary teaching appointments.[80]

The next step was to assemble an academic staff to take on these tasks. Columbia's criteria were simply stated if difficult to achieve: faculty members should have "technical competence; knowledge of the subject matter in a particular part of the Russian field; and scholarly objectivity." While Robinson had worked with a polyglot and cosmopolitan group of analysts at the OSS, including members of the Frankfurt School and émigrés like Vera Sandomirsky Dunham and Alexander Gerschenkron, his Russian Institute relied on American-born scholars. A side benefit of establishing a Russian Institute, as Mosely had astutely noted in 1943, was the chance to gather a concentrated group of Russianists in a single university rather than letting postwar demobilization scatter the scholars across the groves of academe.[81] Columbia's need for Russianists was high indeed. Two émigré economic historians, Vladimir Simkhovitch and Michael Florinsky, were barely connected to their department or to other Russianists; Robinson was likely referring to them when he complained of the "mixed...quality" of émigré scholars. They would play no part in Robinson's enterprise, save for mentions in the RF application for appearance's sake.[82] Abram Bergson, leader of the OSS economists, quickly received an invitation to Columbia.[83] Columbia administrators hired Ernest Simmons for the Slavonic Department, but not without reservation; the letter proposing his tenured appointment called him "probably the best man available," praising his organizational talents while noting the limits of his scholarship. The RI also needed a scholar of Soviet foreign relations, and Robinson briefly considered E. H. Carr before settling on Philip Mosely.[84]

While Robinson and the Rockefeller staff agreed that "there is only one Mosely," the extent of his wartime activities gave reason to wonder if there were not in fact multiple Moselys. On leave from Cornell, Mosely joined the State Department as a political advisor and was present at key Allied conferences in Paris, Moscow, and Potsdam. At the same time, he continued consulting for the Rockefeller Foundation, with an agreement to work there full time after the war.[85] Mosely's advice during this whirl of diplomacy was subtle but consistent: he favored joint Allied control over Germany ("the real touchstone of Allied post-war cooperation") as opposed to unilateral American action. He wanted to continue working with the Soviet Union, even as he grew increasingly wary of its representatives. Looking back a decade later, Mosely still saw the work he had done on Germany as the only "real chance...to lay a basis for some enduring measure of postwar cooperation" between the Soviet Union and the West.[86] Perhaps frustrated by his lack of influence, Mosely plotted his departure from the State Department, and Robinson was able to woo him away from the Rockefeller Foundation.[87]

Finally, Columbia administrators saw the need for a faculty expert in Russian/Soviet law. John Hazard met all of the criteria: native-born American, a doctorate, plenty of Russian experience (including a law degree from the Moscow Juridical Institute), and wartime work with the Lend-Lease administration.[88] By 1947, then, the RI roster was complete; as Robinson boasted in the newspaper article announcing the RI's debut, all five core faculty had scholarly training in an academic discipline, interest and experience in interdisciplinary work (primarily in government), and extensive experience in Russia.

As Mosely and his Rockefeller colleagues proposed, the RI would be a central node for the development of the field at the national level, taking full advantage of demobilization to snare senior and midcareer scholars as well as prospective students before they returned to more traditional departments and pursuits. The institute would be closely tied to government work—hardly a surprise given its institutional origins and its faculty members' experiences. What Secretary of State William P. Rogers wrote about Mosely was true for his involvement in RI; there would be "no line between government and academic work."[89] The area studies approach—organized to solve problems, not to advance disciplines—was the reigning principle at RI and soon enough at the other regional institutes at

Columbia. The focus shaped its priorities as well as its ties to national security for decades.

The RI got off to an impressive start from the time it moved into its brownstone in the fall of 1946. One office, however, remained unfilled: that of a visiting Soviet scholar. The notion of appointing a Soviet scholar to an American university was first proposed to the RF's Humanities Division in 1942; the original hope was for a permanent appointment. Rockefeller gave the go-ahead to identify an appropriate scholar, cautioning that the RI should be sure to confirm that "these men are acceptable to the Russian embassy." The ACLS soon got involved, contacting the Soviet embassy for suggestions on whom to invite to the United States. As was the case earlier, the efforts became serious only when Columbia got involved. Simmons endorsed the idea as "one of the most important things we can do." Robinson, hoping that a visiting scholar would improve the "foreign relations" of the institute, was willing to relax his political criteria. Core RI faculty corresponded almost daily about possible Soviet visitors. The resulting list was something of a who's who of Soviet scholars. Historians I. I. Mints, A. M. Pankratova, and E. V. Tarle joined economists P. I. Liaishchenko and E. E. Varga on the list; also included was A. Ia. Vyshinsky, the reviled prosecutor of many 1930s show trials. The attempts to bring Soviet scholars were hampered by Soviet inaction as well as by American action, namely, the Alien Registration Act, which required the fingerprinting of Communists coming to the United States.[90] In any case, the Soviets did not welcome Columbia's inquiries; Soviet newspapers described the Russian Institute as a key node in a system of "total espionage."[91]

Even though the institute's "foreign relations" with the USSR were not working out, things were better at home. Bolstered by postwar enthusiasm and by RI students, enrollment in Russian language courses quadrupled in a single year. Simmons set about rebuilding the language department to serve dual purposes: meeting the language instruction needs created by RI students and becoming a serious research and training program in its own right. The fit between RI and the Slavic Department was not perfect, as Simmons complained to whoever would listen. The institute focused, not surprisingly, on Russian, while a serious Slavic Department needed a broader range of offerings, including languages like Polish, Serbo-Croatian, and Czech.[92] Rockefeller staffers were enthusiastic, quickly approving a grant to improve "the humanistic phase of Slavic Studies" in order to ensure that Columbia's Slavic Department would rise above "mere 'usefulness.'" And Simmons also got a Rockefeller grant for a "five-year program" to create teaching aids, primarily for elementary Russian.[93]

At the same time, Simmons contacted Polish and Czech government officials in search of scholars from those countries. In 1947, Simmons obtained a Czech government subsidy to create a Tomas Masaryk Professorship. Named for the father of independent Czechoslovakia, the chair was soon

filled by an émigré scholar, the linguist Roman Jakobson.[94] Born and educated in Russia, Jakobson was friends with the most important Russian poets
and literati of the early Soviet period. He spent the 1920s and much of the
1930s in Czechoslovakia, where he founded the Prague Linguistic Circle.
Escaping the Nazi advance in 1939, he eventually landed a job teaching at
a French-language university-in-exile in New York, soon adding work at
Columbia.[95] By the time he took the Masaryk chair, he was working with
a dozen graduate students on a range of literary and linguistic topics. But
Jakobson never set down roots at Columbia; by 1947, he was already talking to
Harvard. When he left in 1949, he took fifteen students (and one junior colleague, Horace Lunt) with him.[96] The Masaryk chair folded soon thereafter.
A similar chair in Polish, named after nineteenth-century poet and nationalist
hero Adam Mickiewicz, came about with the help of Polish cultural attaché
Czeslaw Milosz. It soon was mired in controversy—rooted not in the prospective chairholder, linguist Manfried Kridl (then at Smith College), but
in Columbia's Polish instructor, Arthur Coleman. Coleman launched a very
public anti-Communist attack on Kridl, Columbia, and Simmons. Columbia's
president, Dwight D. Eisenhower, no Communist sympathizer, defended the
appointment; he noted that the State Department had called the program
"a real service to both cultural relations and the government." Coleman soon
decided to "resign for [his] country."[97] Despite Jakobson's rapid departure for
Harvard, Simmons had set Columbia on course to becoming a premier Slavic
department in the country for decades to come.

Meanwhile back at the institute, Robinson's newly assembled group was
poised to provide a well-rounded view of Russia. Columbia's institute emphasized what Robinson called, in his debut announcement, the "extraordinary
degree of uniqueness" of the Soviet Union; in contrast, Harvard's Russian
Research Center would emphasize universal social science. His public and
classroom lectures of the late 1940s expounded and expanded upon this theme.
Russia and the West, he told one class, "stand at the end of two largely different streams of history." He extended this message in telling navy plebes
about Soviet foreign policy; the talk described a variety of East-West binary
oppositions (Russian mysticism versus Western rationalism, Russian collectiv-
ism versus Western individualism, Russian autocracy versus Western democracy) and identified the "Byzantine-Asiatic" inheritance as a key to Soviet
ideology and mindset. His emphasis on Russian distinctiveness did not always
translate directly into a harsh Cold War attitude; his writings about the USSR,
especially in the immediate postwar period, held out some hope for peace. His
public interviews echoed the OSS's "Capabilities and Intentions" report, calling for "foresighted adjustment and compromise" and expressions of "goodwill"
toward the USSR.[98]

Soviet condemnations notwithstanding, this relatively soft line on the USSR was indicative of the RI faculty's politics. Simmons, after all, had served as vice president of the New York state branch of the American Labor Party, a party of liberals, socialists, and Communists.[99] Robinson had long since shed the Greenwich Village radicalism of his youth, but was far from a hardline Cold Warrior. Mosely's leftish tendencies, too, had receded by the 1940s; he certainly never supported Henry Wallace as he had Debs. Students later recalled the wide range of student political views, including classmates thought to be Communist Party members. Political diversity ruled among senior fellows, too; Marxist Herbert Marcuse shuttled between Columbia and Harvard before settling into a teaching post at Brandeis.[100] Columbia offered William Mandel a senior fellowship at the RI after his Hoover fellowship. One memorandum praised Mandel's "impressive" record "in spite of his lack of formal education," thus evading the fact, well known to RI staff, that Mandel had built up this record as a member of the Communist Party.[101] That he was even considered suggests just how slim were the pickings of Soviet experts in the aftermath of World War II—and just how many of those knowledgeable about the USSR had come to the topic through political as well as intellectual commitments.

It was this dearth of Soviet experts that brought the RI into being. Though RI's original mission emphasized both training and research, publication clearly took the back seat to building up a cadre of experts. By 1953, more than 250 students had passed through the institute, with most completing two years of coursework and an independent research project. In the RI's first year, over 150 enrolled in Bergson's basic course on Soviet economics, almost 100 in Simmons's Soviet/Russian literature. Historical topics had similarly strong showings: 112 took Robinson's course on imperial Russian history, and 86 took Mosely's course on Russian foreign policy before 1900. Advising the independent research projects required of all M.A. students took much faculty time. Even so, almost three-quarters of the students complained about the lack of faculty contact.[102] Robinson's excessive demands on students and staff did not help morale. His perfectionism—a two-paragraph memo to his secretary on how to address envelopes, for instance—distracted him from letting students develop on their own and, all too often, from completing their dissertations. Only Robinson, one student bitterly recalled decades later, could offer fifteen pages of criticism on a fifteen-page paper.[103]

The training program was a success, however. The M.A. program boomed in enrollment, and these students were soon joined by senior fellows—thanks to grants from Carnegie and Rockefeller. The senior fellows had diverse backgrounds. Some, like Duke's John Curtiss (the only student to survive Robinson's grueling regimen before World War II) and Princeton's Cyril Black, had training in Slavic fields. Others (Dartmouth's Gordon Skilling and Berkeley's Julian

Figure 1.2. Geroid Robinson lecturing at the Russian Institute, 1947. Note
the copy of George Vernadsky's textbook on a student's desk, and the name of
Russian liberal Pavel Miliukov on the board.

Towster) had already remade themselves as Soviet specialists. And a few came
to the institute precisely in order to retool themselves as Soviet experts: Herbert
Marcuse (straight from OSS), Bertram Wolfe (from New York's radical circles),
and Rutgers's Robert Byrnes (originally trained as a French historian).[104]

Early students in the RI program included a number of future leaders in
the field, especially among historians (Samuel Baron, Ralph Fisher, Michael

Petrovich, John M. Thompson, and Theodore von Laue). Economist Hans Heymann was an early RI graduate, as were literature scholars Deming Brown and Rufus Mathewson and political scientists Alexander Dallin and Marshall Shulman. These scholars would have distinguished careers, advancing the field and helping to build its infrastructure. In quantitative terms, RI's greatest contribution would be government experts, not academics. Roughly 40% of the M.A. graduates between 1948 and 1952 ended up in some form of government service, half again as many as those pursuing doctorates. The State Department and CIA absorbed most of those going into government, with others going to work for military intelligence, Voice of America, or similar organizations. By 1953, Columbia had trained four times more Russia specialists in government service than the other centers combined. The RI also enrolled some two dozen students from government agencies, mainly from the uniformed military, though the United Nations and even an airline sent students to RI. These students were featured prominently in RI correspondence, both because the negotiations with the armed services were so difficult and because the students were proof of RI's commitment to serving the nation—which it defined, seemingly, as the national security apparatus.[105]

One aim of RI faculty research was to use scholarly information to calm the politically charged public discussions of the USSR. Here, the faculty lagged behind the initial expectations. Rockefeller staff were disappointed but not surprised. They had provided funds earmarked for faculty research projects after Robinson convinced them that the Russian field "teems with projects of major significance." For its first decade, though, Columbia administrators had to make excuses for the fact that they could not spend all the research funds nor show significant results. Faculty members were busy catching up on new books, said the dean, while Robinson instead cited the "heavy duties of training."[106] Academics elsewhere concurred: Harvard's Merle Fainsod called the RI "primarily a teaching institution." His colleague Clyde Kluckhohn offered the backhanded compliment that Columbia had done well "on the less exciting" tasks like teaching, leaving Harvard to take the lead in research. A dozen years later, Rockefeller staff sadly noted that Columbia's record remained "quite unimpressive."[107]

Robinson's publication record was the slimmest. He did not complete another book and published one article on Soviet "ideological combat," which had a wide readership in policy circles but was not an academic work.[108] Robinson's colleagues were only slightly more prolific. Mosely's articles in the 1940s and early 1950s were primarily non-academic discussions of current world events or thoughtful reflections on his wartime activities. His true métier was the government report, of which he wrote many even while working at Columbia. Hazard devoted the postwar period to preparing classroom materials, including a broad overview on Soviet government and a casebook on Soviet and international law. Simmons was more energetic, setting up an enterprise that shared Robinson's focus on ideology. His teaching—and, not coincidentally, his students' research—focused on the "social and ideological aspects of Russian [i.e., Soviet] literature." Together, the RI's literature group plumbed Soviet writings for indications of shifting political winds.[109] By far the most productive was economist Abram Bergson, who had received funding from the air force's RAND Corporation for his work on the Soviet economy. While the totals of scholarly production were impressive (sixteen books by RI staff and fellows in seven years), the numbers were not matched by influence.[110]

Even without tremendous research achievements, Columbia's RI rightfully claimed to be the founder of modern Russian Studies in the United States. Columbia faculty often celebrated less-visible training contributions over more visible ones like published (or classified) research. Another key contribution was even less visible than the legions of experts it sent into academe or government: Columbia and its staff built the basic infrastructure of the field that made future success possible. Working together with a broad network of Russia experts, Russophiles, and foundation officials, Columbia staff did the heavy lifting in some of the least glamorous and most important work of Cold War Sovietology.

Robinson and Mosely, in particular, envisioned Soviet studies as a coordinated national enterprise and invested a great deal of time and effort toward that end. Robinson proposed to John Gardner of the Carnegie Corporation that the field needed a national Council of Russian Studies to coordinate the field's activities, citing the prior history of "defeat, defeat, defeat."[111] Mosely agreed, emphasizing that it would also allow better coordination between academic and government work. The prewar ACLS Committee on Slavic Studies was clearly not up to these tasks; in spite of Mosely's efforts, the committee had few concrete accomplishments and needed broader and more active membership in order to meet the ambitious goals set for it.

The Rockefeller Foundation did not wait for war's end in order to invest in an expansion of Soviet studies. In early 1945, the foundation gave ACLS a $50,000 grant for the development of Slavic studies, the primary purpose of which was to send Ernest Simmons to the Soviet Union and Eastern Europe.[112] Simmons waited two years for a visa to enter the Soviet Union. When he finally could depart in June 1947, he traveled through Western and Central Europe, visiting many Slavic programs. He interpreted his job broadly: to develop "cultural relations" among the Slavic world, the United States, and Western Europe. Simmons's main hope had been to engage the Soviet Union in discussions, but wartime and postwar U.S.–Soviet cultural relations had been defined by "maddening frustration and lost causes"—to which Simmons

Figure 1.3. Philip Mosely and Fred Stolling, the associate editor of *Current Digest of the Soviet Press*, 1953. The editor, Leo Gruliow, was not photographed.

added many of the latter. He had hoped to send American students and scholars to the USSR, bring Soviet scholars to visit American universities (he had assembled a wish list from almost a dozen American universities), and obtain Soviet publications. The first two were ruled out, a Soviet official told him, because the universities there were already bursting at the seams with students. There was "virtually no hope," Simmons glumly reported, that scholarly materials would improve beyond their "present insufficient and often impractical level." He proposed stationing scholars in the American embassy—much as Tucker and Ruggles had done for OSS—but made little headway with the State Department. More successful was Simmons's plan to develop a "reading service of the Soviet newspaper and periodical press." Here, Simmons had the support of diplomats in the Moscow embassy, who had already been lobbying for the creation of a public translation service—and indeed, had already discussed the possibility with ACLS staff.[113]

Thus, the *Current Digest of the Soviet Press* (*CDSP*) was born. Its monthly (later, weekly) publications contained translations of articles from the major

Soviet newspapers, *Pravda* and *Izvestiia*, as well as a host of others, including not just dailies but important weeklies. As it expanded, *CDSP* produced
indexes that provided ready reference to past articles, all the more important
because there were no Soviet indexes with the same scope. Started in the garage
of the ACLS building in midtown Manhattan, it soon moved near the Russian
Institute. In spite of significant support from the Rockefeller and other foundations, it spent its early years in fiscal distress. The *CDSP* was supported more
by hard labor than soft money; editor Leo Gruliow reported working 62 con-
secutive hours in 1951 and even the "laziest" staff member logged 160 hours over
two weeks.[114] By 1951, the long-suffering Gruliow was writing daily missives
of complaint about the *CDSP*'s problems. He tried to interest the Associated
Press wire service, to no avail. By 1952, expenses ran $75,000 per year and income
only about two-thirds of that. Problems worsened by the late 1950s, as sponsors raised questions about financial irregularities.[115] There are scattered hints
that "government agencies" (i.e., CIA) were supporting the *CDSP* by the early
1960s if not before. The ACLS solicited "government support" to index the
CDSP and soon received broad assurances from CIA that it "would not allow
the *Digest* to go under."[116] The *CDSP* managed to survive its original subject,
existing today as *Current Digest of the Post-Soviet Press*. The *CDSP* soon left
Columbia's Russian empire and came under the aegis of the most important
organization of early Soviet studies, the Joint Committee on Slavic Studies
(JCSS).

Columbia hosted the new joint committee, a collaborative effort between
the ACLS and the SSRC. Its link to the ACLS's inactive prewar committee
was Philip Mosely, who served as the first JCSS chair; Simmons became secretary. Founded in 1948, the JCSS became a sort of executive committee for the
field, focusing on the unglamorous but all-important scholarly infrastructure.
In addition to sponsoring *Current Digest*, the committee took on numerous
dull tasks: dispersing surplus holdings of the Library of Congress, pursuing
library acquisitions from the USSR, petitioning the post office and customs
service to be sure that the American universities received those few books and
periodicals that were actually sent from Moscow, and preserving historical
materials on Russia already in American libraries.[117]

The JCSS also helped to create the U.S.–based *American Slavic and East
European Review* (*ASEER*). The *ASEER* actually began in World War II as a
foster child. With Britain at war in 1941, the British *Slavonic and East European
Review* relocated to the United States; the journal appeared between 1941
and 1945 as an "American series," edited by Mosely, Cross, and S. Harrison
Thomson at the University of Colorado (like Cross, a medievalist with some
Slavic interests). The other two editors quickly left, however, leaving the over-
burdened Cross as the sole managing editor—and he was barely managing,

overwhelmed by his editorial work for the medievalists' *Speculum* and by ASTP teaching. From the start, the arrangement was a temporary one, with the British organizers entitled to reclaim the journal when circumstances changed.[118]

To make matters worse for *ASEER*, it had to reckon with a competing journal, the new *Russian Review*, founded in 1941. The *Russian Review* began as an American version of a Russian "thick journal," combining memoirs, belles lettres, and translations alongside occasional scholarly articles. While the founders wanted the principal editor to be an American, one purpose of the review was to "utiliz[e] the many-sided talents of Russian émigrés." After Edmund Wilson declined the editorship, journalist W. H. Chamberlin agreed—so long, he insisted, as he did not have to edit anything. So Chamberlin's two assistants, Harvard historian Michael Karpovich and Dartmouth comparative literature professor Dimitri von Mohrenschildt, ran the journal, especially after Chamberlin was forced out in 1946 for being excessively anti-Soviet. Its nonacademic emphasis precluded support from ACLS.[119]

The end of European hostilities changed the landscape of American Slavic publications. The British reclaimed their journal in 1945. The Americans' new journal, *ASEER*, was immediately burdened with a shortage of submissions and a surplus of bills. Harvard agreed to continue hosting the journal, even after Cross's death in 1946, but discontinued its subsidies. The journal was essentially in receivership; ACLS had to pay for an editorial board meeting to plot the journal's future. Simmons became editor and had to scare up both scholarly and financial contributions. Four weeks before the closing date, he had not a single article or book review for his first issue and was still seeking to erase $5,500 in arrears. Mosely imposed on his friends at the Rockefeller Foundation, which reluctantly gave $6,000.[120] In spite of Simmons's own specialization, the journal would tilt toward the social sciences (roughly two-thirds of all articles) rather than literary topics. The *ASEER* survived its early scares, though it was hardly an instant success. John Hazard soon took over for Simmons, extending Columbia's responsibility for the journal. The shift away from literary studies was almost complete; history and political science dominated the journal, so much so that even the political scientist Hazard complained to a colleague about the near-total absence of literary scholarship in the pages of *ASEER*.[121] Yet the journal provided a means of building an intellectual community of Russian Studies scholars from different departments.

The JCSS also worked with government officials. In the late 1940s, it debated what it could do for former Soviet citizens in the United States. S. Harrison Thomson wanted the committee to help with the "hundreds of scholars or near-scholars from the countries that have been overrun by the Soviet brand of absolutism." Could they make a contribution to American Sovietology? he asked.[122] George Kennan had been asking the same question—and indeed, was promoting an organization that could be a "processing center" for émigré scholars, "fit[ting] them into American academic life." He worked with the CIA, State Department colleagues, and military intelligence to design a Eurasian Research Institute. It would be located in Washington for proximity to the Library of Congress and to the intelligence agencies it would advise.[123] Government officials like former OSS head William "Wild Bill" Donovan and Evron Kirkpatrick (State Department) were enthusiastic. Kennan had hoped that JCSS would sponsor such an outfit, but met with a vehement reaction: "American scholarship in Slavic Studies must now be developed by Americans [because] reliance upon Eastern Europeans was now a thing of the past," Mosely declared. Robinson, too, worried about recent émigrés; without "contact with liberal civilization," they would not be sufficiently objective.[124] Even as the network tried to build an academic field in the nation's service, it recognized the divide between academic and government work. While foundations were sympathetic, none would support it; the most compelling aspect, the head of the Rockefeller Foundation told Donovan, was the intelligence value—and this could be more appropriately handled in Washington.[125] Lacking funds, the Eurasian Research Institute died before it was born. By 1951, its proponents had created a similar institute in Munich with covert CIA funding and no academic cover.[126]

While shying away from CIA work with new émigrés, Philip Mosely nevertheless set up a similar operation as part of Columbia's growing Russia operations, what one friend called a "descendant" of Kennan's planned Eurasian Institute. The Research Program on the USSR, directed by Mosely, derived financial support from the Ford Foundation through another Mosely entity, the East European Fund. The bulk of the organizational work was done in the 1950s by two Columbia graduate students, Alexander Dallin and Robert Slusser.[127] The program paid émigré scholars relatively small amounts for pamphlets (in Russian) or monographs (in English) based on their expertise. About eighty short works appeared in Russian and about twenty in English (including titles on Belorussian theater and on Soviet peat moss). Only a few of these reports were cited widely, and those generally garnered praise as personal narratives rather than as research monographs. The final three English-language books were by far the best; edited by American scholars, they gathered shorter pieces by émigré scholars on Soviet historiography, the secret police, and education.[128] Even George Kennan, one of the research program's leading proponents, admitted that the program's main purpose was the "adaptation of these [émigrés] to life in this country."[129]

The final territory for Columbia's expanding Russia empire was gathering source material. Rockefeller staff strongly supported this aim, insisting that Columbia enumerate its plans for library holdings on Russian topics before receiving the grant that established the RI. When that grant was renewed in 1950, Columbia wanted to spend almost 20% of the total on books and periodicals.[130] Mosely also helped Harvard's Karpovich to gather the papers of distinguished Russian émigrés in Europe and the United States. With support from Kennan and others, these collections provided sources on the cultural and political history of modern Russia.[131] These materials were significant when Soviet archives—and indeed, the Soviet Union as a whole—remained off-limits to scholars in the 1950s.

A year after Stalin's death, America's academic Russia experts took stock of the field they had created. The assessment was spurred by a new entrant into the field of area studies, the Ford Foundation, which quickly outspent Carnegie and Rockefeller combined. After Henry Ford's death in 1947, it expanded dramatically and soon began investing heavily—to the tune of $1 million per year—to support area studies at American universities. Ford's International Training and Research programs quickly dwarfed all public and private funding sources for international studies in the United States. Ford officers consulted with the JCSS in October 1953 to help shape its new Slavic programs.[132] The tone was not especially celebratory: the assessments of area studies written in 1947 and 1948 still applied, the JCSS concluded; there were still insufficient resources for "dealing with the problem of foreign areas in general, as these relate to our national well-being." The OSS model of cooperative research had not been carried into the postwar years; "programs of systematic research" had yielded to individual research projects. On the training front, the results were more promising, with almost 100 Russia area specialists on university faculties and over 300 graduates of area programs. Yet there were still few if any experts on non-Russian nationalities in the USSR, let alone on the peoples of "satellite Europe."[133] Disciplinary range was similarly confined, with few economists, sociologists, anthropologists, and experts on Slavic art and music.

The field faced another, especially delicate, problem: political suspicions. Sovietology rose to prominence at almost exactly the same time as Senator Joseph McCarthy. By late 1954, three of Columbia's five core faculty faced accusations of disloyalty. McCarthy condemned Ernest Simmons as "a Communist at the time" he had led the wartime program at Cornell. In the next breath, he fingered John Hazard as "a member of the Communist conspiracy." Mosely defended the pair by saying that they may have made comments "that now appear unfounded," but were loyal Americans.[134] Beyond the glare of public hearings, Mosely lost his security clearance in 1954, probably for his involvement in the Institute of Pacific Relations. Like the more famous security case against atomic physicist J. Robert Oppenheimer, the loss of his clearance would endanger Mosely's work. He could still conduct academic research, but would have to cut his ties to the nine or more agencies for which he regularly consulted.[135] Thanks to support from a who's who list of the foreign policy establishment, Mosely's clearance was quickly reinstated. By the end of 1954, America's Soviet experts had survived the security inquests—indeed, better than the Grand Inquisitor himself, who faced censure from his colleagues only months after haranguing Simmons and Hazard. These political problems were a direct by-product of Sovietologists' government work; after all, McCarthy wreaked havoc from his post on a subcommittee of the Senate Committee on Government Operations. The investigations hardly dissuaded the scholars discussed here—even those with well-documented involvement in left-wing organizations—from taking on government work. Later historians have contemplated the effects of the security inquisitions: scholars opting for "safe" topics, students opting to study different regions, or seminar participants taking extra care not to appear pro-Soviet. These decisions, which reflected a climate of fear, were unfortunately the sorts that left few written traces.

In 1954, Robinson had opened a report to the Rockefeller Foundation as follows: "If the Second World War had not brought the Russian Institute into being, it would surely have to be created now."[136] He was surely right. The need for Russia experts in government and academe was, if anything, more important in 1954 than it was in 1944. Yet it was the wartime work that determined the priorities and shapes of the key institutions of what would become Cold War Sovietology. Columbia's Russian empire, centered around the extraordinary training programs at the Russian Institute, learned from the wartime experiences and built on wartime foundations (and Foundations).

CHAPTER 2

SOCIAL SCIENCE SERVES THE STATE IN WAR AND COLD WAR

World War II cast a long shadow over research, not just teaching, in Soviet Studies. As American-Soviet tensions escalated in the 1940s, the demand for more immediate research results, closely tied to government needs, was all the more pressing. The Sovietization of Eastern Europe gave rise to fears of Soviet power encompassing all of Europe. Soviet propaganda became increasingly belligerent, predicting (even welcoming) imminent conflict with the capitalist world. The handful of Russia experts were scattered throughout the government. George Kennan went from the Moscow embassy to the National War College and then to the State Department's internal think tank in a matter of months, his peregrinations a sign of the desperate need for people who understood the emerging opponent. Journalists covered the flow of daily events, but few of them had the exposure or the experience necessary for a thorough understanding of what was behind Stalin's decisions. Soviet life was even more of an enigma, as the few Westerners in the USSR were almost totally isolated from Soviet officials, let alone ordinary citizens. The need for good information about the Soviet Union was as great as the obstacles to obtaining it.

Veterans of wartime social science projects were unfazed by these challenges and sought to use the techniques they had developed during the war to understand the new antagonist. During World War II, scholars had poured into Washington, D.C., from all over the country, joining large-scale research projects that were oriented toward solving practical problems rather than advancing knowledge. Harvard social scientists were well represented in this group. The lofty aspiration to use social science to improve society had long been a part of American life, but in few moments and in few places was that aspiration as fervently held as at Harvard in the 1940s. Sociologists and anthropologists joined physicists and doctors in the war effort. Samuel Stouffer, for instance, worked in the U.S. Army's Research Branch, producing a multivolume study of American soldiers. A landmark in the application of social science to military issues, it relied on surveys administered to enlisted personnel to describe the sociology of army life and, importantly, to propose changes in how to organize the army.[1] After the war, Stouffer returned to Harvard to run a new organization, the Laboratory of Social Relations, created to host contract research projects like those undertaken during the war. It became only one node of a growing network of social scientists in government, foundations, and universities that was dedicated to the belief that social scientists could and should serve their country.[2]

Stouffer's colleague Clyde Kluckhohn headed another famous wartime research project. Though originally a specialist on the Navajo, Kluckhohn spent the war trying to understand Japan; he was on a team that included anthropologists Ruth Benedict and Margaret Mead at the Office of War Information's Foreign Morale Analysis Division. He and his colleagues boasted that their knowledge of Japanese culture had saved untold American lives at the end of the war. They concluded that Japanese attachment to their emperor was a major factor in civilian and military morale and argued that American propaganda should suggest that the emperor would survive the impending U.S. victory.[3] This heady experience encouraged confidence bordering on hubris. Kluckhohn and his colleagues concluded that cultural and linguistic knowledge mattered much less than the techniques they applied. His work on Japanese culture, after all, had not required any area-specific or language competence, only a good background in anthropology.

In the immediate aftermath of World War II, Kluckhohn and his colleagues celebrated their field's contributions to the war effort and lobbied for its expansion in the postwar period. They breathlessly proclaimed that the "new social sciences" could shape the postwar period as much as atomic physics had shaped the war itself.[4] The goal, as Margaret Mead put it, was for scholars to help in "devising new [social and political] forms to keep human beings safe in a narrowing world." Scholars needed government help to fulfill this promise, Kluckhohn's colleague Talcott Parsons noted in a letter to the *Washington Post*. In urgent but awkward prose, he called on President Harry S Truman to "most vigorously explore the needs which social science must fill in a world equipped for suicide." The new social sciences, Kluckhohn agreed, could have "consequences as revolutionary as those of atomic energy."[5] After the war, this new form of social science (known variously as behavioral science, social relations, or human relations) became a fad among policy makers; as one cynical academic noted after a trip to Washington a few years later, "everybody, sans exception, is doing Human Resources Research. Human Resources research, in fact, has become, next to mink, the greatest single Washington enterprise."[6] Mead, Parsons, and Kluckhohn took important lessons from their wartime service: the need to relax disciplinary boundaries; the value of collaborative work, often on a large scale; and the importance of applied projects. These lessons shaped the work climate at Harvard's new Department of Social Relations, its adjunct laboratory, and, soon enough, the Russian Research Center.

Parsons was the leading ideologue and chief impresario for these new social sciences. He called for combining the insights of social psychology, cultural anthropology, and sociology in order to understand the structures and functions of modern institutions. The foremost question for Parsons was social stability: under what terms, and in what institutions, would individuals put aside their own narrower interests in the name of social cohesion? Behavioralists explained with a reassuring circularity that the existence of a certain institution—family, school, political party, even a way of thinking—meant that it must help to promote stability.[7] Parsons perfected the sociology of the status quo; the job of the sociologist was to study the "*consequences* [of modern society] for the individual," not vice versa. Individuals who failed to adjust to their prescribed role might cause social friction, though their challenges to the social order stood little chance of success. Conflicts over resource allocation or political ideas (perhaps even conflicts in general) were atavisms—as were the older disciplines, like economics or political science, that studied them. Only by integrating the social sciences around the behavioral approach could scholars solve the major social and political problems of the day.[8] Harvard's behavioralists pursued an ambitious research agenda that transcended older disciplinary boundaries. They worked on many fronts, from theoretical (developing a "general theory of action") to applied (inventing the field of cognitive psychology). There was a general feeling of excitement in the Department of Social Relations in those years, a sense that its scholars, individually and collectively, were on the verge of major innovations that would reshape not only social science but society itself.[9]

The idea of applying behavioral science to study America's postwar antagonist emerged as early as 1946—but not at Harvard. The initial spark came from Frederick Osborn, a trustee of the Carnegie Corporation of New York. Osborn had parlayed his family connections to Franklin Roosevelt and his interest in social science into a post overseeing army research like Stouffer's during the war. Afterward, he served on the U.S. delegation to the United Nations Atomic Energy Commission, then debating the international control of atomic technology. Perplexed by the intransigent behavior of his Soviet counterparts, Osborn hoped (as he later recalled) that "a psychologist might be better able to comprehend" what the Russians were doing. He turned to an energetic young program officer at Carnegie, psychologist John Gardner, for help; Gardner soon joined the U.S. delegation as an advisor.[10] Even psychological help was not enough to help the UN commission, however. The problem was not related merely to the psychology of the Soviet negotiators, but to the growing antagonisms between the superpowers; more than one historian has identified the UN atomic debates as the starting point of the Cold War.[11]

Neither Gardner nor Osborn were deterred by this failure. Both held steadfast in their belief that behavioral sciences would help to solve world problems.[12]

Gardner sought an opportunity to demonstrate the value of these behavioral sciences by analyzing the actions of America's ally-turned-adversary. He spent the spring of 1947 seeking advice from psychologists and anthropologists coast to coast about where to establish a center for the study of Russian behavior and whom to hire. From the start, Gardner and his correspondents looked for people like themselves, valuing intelligence and wartime service over area expertise; economist John Kenneth Galbraith, for instance, was one of many non-experts suggested. Gardner also went to Washington to survey classified government work on Russian behavior, finding a warm reception but little research of note.[13] His proposal: Carnegie should move right away to take on the "problem of understanding Russia and the Russian"; the best path toward understanding, he believed, was to focus on the new behavioral sciences. By July 1947, he had settled on Harvard to help meet his goal, which was to take the study of Russian behavior "from a free-floating idea into a working program with a roof (presumably ivy covered) over its head and identifiable figures scurrying around it, and one or more men of sense and wisdom to lead it gently by the hand." True to his enthusiasm for behavioral science, Gardner consulted Parsons about the project and wanted Kluckhohn to serve as the director. Harvard administrators, though generally enthusiastic about the project, refused to call it an institute for fear it might become permanent.[14] These minor issues quickly solved, Carnegie sent $75,000 to Harvard as an exploratory grant, with the promise of ten times that sum should the explorations pan out.

The center's new leaders were certainly "men of sense and reason"—and good connections. But they were not, by any stretch of the imagination, Russia experts. Harvard's faculty included many scholars with knowledge of and experience in Russia: political scientist Merle Fainsod and émigrés like historian Michael Karpovich and sociologist Pitirim Sorokin (whose thorny relations with Parsons would have excluded him in any case). Yet none of these scholars was involved in the creation of the Russian Research Center. Instead, Parsons served on the center's executive committee alongside Kluckhohn, economist Edward Mason (dean of the Graduate School of Public Administration), and Donald McKay (French history and chair of the International and Regional Studies Program). All had served in one or another capacity in wartime Washington (except Parsons, who did his wartime work on campus), but none had been to the USSR nor engaged in serious study of Marxism, Communism, or Russia.

The Department of Social Relations and its related Laboratory soon became the intellectual inspiration for the Russian Research Center. The founding director of the RRC was Kluckhohn, a leading member of the department. And the department's founder, Parsons, was only the second-greatest contributor to the center in his own household; he served on the center's executive committee but his wife, Helen Parsons, was the chief RRC administrator for some two decades.[15] From Kluckhohn's perspective, though, the Russian center was an important adjunct to the department; both existed to further the behavioral sciences. The RRC would have projects on Soviet economics and Soviet politics, but its main purpose would be to seek insights about the USSR available through social psychology, cultural anthropology, and sociology. Envisioning their own work as uniting the best attributes of these disciplines, behavioral scientists modeled their academic research on the faculty club lunches and sherry hours with colleagues in other departments. They would use the study of Russia as a chance to hone—and to teach—behavioral science techniques. The training emphasis meant that the center had a reserve army of graduate student affiliates, which facilitated large-scale research projects. In this context, Kluckhohn's cheerfully acknowledged lack of expertise on Russia and Communism was barely an issue. His appointment as director of the RRC over many Harvard faculty members with closer personal and academic acquaintance with Russia exemplified the preference (in Parsons's condescending phrase) for "general social scientists" over "experts in [an] older sense."[16]

The speaker at the center's inaugural research seminar was Geoffrey Gorer, a British psychiatrist best known for his swaddling theory. He argued that the tight swaddling of Russian infants resulted in either a propensity to violence or feelings of helplessness and passivity; this explained both Stalin's personality and his success in cowing a nation. Gorer, without visiting Russia, made broad claims for a timeless Russian character, the same in 1866 as in 1948, he told his Harvard audience. In spite of Kluckhohn's enthusiasm for this sort of work, seminar participants were unconvinced; they criticized Gorer sharply in his presence and rarely mentioned him thereafter. Subsequent seminars instead established the primacy of sociological analysis over psychology in the center's studies of the Soviet Union.[17]

Kluckhohn envisioned his job as equal parts scholarship and government service. "Both from the point of view of scholarship and of the national interest I can think of nothing that is more urgent or important" than the RRC, he wrote to Gardner as the discussions began. Gardner and Osborn, meanwhile, had already confirmed that government officials would "cooperate" with Harvard's new center.[18] The center frequently performed small research/analysis tasks for outsiders, including officials from the military, the State Department, and "other government agencies" (which, in the argot of the field, usually meant the CIA). Even before it opened its doors, key faculty members met with the CIA director, who hoped to "establish [a] continuous relationship between their organization and ours."[19] The relationship may have been a little too continuous; two years later, the center was swamped by government queries. "In some weeks the deluge has been so heavy," complained Kluckhohn to Harvard's provost, "that the research of six or seven members [i.e., more than half] of the staff has been virtually brought to a standstill." Kluckhohn proposed that President Truman's National Security Council circulate a directive that would require all government contacts with the Harvard center to go through the CIA office in Boston—with which RRC relations "have been uniformly pleasant." One Harvard administrator worried, however, that relying on the CIA as a gatekeeper might "cause general resentment" at other agencies. Nevertheless, even that skeptic agreed that, "in view of the confidential nature of much of the Research Center's work," having the CIA serve as a conduit was "most reasonable."[20]

At the same time that the RRC maintained close but informal ties with the CIA, some of its members also joined a large-scale classified research project. The project began when the State Department asked Harvard's neighbor the Massachusetts Institute of Technology about ways to improve Voice of America transmissions to Eastern Europe and the USSR and to overcome Soviet jamming of American radio. The scholars at MIT had broader aims than merely solving the technical problem of jamming, however; its leaders wanted to shape the broadcasts themselves. Project Troy, as it came to be called, would build the wooden horse of myth and also determine its contents—the ideas to be smuggled through the Iron Curtain.[21] While MIT was the official State Department contractor, it was in most other ways an equal partner with its Cambridge neighbor. Especially as Troy looked beyond narrow technical questions, it needed social scientists. Kluckhohn and his social relations colleague Jerome Bruner were members of the Troy staff, while Alex Inkeles (social relations) and two historians, John King Fairbank and Robert Lee Wolff, were consultants.[22] Project Troy's goal was to develop the ways and means to "induce the dissipation [*sic*] of the Soviet Union from within, with or without war." An ulterior motive was to support the cause of social science, both at the State Department and at MIT. State had yet to establish close connections with universities but did not want to cede the ground to Defense.[23] In mid-February 1951, the Troy staff completed an eighty-one-page final report, with appendixes covering everything from "coherent transmitter arrays" and "moon relays" to population problems, advance planning for Stalin's death, defector policy, and a broad outline for "political warfare" against the Soviet Union.[24] For all of its range and heft, though, the Troy report was maddeningly vague about the next steps.

Take, for instance, Clyde Kluckhohn's outline of a program to deal with high-level defectors from Eastern bloc nations. Kluckhohn promoted his defector policy to a captive audience at the Pentagon's Research and Development Board (RDB). Kluckhohn's panel called for a policy regarding defectors—their treatment in American hands, their use for intelligence purposes, and political warfare strategies that might spur defection.[25] State Department officials dismissed Kluckhohn's ideas as "delightfully vague" because they did not take into account current defector programs.[26] Fair enough, but that was undoubtedly because those programs were so highly classified that even Kluckhohn's Top Secret clearance was insufficient; indeed, all twelve pages of the policy document NSC 86/1, have remained classified into the twenty-first century. The redaction of NSC 86/1 and related documentation prevents any conclusive determination about Kluckhohn's influence but one sociologist with strong Pentagon connections credited this work on defections for a successful tactic during the Korean War.[27]

Even without full access to essential information, Troy scholars felt the lure of doing policy-relevant work for senior government officials. They recalled the project as a remarkable, even life-changing experience, and they wanted more. Bruner, for instance, recalled the group of scholars who convened in MIT's suburban "bunker," with frequent visits from Washington dignitaries, as "the best club I ever belonged to."[28] They were pleased, then, when a new program, Troy Plus, followed from their initial work. This Troy Plus would carry out some of the research proposed in the original report and would experiment with a new form of organization, one that would be (in the words of the MIT president) an "MIT Project" yet would have a "direct link with the State Department through the Under Secretary" and his staff. The president of MIT, James Killian, appointed economist Max Millikan to lead the new Center for International Studies. One of the contending titles—Cambridge Institute of Advanced Studies—was perhaps more accurate.[29] It would be a joint Harvard-MIT affair, but housed at MIT to evade Harvard's restriction on classified research.

Troy Plus developed a project on the susceptibility of the Communist world to political warfare, the Soviet Vulnerability Project. Though the project was originally sponsored by the State Department, the transition from Troy to Troy Plus also involved a shift to CIA responsibility, likely because the agency was better shielded from the quickening drumbeat of congressional investigations.[30] Economic historian W. W. Rostow led the Soviet Vulnerability Project, with most of the expertise coming from Harvard's RRC. The Massachusetts Institute of Technology served as the conduit for funds, paying the RRC a portion of the academics' salaries to "buy" their time away from teaching and other Harvard duties. The amounts varied over the next three years, but MIT paid the Harvard center well over $10,000 per year.[31] The arrangement was regularly approved by presidents, provosts, and deans; indeed, Harvard provost Paul H. Buck hoped to participate in the center work himself, even though his scholarly work was on nineteenth-century America.[32] The Soviet Vulnerability Project reflected Rostow's boundless energy, ambition, and confidence. No Soviet expert himself, Rostow would nevertheless lead a large study of that country—much like Kluckhohn was doing at Harvard. Rostow convened an Advisory Board on Soviet Bloc Studies, consisting of the ubiquitous Philip Mosely, diplomat Charles

Bohlen, Vice Admiral Leslie Stevens, and Director of Central Intelligence Allen Dulles.[33] The roster of RRC faculty and advanced graduate students working on the project included social relations faculty Raymond Bauer, Alex Inkeles, Clyde Kluckhohn, and Barrington Moore Jr. as well as historian Richard Pipes and political scientist Adam Ulam. History student Robert Daniels served as one of Rostow's chief assistants, assembling materials, drafting chapters, and fact checking. "It cannot be too strongly emphasized," read the preface of the final report, "that this report is a joint product of Harvard and MIT."[34]

The Soviet Vulnerability Project's report combined analysis and policy recommendations. The main task, following from the Troy report, was to develop a strategy to undermine the Soviet government's control over its population and territories through a combination of propaganda and diplomacy; there was also a brief section on how political warfare might evolve in the case of armed conflict. In spite of the assertive, even aggressive, tone of the report, it also laid to rest one notion frequently bandied around Washington: the idea that the United States might be able to encourage the secession of some of the key Soviet republics, especially Ukraine and Armenia.[35] Supporting these classified recommendations were a half dozen reports that summarized various policy options: efforts to pry Eastern European satellites away from the Soviet grasp, the expansion of radio programming, and planning for the death of Stalin. This last item was based on an informal exercise at the Russian Research Center predicting what would happen after Stalin's death.[36] Underlying the recommendations was a fifty-page report on the past, present, and future of Soviet society. The key to Soviet history, Rostow argued with more certainty than evidence, was the Bolshevik regime's pursuit of power, the "maintenance of its own absolute internal power over Russian society, and the maximization over time of its power vis-à-vis the external world."[37] Ideology, Russian nationalism, and economic goals did not matter; they were merely justifications for a single Soviet leader to pursue power. Just as the Soviet past was defined by this single-minded pursuit, so too was the Soviet future dependent on "the evolution of Soviet power" during the remainder of Stalin's life and especially after his death. The report, "The Dynamics of Soviet Society," after some editing, appeared as a book in 1953. The title is misleading; Soviet "society" appeared primarily as an object of Politburo activities, or at most as providing a problem that the Politburo needed to solve. Soviet society, furthermore, did not seem to be dynamic at all; it was defined primarily by apathy and inertia.[38] Title aside, Rostow wrote a book about Soviet politics, not Soviet society. If later scholars were looking for the ultimate top-down approach to the study of the Soviet Union, *The Dynamics of Soviet Society* was it.

Rostow used the report to develop a contingency plan for U.S. policy after Stalin's death, one that he would help to implement.[39] Daniels was so appalled with the final result that he tried to submit a "minority report" attacking

Rostow's work and then insisted on having his name removed as a coauthor. His fight with Rostow sparked a year-long controversy that led to Kluckhohn informing Daniels's employer, Indiana University, about behavior he considered inappropriate.[40] Mosely more discreetly disavowed any involvement in the project, asking to be excluded from the advisory board and from any public acknowledgment.[41] The Troy and Soviet Vulnerability projects hardly provided successful models of government-academic relations; the former was of limited policy use, and the latter did not generate meaningful scholarship. Whatever use the results were for policy (and those are questionable), the final product made no scholarly contribution; even its main author called the work a "child's guide" to the USSR.[42] Rostow's Troy Plus work bore striking similarities to Kluckhohn's during the war. Both were short-term, intensive projects by ambitious scholars unencumbered by fear or expertise, conducted for a government agency. Each produced both classified and unclassified results. Kluckhohn's most important contribution to Soviet Studies, the Refugee Interview Project (RIP), would share these traits while achieving far greater success.

Harvard's behavioral approach required detailed evidence about Soviet institutions and individuals. Such information, however, was especially hard to come by. The RRC opened near the nadir of Soviet openness to the rest of the world. Stalin's culture tsar, Andrei Zhdanov, was leading a vicious attack, the *Zhdanovshchina*, against "cosmopolitanism," which came to mean any sort of connection with the outside world. While Jews were special targets of this campaign, any hint of contact with the West was suspect. Newspapers fulminated fiercely if inconsistently about Western poverty, decadence, imperialism, and exploitation. American diplomats in Moscow felt embattled and alone, with few contacts outside their own compound. This was hardly a propitious moment for fieldwork in the USSR.

Harvard scholars activated their Washington connections to pull back or peek around the Iron Curtain. Their first hope was to send Fainsod to Moscow under the cover of "temporary cultural attaché" in the U.S. embassy there. The effort reveals not just the scholars' creativity in order to study Soviet life first-hand, but also their belief that the RRC had the power and status of a government agency. State Department officials did not share this belief and scuttled the plan.[43]

With entry to Moscow blocked, RRC staff looked for other sources to learn about Soviet life. They quickly fixed on displaced persons (DPs) from the USSR living in the western zones of Germany. The paths of Soviet citizens to DP camps in Germany were diverse. Some were Red Army deserters, prisoners of war, or soldiers detached from their units in the chaos of the war's closing days. Other DPs came to Germany as forced laborers (*Ostarbeiteren*) from among the 8 million living in Soviet territories occupied by Germany. While estimates of the number of DPs varied widely, there were likely as many as 40,000–50,000 former Soviet citizens in Germany. Most were in Bavaria, in the American occupation zone.[44] Occupation authorities made intelligence gathering among war refugees a high priority at the start of the occupation in 1945. By 1948, army intelligence was finished with the vast majority of DPs, who were still living in DP camps.

The University of Michigan's Survey Research Center (SRC) soon started conducting research with these DPs. Run by sociologists who had worked in wartime Washington, SRC signed a contract with the U.S. Air Force's classified Air Research Unit at the Library of Congress to "prepare basic social-psychological guides to air attack on the Soviet Union," helping to determine both post-attack propaganda and (as the report eerily put it) "propaganda of the deed," the air attack itself. Planning these attacks, the scholars argued in their air force report, required detailed knowledge about the fabric of Soviet society, the forces of cohesion as well as division.[45] Scholars planned to interview 150 Americans who had worked in the USSR and an equal number of DPs who had ended up in the United States. With the help of Menshevik historian Boris Nicolaevsky, SRC also planned to administer surveys to "old émigrés" who could speak about Russian culture more generally. Michigan staff also managed to interview about 100 Soviet DPs in Germany. The Michigan staff faced formidable obstacles. Only a small percentage of potential informants agreed to speak to the researchers, and most of them spoke with a mood of great distrust.[46] More important were the divergent goals. While SRC staff wanted to produce a classified work of social science, the air force sponsors seemed interested only in targeting, including seeking information about a list of thirty Soviet cities "which ought or ought not to be bombed."[47]

The RRC leaders viewed the DP population with cautious curiosity at first; they were "not convinced" that DP interviews would yield sufficient information to justify the "large assignment of personnel" required. Even though Kluckhohn had consulted with the Air Research Unit about the SRC work, Harvard staff ignored the study.[48] In dozens of boxes of correspondence and reports, there is no evidence that they drew any lessons, positive or negative, from the Michigan work. Perhaps that confidence was justified; the Harvard model of "big social science" was successful on its own terms. It highlighted social science techniques and large-scale research to provide useful information for U.S. policy.

As the Michigan project concluded, Harvard began its own work with displaced persons in Germany. Parsons spent the summer of 1948 touring Germany, investigating both the Eurasian Institute and the possibility of larger-scale work interviewing DPs.[49] On a related mission was George Fischer, a rising star among Harvard graduate students. Fischer had fluent Russian from living in Moscow as a child, the son of journalist-cum-sympathizer Louis Fischer.

He knew a great deal about the Soviet refugees in Germany through his work with the army's Counter-Intelligence Corps immediately after the war. And he was up to date on the latest developments thanks to his mother's work for the International Refugee Organization in Munich.[50] The young Fischer dove into émigré life in Munich, where monarchists and Social Democrats fought bitterly to represent the "true" Russia. Going to the camps that a colleague called "cold" and "squalid," Fischer found "bedraggled refugees" who were scared, cut off from their old society, and unable to integrate into their new one.[51] Amid this confusion, Fischer saw great promise for an institute of émigré scholars and also for a large-scale interview project. He served as the advance guard for Harvard's interview work and as the "spiritual father" of the Institute for the Study of the History and Culture of the USSR in Munich, funded by the CIA.[52]

Fischer's and Parsons's German sojourns were successful enough that the RRC soon sent another pair of scholars. With a grant from the air force, political scientist Merle Fainsod spent the summer of 1949 "interrogating non-returnees and recent escapees" in Germany with the help of Paul Friedrich, the son of Fainsod's colleague Carl. Fainsod wrote about the DPs with uncharacteristic enthusiasm: "they provide a living reservoir of fresh data on the Soviet Union...for which there is no parallel in the world today." Kluckhohn was not convinced. He shared his colleague's excitement, believing that the RRC was in a position to take full advantage of the "psychological, sociological, and to some extent the political and economic intelligence potentialities" of DP research, but still wondered if his World War II work on Japan—a handful of senior scholars studying "culture from a distance"—might be a better use of time and money. Kluckhohn proposed "setting up a branch" of the RRC on an air force base.[53]

Kluckhohn's approach to the air force was well timed and well directed, confirming his reputation as a Washington operator. Kluckhohn's appointment to the Pentagon's RDB introduced him to air force personnel who shared his enthusiasm for applied behavioral science. Founded in 1947, the air force was enthusiastic about social science in general. It was by far the most consistent military customer for civilian expertise—so much so that some old-line brass fretted in the 1940s about a "long-haired air force." This interest in social science led to the creation of the U.S. Air Force's Human Resources Research Institute (HRRI), two related institutes, the RAND Corporation (originally part of Douglas Airline Corporation), and the Air Research Unit at the Library of Congress.[54]

The push for social science came not just from Harvard but from two air force officials with sociological training. The first, Lt. Col. Raymond Sleeper, had earned a master's degree from Harvard's Department of Social Relations in 1949, having taken social theory courses with Parsons and anthropological theory with Kluckhohn. Sleeper wanted to apply his Harvard education to air force strategy, envisioning an aerial contribution to psychological warfare—a growth industry in early Cold War military doctrine.[55] Sleeper coined the term "air persuasion," which amounted to an escalating bombardment strategy to "encourage international behavior that will build toward a solid world peace."[56] His Project Control convened a classified panel of academic advisors, including Frederick Barghoorn (Yale), Alexander Dallin (Columbia), and Kluckhohn, and earned an endorsement from John Gardner at the Carnegie Corporation. Nevertheless, many government officials remained deeply skeptical. Diplomats George Frost Kennan and Charles Bohlen objected (as Sleeper recollected) "violently" to the notion of air power as an aspect of psychological warfare. Project Control required detailed information on the "political-psychological vulnerability of Russia," so he spoke with his "friends at Harvard," and suddenly the Russian Research Center's small and tentative forays into DP interviews had found a major sponsor.[57]

Raymond V. Bowers, director of the air force's HRRI, shared Sleeper's faith in the military use of social science. Bowers, too, had been inspired by behavioral science research. He received his Ph.D. in sociology from the University of Minnesota in 1934 and had received advanced training in social psychology at Columbia and in "experimental sociology" at Yale. In 1942, he joined the war effort, moving after the war to the Pentagon's RDB and then to HRRI.[58]

Together, Sleeper and Bowers helped to stake out a wide swath of common ground between the air force and Harvard. These two, along with Kluckhohn, desired the direct application of behavioral sciences to the pressing international problems of the day. Kluckhohn praised the interview project as representing "just about the best chance our kind of social science has to prove itself for the Air Force." As another air force officer noted, the planned interview project would be the "largest and most important" work ever undertaken by the air force's social science wing. The stakes went well beyond pure knowledge. As Sleeper wrote to Kluckhohn, "if our utilization of the social sciences in combating communism is not immediate and at once," atomic Armageddon would surely follow.[59] Bowers and Sleeper shared Kluckhohn's broad mission, treating with utmost seriousness the aspirations to develop new social scientific methods while at the same time providing support and hands-on training for cadres of graduate students.[60] The Refugee Interview Project thus reveals as much about the academicization of military life as it does about the militarization of academic life.

While Kluckhohn was the titular head of the RIP, the day-to-day work was in the hands of two junior scholars who were more knowledgeable about Soviet affairs. Alex Inkeles was a perfect fit: trained in sociology, Inkeles picked up Russian in the Cornell summer intensive program. He had already learned about Soviet politics "on [his] father's knee," as he put it, while growing up in radical circles in Brooklyn. Inkeles was an ambitious young scholar trying to understand the whole world at once. A lifelong friend recalled his "turbine mind, with endless facts at his fingertips [as he] professed opinions on all subjects" at great speed. This combination of talent, training, and ambition helped Inkeles to land a position in the USSR Division of the Office of Strategic Services, where at twenty-four he was among the youngest analysts on the staff.[61] After the war, his OSS boss, Geroid Tanquary Robinson, brought him to Columbia, where he finished his Ph.D. in sociology in 1949—by which point he was already employed at Harvard. Only two years later, Harvard granted him tenure outside of any department—a move that President James Conant made, in his own words, "with extreme reluctance" because of its unprecedented nature. Conant was greatly impressed with Inkeles, whom he considered a "sociologist whose special interest is in comparative work," making no mention of his Russia expertise.[62]

Inkeles would have approved of this portrayal since he too rejected the claim that he was a Soviet specialist; he was instead a sociologist who happened to study the Soviet case.[63] Such broad aspirations were not fully apparent in his first book, *Public Opinion in Soviet Russia* (1950). An analysis of the "structure and functioning" of Soviet media, including radio, press, television, and agitation, it was of primary interest to Soviet specialists. Though Kluckhohn praised the book (the first in the RRC monograph series) as a contribution to "pure science" as well as Cold War knowledge, the book contained little of the generalizing interest that would define Inkeles's later works.[64] *Public Opinion* was more about Soviet efforts to shape public opinion than about its role in Soviet politics. Its principal contribution—no small one—was to identify the extent to which the Soviet regime relied on persuasion, and not just coercion, to garner support. Inkeles then prepared what appears to be a government briefing based on his book. Entitled "The Soviet Union as a Psychological Warfare Target," it outlined Soviet media organization, emphasized the general stability and cohesiveness of the Soviet system, and suggested messages that might separate party elites from the rest of the population.[65]

Inkeles owed his position to his ambitions—in line with Harvard's—to develop a sociology of modern society. He was not alone; Barrington Moore Jr. received nondepartmental tenure at the same time as Inkeles for similar reasons and with the same reservations. Their success shows just how closely the center's work on Russia was tied to the behavioral sciences. Talcott Parsons, the chief promoter, expected from the start that the study of Russia would contribute to social scientific knowledge. What, he asked at one of the first sessions of the RRC seminar, can we learn from Russia about the process and impact of industrialization more generally? A better understanding of the Soviet Union

Figure 2.1. Alex Inkeles lecturing to the Social Relations Club at Harvard on "Letters to the Editor, Soviet Style," early 1950s.

would feed the grand integration of social knowledge that Parsons believed to be imminent.[66] This intellectual goal was not an academic cover story for nefarious classified work, but a central element of RRC's identity and aspirations, at least during Kluckhohn's six years as director.

The fact that the RRC accepted large government contracts and that its faculty maintained long-term consulting arrangements with military services and intelligence agencies did not undercut this self-conception of the high academic purposes of the center. Indeed, the model of applied social sciences that Kluckhohn promoted in the late 1940s encouraged scholarly connections to such agencies. The newly created CIA and the newly independent air force, by Kluckhohn's logic, were more advanced in their thinking than those backward agencies that only cared about economics. Insouciantly believing that like-minded men (and a small handful of women like anthropologists Benedict and Mead) could promote both scholarly and national interests, Kluckhohn and his staff could not imagine government work as presenting any challenge to academic autonomy.

This happy innocence would soon be tested by the interview project's operations. Even with common purposes and perspectives and even with the high stakes that participants saw for their work, military-academic cooperation required intensive negotiation. One initial sticking point involved the classification of project work. Kluckhohn insisted that the reports should be unclassified, allowing project staff to publish and therefore advance their academic careers; open research would be a "condition of our acceptance of any contract." He recognized that the air force would benefit from recommendations and analyses that went beyond journal articles. He compromised by insisting publicly that all of the work of the project—first called, portentously, the "Working Model of the Soviet Social System"—would be open. At the same time, the air force would hire these same scholars as consultants to write "certain classified reports."[67] Kluckhohn saw this arrangement as the best way of "avoiding a somewhat embarrassing situation in terms of general university policy." This compromise allowed Harvard to meet the air force's demand for "operational" information while meeting Harvard's demand that the project would be "general social science." Kluckhohn would spend the summer of 1953 using RIP data to write classified reports for HRRI and air force intelligence.[68] Potential embarrassment avoided, the tension between open social science and intelligence work nevertheless came to define the Harvard project.

The question of security clearances for interviewers soon followed the dispute over classification. As Inkeles and Kluckhohn recruited Russian-speaking graduate students and young professors to conduct the interviews, they had to negotiate access to the DPs. Entry into the DP camps required military permits, which in turn required a security clearance at the level of Secret. Unlike Kluckhohn and Inkeles (who would remain stateside), most of the interviewers had no such status. After determining that clearances were "unavoidable," the RIP leaders dealt with the situation by marrying their experience in government agencies with their knowledge of bureaucracies. The U.S. Air Force would grant temporary clearances just before the group departed for Germany—permissible so long as they had submitted personal security questionnaires seeking permanent clearances. Given the long processing time, the group would already be home from Germany before the investigations had concluded.[69]

The solution to the security dilemma worked perfectly, but inadvertently revealed something about the leftward political leanings of early Sovietologists. While none of the interviewers' security questionnaires listed memberships in the Communist Party or other left-wing parties of the 1930s and 1940s, almost half had a connection to one or another group whose history was intertwined with that of the Communists. Two groups in particular attracted the attention of authorities: the American Student Union and the American Veterans Committee. About half of the interviewers who had attended American universities belonged to one or the other. The two organizations encapsulate the trajectory of the Communist Party's "Popular Front" policies in the late 1930s and beyond. The student group was born of a joint Socialist-Communist effort in 1935; it split into factions within two years and came under Communist control in 1939. (Some of the Sovietologists involved in the ASU had left by this point, while others remained until the organization's final collapse in 1941.) The American Veterans Committee went through a similar process about a decade later and slightly faster, split apart by Henry Wallace's presidential campaign in 1948. A handful had been members of other groups deemed suspicious in the environment of heightened loyalty concerns of the late 1940s: Americans for Democratic Action, the National Association for the Advancement of Colored People, and the ACLU. These scholars' connections to these Popular Front organizations hardly prove that their field was rife with card-carrying Communists—but it does suggest that pioneering scholars came from a wide range of political perspectives, including some on the further side of the left.[70]

The case of the project's third-in-command, psychologist Raymond Bauer, suggests how security problems could arise. Born in Chicago, Bauer studied at Northwestern University, where he was inspired by the racial liberalism of anthropologist Melville Herskovits. His involvement in student politics grew out of these concerns: he joined the American Student Union, as a classmate later reported, in order to "solve the racial housing problem on campus." Yet the very source of this friend's recollection indicates the problem at hand: it is among the nearly 200 pages of Bauer's FBI file. Bauer faced a major security inquisition in 1954, forcing him to abandon the prospect of doing the kind of classified consulting that Kluckhohn and Inkeles did. He defended his college record by telling his boss that he joined the ASU in order to fight Communist control, but at the same time worried that "a careless reader might interpret" an article in the student newspaper "as a 'Party-line' argument." After leaving Northwestern, Bauer joined the U.S. Navy and was soon sent to the navy's Oriental Languages School in Colorado. His navy experience, too, concerned security investigators; he had been friendly with a classmate, William Remington, who was later convicted of perjury for lying about his membership in the Communist Party. Such a friendship was not a crime even in those years, but added to suspicions about Bauer. As if the ASU and a brush with an actual Communist were not enough of a problem for the FBI, Bauer joined the American Veterans Committee at Harvard just after the war, staying with the group until its collapse. Bauer was hauled before the House Un-American Activities Committee in the summer of 1950; though he testified in private, his visit made the national news.[71] Bauer and all of his coworkers made it through the clearance process irrespective of the number of black (or red) marks in their past—thanks, perhaps, to the clever delaying tactics. While there was absolutely no evidence of any act of "disloyalty," even given the era's dangerously capacious and capricious definition of that term, the project's close ties to the government revealed vulnerabilities.

Contract in hand and security questionnaires languishing in the air force security unit, Bauer and the rest of the RRC staff devoted the spring of 1950 to a crash course in project design. Kluckhohn defined the main product as a "conceptual model of the Soviet social system," but one with direct military application: this model would identify elements of Soviet society "which, if damaged, will most impair efficiency." Bauer disagreed strenuously, using the language of behavioral science. He wanted instead a "description of the structure and functioning of the major institutions of the system" in order to build a "description of the structure and functioning of the total system." Bauer considered military applications such as assessments of systemic strength and weakness to be a "relatively minor job," to be completed only after the scholarly exercise was complete.[72] Only a few months later, hounding from air force officials led Bauer to retract, or at least restate, his priorities. In an all-points bulletin to RIP staff, Bauer worried that initial reports paid "inadequate or no attention to the fact that the Project is being sponsored by Air Force funds." While he did not direct staff members to work exclusively on issues for "Air Force and U.S. policy in general," he implored them to flag anything that might have military implications.[73] The supposedly seamless interweaving of scholarship and intelligence was already fraying—even before the ink on the contract could dry.

The interview instruments themselves were compendia of behavioral science topics, not air force needs. They included dozens of questions about key Soviet institutions—workplace, family, education, party, and the like. Well aware of contemporary interpretations of Soviet behavior—including Gorer's swaddling hypothesis—the questionnaire sought to test these theories as well. Inkeles warned prospective interviewees that some questions might appear "strange and even illogical to non-specialists"—but they were, he reassured, in accord with the latest precepts of American social science.[74]

Some of the project's multiple aims left clearer marks on the questionnaire than did others. Its efforts to advance knowledge of Soviet society are evident in the wide range of questions about social structure, work life, leisure, and family. The interest in psychoanalytic techniques are visible in the sixty "depth interviews" performed by staff psychologists. The questionnaires indicated an ancillary mission of the project: training the next generation of Soviet specialists in the United States by providing them with data for their own dissertations as well as the experience of doing interviews (and, of course, with wages). The project functioned, as RRC reports happily noted, as a "training ground" for young social scientists.[75] And indeed, graduate-student interviewers soon published path-breaking books and articles on Soviet factory management, health care, family structure, and other topics. Looking over the interviewers' shoulders were staff from Columbia's Bureau of Applied Social Research, contracted by the HRRI to study interviewing techniques.[76] Even as they emphasized the scholarly potential for their work, Kluckhohn and his collaborators did not stint on national security elements. One report to HRRI proclaimed that the "working model" would compare the likely impacts of internal and external events, including the "simultaneous atom-bombing of twenty major cities."[77]

One of the key analytical categories that united the scholarly and intelligence aims of the project was political allegiance/disaffection. For behavioral scientists, knowing Soviet attitudes toward the regime would help to measure the extent of adjustment to social norms. And military officials wanted to know the extent of home front support in a military conflict. Which Soviet citizens were most likely to grow disaffected with the Soviet system—or already had? What events might attract popular support to the regime? What might increase animosity? The question of political allegiance was a particularly complicated one for the population of DPs in Germany.[78] They were in no way a representative sample of Soviet citizens: the sweep of the Wehrmacht meant that the western regions of the USSR (under German occupation) were disproportionately represented. Rural dwellers were underrepresented in comparison with urbanites. And political allegiance—the central question—was even harder to measure. Because of the large number of AWOL soldiers, escapees, and those fleeing Soviet rule, critics of Stalin were more heavily represented in Germany than in the Soviet population; Soviet "true believers" were few and far between. The DP experience heightened political sensibilities as the menagerie of Russian groups fought among themselves. Compounding the problem was the fact that interviewees were volunteers, not randomly selected. Recruiters worried that DPs chose to participate because they sought an outlet for pent-up hostilities or simply for the remuneration and a free trip to Munich.[79] (A subsequent analysis of the RIP sample indicates that two political groups were overrepresented in the interview pool, both staunchly anti-Communist with strong contingents of Ukrainians and other non-Russians.)[80]

The question of sample bias was a nagging one for the interview project. One solution was to recruit interviewees according to basic demographic data like age, sex, nationality, and involvement with party or police (an advertisement might read: "Wanted: one young Ukrainian woman, non-party, never been arrested.") In their internal correspondence and in their published work, Harvard authors knew that this process was primitive; they made the question of bias into a constant refrain. "No statements made in any portion of this document," Kluckhohn repeatedly warned his air force sponsors, "should be interpreted as meaning we assume that we have a representative sample of the Soviet or even of the émigré population." Well aware of these concerns, the researchers were determined to focus on the causes of discontent even if they could not measure its extent.[81]

In the fall of 1950, the research team departed for Germany, where they spent nine months conducting interviews. George Fischer was part of the advance team working in the DP camps and was joined by Fred Wyle, a Harvard undergraduate then touring Europe. Quickly, a routine developed: Wyle would visit a DP camp, speak privately with camp "elders," and then ask to make a public invitation to the residents. Wyle generally found a great deal of interest, not all of it positive. On one occasion, he required a military escort to rescue him from a group of DPs convinced that he was working undercover for Soviet authorities.[82]

To reassure interviewees that Harvard was not in fact a front for the Soviet secret police, the RIP never learned the names of most of its subjects and did not record the actual interviews. Instead, the interviewers would converse in Russian, take notes in English, and later, while the DP was completing a written questionnaire, record observations into a tape recorder, a rare item in postwar Germany.[83] Though this approach may well have reassured the interviewees, it also introduced opportunities for errors into the process. While many of the interviewers had strong language skills, only five of the twenty-two spoke native Russian; perhaps one indication of their proficiency comes in an interviewer's comment that the work "improved our Russian immensely."[84]

In the course of its work in Germany, the project maintained connections to military intelligence. Inkeles reassured an air force intelligence officer that "we will be able to undertake fairly close collaboration" with the air force's "interrogations." The intelligence staff took this promise seriously, presenting Harvard with a fourteen-page wish list; it focused almost entirely on military topics, touching on semi-scholarly concerns only in its desire to "determine secret Soviet doctrine as distinguished from those doctrines proclaimed by Lenin and Stalin."[85] These queries suggest that Sleeper's ambitions for the behavioral sciences had more adherents at Harvard than among the air force brass. By midsummer, Inkeles and Bauer wrote increasingly distraught, even desperate, entreaties to Sleeper, hoping that he could convince his fellow officers to keep the project on a social scientific footing rather than having it become another sort of intelligence gathering. They summed up the problem with a wit born of frustration, telling their staff that they were busy rebutting the military's "notion that some good friend … bought a piece of Harvard University and is sending it over to them so they can get some service from it." The pair sought to satisfy the air force by promising to hand over "things that are useful" for military intelligence as long as it did "not interfere with our prime mission."[86] Yet air force intelligence officers, who placed little value on social science, saw that prime mission differently. Presaging the eventual ascendance of military brass over academic sheepskin, they noted with malicious pleasure that "the age of Raymond V. Bowers [has] passed."[87]

The interview project had other opponents as well, some of whom came within one well-placed telephone call of shutting it down. In the course of routine congressional appropriations hearings that began in June 1953, a small group of senators and representatives anxious to ferret out what they saw as government waste questioned the Harvard project. A House appropriations subcommittee responded with incredulity when a senior air force officer tried to explain what a "working model of the Soviet social system" was. Apparently, Representative Erret Power Scrivner (R-KS) envisioned a "working model" of a society—which he considered "far-fetched"—along the lines of a working model train or airplane. Scrivner, who prided himself on saving taxpayer dollars, called for the elimination of not just the Harvard RIP but all air force work in the social sciences.[88] Only a few weeks later, Senator Homer Ferguson (R-MI) harshly questioned air force research spending, singling out the Harvard contract. He wondered why the service had sponsored a study of Soviet society—"not targets," he reiterated incredulously, but "the Soviet Union social system." On an NBC talk show, Ferguson insisted that cutting air force research would not impair U.S. security, but merely bring "sanity and efficiency" to defense spending.[89]

Kluckhohn proved better at fighting this charge than his social science counterparts in the military. He went right to the top, explaining the situation to Robert Cutler, President Eisenhower's national security advisor, who considered the congressional complaints "absurd" and promised to sort them out.[90] Cutler's intervention, however, did not prevent a return of congressional inquiries two months later, this time igniting a small-scale newspaper war in Boston. The opening sally appeared in late September 1953, after Ferguson heard additional testimony about air force research. The issue was complicated by Harvard president Nathan Pusey's announcement over the summer that the university would not fire faculty members who refused to testify before congressional committees investigating Communism.[91] Ferguson castigated the military:

> I think personally we are just becoming ridiculous. We are just so extravagant that it shows a form of insanity.... I think it is one of the terrible examples of what the agencies are doing, to go to an institution, of all institutions, Harvard, to find a working model of Soviet thinking when they have criticized Congress for trying to get really at the roots of the thing under oath as to how a communist thinks.

Ferguson's colleague Senator John J. McClennan (D-AR) accused the Harvard program of "throwing money away." If military leaders "have not sense enough to know how to counteract Soviet propaganda without hiring a bunch of college professors...this defense establishment is in one darn bad shape in my opinion."[92]

The *Boston Post*, never a friend of Harvard, made these criticisms into front-page news. A week later, the paper reported that a group of self-appointed crusaders against Communism wanted a list of Harvard faculty and students who had worked on the interview project so it could investigate the researchers' loyalty. Meanwhile, Kluckhohn prepared a counterattack. The *Boston Traveler* slammed Ferguson and other critics for being shortsighted, concluding that Harvard research has been "a mighty good deal for all of us." And the *Boston Herald* launched a three-day series of editorials praising the air force for making full use of "the weapon of knowledge," which was based on information from an air force general that Kluckhohn discreetly provided to the newspaper. Cub reporter David Halberstam, then a Harvard undergraduate, honed his style while praising the RRC in the *Harvard Crimson*:

> During an age when distrust and hatred hang over mention of Russia, when investigations into Communist activities have descended upon American government, education, and churches, when the nickname of the Cincinnati baseball team is changed, a group of scholarly men, working out of dark offices...are heading the study of modern Russia.[93]

This moment in the limelight also faded away—perhaps thanks to another high-level intervention—and the Harvard staff continued the wearying task of data analysis.

The project's sponsors, however, had no such luxury. After a long, hot summer of congressional controversy, the air force quietly dissolved its Human Resources Research Institute and, with it, all such ambitious social science research. Bowers was fired because, as one draft memorandum noted, he promoted more and more research "with less and less application to our military needs."[94] The unhappy fate of the HRRI, even if its largest project survived, revealed one of many ironies in this case of government support for university-based research. Historians of science have long explored the explosion of large-scale research projects ("big science") housed in academic institutions with the government (often the Pentagon) footing the bill. As one leading historian acknowledged, though, these scholars have focused more on the scientific end of things than on military sponsors' interests and needs. The Harvard Refugee Interview Project, as an example of "big social science," showed how divisions within the military could be as devastating as tensions between the military and academics. Indeed, Bowers, Sleeper, and a handful of others represented an academically oriented colony within the air force, one that ultimately faced troubles from above and outside.[95]

Figure 2.2. Air Force employee Herman Sanders surrounded by reports from the Refugee Interview Project, 1955.

For whatever else it meant to be "big social science," the RIP played up its size. Modesty was in short supply in the final products of the project, which bristled with confidence in the project's scale. Every publication listed the scope of the data (often with varying numbers, but the overall effect was the same). One report from early 1952—before the congressional inquisition— estimated that the RIP had already generated 30,000 pages of data. (One administrator with the project worried about this scale from a budget perspective, calculating that the project had consumed 600 reams of paper in a single month.)[96] As the project continued, the numbers mounted rapidly. Graphic depictions were even more impressive: a plug for the RIP in a general-interest magazine showed air force personnel surrounded by reams of data—or, in one dangerous case, dwarfed by piles of paper looming precariously overhead.[97] Similarly, published reports from the RIP opened with a description of the sources: 764 "long interviews" and close to 3,000 "detailed questionnaires," counted one report; 9,748 "written questionnaires on special topics," 2,718 "general written questionnaires," and 329 "extended life-history interviews," reported another.[98]

These mountains of information provided the basis for air force reports as well as scholarly monographs. Interviewers using the data for their own work were especially productive, discharging their obligations to the RIP and writing their dissertations at the same time. Economist Joseph Berliner turned his project reports into his dissertation, soon published as *Factory and Manager in the USSR;* he analyzed former managers explaining their jobs in their own words, at once humanizing the work and offering insights unavailable from published sources. He supplemented his forty-one DP interviews with journal citations ranging from the humor magazine *Krokodil* to the straitlaced *Ferrous Metallurgy;* the end result was a masterpiece of descriptive economics. Berliner introduced the concept of *blat* (connections) and *tolkach* (which Berliner translated, in those days before the war on drugs, as "pusher") to a wider audience.[99] Berliner also argued that the Soviet leadership's pressure for rapid industrial growth spurred the evasive management tactics pursued by *tolkachi* and others throughout the economy. This insight was eerily prescient. The economic reforms of 1957, announced just after his book went to press, reduced target growth rates and reorganized managerial structures, as if following logically from Berliner's criticisms of Soviet management practices.[100]

One of Berliner's major contributions derived from a relatively narrow point. He demonstrated the effectiveness of bonuses paid to managers who had fulfilled their plan allotment; he expanded on this to argue that material incentives were central to the Soviet economy. While this point may have seemed self-evident, it found few predecessors in previous analyses of the Soviet economy. But to Berliner, the success of these premiums suggested that Western economic theories could help to analyze a planned economy—thus bucking conventional wisdom that the Soviet system was beyond the reach of Western economic principles. The substantial edifice of economic Sovietology was built on microeconomic foundations like Berliner's.[101]

Other scholars made similarly good use of the interviews. Mark Field and Kent Geiger wrote sociology articles on Soviet medicine, demography, and family dynamics. Others published dozens of articles on clinical psychology and psychiatry.[102] Though he completed only four interviews, Barrington Moore attempted an overview ostensibly based on interview data. Focusing on Soviet strengths and vulnerabilities, his report would become the core of

his second book, *Terror and Progress* (1954).[103] Works on military topics—
George Fischer's *Soviet Opposition to Stalin* and interviewer Alexander Dallin's
German Rule in Russia—also owe their existence to the RIP.[104] Before any of
these works became dissertations, however, they were reports to the air force,
which collectively reveal the project's priorities. Social and economic topics
accounted for half of the reports, followed by politics and then medicine and
nationality (ethnicity).[105]

The directors teamed up to write a summary analysis that became the project's final report to the air force and the book *How the Soviet System Works* (1956).
They began with a sociological view of the USSR as an industrial society, analyzing Soviet social activities and solidarities as if they differed little from those
in the United States. Both the report and the eventual book concluded with
a discussion of the Soviet threat to the United States. The authors painted a
picture of the Soviet Union wholly at odds with the vision of a totalitarian state
that controlled all aspects of life while its subjects cowered in fear, too atomized
to find common bonds with each other. Not that the authors dismissed state
power; they characterized the Soviet political system as a "dictatorship" and frequently used the word "totalitarian." Yet their implicit definition of that term
did not relate to that of political scientist Carl Friedrich, who promoted the
concept of totalitarianism. The RIP authors noted that the needs of its citizens
stood relatively low on the regime's list of priorities, well below maintaining its
own power, eliminating alternative centers of power, and expanding its international reach. Yet Kluckhohn, Bauer, and Inkeles described Soviet life in broader
terms: the Soviet Union was "a social system existing in a state of imperfect
integration of which the most general form is the clashing between the aspirations and expectations of the people and the demands of the dictatorship which
rules over them." While the authors hardly ignored the "elaborate machinery
for reporting and suppressing deviant behavior," they devoted more space to
understanding citizens' "techniques of accommodation."[106]

In spite of its lack of attention to citizens' interests, Kluckhohn and his
colleagues emphasized, the system won adherents on many different levels.
The interviewees expressed much less concern for individual freedom and personal liberty than Westerners did. Even the DPs most vociferously critical of
Communist rule praised the "social-welfare aspects" of Soviet society, including
education and literacy, health care, and job security; such support was unam-
biguous across all categories of respondents. Similarly, many of the DPs, even
the most critical ones, expressed great pride in the USSR's economic and military achievements.[107] The report devoted a large section to possible divisions
within Soviet society, identifying cleavages that could be of potential use in
psychological (or military) warfare and were also important to understanding
social structure and functions. Kluckhohn, Inkeles, and Bauer concluded that

only one social group was uniformly hostile to the Soviet Union: the peasantry. The workers and intelligentsia, to be sure, had a litany of complaints about the Soviet system—but nevertheless offered general approval of the Soviet welfare-state provisions and new superpower status. Even those who were, in the report's terms, "better adjusted" to Soviet life saw the collectivization of agriculture in starkly negative terms.

To the extent that the sample allowed, the authors explored differences in attitude by nationality group—which meant a special focus on Ukrainians (35% of the total respondents). Their conclusion that nationality was simply not an important factor accorded with the sociological precepts they held. Modern industrial societies like the USSR should have no place for ascriptive categories like race and ethnicity. Thus, they observed, "the basic social and political values of our respondents, their attitudes toward the Soviet regime, and their life experiences and life chances were on the whole *strikingly little determined by nationality* as compared with their social origins or their class position."[108] The RIP data suggest other possible conclusions: the intelligentsia, white-collar workers, and collective-farm workers from Ukraine were about twice as likely to endorse "a-bombing Moscow" as were their Russian counterparts— with over half of the *kolkhozniki* favoring such a violent action. Nevertheless, the authors concluded that the future of (non-Russian) nationalism looked bleak, thanks to the rapid pace of Russification in the Soviet Union.[109] The authors recognized that nationalism might become a mobilizing force that could channel general dissatisfaction into disloyalty and perhaps even active dissent, though they did not anticipate such a turn of events. While American scholars devoted much of the 1950s to hand-wringing over the need for more work on non-Russian (and especially non-Slavic) peoples in the Soviet Union, the data from the RIP offered evidence that nationality was a minor issue in the USSR. For all of the hand-wringing, the view that nationality was not a key factor in Soviet life held sway for decades.

The book *How the Soviet System Works* was, in all major ways, identical to the air force report. The report included an executive summary for officers too busy to wade through the 400-plus pages, and the book changed a handful of chapter titles. The only chapter removed in the transformation from report to book was a lengthy one on the military, which received briefer treatment elsewhere in the book. The excised chapter discussed "cadre officers" (company commanders) in terms identical to those for other professionals. They resented interference from the political deputies assigned to each army unit, but were "by and large supporter[s] of the Soviet socio-economic system." The notion that the Soviet brass might be a source of future political leadership—a hope of some of their U.S. counterparts—found little support from the RIP evidence. Soviet officers did "not conceive of the military organization as even a source of national political leadership."[110] Thus, the Harvard project cast doubt on two American hopes for the dissolution of the USSR—a military coup or the secession of minority nationalities.

A second round of edits played down the air force's role in the project. At first, the air force demanded that none of its employees be mentioned by name. It then relented, allowing the mention of Bowers and other HRRI staff while still forbidding any discussion of intelligence personnel as "likely to lead to misunderstanding" of the project's aims. Readers of the book, therefore, did not have the opportunity to "misunderstand" that the air force had a liaison officer working with the interviewers in Germany, nor that the military interest in the RIP went beyond its social science outfit in Alabama to include intelligence officers and others in the Pentagon. While these omissions hardly constitute a full-scale rewriting of the historical record, they ultimately make the project seem less oriented toward military interests than its original conception or actual operation.[111]

Was the RIP worth its high costs? Or was Kluckhohn's initial skepticism about the value of such a large-scale project well founded? The costs were, by any accounting, impressive. Once the classified consulting arrangements were included, the total price tag neared $1 million (roughly $8 million in 2008 terms) at a time when even well-paid Harvard professors earned $12,000 per year. The RIP revealed both the possibilities and the limits of collaborative work oriented around problem areas under government contract. Generous funding paid for a large staff of junior scholars, many of whom recalled the experience as a signal moment in their careers. With substantial Russian expertise and language skills, the project staff produced scholarship that provided insights into the Soviet economy and society and helped to shape Soviet Studies. The overarching view, that the USSR was a modern industrial society sharing much with Western Europe and the United States, received some play in the academic world. But it was not as influential, especially in the short term, as Merle Fainsod's *How Russia Is Ruled* (1953), which stood for decades as the standard work on Soviet politics. Though peripherally involved in RIP, Fainsod rarely cited the interviews, and his view of Soviet politics emphasized control more than did *How the Soviet System Works*. Nevertheless, compared with other government-funded projects—the failed Eurasian Institute, Michigan's SRC work, the Munich institute, or Troy Plus/Soviet Vulnerability—the RIP was clearly superior in both quantitative and qualitative terms.

The RIP, unlike these other government-supported projects, had a significant impact on the field even outside of scholarly production. The interview "transcripts" (actually summaries) themselves became an indispensable source for the study of Soviet history. Important analyses of nationality policy, consumption practices, and dozens of other topics have all made use of project materials, which comprise thirty-seven volumes and two large file cabinets and are now available in digital form.[112] The goal of training new cadres of scholars was also fulfilled. When the American Association for the Advancement of Slavic Studies (AAASS) came into being, three of its six founding board members had been involved in the interview project: Berliner, Fainsod, and Inkeles. Two project alumni (Berliner and Dallin) served terms as president of the association. "Big social science" projects like RIP had many avenues of influence.

The project also revealed just how problematic government-funded research could be. There were many factors working in RIP's favor, most notably the strong personal relationships between sponsor and contractor and a general agreement about the project's principal aims. Skepticism about social science within the air force (and among congressional overseers) led to conflicts with program staff over administrative issues like security and classification. The marriage of policy and scholarship, which people like Kluckhohn took for granted, was riven with tensions that suggested just how hard it would be to apply the World War II model of research in the Cold War. Within Sovietology at least, RIP represented the final effort to apply this model of collaborative interdisciplinary work, which could advance U.S. policy and scholarly knowledge. Other projects, even at the Russian Research Center, quickly abandoned this model.

With the end of the interview project in 1954, the enthusiasm that had characterized the heady years of the RRC's founding began to wane; one alarmist worried that it was "falling apart." Carnegie dispatched a program officer to assess the situation. He agreed that there was a real change taking place at Harvard, even if fears of collapse were exaggerated. Kluckhohn resigned the directorship in 1954 and was replaced by the European diplomatic historian William Langer, Geroid Robinson's OSS boss.[113] The social relations scholars at the center feared, with some justification, that its original mission—applying behavioral sciences to the Soviet Union—faced extinction. For its first six years, the RRC had echoed the Carnegie Corporation's emphasis on social relations. One calculation had the field accounting for 25% of the RRC spending from the Carnegie grant, with economics (23%), political science (20%), and history (18%) being the major competitors. After Kluckhohn's departure, the center's social relations program steadily shrank. Both Inkeles and Moore embarked upon broad comparative projects in which the USSR would be one of many cases. Carnegie put a positive spin on the center's supposed crisis; the fact that ambitious scholars wanted to tackle broad and ambitious issues was "the healthiest kind of intellectual development."[114]

Clyde Kluckhohn was not sure. When he left the director's post, he severed all formal ties to the Russian Research Center. Although he remained on

good terms with individual scholars, he looked with displeasure at the direction of the center under new management. In typically polite and precise language, he wanted the new leaders to "recall that one of the explicit purposes"
for the RRC was "the development of scholars and scholarship in the 'Social
Relations' area." Such a focus was almost entirely missing, thanks to Inkeles's
and Moore's new projects and the impending departure of Bauer to MIT. The
new guard treated social relations gingerly at the center's tenth anniversary in
1958. The associate director, political scientist Marshall Shulman, called social
relations "one among a battery" of approaches at the center, but by that time,
it had almost no connections to social relations as an intellectual approach or
academic department.[115]

These changes took place over the RRC's first decade. It had originally
appointed project directors to coordinate research on economics and politics
much as Kluckhohn was doing for social relations. But these directors—Wassily
Leontief Jr. and then Alexander Gerschenkron in economics and Fainsod in
political science—advised individual research projects, mostly dissertations,
rather than leading collaborative projects. By 1955, it was no longer a place
that "did research," as one historian later put it, only a place "where research
was done."[116] While social relations students labored in Kluckhohn's model of
"industrial social science," Gerschenkron's acolytes did their writing in a more
guild-like "workshop."[117] As early as 1952, the center's visiting committee concluded that the center ran like a loose "federation of disciplines." More interdisciplinary conversations took place around the lunch table, the committee
concluded, than the seminar table. At first, a wide mix of scholars participated
in the seminar, fulfilling the interdisciplinary dreams of starry-eyed area studies proponents. But by the time the interview project was winding down, it had
become more of a revolving disciplinary seminar, with economists showing up
to hear economists, historians to hear historians, and so on.[118] Before long, the
same fate befell the subsidized lunches that had encouraged interdisciplinary
conversation as well as community building; the cafeteria became the province of cash-starved graduate students.[119] The esprit de corps and the spirit of
excitement that had defined the center's early years had passed, replaced by an
institution that became a vehicle for the advancement of individual disciplines
and careers. At the same time, the direct connections to national security loos-
ened substantially in the first decade; the transition from interdisciplinary to
disciplinary coincided with the demise of large-scale research projects and the
loosening of institutionalized government-academic ties. The same tendencies
would shape the field as it expanded beyond Harvard and Columbia in the late
1950s and into the 1960s.

CHAPTER 3

INSTITUTION BUILDING ON A NATIONAL SCALE

As the Columbia and Harvard institutes celebrated their tenth anniversaries in the mid-1950s, their leaders could take great pride. Each was a thriving enterprise that hosted scholars and teachers in a variety of disciplines. Each housed more first-rate Russia experts than had existed across the whole country before World War II, along with many times the number of graduate students. Each center had its own monograph series, which together had already published more scholarly works on Russian topics than had appeared ever before. Neither center lacked for resources; between Carnegie, Ford, and Rockefeller, the two institutions had received over $2 million over their first decade—close to $16 million in 2008 dollars. Both trained doctoral students in all fields, but each had its own specialty. The close-knit network of scholars, government officials, and foundation officers, working through ad hoc advisory groups, personal friendships, and groups like the Joint Committee on Slavic Studies (JCSS), had created a field.

In both quantitative and qualitative terms, then, the state of Russian studies was strong. But in geographic terms, the state of Russian studies was either New York or Massachusetts; there was an extraordinary concentration of the field's financial and (to a lesser degree) intellectual resources in these two universities. Columbia accounted for roughly half of the 500-plus master's degrees in the Russian field's first decade, with Harvard accounting for about half of the remaining degrees. A similar pattern held for doctoral degrees. By one count, Columbia and Harvard granted 75% of the eighty-two Ph.D.'s on Russian topics between 1945 and 1955, with Columbia responsible for roughly twice as many as Harvard.[1] Another source with a much broader definition of Russia-related topics counted 405 Ph.D. dissertations completed on Russian topics—with Harvard and Columbia together producing over half. While this broader census identified fifty-six universities granting at least one doctorate on a Russian topic, almost half (twenty-three) of those had granted only a single degree.[2] There was an even greater concentration of ruling structures. The all-important JCSS had a dozen members in the late 1950s; eight of them had Columbia connections (for training or employment), and six had Harvard connections. There were more members who had *both* Columbia and Harvard connections than there were with *neither* Columbia nor Harvard connections.[3]

In its second decade, Slavic studies would expand on the achievements of its first, creating a national enterprise out of one that been heavily concentrated in two universities. From the mid-1950s onward, but especially after 1957, the field's leading institutions, from JCSS to the Ford Foundation, devoted a great deal of time and money to extensive growth. By the early 1960s, the field looked dramatically different than it had only a half dozen years earlier. There were more scholars working at more universities on a wider range of topics; invitation-only meetings soon gave way to national conferences; self-perpetuating steering committees (like JCSS) yielded some—but definitely not all— power to a new membership organization, the American Association for the Advancement of Slavic Studies (AAASS, read as "triple-A, double-S").

These transformations of Soviet Studies paralleled other area studies programs at the time. The National Defense Education Act (NDEA), a congressional response to the launch of the Soviet Sputnik satellite in 1957, was as much a symbol as a source of the expansion; for Russian Studies, at least, the expansion and reorganization were well under way before the launch. The NDEA raised the profile of area studies out of proportion to its funding, which was far exceeded by Ford Foundation grants in the ensuing years. Perhaps the greatest innovation of the era was the rise of academic exchanges with the USSR. In keeping with the times, the sponsors wanted the exchanges to both improve the quality of the field and spread its institutional base. The exchanges also forged a new (and not entirely happy) relationship between academic and government work in Soviet Studies. The expansion of the field diffused the area studies emphasis as scholars, especially political scientists, followed disciplinary trends more closely. The next generation of centers became vehicles for the pursuit of individual disciplinary interests. The result was a field that spread not just geographically but also intellectually.

Even before the quantitative expansion got under way, some of the field's leading impresarios had begun to consider reorganization. Rockefeller and Carnegie had created and sustained the field in the late 1940s and early 1950s, giving major grants to the two centers and much smaller ones to a handful of other institutions. Berkeley, Stanford/Hoover, Dartmouth, and Bryn Mawr together received roughly 10% as much as Columbia and Harvard.[4] As the Ford Foundation entered area studies, it took a different approach, setting up a national competition—the Foreign Area Fellowship Program (FAFP)—and allowing the recipients to choose where they would take their fellowships. The fellowships, begun in 1952, were originally for graduate training related to Asia and the Middle East, but soon included Africa and the USSR/Eastern

Europe.[5] The early years of FAFP were national in principle but heavily concentrated in practice; Columbia and Harvard accounted for 88% of eighty-one early career awards in Soviet/East European studies.[6] Postdoctoral fellowships were slightly more dispersed, with "only" 75% of the fellows who went to a university (as opposed to a library) ending up at one of those two institutions.[7]

By the mid-1950s, Ford was looking beyond the immediate training needs toward the professional careers of area experts. For the Soviet/East European area, the solution was to offer grants-in-aid to scholars outside the major area studies centers; "isolated individual scholars," the foundation concluded, could "increase and improve their research production" with small grants aimed explicitly to provide them with opportunities more readily available to scholars at the major centers. Rather than administer these grants directly, Ford officials preferred outsourcing to JCSS, with an explicit charge to favor scholars remote from centers and sources. Ironically, every member of the group charged with diversifying the field's institutional base had taught or been trained at Columbia or Harvard.[8] Yet this group, along with other key leaders in the field, thought that the field could not remain centered at these two institutions no matter how prolific the scholars, how good the training, how well funded. Thanks to a hefty grant from the Ford Foundation in early 1957, the JCSS undertook an extensive review of the field, examining everything from infrastructure to intellectual content.

The JCSS appointed a review committee, which convened in May 1957 to design its assessment of the field. Of its eight members, only Berkeley historian Charles Jelavich had no ties to either Columbia or Harvard.[9] The time was ripe. A number of universities were contemplating new programs in Russian studies. At the same time, the rationale for the field's existence was shifting. For its first decade, the field's raison d'être was expressed in terms of the national interest—"in a catchword," the minutes noted, "the 'know-your-enemy' approach." This rationale had become "somewhat outmoded," and the field needed to define a broader mission. Thus, aside from focusing on training and research, the review would also cover "general education and public information." Rather than letting knowledge of Russia trickle down from specialist publications, the field needed to demonstrate that Russia was an essential part of a college-level liberal arts curriculum and even of secondary education. Similarly, the group sought to elevate public discussions about the Soviet Union; it cited French sociologist Raymond Aron, who observed that the high quality of American scholarship on Soviet topics contrasted sharply with the "shockingly primitive level of public information." The field also considered more general matters of organization—was the JCSS the most appropriate body to lead the field in this new phase?—and, finally, the relationship of the academic field to government agencies.[10] The field, members of the committee believed, was "on the threshold of a great expansion, which could carry its impact into unaccustomed fields and remote corners of the country." All of this happened in early 1957, while Sputnik was still on the launching pad, if not still in the assembly facility. Indeed, the review committee's discussions often highlighted its differences from NDEA and post-Sputnik concerns, to the point of explicitly countering some of the central justifications for federal action. Meeting two months after Sputnik, it warned against letting fearful responses to the satellite drive the field's transformation. Russian Studies was only "one component of recently realized national needs in education." To the extent that Sputnik brought increased attention to the need for knowledge about the USSR, so much the better. But it was important to study "the whole of Soviet society, not just Soviet science and education." Seeking an integrative intellectual framework that would encourage a wide range of work, it proposed a framework of modernization theory, then just coming into social scientific vogue. Committee chair Cyril Black (Princeton) was particularly enamored of modernization theory and saw it as a means of bringing together scholarship on Russian history, culture, economics, and politics.[11] The review committee still insisted on a broader vision of area studies, one that served training, research, and national security rather than concentrating narrowly on any one of these.

The review committee also remained focused on developing the field of Slavic studies on a national scale. It sent its staff assistant, historian John M. Thompson, on a fact-finding mission, and he visited the dozen or so universities not on the eastern seaboard with interests in the field. The findings were not encouraging; few institutions, Thompson reported, had any coherent idea of why they were active in the Russia field. There were, however, strong and clear views on the state of the field: scholars at these institutions "almost without exception ... complained bitterly" of feeling isolated. Similarly, "resentment against alleged domination of the field by the East and specifically Columbia and Harvard almost invariably cropped up." Harold H. Fisher, the historian who ran the Hoover Institution until being run out on political grounds, summed up this sentiment nicely:

> [There is] a kind of academic colonialism in the underdeveloped spaces that lie north of the Charles, west of the Hudson and south of the Potomac. The metropolis draws away from the colonies and semi-colonies some of their best products and returns less than it receives. The metropolis, in the mind of the colonial, [has] ... a perfunctory interest in and lack of knowledge of the hinterland.[12]

Those on the periphery did not desire independence from the metropole, only a fair share of the responsibility for running the whole empire. Thompson attributed this "alleged" resentment to "emotional" rather than "rational" factors.[13]

The final report of the review committee covered the primary topics on the JCSS docket for the previous decade, ranging from research to professional organization. It evaluated scholarship in a series of discipline-by-discipline assessments, symbolizing perhaps an inflection point for the field, when it was already too large and too diffuse to be evaluated as a single body of work.[14] On the one hand, this breadth spoke very well of the range and productivity of Russian Studies scholars, but on the other, it suggested the limits of the inter-disciplinary aspirations of the field's founders. As Harvard's Russian Research Center had increasingly dissolved into disciplines, so too had the field writ large. The authors of essays on the least populous disciplines were, by and large, on the margins of the academy. Indeed, the sociologist of the group had left academe to work at CBS News, a hint of the increasing irrelevance of sociology/social relations to Russian Studies.[15]

The report devoted the most attention to discussing how to incorporate Russian Studies into undergraduate and even secondary education, revealing its high aspirations.[16] It "envisage[d] a time when...every university and almost every college will teach the Russian language and will have faculty members in several disciplines who are well acquainted with the Russian area, and when every secondary school and college graduate will have a basic understanding of modern Russia." Knowledge of Russia was essential on two counts, the committee argued: it was important for students to appreciate at least one foreign culture; at the same time, given the centrality of the USSR in the international sphere, knowledge of the country was essential preparation for "responsible citizenship."[17] This two-pronged educational approach was hardly new; indeed, the original premise for building area studies programs in the 1940s revolved around deprovincializing American education and also training future policy makers.[18] While the area studies discussions of the 1940s focused on higher education, the review committee sought to reach younger students through teacher preparation programs and the development of appropriate classroom materials. These efforts, incorporated into NDEA, probably accounted for the fivefold increase in high school Russian-language enrollments between 1958 and 1965 (at which time it began an equally precipitous drop).[19]

The review committee also took up the question of government-academic relations, noting that the "rapid growth and increasing complexity" of Russian Studies in government and academe required new approaches to cooperation. The initial charge to the committee included eleven questions about the relationship of government and academic research, most of which were oriented toward improving the training of future government researchers. Only the last of these questions suggested any concern about the involvement of government research funds in the field: "Has independent research been deflected and influenced by government demands and contracts?" This question, which ten years later would divide the field, was far outnumbered by questions along the lines of what universities could do for the government, for instance, "What are the major research needs...which the government would like to see the universities fill?" The group also sought to ensure that "scholars in academic institutions [could] derive as much benefit as is desirable" from the government's Soviet research.[20] The JCSS soon created a subcommittee chaired by Indiana historian Robert Byrnes with Sergius Yakobson (Library of Congress, brother of the linguist Roman Jakobson) and John Michael Montias (then an economist at Yale and a government consultant).[21] The subcommittee was not active, suggesting perhaps the difficulty of reformulating government-academic relations in a rapidly expanding field.

The most revealing portions of the report related to graduate training and professional organization. The committee was candid about the field's failures: "not much [had] been achieved in genuine interdisciplinary training even though this had been an important objective."[22] The committee members praised the success of interdisciplinary research projects during World War II—especially those with the Office of Strategic Services (OSS)—but acknowledged the obstacles in postwar projects. The first generation of scholars had been more fully interdisciplinary thanks in large part to historical accident: they were trained in a single subject before the existence of Soviet Studies centers and then, typically, served in problem-oriented wartime programs—especially OSS and military intelligence—that valued regional expertise but cared little about academic discipline. But such a background was hard to replicate. The object of area training, as the report put it, was to add area competence to "a basic disciplinary skill, not to substitute area knowledge for disciplinary competence."[23] Promoting a multidisciplinary approach meant that the field's great expansion in the early 1960s left Slavic studies in a paradoxical position. The progress of the field would emerge through scholars in the disciplines, even as the disciplines themselves made little room for the Russianists in their midst. Russian centers new and old most often served as vehicles for the pursuit of individual disciplinary goals rather than as truly interdisciplinary organizations. Even those centers founded with different aims—most notably those in Cambridge and Seattle—had relinquished them by the late 1950s.

A similar contradiction emerged in the arcane topic of organization. While those outside the major centers complained about being ignored, those within them complained of overwork. The JCSS portfolio had expanded in the 1950s as it organized conferences, sponsored *Current Digest of the Soviet Press* (*CDSP*), aided the *American Slavic and East European Review* (*ASEER*), and administered grants-in-aid.[24] The JCSS members hoped, therefore, that reorganization might produce a more equitable "distribution of administrative burdens" among scholars in the field.[25] Recognizing the unpopularity of this dominance but unwilling to yield completely, a substantial portion of the JCSS proposed expanding the committee and agreeing to sponsor larger conferences. The ultimate goal was to create a national organization with "as broad a membership as possible," which could sponsor a revived journal and perhaps hold national meetings.[26] As Ralph Fisher gently noted, JCSS was ready to shed responsibility for planning and communication, but refused to hand over the reins for research, publication, and conferences.[27]

This new national organization would have an ambiguous relationship to academic disciplines. As Marshall Shulman noted in his draft recommendations to the review committee, Russian Studies "does not fit into the conventional pattern of organization familiar to the established disciplines." Scholars had "primary allegiance" to their own disciplines. Yet without other Russia experts around, they felt a "sense of isolation and lack of invigoration of their work and their interest."[28] The review committee hoped that the association could promote "closer cooperation among the disciplines"—effectuated by having representatives from five major disciplinary organizations on its board.[29]

One of the most direct and immediate results of the review committee was the AAASS. Technically speaking, the organization was not new at all; it had come into being as the legal entity that owned *ASEER*. The title of the journal and its owner had to meet unusual criteria, a sign of the concerns that at least one member of the field held in 1948. As John Hazard, a one-time practicing lawyer and future *ASEER* editor recalled in a third-person memoir:

> Robert Kerner of Berkeley insisted that the name "Russia" be omitted from any titles, and that the word "American" begin any title. He wanted it clear that this was not a front organization to insinuate Soviet propaganda into American scholarship....To avoid "Russia" in the title, the names of both [association and journal] became lengthy, so much so that Hazard's former colleague in his law office questioned whether any organization could endure, without ridicule, a title of AAASS.[30]

The JCSS saw an opportunity to build a national organization without extensive new paperwork by upgrading the journal and making it a part of a national membership organization. Perhaps fittingly, the organizing committee charged with rebuilding AAASS was heavy on Columbia and Harvard affiliates.[31] This organizing committee worked quickly to build AAASS, which would take control of *ASEER* and take on the general task of the development of the field; these tasks ranged from administering *CDSP* (which was running significant losses under JCSS sponsorship) to organizing grant programs and representing the field to foundations and government agencies.[32] It would also sponsor national conferences and help to produce the *Annual Bibliography of Slavic and East European Studies,* then run by William Edgerton at Indiana University.[33] Having transferred all of its operations to a broader membership-based group, JCSS could then wither away. Or so it hoped.

The AAASS grew quickly as a membership organization. Starting with roughly 600 members in 1960; it hit 1,300 in December 1962, 1,831 in 1966, 2,260 in 1969.[34] The core of the membership was made up of historians and political scientists, who accounted for half of the 1961 members. The numeric strength of these disciplines would continue through the remainder of the decade and well beyond.

The transfer of the journal was also a success; it became *Slavic Review* and relocated from Columbia to Seattle. Under the dynamic editorship of Donald Treadgold, a historian at the University of Washington, the journal's quality and reach improved markedly. Between 1960 and 1962, the journal's circulation went from 900 to 2,100, vaulting ahead of its one-time competitor, the *Russian Review,* but still far behind the flagship disciplinary journals (which had circulations ranging up to 16,000).[35] Selectivity also increased; whereas Simmons scrambled to find articles in *ASEER*'s early years, Treadgold rejected three of every four submissions. Treadgold introduced a "Discussion" section, in which he solicited individuals to write on topics of broad interest. These articles were among the most interesting in the journal and included a number of widely cited articles: Zbigniew Brzezinski on "the nature of the Soviet system," Cyril Black on modernization theory and Russian history, Georges Florovsky on old Russian culture, Gregory Grossman on Soviet economic prospects, Hugh McLean on modern Russian literature, Karl Wittfogel on Oriental despotism in Russia, Victor Erlich on post-Stalin literature, and most cited of all, Leopold Haimson on social stability in early twentieth-century urban Russia. For all of Treadgold's innovations, though, the *Slavic Review*'s finances continued the *ASEER* tradition of losing money; the new journal received support— over $12,000 per year—from nineteen university "angels," but still operated at a deficit. Donations from ACLS, Ford, and the Slavic Publications Fund (a joint project of Indiana University and the ACLS) kept the journal afloat.[36]

Getting the AAASS to take on the more difficult task of development was tougher going. As early as the association's fourth year, Treadgold, also a member of the JCSS, proposed three-year presidential terms (with presidents elected by the board, not the general membership) and a stronger board of directors as a way to encourage innovation by the officers. He also defended the JCSS in language both provocative and evocative:

> In the long run, [JCSS] provided leadership not in the sense of doing what certain people at (hypothetical) St. Blasius or North Dakota State Teachers

or Quakers' College for Bright Boys would like representatives they had
elected to have done, but in the sense of setting rather uncompromising academic standards which had to be met by people throughout the field....The
fact is that the Fainsods and the Moselys, to mention only two of many
names, attempted to judge on the basis of solid standards, and it was better at that stage to leave out some people or places they thought they really
couldn't judge rather than to take a chance.[37]

A self-perpetuating committee like the JCSS maintained standards, he suggested, while a large and democratic organization might not. Treadgold's complaints seem to have carried the day at JCSS, though his proposal to strengthen
the AAASS leadership did not have the desired effects. By 1966, JCSS members seemed disappointed that their committee still existed.[38]

The JCSS implemented the proposals from its review committee in a flush
moment for international education, what one historian aptly called "the
bonanza years."[39] The quantitative and financial expansion of Slavic studies
was part of a larger trend reshaping area studies. Like the field's pioneers in
the late 1940s, those working for its expansion in the late 1950s saw Slavic
studies as an exemplar for the study of other world areas. This high aim was
something of a conceit since Slavic studies programs were by this point no
longer the cutting edge of area programs, nor even the largest; Asian studies
had caught up with and in some cases surpassed Slavic programs. Unlike its
original incarnation, when the field had closer and denser ties to government
agencies and foreign policy formation, this newly expanded field was simply
one more world area—or, in the nomenclature of the day, one component of
"the non-Western world."

The changing of the guard of Slavic studies was also marked by a changing of the guardians. Starting in the late 1950s, Rockefeller and Carnegie were
dwarfed by Ford and the federal government, each of which supported Russian
Studies much as it did the study of other world regions. The JCSS had already
reckoned with these new circumstances by justifying the study of the Soviet
Union by the need to teach cosmopolitan citizens, not to know the Cold War
enemy. Both the federal NDEA and Ford funneled significant funds to Russian
Studies, but these were far from their central concerns. Only about five cents
of every NDEA dollar went for Title VI (language and area studies)—and
roughly half of that sum went for summer language institutes that were taught
on college campuses but aimed to improve language skills for elementary
and secondary school teachers. A similar sum went to vocational education
and high school guidance testing.[40] The Office of Education calculated that
roughly $8.6 million went to language and area centers over the first five years
of NDEA; of this, Slavic and Eastern European centers received $1.9 million

(22%); this was the largest sum for any world region, to be sure, but hardly an earth-shaking commitment.[41] The NDEA had a matching requirement that ostensibly doubled the dollars going to Slavic studies, but its more important impact came through the publicity it generated for area studies in general.

Ford monies quickly overwhelmed federal spending, as the foundation allocated well over $100 million to international studies in five years. The FAFP accounted for $6 million, but the rest went to about sixty grants to universities to build "non-Western and international studies."[42] The nature of the Ford grants—which provided as much as $12 million to a single institution for a variety of purposes—disguised the contribution to Slavic and East European studies in particular.[43] Anecdotal evidence from a handful of Slavic centers makes it clear that ample funds trickled down to Slavic programs through the various Ford programs. Columbia, for instance, apparently devoted roughly 28% of its $10.9 million block grant to its Russian and Eastern European centers. Berkeley, in contrast, spent only 15% of its region-specific funds on Slavic studies, with Chinese and African studies getting more.[44] While there are no figures for the total extramural support for Slavic studies, one analysis of Chinese studies calculated that Ford provided 60% of all support for Chinese studies between 1933 and 1970, even though Carnegie and especially Rockefeller had been awarding grants for decades longer.[45] In Slavic studies, too, Rockefeller and Carnegie provided the initial organization, and NDEA was better known, but Ford did the heavy lifting.

Though they differed in size, the Ford and NDEA programs had some common aims. They both defined their purpose in terms of national interest, but construed that term broadly to encourage higher education and advanced research. The desired product was not actionable intelligence or action-oriented intelligence officers (or even the desk-bound type); the hope was to produce and disseminate knowledge about the rest of the world. Both NDEA and Ford focused on higher education's elite tier but also sought to spread the wealth. One-third of the $70 million Ford spent on "the expansion of international studies" went to Columbia and Harvard alone. A handful of other institutions were able to use these funds to improve their general standing in international studies—the Universities of Illinois and Pittsburgh, for instance. The NDEA and Ford programs both accepted the organization of knowledge of the world into existing disciplines. As an official report on the NDEA noted in classic bureaucratese: "It was generally accepted by the late 1950s that language and area studies could not, and should not supplant the disciplines. Each of the several related disciplines had a unique contribution that could be realized only if its separate identity and character were retained."[46] By giving large sums of money for faculty appointments and graduate fellowships in non-Western and international studies, Ford poured funds into existing departments and

graduate programs. The impressive quantitative growth of area studies programs also contributed to growth in the disciplines.

In a general climate of expansion, funding sources like NDEA and Ford
provided the impetus for some but by no means all Slavic studies programs.
Their funds more often contributed to the transformation of a university program, especially one organized at a large state university invested in international studies, than to the creation of a new center from scratch. National
funding patterns mattered, but so too did institutional and even individual
particularities.

The University of California, Berkeley, for instance, opened its new Center
for Slavic Studies in 1957, weeks before Sputnik. Home to one of the oldest
Slavic programs in the country, it had regularly offered Russian-language
classes since the turn of the twentieth century. By the start of World War II,
Berkeley mounted forty-one courses on the Slavic world, ahead of Columbia
and almost twice as many as Harvard.[47] Historian Robert Kerner had established an Institute of Slavic Studies in 1948, but it never achieved the support
or status he desired.[48] After Kerner's death in 1956, the new Center for Slavic
Studies became part of Berkeley's new Institute for International Studies;
Charles Jelavich, historian of the Balkans, served as the first director. By 1960,
the center had newfound resources from NDEA and the Ford Foundation. The
NDEA paid $196,000 over four years, while Berkeley's initial Ford block grant
provided roughly $450,000 over eight to ten years.[49] The funds helped, but it
was really the departure of the cantankerous Kerner that allowed Berkeley to
regain its prewar prominence.

Indiana University, too, had established programs in Russian and Eastern
European studies before the arrival of Ford and NDEA funds. It had begun its
area programs with the Army Specialized Training Program (ASTP) in 1942;
its principal task was to cover Eastern Europe from Finland to Turkey, offering
courses in Finnish, Polish, Czech, Hungarian, Serbo-Croatian, Albanian, and
Russian. After the war, the ASTP group, led by linguist Thomas Sebeok, was
reconstituted as a program in Uralic and Altaic studies. Soon thereafter, the
university hired its first full-time Russian professor, who was assigned to the
French Department until the creation of a multidisciplinary Department of
Slavic Studies in 1949. The arrival of historian Robert Byrnes in 1956 soon led
to a struggle between the Department of Slavic Studies and the Uralic/Altaic
studies program for control over an underfunded Institute of East European
Studies. The end result was that Uralic/Altaic studies went off on its own;
Sebeok soon focused more on semiotics than regional studies. Before long,
NDEA grants supported both centers—though the Russia/Eastern Europe
center, led by Byrnes and then William Edgerton, had substantially more support. Indiana's aspiration to be the best Slavic program "between the coasts"

dated back to the early 1950s. Outside funding helped the university to move toward that long-standing goal.[50]

The support of NDEA led directly to the creation of centers at the Universities of Illinois and Michigan. Michigan had offered Russian instruction in the interwar years and created its Slavic Language Department in 1952. Its Slavic Center came into being only after receiving an NDEA grant in 1959, which helped Michigan to expand its offerings in Russian and Eastern European languages, politics, economics, and history.[51] The University of Illinois also opened the doors of its center in 1959 in the hopes of garnering an NDEA grant. Even after its first NDEA application was rejected, historian Ralph Fisher managed to get the library's Slavic acquisitions budget quadrupled in only two years. A reapplication to NDEA in 1960 was successful; the proposal was heavily oriented toward the library. But the biggest boon for Illinois's impressive Slavic collections was a renewable $150,000 gift from Doris Duke. Fisher enhanced the school's profile by hosting the national office of the new AAASS. What was most impressive about the Illinois program was that it started essentially from scratch in the late 1950s, invested heavily in less visible items like library purchases, and soon attracted a diverse and strong faculty.[52]

All told, the number of Russian area centers almost doubled between 1959 and 1964, from seventeen to thirty-three. Yet extramural support was not the only factor here; of twelve centers in Slavic (or Slavic/Asian) studies that received NDEA support in 1964, over half dated back to 1956 and some beyond then. Or, considered differently, only five of the sixteen Slavic centers created between 1959 and 1964 were supported by NDEA.[53]

As new centers came into being in the early 1960s, the number of graduate students working on Russian and Soviet topics grew rapidly. The number of completed doctoral degrees doubled between 1953 and 1965 (though there was a slight decline in the late 1950s) and doubled again between 1965 and 1972. The trend suggests that there was a first surge of student interest in about 1949 (completing in 1954), with another one beginning in about 1958 (completing in 1963–1964).[54]

Thanks to NDEA and Ford—plus the aims of the JCSS review committee—the dominance of the older programs diminished over the 1960s. An inclusive list of doctoral dissertations on Russian topics shows a dramatic spread, as well as some changes among the leaders. Columbia and Harvard combined for about 100 of the 332 Russia-related doctorates in the early 1960s and about 100 of 900 a decade later. Newcomers like Indiana, Wisconsin, and NYU joined the top ranks in the 1960s. The top four institutions were far less dominant in the early 1970s (roughly 23% of doctorates) than they had been in the early 1960s (roughly 42% of doctorates). And far more institutions graduated Ph.D.'s on Russian topics than had in earlier years.[55]

Increased numbers of graduate students were matched by increased undergraduate interest in Russian language and Soviet topics. Enrollments in Russian
had jumped during the latter part of World War II; some teachers credited the
Red Army's success at turning back the German invasion in 1943. Offerings in
Russian increased for the next decade, through the end of the Grand Alliance
of World War II into the early years of the Cold War. Enrollments reached a
plateau and started to decline in the early 1950s; the *New York Times* estimated
that the number of undergraduates studying Russian fell by one-third between
1950 and 1954.[56] These declines were short-lived. By the time the first reliable
data became available in 1958, enrollment in Russian courses topped 16,000.
Sputnik and NDEA had an immediate effect: between 1958 and 1959, enrollment in Russian courses shot up by 56.5%. Enrollments in other languages
went up too, but by a modest 13.7%. After that point, Russian enrollment
growth tracked slightly behind growth in foreign language enrollments more
generally. For example, enrollments in Russian doubled in the five years after
1958, but enrollments in Spanish were not far behind. By the time of the 1965
survey, other foreign languages had booked more growth than Russian, which
reached a plateau in the mid-1960s and began a decline in absolute terms after
1968, even as overall college enrollments continued to grow.[57]

Undergraduate degrees in Russian language and literature also climbed dramatically in the 1960s, from a measly 7 in 1958, to 54 in 1953, 107 in 1957, and 446
by 1964; this far outpaced enrollment growth in other foreign languages. The
most striking trend in bachelor's degrees in Russian is the gender skew: while
women accounted for about 65% of all foreign language majors throughout the
1950s and 1960s, they accounted for a much smaller share of Russian-language
B.A.'s—somewhere between 35% and 50% of majors before 1960, and then
50–60% for the rest of the 1960s.[58] These figures, together with the paucity of
women studying Russian topics in graduate school in the 1950s and 1960s suggest that men were especially likely to use the language major as preparation
for advanced work in Russian Studies.

There was a virtuous circle of expansion that began well before 1957 but followed Sputnik into the stratosphere. More undergraduate students in Russian
meant more graduate students in Russian, which meant more future faculty
members in Russian topics. The trend in Russian Studies mirrored the national
growth in American higher education, especially in international studies. As
table 3.1 shows, the decade of the 1960s saw an extraordinary expansion of
American universities; the rising tide floated the Russian Studies boat as it did
many others.

This pattern of growth shaped the nature of government-academic relations,
at least in Russian Studies. The JCSS review committee perspicaciously took
up this question in the late 1950s, faced not with any major scandal but aware

Table 3.1: Growth of Russian Studies in Comparison to National Trends, 1960s

	1969–1970 as % of 1959–1960	
Category	Russian Studies	National Trends
Faculty members	226	118
Doctoral degrees	277	305
Language enrollment	250	252 (foreign-language enrollment) 305 (overall enrollment)

Sources: National data on degrees, faculty members, and overall enrollment from U.S. Department of Education, *Digest of Educational Statistics 2006* (online at http://nces.ed.gov/Programs/digest/, accessed May 2008), table 174. See note 55 for source on Russian Studies doctorates. Russian Studies faculty based on AAASS membership data from Ralph Fisher, "The American Association for the Advancement of Slavic Studies: From Its Origins to 1969" (AAASS Records), 21, 24, 32. Language enrollments from Richard I. Brod, "Foreign Language Enrollments in US Colleges, Fall 1970," *ADFL Bulletin* 3:2 (December 1971), 50.

that much had changed in the field's brief life. There is no extant evidence that the JCSS Subcommittee on Government-Academic Relations accomplished anything, or even that it met. By 1961, it was a rump group consisting solely of Robert Byrnes; he used the subcommittee to advance his interests in academic exchanges.[59] The JCSS chair, Donald Treadgold, awakened the committee from its slumbers in 1962 to deal with a proposal by Columbia political scientist Alexander Dallin. After spending a good portion of 1961 working in Washington, Dallin called for "significantly closer…relations between parts of the government and academic communities." Closer ties, Dallin argued, could help to improve graduate training, academic research, and government "political intelligence" regarding the Communist world. He offered a list of five areas for which the exchange of information between scholars and analysts would be especially fruitful; they tended toward operational concerns more directly useful for intelligence than scholarship, for instance, the comparative effectiveness of Communist appeals and "how to 'read between the lines' of Communist documents." Dallin also wanted the leaders of Communist studies to be better acquainted with the information available within the U.S. government. Based on his own experience with the CIA's senior research staff on international Communism, Dallin favored informal contacts and temporary personnel exchanges rather than advisory committees or other formal mechanisms. Finally, Dallin wanted better flows of information; he proposed reevaluating government classification systems to make available a wider range of primary sources, especially those with low levels of classification or those that were "unattributed" (published by the government, though not identified as such).[60]

The memo piqued Treadgold's interest, and he set out to create some of the links that Dallin had proposed. He had hoped that AAASS would be ready to take on some of the tasks of this sort, but in this case he worked through JCSS.

Treadgold reactivated the Subcommittee on Government-Academic Relations by stocking it with scholars who had appropriate clearances (he proposed Chicago geographer Chauncy Harris and political scientist Marshall Shulman, then relocating from Harvard to Columbia) and convening a meeting with a handful of government officials.[61] The meeting, in October 1963, brought Treadgold, Harris, and Dallin together with three State Department representatives. They concluded that a new journal of political analysis, with authors from the intelligence community as well as the ivory tower, would provide a venue for intellectual exchange; the participants hoped that AAASS would take the lead in exploring such a journal. Surprisingly, no mention was made of the State Department's journal, *Problems of Communism,* which served a similar function. Long edited by Abram Brumberg (a Polish émigré and Social Democrat), the journal provided a venue for academics to write on broad issues of potential policy concern while giving government experts the opportunity to reach a larger (unclassified) audience. One government official hoped to "make doctoral dissertations more responsive to matters of government interest," but he got a decidedly mixed response from the academics. Academics and government officials alike rejected formal "internships" in government agencies as unfeasible. Most of the meeting was devoted to the issue of broadening the circulation of unclassified government publications, and it ended with a desultory discussion of joint academic-government seminars.[62]

The fact that Dallin's proposals yielded so few results demonstrated that a new era of government-academic relations had arrived. The individual contacts between intelligence officials and academics (along with foundation officers) that had shaped the field in the 1940s and early 1950s had faded with the passage of time; younger scholars no longer had such ready access to involvement in government work. The academics' desire to expand relations with government had not yet disappeared, but the mechanisms for continuing the work were in flux. Too large and too diffuse to work with government officials in the same informal way that it had earlier, the field of Slavic studies had yet to develop a system of formal contacts, despite Dallin's best efforts.

Such formal government-academic contacts were apparently stronger in infrastructure programs than in intellectual ones. By the time that scholars and government officials met to discuss Dallin's ideas, government-academic cooperation had generated one of the most important changes in Russian Studies in the 1950s: scholarly exchanges. Short- and long-term exchanges had been under discussion since World War II, with scholars, foundation officials, and diplomats all seeking opportunities for American-Soviet interchange. The failure of Columbia's Russian Institute to host visiting Soviet scholars did not deter its faculty from seeking short- and long-term visits to the Soviet Union and reciprocal visits by Soviets. While accompanying the American secretary of state to the Moscow Conference of Foreign Ministers in 1943, Philip Mosely had proposed an exchange to Andrei Vyshinskii, the Soviet deputy commissar for foreign affairs. Vyshinskii's reply was positive but noncommittal and ultimately fruitless. The University of Washington's George Taylor, who like Mosely also served in wartime diplomacy, had proposed a similar plan to the Rockefeller Foundation in the final months of the war. Columbia literature scholar Ernest Simmons made similar (and similarly unsuccessful) overtures to the Carnegie Corporation of New York.[63] And John Hazard and Geroid Robinson hoped to include educational exchange in the final settlement of U.S. Lend-Lease aid to the USSR, but as the negotiations over the Lend-Lease "tie-off" grew bitter, talk of exchanges quickly evaporated.[64]

American diplomats took a cautious approach to academic contacts with the Soviet Union. While the State Department discouraged undergraduate programs, it pursued graduate student and scholar exchanges with some vigor; in six separate initiatives between 1945 and 1947, the department reported, it had "consistently taken the position that by broadening the base of contact, mutual understanding and cultural appreciation may be increased."[65] But these programs foundered on Soviet xenophobia and American anti-Communism. The McCarran-Walter Immigration Act of 1952 added an additional hurdle: any nondiplomatic personnel coming to the United States from the Soviet bloc would face stringent tests, and those passing those tests would still need to be fingerprinted upon arrival in the United States. The Soviet position softened slightly after Stalin's death in 1953, as various initiatives led to ad hoc visits, including Soviet participation in the World Congress of Cardiologists (1954) and an American production of *Porgy and Bess* in the USSR (1955). These cultural exchanges were small and tentative efforts that entailed extensive support from the State Department and private organizations.[66]

The Geneva Conference of 1955 prompted a full-scale assessment of Soviet-American cultural relations in the U.S. government. The result was a foreign policy statement, NSC 5607, that outlined a broader and more intensive effort to establish cultural exchanges with the Soviet Union. The aim was to "promote…evolution toward a regime" that was less despotic at home and less aggressive internationally. The report termed cultural relations as an explicitly "*offensive*" act that would be part of the implementation of a "positive…foreign policy."[67] Ambassador William Lacy, the State Department's point person for East-West exchanges, lobbied Congress to waive the fingerprinting requirement. He favored exchanges for their role in promoting regime change as well as the "intelligence gain" they could provide.[68]

The first cultural exchanges emphasized technical experts and performing arts, though a handful included academics. The Ford Foundation sent a hundred or so scholars-in-training to various Eastern European nations in the three years after Stalin's death.[69] After receiving dozens of requests for travel grants to the USSR in 1954 and 1955, Ford wanted to work out a formal grant program. Ford program officer David Munford argued that "every superior advanced" graduate student should be eligible for travel support, on whatever terms possible.[70] Individual universities sought to establish bilateral exchanges with their counterparts in the USSR but met resistance from the Ford Foundation and the State Department. Ford officials believed that supporting bilateral academic exchanges would further concentrate Soviet Studies at the very moment when the foundation was seeking to expand it. Diplomats were reluctant for very different reasons; one admitted to an "instinctive revulsion against" having Soviet scholars in "our great universities."[71] When Munford approached State about a national program, diplomats wanted to send Americans to the USSR but not receive Soviets in the United States, which would provide the USSR with positive publicity.[72] The JCSS sought to parlay these explorations into a systematic program of travel grants. In late 1955, it discussed "proposals for the piercing of the Iron Curtain."[73] Munford worried that the joint committee itself was too narrow to manage the exchange. He envisioned a group representing a wider range of universities and disciplines and also insisted that each member have "a background of close relationships with government."[74] The group, representing ten universities, first convened in February 1956, only two days before Nikita Khrushchev's Secret Speech signaled a new era of Soviet openness.[75] Opting for a nondescript label that would not raise suspicions, they constituted themselves as the awkwardly named Inter-University Committee on Travel Grants, known as the equally awkward IUCTG. With start-up funds from Carnegie, IUCTG did not begin with exchanges, but was only a one-way operation, sending Americans to the USSR on thirty-day tourist visas.[76]

This program of tourist visas set patterns that would not change even as the one-way trips gave way to a reciprocal exchange. Foundation officials worked closely with scholars and government agencies to establish these exchanges. They organized a stand-alone group, in part to ensure a national body—and yet its administration was centralized (initially hosted by Columbia) and benefits accrued disproportionately to Harvard and Columbia. The 122 IUCTG travelers between 1956 and 1958 included 19 from Harvard and 10 from Columbia (plus many more who had trained at one of those institutions); only Berkeley (with 8) approached these figures.[77] The autonomous IUCTG also protected existing enterprises from public or congressional criticism for consorting with the Cold War enemy; even as Soviet conditions changed, American academics feared reverberations from sending innocent American youth into a Communist country. As further insurance, the committee also cultivated American journalists, especially those at the *New York Times*. The purpose, according to one early IUCTG administrator, was to have good contacts in place "just in case something happened."[78] The organization gave priority to younger scholars—advanced graduate students and junior faculty members— and to Soviet experts. This emphasis on training suggests the long-term vision of the field's early leaders and would also set an important precedent for future programs. The emphasis on youth and training also locked the IUCTG into dealing with the Ministry of Higher Education, a low-ranking institution in charge of universities, rather than the more powerful Academy of Sciences.[79]

The IUCTG grantees who went on month-long trips to the USSR between 1956 and 1958 garnered treatment akin to that of explorers of unknown lands. And with good reason; these were among the first American experts to visit the Soviet Union, excluding diplomats, for almost twenty years. There was wide interest in participants' experiences, leading many to publish newspaper articles and to give informational seminars describing their visit. The IUCTG convened debriefing meetings of the early participants, inviting State and CIA representatives to unobtrusively observe the discussions.[80]

The trips to the USSR provided what one participant called "the shock of the concrete." Especially once the year-long exchanges started in 1958, participants had a chance to meet Soviet students, scholars, archivists, and others and to learn more about individual Soviets' lives rather than aggregates; as one exchange student put it, this accumulation of mundane experiences provided the chance to "see how ideology is thought and felt and experienced" on a daily basis. Ideology as experienced was drastically different than the ideological slogans plastered on posters or enumerated in official directives. For historians Samuel Baron and Nicholas Riasanovsky, visiting Moscow provided their first chance to see the contrast between official portrayals of Soviet life and the lives actually lived. Marshall Shulman was able, after his trip, to draw "a wholly more differentiated map of the Soviet universe," one full of divisions, tensions, and conflicts. And Merle Fainsod, one of the few senior scholars to participate, found optimism about changes in the Soviet system after observing "dissident students" during his 1956 trip. Participants' experiences did not automatically incline them to sympathy for the Soviet system; indeed, students reported (especially in the early years) that their time in the USSR had taught them the "true meaning and worth of freedom" and given them a sense of the reasons for "the struggle between East and West." Another generalized that he knew no one "whose views weren't hardened against the Soviet Union" as a result of the exchange experience.[81] The difficulties of everyday life also shaped scholars' attitudes toward the USSR. There were few Sovietologists who held the same love for their subject country as scholars specializing in, say, English literature, European history, or African cultures. While the experience of extended work in the USSR was crucial to success in the field, it was rarely something to be relished until it was in the past tense.

The U.S.-Soviet agreement on cultural exchange, signed by Lacy and the Soviet ambassador in Washington G. Z. Zarubin in 1958, established a reciprocal academic exchange with visits ranging from four to twelve months. The IUCTG sent twenty American scholars to the USSR for the 1958–1959 academic year and placed a similar number of Soviet scholars in American universities; the initial agreement called for increasing to thirty scholars each way in 1959–1960. Munford reported to the State Department in the spring of 1959 that it was unable to meet the thirty-student goal without lowering its standards. In the first three years of the exchange program, IUCTG sent sixty-eight students to the USSR and hosted a similar number in the United States. To the constant frustration of the Americans involved, the USSR sent laboratory scientists who had little direct bearing on Sovietology as practiced by social scientists and humanists. Another frustration for IUCTG was its effort to decentralize Sovietology, which was at best a partial success in the early years; close to half of the participants came from Columbia and Harvard.[82]

The late 1950s saw widespread interest in academic exchanges with the USSR, in which IUCTG was only one player. President Dwight Eisenhower called for a program to send 10,000 students to the USSR, but that proposal soon fell victim to bureaucratic in-fighting.[83] Individual universities tried again to mount bilateral exchanges with Soviet institutions. The Ford Foundation, in a brief but expensive flurry of enthusiasm, supported at least three efforts in 1959, granting a total of $265,000 to Berkeley, Columbia, and Harvard. None of the three got much beyond exchanging delegations, and even these efforts were, in the words of participants, "mutually disastrous," even "hilarious" in their failures.[84]

The brief moment of optimism also sparked the interest of the American Council of Learned Societies (ACLS), which initiated an exchange with the Soviet Academy of Sciences. Unlike the junior scholar exchange, which dealt primarily with teaching-oriented universities in the USSR, the ACLS program would work with the premier Soviet academic institution, under whose auspices the bulk of scholarly research, in all disciplines, took place. The ACLS senior scholar program was smaller in scale but broader in approach than that of the IUCTG. In its first two years, the ACLS sent thirteen American scholars and hosted the same number of Soviet scholars. The program encouraged a wider range of purposes, from long-term research visits to exchanges of lecturers not specializing in Soviet (or American) affairs.[85] The ACLS staff members were initially optimistic, thanks in part to almost $200,000 in grants from Carnegie, Ford, and Rockefeller.[86] For the exchange in 1962–1963, they nominated fifteen scholars, almost all of whom were Russia/Soviet experts hoping to conduct research for three months or more.[87] Yet months later, the Academy of Sciences had approved fewer than half of the American nominees, including many working on innocuous topics of pre-1917 history.[88] Soviet inaction amounted to a pocket veto of prospective participants, both those in the ACLS program and in the IUCTG senior scholar program that began, on a larger scale, in 1962. In the first two years of the IUCTG senior scholar program, ten of the eighty-seven nominees were rejected by the Soviet Ministry of Higher Education, and another forty-four were subject to the pocket veto. Predictably, applications plummeted, falling by half between 1963 and 1964 and shrinking further after that.[89] Tortured negotiations, last-minute changes, and constant confusion became hallmarks of early exchanges.

As troubles mounted with Soviet authorities, academics needed ever-greater cooperation from U.S. government officials. Because the exchange program took place under the auspices of an intergovernmental agreement, the State Department was involved in the everyday operations, a process that both deepened and tested government-academic relations. The Bureau of Educational and Cultural Affairs (known by its State Department acronym, CU) gave substantial grants to IUCTG for operations—from a start-up grant of $6,000 in 1958 to over $300,000 by 1962. The Moscow embassy provided on-site logistical support for the exchangees, from use of the PX and mail facilities to help in sorting out the myriad daily problems of life in the USSR. Difficulties with Soviet authorities more often than not threw the American academics together with State Department officials, but they could just as easily create conflicts. The CU staff were also intimately involved in negotiations with the Soviet authorities, to the frequent frustration of all involved.[90]

Though the exchange programs owed their success to cooperation between government and academe, problems soon mounted in this sphere as well. Other aspects of cooperation—especially security checks of participants—would soon generate significant conflict. From the outset, IUCTG provided advance notification to the State Department so that it might get an "early impression of what might be the final composition of the [student] group."[91] State would then run "name-checks"; these were not full-scale security clearances, but entailed an examination of FBI records. What exactly the State Department and IUCTG would do with information gleaned from the name-checks was not clearly spelled out at first, but evolved as individual cases arose.[92] Early on, IUCTG staffers confirmed and endorsed the process, with Stephen Viederman calling it essential to "insure the integrity of the program."[93] They would allow the committee to screen for applicants with "political maturity and emotional stability" who were "steeped in the American tradition"—criteria reflected in the form for applicants' recommenders. The IUCTG sent lists of finalists to the State Department, which ran the name-checks and flagged applicants that it considered a security risk. If the selection committee, kept unaware of the name-check results, chose someone who had been flagged, IUCTG would send a faculty member to Washington to examine the applicant's file. Such a faculty member needed a security clearance. In the first decade of the junior scholar program, the department flagged five of roughly a thousand applicants.[94]

The name-check process continued after IUCTG headquarters moved to Bloomington, Indiana, in 1960. Historian Robert F. Byrnes became the chair and led the IUCTG during its heyday in the early to mid-1960s, when applicants were numerous and well qualified, when conflicts between Soviet and American educators did not create existential crises, and when financial support flowed readily from the Ford Foundation and the State Department. Originally trained as a historian of France, Byrnes undertook a year of retooling as a Russianist at Columbia in the late 1940s. His late arrival in the field, however, left him at a distinct linguistic disadvantage; colleagues remember that he relied on fury more than fluency during exchange negotiations in Moscow, and he later recalled his "struggles" with Russian. He had difficulties finding a suitable job in the early 1950s, a fact he attributed to anti-Catholic sentiment at elite universities. Byrnes opted to work for the CIA for three years. The CIA work gave Byrnes the necessary clearance to evaluate the dossiers of students flagged in the name-checks, which he did even before becoming chair.[95] By virtue of his various roles at IUCTG, he quickly became a lightning rod for criticism. Other factors mattered, too. Some felt that his organizational contributions far outweighed his scholarly ones. And many colleagues recalled his deeply held and vehemently expressed moral and political values, which were more conservative than much of the profession and would grow from watercooler grumblings to public protest.

All of these exchanges, junior and senior, ultimately intensified divisions between the disciplines in Soviet Studies. The grants for thirty-day trips (1956–1958) went to scholars across the disciplines of Russian Studies: 39% to social scientists, 31% to historians, and 26% to humanists. But political scientists, economists, and the few sociologists, driven by broader trends within their disciplines, made less and less use of the IUCTG exchange, together accounting for only 15% of the long-term exchangees between 1958 and 1968. Historians and literary scholars quickly came to dominate, sending roughly 36% each.[96]

While the IUCTG became almost the exclusive province of humanists and historians, institutions like Ford's Foreign Area Fellowship Program tilted toward the social sciences. By 1960, history emerged as dominant, accounting for 49% of the fellows, with 41% from social science and fewer than 10% from the humanities.[97] The contrast between Ford and IUCTG distributions suggests the growing differentiation between Slavic studies graduate students in various disciplines; they received support from different sources and attended different programs. This would prove to be problematic for the field as a whole as the bonanza came to an abrupt end in the late 1960s. The IUCTG and Ford grants did not create the growing divisions between the disciplines of Russian

Studies, but they did help to distance the humanists and historians from the social scientists. By any measure—membership in AAASS, participation in AAASS conferences, course offerings, doctoral degrees—the core of the field remained history, political science, and literature. Yet the components of this core were increasingly distinct, with scholars having different graduate experiences and different opportunities for support.[98]

Paralleling trends in AAASS membership, there was a substantial increase in the number of doctoral degrees on Slavic topics in the 1960s, with a generally stable distribution. There was only one noticeable shift in the 1960s: an increasing number of dissertations oriented toward foreign policy. While most social science fields grew little from 1960 to 1970, degrees on Soviet foreign policy or international relations almost doubled.[99] These students were less inclined to study in the Soviet Union; many key sources were available in translation through the *Current Digest of the Soviet Press,* devaluing language expertise; and scholars of international behavior had fewer prospects of gaining entrance to the USSR on an exchange program, and little research they could do even if they were admitted. They focused less on the internal dynamics of Soviet society than on Soviet foreign policy, which was just as easily studied from Washington as from Moscow.

At least one scholar expressed his concerns about these changes in the field. Columbia historian Henry Roberts put a damper on an otherwise celebratory event, the first national AAASS conference in 1964. He criticized the graduate students whose applications for funding and travel he had read. Many, he noted, showed "intellectual shabbiness."[100] Roberts's brief and eventful tenure at the helm of *Slavic Review* did little to improve his evaluation of the field. In the midst of giddy talk of expansion, Roberts sounded a cautionary note:

> [We] persist in the notion that we represent a "field."...Is this simply a delusion?...It would probably be well to admit that ours is a singularly disheveled field, comprising partially overlapping but by no means congruent interests. Indeed, this may be its salient feature.[101]

Roberts's doubts about the direction of Slavic studies were shared by Walter Laqueur in London. Writing in *Survey* in 1964, he bemoaned in even stronger terms the tendency toward specialization in research; there was a "false image of scholarship" that measured success by counting footnotes and using jargon. The end result was that "scholarship and academic standards have often become synonyms for sterility and irrelevance."[102] Roberts and Laqueur both acknowledged the benefits of expanding the field's geography and intellectual scope but emphasized the costs.

Roberts's and Laqueur's concerns identified some of the intellectual effects of the transformation of Russian Studies. The expansion of the field had created remarkable new opportunities—the exchanges, for instance, and the creation of new Slavic and Russian centers. Yet it also led to diffusion; indeed, Ford officials would later characterize international studies in these years as undergoing "growth by dispersion."[103] More and more scholars who completed their degrees at institutions with Slavic centers soon found themselves working at universities without a critical mass of Slavicists. Not surprisingly, concerns of discipline competed with, and frequently won out over, concerns of area expertise.

The justifications for area studies programs in general, and for Russian Studies in particular, shifted. Scholars sought to advance knowledge through disciplinary channels, working individually rather than on collective and interdisciplinary projects. The training imperative was maintained as area studies centers blossomed in the decade after 1957. They provided a meeting place for scholars in various disciplines, plus funding for graduate students. With rare exceptions, though, they were not truly interdisciplinary.

These changes created a field markedly different from the interdisciplinary—or better, perhaps, the nondisciplinary—early days of Russian Studies. Many of the pioneers had themselves changed fields. Political scientists Philip Mosely and Frederick Barghoorn both earned doctorates in history while Michael Karpovich, Barrington Moore Jr., and Alex Inkeles were sociologists before they were Russia experts—and afterward, too. Economists Abram Bergson and Alexander Gerschenkron were well trained in their discipline before they began to study Russia. And so on. The early experts, who were rooted as much in area as in discipline, trained students who were increasingly responsive to the siren song of disciplines—in part because they would be hired, promoted, and tenured in departments, not area studies programs.

The quantitative growth made Russian Studies scholars more attuned to their disciplines at the very moment when the universalistic aspirations of postwar social science made it harder to focus solely on Russia. Social scientists felt especially keenly the tensions between discipline and area. Even as experts on the Soviet economy sought to employ the mathematical techniques coming into ascendance in the discipline, they found themselves on the margins. The Soviet Union fit well into sociologists' grand theorizing about industrial societies, though the discipline was woefully underrepresented in Soviet Studies. Political scientists, meanwhile, faced an uphill battle as they tried to contribute to broader disciplinary currents. Nor were humanists exempt from concerns about discipline. Scholars of Slavic literature undertook a variety of contradictory experiments to bring their subject to broader audiences. Historians of Russia, energized by the exchange programs, similarly sought to apply the ideas of their discipline. The quantitative and organizational changes of the late 1950s, in other words, offered intellectual opportunities as well as intellectual challenges, and each discipline within Russian Studies took advantage of the opportunities and faced the challenges in different ways.

PART II

GROWTH AND DISPERSION

CHAPTER 4

THE SOVIET ECONOMY AND THE MEASURING ROD OF MONEY

Even before academic Sovietology began, key sponsors in the U.S. government stressed the need to improve American understanding of the Soviet economy. During World War II, U.S. intelligence and military officers sought to measure the economic strength of their Soviet ally. These calculations shaped economic and military strategies in fighting the Nazis; strategists needed to know if the Soviets would be able to hold off the German invasion, whether they would be able to benefit from Lend-Lease aid (and if so, what kind), and whether the Soviet economy was providing sufficient war materiel. Yet, as analysts in the Office of Strategic Services (OSS) took on the task of measuring the Soviet economy in 1943, they found few scholars and even less scholarship at their disposal. Previous writings on the Soviet economy ran from unsystematic to anecdotal; they left basic questions—How much could the USSR produce? How fast was it growing? What were the obstacles and spurs to further growth?—unanswered and usually unasked. In the words of economic historian Alexander Gerschenkron, to derive even the most basic measures, "a new field had to be built by new people."[1] No new person was more important than Abram Bergson, the prodigy who would set economic studies of the USSR on a course that it would keep throughout the Cold War. That course was profoundly shaped by the circumstances of its wartime birth, as OSS developed some basic quantitative measures of the Soviet national income. The close ties to government agencies, the orientation toward national income accounting, and the reliance on published Soviet statistics were evident in the rushed wartime work as well as in the decades-long Cold War project of computing Soviet national income.

The size and growth of the Soviet economy were not arcane topics confined to specialist academic journals or classified intelligence reports. The Soviet press trumpeted high growth rates—as much as 20% annually at their most extreme—and Bergson and other economists considered public challenges to these exaggerations to be a central part of their work. The fact that such a reserved and

cautious individual as Bergson would publish widely about such highly technical topics suggested the importance of addressing public audiences.[2] Bergson
and his academic colleagues appeared frequently in publications from the *New
York Times* to *Vital Speeches of the Day*—participating in debates that included
high-ranking government officials, scholars, and diplomats.

For all of its importance in the public sphere, the Soviet economy was not
necessarily a central concern of economics departments. As Bergson and others applied macroeconomic techniques to the study of the USSR, other economists were expanding model building along very different lines, ones that
excluded nonmarket economies. Studies of planned economies fit into the subfield of "comparative economics," a subfield that diminished in importance in
the postwar years, marginalized by more mathematically sophisticated analyses that relied on data that were either unavailable for or inapplicable to the
USSR, sometimes both.

There were numerous obstacles to applying quantitative techniques to the
study of the Soviet economy. First was the problem of the country's ever-
increasing secrecy; Bergson summed up the situation nicely in the early 1950s:

> The First Five Year Plan [1928–1932] as published occupies four volumes;
> the second [1933–1937] occupies two. The Third [originally 1938–1942] was
> released in one volume of 238 pages. The Fourth Five Year Plan, the first
> postwar one [1946–1950] has the dimensions of six pages in *Pravda*. The new
> Fifth Five Year Plan [1951–1955] occupies three pages in *Pravda*.[3]

Along with secrecy came myriad obstacles to analyzing the Soviet economy:
statistical practices designed to mislead; different definitions for basic terms;
and a frustrating tendency to shift practices to hide bad news. No less an expert
than Bergson complained, "When I try to make sense of Soviet statistics, I
sometimes feel that I am wandering in a swamp."[4] It was hard to find any solid
ground from which to evaluate the Soviet economy because even bad data on
the Soviet economy were hard to come by.

The challenges first emerged during World War II, as U.S. war planners
tried to determine the dimensions of Lend-Lease aid to the USSR. The initial work borrowed extensively from British Ministry of Economic Warfare
reports, which themselves were informed speculations based on minimal (and
outdated) direct evidence. Geroid Robinson, chief of OSS's USSR Division,
used the outside demand for such information to bring OSS economists into
his division. Better understanding of the Soviet ally, Robinson argued, required
a combination of disciplinary expertise and solid grounding in the politics,
the society, and—not least—the Russian language. Robinson's perfectionism
and desire for control soon drove some economists to the exits. Among those
departing was Simon Kuznets, who went on to produce the "numbers that won

the war," estimates of U.S. national income and product accounts that were crucial for determining the production potential of American industry.[5]

Robinson must have especially rued Kuznets's decision when the USSR Division took on its first serious economic analysis. The initial effort appeared as a Research and Analysis (R&A) report in September 1943, as the Red Army swept the Nazis out of most Soviet territory. It was organized by the USSR Division's chief economist, Wassily Leontief Jr. Leontief had received his education and begun his career in Russia. (Leontief and Kuznets would eventually be among the first recipients of Nobel prizes for the ideas that they applied in the 1940s.) The goal of the paper was to estimate Russian national income and defense expenditures for 1940, the last year of peace. Plucking a handful of useful statistics from stacks of Soviet publications, the report estimated Soviet production for 1940 as about 53% of American production, immediately adding the italicized proviso that this figure was a *"major overstatement."* The report made ingenious use of a few scattered numbers, but otherwise bore little resemblance to the techniques of national income accounting that Kuznets proposed. Indeed, it did not even share the same definition of national income (gross national product) that Kuznets employed—this in spite of opening with a quote from Kuznets himself.[6]

Leontief, working with one of his favorite students, Abram Bergson, and a handful of other economists, tried to develop a systematic quantitative approach to the study of the Soviet economy. The results of the 1943 report on national income suggested the potential of quantitative models of the Soviet economy but also revealed some of the obstacles for national income work. Senior diplomats, especially Russia hand Charles "Chip" Bohlen, began asking for more detailed information on the Soviet economy. After the Moscow Conference of Foreign Ministers ended in November 1943, Bohlen knew that German reparations would become a major issue in postwar international relations. All too aware of the damage that punitive reparations did to German politics after World War I, Bohlen wanted the OSS to calculate Soviet war losses as he prepared to negotiate over German reparations. Leontief set up a more systematic approach to estimating Soviet war losses, employing the input-output matrices that he had developed. Though his tables for the Soviet economy were littered with empty cells, Leontief did produce an estimate: the Soviet economy had lost roughly $18 billion in fixed capital during the war. This would, the report's authors hoped, provide a starting point for the negotiations over postwar arrangements. Midway through the reparations analysis, Leontief returned to the Bureau of Labor Statistics, the result of a high demand for his services and an oversupply of criticism from Robinson.[7] Abram Bergson took over from Leontief and steered the reparations report to completion in early 1944.

Thanks to Bohlen's queries to OSS and his influence in the foreign policy apparatus, R&A soon gained influence in top policy circles. At Bohlen's request, OSS organized research on Soviet economic reconstruction, producing a landmark of economic analysis that helped to shape postwar U.S. foreign relations. The research started by recalculating, on an annual basis, the size and structure of the Soviet economy, including the division of its national income among investment, consumption, and defense. The results were impressive: Soviet GNP had increased fourfold since the start of the Five-Year Plan era in 1928, allowing for a massive expansion of military expenditures, increased investment, and a near-doubling of consumption. The report projected that the USSR would achieve prewar levels of production as early as three years after the war's end. Even more noteworthy was that this rapid reconstruction could take place "entirely out of domestic resources." While foreign trade or aid would lessen the impact of some bottlenecks, Soviet productive capacity, well protected behind the Ural Mountains, would be sufficient to power the country back to its prewar state—and soon, well above that.[8] The report outlined three scenarios for the postwar world and showed how, even amid maximum tensions (which translated into even higher spending on defense), the Soviet economy would quickly catch up with and surpass its prewar levels.

This document circulated widely in Washington, D.C., and a copy made its way to the American embassy in Moscow, where it caught the attention of George Kennan. Kennan echoed the R&A report in his assessments of the Soviet economy, glossing its statistics with his elegant prose. If the USSR could finance its reconstruction without relying on foreign aid, Kennan argued (following R&A), then promises of postwar aid would not provide any sort of bargaining chip for the West. As a result, Kennan argued, the West would be unable to keep the USSR from establishing a zone of influence in Eastern Europe. But Kennan (again following OSS analysts) also argued that the USSR would seek to expand its influence by taking advantage of available opportunities. Kennan hoped to limit Soviet opportunities and to contain the USSR within its existing sphere of influence.[9]

The culmination of USSR Division research was a major report, "The Capabilities and Intentions of the USSR in the Postwar Period," which was produced as background for the Yalta Conference of February 1945. The OSS's fans and skeptics alike praised the report for its apt summation of wartime trends and its projections for the immediate postwar years. The report combined detailed economic analyses with an innovative assessment of Soviet politics and outlined scenarios for Soviet postwar development. At its heart was the connection between capabilities and intentions. The Soviet leaders' primary goal was to rebuild their economy to prewar levels, which would fund enhancements in military capabilities while also allowing civilian standards of living to improve. Dreams of world Communism had not been forgotten, but would be temporarily shelved in the interests of national recovery. Even amid wartime devastation, the Soviet Union had remained a "highly stable" society; it would face a great many "strains" but had little risk of imminent collapse. The wartime experience, in fact, had demonstrated some of the sources of its stability: ideological flexibility along with the steady maintenance of "totalitarian" controls. The report predicted some postwar "relaxation" but few fundamental changes. The implications for postwar Soviet foreign policy were serious but not ominous. At the end of hostilities, the USSR would have neither the "resources" nor the "inclination" for an "adventurist" foreign policy. The focus would be on economic reconstruction, based primarily on its own resources and taking full advantage of its citizens' "traditionally ... Spartan standards of living." At the same time, though, Soviet foreign policy would be opportunistic, seeking "strategic expansion" where it could be accomplished unopposed. Since Soviet leaders believed that "time was on their side," they would be patient, even cautious in their international posture.[10]

The postwar scenarios outlined in "Capabilities and Intentions," as well as much of the evidence within it, reappeared in State Department debates, ambassadorial dispatches, and policy discussions. The report became the basis for an important postwar analysis that Robinson coauthored with Bohlen in 1945. And it shared much with the conclusion Kennan would reach in his long telegram of February 1946. While Kennan put his distinctive mark on American strategy, he was not the only Russian expert to reach the conclusion that Soviet leaders would be focused on internal reconstruction in the short term. The R&A economists, then, helped to shape the postwar debate over Soviet policy. Their conclusions that the USSR would be strong enough to recover on its own and would seek to expand when opportunities presented themselves were basic assumptions for early Cold War policy.[11]

The report on Russian reconstruction was the first Western analysis of the Soviet economy that constructed national income accounts. It built up to national income (using Western GNP definitions) by incorporating the contributions by various sectors: industry, agriculture, transportation, trade, and construction. In each of these cases, it used proxies to estimate sectoral growth—for instance, correlating agricultural production with the size of a year's grain crop. These assumptions and methods became standard operating procedure for the postwar field. And they prompted questions from outsiders that OSS economists themselves had asked: were Soviet data reliable? How did Soviet methods of measurement and accounting differ from Western approaches? What did Soviet prices really mean absent a free market? Bergson and his team sketched out their own answers to these questions amid the stress of their wartime work and stuck to them until the Soviet Union collapsed.

There is no better place to start examining those questions and answers than with Bergson himself. He started graduate work at Harvard at the age of nineteen and spent the 1930s as a star theorist, not a Soviet expert. His work on economic theory, beginning with a paper for Leontief's graduate class, shaped his approach to the study of the Soviet economy but was far broader. As he approached his twenty-fourth birthday in 1938, Bergson—then going by the name Abram Burk, which his parents used to disguise their Jewish heritage—published a signal contribution in welfare economics. It reflected Bergson's deep talents and narrow interests; he described his work in this field as "extracurricular," mere table talk for Bergson and a close friend, the economist Paul Samuelson. Bergson's highly technical article established a new criterion for considering the central theme of welfare economics. Vilfredo Pareto and other scholars focused on the distribution of resources within an economy; for example, a Pareto optimal distribution is one in which no individuals can improve their welfare without others facing a decline in theirs. Bergson argued against considering the distribution of individual welfare, proposing instead that economists consider economic welfare only "through the eyes of an ideal social planner" concerned for the welfare of all members of a society collectively. Welfare economists, Bergson insisted, must concern themselves only with the question of whether a given set of arrangements provided sufficient resources for winners to compensate losers; whether winners actually did compensate losers was, in the words of another economist, "a political question on which the economist had no special authority to pronounce."[12] Even while working in the recondite realm of welfare theory, Bergson was interested in the questions of planning for the social welfare; he also identified the limits of economists' studies.

Bergson hoped to follow up this theoretical interest in the planner's perspective with an empirical analysis of a planned economy. This move would allow him to test his theories while also contributing to one of the most heated economic debates of the interwar period, the so-called planning versus market debate. Some of the most important economists of the time argued over the efficiency of planned economies relative to market ones. Bergson, if he could combine his new measure of efficiency with empirical results, could make a major impact on that debate. As Bergson later recalled, "in the mixed-up world of [the 1930s], how socialist planning functioned in the one country where it was being applied on any scale seemed a rather momentous matter." Bergson started a crash course in Russian and spent the summer of 1937 in Moscow. It was perhaps the most brutal year in Soviet history; purges were going full-speed both at the highest levels of government and among everyday Soviet citizens. Bergson recalled that the fear among citizens affected him deeply. Few Soviet citizens were willing to talk to a foreigner, and he was "utterly terrified" to seek help in research. While it made a lasting impression on Bergson personally, the Soviet journey provided him with little research material.[13]

Once back in the United States, he located some musty Soviet publications in the Library of Congress that would become the basis for his dissertation. These reports from the early 1930s on Soviet wage levels allowed Bergson to apply a primitive measure of wage differentials, comparing the worst-paid workers with those making above-average wages. He concluded that Soviet practices violated Marxist claims of equal pay. Comparing the wage structure of the USSR in 1928 to that of capitalist countries (Russia in 1914 and the United States in 1904), he concluded that they were fundamentally similar. They were so similar, he concluded, that the Soviet wage structure was "capitalist." (As one reviewer pointed out, what Bergson called "capitalist," others might simply call economic: efficiency maximizing.) There were two crucial assumptions embedded in this argument.[14] First was the belief, as economist James Millar later put it, that microeconomic principles applied to the centrally planned Soviet economy. Bergson's logic worked as follows: Soviet wages shared a pattern of inequality similar to those of capitalist economies. Therefore, he concluded, Soviet wages were paid according to "capitalist principles." Among these principles is the notion that wages reflect productivity. Wage differences, after all, are explicable under capitalist principles only by two factors: relative productivity (a more productive task produces more income and can yield higher wages) and relative disutility (a particularly unpleasant job will need higher wages to attract workers than will a pleasant one). The notion that Soviet wages adhered to capitalist principles allowed the application of the economist's full set of economic tools: microeconomic measures of supply and demand and macroeconomic efforts to measure the size and scope of the economy. Wages, after all, are income for the worker, but they are also prices, which are central to both micro- and macroeconomic analysis. Bergson, therefore, was not making "an argument for socialism," Millar later summarized, but "for the general applicability of…microeconomics." Second, Bergson asserted that the Soviet wage statistics that he discovered at the Library of Congress were valid. The 1928 and 1934 data in the book, for instance, came from two reports produced by Soviet central statistical agencies, with few opportunities for double-checking against other sources. Noting that the data he used in his work were also the basis for articles in Soviet academic journals and, more important, appeared to be "the facts on which Soviet administrators base their decision[s]," he concluded, "'double-bookkeeping' is not remotely possible."[15] The wage ratios were similar to his capitalist cases, which would not have been possible if the Soviet figures were inaccurate. This last argument contained a tautology: Bergson used the conclusions he reached using Soviet data to support the claim that the data themselves were valid.

The narrow source base in his book on Soviet wages saved Bergson from having to confront the bigger challenge of measuring the size of the Soviet economy, a task he would take on after World War II. There were differences in definitions; for example, Soviet "net material product" did not include services covered in GNP. Another major problem with Soviet national accounts was the data's presentation in "constant 1926/27 prices." Though economists usually preferred constant prices to account for inflation, in the Soviet case they would lead, as OSS officials well knew, to inflated growth rates.[16] Why is this? Imagine an economy with only two products, videocassette recorders and popcorn. Measuring the production of each item over time would be easy: just count the number of VCRs and the amount of popcorn produced and compare to the previous year's production. But how should one measure the general level of production for this (mini-)economy as a whole? National income statistics like GNP require using the "measuring-rod of money": add the dollar value of VCRs produced to the dollar value of popcorn.[17] But using prices to make comparisons over time can be difficult. First of all, inflation distorts prices: an economy producing the same amount of popcorn one year is not more productive if it produces the same amount at a higher price the next year. So economists use "constant-dollar" data series, multiplying production in one year by prices in the base year. This adjustment to "real dollars" works very well in most cases, but there are some notable exceptions, especially in a rapidly changing economy. When VCRs first hit the mass consumer market in 1976, they were very expensive—around $1,300. Prices soon plummeted as VCRs entered mass production; by 2005, basic VCRs were available for around $50 (and by 2009, they were all but obsolete). So how should one compare the total output of the economy between 1976 and 2005? Using current dollars does not account for inflation. But using constant 1976 dollars would be even more distorting, overvaluing VCRs at the high 1976 prices. Because VCR production skyrocketed (say, 500-fold) in a short period of time, the differences between using constant and current prices would be sharp. National output grew almost 500-fold in constant 1976 dollars, compared with merely doubling in current dollars. Which number is correct? It depends on what measure is desired: in terms of how much videotaping an economy could do, 500-fold is a better measure, but in terms of the overall size of the economy, doubling is a better measure. Comparisons between economies with different price structures present an insurmountable problem for economists, and they have discussed the so-called index number problem since the 1920s.[18] The OSS economists were well aware of the problem as they used Soviet data; most were expressed in 1926/1927 constant ruble prices, which produced an "upward bias" in Soviet national income data, especially data related to industry.[19] The OSS economists had no easy solution to the problem, which would vex Western economists for years to come.

The issue of prices was even more complicated than merely the problem of which year's prices to use. In the economists' hypothetical free market, prices represented, on the one hand, how much something was worth to the buyer and, on the other, for how much it could be profitably sold. While no market corresponded exactly to the hypothetical free market, it is safe to assume that the Soviet economy was a greater deviation from the market than any other economy of the day. What, then, did Soviet prices represent? They were set by planners, presumably to reflect the planners' preferences—subsidizing some products (such as bread) while overvaluing others. A hefty turnover tax, in addition, kept the data from accurately reflecting scarcity conditions—the conditions would make prices bear useful information about the costs of production and the extent of demand. The OSS economists had recognized these problems, but lacked the time or resources to solve them.

Bergson, who had come to OSS from a post at the University of Texas, followed his boss Geroid Robinson to Columbia University, where he taught until he was hired away by Harvard in 1956. In the meantime, he stayed involved in efforts to calculate the dimensions and structure of the Soviet economy. Before OSS economic work ended up at CIA, it migrated first to the RAND Corporation, which funded an exercise in competitive economic intelligence. An agenda-setting session of social scientists in RAND's first month, September 1947, demonstrated special interest in an "economic prospectus for Russia" that would develop the procedures for computing Soviet national income in order to "provide a rough estimate of the economic power with which we may have to contend." The assembled group responded enthusiastically to the proposal, citing specifically a recent study by émigré economist Naum Jasny that surveyed the available Soviet data on national income. That article argued that national income estimates would be technically demanding but essential both for the economics profession and for national security.[20] RAND sponsored three distinct approaches to measuring the Soviet economy: Norman Kaplan calculated Leontief-style input-output tables for the Soviet economy; Alexander Gerschenkron produced dollar-denominated estimates; and Bergson worked on ruble-denominated estimates. The OSS veterans cornered this miniature marketplace of ideas: Bergson, of course, had been chief economist in the USSR Division, Gerschenkron briefly served on Bergson's staff, and the input-output tables were the brainchild of Bergson's professor and predecessor, Wassily Leontief Jr.[21]

The three RAND projects of the late 1940s and early 1950s shared one central assumption: that Soviet economic statistics had economic meaning. This was not the same thing as assuming that the Soviet data were correct; few serious scholars believed that Soviet data as published provided an accurate accounting of Soviet economic achievements.[22] Even long-time critics of the Bergsonian approach to the study of the Soviet economy—like British economists Colin Clark and Peter Wiles as well as Jasny—made use of Soviet statistics with various adjustments. Their many disagreements revolved around how best to adjust the published Soviet data, not about whether they were suitable as starting points for analysis. Bergson was far from alone in wanting to work with Soviet data. Gerschenkron emphasized that the Soviet strategy was to withhold information rather than to falsify it. At one of a handful of scholarly symposia, even critics like Clark accepted this premise; he enumerated dozens of problems with the data, but implied that valid data lay beneath the published reports. "It is not permissible," he had concluded earlier, "to accuse the Russian statisticians of deliberate distortion"; with proper adjustments, therefore, economists could compute usable data. Beneath his bilious attacks on Bergson, even Jasny relied on published data after trying to undo Soviet statistical shenanigans. He offered strictures similar to those of Bergson and Gerschenkron: all Soviet figures required "thorough check[s]"; data corresponding to physical quantities (acres sown, tons harvested, or number of items produced) "seem[ed] in general to be correct"; but the index data and long-running data series were especially suspect.[23]

Bergson's defense of Soviet data was much more detailed than Jasny's, which is no surprise given his extremely cautious personality and his deep professional investment in using Soviet statistics. While Bergson had offered some defenses of Soviet statistics in *Structure of Soviet Wages,* by 1953 his explanation was quite elaborate. He first defined falsification narrowly as "free invention and double bookkeeping" and then enumerated the reasons that he thought Soviet data were not falsified:

1. Soviet data held up "tolerably well" to tests of internal consistency, that is, they corresponded closely to other Soviet data;
2. Soviet data were consistent with other Soviet evidence—for instance, low growth rates in a certain industry were often followed by personnel shake-ups in that industry;
3. Soviet data were broadly consistent with reports from foreign observers;
4. Soviet data about World War II were definitely not overstated since they were so little above the nation's military requirements;
5. Soviet authorities preferred to withhold data, as "an alternative" to outright falsification; and
6. classified and unclassified Soviet versions of the 1941 economic plan "check[ed] closely, item by item."[24]

The strongest evidence came from a detailed comparison of two versions of the 1941 plan, an English-language pamphlet published as "The Growing Prosperity of the Soviet Union" and the statistical attachments for a classified version of the 1941 plan that was distributed in the Soviet *apparat.* The plan documents remained classified by the U.S. Army through the 1940s; much to his frustration, Gerschenkron was unable to see the plan until 1950, but it had come to RAND's attention at least a year earlier. For Bergson, the classified version of the 1941 plan proved that there was no "double-bookkeeping" in the Soviet economic system.[25] Yet here, too, questions arise. The 1941 plan documents were at the lowest possible level of classification, *ne podlezhit' oglasheniiu* (not subject to publication)—roughly equivalent to "restricted" or "confidential" and well below top secret. There were tens of thousands of economic documents more highly classified; indeed, one scholar estimates that only 12% of Soviet economic decrees between 1930 and 1941 were unclassified, while more than 18% were "top secret."[26] So the existence of a document with such a low level of classification is hardly conclusive evidence that there was no double bookkeeping; the "real" books could very easily have been more highly classified than the 1941 plan that fell into American hands. Bergson devoted less time to demonstrating that Soviet data were not "freely invented," but ultimately let the argument rest on the issue of consistency: it would be very difficult to create fictional data in one field (say, bread production) without similarly making up data in another (say, grain harvest). The complex relationships inherent in economic data ruled out invention. Yet, as economists well knew, there were plenty of forms of distortion aside from outright invention.[27]

Even if Bergson was right that there was no double bookkeeping or free invention, that hardly constituted proof that the data were accurate. Indeed, Gerschenkron speculated that the inaccuracies could easily wend their way up the statistical system, so that even if the central agencies reported the data with perfect accuracy, they would incorporate significant distortions from lower reporting levels. His argument to continue using Soviet data rested on the claim that "the tendency to understate is no less real than the tendency to overstate. Both are inherent in the very nature of industrial enterprises in Soviet Russia."[28] Gerschenkron may have based this claim on the work of his student Joseph Berliner, who was using Refugee Interview Project (RIP) data to examine the management of Soviet industry. Berliner used the gentle term "simulation"—"dissimulation" might have been more apt—to describe a form of what Soviets called *ochkovtiratel'stvo* (literally, rubbing someone's eyeglasses); he recognized that it polluted Soviet published statistics, though he minimized the overall impact.[29] Ultimately, Bergson admitted candidly, if Soviet officials were falsifying their data, then "research on the Soviet economy today would be entirely out of the question."[30] For good calculations, he insisted, Soviet statistical information did not have to be accurate, only inaccurate in systematic ways, for which scholars could make appropriate adjustments.

The RAND projects headed by Kaplan, Gerschenkron, and Bergson all sought to adjust Soviet data in an effort to see which approach to the Soviet economy would yield the most useful results. The input-output tables quickly foundered. Leontief was unwilling to run the project, so it ended up with the RAND junior economist Norman Kaplan. His input-output table examined twenty sectors, a paltry number compared with Leontief's prewar table for the American economy (forty-two sectors) or his wartime work for the Bureau of Labor Statistics (ninety-five sectors).[31] Compounding the problems of analysis—with far too many blank cells in the input-output matrix—was the fact that the table analyzed the Soviet economy in 1941, a year that had a uniquely rich data source. Far more information was available for the 1941 plan, a classified copy of which the German army took when fighting in Soviet territory, and which came into the hands of U.S. intelligence after the war. But as difficult as it was to develop an input-output table for 1941, it would have been significantly more complex to do so for any other year with substantially less data available. Kaplan's final result, titled with due modesty "A Tentative Input-Output Table," was rarely cited and did not become a significant part of the growing literature on economic Sovietology.[32]

The other two approaches both relied on national income accounting. They differed only in denomination: Gerschenkron indexed changes in the economy in terms of dollars while Bergson used rubles. This difference was far from trivial, as Gerschenkron emphasized. Using dollar weights would only replace one form of the index-number problem with another. After all, applying the price structure of a highly industrialized country (the United States) to one just starting rapid industrialization (the USSR) would still distort national accounts. There were added complications, too, that turned the dollar-valuation project into an exercise in engineering and marketing as well as re-indexing. To assign dollar values to Soviet machine tools—the first type of goods that Gerschenkron tackled—he had to speak with industry officials who could estimate the dollar costs of producing each tool; differences in productivity and durability further complicated such comparisons. Gerschenkron made the case for the dollar-valued approach at the same time that he sought funds for it: "the task," he implored in a journal article, "could hardly be undertaken without the assistance of a generously staffed research organization." RAND provided the generous funding to hire a small staff of research assistants. The result was a thick research paper on a seemingly narrow topic: "A Dollar Index of Soviet Machinery Output, 1927–28 to 1937." The report tracked the production of 128 different machines, including more than 40 types of farm machinery, using machine production as a proxy for overall economic growth.[33] He concluded that the overall Soviet growth rate barely reached half of Soviet claims, and even these rates were achieved for only a handful of years in the 1930s. Scholars started to refer to the "Gerschenkron effect" of using constant currencies to measure the growth of rapidly changing economies, to the delight of its namesake, who gleefully told his student Nancy Nimitz, "I'm an effect!"[34] Though this nomenclature significantly overstated Gerschenkron's role in describing the index-number problem, it did at last provide a convenient name—but no solution—for a difficult problem. At the same time, it deflated Soviet claims about rapid economic growth, an intended consequence of the Gerschenkron effect.[35]

After producing a handful of dollar indexes for RAND, Gerschenkron moved away from measurements of the Soviet economy and toward a broader historical perspective. One reason for this shift related to the dollar indexes themselves, which were ultimately less useful measures of the Soviet economy than the ruble-denominated data that Bergson was developing. Converting from rubles to dollars introduced new distortions related to differences in productions costs and product quality, among other things. The conversion also created a new form of the Gerschenkron effect by applying the price structure of a highly industrialized economy to an industrializing one. The end result was a calculation that may have been even more distorted than those relying on "constant 1926–1927 prices." When one colleague criticized the dollar indexes—they "will not help"—Gerschenkron pleaded only for a revision that they "will not help much."[36] He grasped the limited utility of the dollar indexes, praising one book for "avoiding the use of weights pertaining to some non-Russian economy (such as dollar prices and so on)"—that is, for avoiding precisely what Gerschenkron himself had been doing.[37] If the limits of the dollar-based analysis were clear to Gerschenkron, it is also likely that he was increasingly aware of his own analytical limits. The work of Bergson and Kaplan quickly overtook and surpassed Gerschenkron's skills in formal, quantitative economic analysis. Gerschenkron lacked training in and aptitude for quantitative methods and also lacked the patience to spend weeks mulling over a single number, which defined Bergson's work.

Gerschenkron's greatest influence on economic Sovietology, aside from his effect, was through graduate training. While he advised only seven Ph.D. students in economic Sovietology, six of them went on to great success. Most landed at the premier Russian Studies centers: Columbia (Alexander Erlich), Berkeley (Gregory Grossman), Illinois (Donald Hodgman), and Indiana (Robert W. Campbell). Others, Joseph Berliner (Brandeis) and Franklyn Holzman (Tufts), were at teaching institutions but maintained close connections to Harvard's Russian Research Center.[38] Few of them worked on the sort of painstaking quantitative reconstruction that Bergson did. Berliner's dissertation, for instance, was just as much ethnography (using RIP sources) as economics, as he described the behavior of Soviet managers.[39] Only Hodgman did serious measurement work, but he soon turned away from Soviet topics to write about banking and monetary policy in capitalist economies.[40] Grossman shifted between more quantitative analysis and work on original topics like the functioning of the "second economy" (black and gray markets) in the Soviet Union. Erlich (who earned his Ph.D. from the New School, but was connected to the Russian Research Center for most of his graduate school career) attempted to apply formal economic theory to the Soviet economic debates of the 1920s. It was an impressive and insightful analysis but was not, in any sense, an analysis of Soviet economic growth.[41] In all of their innovative work, Gerschenkron's students ultimately emulated their advisor's breadth and his avoidance of Bergsonian quantification. Their work was invaluable for bringing an economic approach to the study of the Soviet Union, but it did not tackle the questions of measurement that animated Bergson, RAND, and eventually the CIA.

In contrast to Gerschenkron's intellectual restlessness, Bergson's patience and caution suited him well for the task of measuring the Soviet economy. His writing style was a reflection of his personality. Campbell may have penned the cleverest of many references to Bergson's prose: like "instant coffee," he noted, it required "considerable dilution before it can be easily absorbed." Another economist rightly called Bergson's prose "ever on its guard with a well-stocked arsenal of qualifying phrases." Bergson was overqualified in both his writing and his talents: a theorist with an excellent head for numbers, extremely patient, and even more cautious. Generations of Harvard students came through his classes without the enthusiasm for their professor that others felt for his erstwhile Columbia colleague Philip Mosely and without the sense of mystique and loyalty that Gerschenkron triggered in others—but they completed their degrees knowing a great deal about how to use economic theory, statistical techniques, and limited data to measure the Soviet economy. Colleagues described his personality, politics, and scholarship alike as abstemious and cautious.[42]

By 1949–1950, as Gerschenkron's and Kaplan's RAND projects ran into difficulties, Bergson's RAND project on ruble-denominated estimates was beginning to bear fruit. The basic approach was to use data that were as "unprocessed" as possible; physical measures of output were best. These data, in which Bergson and others placed more faith, were at the maximum possible level of disaggregation. Earlier estimates of Soviet national income started with Soviet aggregate data and made a handful of adjustments to account for definitional differences. Bergson, in his Soviet National Income and Production (SNIP) project, instead tried to construct Soviet national accounts from the ground up—what would later be termed the "building block" approach. It was a painstaking process that required extensive research in the spotty Soviet data about production, the determination of prices, and ultimately a huge arithmetic exercise, multiplying production by price for hundreds of items produced. All of this work, if handled properly, would result in the Soviet national income for a single year.

There were, however, many challenges—in data gathering, conceptualization, and computation—to producing these national income and product data. One of the first items on Bergson's agenda was to develop prices that would allow the proper weighting of production figures. The main reason to make this adjustment was to ensure that prices reflected productivity, just as they would in a free market. Bergson ultimately settled upon the adjusted factor cost system (AFCS), which took into account two of the most obvious distortions of Soviet prices: the use of government subsidies and taxes. Bergson's adjustments would yield the producer's price for a given item—how many rubles' worth of the three basic factors of labor, capital, and materials were used in creating that product. The AFCS used prices primarily as weights to calculate national income, which allowed him to convert physical units into the measuring rod of money. Bergson developed these adjusted prices to use as weights for calculating national income, not as determinants in standard of living. The AFCS was an accounting category, and as he wrote in his dissertation, "workers do not eat accounting categories."[43] This use of prices was well understood in economics departments, but not so widely outside them.

Beyond this limitation lay an assumption about prices. Bergson argued that, by adjusting for subsidies and taxes, he could derive prices that would be useful for determining the factor costs of producing a given item. Yet he was not actually deriving the price from those costs, only assuming that the adjusted price equaled those factor costs. On what basis could he assert this? He argued that prices were set by "planners' preferences," which might reflect political goals, but aimed for maximum production at minimal cost given those goals. Ultimately, he imputed market-like behavior to planners, which would lend validity to the AFCS-based prices; AFCS thus became "what would be recorded if factor prices were uniform as between industries and at the same time corresponded to relative factor productivities *on the average* in the economy generally." That is, AFCS would mark equilibria between different products and industries as if they had been prices set in a free market. As one economist put it succinctly, "the underlying assumptions [of Bergson's work] were that the dictator controlled the economy and sought what was 'best' for the economy." Bergson did not imagine Soviet planners to be a "committee of supermen," but saw them as in charge of a system that could function in its own best interests.

This sort of system-wide thinking is evident even in Bergson's views of welfare economics, where he redefined welfare at a collective rather than individual level. This assumption, too, is evident in his AFCS analysis; it assumes that planners are maximizers even within political constraints—that they are looking out for the best results for the economy as a whole rather than any one of its components. Yet, one economist noted, evidence from the Soviet archives (available in the 1990s) painted a very different picture of the functioning of the

Soviet economy: "planners' preferences were exercised weakly," creating short-ages and misallocations.[44] This archival information, of course, was unavail-able in the 1950s, but it highlights just how many assumptions were built into Bergson's estimates of the Soviet economy. While he made some adjustments, he did not devote significant attention to the institutional mechanisms and informal operations that would prevent a planned economy from functioning according to planners' preferences.

The first preliminary product of Bergson's work came in the form of tables of the adjusted Soviet GNP for 1937, broken down by sector of production and by use. Aside from using AFCS to adjust for subsidies and turnover taxes, Bergson set up a series of separate adjustments related to farm prices. All told, Bergson computed the Soviet GNP for 1937 at 224.9 billion rubles, about 25% below official Soviet statistics. By his calculation, defense spending accounted for almost 8% of GNP. Compared with the United States, the Soviet economy was more agricultural (30%, three times the U.S. share) and at the same time more oriented toward investment (21% versus 13% for the United States).[45]

As this first monograph of Bergson's SNIP project moved toward publication, he also organized a conference on Soviet economic growth that projected Soviet prospects for growth over the next two decades—and represented the state of the art in Sovietological economics in the early 1950s. The main purpose was to evaluate Soviet production potential, a key indicator of the success of central plan-ning as well as the extent of the Soviet military threat. The bulk of the contribu-tions came from scholars connected to RAND, leading Colin Clark to compare the event to "the most oleaginous type of Mutual Admiration Society." Jasny was even more hostile, insisting that Bergson step down in favor of a "neutral (non-RAND)" chairperson; when the Joint Committee on Slavic Studies refused this request, Jasny refused, on principle, to participate. Perhaps the only surprise was Jasny's desire to be involved at all; he accused RAND economists, variously, of stealing credit for his work, harassing him, and letting a pro-Soviet bias shape their work. Perhaps Jasny's exclusion from the network of economists centered around RAND played a role, too. He had tried to join the OSS and then Harvard's RRC, to no avail. Outsider Alec Nove summarized Jasny's frequent controversies:

> Dr. Jasny might perhaps be aptly described as an angry scholar. In this field a dose of anger is not unjustified with regard to the deliberately misleading nature of much of the statistical material and to its use by some of the more uncritical Western commentators (though this should not lead him to imply that views different from his own, even if mistaken, have a necessary connec-tion with the Hand of Moscow, as from time to time he tends to do).

Though the conference organizers had long anticipated Jasny's involvement, they shed few tears after his withdrawal.[46]

The published volume, which aimed to project the state of the Soviet economy from the early 1950s until 1970, depicted an economy better suited for brief bursts of rapid growth than for long-term steady expansion. Gregory Grossman set out the basic groundwork for the volume in his opening essay on national income; he recognized that the Soviet Union might be able to maintain a high growth rate through the 1950s, in the neighborhood of 6.5–7% annually, at a time when the U.S. economy rarely topped 3%. But he cited numerous obstacles to continued growth at that pace, the most important being the problems of the agricultural sector, which would hold back growth through its remarkable inefficiency; further growth required a shift in labor resources from agriculture to industry, which in turn required increases in agricultural productivity. Other economists reached similar conclusions through their examinations of capital formation, labor productivity, and trade. Given Bergson's and RAND's focus on GNP as production potential (and not as an indicator of individual welfare), it is not surprising that the conference had omitted serious discussion of standards of living, though of course the topic emerged in a handful of the published essays.[47]

Taken together, *Soviet Economic Growth* (1953) and *Soviet National Income in 1937* (1953) marked the arrival of Bergson's approach to studying the Soviet economy. While earlier work had appeared in purple-dittoed RAND reports and research memoranda, these widely distributed books summed up knowledge of Soviet economic history, described in detail the methods of calculating key Soviet economic indicators, and offered projections into the Soviet future. Jasny, not surprisingly, was aghast at the proceedings; scholars did not know enough about the past or present, making any projections to 1970 "remote…from science." But even Peter Wiles, a once and future critic of Bergson and RAND, celebrated the volumes: "The free world is heavily in debt to the simple frontiersman's spirit and the large bank balances of American research, especially the RAND Corporation." But he had in mind a peculiar form of frontiersman, one more inclined to the cubicle than the canoe; Wiles noted that statistical data tended to be "compiled rather than used," suggesting that this was just what the field needed: "not brilliant and novel interpretations but quantification." Not brilliance but lots of rote calculations—just the sort of task for a government agency. Jasny concurred: "since almost all the money comes from the [government] treasury, the government might as well take the task into its own hands."[48] Indeed, the work that RAND sponsored soon found its way to the Central Intelligence Agency, which was just at that moment beefing up its economic intelligence work under the leadership of economist Max Millikan (MIT), a long-time consultant to the RAND project.

By the time of the Soviet economic growth conference in May 1952, Millikan had just returned from a yearlong stint as the founding director of the CIA's Office of Research and Reports (ORR). Millikan had made the most of his brief stay at ORR, expanding the group's mandate, building up its staff (from roughly 100 in economic intelligence when he arrived to more than 400 a year after his departure), and most important, establishing the methods and approaches that would guide the ORR for decades. Despite its vague name, ORR was the centerpiece of CIA efforts at economic intelligence and focused on the Soviet bloc.[49] Not surprisingly, Millikan, who had consulted with all three of RAND's Soviet economy projects, built on the RAND experience.

Early on, Millikan promoted a two-pronged approach to studying the Soviet economy, one for measuring the Soviet economy as a whole and another for military spending in particular. For general indicators of Soviet growth, ORR would estimate growth by sector of origin to produce an overall estimate of real Soviet national income and product much like Bergson's work did. Millikan expected that ORR would start with large sectors (like industry and agriculture) and then try to disaggregate each sector into smaller and smaller units. This building-block approach would stay with CIA for the whole Cold War. Millikan's key phrases—starting with an "inventory of ignorance" and then proceeding by "successive approximation"—would become mantras for CIA economists, appearing in almost every historical account.[50] The ORR would move well beyond Bergson's level of analysis, focusing especially on factor productivity (how much labor and capital went into making a given product); this would prove to be a key method in projecting long-term economic growth.[51] Millikan promoted a Bergsonian approach for macroeconomic studies of the Soviet Union, which incorporated that scholar's assumptions and limits. The CIA estimates would rely heavily on Soviet data, assuming them to be inaccurate, but in systematic ways that could be accounted for; they would focus on real GNP as a measure of production potential (not individual welfare); and they would measure Soviet GNP in real rubles, adjusting for inflation but avoiding conversions into dollars. All of these assumptions would prove to be controversial in later years.

The ORR's estimates of Soviet military spending differed from this sectoral approach. Millikan was left with two choices for computing Soviet military expenses: relying on the Soviet public figures or calculating military spending as a residual—that is, what was left after civilian production and services were accounted for. The former approach had little to recommend it; Soviet authorities used obscure definitions of what constituted a military expense and, more important, were even stingier with the release of military data than they were with general economic data. And there was little reason to be confident enough in estimates of the Soviet economy to believe that the residual figure was sufficiently accurate. Neither of these methods allowed any possibility of breaking down Soviet military expenditures by mission, function, or location—which would be necessary to meet Millikan's ultimate goal of estimating "the character and location of possible military threats."[52] The ORR broke down the Soviet military into functional units and then estimated both ruble and dollar costs for each entity. This approach fit perfectly with Millikan's oft-cited ideas about inventorying ignorance and then repeating estimates with more and more precision; starting with only a handful of building blocks, the CIA's estimates of Soviet military spending eventually incorporated almost 1,800 items.[53]

The CIA estimates on Soviet economic growth found almost immediate application after the inauguration of President Dwight D. Eisenhower in 1953. America's Soviet policy had featured prominently in the election campaign, and a wing of the Republican Party promoted "rollback," forcing the Soviet Union back within its own borders and out of Eastern Europe. At the same time, another wing of the Republican Party shared Eisenhower's view that military spending had become an unmanageable burden for the American economy. Two weeks after taking office, Eisenhower embarked on a thorough review of America's defense posture, calling on his National Security Council to "figure out a preparedness program that will give us a respectable position without bankrupting the nation." He hoped to make good on his campaign pledge to solve the "Great Equation" by "balanc[ing] requisite military strength with healthy economic growth." The president wondered "whether we can afford to keep absorbing our resources [in military expenses] at this rate and maintain our free and democratic way of life." His budget director believed that the USSR was trying to "destroy our capitalist economy by means of economic warfare," forcing an increase in U.S. government expenditures.[54] Eisenhower was looking for a new foreign policy and military posture that would allow him to reduce defense spending without increasing American exposure to world threats, most notably the USSR.

Eisenhower envisioned Operation Solarium (named for its initial meeting place in the White House) as an exercise in competitive policy determination. He convened three task forces of outside experts, each charged with analyzing one policy option. In the broadest terms, these options were isolationism, containment, and rollback (which included the "explicit use of nuclear weapons"). These three teams included luminaries like George Kennan (heading, not surprisingly, the containment team) and Dean Rusk (then head of the Rockefeller Foundation), a dozen senior military officers, and a sprinkling of academics with policy and intelligence experience, including Mosely. Overseeing the whole exercise was the troika of Secretary of State John Foster Dulles; his brother, Director of Central Intelligence Allen Dulles; and the president's national security advisor, former banker Robert Cutler.[55]

As background to the Solarium exercise, the CIA prepared an estimate of "Probable Long-Term Development of the Soviet Bloc and Western Power

Positions." Though the report complemented and extended a recent national intelligence estimate (NIE 65) that predicted Soviet capabilities through 1957, its tone was less alarmist. The NIE 65 had predicted Soviet economic growth in the neighborhood of 5–7% annually, but underscored that military capabilities would increase far more rapidly.[56] The special estimate, in contrast, anticipated high growth rates for the next few years but noted that a "leveling off" had already begun; by 1967, growth rates were likely to be in the 3–4% range. While the report predicted that the ratio of U.S. to Soviet GNP would decline, it also expected that the absolute gap between the Soviet and American economies was likely to grow since the U.S. economy was so much larger.[57] According to this later report, then, time was on the American side for economic competition with the Soviet Union—a position open to only one of the three Solarium task forces; the mandate of the others was to assume that time was working on the side of the Soviet Union.

The three Solarium task forces revealed the shared assumptions of the policy elite in the early 1950s. While they differed greatly in military strategy, all three incorporated claims about the Soviet economy into their threat assessments. Though the CIA estimates offered reasons for optimism as well as concern, optimism was in short supply in Operation Solarium. The aggressive Task Force C took as an operating assumption that "time was working against" the United States; the least aggressive Task Force B expressed confidence that the Soviet Union would not catch up with the U.S. economy "in the foreseeable future."[58] Soviet growth from 1945 to 1950 was indeed high—as high as 10% annually, according to CIA. The economic threat of the Soviet Union received less explicit attention than the military threat, yet it undergirded assumptions about the expansion of Soviet military capabilities, in terms of not just atomic weapons but also more costly conventional forces. None of the Solarium task forces called for the reduction of U.S. military expenditures; the only differences came in the rate of increase they proposed. Two of the task forces explicitly noted the need for higher taxes in order to fund increased defense spending. Estimates of Soviet economic growth cast a shadow over the whole Solarium exercise.

The results of this exercise, and the intelligence work that went into it, must have alarmed some senior administration officials. Eisenhower worried about defense spending as a drag on the economy and saw here that the options open to him left few possibilities of reducing the defense burden. This apparently concerned Eisenhower greatly, and the "New Look" adopted after Solarium took more seriously the need to provide (as a campaign slogan had it) "security with solvency." The official policy, outlined in NSC 162/2 (October 1953), said little about Soviet economic growth, focusing instead on the dual threats of Soviet expansion and Soviet atomic capability. But the document emphasized—perhaps ten times over its twenty-nine pages—the need to maintain American economic strength; typical is this claim:

> The United States must maintain a sound economy based on free private enterprise as a basis both for high defense productivity and for the maintenance of its living standards and free institutions. Not only the world position of the United States but the security of the whole free world, is dependent on the avoidance of recession and on the long-term expansion of the US economy....Expenditures for national security...must be carefully scrutinized with a view to measuring their impact on the national economy.

The document sought to navigate between the Scylla of Soviet atomic-backed expansion and the Charybdis of big government and "repressive taxation." Indeed, Cutler made sure that this new national security doctrine treated the threats of Soviet aggression and American overspending as "co-equal."[59] If the economic basis for the Soviet threat was less than the CIA calculated, then Eisenhower would have an easier time steering clear of what he later called the "military-industrial complex."

While taking seriously the reports of the Solarium task forces, Eisenhower also worked in a time-honored tradition of policy: if facts do not fit the theory, change the facts. In this case, he wondered how it was that a planned economy could possibly outperform free enterprise. The defenders of free enterprise believed in that system instinctively; Eisenhower, Cutler, and the secretary of state shared similar views, characterized here by Townsend Hoopes:

> American economic and technical superiority rested in large part on the *moral* superiority of the free enterprise system. Only men operating in political freedom could achieve spectacular industrial progress....To acknowledge that the Soviet system was now an emergent industrial power, capable of generating [a] vast economic surplus...was to yield the moral foundations of [this] policy.

Eisenhower worried greatly that defending against the Soviet economic threat would itself endanger the American economy and ultimately its "basic institutions."[60] Theories firmly in place, John Foster Dulles and Eisenhower set about to challenge the facts.

The White House responded to this dual threat to its policies and principles by doing what one historian aptly termed an "end-run" around the CIA to investigate the agency's estimates and perhaps to develop ones that deflated Soviet growth predictions. This process started just as the Solarium task forces disbanded. Robert Cutler, who had managed the whole Solarium process, wrote to Dean Rusk with a request. While the letter was marked "personal and confidential," it was hardly a letter to a friend. It first noted the official and private estimates of Soviet growth—presumably by the CIA and Bergson, respectively. Calling attention to the "great scientific interest" of such estimates as well as their "immediate relevance to national security policy," Cutler hinted that Rusk's Rockefeller Foundation "may wish to take some leadership" in organizing an alternative study of Soviet economic growth.[61] Mosely objected but was overruled, so plans sped ahead; at the invitation of Rockefeller staff, the National Bureau of Economic Research (NBER) applied for a major grant to study "the performance of the Russian Soviet economy," citing in particular its value to "the military, political, and economic policy of…the free world."[62] The NBER was an unusual place for Rusk to ask for help. Founded in the 1920s with Rockefeller support, it aimed to provide apolitical economic expertise for policy purposes. It was NBER, for instance, that had sponsored Kuznets's pathbreaking work on national income accounts like GNP. Yet the NBER decided to focus domestically and to leave international calculations of GNP to others. So why did the White House and the RF turn to NBER for this project? Most likely, because of personal connections; the chair of Eisenhower's Council of Economic Advisors, Arthur Burns, had served as NBER president before coming to Washington. He shared Cutler's skepticism that a planned economy could outperform a capitalist one; indeed, he had lobbied for an outside challenge to CIA estimates of Soviet growth well before Solarium. Cutler, after the RF grant, promised Rusk that he would inform only two people of the real nature of the NBER work: Burns and a senior CIA official.[63] The idea was to produce an alternative assessment, and preferably a less impressive result, than the classified work by CIA analysts and the public work of Bergson and his RAND colleagues.

The NBER officials understood the political stakes of this grant. The proposal to the Rockefeller Foundation noted that high estimates of Soviet growth presented "a great challenge to believers in the productive powers of the private-enterprise system."[64] To work on the project, the bureau hired G. Warren Nutter, whose scholarly experience made him a far from obvious selection. Milton Friedman's first graduate student, Nutter wrote a dissertation concluding that there were few monopolies in the recent American past—and those resulted from government intervention; the market, in other words, functioned properly until government got involved. He knew no Russian and his only claim to Russia expertise was that he had served as one of a half dozen consultants to Norman Kaplan's unsuccessful work on a Soviet input-output table.[65] Nutter later admitted that he "was almost a blind man seeing through the eyes of others" when it came to examining Soviet data; he relied heavily on assistants like the brother-sister team of Murray Feshbach and Charlotte Wasserman. In political terms, at least, Nutter's selection was logical; his early work had demonstrated his belief (in the words of a former student) that the growth of government was "perhaps

HERBLOCK'S CARTOON

"Pst! Want To See Some Hot Statistics?"

Figure 4.1. Herblock cartoon on the public significance of Soviet economic statistics, 1964.

the most ominous development since World War II." Perhaps it was not a coincidence that both Burns and Nutter would hold senior posts in the Nixon administration—in Nutter's case, after a stint with Barry Goldwater's 1964 presidential campaign.[66]

Nutter managed to reach some preliminary conclusions by the time his Rockefeller grant concluded in late 1956. In an academic article circulated in the White House before publication, Nutter put the question of Soviet economic growth in a competitive framework: "How successful has the Soviet Union been in matching the industrial achievements of the United States?" He opted for a disaggregated approach, undertaking three dozen industry-by-industry comparisons with the United States and computing the Soviet lag behind the United States, measured in years, for each one.[67] Nutter had already offered a theoretical challenge to index numbers as a basis for comparison; he made no direct reference to the Soviet Union until the penultimate page, but it was clearly an effort to challenge the Bergsonian approach. He rejected the whole approach of production indexes in rapidly changing economies, which he compared with "measuring how much the caterpillar grows when it turns into a moth." Nutter was not the theorist that Bergson was, but quickly surpassed Bergson in public relations. He wrote an article for *U.S. News and World Report* that proclaimed to tell "the true story of Russia's weakness." Introduced in gushing language as a "trained economist who went to Russia to see for himself" (it did not report that he went for a few weeks only, as a tourist), Nutter argued that there "would have been remarkable growth of the Russian economy over the last forty years"—if only "there had been a significant area of private enterprise." But the lack of economic incentive and the dead weight of bureaucracy meant that there was a "hollow shell" behind the "impressive façade" of rapid Soviet growth.[68]

The CIA officials responded aggressively to this challenge. Through the mid-1950s, the national intelligence estimates (NIEs) coordinated by CIA calculated Soviet postwar growth rates as high as 10–11% annually in the late 1940s, slowing to 6–7% in the mid-1950s and to 5–6% for the late 1950s.[69] One CIA analysis considered it "unlikely" that the Soviet Union could maintain even a 5% growth rate into the 1970s, but nevertheless saw 4.5% as both likely and readily attainable.[70] With U.S. growth rates hovering at 3–3.5%, the difference between the long-term rates seems relatively small. But over time, even small differences would compound: if the USSR maintained, for instance, a 4.5% rate from 1955 to 1975, it would grow by a factor of 2.4. Over a decade, the Soviet Union could make rapid progress relative to the United States; the CIA estimated that the Soviet economy was roughly 33% of the American one in 1953, 40% in 1959, and could reach 45% by 1962.[71] The CIA's director, Allen Dulles, used economic data to further CIA's own expanding mission in the 1950s; according to the CIA official who oversaw the Soviet NIEs, "it was probably this economic expertise more than anything else" that gave CIA a leg up on military agencies in the bureaucratic struggles for supremacy.[72]

Allen Dulles also took his case to the public. In a series of public events starting in 1956, he warned of the dangers of rapid Soviet economic growth. A strong Soviet Union, and one gaining economic and military strength with each passing year, posed a direct threat to the United States. Thanks to its centrally planned economy, Soviet leaders were better positioned to expand further their country's economic and military strength by diverting even more resources to investment or to defense. Second, underdeveloped countries all over the world looked to the Soviet Union as a model of rapid industrialization; continued growth would bolster Soviet prestige and Soviet global influence, which then posed an indirect threat to American interests.[73] Comparing U.S. and Soviet economic growth became a growth industry of its own in the late 1950s, with articles appearing in major newspapers and magazines. Soon, Congress got in the act; in 1959, the Joint Economic Committee held its first hearings on Soviet-American comparisons. Volumes based on these hearings were produced every three to five years; nicknamed the Green Books, they became indispensable sources of the latest Western analyses of the Soviet economy.

Perhaps fittingly, Dulles was the first to testify at the Joint Economic Committee hearings. The CIA chief took a calm tone although his predictions were dire; he claimed that Soviet production was already nearing half of American production—up dramatically from just over one-tenth of American production in the final years of the Russian empire. Echoing the testimony of economist Morris Bornstein (who had close ties with CIA analysts), Dulles estimated Soviet growth in the neighborhood of 7% per year, presenting an increasing danger to American interests.[74]

The public battles continued, and Nutter was among the other experts appearing before the Joint Economic Committee. The publication of his full monograph prompted snide "I told you so" responses from conservative editorial pages, one of which accused the CIA of "using exaggerated estimates of Soviet growth to create political panic."[75] Nutter's congressional appearance and the subsequent publication of his book showed the success of the White House's end-run around the CIA. A free-marketeer with minimal Soviet experience was using the imprimatur of NBER and money from the Rockefeller Foundation to challenge the estimates of CIA experts. The biggest test would come when Nutter's magnum opus on Soviet growth went up against major works by Bergson and Jasny, all of which appeared in the early 1960s.

The early 1960s saw the highest stage of economic Sovietology in the United States—perhaps in exactly the way that Lenin meant when he called imperialism "the highest stage of capitalism." That is, the early 1960s marked both the blossoming of the field and the moment before its decline. The three competing estimates of Soviet economic growth—by Bergson, Jasny, and Nutter—appeared within a year of each other. The books employed different methods, responded to different political agendas, emphasized different aspects of the Soviet economy, and were full of criticisms of the others' work.

As table 4.1 shows, the differences between Bergson's and Jasny's overall figures were relatively small, and both authors painted a roughly similar picture: the Soviet economy grew rapidly, led by industrial production, during the first two Five-Year Plans (1928–1937); it managed to recover quickly from the destruction of the war and was on track for slower and more balanced growth in the 1950s. This common ground was barely visible in the books, however, thanks to their dramatically different tones and predictions. There were wider discrepancies in their comparisons of the Soviet and American industrial programs, as table 4.2 suggests. Bergson, Jasny, and Nutter devoted years of work, crunched tens of thousands of numbers, and (in the case of Bergson and Nutter) employed extensive research teams costing hundreds of thousands of dollars—all to reach conclusions closely related to their starting assumptions.

Bergson, for instance, took as his starting point 1928, the opening year of the first Five-Year Plan, when central planning was dominant. Since he was interested in the overall performance of the economy, not the welfare of individuals, Bergson chose to emphasize national income, which measures production potential rather than standard of living. His claim that "1937 was for the Soviet consumer a year of relative prosperity"—which Jasny relished the chance to cite incredulously—is misleading precisely because Bergson's measure of

Table 4.1: Comparison of Estimates of Soviet National Income Growth

| Source | Annual % Growth Rate | | | | |
	1928–1937	1937–1940	1940–1950	1950–1955	1928–1955
Official Soviet data	16.2	9.9	5.1	10.9	10.3
Noam Jasny	6.1	3.4	2.6	8.9	5.0
Abram Bergson	5.5	6.7	2.1	7.6	4.7
G. Warren Nutter	(rejected national income measures)				

Source: Calculated from data in Mark Harrison, "Soviet Industrial Production, 1928–1955: Real Growth and Hidden Inflation," *Journal of Comparative Economics* 28 (2000), 137–138.

Table 4.2: Soviet-American Comparisons

Source	Soviet Industrial Production as % of U.S. Production (Year)
Official Soviet data	60 (1959)
CIA/Allen Dulles	40 (1955)
Noam Jasny	33 (1955)
G. Warren Nutter	20 (1960)
Abram Bergson	(rejected direct comparisons between the economies)

Sources: Jan Prybyla, book review, *RR* 22:2 (April 1963), 190–192; Noam Jasny, *Soviet Industrialization, 1928–1952* (Chicago, *1961*), 24.

production potential leaves little room to calculate the purchasing power of individual workers and *kolkhozniki*.[76] Bergson avoided a direct comparison between the Cold War antagonists because of their different price structures. He was willing to compare growth rates across the two countries because these kept ruble-denominated and dollar-denominated accounts separate—but that was as far as he would go; he had just as little faith in an estimate of Soviet GNP in dollars as in an estimate of American GNP in rubles.

Nutter, too, selected his starting points on the basis of his own intentions— in his case, a determination to deflate Soviet claims (as well as Bergson's). Proclaiming an interest in measuring the performance of the Soviet economy over its whole lifetime—and not just in the era of planning—Nutter insisted on starting his account in 1913, the last full year before World War I. He took direct aim at those starting with the implementation of the planned economy, professing confusion at the "deliberate refusal of some western scholars to expose or examine the Soviet and Russian economic record before 1928." Similarly, Nutter deemphasized national income figures like GNP, claiming that it was a "delusion" to believe that "there is some single-dimensioned, neutral measure of growth, equally meaningful for all types of economies." Nutter instead focused on industry, with the logic that the Soviet industrial production index "embodies a myth that should be dispelled from the popular mind." This statement also revealed Nutter's desire, shared by those who prompted his study in the first place, to recast the public debate about the Soviet economy to emphasize American superiority. Nutter used Soviet data of physical quantities (for instance, tons of pig iron produced), looked back to see when the United States first achieved that quantity, and then calculated a lag time. By his reckoning, the Soviet Union was not only lagging behind the United States, but was falling further behind as time went on. Even with a goal of "catching up with and surpassing" the United States, the Soviet Union was facing instead Jay Gatsby's green light, the "future that year by year" receded before it. Nutter himself preferred a parental metaphor: "A son will get closer and closer percentagewise to his father in age but will never catch up."[77] Yet there was a basic flaw in that analogy: unlike age, economic growth could differ—one year could bring a larger increase in one country than in another. Nutter's parental analogy implicitly equated Soviet and American growth rates, which was empirically incorrect for the 1950s by almost any measure, including Nutter's own. Other adjustments—for the inferior quality of Soviet goods, for instance—further reduced Nutter's estimates of Soviet growth. As one reviewer noted delicately, Nutter was "more sensitive to the possibility that his data are too high than that they are too low." In the end, Nutter's work cast significant public doubt on Soviet economic growth not by identifying errors in prior estimates, but by changing the time frame (starting in 1913 rather than 1928) and by using spurious comparisons like time lags. Professional Sovietologists had already rejected this approach, with Gerschenkron concluding a decade earlier that "the statement, 'Russia is now where the US was in this or that year,' is hardly a meaningful one," and he saw little to change his mind in the ensuing years.[78] These questionable techniques overshadowed all the real work that Nutter did in calculating Soviet production over some four decades.

Nutter found himself in good company with his denigration of Soviet economic growth. No less an economist than Simon Kuznets, the father of national income accounting, offered a similar round of attacks on Soviet growth in his one brief article on the topic in 1963. Like Nutter, Kuznets defended a pre-1928 starting date on political grounds, arguing that Soviet planning could not have begun without the destruction in the first decade of Soviet rule: "Does not every case of Communist economic growth begin with a breakdown of libertarian social and economic institutions followed by recovery, in the process of which opposition is reduced and the way cleared for the forced programs that follow?" Similarly, Kuznets compared Soviet growth in the 1950s—using Bergson's data—to that of a broader range of countries. The USSR was outpacing the United States, but it was still on a par with the economic miracles of West Germany and Japan, as well as with underdeveloped countries like Venezuela and Rhodesia. Finally, Kuznets tallied the costs of Soviet economic growth in both human and financial terms. His point that "economic success, as measured, is irrelevant or makes only an insignificant contribution to the total positive performance in terms of the whole complex of goals of the societies that are being compared" was better suited to a critic of national income accounting than to its inventor.[79]

While Jasny took pride in attacking Bergson's work, his quantitative results were quite similar. He undertook calculations of Soviet industrial growth because he felt that Bergson's were "biased in favor of Moscow" and "out of place" in the Cold War conflict, even though some of Jasny's estimates of national income were actually higher than Bergson's. Bergson and most of his students expressed frustration with the opacity of Jasny's estimates. If Bergson's prose was dense, it nevertheless included all of the essential explanations and assumptions involved; Jasny's, in contrast, often omitted any description of his estimating process. Jasny's approach, one critic wrote, was an "art" not a science. He relied, according to another colleague, very heavily on the "rule of thumb" rather than precise derivations. Others were less subtle; RAND's Norman Kaplan had early accused Jasny of replacing Soviet data with inventions and unsubstantiated estimates of his own unexplained derivation. In Kaplan's view, Jasny's estimates amounted to arithmancy, divination through numbers.[80] For instance, one of Jasny's data tables included the caveat that explanations of "the details of some of the calculations" had been omitted for "technical reasons"—an inadvertent echo of Soviet excuses. Jasny ignored the Gerschenkron effect (perhaps because of its namesake's RAND links) and kept all of his data in 1926/1927 prices.[81]

For all of these problems, Jasny provided by far the most fully historical account of the Soviet political economy. Considering the plans to be mere propaganda, Jasny organized his data around more meaningful periods of Soviet economic history—shaped by economic trends, not political goals. A key part of this reperiodization was to emphasize the difficulties of the first Five-Year Plan—a point rarely evident from Bergson's data, since he lumped the first two plans (1928–1937) into a single period. Jasny used three different periods to cover the same years: Warming Up (1928–1931), All-Out Drive (1932–1934), and Three "Good" Years (1935–1937). He used scare quotes in this last category to emphasize just how bad the preceding years were—not only in terms of consumption and food production, but even in terms of industrial growth. This periodization offered many new insights not evident from Bergson, especially in demonstrating the "disaster of the large part of the first Five-Year Plan." Starting from his original expertise in agriculture, Jasny was better able to handle estimates in this sector (even if they were off the cuff) and to account for shifts in population. He concluded that much of the increased production of Soviet industry was simply a result of shifts in the labor force, draining the agricultural sector and leaving it ill suited to feed the country. At root, Jasny did not accept Bergson's imputation of economic rationality for Soviet planners; he instead emphasized the political nature of Soviet goals. Even sympathetic outside observers like Eugène Zaleski doubted Jasny's "purely political explanation" of economic trends.[82] Jasny also placed a heavier emphasis on the costs of Soviet industrialization; while Bergson did not ignore the costs, he focused on the production potential of a planned economy rather than on the standard of living of its citizens.

Taken together, the major works of the early 1960s by Bergson, Jasny, and Nutter marked the culmination of the first stage of Sovietological economics, especially in the United States. Some reviewers expressed relief that the basic task of recalculating key statistical series was complete; the next task would be subjecting these data to standard economic techniques and theories.[83] This was hardly the first time such hopes had appeared in print; Gregory Grossman, a Gerschenkron student, had five years earlier called for a shift from "description and measurement" to "analysis, cognition, interpretation and explanation." By the late 1950s, the basic tasks of calculation and adjustment were taken over by the CIA; this should have freed academic economists to explore the broader theoretical implications of understanding the Soviet economy. The early 1960s, therefore, should have marked the field's intellectual coming of age.[84] After a long period of bringing together detailed knowledge of the Soviet Union and borrowing the latest techniques of economic analysis, the field should have been ready to return the favors, helping other Soviet experts to deal with the broadest outlines of the Soviet economy and at the same time contributing to mainstream economics. Yet neither would come to pass.

Economic Sovietology went quickly from a series of successes in the early 1960s into a stasis and then a steady decline that long preceded the Soviet Union's. Alexander Gerschenkron feared such a future in 1964, writing that the field's chances of doing original work in the future were "less than excellent." He cited in particular the declining number of students entering the field and the difficulty of getting sufficient training in Russian language and economic analysis to make future contributions. While there were still economics graduate students entering the field in the mid-1960s, they were fewer in number and mostly outside of the places that had trained the first generations—notably, Harvard and Columbia.[85] These students faced increasing difficulty in getting academic jobs. The oldest programs—at Harvard, Columbia, Berkeley, Indiana, and Illinois, for instance—had stocked up on Soviet economic experts with the first student generation in the 1950s and were not in the market for a second. Universities without major Soviet centers might still hire Soviet specialists to cover comparative economics, though this field, too, was declining in the 1960s.

What led to the field's plateau and subsequent decline at the very moment it had achieved its crowning success, in terms of policy influence and public attention? First, economic Sovietologists were, in some ways, victims of their own success. The efforts to recompute the extent and shape of Soviet industrialization efforts in the Five-Year Plan era culminated with Bergson's, Nutter's, and Jasny's magna opera in the early 1960s. Second, these scholars' success at deflating Soviet achievements meant a corresponding decline in the perception of a Soviet economic threat in the 1960s. Soviet growth rates were indeed impressive in the 1950s—but as Kuznets and Nutter both pointed out, so too were the market-oriented recoveries of West Germany and Japan. Indications of a Soviet slowdown in growth—even as it still exceeded American growth—made the notion of the Soviet Union surpassing the United States less likely. Third, the nature of their subject was itself changing. Most Western analysts agreed that Soviet economic growth began to slow in the early 1960s due to system inefficiency, the limits of the agricultural sector, and the exhaustion of extensive growth possibilities. What should have been a triumph for the estimators—identifying the limits to Soviet growth, dating back to Grossman's projections of 1953—instead rendered their work less important, at least for public discussion.

Just as important as all of these issues specific to the study of the Soviet economy were trends in the economics profession as a whole. The growing dominance of modern economic analysis—pioneered by Bergson's classmate Paul Samuelson—gave full expression to the universalistic sentiments long latent in economic analysis. The discipline's advances in the 1960s had more to do with quantification and systematization—which required assumptions of common trends across all countries—and gave short shrift to historical, regional, and institutional specifics.[86] As one economist summarized in 2001, "Over the course of the Cold War many economists came increasingly to conclude that all deviations from the competitive market norm were simply short-term aberrations and unworthy of serious scholarly attention."[87] The increasingly mathematical nature of economics ultimately had no place in its formulas for context. Economic laws were universals and could be universally applied. The result was ironic. Bergson's early work had devoted special attention to arguing that even a centrally planned economy was susceptible to the analytical tools of market economics. Future generations of economists would agree with him so staunchly that they would see little reason to explore the different organizations and institutions in different economies.

Economic Sovietology was hindered by its own success in combining technical economic tools and country-specific expertise. In training scholars who would be both professional economists and area experts, Bergson had hoped to bridge the schools of disciplinary and regional expertise. The success of this approach is evident in the tremendous advances in the sophistication of Western knowledge of the Soviet economy—a success acknowledged occasionally by the Soviets themselves, who apparently used published Western estimates in their own classified reporting.[88]

As Russian Studies expanded in the 1960s, some of the most important institutions, like the IUCTG exchange programs, had only minimal representation from economists. Few economists applied and even fewer (barely a dozen) were accepted into the IUCTG program—and half of these were denied entry by Soviet authorities. So few Russianists had the requisite economic expertise that some economic aspects of Russian/Soviet history remain underexplored to this day.[89] In the same way that economic Sovietology's success in revising estimates of Soviet growth made the field less relevant to public discourse, its arcane tools and extensive "local knowledge" made connections to adjacent fields—in economics departments and area studies centers—more difficult to maintain. As the field of economics came to value technical expertise over nation-specific knowledge, a whole group of area specialists and comparative economists found their place in the profession shrinking.

Economic Sovietology always had an active following in Washington, as many of its practitioners consulted with or talked informally to their counterparts in government, especially in the CIA. The production of the so-called Green Books, based on hearings of the congressional Joint Economic

Committee, brought economists from all branches of university and govern-ment life together, as did occasional seminars that accompanied the release of new Soviet data.

In 1980, nearly all of the Soviet economy experts in academe and a good portion of those in government convened to reprise the exercise that Bergson had organized almost three decades earlier. That first conference on Soviet economic growth had tried to look ahead twenty years from 1953; this new event, subtitled "Toward the Year 2000," did the same from the perspective of 1980. Douglas Diamond led a contingent from CIA; Herbert Levine, one of the organizers, made predictions based on his SOVMOD computer model; and a handful of participants in that first conference (including Bergson and Berliner) were present again. The resulting book highlighted many of the prob-lems of the USSR under Brezhnev; essays utilized sophisticated modeling (much of which used mainframe computers) to reveal deep knowledge of the innards of the Soviet economy and a strong sense of professionalism in assess-ing possible and likely outcomes. Yet the volume also could serve as an epitaph for the field. A photo of the conference participants—including Bergson, still on the Harvard faculty—revealed some of the concerns that Gerschenkron and Millar had raised about the future of the field; it was relatively small, com-fortably fitting in the frame of a photo, and top-heavy, with plenty of gray hair.[90] By the time reviews of the book appeared in academic journals, Mikhail Gorbachev had become general secretary, and major changes were afoot in the USSR. And eight years after the book appeared, in 1991, its subject—the Soviet economy—ceased to exist. The combination of quantitative and linguistic knowledge required for the field had led to its slow decline in the 1960s, while the rest of Russian Studies was still on the rise, but economic Sovietology soon mirrored the rest of the field in its decline.

THE LOST OPPORTUNITIES OF SLAVIC LITERARY STUDIES

American scholars of Slavic literature had, in the 1950s and 1960s, unprecedented opportunity to address fellow students of literature, scholars in other disciplines, and a wider public. Events in the Soviet Union attracted broad attention to their subject, giving them the same entrée to public discussions that Soviet economic experts had. Trends within their discipline were not merely amenable to the Slavicists' work, but were the product of collaborations involving some of them. A world of literary criticism that straddled university gates celebrated the very authors who had been the mainstay of their teaching and research. Conditions within Slavic studies had changed dramatically, too. A dramatic upswing in language enrollments after Sputnik expanded the Slavicists' ranks; the American Association of Teachers of Slavic and East European Literature booked a fourfold increase in membership between 1958 and 1962, growing more than twice as quickly as language enrollments.[1] Academic exchanges offered American scholars unprecedented opportunities to spend time in the USSR, which was crucial for perfecting language skills and also for meeting Soviet scholars, learning more about Soviet culture and everyday life, and expanding the source base to include materials stored in Soviet libraries and (eventually) archives. These were propitious times for scholars of Slavic literature to make a major contribution within and beyond the academy.

Slavicists experimented with ways of reaching these broader audiences, trying to show not just the value but the necessity of their pursuit. These experiments ranged widely. At Columbia's Russian Institute, Ernest Simmons endeavored to show what the study of literature could do for area studies programs. Across the country in Berkeley, Gleb Struve sought to both document and shape the Russian literary tradition in the twentieth century. Simmons's erstwhile colleague Roman Jakobson (who then decamped to Harvard) inspired many in his efforts to develop a universal theory of language that could also shape literary scholarship. And Yale's René Wellek attempted to place Slavic literatures firmly within the European tradition, an effort shared by other critics less professionally invested in Slavic literature. These experiments spurred the growth of a robust and dynamic field of Slavic literary studies. Yet this enterprise—larger, broader, and deeper than it had been before World War II—had difficulty reaching those outside it.

Indeed, it is striking how low a profile professional Slavicists maintained in the field's early years. Soviet events attracted the attention of many non-experts: ideological orthodoxy, exemplified by postwar culture purges known as the *Zhdanovshchina*, gave way to a sporadic and tentative thaw after Stalin's death in 1953. Translations, anthologies, and reportage on thaw literature abounded, especially after 1958, when Boris Pasternak won the Nobel Prize in Literature but provoked an official Soviet backlash: his novel *Doktor Zhivago* was not published in the USSR, and its author was banned from attending the Nobel ceremonies. All the same, the main commentators on these events were not necessarily from Slavic departments.

The emergence of a modernist canon, the culmination of decades of work, brought new attention to many of the classic Russian novels of the nineteenth century. Important critics included Dostoevsky and Tolstoy in their canons and their criticism. Yet their discussions seemed to exist in a different universe than that of the Slavicists, with only rare citations from one to another.

The New Critics who dominated formal literary study shared much with Russian formalists. Both groups promoted a research agenda focused on the exposition of literary technique instead of social, political, and biographical context. But even this opportunity did not bring broader attention to the Slavicists. They were connected with formalists, or studied them, but remained on the sidelines of general discussions of literary theory.

How could a group of scholars whose subject matter was of such wide academic and public concern fail to ride that wave to prominence outside their own precincts? Émigré scholars, many of whom led Slavic programs in major American universities, saw little problem with their own resolute focus on their own countries and had varied exposure to and interest in the main trends of literary scholarship in the United States. Émigrés held a wide range of posts in Slavic departments. Many, especially women, ended up as drill instructors who, in Vladimir Nabokov's pointed description, "manage[d] somehow, by dint of intuition, loquacity, and a kind of maternal bounce, to infuse a magic knowledge of their difficult and beautiful tongue into a group of innocent-eyed students in an atmosphere of Mother Volga songs, red caviar, and tea."[2] Yet émigrés were also an important presence in literary scholarship. Vera Sandomirsky Dunham, for instance, was a Russian émigré with a German doctorate who went from the Office of Strategic Services to Wayne State University in Detroit. Yet perhaps the teaching responsibilities there took their toll; only when she retired in

1976 did she publish her influential book, *In Stalin's Time*. Elite departments, too, relied on émigrés; Dunham taught intermittently at Columbia after leaving Detroit. And there were so many émigrés in Harvard's Slavic Department that it conducted its meetings in Russian, much to the dismay of Italian Renato Poggioli, who struggled with spoken Russian.[3]

There were a number of conceptual and practical limits on Slavicists' work as well. Studies of Soviet culture meant, with rare exceptions, studies of Russian literature and were limited almost exclusively to works in Russian. A few books and articles on Ukrainian culture appeared, but most dealt only minimally with Ukrainian cultural life in the Soviet period.[4] Next to nothing appeared on literature in other Soviet languages. Before Western scholars could travel to the USSR in 1956, they were limited to the materials that the Soviet authorities published. Work on Soviet theater could rely only on reviews and other published accounts of the plays; in many cases, the scripts were unavailable, and of course attendance was impossible. Similarly, any scholarship that relied on art works held in Soviet museums was hindered by scholars' inability to see the original works. The exchange programs expanded opportunities for American scholars, though plenty of impediments remained for those seeking to study Soviet theater and art. Most Slavic departments focused heavily on Russian texts, especially those by the great novelists of the nineteenth century.[5] Studies of the Soviet period tended to focus on the politics of cultural production rather than on the texts themselves.

From his posts at Columbia's Russian Institute and Slavic Department, Ernest Simmons was perhaps the most influential American Slavicist organizer of his generation. He advised dozens of graduate students, served as a member of the Joint Committee on Slavic Studies, and edited the leading Slavic studies journal, *American Slavic and East European Review*. Rather than teaching aspiring political scientists and sociologists how to analyze literature, Simmons applied his knowledge of literature to understanding Soviet society and politics.

Simmons came to Russian Studies after training in German literature at Harvard. While teaching there, he began writing about some of the classic Russian authors of the nineteenth century. Running the intensive seminar on the Soviet Union at Cornell may have spurred Simmons's new interest in Soviet literature. He wrote a primer on modern Russian literature from 1880 to 1940 (published in 1943) that revealed a strikingly supportive view of Soviet literary politics. The book offered a spirited defense of the reigning doctrine of socialist realism for its "attempts to integrate literature and life," which assured it of a "great future."[6] The repressive cultural policies of the late 1940s dulled Simmons's enthusiasm for socialist realism. When Andrei Zhdanov blasted the literary journals *Zvezda* and *Leningrad* in 1946, it marked the arrival of a new

cultural orthodoxy more stringently upheld (if less brutally enforced) than that
of the 1930s. Simmons became less concerned with socialist realism per se and
more concerned with the politics and administration of Soviet culture.

Simmons sought to bring literary scholars to the area studies table by using
literature as a means of studying Soviet politics. His book *Through the Glass
of Soviet Literature* (1953) exemplified his approach and modus operandi. The
book collected essays by a number of his students covering a range of topics,
from single-author studies to the treatment of Jews and of women in Soviet
literature to post–World War II battles over Soviet ideology and literature.
Simmons added an introduction, making the case that literature could be a
useful tool for understanding Soviet society—so much so that he cited patron
saints of sociology like Max Weber and Thorstein Veblen but no literary critics or scholars. While Simmons did not assume that Soviet literature was an
accurate reflection of Soviet reality, he believed it could shed important light
on ideology and politics in the Soviet system, illustrating the "idealization of
life which the Party foists upon the public both as a mirror of Communist
aspirations and as an opiate to minister to discontent."[7]

A similar inclination toward the social scientific is visible in a more ambitious
project that Simmons organized with support from the JCSS. Simmons edited
a volume called *Continuity and Change in Russian and Soviet Thought* (1955)
that brought together an interdisciplinary group of almost thirty contributors,
including many of Western Sovietology's leading lights. Strikingly, there were
more historians (eleven) and social scientists (ten) than humanists (eight).[8]
The book's central questions were key for Sovietology: To what extent should the
USSR be seen as primarily Russian in nature, and to what extent Communist?
Who were the predecessors to Lenin and Stalin: Ivan the Terrible and Peter the
Great, or Karl Marx and Friedrich Engels? The book's contributors took these
questions seriously in economic, political, philosophical, and literary realms,
searching for continuities across the divide of 1917. The book encapsulated the
state of the field at this early stage in its development, with many articles by
younger scholars debuting their work. But among its weaknesses must surely
be the narrowness and nonliterary nature of the contributions in Simmons's
own field, literature. A pair of essays allowed a comparison of censorship in
nineteenth-century Russia and in the USSR, but never dealt with literature per
se.[9] The two essays on literary criticism, by Wellek and Victor Erlich, examined
the nature of Russian and Soviet literary criticism at two crucial moments in
modern Russian history, the 1840s–1860s and 1920s–1930s. The essays offered
handy excerpts of larger works by each author. In his commentary, Simmons
considered Russian formalism's attempts to "coquette with Marxism" to be
more significant than the sociological stance taken by nineteenth-century critics like Vissarion Belinskii, whom Wellek discussed.[10] Simmons revealed his

principal scholarly interest: the contribution that literary studies could make to understanding Russian society and politics.

Simmons's focus on literature's contributions to social science shaped the work of his students in the 1950s. Especially in the first half of that decade, Columbia was the predominant program in quantitative terms, accounting for about 40% of the forty-three doctorates in Slavic literature in the postwar decade.[11] Students enrolled in Simmons's two graduate seminars, which comprised the main offerings on literature in the Russian Institute: Marxism and Literary Theory in the Soviet Union and Social Control of Soviet Literature.[12] Neither emphasized literary topics.

Most of Simmons's graduate students wrote their dissertations on Soviet topics, but few focused directly on literature.[13] The works of Deming Brown and Maurice Friedberg, for instance, focused on literary production but not with Russian-language fiction itself. Brown devoted much of his career to studying the reception of American literature in Soviet criticism. His first book, *Soviet Attitudes towards American Writing* (1962), was full of interesting commentary on the American writers most widely published and respected in the Soviet Union, including the generally approving attitude and large print runs for Jack London, O. Henry, and Upton Sinclair and the debates over John Dos Passos. Brown touched on an important aspect of Soviet culture: Soviet publishing houses produced more than 50 million volumes of translated American writings in the USSR's first forty years. Each chapter had a variation on the same theme: how the acceptance and acclaim of a given American author fit into a specific ideological moment in the USSR. While Brown did analyze Soviet critical commentary on American authors, the book paid little attention to the actual texts. Brown's work revealed a certain animus. Even where Soviet reception accorded with American critical opinion—favoring, for instance, Theodore Dreiser over Sinclair Lewis—Brown saw nefarious forces at work; any common ground was "interesting but beside the point" because Soviet assessments were "largely vitiated by the[ir] political tendentiousness."[14] This last word appeared frequently in the works of Simmons and his students, as they set up a dichotomy between tendentiousness and true art—and applied the term not only to all literature produced in the Soviet Union but also to nineteenth-century Russian literature used to promote one or another political cause. The response was a perfect rebuttal of Soviet literary trends. At the Soviet Congress of Writers in 1934, Zhdanov had called for an end to literary experimentation in favor of an embrace of the "tendentious." Brown was not the only Columbia scholar to rebut such pronouncements.

Maurice Friedberg emphasized this corrective agenda in scholarship on Soviet literature. His book *Russian Classics in Soviet Jackets* (1962) described the fate of an ideologically suspect literary canon in an ideological state. Friedberg's

book, like Brown's, contained a great deal of useful information about the works'
publication histories—as mass-market books, in prestigious complete editions,
and the like. Friedberg seemed to glean more from the "Soviet jackets" and
front matter, where the print runs are listed, than from the texts themselves.
He devoted little attention to the Soviet scholarly enterprise that was typically responsible for producing the classics themselves—what Friedberg dismissed as providing the "necessary Marxist forewords." Based on data from the
Refugee Interview Project (RIP), Friedberg argued that Soviet citizens read
Tolstoy and Chekhov to get "a glimpse of the outside world in the middle of
the twentieth century" or to gain "moral support in an otherwise hopeless conflict with an omnipotent state."[15] Citing Simmons extensively, Friedberg followed Simmons by writing about literary topics in the Soviet Union without
writing about literature.

Other Simmons students were more determined to focus on literary topics or at least literary figures. Edward J. Brown's *Proletarian Episode in Russian
Literature* (1953) was an institutional history of the Russian Association of
Proletarian Writers (RAPP). It offered a serious discussion of the critical theories at stake in the 1920s, elaborating upon the institutional history with an
intellectual history of some pressing questions in the organization and orientation of Soviet culture. The RAPP had struggled to promote its own vision of
proletarian literature as the Bolshevik Party sought to define the term strictly
for the promotion of its own interests; RAPP was "neither the author nor the
willing executor" of the destruction of Russian literature in the era of the first
Five-Year Plan. Brown's evaluation of RAPP criticism was sympathetic but
hardly sycophantic; he took the critics' intentions on their own terms while
concluding that their literary criticism was, in the end, "narrowly derivative."[16]

Even more focused on literature was Rufus W. Mathewson Jr.'s *The Positive
Hero in Russian Literature* (1958). While the book opened with a nod to recent
Soviet cultural politics, the book was original and wide ranging in its analysis
of depictions of heroes in Russian literature and criticism in the century or
so after 1840. Moving from radical democrats like the 1840s critic Belinskii
through socialist realism in the 1930s, Mathewson addressed the central question of Simmons's best work: the continuities and discontinuities between
tsarist and Soviet Russia. Mathewson noted, almost apologetically, that this
focus emerged fairly late in the project; he had originally hoped to "define
one of the literary archetypes of our time" and "gain insight into the moral
condition of the Soviet Communist" by studying the hero figure. Yet the focus
on Soviet heroes failed because the heroes themselves did; they were shaped
by "Party policy" not "literary imagination."[17] *The Positive Hero* was a work of
careful scholarship, dealing with both literature and literary criticism over a
very crowded century of Russian history and culture. The tone combined irony

(the dominant mood of RI faculty, according to Edward Brown) and condemnation, tracing the transformation of the social commitment praised by radical democrats like Belinskii into the two-dimensional party puppet of the Soviet years.[18] Having no truck with modern Soviet literature—which would be better left to "social scientists or propaganda analysts"—Mathewson nevertheless acknowledged the origins of a central Soviet archetype in nineteenth-century dreams of liberation. The flaw of these early radical democrats was a fatal one, but was not visible until the Soviets turned the pursuit of a "radical aesthetic" into "the incomplete portrayal of incomplete men."[19] Investing art with social meaning would eventually destroy it.

Even the most ambitious and successful of these works of the 1950s, like Mathewson's *Positive Hero,* demonstrated the serious limits of the area studies approach. Simmons deployed many of his graduate students as if he were directing a collective social scientific research enterprise like Harvard's RIP. Assigning topics to his students, he then incorporated their ideas into his own publications, as in *Through the Glass of Soviet Literature.* Simmons had come a long way from his dissertation research into European folktales in the 1920s and from his writings on Pushkin in the 1930s. The literary value of texts was more and more deeply submerged in his writings; they mattered, in much of his teaching and scholarship, primarily as objects of political control or imperfect reflections of social conditions. By 1958, he saw Soviet literature as a morality tale of "national genius in…fiction and verse" destroyed by political and ideological controls.[20] Even his works oriented around authors, including full-length biographies of Tolstoy, Chekhov, and Dostoevsky, focused more on life than on art. The value of Russia's literary geniuses inhered in what they revealed about their times, not in their fictional investigations of pressing questions of human existence. Simmons focused instead on the politics of culture, investing it with the same meanings as did the Soviet censors and cultural authorities themselves.

Simmons's dismissal of meaningful cultural production in the Soviet Union—a claim dating back to Max Eastman's *Artists in Uniform* (1935)—became a challenge to others. Some tried to defend Soviet literature as the authentic expression of a new way of life that the Soviet Union embodied; Simmons was in this camp in the 1940s, at least until the *Zhdanovshchina.* But some of the Soviet Union's staunchest opponents wanted to break the notion that Soviet culture was an oxymoron; one émigré wanted to show not "what literature in Soviet Russia was *unable* to achieve…but rather what it *has* achieved" in spite of the political efforts to control it.[21] That émigré, Gleb Struve, wrote this line in the 1930s, in response to *Artists in Uniform.* At the time, Struve was still in Europe. But his arrival in the United States in the aftermath of World War II marked a new direction for the study of Russian/Soviet literature—yet not one that drew Slavicists into the mainstream of literary scholarship.

The name Gleb Petrovich Struve revealed his importance. His father, Petr Struve ("Petrovich" means "son of Petr"), was one of the most interesting and astute intellectuals in imperial Russia's final decades. His geographic trajectory was as wide ranging as his political one: he moved from provincial Perm' to the capital, St. Petersburg, to punitive exile in Paris, and from conservative to Social Democrat to liberal Kadet. After holding a senior post in the provisional government (which came into being after the collapse of the imperial government until it was overthrown by the Bolsheviks six months later), Struve took his family, including his teenage son, into exile in Paris. There the younger Struve spent many years working with his father, who knew everyone there was to know in Russia Abroad—which would become especially useful when Gleb wrote a literary history of that group.[22]

In 1946, Struve arrived as a visiting professor at the University of California's Berkeley campus, where the nation's oldest Slavic Department was in disarray, depleted by the recent deaths of its stalwarts. His temporary appointment soon became a permanent one, and Struve would be one of the department's pillars for the next two decades.[23] Already well published—his *Soviet Russian Literature* had appeared in England in 1935—Struve exemplified the multiple "careers" of American Slavicists. He translated and edited literary works in addition to analyzing them. Indeed, his first publication was a translation of the most famous work by the most famous writer in the Russian emigration, Ivan Bunin; Leonard and Virginia Woolf were his editors for the volume. He also took on more miscellaneous projects in London in the 1930s: translating a Russian *bylina* (folktale) along with the doyen of British Soviet Studies, Sir Bernard Pares, and writing a textbook on "practical Russian." His first projects in Berkeley included a translation of George Orwell's *Animal Farm* into Russian. He also edited primary sources on eighteenth-century Russian diplomat P. B. Kozlovskii.[24] The title Struve chose for this last book—*Russkii evropeets* (Russian European)—was a telling one. Struve's vision of Kozlovskii fit Struve's vision not just of himself but of his whole generation of the Russian emigration; he and his fellow exiles were "Russian Europeans" not just by virtue of nationality and adopted homelands, but by inclination and cultural inheritance. They celebrated the Russian culture of the silver age (1890–1914), a great efflorescence in scholarship, literature, and the arts second only to the golden age of Pushkin and Belinskii. Even more than the earlier era, the silver age was defined by intimate connections to Western European culture. Their Russia, at least in cultural terms, was a full member of the European cultural milieu and traditions.[25] Ironically, though, Struve's work did little to strengthen the links between Russian and European writers and ideas.

Struve's first major contribution to American Slavistics was a substantially overhauled edition of his 1935 survey of Soviet literature. The book's introduction stated Struve's intention to "consider Soviet literature as objectively as possible, and to consider it, above all, as literature." Struve sought to maintain an objective stance, free of the polemics that defined most writings on the topic, from Eastman in 1935 to Simmons in 1943. Struve sought to put discussion of literary qualities at center stage, with mixed results. The book was full of condemnations of Soviet cultural politics and was dedicated to "victims of Soviet thought control." His discussion of Soviet literature aimed for evenhandedness; to the extent that socialist realism "helped raise literary standards," he wrote, it had a "progressive face." Unfortunately, this face rarely appeared, as Soviet culture became more tightly controlled and increasingly "reactionary" in the 1930s. Similarly, Struve praised the "new impetus" for theatrical life provided by the revolution, even while noting that the party's revival of theater was a recognition of its "power...as a weapon of propaganda." His aspiration to treat Soviet literature "as literature" was further undermined by the book's organization around political events. While the chapters were much more focused on literary production than were Simmons's works, the book's central narrative was driven by political events, not literary trends. Indeed, Struve tended to focus on the political implications of the various works of literature over their artistic qualities. Evgenii Zamiatin's dystopian novel *My* (*We*, 1927) mattered more for its foreshadowing of "conservativism [*sic*] and stagnation" in Russia than for its literary qualities. Struve devoted more space to Iurii Olesha's recantation of his novel *Zavist'* (*Envy*, 1927) in 1934 than to the novel itself. The same focus on politics emerged in his few discussions of literary criticism. He concluded that the Russian Formalists of the 1920s were of interest mainly because of their position as "the most consistent and active opponents of [the] officially sponsored Marxist, sociological approach to literature."[26] Struve's focus on the politics of Soviet literature, in spite of his attempts to do otherwise, demonstrates the obstacles to bringing studies of the topic into conversation with scholars of other twentieth-century literatures.

While Simmons and Mathewson explored the continuities in Russian culture before and after 1917, Struve made little effort to do so, as if Soviet/Russian literature was born with the revolution. His book opened with four pages "on the eve of the Revolution," but these focused on the portrayal of contemporary politics, not broader literary trends. Thus, the writer Maxim Gorky, a close friend of Lenin's and a favored Soviet author in the 1920s, appeared as a Bolshevik, not a novelist. Struve dispensed with Gorky's rich prerevolutionary oeuvre in a single paragraph, though it was these works (including his autobiographical trilogy) that made him a cultural icon in Russia and the West. Struve's discussion of later works, including those of the thaw, had a similarly political bent. For instance, he called one of the first post-Stalin novels,

Vladimir Dudintsev's *Not by Bread Alone* (1956), a "kaleidoscopic illustration" of a Sovietological treatise, *The New Class* (1957).[27]

The book had the feel of an annotated bibliography; it was organized around brief and self-contained sketches of dozens of authors, with few connections or arguments that addressed the nature of Soviet literature. A leading scholar of the next generation, Robert Maguire, praised Struve's "compendiousness," but considered him a "chronicler" not a critic. Robert Hughes, a student of Struve's, similarly noted his advisor's preference for "recovery" over analysis. A long-time collaborator celebrated Struve's principal accomplishment as the "resurrection [*voskreshenniia*] of the forgotten."[28] Struve was haunted by the need for comprehensiveness, much as a dictionary editor might be. "No history of Soviet literature can be complete," Struve noted in his first book, "without at least a brief mention of Demyan Bedny," which he dutifully provided. The World War II works of two great Russian poets, Boris Pasternak and Anna Akhmatova, garnered one long paragraph, most of which was devoted to critical reception. Akhmatova's return into print earned only grudging recognition along the lines that "mention should be made" of the work.[29]

Struve's documentary impulse and fierce defense of Russian culture were both evident in his second major monograph, *Russian Literature in Exile* (1956, in Russian). His preface suggested an important motivation for Struve: "it will be useful…as material for the future historian." In the closing section, Struve reiterated his goal of "register[ing] important facts." And the intervening 390 pages did just that, noting the multifarious forms of literature, broadly construed to include "philosophical prose" and *publitsistika* (journalism on contemporary affairs). Struve organized the book around individual authors and provided no index, only a list of authors annotated with pseudonyms and dates of birth and death. Struve wanted his book to serve a "reference" function. As historian and fellow émigré Michael Karpovich noted, the book served more as a "preliminary inventory" than any sort of analysis. Struve had a narrow conception of his subject. For instance, he summarized Nabokov's works written in Europe, but provided only bibliographical information on Nabokov's works that appeared after he arrived in the United States in 1940. Struve noted with disappointment that the novelist then "became an American writer"— and with that, Struve abruptly ended his analysis. Struve had earlier protested that Nabokov exhibited an "un-Russianness" in "his utter unconcern with any ethical, religious, philosophical, or social questions" and in "his aloofness from, and indifference to, the ultimate problems of being." Struve, writing a year after *Lolita* propelled Nabokov to fame, cast the novelist out of the emigration.[30] The book focused exclusively on the wave of émigrés that had fled the revolution, not the new emigration arriving in midcentury. The writers of the new emigration, Struve concluded, offered only "documentary interest" about life in the USSR, "fictional form being purely accidental."[31] Struve's aim was to document the contributions of emigration, including those of himself and his father.

Like his *Soviet Russian Literature,* Struve's book on the emigration was heavily weighted toward the 1920s. It was then that the "two branches of Russian literature"—separated by the Soviet border—were "in close contact."[32] But Struve concluded glumly that "the literature of Russia Abroad, as a special chapter in the history of Russian literature, is coming to its inevitable end." By the 1950s, Struve was actively engaged in trying to alter émigré literature's status as a "special chapter"—not by hastening its "inevitable" decline but by ending its separation from the rest of Russian literature. This was undoubtedly Struve's greatest accomplishment.

By force of hard work (and with the courageous help of a number of his friends and colleagues), Struve managed to bring dissident Soviet literature to the West and to make émigré literature available in the Soviet Union. His project began during his European exile, but grew into a full-fledged enterprise after he settled in California. The establishment of the Chekhov Publishers in New York in 1951 greatly facilitated this expansion. Receiving its principal support from the Ford Foundation, the publishing house hoped to join the interests of the Russian emigration and American politics by distributing key texts of Russian culture in Russian. The press would thereby demonstrate American commitment to preserving the important artifacts of Russian culture, in contrast to Soviet efforts to ban these works.[33] After Ford refused to renew its grant in 1954, George Kennan spoke with his friends in Washington and sought quiet support from the American Committee for the Liberation from Bolshevism, which in turn received quiet support from the Central Intelligence Agency. Chekhov, Kennan argued unsuccessfully, was important both "from the standpoint of Russian literature" and "from the standpoint of the struggle against Communist influence in the cultural world."[34] His effort failed and, by 1956, Chekhov Publishers had disappeared. In its short life, it republished many classic Russian novels of the nineteenth century, some of the novels of the new emigration, and Struve's own *Russian Literature in Exile.*[35]

Chekhov Publishers' most important products were undoubtedly its editions of previously unpublished (or long unavailable) works by Russian writers who had fallen into official Soviet disfavor. Struve here was a pioneer; he gathered and annotated works of silver age poets like Osip Mandelshtam and Nikolai Gumilev (the husband of Anna Akhmatova). Both had died at the hands of the Soviets and were symbols of the heights of silver age Russia brought down by the Bolsheviks.[36] Aided by the Inter-University Committee for Travel Grants (IUCTG) exchanges, Struve's work in recovering texts banned by the Soviets continued even after Chekhov Publishers collapsed. With the presence of American scholars in Moscow and Leningrad, Struve had little trouble establishing contacts with Soviet intellectuals. Struve never met directly with these Soviet scholars; as one colleague put it, he "refused to accept the Soviet system even to the extent of paying it a visit."[37] From afar, though, he produced editions of writings by living Soviet authors who survived on the outskirts of official Soviet life, such as the critic Iu. G. Oksman and the poet Akhmatova. Oksman was a distinguished literary scholar who had survived many years in the camps and had slowly worked his way into official Soviet literary institutes by the 1950s. A powerful intellect, Oksman had known some of the leading Soviet intellectuals of the 1920s, many of whom had become personae non grata.[38]

Struve was happy, however, to work with his younger colleagues and students to get illicit writings in and out of the Soviet Union. When Berkeley historian Martin Malia left for a research year in Moscow in the winter of 1962, for instance, he was carrying detailed instructions that introduced him to Moscow's important literary circles. Thanks in part to a sympathetic diplomat in the U.S. embassy (Jack Matlock, who had studied Russian literature at Columbia before joining the Foreign Service), Malia made extensive use of the embassy facilities to bring in writings banned in the Soviet Union and to send out letters and writings by his Soviet contacts. Malia's first gift to Oksman was Boris Pasternak's *Doktor Zhivago*.[39] In return, Oksman gave Malia rare finds, like an early edition of Mandelshtam's works, which the American then shipped to Struve via the embassy. Malia insisted on great secrecy, using code names rather than any specific details, putting pillows over telephones to prevent authorities from listening in, and other such precautions.[40] He considered his year in Moscow a great success, though he did little research during his exchange. He frequently recounted his visit to Anna Akhmatova, whom he was shocked to discover writing poetry (as she did every day) during the Cuban missile crisis.[41]

In spite of his precautions about Oksman, Malia worried that the authorities were suspicious. He warned Struve that Oksman had become "increasingly a compromised and compromising individual," suggesting that no more Americans should visit Oksman for a time.[42] Ignoring that warning, Struve sent a friend and protégée, Kathryn Feuer, to continue his connection to Oksman after Malia's departure.[43] Shortly after arriving in Moscow, Feuer, presumably ignorant of Malia's cautions to Struve, made contact with Oksman. Struve had heard rumors about a poem by Akhmatova, which he needed for an edition of her poetry he was editing. (The poem, "Rekviuum [Requiem]," is now considered a masterpiece.) Akhmatova complied with Struve's request, perhaps because (as Malia reported) she believed that she was a "strong contender" for a Nobel Prize and wanted her works available in the West.[44]

Unfortunately, Malia's concerns about Oksman proved to be well founded. When Feuer and her teenaged daughter left the USSR, her handbag (including a letter she was writing to Oksman) was confiscated, along with some notes from Oksman himself. At the Soviet-Finnish border, the two were removed from their train and questioned by security officials.[45] Just as Malia had suspected the previous winter, Oksman was compromised. Soviet authorities appear to have been well aware of his connections to Malia as well as Feuer, whom they accused of possessing "materials of a slanderous nature" given to her by Oksman, including a draft of an article of his that would soon be published abroad. Shortly after Feuer's troubles at the border, Soviet officials searched Oksman's apartment and found banned "foreign literature." Questioned about his contacts with Struve, Oksman insisted that he wrote to the American for two reasons: Struve held "invaluable literary materials" important to his work, and through this contact (Oksman claimed to his interrogators) he could try to "get Struve to drop his boycott of Soviet literature." Oksman also denied giving Malia or Struve permission to publish a highly critical article, "'Stalinists' among Soviet Writers and Scholars," that appeared in the émigré press in 1963.[46] Oksman's dossier at the Soviet Procuracy noted the final disposition of the case: the criminal investigation was closed, party officials at Oksman's institute were notified, and the "anti-Soviet literature" once in Oksman's possession would not be returned.[47]

Almost a decade later, in 1973, Struve published a survey article on recent Russian literature. Like so many of his writings, it was addressed to "future historians of twentieth-century Russian literature." Yet it differed in tone from his earlier works, concluding on a sanguine note. The last few years, he wrote, had seen the interpenetration of Soviet and émigré literature, as works by Pasternak (in 1958) and Alexander Solzhenitsyn (in 1962 and again in 1975) had become political sensations in the West. He also acknowledged, delicately, the arrival of émigré literature into the Soviet Union; it is "unofficial," he conceded, "but it does go on all the time, and…foreign editions of Russian writers find an enthusiastic response on the other side of the curtain." In a display of modesty and perhaps self-protection, Struve did not claim credit for the interpenetration he observed.[48]

Struve wielded influence within the United States. He trained an important generation of Russian literature scholars, many of whom spent their careers at Berkeley and helped to maintain it as a top Slavic department. His books documented long-forgotten authors (some of whom, as one reviewer noted, may be eminently forgettable).[49] But his lasting contribution is the one that is hardest to specify: he helped to build connections between American and Soviet intellectuals and thinkers that brought the best Soviet work to American audiences. This work made him important, even crucial, within Russian Studies but attracted little attention from others.

Struve could claim, by virtue of his travels and his knowledge of languages, to be a cosmopolitan—but his work was doggedly focused on the country of his birth. Another émigré arriving in the United States in the 1940s, however, brought with him an even longer itinerary, even broader language skills, and an intellectual agenda that was not merely cosmopolitan but universal in aspiration. The linguist Roman Jakobson was, without question, the Slavic specialist most widely read outside Slavic departments from the 1940s at least through the 1990s. He was also the central figure in American linguistics in the late twentieth century, and his impact spread into anthropology, architecture, semiotics, and indeed any field engaged in the systematic analysis of culture.[50] His intellectual contributions predated his arrival in the United States in 1941, as the writings of the Moscow and Prague linguistic circles, both of which he helped to found, made their way into specialist publications, primarily in his two native languages (Russian and French) or in Czech or German. He could also give extemporaneous academic talks in heavily accented English and Polish, leading one colleague to quip that Jakobson "speaks Russian fluently in six languages."[51]

In whatever language, Jakobson was the rare Slavicist who had an impact both within his field and beyond it. He wielded this influence from the center of early Sovietology. Simmons had recruited him in 1946 to join Columbia's new Slavic Department, where the two worked together on departmental matters and on joint research on Russian epics. As his relationship with Simmons soured, Jakobson left for Harvard's new Slavic Department. He soon thereafter joined the Linguistics Department at Harvard and eventually moved to MIT.[52] From the moment of his arrival in Cambridge in 1949, he headed a massive training program, bringing with him some seventeen junior scholars from Columbia, including assistant professor Horace Lunt.[53] As Lunt's classmates completed their degrees, they fanned out to create a half dozen or more graduate training programs in Slavic linguistics—at Michigan, Washington, Chicago, Indiana, Stanford, Brown, and Princeton. All of these departments had a Jakobsonian orientation.[54] Jakobson also had a hand in the creation of two academic journals of Slavic linguistics, first *Slavic Word* (1952–1955) and then the *International Journal of Slavic Linguistics and Poetics* (1959–).[55]

At the center of Jakobson's intellectual agenda and academic legacy was the relationship between structure and meaning in language. His explorations of this relationship ranged from brilliant expositions of poetry by Pushkin and Shakespeare and prose by Pasternak to studies of language disabilities in children to detailed studies of verb declensions. What was most impressive about Jakobson's writings on these topics was not their breadth but their connection;

virtually all of his writings sought to understand language as part of a single grand theory of meaning. These interests, of course, hardly made him a Slavicist—though most of his examples came from the Slavic world and from Russia in particular.[56] Jakobson made the study of Russian language, literature, and criticism an absolute essential for modern humanists—and also made a singular contribution to the study of Russian literature within the narrower precincts of Slavic studies. Jakobson showed how the expansion of area studies programs like Russian/Soviet Studies could promote the arrival of European ideas in the United States. While scholarly pursuits in the postwar years might have been American in scale, they could be European in content thanks to scholars like Jakobson.

Jakobson's early years contained, in miniature, the germs of the ideas for which he would later become famous. Born into a well-off family, "Roma" Jakobson's university years at the Lazarev Institute of Oriental Languages in Moscow coincided with the peak of silver age intellectual excitement before the Russian Revolution of 1917. His social and professional circle included some of the most interesting radical politicos, artists, writers, and thinkers of imperial Russia's final years: poets Vladimir Mayakovsky and Velemir Khlebnikov; artists Osip Brik, Vasilii Kandinskii, and Kasimir Malevich; critic Kornei Chukovskii; and Bolsheviks ranging from a future commissar of enlightenment, Anatolii Lunacharskii, to future diplomat Konstantin Umanskii. Jakobson spoke, drank, argued, and worked with this impressive circle of artists and writers, some on the verge of international recognition, others already well known. Poetry, he later recalled, was his "first passion" in these years, but he was also drawn to pursue scientific explorations of poetic work.[57] He recalled browsing through the *Bulletin* of the Academy of Sciences—not exactly light reading—to find an article by the mathematician A. A. Markov applying his chain theory to an analysis of Pushkin's *Evgenii Onegin* by studying vowel-consonant alternation in the first 20,000 letters of that poem. "It was hard to understand," Jakobson recalled, "but I was instantly fascinated by it."[58]

It was a propitious time and place to be studying the relationship of language and meaning. Russian symbolists Andrei Belyi and Alexander Blok were experimenting with neologisms and other poetic devices that would link sound and meaning. And the Russian Futurists, some of whom Jakobson knew personally, carried these experiments further, trying to use "nonsense" sounds to impart both emotional valence and semantic meaning. Futurist poetry used words as sounds rather than as carriers of semantic meaning.[59] In early essays on art, Jakobson dismissed the notion that verisimilitude was the only criterion for artistic work; indeed, he castigated those critics who evaluated a work of literature or art in terms of its being true to life.[60] He wanted instead to understand the artistic qualities of a work of art. Jakobson's interests in criticism and poetry were closely linked, as formalists and futurists shared a common interest in the relationship between sound and sense.[61] Both rejected the distinction—so often made in both linguistics and literary scholarship—between form and content, which were intertwined in the Futurist poetry that had so engaged the teenaged Jakobson. Only in verse did the "poetic function" of language (i.e., the function of imparting meaning) dominate; in other genres, it jostled with other functions. It was in verse, as Jakobson approvingly quoted the English poet Alexander Pope, that "the sound must seem an echo of the sense."[62] Understanding a poem's sounds was the first step to understanding its meaning.

How exactly does sound impart meaning? Here, Jakobson and the formalists pursued two related agendas. Jakobson revised Ferdinand de Saussure's distinction between *la langue* (existing language norms) and *la parole* (the specific utterance). To Jakobson, the ways in which *la parole* did—and did not—adhere to the guidelines of *la langue* were especially significant. Literary devices produced "deformations" of the strictures of *la langue;* these deformations were the key devices that imparted meaning. What mattered to Jakobson, then, was neither the genealogy nor the systems of *la langue* but "the multiform relationship and interplay between the two sides of any verbal sign—its sensuous, perceptible aspect…and the intelligible, or properly, translatable aspect."[63] The poet's *choice* to depart from the conventions of *la langue* was what made meaning in art.

As a result, Russian Formalists in the 1920s sought to move the focus of literary scholarly inquiry from the poet to the poem. Challenging a century of Russian criticism that emphasized the social and political meanings of art, the formalists wanted to focus on the artistic qualities of art—what Jakobson called *literaturnost'* (literariness). In the words of one formalist, art's "color never reflect[ed] the color of the flag waved over the fortress of the city."[64] The proper reference point for understanding literature, therefore, was past literature, not extraliterary events. Critics and historians too often studied everything—"everyday life, psychology, politics, philosophy"—except the work itself. As a result, they treated literary works as "second-rate documents" and turned literary scholarship into "a conglomeration of homespun disciplines."[65] Jakobson wanted to study *literaturnost'* in scientific terms, not in the form of haphazard critical commentary.[66]

By the end of the 1920s, the Formalists, including Jakobson (by then in Prague), drew away from the extreme formulations of the study of literature abstracted from social context. One of the most significant signposts of the new direction was a short piece that Jakobson coauthored in 1928, "Problems in the Study of Language and Literature." This manifesto expanded upon the formalist agenda of the 1920s and broadened the range of scholarly inquiries into literature and art; it marked the first major step from Russian Formalism to what came to be called Prague Structuralism. The main task of "Russian literary and linguistic science," as the manifesto put it, was to "establish in a scientific manner the correlation between literary series [of data] and other historical series." Literature, it continued, could not be properly understood with a "functional point of view" that traced literature back to extraliterary causes.[67] Continuing in his formalist polemics into the 1930s, Jakobson criticized the "vulgar *biographism*" of scholarship, which took "a literary work [to be] a reproduction of the situation from which it originated." But he also began to attack "vulgar *antibiographism*, which dogmatically denies any connection between the work and the situation."[68]

While he completed a handful of literary studies, Jakobson never applied Prague Structuralism systematically. As one biographer noted, "Despite his warnings that the poem is not self-contained, Jakobson essentially treated it as such."[69] Describing the "intrinsic values" of literature meant a detailed and careful study of language itself. And here Jakobson's linguistic interests came to the fore; his ultimate goal was to create a universal science of language, a set of rules that did not merely document exceptions and variations, but that could both organize and explain the variations in sound patterns between different languages.[70]

Jakobson's remarkable contributions to the study of language and literature generally took place at a high level of generalization. Yet his greatest contributions were to Slavic studies. As student Hugh McLean noted, Jakobson "kept returning to his native Russian for specimens on which to demonstrate poetry's fundamental features." Similarly, many of Jakobson's most significant linguistic articles—such as his "epochal" article on verb cases—relied on Russian examples. As student-cum-colleague Horace Lunt, put it, Jakobson "made Slavists take account of general linguists, and forced general linguists to deal with Slavic problems." The latter issue, Lunt continued, was a particular concern since it required convincing generalists that both general linguistics and Slavic studies were "profoundly serious matters, worthy of the full attention of first-rate minds."[71]

Jakobson had a substantial impact on studies of Slavic literature, even though his own writings on that topic were relatively few and unsystematic. His passionate account of his friend Vladimir Mayakovsky, written in the aftermath of the poet's suicide, became essential reading in Slavic literature; that work, "On a Generation That Squandered Its Poets" (1931), for all of its intellectual brilliance and personal energy, stood outside the trajectory of Jakobson's thought. His work in the 1940s was important to Slavicists, but had little relation to his linguistic theories. Together with Simmons, Jakobson wrote on the Igor' tale, addressing (but not resolving) a perennial debate over the provenance of the most famous Slavic epic.[72] Jakobson's seminal contribution was in the development of structuralism, which had its heyday in Slavic studies when the cutting edge of American literary scholarship was focused on New Criticism.

Structuralism had another proponent in American academic life in the 1950s, the literary historian René Wellek. Like Jakobson, Wellek brought Eastern European theories and sensibilities into American thought and criticism. Like Jakobson, Wellek also had something of a side career in Slavic, particularly his native Czech, literature. Torn between the cosmopolitanism of his education in Prague and the "ardent" Czech nationalism of his father, Wellek gave priority to the former. He spent the 1930s teaching at London's School of Slavonic and East European Studies until the Nazi invasion of Czechoslovakia cut off the external funding for his post. He soon landed at the University of Iowa—in a state he had never heard of—where he taught English literature to graduate students and Czech language to undergraduates and (soon enough) to U.S. soldiers through the Army Specialized Training Program.[73] Wellek's landing in Iowa City was extremely fortuitous; he quickly made common cause with English professor Austin Warren, who was promoting New Criticism in the United States. Wellek contributed to a 1941 volume that helped to introduce New Criticism to an academic audience; his contribution insisted that literature scholars cease using literature to explain society and vice versa. Instead, scholars should "first and foremost, concentrate on the actual works of art themselves" and give up their "attempts to account for literature in terms of something else."[74]

Wellek's engagement with the New Critics marked a confluence of two very different streams of thought, each with its own distinct history and concerns—but which, for a moment in the 1940s, provided a powerful argument for the reorientation and reorganization of literary studies. New Criticism was an indigenous American movement, led by critics who rejected the critical trends of the 1930s, especially the arguments of Marxist-inspired critics, and who wanted to direct their attention to the intrinsic literary qualities of texts. The typical English professor, one New Critic wrote mockingly, "diligently devoted himself to discovering 'what porridge had John Keats,'" resulting in knowledge of "what the poet ate and what he wore and what accidents occurred to him and what books he read"—and yet total ignorance of "his poetry." "We rarely know," he implored, "as much as the poem itself can tell us about itself."[75] The job of the New Critic was to study the poem, not the poet. This emphasis on the intrinsic literary qualities of a text, rather than its extrinsic circumstances, resonated with Wellek's own interests. A tangential member of the Prague Linguistic Circle—in which Jakobson played a crucial role—Wellek imbibed Russian Formalism and Prague Structuralism long before arriving in Iowa. He praised Russian Formalists for insisting that "form" was "not a mere container into which ready-made 'content' is poured."[76] The structuralists "made literary scholarship centrally literary," Wellek wrote; they jettisoned the "factual anti-quarianism and flimsy aesthetic appreciation" that he had so hated during his year of graduate study at Princeton.[77]

In 1946, Wellek was "called to Yale" to establish its Department of Slavic Literature, yet his contributions to the Slavic field were secondary.[78] He wrote a set of brief essays on Czech literature for reference works, shedding the cosmopolitanism of his other scholarship and resorting to special pleading; he complained how poorly Czech literature was known in the West, even though it was comparable to any of the "major and minor literatures" of medieval Europe.[79] Wellek's service to the Slavic profession was more significant. He became a founding member of the Joint Committee on Slavic Studies and worked closely with a small outfit called the Committee for the Promotion of Advanced Slavic Cultural Studies. This latter organization, run by George F. Kennan, Philip Mosely, and Roman Jakobson, spent the funds of a wealthy businessman-cum-mycologist, R. Gordon Wasson, whose interest in things Russian grew out of his enthusiasm for Russian mushrooms. Wellek also served on the editorial board of the *Slavic and East European Journal* for many years and was an honorary editor of *ASEER*.[80]

In spite of these connections, Wellek focused primarily on the latter half of his title as professor of Slavic and comparative literature. His collaboration with the New Critics reached its high point with the appearance of *The Theory of Literature* (1949), coauthored with erstwhile Iowa colleague Austin Warren. The book stressed the distinction between the intrinsic and extrinsic elements of literature and considered the extrinsic realm—history, biography, psychology, politics, sociology—as unworthy of the attentions of the literary scholar.[81] *The Theory of Literature* seemed to be a perfect vehicle for bringing the concerns of the Prague Linguistic Circle to the United States. A broad manifesto calling for a new approach to literature, the book was required reading in all language and literature departments for much of the next decade. The book contained within it virtually all of the issues Jakobson had raised in his manifesto two decades earlier. It was, as one Slavicist noted excitedly, the very first English-language work of any substance and significance to deal with Russian Formalists at all.[82] And yet the book hardly mentioned Russian formalism or Prague Structuralism; key authors and works appeared in the footnotes, but only rarely in the main text itself. The time was apparently not ripe for a Slavic approach to the study of literature, even one so closely aligned with reigning American notions.[83]

Wellek and Warren's aspirations for literary studies might explain the marginal role of Slavic literature in Wellek's career. The coauthors aimed to create a field independent of national tradition, frequently deriding the provincialism of those who focused on a single national literature. The essence of comparative literature was to fight the "false isolation of national literary histories." Instead, Wellek and Warren wanted literature departments to hire faculty by "types of mind and method," not by conventional divisions like nations or periods.[84] Wellek ultimately sought to stress the universality of the human experience; his approach to literary study would at last reveal "man, universal man, man everywhere and at any time, in all his variety."[85] This intellectual world would not be organized into geographic or linguistic units.

With this modest goal in mind, Wellek embarked on his magnum opus, *A History of Modern Criticism, 1750–1950* (1955–1992). Each of the eight volumes covered a different, if loosely defined, period, with the crux of the series a volume on the "Age of Transition" in the middle of the nineteenth century. Each volume, in turn, was organized around national traditions and then individual authors. The chapters themselves tended toward textual summaries, especially when moving away from the most prominent critics of a given time and place. Wellek's materials on Russian criticism were revealing in this respect—though, no doubt, the same points apply to almost any section of the *History*. The book devoted four pages to a handful of articles about Tolstoy written by Vladimir Lenin, for instance, but gave short shrift to the authors of some of the most interesting literary criticism. The silver age critic Vasilii Rozanov merited only one paragraph to describe his wide-ranging views of nineteenth-century novelists like Tolstoy and Dostoevsky.[86] The *History* was remarkably broad, but frequently seemed to contradict Wellek's agenda for the study of literature. For a scholar emphasizing the cosmopolitan enterprise of criticism, his emphasis on national boundaries and on "individual initiatives rather than collective trends" was similarly unexpected. And his promiscuous definition of criticism as "any discourse on literature" was hardly what one would expect from someone who had learned so much from structuralism and New Criticism, both of which were highly discerning in their selection of appropriate texts.[87] The result was a work that claimed cosmopolitan insight but achieved only catholic inclusiveness. Much like Struve's works, Wellek's *History* was more encyclopedic than analytical. This point was politely noted even by those reviewers who admired the books; one Slavicist called the *History* a "tour de force of erudition, industry and refined critical judgment," but concluded that it "is not a history; it is a collection of studies of creativity in criticism." Aiming to be a historian, Wellek ended up as an archivist—or, according to one critic, an "antiquarian."[88]

Adding to the ironies of Wellek's *History of Modern Criticism* was the trajectory of his career. Trained as a specialist in English literature, he was hired by Yale to build up a Slavic literature program in the height of the Cold War to support a new research program in Soviet Studies.[89] Instead, Wellek all but abandoned Slavic concerns, other than his sideline in Czech literature, and propounded literature as a human universal. Yet Wellek's service to the higher calling of comparative literature did not include any effort to link Russian literature to literary studies more generally. As a result, Wellek did not bring Slavicists into the mainstream of literary scholarship.

The loss for Slavic studies was particularly acute because Wellek was the individual most likely to bridge the gap between specialists in Russian/Slavic literature and the broader discourses of literary criticism. A key agenda—perhaps even *the* key agenda—of midcentury American literary criticism revolved around defining, analyzing, and disseminating a modernist literary canon.[90] The discussions took place not in academic journals but in literary magazines like the *Hudson, Partisan,* and *Sewanee* reviews. By the 1940s, the efforts to create a modernist canon were advancing quickly—and in a way that should have brought more prominence to the Slavicists, but ultimately did not. Critics defined modernism as a sensibility: modernist literature was suspicious of human motives; it discarded all traditions, especially literary ones; it valued expressiveness over unity—indeed, it valued just about anything over unity; and it expressed disenchantment with contemporary culture.[91] They found all of these traits in Russian novels.

Columbia's Lionel Trilling, for instance, considered Dostoevsky's *Notes from the Underground* (1864) to be among the central "prolegomenal books" for his course in modernist literature. Dostoevsky suited Trilling's definition of modernism almost too well; modernism was subversive, but *Notes from the Underground* "made all subsequent subversion seem like affirmation, so radical and so brilliant was its negation of traditional pieties."[92] Irving Howe also defined modernism in relation to Dostoevsky's short novel; indeed, he gave his most succinct description of modernism in an essay about *Notes from the Underground*.[93] Both Trilling and Howe also celebrated Tolstoy's *Death of Ivan Ilyich*—which, as Trilling put it, "destroyed the citadel of the commonplace life in which we all believe we can take refuge from ourselves and our fate."[94]

Others contemplating the modernist canon similarly gave classic Russian authors like "Tolstoevsky" pride of place. Princeton critic R. P. Blackmur, for instance, conceived a study of the European novel that featured Dostoevsky alongside James Joyce and Henry James. In making them European, though, these modernist critics ran the risk of abstracting them from their Russian setting.[95] The critics relied little, at least according to their footnotes, on any of the burgeoning specialized scholarship on Russian literature, which seemed to occupy an entirely distinct plane of existence. Edmund Wilson and Howe came into their subjects with knowledge of Russian language, but Trilling and Blackmur did not.[96] Another critic, Joseph Frank, grew interested in Russian literature as a result of his research on French existentialism, teaching himself Russian in the late 1950s so he could better understand Jean-Paul Sartre's writings on Dostoevsky. Frank then embarked on a dissertation that situated Dostoevsky's "modernist" elements in their Russian milieu. In doing so, he resisted both the decontextualization of New Criticism and the move to emphasize the universal, rather than the centrally Russian, aspects of Dostoevsky's career. The dissertation grew into a five-volume biography of Dostoevsky that doubled as a cultural history of nineteenth-century Russia.[97]

The fate of Dostoevsky in America illustrates the dramatic change in the status and stature of Russian literature in the United States. Well into the twentieth century, those few American writers who read Dostoevsky did so as a window into the supposed Russian soul, feeding the general sentiment (as a pioneering American scholar of Russian literature put it) that Russia earned not Americans' respect but their "condescension or even contempt."[98] Or, as Wellek noted: "By determined blindness...many western writers...insist on seeing Dostoevsky as completely outside the western tradition—as chaotic, obscure, and even 'Asiatic' or 'Oriental.'"[99] Nineteenth-century America, in the apt words of one scholar, "was not ready to understand and accept Dostoevsky."[100] In the interwar period, Russian literature was relegated to the margins. A handful of Soviet experts (no literary scholars among them) quoted haphazardly from Dostoevsky or Tolstoy to describe Russian peasants' passivity or the Russian soul.[101] Essays on Russian works often began with acknowledgments of ignorance, either the critics' own or that of their readers. Lionel Trilling introduced a 1955 edition of Isaac Babel's *Red Cavalry* (1923) by noting that, when he first encountered the book in 1929, he had never heard of the author and "nobody had anything to tell me about him."[102] Edmund Wilson devoted the first three pages of a 1937 essay celebrating the centenary of Alexander Pushkin's death by acknowledging that Pushkin was "little appreciated in the English-speaking countries." Wilson then went on to make the case that Pushkin "belongs among those figures of fiction who have a meaning beyond their national frontiers for a whole age of Western societies."[103]

Wellek made a similar point. He considered Dostoevsky to be a European novelist offering "deep insight into human conduct and the perennial condition of man," not a cultural curio valuable only to show Russia's difference from the West. Wellek edited a classroom reader of ten critical essays on the novelist; it included only one by a scholar who had served in a Slavic literature department in the United States—and that lone scholar, Dmitri Chizhevsky, had long since left the United States.[104] Wellek's compilation of Dostoevsky criticism offered commentary on the place of Slavic literary studies in postwar America. For all the attention that America's most important critics lavished on "Tolstoevsky," Slavic experts were all but ignored.

The evolution of Slavic literary studies, even as it remained out of step with mainstream literary scholarship, had been remarkable in quantitative terms and in the rapidity with which a field once replete with amateurs had become a full-fledged scholarly discipline. Reviews of the field in the late 1950s and early 1960s praised numerous books, articles, and dissertations—but nevertheless maintained a critical view of the discipline's accomplishments as a whole.[105] The professionalization of the field can easily be traced through American contributions to the International Congress of Slavists, a group that met every five years. The volumes themselves give testament to the steadily increasing quantity, degree of specialization, and language facility in the discipline. Each volume was larger than the previous one, each contained more articles that were narrowly focused on a single author or single text, and each contained more articles written in Russian or other Slavic languages (this last feature was only in part a result of the number of émigré scholars in the American delegation). The presence of American scholars at the 1958 congress—the fourth international confab but the first to include Americans—marked a "coming of age of Slavic linguistic and literary study in the United States," according to one reviewer. The 1963 publication celebrated the "variegation and vital initiative in the United States." The 1968 congress—held in Prague during the Soviet crackdown on "socialism with a human face"—also indicated an "optimistic feeling that serious scholars in the American academic world" were achieving "considerable success in arriving at new and interesting critical perceptions." By 1973, however, the optimism about quantity had turned to dissatisfaction about quality. Linguists, one reviewer noted, "are extremely wary about venturing onto new theoretical ground," leaving their contributions to the congress "bland." The contributions of American scholars of literature, similarly, amounted to a "rather prodigious miscellany." This prompted a reviewer's "sad reflection" that Slavic studies had been "well entrenched in the academic establishment," producing more essays with more polish but less panache. "It all seems well done," he noted, and "well presented. With hardly an erratum. I only wish I could remember something! But perhaps that is genuine academic respectability."[106] Success at becoming a field of study meant, apparently, a failure at innovation within that field. And those successes had done little to build connections with other literary scholars.

One example of the fate of Slavicists in professional literary studies is the reception of Mikhail Bakhtin. Wellek's compilation on Dostoevsky, for instance, did not include Bakhtin's 1929 study of Dostoevsky; Wellek considered it "a Marxist enterprise written to make Dostoevsky seem irrelevant and innocuous," and earlier he had made passing reference to Bakhtin's "brilliant but extravagant" criticism on Dostoevsky. Only after French theorists of the 1960s rediscovered structuralism did Bakhtin make his way into mainstream American literary scholarship. And yet, as late as 1972, Frederic Jameson protested that American literary scholars treated the Russian theorists of the

1920s as "the spiritual property of the Slavicists."[107] The French were led by
Claude Lévi-Strauss, who had been Jakobson's colleague and coauthor during
World War II.[108] Julia Kristeva and Tzvetan Todorov looked back to Bakhtin's
ideas, turning them into what one Slavicist called "the latest Parisian fashions."
Enthusiasm for Bakhtin in the 1980s and 1990s would provide Slavicists with
another chance to join the mainstream in the field. By then, though, Slavicists
had grown enthusiastic about Russian formalism, seeing it in the political terms
that Struve had earlier—"not as the cerebral play of a few armchair theoreti-
cians," as one commentator put it, "but as a clear-cut political stance: the voice
of dissent against the monopoly of official Marxist criticism." The result was
that Slavicists were "simultaneously behind and ahead of what their colleagues
[were] doing, but almost never in sync with them."[109]

The first decades of the Cold War saw an expansion and a deepening of
scholarly work on Slavic literature in the United States, the result of the post-
Sputnik language boom and the direct and indirect effects of the thaw. These
headlining events coincided with intellectual trends like New Criticism to
make fertile ground for the growth of Slavic literary studies as a central element of American literary scholarship more generally. Yet experiments to bring
Slavic studies into the mainstream of literary studies withered. Simmons's area
studies approach had little to offer literary scholars, and even by the late 1950s
it was on the defensive within Russian Studies.[110] Struve's acts of recovery and
discovery built bridges to Soviet writers, not to American scholars. Wellek's
cosmopolitan approach to comparative literature had little place for special
regional expertise; his professional success was directly proportional to his distance from Slavic studies. It took a scholar with the originality of Jakobson
to have an impact both within and beyond the field, and his influence—like
the popularity of Bakhtin—was shaped in part by other trends. The failure of
American studies of Slavic literature and language to become part of broader
conversations was matched by an intensive internal growth that ultimately
produced a remarkable range of scholarship.

CHAPTER 6

RUSSIAN HISTORY AS PAST POLITICS

The American study of Russian history, like the study of Russian literature, orbited around émigrés. For two decades after World War II, the field was Russian in many dimensions. Many of the pioneering historians were émigrés, as were many of their students. More important, the study of Russian history was dominated by Russian arguments and approaches. These participant and partisan accounts of 1917 slowly gave way to ones that took advantage of a wider range of primary sources, eventually including archival materials. This trend was the result of demographic change, to be sure, but more important was the rise of scholarly exchange programs, which profoundly altered American studies of the Russian past. These changes brought the study of Russian history closer to the mainstream of historical scholarship in the United States. The partial convergence with the broader discipline took shape in an environment focused on, even obsessed with, 1917. Liberals sought out alternative historical trajectories that would bypass the revolution, while radicals refought the battles of the revolution itself.

As Russian Studies got off the ground in the late 1940s, émigrés dominated the history field. Moscow University classmates Michael Karpovich and George Vernadsky taught at Harvard and Yale, respectively. Alexander Gerschenkron soon joined Karpovich at Harvard, while émigré historians also were on the faculties of Stanford and Columbia. Across the Atlantic, Isaiah Berlin (Oxford) and Leonard Schapiro (London School of Economics) held the most prominent posts.[1] While their perspectives on Russian history varied widely, looming behind them was a strong, even visceral, response to 1917.

Many, perhaps most, émigrés shared the views of the Russian liberals, especially the Kadets (Constitutional Democrats), who were often a part of their political upbringing. Reaching maturity in Russia's silver age, the émigrés had imbibed the flowering of artistic expression—in poetry, dance, literature, and scholarship—that coincided with a period of intense interaction with the West. Raised by French governesses and tutors, with wide experiences in Europe, this generation of émigrés declared themselves to be Russian Europeans, a term not coincidentally included in the titles of multiple biographies and autobiographies. They emphasized the robustness of Russia's cultural life, as well as the dramatic changes in its economic and political life in the decades preceding World War I; in doing so, they identified a historical path that might have avoided the Bolsheviks. Only a series of miscalculations during World War I, the argument went, weakened the otherwise healthy body politic and allowed the Bolshevik contagion to take over.

Foremost in this group was Karpovich, the doyen of Russian historians in the United States. Though he published little, he imparted his historical sensibility to his students and through them to an expanding penumbra of American-educated historians of Russia. Karpovich believed that Russia was a full interlocutor with European culture and a constituent part of European diplomacy and economy. He disliked the Bolsheviks not just because they had displaced him and his family, not just because they were Communist, but because they took Russia off the path toward European liberalism that Karpovich imagined. Born in Tiflis to prosperous Russian parents, Karpovich attended schools in Georgia. It reflected both the demeanor and the wealth of his family that they spent the summer of 1905, as protests paralyzed Moscow and St. Petersburg, vacationing in Geneva. Returning to Georgia, Karpovich felt a teenager's urge to make history rather than simply study it, so he joined the local Party of Socialist Revolutionaries. The imperial government rewarded him with a month-long prison term, after which he enrolled in Moscow University, studying history like his uncle A. E. Presniakov.[2] These studies, too, were interrupted by Karpovich's continuing work for the Socialist Revolutionaries and then by a year of study at the Sorbonne. While in Moscow, he attended the lectures of the towering figure in silver age historiography, V. O. Kliuchevskii, but (as he later recalled) he learned from others how to become a historian.[3]

Karpovich's students and successors often considered him to be a crucial link to Kliuchevskii and the grand tradition of Russian historiography. Thanks in part to Karpovich, Kliuchevskii's *Course in Russian History* was required reading for generations of American graduate students. Yet the lectures' importance for Karpovich inhered less in Kliuchevskii's arguments than in his artistry; his aphoristic style offered useful quotations, for instance, "the state swelled up and the people grew lean."[4] Though Karpovich believed that his teacher "did not know Marx," he thought that Kliuchevskii, like Marx, was determined to get "beyond the surface of laws and institutions...to the economic and social stuff of history."[5] Kliuchevskii described his own dissertation as a "history of society" focused on dominant "classes and interests."[6] His early work shared much with the New Historians in the United States, as he also studied the relationships among state, economy, and society.[7]

Kliuchevskii had little interest in the history of ideas, denigrating it as "metaphysics." He tended to evaluate cultural and intellectual life in terms of social and economic forces.[8] He found the Russian intelligentsia at times a source of ridicule; one diary entry praised Russians for belatedly recognizing, after the debacle of the Japanese War (1904–1905), that their government and their intelligentsia were "worth nothing."[9] Karpovich attended Kliuchevskii's lectures, but wrote his dissertation, with a different advisor, on nineteenth-century foreign policy. Even in Karpovich's student days, Kliuchevskii may have been his teacher but was not his guiding light.

Karpovich's arrival in the United States came about through a time-honored tradition of Russian elites: family connections. After the abdication of the tsar, the provisional government took power and appointed engineer Boris Bakhmeteff as its ambassador in Washington, D.C. Karpovich, a family friend, became the embassy's secretary. By the time the ambassador and his secretary reached their posts in June 1917, the government they represented was barely functioning; it was liquidated after the Bolshevik takeover in November 1917.[10] The ambassador's determined hopes that the Bolshevik regime would soon fail—widely shared in Washington—kept the embassy open until 1922. After conceding that this was not imminent, Bakhmeteff joined the faculty at Columbia and set up a lucrative engineering business. He channeled much of his sizable wealth into the Humanities Fund, which supported numerous Russian-related causes, from the *Russian Review* to Columbia's Russian archive, later named after him.[11]

Karpovich ended up at Harvard as a last-minute replacement in 1927. Though adored by his students, he found fewer admirers on the faculty, attaining the rank of full professor only in 1947, his twentieth year at Harvard. By then, his political leanings had shifted, from socialist revolutionary in his youth to an Eisenhower Republican by the early 1950s.[12] Beyond Harvard Yard, Karpovich was one of the pillars of the Russian emigration in the United States, editing *Novyi zhurnal* and working on *Russian Review*, in both cases shouldering a heavy burden to keep up the spirits of the Russian emigration in the United States. He also gave generously of his time and money to émigrés.[13] It was this generosity, perhaps, that kept him from the writing he promised to undertake; he left only miscellaneous articles and a set of transcribed lectures.

His scattered writings revealed Karpovich as a thoroughgoing Westernizer. Like most Westernizers, he saw Peter the Great (1688–1725) as the source of Western techniques and ultimately Western ideas, including constitutional government, civil equality, and personal liberty. He often extolled the golden age of the early nineteenth century; Russia then had not just a cultural life as vibrant as any other in Europe, but an economy that he called the most "dynamic" in Europe.[14] Karpovich railed against those who took seriously Dostoevsky's musings on the Russian soul; the best writers of his homeland revealed universal truths, not national particularities. By the turn of the twentieth century, Russia was "in the process of a profound internal transformation." It had begun as a "constitutional experiment," albeit with no written constitution. Its vibrant culture was the sign of a "stronger and healthier soul." The eruption of World War I, however, derailed Russia at its most hopeful, yet most vulnerable, moment.[15] The Bolsheviks took advantage of the war-weakened Russian state, throwing out the liberal provisional government that had succeeded Tsar Nicholas II in March 1917. The Bolshevik takeover marked, he said ruefully, the end of Russian history. His history courses reflected this belief; they, too, ended with the revolution, which was presented as an external force interrupting authentic Russian development.[16]

Karpovich's view of late imperial Russia drew more on his hopes than on his historical research. He spent much of the late 1940s expounding optimistic views of Russia in lectures to university audiences nationwide. He criticized scholars for focusing too much on the conditions underlying the revolution rather than on its immediate causes. This approach, antithetical to Kliuchevskii's sociological history, redirected attention away from the weaknesses of Russian society and toward Bolshevik intrigue. There was little in Russian history, he believed, that led to the Bolsheviks.[17]

The late 1940s were a time of great change for Karpovich. Finally promoted to full professor in 1947, he became the founding chair of the Slavic Department the following year. Karpovich had an uncomfortable relationship with the new Russian Research Center. Clyde Kluckhohn was happier to advertise Karpovich's expertise than to involve him in the center itself. In his few contacts with Kluckhohn, Karpovich tried unsuccessfully to bring Russian émigrés, especially those with "direct experience in Russian political and social life," into the RRC orbit.[18]

Karpovich's greatest legacy was a cohort of Russian history graduate students whom he trained in his remarkable decade after 1948. Most of his students focused on intellectual history, a field distant from his own scholarship in diplomatic history and from Kliuchevskii's interest in sociological history.[19] Karpovich had an advantage in teaching Russian intellectual history, even though it was the topic of neither his training nor his research: he was, in effect, transmitting an émigré's knowledge of his homeland when he taught the topic. This breadth helped to attract top students, as did the sharp contrast in personality between Karpovich and Columbia's Geroid Tanquary Robinson, whose demeanor became Harvard's best recruiting tool.[20] This interest in intellectual history was in line with trends in the American historical profession. Rejecting the prior generation's focus on socioeconomic causes, economic interests, and top-to-bottom histories of a whole society, historians of the 1950s—not just Russianists—wrote classic syntheses that emphasized a broad American consensus or Europe-wide trends. The 1950s historians focused on the ideas themselves, rather than on the societal origins or social functions of those ideas, sharing something with New Criticism's approach to literary works.[21] For Russianists in the 1950s, intellectual history had many advantages over other approaches. First was the availability of sources at a time when it was impossible to travel to the USSR; as student Nicholas Riasanovsky put it, "it's much easier to write on Slavophiles without archives than, let's say, on medieval land holding."[22] The Harvard library had perhaps the best American collection on Russian history, dating back to the nineteenth century and augmented by the bibliophilic tendencies of historian Archibald Cary Coolidge (1866–1928).[23] Other librarians had built up Russian collections at the Library of Congress, the New York Public Library, and the Hoover Institution. Historians also went to London and Paris to use collections there. The Russian Imperial Library in Helsinki would only later become a regular destination for American scholars.[24]

The cause of Russian intellectual history in America, especially at Harvard, was advanced by the intermittent presence of the British historian/philosopher Isaiah Berlin. The RRC had been trying to wrest Berlin from Oxford's All Souls College from the start, finally enticing him to teach a course on the development of revolutionary ideas in Russia in 1949. Martin Malia reported that he and his classmates (who included Richard Pipes and George Fischer) were all "dazzled" by Berlin's presence in and out of the classroom.[25] He brought not just the ideas but the thinkers to life. He seemed so at home among nineteenth-century Russian *intelligenty* that his letters referred to them in the present tense, reporting on their ideas and personalities in the manner of high table gossip. He focused especially on the ways that great Russian thinkers like Vissarion Belinskii, Mikhail Bakunin, Leo Tolstoy, and Alexander Herzen reconciled European thought and Russian circumstances, producing a remarkable body of ideas that inspired later generations to opposition and, eventually, revolution.

Berlin used his writings, which roamed well beyond Russian intellectual history, to muse on broad philosophical questions. In his most famous essay, originally entitled "Lev Tolstoy's Historical Skepticism," Berlin borrowed from a minor Greek author the comparison between the fox, who knows many little things, and the hedgehog, who knows one big thing. Tolstoy, Berlin wrote, was "by nature a fox, but believed in being a hedgehog"—that is, he took pleasure in the multitude while yearning for a singular vision.[26] Berlin seemed to be a fox. His many efforts to write a monograph all failed, but he assembled a remarkable oeuvre of stand-alone essays that he produced as occasions arose; he compared himself to a taxicab, moving only when summoned.[27] Berlin careened from commission to commission, from topic to topic: here on Tolstoy's view of history, there translating a Turgenev story, here analyzing European Romanticism, there enumerating two kinds of liberty. Yet through all of this "foxy" behavior, there was one big hedgehog-like idea, which was rooted in his own experience as an émigré from Bolshevik Russia: the relationship between the individual and the collective.

Berlin broadcast his credo in *Foreign Affairs,* the official organ of the U.S. foreign policy establishment. His essay, no doubt commissioned by friends he had made during his wartime service in Washington, provided a stunning survey of "Political Ideas in the Twentieth Century" (1950). It traced the two evils of his time, Communism and fascism, to the nineteenth century's responses to Enlightenment universalism: humanitarian liberalism, on the one hand, and Romanticism, on the other. These positions, as they later evolved, gave rise to Communism and fascism which, for all of their differences, both valued collective welfare over individual freedoms. But, Berlin noted, since there was no single solution to the problem of collective versus individual welfare, the world needed "less Messianic ardor [and] more enlightened skepticism." Well before Edward Shils and then Daniel Bell celebrated the "end of ideology," Berlin outlined the case against utopian ideologies and for incremental change.[28]

Subject, country, and politics came together brilliantly for Berlin. Russian history provided him with an "object lesson in the enormous power of abstract ideas," a theme well explored by the nineteenth-century writer Alexander Herzen. And as his friend Andrzej Walicki put it, Berlin's genius was not simply in reviving Herzen but in repackaging him. Berlin found in Herzen much that intrigued him: the tensions between individual and collective and between the present and the future. Herzen had become a Soviet icon on the basis of Lenin's frequent praise of him as the founder of the Russian revolutionary movement. Berlin emphasized not Herzen's call to revolutionary action but his belief in the sanctity of the individual and in the need to focus on the present rather than sacrificing the current generation for the future—a process which would, famously, turn its members into "caryatids holding up a floor on which future generations will dance."[29] Berlin wrote to a friend that Herzen "altered [his] life and became a point of reference both intellectually and morally." He admired other thinkers, but he became (as his nemesis E. H. Carr had it) "Herzen writ large."[30] Carr had a point; Berlin introduced Herzen's famous memoirs with a paragraph that suited its author as well as its subject:

> He believed that the ultimate goal of life was life itself; that the day and the hour were ends in themselves, not a means to another day or another experience....He believed in reason, scientific methods, individual action, empirically discovered truths; but he tended to suspect that faith in general formulae, prescription in human affairs was an attempt, sometimes catastrophic, always irrational, to escape from the uncertainty and unpredictable variety of life to the false security of our own symmetrical fantasies.

Berlin relished the immediacy of conversation—he was a famous raconteur—more than the delayed gratification of research. His view of Communism was shaped not only by his enthusiasm for nineteenth-century Russia but also by the pain of separation from the country and the language of his birth, a pain he felt especially acutely after meeting the legendary silver age poets Boris Pasternak and Anna Akhmatova in 1945. He expressed his views with emotion, not scholarly abstraction, in cascades of words so rapid that even his admirers struggled to follow him; he dazzled not just Harvard students but the likes of Winston Churchill and John F. Kennedy.[31]

The closest thing Berlin had to an American doppelgänger was Alexander Gerschenkron, an Odessa-born economic historian. Gerschenkron, like Berlin, would be better known for essays rather than books. Gerschenkron also was a noted conversationalist, usually with a competitive edge.[32] He was famous around Harvard for his ability to master languages in pursuit of some passing interest, for the breadth of his knowledge, and for his passionate if painful devotion to the Boston Red Sox. He cultivated a reputation as an expert in everything; his occasional forays into Russian literature led to persistent, if almost certainly false, rumors that he had been offered the Samuel Hazzard Cross Chair in Slavic Literature.[33] If Berlin's foxlike behavior hid his hedgehog nature, Gerschenkron was a fox through and through. His historical writings, however, frequently returned to a theme that he shared with Berlin and Karpovich: the insistence that Russia was fully a part of Europe.

Gerschenkron insisted on the viability of tsarist Russia up until World War I, when Russia's promise was stolen by the Bolsheviks. His best-known essay, "Economic Backwardness in Historical Perspective," contained all of his trademarks: it wove together economic and intellectual history to make confident and sweeping generalizations across all of Europe; it dropped literary references from Matthew Arnold to Emile Zola; and, surprisingly for an economist, it did not cite a single statistic. It defined *backwardness* as the tension between, as he later put it, "what is" and "what can be."[34] Latecomers to industrialization, he argued, relied on substitutions to close the gap. Moderately backward economies like France and Prussia developed banking systems to facilitate capital accumulation. Turn-of-the-twentieth-century Russia, with a far greater gap between what was and what could be, needed more than banks; only the government could spark industrialization. Ultimately, even backward Russia would catch up. Gerschenkron saw this dynamic in late imperial Russia; on the eve of World War I, he argued, Russia had "graduated from the government-instituted…school of industrialization" and was becoming more European in form; the government role in the economy waned while the private financial sector expanded.[35] Gerschenkron shaped the next generation of Russian historians; classmates-cum-colleagues

Nicholas Riasanovsky and Martin Malia concluded that Gerschenkron was the greatest influence on the cohort of historians trained in the 1950s.[36] While some of this influence is undoubtedly due to his outsized reputation, his articles on Russian history—his broad analysis of Russian industrialization, his argument (however wistful) about the Westernization of the Russian economy, and his linkage of economic and intellectual history—carried a great deal of weight. It helped, too, that Gerschenkron's views echoed Karpovich's and Berlin's.

Gerschenkron, much like Karpovich, had a rose-tinted view of silver age Russia. He expressed the wistful, even longing, counterfactual claim, "if not for the war…" The notion that the war diverted Russia from a path toward the West—whether via Karpovich's "constitutional experiment" or Gerschenkron's economic "Westernization"—was tenuous at best. Failings abounded: the lack of democratic institutions (or even a constitution), the unevenness of economic development, and the limited capacity of the tsarist government and the tsar himself. Yet this wistful counterfactual was omnipresent in American historical scholarship on Russia. It served both to portray tsarism in the best possible light and to delegitimize the Bolshevik regime.

George Vernadsky should have, by all indications, ended up in the camp of Russian liberals nostalgic for the silver age and wistfully imagining alternatives to 1917. Vernadsky, after all, was the son of a distinguished Russian physical scientist, V. I. Vernadsky, at a time when the Academy of Sciences was a bastion of liberal thought. He studied history at Moscow along with Karpovich and was even more cosmopolitan than his classmate, publishing articles in at least seven languages. In the 1910s, Vernadsky's political sympathies lay with the liberal Kadets, whose student organization he joined; he later worked as an assistant to A. A. Kornilov, a leading Kadet.[37]

Vernadsky's Westernizing tendencies, however, waned in a peripatetic decade of emigration before he landed at Yale in 1927, made all the more difficult by his father's decision to remain in the Soviet Union. George Vernadsky fell in with a circle of émigrés of Eurasianist proclivities who celebrated Bolshevik rule as the best opportunity for the fulfillment of Russia's historical destiny. Like his father, then, he reached some sort of reconciliation with the new order. Russia, in the Eurasianists' imagined geography, did not straddle Europe and Asia but formed a distinct continent and culture with its own unique qualities. With a strong dose of geographic determinism, they suggested that the characteristics of the land defined the character of the people and of their government. The era of the Tatar yoke (1238–1471) held the key to Eurasian history: the Mongols under Chengiz Khan tried to unite the vast Eurasian plain under a single ruler. This period bequeathed to tsarist Russia a strong centralized government and a deep suspicion of Europe. The Soviet Union, in their view, came a long way toward the goal of a single, centralized government over all of Eurasia. They dismissed Marxism as a European import; once free of it, the USSR would be "the base of a new order."[38] With this circumlocution, Eurasianists accepted the Bolsheviks as a force bringing the whole region under central rule.

Vernadsky became the leading U.S.–based exponent of Eurasianism. His massive oeuvre constantly struck Eurasian themes; it measured the great cultural differences between Russia and Europe and extolled the virtues of Russian development according to its own unique character. His historical scholarship on early Russia revealed his Eurasianist views most clearly. He was commissioned to write the first six volumes of a projected ten-volume *History of Russia,* supported by Bakhmeteff's Humanities Fund.[39] From the opening sentences of the first volume, *Ancient Russia* (1943), Vernadsky defined his topic as "Eurasia," the "final stage" of Russian expansion. The very notion of "ancient Russia"—that is, a Russia existing long before there were Slavic peoples on those lands—was itself a Eurasianist concept. It undercut the claim that modern Russia emerged only from Kievan Rus' (880–1150). His volume on that period opened with a brief discussion of the question "Is Russia Europe?"; he concluded that medieval Russia was "obvious[ly]...a unit by herself."[40] Vernadsky's volume on the Mongol years stressed the importance of this era, which established an "entirely new concept of society and its relation to the state"; it featured the Mongols over the Russians by a ratio of seven to one, a disappointed reviewer calculated.[41] Vernadsky differed from Western-oriented historians like Valentine Riasanovsky (Nicholas's father), who argued that there was little Mongol legacy in Slavic legal codes.[42]

Eurasian themes also shaped Vernadsky's widely read single-volume textbook, *A History of Russia.* "Eurasian Russia" since "time immemorial," he said, had been united as a single state. He stressed the historical significance of the Mongol period in establishing the geographic and political parameters for Eurasia's future. Peter the Great, Westernizer par excellence, came in for heavy criticism in Vernadsky's text. The tsar "completely overlooked the national psychology of the Russians," dividing Russian culture into the Western-oriented elite and the Eurasian masses. This division grew over the decades, leaving a great chasm between elites and masses and contributing to the weakness of the tsarist regime at the turn of the twentieth century. When the parliamentary system ("borrowed from the west," stressed Vernadsky) collapsed in 1917, Eurasian influences once again came to the fore. The book's discussion of the USSR combined Eurasian appreciation of the Bolsheviks with a general defensiveness about the Soviet system. He devoted, for instance, less attention to the purges themselves than to the ways in which "the enemies of the Soviet Union" used the purges for their own advantage. He mentioned the Nazi-Soviet Pact after devoting two paragraphs to describing Soviet feelings of betrayal at the hands of the British and Americans. And his chapter on Soviet culture had a distinctly rosy hue.[43] In public speeches and opinion pieces, he offered similar defenses of Russia during and after World War II. These public pronouncements attracted the close attention of J. Edgar Hoover, whose FBI agents opened Vernadsky's mail and searched his luggage when he traveled.[44]

Given his impressive scholarly output, Vernadsky attracted more attention from Hoover than from Yale. He languished for two decades there as a "research associate" before being promoted to professor—and then only because of an outside job offer.[45] While many of his colleagues went to Washington during the war, Vernadsky taught in Yale's ASTP program—a poor fit, given that he was, according to a colleague, "an uninspiring lecturer in any language." His classes nevertheless became a "Mecca for specialists in Russian history," in one historian's phrase, and he became an informal advisor to dozens of young scholars in Russian history.[46] Visitors would come to his home office, cluttered with books and bursting with papers, to get bibliographic advice; he served as a reference librarian more than as an interpreter of Russian history for American audiences. It is therefore hard to trace the specific impact of Vernadsky's ideas. The students who read and praised his ubiquitous books were more likely to stress Russia's similarities to Europe than its differences, more likely to revel in Russia's silver age, and more critical of the Bolsheviks. If, as one historian wrote, all Russianists in the United States were taught in the Vernadsky school, then it is not exactly clear what they learned in class.[47]

Vernadsky's Eurasian emphasis found few adherents among American scholars, most of whom shared the Western orientation of Berlin, Gerschenkron, and especially Karpovich. Between them, these three Westernizers inspired and trained the majority of American scholars in Russian intellectual history. Their special talent was, to use Berlin's words, "not inventiveness but a unique degree of responsiveness to others."[48] They preferred Westernizers like Turgenev to Dostoevsky's musings on the Russian soul, and they insisted that Russia was part of Europe.

Together, they translated the Russian liberal framework into a scholarly agenda that defined their careers and those of their students. Berlin supervised at least three dissertations by Rhodes scholars who would go on to teach Russian history: James Billington (Harvard and Princeton), Nicholas Riasanovsky (Iowa and Berkeley), and Donald Treadgold (Washington). Karpovich worked with these three and many others, both American-born (Robert Daniels and Martin Malia) and those born overseas (Leopold Haimson, Richard Pipes, Marc Raeff, and Hans Rogger). Many students wrote biographies or collective studies of nineteenth-century radicals. Some of Geroid Robinson's students at Columbia, like Samuel Baron and Michael Petrovich, also mined this rich vein of Russian history. Not surprisingly, given Karpovich's Georgian upbringing, his students wrote many works dealing with the imperial dimension of Russian history, whether in Poland, Siberia, Central Asia, or North America, or in terms of relations with China or Korea; none of these authors working on nationality questions, however, would rise to the top of their profession.[49] The students who came to dominate their generation shared common themes and topics: all wrote important works on intellectual history.

The 1950s generation of Russian historians clustered around different ways to link their nineteenth-century topics to 1917. Some scholars looked for paths not taken in the late nineteenth century, ones that would have led away from tsarism but not in the direction of Bolshevism. Berlin's writings on Herzen provide an example of this approach. Nicholas Riasanovsky sought to rescue the Slavophiles from the accusation that they gave succor to conservative and monarchist politics. He pointed out, with understated irony, one of the central paradoxes of Slavophilism: in proclaiming the distinctiveness of Russia, the Slavophiles sounded just like other European Romantics then celebrating their own countries' special qualities.[50] Following Karpovich—and also his own father, a distinguished legal historian—Riasanovsky placed Russia squarely within Europe. He also followed his advisor in emphasizing the growing alienation of Russian intellectuals, entranced by Enlightenment ideals, and an increasingly insular government.[51] Riasanovsky's classmate Marc Raeff traced that alienation back to the eighteenth century and in other work would similarly insist on Russia's place in Europe. Raeff, more than any scholar of that cohort, took an explicitly comparative view of Russian history, writing a seminal comparison of political institutions—what he called "the well-ordered police state" in Russia and in the German lands over the seventeenth and eighteenth centuries. He modestly attributed this comparative focus to his "scant work in the archives," though Raeff did conduct research there on several occasions.[52]

Other students ultimately challenged their advisors' views, identifying the origins of 1917 in the nineteenth-century thinkers whom their advisors so adored. Challenging Berlin's portrayal of Herzen as the anti-Bolshevik, Martin Malia presented Herzen as the ur-Bolshevik, a "gentry revolutionary" who "invented socialism" in Russia.[53] Many of Malia's cohort shared his view that the events of 1917 emerged from the ideas of the nineteenth-century Russian intelligentsia. For James Billington, the populist Nikolai Mikhailovskii wrestled with important intellectual questions in European thought—including the role of science in public affairs—but ultimately answered them in a way that brought Russia one step closer to revolution. Similarly, the biography of "the father of Russian Marxism" by Columbia student Baron stressed Georgii Plekhanov's reworking of Marxist ideas in the context of backward Russia.[54] Both Baron and Billington saw Russian radicalism emerging from Russian intellectual life. This generation of students produced works of great erudition and careful reflection, generally working within the liberal Russian matrix that looked back to the high points of Russian cultural life to argue over the possibilities of avoiding 1917.

Two of Karpovich's prominent students bucked this trend toward intellectual history and engaged more directly with the battles over 1917. Richard Pipes first envisioned his dissertation as an intellectual history of Marxism and nationality, but instead wrote about Soviet nationality policy in its first decade. Pipes relied heavily on ephemera, periodicals, and especially published Soviet proclamations on Soviet policy. Pipes's overall framework took much from the members of the non-Russian imperial diaspora whom he interviewed in Europe, thanks to support from MIT's Center for International Studies. Like his interviewees, Pipes blamed Soviet policy for destroying the possibility of the autonomous development of minority areas of the USSR; he evinced a special appreciation for those groups that lost out to the Bolsheviks. He credited his advisor with much support but recognized the vast differences between teacher and student in outlook.[55]

Robert Daniels, like Pipes, was not persuaded by Karpovich's focus on prerevolutionary alternatives to 1917. After completing his degree in 1950, Daniels worked unhappily on MIT's Soviet Vulnerability Project but soon returned to his grandparents' home on the campus of the University of Vermont, where he would teach for some four decades. Daniels completed an impressive study of the "Communist opposition" in the 1920s, *The Conscience of the Revolution* (1960). In it, he explicated a variety of possible interpretations of Leninism that had lost out in the USSR; most were more democratic than Bolshevism, and none would have resulted in Stalin. Daniels relied on the Trotsky Archive, by then open to researchers at the Harvard library, and other published sources. His title suggests the tragic tone that suffused the book; "there is a certain romance in lost causes," he wrote. The debates of the 1920s, in Daniels's telling, were between the oppositionists, who became the "conscience of the revolution," and the Bolsheviks, who sought only the "enlargement of a system of power"—in short, between principle and power, with the latter winning out.[56] Early Soviet history became, as one historian put it, "the record of the betrayal and perversion of great ideas." The betrayal began with Lenin, who failed to recognize how Russian backwardness would transform revolutionary aspirations.[57] Daniels rarely wavered from his view that the Menshevik perspective on the Soviet Union was the most accurate, a position he held while befriending Mensheviks like George Denicke in the United States.[58]

There was a handful of more senior Anglophone scholars writing about Soviet history, but none in the United States; the most prominent were based in England: E. H. Carr, Isaac Deutscher, and Leonard Schapiro. Though

Schapiro and Berlin had similar backgrounds—Riga, Petrograd, and eventually London—Schapiro was technically not an émigré; he was born to Latvian Jewish merchants who had briefly lived in Glasgow. He came back to the British isles after 1917, never losing antipathy for the Bolshevik Party that had uprooted him. He worked as a barrister before publishing his way into a position at the London School of Economics and Political Science in the mid-1950s.[59] Though his post was in political science, his inclination was historical, in keeping with the orientation of the field in the 1950s. The English academic system had looser boundaries and more flexibility than the American one; neither Schapiro nor any of the other leading scholars teaching Soviet history in the U.K. held Ph.D.'s.

Schapiro's views of the Soviet Union are especially evident in his early writings on contemporary affairs. He published a pamphlet on *The Future of Russia* (1955) that emphasized the grave threat of Soviet materialism to Western humanism; he hoped to rally his readers, he told his editor, behind their "moral duty" not to "barter [freedom] for the temporary illusion of security." Though the book dispensed with this apocalyptic language, it made the same point forcefully. Directing his ire toward Europeans who were calling for engagement with the USSR as a means to effect internal change, Schapiro called upon the West to confront actively Soviet expansion. Well before this book, he had also begun work on factional politics in the early Soviet state. After numerous publication delays—the result of E. H. Carr's effort to squelch the book—*The Origin of the Communist Autocracy* appeared in 1955.[60] It explored the fate of the Mensheviks and socialist revolutionaries in the aftermath of the Bolshevik takeover. While paying close attention to the doctrinal and tactical disputes that dominated radical arguments after 1917, Schapiro rejected the claim that the Bolsheviks were driven by doctrine. Opposition groups, he wrote, "were not eliminated...because they were counterrevolutionary. They were described as counterrevolutionary in order to justify their elimination." Excoriating Lenin and the Bolsheviks for their tactics, Schapiro hardly shared Daniels's sympathy for their victims; other radicals had worked with Lenin and had therefore "started [Stalin] upon his path."[61] The book made impressive use of a wide range of sources, mostly political pamphlets and Lenin's writings. Even as Schapiro's lifelong conservatism moderated over time, he maintained a palpable anger toward the Bolsheviks, which he acknowledged in the opening pages of his book: "The position of a historian becomes even harder when he has to deal with a revolution which has had a deep, emotional impact on his generation."[62]

The Origin of the Communist Autocracy brought Schapiro attention and job offers in both the United States and the United Kingdom. Philip Mosely then commissioned Schapiro to write a comprehensive history of the Soviet Communist Party for the Research Program on the History of the CPSU, another Mosely entity. With ample funds from the Ford Foundation, the program supported research on party history, including grants to young scholars and a three-volume reference work on CPSU history.[63] Mosely nicknamed the project the "Long History of the CPSU," hinting at its purpose: rebutting the Stalinist "Short Course" party history of 1938. Like so many of Mosely's projects, the CPSU history existed at the intersection of scholarship, philanthropy, and government; the CIA provided sources and advice to program authors, and Mosely kept his agency friends well informed.[64]

With time, money, and sources from Mosely's project, Schapiro wrote his *Communist Party of the Soviet Union* (1960), which he called a "biography of the party." It placed a significant emphasis on the formative years, arguing that the Bolsheviks' key aim was the pursuit of power, which dominated Lenin's actions in the 1920s and Stalin's in the 1930s. For instance, Schapiro saw the pursuit of power, not production, behind what he called the "Third Revolution," collectivization. Reducing politics to the pursuit of power—with no role for ideologies or beliefs—Schapiro stood accused by one reviewer of writing party history by reading leaders' memos but not their books, focusing on their tactics but not their ideas.[65] Schapiro looked at 1917 much as the Russian conservatives had, focusing on Bolshevik wrongdoing as a symbol of what was wrong with radicalism in general.

Schapiro's book remained in the tradition of fighting over 1917, a tradition that was still a part of classroom teaching in the 1950s. William Henry Chamberlin's two-volume history of the revolution, already twenty years old by the late 1950s, remained the only classroom standard that was not strictly partisan; but even that book was shaped by Chamberlin's enthusiasm and then disillusionment about the Soviet regime.[66] John Reed's *Ten Days That Shook the World* (1919), sympathetic to the Bolsheviks, was still a regular on undergraduate reading lists. Graduate students typically chose between accounts by the Menshevik Fedor Dan (Russian 1946, English 1964) or by the former head of the provisional government, Alexander Kerensky (1927). Foreign party members also took a stab at writing on 1917, thus adding to the feeling that the revolution, long since resolved in the streets, was still being fought in classrooms and libraries. The most widely read of these partisan works was Bertram Wolfe's *Three Who Made a Revolution* (1948). A founding member of the American Communist Party, Wolfe fatefully argued against Stalin at a Comintern session in 1927, for which he was expelled from the party. By the time his book appeared, Wolfe had become an outspoken critic of the USSR from posts at Radio Free Europe and the Hoover Institution.[67] Wolfe's account of Lenin, Stalin, and Trotsky was written with the dramatic zeal of the apostate. It paid due attention to their personalities as well. Wolfe's radical past was little obstacle for his involvement in Russian Studies: his book was widely assigned by academic experts; he frequently reviewed books in scholarly journals; and he maintained regular contact with the university establishment, especially at Columbia.

Wolfe's closest British equivalent was Isaac Deutscher, who also continued fighting over 1917 in his books. Deutscher had been a Communist in his native Poland; like Wolfe, he found himself arrayed against Stalin over Comintern policy, after which he joined the Trotskyite opposition.[68] He completed in 1949 a masterful biography of his nemesis, which held on to his revolutionary tenets; Deutscher was quick to criticize Stalin for cruelties great and small, but he justified the greatest ones—famine and the purges—on the grounds of historical necessity. His next project was a dramatic and sympathetic biography of his hero, Trotsky, following him through three volumes as a prophet armed, unarmed, and outcast. After Stalin's death, Deutscher argued for precisely the engagement with the USSR that Schapiro and Wolfe rejected; he predicted that the USSR after Stalin would evolve toward the democratic socialism he associated with Lenin.[69] Though at the margins of academic life, Deutscher's works were widely read by American scholars; for instance, the Inter-University Committee on Travel Grants (IUCTG) recommended his books to participants in its exchange.[70]

Diplomat-turned-historian Carr rejected the partisanship of Wolfe and Trotsky in the 4,000-plus pages of his series on early Soviet history. Carr's *History of Soviet Russia* was a diplomat's history that treated Bolshevik leaders as officeholders rather than as people, recounting in numbing detail the ins and outs of governing Russia after the tsars. Gathering materials from a mass of published sources, Carr took the perspective of the Bolshevik regime; almost every other account of the era, from Schapiro to Dan to Daniels to Deutscher, took the perspective of those who had lost in 1917. Carr's history, as his friend Deutscher put it, was a "history of the ruling group" that treated society only as "an object of policies made and decreed from above."[71] The volumes had an air of inevitability to them: policies won out because they were superior; oppositions lost because they opposed; Politburo members were removed when they outlived their usefulness. He replaced Wolfe's and Deutscher's high drama of idealism gone awry with bloodless bureaucracy.[72] Carr took 1917 not as a moment of historical contingency, but as merely one inevitable step on the Bolshevik road.

British studies of the USSR were distinguished by their venom as well as by their variety. Carr and Deutscher, for all of their differences, typically lined up against old friends Berlin and Schapiro in a complex argument combining politics, personality, and philosophy. Berlin and Carr frequently sparred over their philosophies of history. Berlin complained that Carr saw "history through the eyes of the victors, the losers have for him all but disqualified themselves from bearing witness." Carr retorted that his "History of Cricket" would focus on winners, not "the nice young man who muffed that catch"; to focus on what might have been was to engage in "idle curiosity," not history. Berlin scuttled a professorial appointment for Deutscher on "moral grounds," while Carr did his best to quash Schapiro's *Origin of the Communist Autocracy*.[73] Schapiro declined offers from Yale and Columbia because he felt it imperative not to leave the British field of Soviet history to Carr and Deutscher.[74] These debates may have been all the fiercer because there was little opportunity to exploit new sources on 1917 or on Soviet history. Even as they declined job offers in the States, Britons like Schapiro and Carr made frequent trips there to utilize sources on Soviet history at the New York Public Library, the Hoover Institution, and Harvard.[75]

In both Britain and the United States, histories of 1917 and the USSR were highly contentious, reflecting the general mood of Russian partisans. Emotions ran high, while sources were limited to published materials and personal experiences. The varied approaches to the revolution, for all of their differences, remained within the parameters of debates that had been raging since 1917—about the future of Russia, the mistakes of that fateful year, and the consequences of Soviet rule. The debates took place in cafes frequented by émigrés and also in lecture halls and around seminar tables, and the distinction between politics and scholarship was at times hard to identify. This would slowly start to change in the 1960s, as distance from 1917 grew and especially as new sources became available to Western historians.

The crucial transition from a Russian matrix to a Western one began, ironically, with a work closely tied to partisan statements on 1917 written by a Karpovich student. Leopold Haimson was different from most of his classmates—in terms not so much of background (raised by Russian émigré parents in Belgium) as of intellectual interests. Alone among Harvard history students, Haimson drew inspiration from the social relations approach, especially its psychological aspects, that had dominated the early work of the Russian Research Center; he was influenced more by Margaret Mead than Michael Karpovich.[76] He spent the late 1940s in New York working for Mead on navy-sponsored research on the psychology of Russian behavior and participating in the city's lively psychoanalytic community. Haimson's dissertation explored Russian Social Democracy before it split into Bolshevik and Menshevik factions.[77] In political terms, Haimson's central focus, the debate between "consciousness" and "spontaneity," was about tactics: would the revolution spring from the spontaneous uprising of oppressed workers, or would it come from the organized efforts of radical intellectuals? In a psychological sense, the terms represented the battle between the id and superego within an individual leader.[78] Some historians were unconvinced. "It is an interesting exercise," wrote one, "but is it history?" Another complained that Haimson privileged the Mensheviks over the Bolsheviks.[79]

This interest in social democracy provided Haimson with many opportunities. From his post at the University of Chicago, Haimson soon joined the Inter-University Project on the History of the Menshevik Movement. The Menshevik project was a typical Mosely one, with multiple constituencies and purposes: it supported Menshevik émigrés living in the United States while at the same time building a primary-source base of information from contemporaries involved in the revolutionary movement in 1917. Just as the Refugee Interview Project used Soviet DPs to get closer to life behind the Iron Curtain, the Menshevik project provided access to history by proxy. Mensheviks in exile were obsessed with their defeat at the hands of the Bolsheviks and combined left-wing politics with a fierce anti-Bolshevism. Having lost the battles of 1917, the Mensheviks hoped to win the history of 1917. After disappointing the Mensheviks who wanted to run the CPSU history project, Mosely obtained Ford Foundation funding for the Menshevik history project—the fulfillment, as one émigré put it, of "our fantasy." As the director of the project, Haimson oversaw the publication of many specialized monographs and memoirs on Russian Social Democracy.[80]

Haimson's immersion in revolutionary Menshevism shaped his landmark articles on social stability in urban Russia. These articles, appearing in 1964–1965, repeated Menshevik explanations for losing the revolutionary leadership. Challenging the liberal claims of orderly and Westernizing economic growth, Haimson and the Mensheviks emphasized its destabilizing effects, especially upon workers. The Mensheviks believed that the failure of their revolution was not their own fault; the problem lay with the workers, who were unready for the sophisticated political lessons that the Mensheviks had to teach. While Bolsheviks appealed to the basest instincts of the most primitive workers, only the most sophisticated workers properly understood the Menshevik call for patience. The main problem with the Menshevik message was that the urban proletariat was more greenhorn than red. An influx of peasants into the expanding industries of Moscow and St. Petersburg had created a working class but not working-class consciousness. New workers were "instinctive," not rational; their mood was one of *buntarstvo*, which Haimson translated as "violent if still diffuse opposition to all authority." Haimson echoed the Mensheviks' argument that workers were "driven by instincts and feeling"; they were not a class but a mass with a "disorganized and primitive elemental character." Following his Menshevik sources, Haimson portrayed the Bolsheviks as opportunists, whose "slogans...were calculated to sound a deep echo" among new workers. "Naturally," Haimson concluded, "these 'unconscious' masses proved most responsive...to the Bolsheviks." The workers' immaturity was responsible for the Mensheviks' irrelevance.[81]

Social stability was threatened by two dangerous chasms that emerged in Russian society in the early twentieth century: one between workers and so-called census society (the small educated elite in Russia's highly stratified society), and another between "the vast bulk of privileged society" and the government. Haimson's discussion of the "dual polarizations" in late imperial Russia—the growing distance between workers and elites, on the one hand, and between elites and the government, on the other—would define much of the next generation of historical scholarship. Challenging the vision of the stable and Westernizing society promoted by Karpovich and Gerschenkron, Haimson argued that, by 1914, Russian society was on the verge of collapse or perhaps explosion. World War I further strained both polity and economy, but the systems were doomed even before the war began; World War I "accelerate[d] substantially" the collapse of tsarism but did not "conceive" it.[82] Haimson answered Karpovich's wistful counterfactual "if not for the war..." with certainty: war or no war, tsarism was doomed.

One scholar criticized Haimson for following the Mensheviks' assumptions about the instinctual nature of Russian workers. Haimson readily confessed his sympathies, defending himself with the claim that the "Mensheviks' stereotype [came] closer to contemporary realities" than anything else. Over the years, however, he came to question his initial assumptions. Reflecting on the articles decades later, Haimson recalled being "impressed—in retrospect, overly impressed—by the explanations that the [Menshevik] authors...advanced about the factors that contributed to the explosiveness of this labor unrest."[83]

Unlike his Menshevik subjects, Haimson soon attracted a substantial and productive following. His social stability articles remained on reading lists for graduate students for decades, even after Haimson's retirement from Columbia in 1995. As they near the half-century mark, the articles remain the most popular items in the sixty-year run of *ASEER* and *Slavic Review*.[84] Dozens of historians who began their careers in the two decades after the articles appeared have cited Haimson's essays as among the most influential in their scholarship. While remaining well within the Russian matrix—specifically, the Menshevik position—for understanding 1917, those inspired by Haimson's work would move out of the partisan framework in order to understand early Soviet history as history.

Haimson's call for a reconceptualization of late imperial Russia and 1917 came at a propitious time. By 1965, the IUCTG exchange program was sending to the USSR annually about thirty American graduate students and junior faculty, at least one-third of whom were historians. Indeed, historians were by far the best-represented discipline among exchange participants. By enabling access to sources, the exchange program contributed handily to the professionalization of the study of Russian history in the United States. Historians could obtain more direct academic benefit from their time in the USSR: access to libraries and some archival collections allowed not just new sources but ultimately new topics and new approaches to Russian history. No longer limited to intellectual histories with published sources, or to political histories that relied on the memoirs and experiences of participants, American historians of Russia became more like their Europeanist colleagues.

Of course, there were numerous obstacles and filters that limited the work that American scholars could do. Those who made it through the IUCTG selection process were occasionally turned away by Soviet authorities for reasons ranging from humorous to bizarre. For instance, historian John Thompson applied to spend 1963–1964 researching the Russian Army during the 1905 revolution. The Soviets initially declined his invitation, declaring that "no real military problem existed" at that time—as if the Russo-Japanese War was not going on in that turbulent year. After protests from American organizers, the Soviet authorities reconsidered; they then declined his application because the subject "had been decisively covered in Lenin's works."[85]

To get around the problem of working on forbidden topics, American scholars couched their research projects in less controversial terms. For instance, political scientist Stephen Cohen described his research on Nikolai Bukharin—then an official (if posthumous) enemy of the USSR—as an inquiry into a less important and less controversial figure, Commissar of Foreign Trade Leonid Krassin. Even then, he was rejected.[86] Literary scholar Andrew Field proposed a topic in eighteenth-century literature, but once in the USSR tried to study Russian symbolists of the 1920s, then taboo.[87] Misdirection could easily backfire because students' topics became part of their Soviet academic record, dictating everything from the selection of their advisors to the archives they could enter to the specific materials they could see.

Students who made it to the USSR faced other obstacles, too. Richard Stites's advisor told him that he was unfit (as a man) to write a dissertation on feminism in nineteenth-century Russia, while Laura Engelstein was informed that the 1905 revolution was not an appropriate topic for a woman.[88] To find citations to useful primary sources, exchangees relied heavily on Soviet dissertations. The IUCTG participants requested more than forty dissertations from the Lenin Library (the official repository for all dissertations) in 1961 and received exactly one. Then, citing space constraints, library officials moved all of the dissertations to a new location outside of Moscow that was off-limits to foreigners.[89] Archives were even harder to use than libraries. One student spent his entire semester in the USSR waiting for a reply to his application to use a state archive.[90] Once granted entry to an archive, students were sometimes told that it held no documents related to their projects; if they pointed out citations to materials from Soviet scholars, they were informed that they had all the material they needed. In spite of support from IUCTG staff and especially the cultural affairs staff at the Moscow embassy, these problems persisted throughout the existence of the USSR and, in some cases, long beyond.

In spite of these obstacles, however, a great deal of excellent scholarship was made possible by IUCTG. Scholars of early modern Russia had plenty of opportunities to work in the archives, examining codexes, chronicles, and other documents; they also had a relatively easy time establishing contacts with Soviet scholars. The result was a rejuvenation of early Russian history, with articles and books on a range of political, economic, and cultural topics. Edward Keenan, one of the most important early Russianists of his generation, emphasized longstanding continuities of Russian culture, seeking to explain aspects of Soviet political culture with reference to what he called Muscovite political folkways.[91] And even for those working on the nineteenth century, conditions improved over the 1960s and 1970s, with more scholars gaining access to more archival documents. They never had the same freedom and opportunities of their colleagues studying Europe or the United States, but they saw a noticeable improvement nonetheless.

These impediments aside, the exchange programs allowed historians to move beyond the scholarship on politics and intellectual life that dominated the 1950s. Historians swayed by Haimson's articles or by the trends in social and labor history epitomized by E. P. Thompson's *Making of the English Working Class* (1963) had hopes of visiting the USSR to conduct research along these lines. But the obstacle course that was Russian historical research helped to maintain the differences between historians of Europe and those studying Russia. Take, for instance, labor historian Reginald Zelnik, trained at Stanford by "Uncle" Wayne Vucinich. He had originally hoped to write about the revolutionary era, but Philip Mosely, a family friend, doubted that Soviet authorities would allow him to make a meaningful study of 1917. Zelnik then chose to study "social composition, class structure, and economic development" in St. Petersburg after the emancipation of the serfs in 1861.[92] While on the IUCTG exchange in 1961–1962, he examined published and archival materials dealing primarily with the debates over labor policy in the 1850s and 1860s. Thompson's landmark labor history appeared as Zelnik was sorting through his research materials and writing his dissertation. Based on the materials he found and influenced by Thompson's view of class consciousness as a process rather than an objective reality, Zelnik shifted gears. He sought to examine mid-nineteenth-century workers' consciousness and commitments before they were shaped by intelligentsia hoping to radicalize them; studying St. Petersburg workers before 1870 afforded the "only opportunity…to study the situation of urban workers independently of the history of revolutionary politics."[93] This would become a recurring pattern for Zelnik: he would seek out workers' authentic identities and world views before they had been shaped by others. He sought to remove what Haimson called "the layers of distortion imposed…by the values and prejudices" of outsiders. This led Zelnik to study workers' memoirs, including a translation of one which he tellingly entitled "Before Class"—that is, how a worker understood himself before learning about abstractions like social class.[94]

For all of Zelnik's interest in workers' consciousness, his first book, *Labor and Society in Tsarist Russia* (1971), did not deal with individual workers, let alone their inner beings. Zelnik instead traced the "labor question" in mid-nineteenth-century Russia, documenting official efforts to avoid the violent labor relations of Western Europe. The failure of these piecemeal efforts became clear by the time of the Nevskii cotton mill strike in 1870 and the radicals' "Movement to the People" the subsequent year. Russia's window of opportunity had slammed shut, Zelnik concluded, and a "new era of urban class conflict had begun." Labor struggles, then, grew out of the inability of the tsarist government to find effective means of amelioration—not (as Thompson would have it) out of the emergence of working-class consciousness. As his good friend Terence Emmons put it, Zelnik wrote not about workers, but only what the "educated minority…thought about them."[95] Pipes, meanwhile, accused Zelnik of holding a "romantic view of the working man" and of relying on Marxist concepts and language.[96]

Zelnik's early work owed its sources to his research in the USSR, but owed its framework to Haimson. Though his book covered a period remote from the revolution, 1917 was clearly on Zelnik's mind; the book opened by asserting the "decisive role" of industrial workers in the Bolshevik ascent—and its first citation was to Haimson's social stability articles. The two had grown close in 1968–1969, while Zelnik held a fellowship at Columbia. Unlike Haimson's early work, Zelnik's was doggedly archival; one protégée called him a "die-hard empiricist" driven by historical data.[97] Thanks to the exchanges, Zelnik was able to place the origins of Haimson's polarization between workers and elites long before 1900.

William Rosenberg, a Harvard graduate student, shared Zelnik's interest in the polarization between workers and elites. Both were, in Rosenberg's words, determined to study *"aktuel'nye* problems"—vital issues of the day—which covered a broad range of topics in the tumultuous 1960s. Zelnik became a leading faculty ally of the free speech movement that rocked Berkeley in 1964; he also agitated against the Vietnam War.[98] Rosenberg had been involved in the Student Nonviolent Coordinating Committee, a leading civil rights organization that was becoming increasingly radical. He chose his dissertation topic, he later recalled, in part because he wanted to investigate "the pressing struggles of material and individual welfare that affect so many societies at time[s] of conflict and stress" and "the dilemmas of liberal and social democratic values in certain socio-economic contexts." He studied Russia's liberal party, the Kadets, which included many of the leading lights of Russia's silver age who had come together to promote a liberal democratic alternative to tsarism. An added advantage of this topic was ready access to émigré Kadets' papers, many of which ended up at American and Western European libraries.[99]

Rosenberg saw a poor prognosis for liberals in revolutionary Russia; their "faith in reason" and "sense of justice, legality and freedom" had little chance against the "armed strength" of radicals. His book *Liberals in the Russian Revolution* (1974) emphasized the liberals' growing alienation from both the tsarist regime and workers. Unwilling to work with the Right and unable to join forces with the radical Left, the Kadets were left only with their dreams of a liberal democratic Russia. As a historian reconstructing the Kadet Party's downward trajectory through revolution and civil war, Rosenberg evaluated Kadet decisions in terms of the limited "alternatives open to them." These alternatives were constrained by the "dramatic political and social changes in Russia" that resulted from the "imperatives of industrial modernization."[100]

His book was professional history, but shaped by what he later called *"aktualn'nye voprosy,"* meaning "problems that have some immediacy and urgency in terms of central issues of order and change." Many of his reviewers responded only within the partisan matrix of 1917. Leonard Schapiro, for instance, criticized Rosenberg for questioning the Kadets' assessments of the peasants, insisting that they were, just as the Kadets claimed, "totally devoid of any political consciousness." Other reviewers similarly engaged the Kadets' positions more than Rosenberg's interpretation.[101] Historical debates continued the arguments, which dated back all the way to 1917.

Such was also the case for Alexander Rabinowitch's efforts to write a history of the Bolsheviks in 1917. Rabinowitch, too, had a hard time breaking away from the partisan matrix of the revolution, a predicament he inherited from his father. Eugene Rabinowitch had been a chemistry student in St. Petersburg in 1917, when he worked with other liberals to elect the short-lived Constituent Assembly; he came to the United States in 1938. Alexander Rabinowitch was immersed in émigré life; he spent summers in Vermont's Green Mountains, where he learned from scholars like Karpovich, politicos like Alexander Kerensky, and lepidopterists like Vladimir Nabokov.[102] Rabinowitch's major influence among the émigrés was Boris Nicolaevsky. A Menshevik from the first days of factional dispute, Nicolaevsky worked as an archivist for the Soviet regime; posted to Berlin as a representative of the Marx-Engels Institute in the 1920s, he broke with the regime and never returned to the land of his birth. He became instead the archivist—even a living archive—of the revolution.

He collected political pamphlets and correspondence obsessively; his collection ended up at the Hoover Institution, where a microfilm edition comprises
some 800 rolls.[103] Nicolaevsky was not the only influence on Rabinowitch,
who was also shaped by his studies with Haimson, then at the University of
Chicago.[104]

Thanks to an IUCTG grant, Rabinowitch spent 1963–1964 reading memoirs, documents, and newspaper accounts of 1917 that were hard to find in the
West but available in Russian libraries and museums; no archival materials
were available on the subject.[105] The center of Rabinowitch's book was the July
Uprising in 1917, mass demonstrations against the provisional government in
Petrograd. Official Soviet histories credited the organizational work of a unified Bolshevik Party under Lenin's brilliant leadership. Liberal historians, too,
held Bolsheviks responsible for the July Days. Rabinowitch challenged this
portrayal: Lenin's role was "secondary"; the Bolsheviks were sharply divided
about the protests, often working at cross-purposes; and they led the protests only "because they follow[ed]" the protestors.[106] While official accounts
credited the Bolsheviks' centralized nature for their success, Rabinowitch
argued that the Bolsheviks won precisely because they were not centralized.
Contrary to standard Western and Soviet histories of 1917, it was not Bolshevik
single-mindedness that mattered: "the phenomenal Bolshevik success can be
attributed in no small measure to…the party's internally relatively democratic,
tolerant and decentralized structure and method of organization."[107] Basing
his work on Bolshevik sources, Rabinowitch worked to overturn common conceptions of 1917.

Ronald Grigor Suny, like Zelnik, Rosenberg, and Rabinowitch, aimed to
write a history of 1917 that would look beyond participants' finger-pointing and
partisan polemics. Suny came to the study of Russian history with more sympathy for the Soviets than his peers had. Heir to a tradition of Armenian radicalism, Suny spent his IUCTG year, 1965–1966 (shortly after Nikita Khrushchev's
ouster), as, in his words, a "kid in a candy shop." He recognized many of the
problems with Soviet life, but he was "never disillusioned" and still appreciated
it for being "non-capitalist." He recalled KGB agents following him around
Moscow and wanting to ask his tails, "I'm on your side; why are you following
me?"[108] Such views, however they were understood by the authorities, did not
help him to obtain access to Soviet archives.

Suny returned to Columbia, where he grew close to Haimson, especially as
student protests began to intensify in 1967–1968. Haimson was deeply involved
in the protests. Viewing 1968 through the lens of 1917, he had hoped to act
more effectively than the Mensheviks had. Arriving at his first job at Oberlin
College, Suny aimed to become the college's "red-in-residence." He published in the magazine of Oberlin's Students for a Democratic Society and in

academic journals.[109] Suny also built up his professional credentials. He published *The Baku Commune* (1972), an important account of 1917 in the Caucasus. The dissertation bore the marks of Haimson, focusing especially on the difficult relationship between workers and intellectuals. In multinational Baku, Suny argued, class consciousness was hard to come by; the workers seemed more interested in improving their wages than in overthrowing the economic system.[110] He was especially interested in showing how the Bolsheviks attracted and then lost the working class. Undergirding the book's explication of party conflicts and policies, the result of prodigious work in Soviet libraries, was the claim that the fate of the Bolsheviks rested on working-class support: "The Bolsheviks of Baku lost power when they lost the workers."[111] As Haimson had argued, social conditions had made the revolution.

Suny later canonized these works, from party histories by Rabinowitch and Rosenberg to his own labor and social histories, as "the social history of October." These accounts argued that successful political leaders of 1917 had "an acute sensitivity to popular moods and desires." Envisioning 1917 as a revolution with popular support rather than as a coup, Rabinowitch added, would allow historians to "understand better the impact of ordinary Russians on the revolution's course."[112] Divining popular moods was a difficult task; most of the scholars ultimately relied on partisan sources rather than on what one historian called "more conventional social historical data" like census tables, diaries, and the like.[113] They proved that the Bolsheviks appealed to the masses by citing Bolshevik accounts of their appeal or Menshevik complaints of their own inability to sway the masses. But social historians of 1917 relished the chance to interpret the Bolshevik takeover "from the bottom up." The Study Group on the Russian Revolution, established in the United Kingdom in 1975, also promoted this perspective; the group aimed to move beyond the partisan disputes that had dominated works on 1917 for a half century or more. According to its founding manifesto, the study group concerned itself with "political radicalism and related social change" in modern Russian history.[114] Storming the academic barricades, social historians fomented a scholarly revolution amid scattered resistance. The exchange program had brought new sources into play and allowed scholarship to move beyond the participant accounts of 1917. But partisanship was still very much in evidence; indeed, these works faced political criticisms with increasing frequency in the 1980s.

The exchanges expanded the possibilities for studying Russian history. They provided access, hard-fought and partial at best, to published and archival materials that allowed Russianists to write histories that more closely resembled the work of their colleagues studying Western Europe and the United States. Intellectual and political histories were on the wane in American history departments in the 1960s and 1970s, for both political and professional reasons.

Under a broad banner of social history, scholars began studying "ordinary people" in Europe and the United States, emphasizing a new approach to labor
history and to the history of women. There was still a great gap between the
social histories of 1917 and the work of E. P. Thompson and Herbert Gutman
in labor history, or John Demos and Peter Laslett in social history, and there
was little scholarship, in these years, on the history of Russian women even
as the scholarship in European and American women's history expanded
quickly. Nevertheless, the desire to examine Russian history from the bottom
up was strong, shaped by scholarly trends and the opportunities afforded by
the exchanges.

These new approaches generated new controversies in the American historical profession. Many scholars greeted the social historians' desire to write
"history with the politics left out" with dismay; some wondered if there was a
political edge, a desire to write history with the politics on the left. Russianists'
versions of these controversies often revolved directly around the exchange
program. Long-time IUCTG chair Robert Byrnes blamed the rise of new
approaches and the increasing focus on what he saw as marginal topics on
Soviet censorship. He reasoned that Soviet authorities prevented American
scholars from working on important topics in Soviet political history, so they
turned elsewhere. Pipes's criticism was more political; he accused the exchanges
of handing the keys to professional success in the field to Soviet authorities,
who maintained control over who could participate in the exchange and what
materials they could see.[115]

Contrary to Byrnes's view, the exchange programs promoted political history as well as social history. He was right, of course, that useful sources,
especially archival ones, on Soviet topics were only rarely made available.
But the political history of the nineteenth century was transformed by the
exchanges. Behind the sea change in American studies of Russian political
history was a Soviet scholar, P. A. Zaionchkovskii, who served as inspiration,
mentor, and bibliographer for a generation of Western and Soviet scholars.
Trained by a student of Kliuchevskii, Zaionchkovskii taught at Moscow State
University from 1951 until his death three decades later.[116] His many protégés
praised his commitment to "scientific" history: aiming for scholarly objectivity, relying as much as possible on archival documents, and accounting
for broad social and economic forces as well as immediate political circumstances as sources of historical change. He was deeply immersed in archival
sources, having served in the 1940s as director of the Manuscript Division
of the Lenin Library. In the words of his leading American acolyte, Terence
Emmons, Zaionchkovskii saw historical work as a calling (*prizvanie*) and not
merely a profession; Martin Malia called him a "missionary." Like Karpovich,
Zaionchkovskii believed that Russia was firmly on a path toward liberalism

in its last decade; the "constitutional experiment" would have borne fruit if
not for the war. Zaionchkovskii aimed to redeem imperial Russian history
from the shadows of 1917 and to redeem Russian historiography from Soviet
ideological blinders.[117] Soviet accounts, true to their Marxist claims, saw the
Russian state as a transmission belt, responding blindly to economic conditions. Western scholars, to the extent that they focused on political history, wrote individual biographies of tsarist ministers that gave short shrift to
institutional context.

Together with his Soviet and Western students, Zaionchkovskii sought to
rewrite the history of late imperial Russia, using extensive archival materials
to trace the institutional forces within the tsarist government and focusing on
the mindsets of individual ministers and bureaucrats. They insisted that government was not driven solely by social forces, but was a historical force in its own
right.[118] While this approach was in line with mainstream Western approaches
to political history, it was a novelty in the study of nineteenth-century Russia.
Zaionchkovskii organized his students as if he were the commanding general of
a military campaign, assigning them to research topics on one or another "front"
of nineteenth-century history.[119] He quickly seized the opportunity to work with
new recruits who came through the exchange program. His "school" included
some three dozen historians, sixteen of whom were foreign graduate students.
The students focused, in their early works, on a period that Zaionchkovskii considered to be a high point of the tsarist regime: the Great Reforms under Tsar
Alexander II (1855–1881). Many of Zaionchkovskii's own writings focused on
that period. The entirety of the Russian government was transformed in one
way or another during the Great Reforms, from military organization to local
government (rural and urban) to the judiciary to the financial basis of the government. Many American students, such as W. Bruce Lincoln, Daniel Orlovsky,
and Elise Kimerling Wirtschafter, wrote on the reforms. Other Zaionchkovskii
students, like Emmons and Daniel Field, wrote about the end of serfdom in 1861.
While he expected loyalty and hard work from his students, Zaionchkovskii
made "heroic efforts" to get them into central as well as local archives and was
deeply concerned with their welfare.[120]

Zaionchkovskii's role in American historiography was unique. While other
Soviet scholars influenced IUCTG historians, in no other case did a Soviet
advisor play such an important role in shaping American studies of Russian
history. The closest competitor may have been N. N. Bolkhovitinov, a specialist in eighteenth- and nineteenth-century American-Russian relations,
who worked closely with American scholars in the 1960s and especially the
1970s.[121] His work was mainly archival and was free of the ideological bluster
endemic to Soviet writings on foreign relations. Access to sources relevant for
Bolkhovitinov's work was more complicated; foreign relations records were not

under the control of central archival authorities, but were managed directly by the foreign ministry. Bolkhovitinov, like Zaionchkovskii, helped foreign students to gain access to historical source material, whether archival or published, and to navigate the Soviet academic system. The exchanges shaped American studies of Russian history by providing at least some access to archives, and by introducing American scholars to their Soviet counterparts.

In the late 1970s, as IUCTG's successor, the International Research and Exchange Board (IREX), sought to promote its work, Harvard historian Edward Keenan evaluated the impact of the U.S.–Soviet scholarly exchange on historical scholarship. Keenan was, in many ways, an unusual choice to celebrate the exchanges; after all, the Soviet authorities had expelled him.[122] He concluded optimistically that the exchanges had "revolutionized the study and teaching of Russian history" in the United States. But when discussing the nature of that intellectual revolution, Keenan was less specific. He admitted that scholarship on Russian history had little influence on the broader discipline and lagged behind leading general historiographic trends.[123] Yet this understated the transformations of the field in the 1960s and 1970s. The exchanges promoted a shift from a partisan to a professional matrix for understanding Russian history, including the history of the revolution. Sources in Soviet libraries and archives, as sketchy and incomplete as they might be, facilitated new approaches to Russian—and, eventually, Soviet—history. These approaches, by and large, put American historians of Russia closer to the work of their colleagues who were studying other countries. In rare cases like Zaionchkovskii's, the exchanges could also put American and Soviet scholars in serious and direct dialogues.

The achievements of U.S.–based historians of Russia were not limited, of course, to the fruits of the exchange program. Intellectual historians, educated in Karpovich's famous seminars, inspired by Berlin's articles and conversations, and deeply immersed in European ideas, produced an impressive range of scholarship. American historians of Russia were also, perhaps, lucky that disciplinary winds blew in their favor: intellectual history was at its peak popularity in the 1950s and into the 1960s, followed by a turn toward histories emphasizing the intentions and actions of ordinary people. The end result was that historians, alone among Russian Studies scholars, were able to move closer to their discipline's mainstream.

CHAPTER 7

THE SOVIET UNION AS A MODERN SOCIETY

The most influential sociologists of their generation made the Soviet Union central to their social theories, yet there were almost no sociologists specializing in the USSR whom these mainstream scholars cited. One 1958 estimate placed the number of sociologists of the USSR at roughly thirty. Even this number seems high when compared with Ph.D. production—only twenty-two sociology doctorates on Soviet topics between 1940 and 1975.[1] As a result, sociological analyses of the USSR generated more intellectual shifts outside Russian Studies than within it. For as much as the study of Soviet society mattered to American academic life, the work came from scholars who could not be considered Soviet experts even in a loose definition of the term. Harvard's Talcott Parsons, though he helped to bring the Russian Research Center (RRC) to Harvard and remained a member of its executive committee for decades, never learned Russian and followed Soviet society only as a sideline to his role as sociological grand theorist and impresario. Columbia's Robert Merton had fewer connections to Soviet Studies but was among the first American sociologists to visit the USSR. His sometime colleague Daniel Bell knew Russian but looked only occasionally across the Iron Curtain in his wide-ranging work. Harvard housed three scholars whose work in the 1950s explored Soviet society, but who rejected the notion that they were Soviet experts: Alex Inkeles, Herbert Marcuse, and Barrington Moore Jr.

Nowhere was the focus on Soviet social structure more resolute than at Harvard's RRC. Its founders at Harvard and the Carnegie Corporation wanted the center to become a laboratory for policy-relevant behavioral science. The connections between the Department of Social Relations and RRC were so numerous that some department members feared that their department would lose its distinctiveness by focusing too much on Soviet topics.[2] Others worried about the opposite problem, fearing that an exclusive focus on behavioral approaches would prevent the center from drawing a more complete picture of the Soviet Union. Such worries were short-lived, as behavioral approaches all but disappeared at the conclusion of the Refugee Interview Project (RIP), which received its last air force check in 1954.

In the 1940s and early 1950s, the guiding light for the center's sociological work was Parsons, America's leading postwar theorist of modern society. He trained many, if not most, of the key scholars in the behavioral sciences and its constituent disciplines, sociology and anthropology. Most of the major scholarship in sociology, social theory, and the behavioral sciences took inspiration (or, later, provocation) from his penetrating but impenetrable prose. His extensive connections to the RRC facilitated the cross-fertilization of the behavioral sciences and research on the USSR. Talcott Parsons's connections were personal as well as professional, as his wife, Helen Parsons, was the administrative hub of the center for many years. With Parsons at the forefront, a generation of American intellectuals reconsidered modern life as they observed the USSR.

The key concept for Parsons was the "social system," the title of his abstract book of 1951 that outlined the assumptions underlying his post–World War II work. In that work, he made the case for a new behavioral science, drawing on social psychology, cultural anthropology, and sociology, that was uniquely able to answer fundamental questions about social stability by investigating the relationship between individuals and institutions. The framework of structural functionalism, which Parsons did much to promote in the field of sociology, contributed to its focus on stability over instability, on individual adjustment rather than institutional change.[3] In the words of one scholar, structural functionalism was "based on the assumption that the social traits existing in a society at a given time are interrelated in a systematic way"; it took as its subject those interrelationships, with the main question being how "the whole system 'hangs together.'"[4]

At the same time that he helped to found the RRC, Parsons made his first systematic efforts to conceptualize industrial society in a comparative framework. Fundamental to that framework was the Soviet Union. At one of the first meetings of the RRC's seminar in March 1948, Parsons posed a question revealing his own interest in Soviet Studies. Ever the grand theorist, he called for an examination of the Soviet Union on a "broad comparative front." Studying present-day Russia, he claimed, would enhance historical knowledge about industrialization and urbanization; processes long since completed in the West could be "caught in an earlier stage" in the Soviet Union.[5] Based on the work of his junior colleagues Moore and Inkeles, Parsons saw the USSR as an industrial society; he noted how the responsibilities of power and the imperatives of economic growth would challenge the primacy of Soviet ideology and reshape the Soviet system as a whole. He fit the USSR into the taxonomies of *The Social System*, using it as one of a very few empirical cases of social change. Even before Stalin's death, then, Parsons identified lines of development for the USSR as an industrial society.[6]

Central to Parsons's grand theorizing were professionals whose expertise gave them special claim to resources and autonomy. The existence of professions was a sign that a society was becoming modern as well as a factor contributing to further modernization. Parsons gave special place to his own profession, social science, as an indicator and as a lever of modernity, celebrating its rise as a victory of scientific rationality over ideology, a battle that he traced back to Karl Marx and before. He carried over his interest in the professions, and especially in the social sciences, when his inquiries turned to the USSR.[7]

Based on these ideas, Parsons believed that the Soviet Union, like the United States, had already been inoculated against the dangerous threat of ideological thinking. "The Communist societies have gone too far in positively institutionalizing science," he wrote, to be seduced by ideological sirens. Scientific thinking, he suggested, would lead Soviet society away from its pursuit of ideological fantasies and toward the incremental improvements appropriate to modern industrial societies. New modes of thinking in the USSR would soon enough subject Marxism to "the kind of critical reexamination which scientific development inevitably entails." His striking prediction, made in 1995, followed from his faith in the power of scientific thinking: "it seems likely that East and West in the present ideological sense…are more likely to converge than to continue to diverge."[8] Soviet social sciences provided not just a keyhole through which Parsons and other American scholars viewed the Soviet Union but also a key with which they sought to modernize the USSR.

While Parsons was only tangentially involved in the RIP, he provided its basic theoretical principles about social stability. The thrust of the official U.S. Air Force report—that the Soviet Union was a stable, modern industrial society not likely to disappear any time soon—appeared even more clearly in the books and articles that appeared afterward. As the published results made clear, RIP sought to understand the Soviet Union as an industrial society. With the conclusion of the air force sponsorship of RIP in 1954, Inkeles and the other project leaders, Clyde Kluckhohn and Raymond Bauer, set about theorizing about industrial society using Soviet data. The first indication of this focus on industrial society came in the published version of the final air force report, which appeared as *How the Soviet System Works* (1956) by Bauer, Inkeles, and Kluckhohn. The authors painted a picture of the Soviet Union wholly at odds with the vision of a totalitarian state that controlled all aspects of life while its subjects cowered in fear, too atomized to find common bonds with each other. Not that they dismissed state power; they frequently characterized the Soviet political system as totalitarian or dictatorial. But they did not use the term systematically, stressing instead the mechanisms of persuasion, forms of accommodation, and sources of support for the Soviet regime. Yes, Kluckhohn and his coauthors noted, the needs of citizens stood relatively low on the regime's list of priorities, well below maintaining its own power and expanding its international reach. Yet as sociologists, they shied away from detailed examination of political rule in order to emphasize the structures and functions of Soviet institutions. They also argued explicitly that the Soviet Union, in terms of social organization, "resemble[d]…the large-scale industrial society in the West." The Soviet Union, the authors wrote, "generated a great deal of dissatisfaction, but very little disaffection and even less active opposition." The authors viewed political repression in terms of social tensions most easily resolved by the "adjustment"—a favorite word of behavioral scientists—of the population. While the book hardly ignored the terror and the secret police, it devoted more space to understanding citizens' "techniques of accommodation."[9]

The book identified social cleavages as well as social cohesion. The workers and intelligentsia, to be sure, had a litany of complaints about the Soviet system, but nevertheless offered general approval of the Soviet welfare-state provisions and the new superpower status. Only the peasants were uniformly hostile to the Soviet system. Even those peasants who were, in the book's terms, better adjusted to Soviet life saw the collectivization of agriculture in starkly negative terms. The report also identified other potential lines of cleavage, especially ethnicity (called, in the Soviet context, nationality). It concluded that such ascriptive factors mattered little in the USSR, having already given way to class divisions.[10]

How the Soviet System Works was a runaway success for Harvard University Press's RRC series and garnered largely positive reviews in newspapers and magazines.[11] It was only the first published product of the interview project; a steady stream of books and articles appeared in the late 1950s. Aiming for a broad public readership, Raymond Bauer wrote a collective portrait of Soviet society by creating nine characters to represent "actual" figures in Soviet life. He wrote the book, he recalled, on "a dare" from Walt Rostow, who challenged him to provide "synthetic portraits of 'typical Soviet types'" for Rostow's Soviet Vulnerability Project. Integrating RIP materials with contemporary Soviet literature, Bauer portrayed composite characters in terms strikingly familiar to Americans: a student, a housewife, a factory director, a "woman doctor." He included a secret police agent (Sergei, who came off as a victim of the Soviet system), but not a party official. The main purpose of the book, Bauer wrote, was to show that "the Soviet Union is a modern industrial society (or at least in the last stages of becoming one), and [that] all industrial societies have many features in common." Social structure, for Bauer, trumped political or cultural differences.[12]

Dozens of other works based on RIP data further enforced claims about the stability of the Soviet system and the focus on social structure over political institutions. Inkeles predicted in 1954 that Stalin's death would not lead to the dismantling of the Soviet system; it had weathered revolutionary upheavals and become a stable industrial society.[13] Monographs also made the same case, emphasizing the USSR as a stable industrial society comparable to any other. Joseph Berliner showed that factory managers adapted to structural incentives much like their counterparts in the West. Mark Field examined the structures and strains of Soviet medical practice, showing how it related to the larger social system. Kent Geiger did the same for the Soviet family.[14]

Inkeles and Bauer published what they saw as the summation of the interview project in *The Soviet Citizen* (1959). The book's opening sentences established its principal contributions to sociology; Soviet Studies was a distant second. The book was, before anything else, the only detailed study of the "general social-psychology of industrial society." Based on the results of the interviews and questionnaires administered to displaced persons in 1950 and 1951, it provided the largest data set for analyzing any modern society. The most important conclusion of the project, the authors declared, was that the Soviet Union "shares many features in common with the large-scale industrial order." This general conclusion was backed, as was every other aspect of the project, with sophisticated rehearsals of quantitative data teamed up with anecdotes to support individual points. First and foremost in the Soviet Union, as in all modern societies, was the role of labor. "In modern industrial societies," they wrote, "a man's 'job' tends to be the most important fact about him." Even amid the promises of the USSR's "classless society," social class was one of the central factors in Soviet life: it shaped prospects for upward mobility, reflected personal and social values, and defined political attitudes. Soviet citizens, like Americans, were not necessarily happy with their circumstances, but rarely connected these to politics: "Despite the high incidence of dissatisfying experiences in the life of the Soviet citizens, their usual response was one of accommodation or even positive loyalty."[15] Even large reservoirs of dissatisfaction would not lead to a flood of active protest.

Would Soviet citizens act on their political beliefs? Were they motivated by a striving for human freedom? Inkeles and Bauer had little expectation of principled action. Even those citizens who reported turning against the regime were unlikely to cite political reasons for their transformation, let alone express principled opposition to the regime. But this hardly distinguished Soviet citizens from anyone else; Inkeles and Bauer insisted that "the main drive of man" is not "ever towards increased freedom." They found that Soviet citizens had by and large adjusted to the society around them. That the society had much less to offer its citizens than the United States did—in terms of material comforts and especially political freedoms—was true but beside the point. The system worked well enough to minimize active disloyalty, even if it did not eliminate dissatisfaction. The Soviet system was, like other industrial societies, a relatively stable one—not unchanging but stable.[16]

As the book neared completion, Inkeles presented his views to the Senate Foreign Relations Committee. While the senators expressed enthusiasm for Inkeles's ideas about the USSR as a modern industrial nation, they seem to have misunderstood fundamentally his viewpoint. Senators J. William Fulbright (D-AR) and Hubert Humphrey (D-MN) asked Inkeles to comment on the eternal Russian nature, with Fulbright citing the Marquis de Custine's recently reprinted travelogue, *Russia in 1839*.[17] Inkeles's argument was the opposite: as a modern industrial society, the Soviet Union shared less with its imperial predecessor than with the United States, its Cold War antagonist. His sociological claims fell on deaf congressional ears. While Inkeles and Bauer rejected claims that Russia might forever be doomed to despotism, they nevertheless offered a deeply pessimistic assessment of political life in the Soviet Union. Even a system as repressive as the USSR would be stable thanks to its ability to elicit individual adjustment. While they recognized that repression played a role in limiting opposition, the authors ultimately focused most intently on individual behavior. The adjustive powers of the population were simply too great to bring about change, so Communism would not give birth to its own grave diggers.

Inkeles and Bauer's views of the USSR were an application of behavioral science's general pessimism about political life in modern societies. Bauer made this point in a paper comparing totalitarian and liberal societies; he concluded that "we will inevitably be … the creatures of our political and social institutions." Citizens adjust their actions and aspirations to their political system, rather than vice versa. "The Soviet experience," Bauer believed, "asserts the strengths of man's disposition to accommodate or to accept any ongoing social system, even one which presents as many negative aspects as does the Soviet system." Bauer did not celebrate such a conclusion—he thought it "somewhat dismaying"—but found it the most fitting theory of politics and social life. Indeed, he used this comparison to criticize McCarthyism; given the power of institutions over individuals, he wrote, "we must be extremely vigilant concerning our own institutions … [especially] those institutions which guard our civil liberties."[18] Bauer's pessimism about Soviet politics, then, mirrored his pessimism about democratic politics.

Bauer was hardly the most pessimistic or the most prominent postwar American social scientist to question the possibility of a truly democratic politics. The behavioral sciences colonized political science departments after World War II, documenting the numerous ways in which democratic societies did not—and, just as importantly, could not—operate according to the collective will of the citizenry. Looking at political behavior, rather than ideas or institutions, political scientists concluded that citizens often lacked the incentive and capacity to get involved in key government decisions, even in local governance. As a result, the real power resided in the hands of those leading institutions; as Robert Dahl famously noted, even the PTA functioned as citizen mobilization in the guise of citizen control, providing the appearance of democracy rather than a democratic process.[19] Talcott Parsons's emphasis on individuals' adjustment to social structures worked in parallel ways; it took the power structures for granted and studied how different groups functioned within them. Bauer and Inkeles, in short, treated political mobilization in the Soviet Union with the same skepticism as their Americanist counterparts treated it at home.

Bauer and Inkeles's pessimism about change from within the Soviet system distinguished them from some Western observers of the USSR who still carried a torch for a progressive politics and society in the Soviet Union. Isaac Deutscher, for instance, hoped that the repressive aspects of the system would attenuate as the Soviet Union reached higher levels of industry and education. By that argument, Stalinist repression had fulfilled an important function— spurring an industrial revolution even though at tremendous human cost— but would fade as that revolution reached a successful conclusion.[20] Inkeles and Bauer rejected Deutscher's optimism, claiming instead that there was no "inherent incompatibility of totalitarianism and industrialism."[21] This question—phrased more broadly as the relationship between political and socioeconomic structures—would dominate sociological writings about the Soviet Union in the 1950s and 1960s.

Only a handful of scholars seemed to accept Inkeles and Bauer's claim that they were writing an analytical sociology of modern industrial society rather than a view of Soviet daily life. Soviet specialists were generally positive about *The Soviet Citizen*, but rarely addressed its central claims; clearly impressed by the project's size, they duly recited the book's argument with little or no critical engagement.[22] Other sociologists were more skeptical. Columbia's Daniel Bell attacked "How the Harvard System Works" in a classic article, "Ten Theories in Search of Reality." Appearing before the publication of *The Soviet Citizen*, his criticisms of *How the Soviet System Works* nevertheless apply. Bell excoriated the RIP approach for ignoring power and for refusing to give priority to any one part of the Soviet system. "Is it not quite clear, really," Bell asked facetiously, "that the Soviet system is characterized, essentially, by the central control of political power, that it is a *command* system, and that all other aspects of the system…derive from that fact?"[23] Reinhard Bendix made a similar criticism of *The Soviet Citizen*, complaining that the authors had assumed the primacy of social forces and thereby excluded the possibility that Soviet policies might fulfill political aims. He charged that Inkeles and Bauer, seeking to dethrone the totalitarian school's primacy of the political, had merely replaced it with the primacy of the social.[24] This question, once raised, touched on some of the fundamental issues of postwar social science. In order to answer a narrower question about the relationship between totalitarianism and industrialism, scholars needed to pursue a much broader line of inquiry. How do economic organizations, political regimes, and social systems interact?

Inkeles's later work would not, presumably, have met the approval of Bell or Bendix. He continued to focus on modern social systems and their effects on individuals; political structures receded into the background in that work. Inkeles began comparing social stratification in different industrial societies.[25] He and a coauthor compared rankings of occupational prestige from a handful of Western societies, added RIP data on the USSR, and concluded that scales of prestige differed little in spite of significant differences in culture, history, and political structures; they concluded that there was "a relatively invariable hierarchy of prestige associated with the industrial system." Any deviation from the norm, they argued, could be explained by the incompleteness of the modernization process in a given country.[26] Speaking at the landmark Dobbs Ferry conference of the SSRC's Committee on Comparative Politics in early 1958, Inkeles hypothesized that "institutional patterns" shape all aspects of human experience, including "perceptions, attitudes and values." The "randomized influence of traditional cultural patterns"—what others might call "culture"— mattered less. What Inkeles called "industrial man" was a single social type, transcending nationality, religion, and ethnicity.[27]

Inkeles soon embarked with fellow sociologist David Smith on a large-scale project, one that fit squarely within the scope of the Department of Social Relations, which he later joined. The two compared the social psychology of modernization in six developing countries. Interviewing roughly 1,000 men in each country, the authors focused less on societies than on individuals, traditional and modern. They used the terms to specify clusters of personality traits. The very scale of the study contributed indirectly to its downfall. *Becoming Modern* might have been a significant contribution to the sociology of modernization in 1964. But by the time it appeared in 1974, it was a monument to 1960s social science that was a decade too late.[28] Inkeles saw the process of modernization as one of convergence: individuals and societies each converged on a single modern type. In a later book, *One World Emerging?* (1998), Inkeles made the case for convergence as the ultimate and inevitable outcome of industrialization; he took seriously the possibility of an individual nation's divergence from this norm, but saw such divergences as temporary detours from the road to modernity.[29]

In contrast to Inkeles's focus on the sociological and psychological impacts of industrialization, his colleague Barrington Moore Jr. was interested in the relationship of politics and society along the lines of Bell and Bendix. Though Inkeles and Moore both rejected the label "Soviet expert," and both earned nondepartmental tenure at the same time, they differed greatly in approach, background, and personality. Most important, they differed in their conception of Soviet politics. Inkeles rarely considered political systems—in *Becoming Modern*, political ideologies and systems were outside his focus. Moore, in contrast, was closely attuned to the relationship between politics and social structures, concerns that would remain evident throughout his long and illustrious career.

Moore cut an unusual figure at the RRC and at Harvard in general. He was independently wealthy, thanks to a family whose name often graced the society pages. One great-grandfather was Bishop Clement Clarke Moore, who wrote "The Night before Christmas"; a grandfather was J. P. Morgan's private lawyer; an uncle married into the Pulitzer family. While his colleagues and classmates joined a raft of political organizations (according to the security clearance applications they filed with the air force before beginning work for RIP), Moore listed only one organization of which he was then or had ever been a member: the New York Yacht Club, following his grandfather, who had been a commodore there.[30] Moore studied sociology at Yale, earning his doctorate in 1941. He learned Russian for his dissertation, which examined social stratification in thirty different societies, including the contemporary USSR. The only Russian items Moore cited were a handful of Soviet novels. He spent most of World War II in Washington, D.C., living on a boat that was docked on the Potomac and working for the Justice Department and the Office of Strategic Services. At the OSS, he met Herbert Marcuse, who convinced him, he later recalled, that there was "quite a lot of utility in the Marxist tradition—if you didn't take it too seriously."[31] Wedding Marx and Weber, Moore published widely during the war, including an article emphasizing the ubiquity of social stratification and therefore "class struggle." He also published two articles on the changing nature of Communism that foreshadowed his later work. Both dealt with the transformation of Communism from a "revolutionary appeal" to a state ideology; one article was based on his Department of Justice work about the CPUSA, the other about the Bolshevik Party.[32]

By 1948, as he was being considered for a Harvard appointment, one scholar expressed the concern that Moore was too biased politically to work at the RRC. His OSS boss, Geroid Tanquary Robinson, worried that Moore was "not as objective as one might hope" since he believed that the American and Soviet systems "were bound to clash." Kluckhohn set aside this concern, arguing that Moore had already made major contributions to Soviet Studies and sociology while at OSS. After earning tenure in response to an offer from Columbia, Moore remained (as students recalled him) "aloof from departmental concerns"; allergic may have been a better term.[33] Thanks to his wealth, he could keep a safe distance from most institutions, a privilege he exercised with some frequency.

Though Moore hated large administrative structures, he loved large intellectual ones; he avoided grand theories but was drawn to grandiose questions. Moore insisted that he was never a Russia specialist, but a sociological theorist who happened to use the Soviet case. That proclamation aside, Moore focused exclusively on the USSR for the decade after World War II. His first book, *Soviet Politics: The Dilemma of Power* (1950), picked up on the theme of his 1945 articles on American and Soviet Communism, studying the transformation of Bolshevism in what he called "an essay in applied social science." Moore intended to determine "which of the pre-Revolutionary Bolshevik ideas have been put into effect in the Soviet Union, which ones set aside, and why." The book argued for the importance of ideology, which "sensitized the new Russian leaders to certain facts and made them obtuse to others." At the same time, he closely traced changes in Bolshevik ideology, especially the increasing irrelevance of Bolshevism's original "anti-authoritarian tradition" and egalitarianism. The shifts in Bolshevism were not the result of abandoning one tenet for another, Moore explained, but allowing one or another aspect of a contradictory ideology to gain prominence.[34] Early Bolshevism contained not just threads of antiauthoritarianism, Moore argued, but also (as he put it at one seminar) "a strong tinge of what today would be labeled with the adjective totalitarian."[35] The argument is strikingly original in suggesting that Soviet rule was neither the terrestrial incarnation of a fixed ideology nor the opportunistic pursuit of power. Bolshevik ideology provided a finite set of options; the specific elements that came into play were then shaped by circumstance. Bolshevik ideology and Bolshevik policy had their own histories, each shaped by the other.

Moore explained the ultimate emergence of an authoritarian Bolshevism that accepted (even encouraged) inequality by the Bolsheviks' need to adapt to "problems that are common to any industrial society." As he had argued in his dissertation, social stratification seemed inherent to modern societies, and central authority was a common way of quelling the tensions that stratification caused:

> The Bolshevik experience...reveals the need for inequalities of power in an industrial society. At the same time, it reveals the need for a functional division of labor and for inequality of rewards. All of these requirements add up to the necessity of a system of organized social inequality.

The Bolsheviks faced, then, not so much the "dilemma of power" of Moore's title as a dilemma of modernity. An industrial economy affected social organization. "Weapons from the capitalist arsenal," he wrote, are "basic requirements for the survival of an industrial society." These weapons would ultimately shape political institutions. The inconsistencies of prerevolutionary Bolshevik ideology were resolved in favor of centralized control, systemic inequalities of power, and traditional great-power foreign policy, all in order to conform to the dictates of modern industrial society. The subtitle, too, was something of a misnomer; the book was less about "the role of ideas in social change" than the opposite, the role of social change upon ideas. Ideology provided the initial set of possibilities, whereupon the imperatives of a modern industrial society did the rest.[36] The book was well received, earning encomiums from Bertram Wolfe and Reinhold Niebuhr for insights about Russia though they had little to say about contributions to the sociology of ideas.[37] A rather amorphous form of social change—industrialization or perhaps modernization—exerted influence over ideology, not the reverse.

By the time he completed *Soviet Politics,* Moore had a variety of different ent projects in mind, including one on the status of Soviet natural scientists (prompted by Lysenkoism and the turmoil in Soviet academe in the late 1940s), another on Soviet social structure, and a third on the Soviet secret police. He also devoted some time to an examination of Soviet-American relations, arguing that the Cold War was both a "struggle of ideas" and an "old-fashioned struggle for territory." He emphasized common outcomes for both antagonists, which were simultaneously "loudly proclaiming" and "sacrificing" their ideals. The conflict "favors the intransigents on both sides of the Iron Curtain"; seeing the Cold War as a dynamic process, Moore identified a seemingly inevitable push toward escalation with little opportunity for calming Cold War tensions. This last point likely prompted Robinson's warnings about Moore's politics; what Moore saw as sociological prediction, Robinson interpreted as political proclamation.[38]

In 1950, as the Refugee Interview Project came to dominate RRC business, Moore joined in—sort of. He completed only four interviews and then launched into increasingly fundamental challenges to the project. At first, he complained only about the process of data acquisition, arguing that interview replies should not be analyzed statistically, as Inkeles was doing; instead, the replies "should be treated in a manner similar to the way a psychoanalyst treats a patient's dreams or free-floating fantasies." Fundamentally, Moore did not trust the interviewees. He worried that the researchers would take the interviews at face value, using them to describe objective conditions in the Soviet Union. Moore, in contrast, wanted to examine them critically for insights into personal subjectivity. Later, however, Moore told the air force sponsors that the whole project was a waste of time; big social science amounted to "pseudo-accuracy based on dubious statistics" watered down by group thinking.[39]

In spite of his deep reservations about the interview project, Moore wrote one of the most insightful of the many dozens of reports completed for RIP. What started in 1949 as a project on "status and motivation in Soviet society"—focusing at the individual level—grew into a broader analysis; he wanted to examine the "interrelationships of the major economic and political positions within the system" to evaluate the "strengths and weaknesses of the Soviet social system."[40] A 1952 report to the air force covered precisely this topic. As he had done in his first book, Moore emphasized the impact of the imperatives of a modern industrial society—in the Soviet context, "the conflict between political criteria of behavior" and those imposed by "technical efficiency." He hypothesized that the "dominant political criteria must at some points yield" to economic criteria in order for the system to survive. Writing in the final year of Stalin's rule, Moore did not see the maintenance of domestic power and the pursuit of international power as the sole factor in Soviet politics. Aside from the emphasis on power for its own sake (the central theme of scholars arguing for Soviet totalitarianism), Moore saw two competing factors: the need to continue industrial development by promoting technical efficiency and a somewhat more vague "necessity for the rulers to make concessions to human values and requirements." He outlined two possibilities: first was the "partial de-politicization" of Soviet life, the regularization of political control, allowing more "orderliness" in Soviet life through the diminution of terror even if it slowed the pace of Soviet economic growth. This would ultimately lead to the "further stabilization of the Soviet regime" by providing more space for "rational and efficient forms." The second possibility would come about if Soviet leaders tightened their grip on power, maintaining a system based primarily upon political criteria in the domestic and international sphere. The ultimate direction of the Soviet system depended on the resolution of these tensions.[41]

Moore soon expanded these arguments in *Terror and Progress* (1954). Much had happened, of course, in the Soviet Union in the two years between the completion of Moore's air force study and the publication of the book: Stalin had died, his favorites Lavrentii Beriia and Georgii Malenkov had been deposed (with the former executed), and the gulags began to empty. Yet the book retained the same topics, key points, and a great deal of the language from the report. The long-term Soviet future looked much the same to Moore in 1954 as it had in 1952. With or without Stalin, the Soviet leaders had to reckon with the challenges of maintaining their power while building a modern industrial system. Three trends shaped the Soviet future, two of which—the pursuit of power and the imperatives of technical rationality—carried over from the air force report. The vaguely expressed third trend in the report, however, had much more specificity in the book; Moore no longer discussed "human values" in the abstract but a resurgent "traditionalism" (including nationalism) as a factor in Soviet life.

Like other Russia experts of the time, Moore saw Soviet terror as a crucial barometer for the future. The new—post-Stalin—regime "still requires terror as an essential aspect of its power," yet terror created such uncertainty that it led to inefficiency. A more rational system would maintain power not through terror but through "conformity to a code of law." While he offered three possibilities for the Soviet future—based, respectively, on power, technical rationality, and traditionalism—he devoted the most attention to the second possibility, that the Soviet system would "adapt to the technical requirements" of modern industrial society "even at some sacrifice in political control." What would a Soviet society more receptive to the demands of industrialism look like? It would replace political aims with "technical and rational criteria," allowing rapid economic growth to continue without maintaining the economy as a "servant" of the political system. It would still be a centralized society, but one that no longer relied on organized terror; social mobility would remain high, and individual and social aims would be expressed increasingly in "secular and materialist terms." It could even evolve into "technocracy—the rule of the technically competent," including a "technocratic aristocracy" in ascendance among political elites. The rise of "technical and rational criteria of behavior and organization," he argued, would "by definition...imply a heavy reduction of emphasis on the power of the dictator." The other challenge to political dominance, Moore argued, came from traditionalist forces in Soviet society— most evident, he argued, in the educational system and in most aspects of rural life. Traditionalism would involve the devolution of power to localities, a strong emphasis on personal connections in personnel decisions, a more rigid class system, and stronger kinship ties. Either traditionalism or rationality could, as the book concluded, "do [the] work of erosion upon the Soviet totalitarian edifice."[42]

The ultimate direction of Soviet society depended not just on the resolution of internal forces (power, rationality, tradition), but also on the international environment. The inefficiencies of a traditionalist system would render it ineffective amid international tensions, while technical rationality was better suited to "a more competitive [international] political environment." A 1956 article dropped some of Moore's initial coyness about the possibilities of technical rationality in the Soviet Union, arguing unequivocally that the USSR was moving in that direction. He also suggested that the best chance for technical rationality to defeat totalitarian elements was a relaxation in international pressure.[43]

Terror and Progress would later become one of the most significant works in Sovietology, though that fate could hardly have been predicted from the initial reviews, which were positive but muted.[44] Many scholars relied on Moore's discussion of technical rationality to describe the evolution of the USSR in the decades after Stalin's death. Given the eventual importance of this work to political scientists, it is worth noting that Moore's vision of technical rationality happened *within* rather than *in opposition to* continued rule by the party. The nature of the party elite might change, but the party would not relinquish the reins of power. Thus, Moore emphasized the extent to which he agreed with Harvard colleague Merle Fainsod.[45] Moore, like Fainsod, saw Bolshevism as an evolving and dynamic system of ideas and practices. It had evolved from an ideology combining antiauthoritarian and centralizing tendencies under tsarism to a totalitarian system (Moore never shied away from that term), an evolution he had traced in *Soviet Politics.* In *Terror and Progress,* he outlined the possibility of an evolution away from totalitarianism, toward a more stable and rational system, but one with the party still firmly in control. Moore suggested that the imperatives of a modern industrial society existing in a complex international environment would not just encourage but even require such changes. These industrial imperatives would yield the demise of totalitarianism by rendering it into a less ambitious despotism—or perhaps into a more stable and rational form of single-party rule. His focus on the interplay of political and economic organizations drove these works on the Soviet Union, making them as useful for political scientists as for sociologists.

The handful of sociologists still active at the RRC in the mid-1950s clearly drew inspiration from Moore's work. They organized a series of talks on "social change in the Soviet Union" that foresaw the transformation of Soviet politics and society by the imperatives of industrial society. They focused especially on the rise of a new cohort of technical elites who were determined to remake Soviet politics. One scholar termed this trend a "revolution 'from below'" in the making. This marked perhaps the first use of a term that would later dominate debates over "revisionism." It also showed just how broad were the hopes for a new Soviet society even before Khrushchev consolidated his power.[46] Among the participants in this RRC series was Moore's friend Herbert Marcuse, an influence since the war. Moore's paper on the "meaning of Soviet experience for industrial society" incorporated Marcuse's ideas. Moore claimed that Soviet events showed how industrialism could have a drastic effect on social organization. Excluding the USSR from sociological analysis "unduly narrow[ed] our perception of the range of actual alternatives presented by advancing industrialism." He then outlined some of the radical changes that industrialization might effect, for instance, "a sharp flattening of the pyramid of rulers and ruled that has characterized most of human history since the dawn of civilization." "With a big enough increase in resources," Moore hypothesized, "the *necessity* for a system of repressive allocation, i.e., dictatorship, nearly disappears." Moore had shifted from his earlier stance on inequality toward the more fundamental critique of modern society offered by Marcuse.[47]

Marcuse came to his studies of the Soviet Union with an imposing set of ideas about modern industrial society that were rooted in the Frankfurt

School's version of Marxist criticism. Like Hannah Arendt, Marcuse thought about the USSR in terms of a framework built around the German experience. The lineaments of his ideas are visible in his writings of the 1940s, well before he learned Russian or devoted serious attention to Soviet affairs.[48] By 1950, after spending half the previous decade in the OSS and its first postwar spin-off, Marcuse won a two-year fellowship at Columbia's Russian Institute, with the sole proviso that he learn Russian. He predicted as early as 1954 that the USSR might be heading toward a "totalitarian welfare state." Marcuse saw a "new adjustment" in the USSR after Stalin that focused on "the growing productive capacity." Marcuse's research project, eventually published as *Soviet Marxism* (1957), emphasized the "interconnection between Russia and the West" in the twentieth century. The connection, for Marcuse, was simple: Western and Soviet societies were both organized around modern industrialism. Socialized industries, he argued, were just as exploitative, alienating, and repressive as capitalist ones. The culprit was technical rationality as an organizing principle for economy and society. The development of a welfare state would not necessarily undercut Soviet rule; Marcuse, like Moore, saw sociological changes but not fundamental political ones. This part of Marcuse's argument paralleled Moore's discussion of technical rationality and was undoubtedly an important inspiration for Moore; the two friends also shared the view that the evolution of social organization would not bring about an end to party rule, only a new mode of it. Finally, both Marcuse and Moore emphasized the dangers of industrial society—in the USSR or the West—to individualism and the individual psyche.[49] Marcuse later offered extensive commentary about the alienating nature of work in industrial societies, most notably the way that the organization of labor hampered the free expression of individuality. The "common features of late industrial society" included bureaucratic rule, centralization, and regimentation—which might diminish not just freedom but the desire for freedom. Marcuse would later focus more intently on the ways in which "industrial society" (which he ultimately used in the singular) restricted individuals in *One-Dimensional Man* (1964). Offering few distinctions between Western and Soviet versions of industrial society, Marcuse railed against the impact that industrial society had upon individual behaviors in democratic and totalitarian societies alike.[50]

As Marcuse moved toward his critique of a singular industrial society, Moore devoted increasing attention to the question of how industrial societies (plural) came to differ from each other. He approached the question through comparative history. The result of this work, *Social Origins of Dictatorship and Democracy* (1966), was a landmark in comparative history and sociology that shaped a generation of scholarship. Moore had embarked on the project that became *Social Origins* in 1953, even before completing *Terror and Progress*. Envisioning a "broader study of the relationship between industrialism and totalitarianism," he affiliated with MIT's Center for International Studies (CENIS). He also declined an apparent offer to become a "full-fledged member" of the Harvard faculty, remaining, for the next forty years, Harvard's sole tenured lecturer.[51] In its first form, Moore imagined the book as addressing the question "how does industrialism affect the structure of authority and the possibilities of freedom in modern society?"—a Marcusian question. He would use case studies of England, Germany, and Russia, coincidentally facilitating his continuing relationship with the RRC. The projected book would contain two chapters of historical background, one on preindustrial "precursors to totalitarianism" and another on the transformation of rural society in the three principal cases.[52] The remainder of the book would examine the modern versions of the three central societies, with chapters on "the structure of authority in industry," violence, the military, science, social classes, religion, and government.[53] Moore's MIT links may have brought him to the study of India, then the subject of a major CENIS project. By 1955, Moore concluded that consideration of "the Asiatic experience" was essential in order to avoid being "utterly provincial." Some of the key themes of *Social Origins* were already evident in this very preliminary (and ultimately peripheral) chapter: emphasis on the imperative of industrialization, but also its high costs, careful attention to the structures of authority, and interest in the agricultural sector.[54]

After drafting the India chapter, Moore began describing his project on "dictatorship and industrialism" in much broader terms. While still focused on modern dictatorships and democracies, Moore greatly expanded the number of comparative cases, especially in the chapter on rural transformation. By 1956, Moore wanted to study rural transformation in England, the United States, France, Germany, Italy, India, Japan, China, and "of course" the USSR. He was still interested in "how the penetration of industrialism…changes the structure of authority" in three institutions: science, military, and industry. But he also argued that "the transformation of rural society to a democratic or totalitarian political system" was a key issue—that is, he wanted to explore the impact of economic change on social and political structures.[55] As he worked on the project, he focused less and less on the structures of modern society and more and more on the divergent processes of modernization. By the time the book appeared in 1966, it had shed any significant analysis of modern institutions, which had constituted the bulk of Moore's original outline, and had expanded the chapter on rural transformation into a 500-page book.

Social Origins examined four paths to modernity in six countries: "capitalist democracy" in England, France, and the United States (where he viewed the Civil War, not 1776, as the revolution); Communism in China; fascism in Japan; and "non-industrial democracy" in India.[56] Unlike modernization theorists who envisioned a single path of economic development—leading perhaps to world government, according to one bold prediction—Moore emphasized varying paths.[57] The decisive factor in determining the path of modernization, Moore concluded, was the relationship between the figures in his subtitle: lord and peasant. For all of the differences among the routes to modernity, there was one common feature: "There is no evidence that the mass of the population anywhere has wanted an industrial society, and plenty of evidence that they did not. At bottom all forms of industrialization so far have been revolutions from above, the work of a ruthless minority." Combining the passion of Marx's critique of industrialization with Max Weber's attention to the articulation of interests, the book was a plea to recognize the violence in which all modern societies came into being.[58]

The absence of German and Russian cases from *Social Origins* is striking, especially after considering Moore's original inspiration for the project. He drew on Arendt's and Marcuse's ideas about Germany as well as his own writing on the USSR; he was influenced also by the long shadow cast by the failures of German and Russian modernization—in the form of Hitler and Stalin—in the postwar West. Moore had planned chapters on Russia and Germany and even drafted one on Russia; one student recalled that he dropped it because it was weak. In the end, Germany and the USSR were not so much written into the text of the book as they were the parchment upon which the book was written. Moore relished, in passing, the irony of a peasant revolution yielding to rule by a Bolshevik Party that had virtually no standing in the countryside, ultimately creating a society that treated the peasants even worse than had the ancien régime.[59] Even as *Social Origins* offered an incomplete account of the conditions and consequences of the Bolshevik revolution, it became the rare case of a social scientific work whose influence grew dramatically as it aged. A twenty-first-century informal survey of American sociologists ranked *Social Origins* at the top of the list of the "most important contributions to scholarship" in that field.[60]

In *Social Origins,* Moore set out to answer two pressing questions of 1950s social science: what were the origins of totalitarianism and of the structures of modern society? More broadly comparative than the works of totalitarian theorists like Arendt and Carl Friedrich, and more historical than the approach of sociologists like Parsons and Inkeles, Moore's *Social Origins* offered an explanation for the course of every twentieth-century tyranny except the one that he had set out to study, the USSR. Moore's work grew out of a determination to understand what the USSR meant for the basic predicaments of modern society: inequality, violence, and injustice, which would all be topics of his future works. Moore's senior colleague Talcott Parsons had the same view of the Soviet Union as a key to understanding the predicaments of industrial society but a radically different vision of what that predicament was.

Parsons began to devote serious attention to the USSR in the late 1940s, as his professional, pedagogical, and familial connections to the RRC grew. Parsons made the connections between his conceptions of the USSR, on the one hand, and industrial society, on the other, especially clear in his contribution to a classic work applying modernization theory to Soviet Studies: *The Transformation of Russian Society,* edited by Cyril Black. Indeed, the original title for the volume was "The Modernization of Russian Society," and it was changed only at Alexander Gerschenkron's insistence.[61] Parsons's contribution outlined "some of the principal features of the structure of that still small, but increasing, group of societies which can be called 'industrial,'" adding a historical dimension to his categories from *The Social System.* Parsons's earlier works were more static and homogenizing than the dynamic and differentiated theories he developed in the 1960s. The first industrializers, Parsons argued, necessarily relied upon "economic primacy." Later industrializers, he continued, could opt for economic primacy or "political agency"; Parsons considered the USSR to be the "paradigmatic example" of the latter. Yet even an industrialization process led by politics would necessarily adopt economic criteria as it continued. This is the reasoning behind Parsons's prediction of a "convergence of the Cold War antagonists."[62] He suggested that Cold War tensions would fade as superpowers' similar structures (and, ultimately, similar values) would mitigate their differences. A talk prepared for Radio Free Berlin offered his most direct statement about convergence: Parsons argued that the United States and the Soviet Union were "very closely related"; they both promoted modernization as well as a general pattern of "'human freedom and welfare' which transcended their differences." What Parsons termed *convergence* might more accurately be described as Soviet capitulation. The economic rationality that he saw in the Soviet future would bring the USSR toward the "core...pattern" of industrialism—and that pattern amounted to an encapsulation of his views of the United States.[63]

Parsons joined his argument about the rise of economic rationality to a belief in the decline of ideology in Soviet life. In the early stages of industrialization, he argued, ideology was an important asset, legitimating new values and norms appropriate to an industrial society. Parsons's latest works no longer set ideology in opposition to industrial progress (as he had earlier), but saw it as a tool for mobilizing masses mired in tradition. Ideology had no place, however, in mature industrial societies. Measuring ideological commitment could therefore provide a barometer of modernity. Western sociologists like Parsons, Merton, and Moore understood Trofim Lysenko's success at promoting a Lamarckian theory of botany as a prime example of the victory of

ideology over science and paid special attention to the role of scientific thinking in the USSR. Looking at the state of Soviet social science, Parsons concluded optimistically that Soviet society itself was on the brink of large-scale
change. Comparing Communism to other ideologies of reform (Calvinism and
Jacobinism), Parsons argued that such radicalism would inevitably fade. And
he saw signs in Khrushchev's Soviet Union: the spread of scientific thinking,
the rise of education, and the growth of administrative (as opposed to political) bureaucracies. "From its own internal dynamics," he wrote, Communism
would soon yield to political democracy, pluralism, and rationalism. "It seems
as certain as such things can be," Parsons concluded with rare clarity, "that
Communism...will prove to be short lived."[64]

Parsons's deepening interest in the USSR led him to travel there twice in
the mid-1960s. These trips brought together his central scholarly concerns: the
importance of the sociological profession, the functions and limits of ideology,
and the convergence of industrial societies, including most prominently the
United States and the Soviet Union.

As if responding to Parsons's proclamations about social science in the
late 1950s, scholars in the USSR began to claim some autonomy for research.
Sociology as a field of scholarship had not existed since the 1930s; what passed
for social research took place in institutes of philosophy, which were, in turn,
devoted primarily to propagandizing dialectical materialism. Even amid the
straitened circumstances of Soviet *nauka* (literally science, but meaning here
scholarship), philosophy stood out as the least serious enterprise and the one
most prone to political manipulation. Starting in the last years of Stalin's life,
natural scientists and economists (the most "scientific" of Soviet social sciences)
sought new avenues of research and new directions of theory under the banner
of science.[65] But, eventually, scientific thinking came even to the barren intellectual tundra of Soviet sociology. By the time scholarly exchanges brought
the first Western visitors to Soviet institutes, glimmers of sociology that went
beyond dialectical materialism were visible. Soviet sociologists argued that
their field was the science of society, not the exegesis of Marx and Lenin. The
Soviet Sociological Association was founded in 1958 to arrange Soviet participation in international scholarly conferences.[66] Other new organizations
facilitated more serious sociological research, especially empirical research
through surveys; institutes and journals of "concrete social research" and "social
measurement" appeared in Leningrad, Moscow, Kiev, and Novosibirsk after
1960.[67] Applied social research units also proliferated in government agencies,
including the security apparatus.[68]

The initial products of this research were rudimentary by American standards; analyses of simple surveys and observational studies predominated.
Staying close to the facts had a clear advantage for Soviet scholars, allowing

them to avoid making interpretations that could later be called into question. Theoretical works would have been even more dangerous, open to accusations of "idealism," obeisance to the bourgeois theorists, or worse. The first inklings in 1956 (before Khrushchev's Secret Speech) emphasized "the unity of theory and practice" and offered scholarly support for the "building of communism."[69] Pioneering sociologists tended to emphasize the practical benefits of their work, especially outside academic circles; concrete social research would provide information to help the Soviet system work better.[70] By the early 1960s, Soviet sociological work was growing in quality and especially in quantity; one source estimated a tenfold increase in the number of scholarly sociology articles between 1960 and 1964.[71] A collected volume in 1966, produced in anticipation of the inaugural meeting of the sociological association, contained dozens of empirical studies on topics like rural transformation and changes in Soviet social structure.[72] The president of the association, G. V. Osipov, served as general editor; he cheered the advances in method and theory, arguing that this justified making sociology an independent discipline.[73] The work of this new field was celebrated in the Soviet press, both as an example of a science-in-embryo and as a practical measure likely to improve Soviet society.[74] Institutional recognition soon followed in 1968, when the Academy of Sciences created its Institute of Concrete Social Research with Osipov in a leading role.[75]

American academics followed the transformation of Soviet sociology closely. Robert Merton, who ranked with Parsons as the most influential sociologists of their time, visited the USSR in 1961 as part of a delegation of behavioral scientists. The delegates met with Osipov and others leading the transformation of Soviet sociology. Merton praised the new scholarly institutions of the late 1950s, but expressed mixed feelings about the work going on there. He welcomed the turn to empirical research but at the same time viewed Soviet research thus far as primitive, atheoretical, and more like market research than American scholarship.[76] After two visits to the USSR, Parsons's student George Fischer celebrated what he called "the new sociology" emerging in the USSR.[77] As Fischer made some of the principal findings of Soviet social research available to his non-Russianist colleagues, others took a more direct approach, inviting Soviet scholars to publish programmatic statements and scholarly reviews in American journals. Daniel Bell, who had proclaimed "the end of ideology in the west" in 1959, was by 1966 wondering about the same trend in the USSR—and citing the emergence of sociology as proof.[78]

Parsons soon joined this chorus and made his own pilgrimage. He received an invitation to participate in a Soviet-American scholarly exchange program in 1964 and spent almost three weeks in Moscow, Leningrad, Kiev, and Yalta. The main purpose of the trip was to inform Soviet scholars about the state of

American sociology. In a series of small seminars and one large public lecture, Parsons described recent American work along both empirical and theoretical lines.[79] While his discussions with Soviet sociologists revealed many areas of significant disagreement, he emphasized common ground in his reports. American and Soviet scholars, he wrote, employed similar methods in their empirical work and could, he noted with hollow generosity, learn from each other. Their research often focused on similar topics, especially those related to industrial sociology or to generational conflicts. Though Soviet sociology had yet to catch up with, let alone overtake, American sociology, Parsons concluded that it had already become a true scholarly discipline. Parsons drew obvious satisfaction from the rise of academic sociology in the USSR, seeing it as a victory of science over ideology. Seeing Soviet sociology "crystallize"—Fischer's term—as a discipline confirmed for Parsons that the USSR was fully modern. There is a certain degree of self-congratulation in Parsons's response; he noted on multiple occasions how many Soviet scholars were familiar with his work and that of his students.[80] Beyond that, he took pleasure in the rise of science, which would further propel the USSR toward modernity.

Changes in the Soviet Union also sparked a reconsideration of some of Parsons's main ideas, leading to a significant deepening of his historical perspective. Evidence of this change appeared in his notes from the trip. At one level, the untitled notes amounted to a simplistic comparison between the liberalization of Calvinism and the transformation of Soviet Marxism. Read alongside his earlier writings on the sociological profession, the notes highlighted the special emphasis that he placed on the social sciences. The differentiation of sociology from the discipline of philosophy held special importance: it amounted to "admitting [the] canons of science…into what had previously been matters of faith." The field of philosophy, the guardian of Marxism-Leninism and official Soviet ideology, was giving birth to a scientific field organized around an empirical research agenda rather than deducing scientific truths from Soviet doctrine. The rise of sociology in the USSR was tantamount to the separation of church and state in early modern Western Europe.[81]

Parsons's increasing attention to the evolution of industrial societies like the USSR also shaped his historical views on the emergence of such societies in the first place. By the 1960s, Parsons was distracted by too many projects to undertake a major theoretical statement like *Structure of Social Action* or *The Social System*. The closest he came to a theoretical statement was a pair of books written for undergraduates, the draft outlines of which he had carried with him to the USSR in 1964. Parsons's description of the history of modern societies in what became *The System of Modern Societies* (1971) revealed how considerations of the USSR had informed his theory of social change.[82] The distance that his social theory had traveled in the previous decade is evident from the two works' tables of contents. Whereas *The Social System* began with a discussion of action theory and its relevance to social theory, his new work opened with a historical section. His view of the nature of modern social systems had not changed significantly over the decade, but he was now attempting to describe their emergence in a historical framework.

When dealing with the evolution of modern societies, he applied his familiar model of social functions in a dialectic mode. Each modern society, he argued, excelled in advancing some but not all of the functions. Thus, the first modern system in Holland, England, and France introduced the dual industrial and democratic revolutions of the eighteenth century. But it took Prussia, in the early nineteenth century, to further increase the "adaptive capacity" by placing duty to the state above democratic rule. The next step came from the United States in the late nineteenth century, representing further technological advance that, in turn, surpassed Prussia without forgoing democracy. But again, a variation emerged from the East—this time, the Soviet Union. It is here that Parsons's analogy between Prussian Calvinism and Soviet sociology becomes most significant. Both Calvinism and Communism represented "counterpoints" to the main (i.e., Western) line of historical development. For Parsons, the Soviet Union further improved modern societies' capacities to organize and mobilize their populations around collective goals. His optimism about the future liberalization of Soviet political control, then, suggested that the USSR, too, would soon incorporate the innovations of the democratic revolution. This roughly sketched analogy shaped the direction of *System of Modern Societies,* as he compared the post-Stalin thaw to religious toleration and predicted an "ecumenical" future for the Soviet Union. It could thus become the lead society in a new stage of modern life. This advancement in the Soviet Union could take place only through the spread of scientific thinking, which was, in turn, the responsibility of social scientists. The differentiation of sociology and philosophy was a harbinger of the "secularization" of Soviet ideology. Political change should soon follow, he argued, and the Soviet Union might "run broadly in the direction of western types of democratic government." The keys to Soviet developments in this direction were twofold: widespread education and the emergence of effective social sciences.[83]

After returning to the United States in 1964, Parsons sporadically pursued research on the state of sociology in Soviet bloc countries—a project hampered by his lack of knowledge of the relevant languages. Reading through the growing number of English-language reports on Soviet sociology and working with a Russian-speaking research assistant, Parsons envisioned a project that would substantiate his high hopes for the future of Soviet sociology. He was especially excited to see how Soviet scholars had adopted many of the elements that he identified with his own work: a determination to shed ideology in the name of science, a desire to undertake theoretical as well as empirical work, and a focus on social stability.[84]

Parsons had high ambitions for continued exchanges with the USSR. He believed that scholarly exchanges sped advances in Soviet sociology, by which he meant the field's Westernization. At the same time, the exchanges provided opportunities for productive contacts across the Iron Curtain, helping to reduce Cold War tensions. Bringing together Soviet and American scholars offered "one way to minimize East-West ideological conflict and polemics," Parsons optimistically proclaimed.[85] Parsons's second trip to the USSR, in late 1967, was far briefer and less involved than the one three years earlier. Traveling with a group of scientists promoting disarmament (an offshoot of the international Pugwash movement), he reestablished contact with the hosts of his 1964 trip and with a handful of Soviet sociologists whom he had met at an International Sociological Association conference.[86] These meetings clearly exceeded even Parsons's high expectations. Writing afterward to the U.S. ambassador in Moscow, he repeated his enthusiastic appraisal of Soviet scholarship. Soviet scholars' determination to master the techniques and approaches of Western social science, Parsons predicted, "may prove to be of very substantial significance in easing some of the tensions inherited from the Cold War period."

Parsons's grand hopes for Soviet-American academic exchanges were best illustrated in a remarkable letter that he wrote to Walt W. Rostow, then in his final year as national security advisor in Lyndon Johnson's White House. Parsons began by updating Rostow, whom he knew personally, on his most recent trip to the USSR. Celebrating the spirit of joint scientific enterprise he had recently experienced, Parsons emphasized developments in sociology as proof of the "'secularization' of the political religion of Marxism-Leninism." Ideology had yielded to science, and there was no going back. Yet the shift in Soviet scholarship toward Western social scientific models faced a grave threat. This threat came not from the Soviet side but from Parsons's own: the American escalation of the Vietnam War might isolate Soviet scholars and thereby prevent their new belief in science from reaching full flower. Already, war-related tensions had scotched one prominent Soviet scholar's visit to the United States; any further delays in the academic exchange programs would be "truly tragic." The answer, he told Rostow, was simple: stop the Vietnam War, which was impeding the efforts of serious scholars to bring about significant changes in Soviet life.[87] The ivory tower, not the Pentagon, was best suited to winning the Cold War.

Parsons's second trip to Moscow was the high-water mark of his efforts to build connections between modern sociology and modern society. From his early focus on modern societies in the 1930s, through his more systematic efforts to theorize modern social structures in the 1950s, he saw the emergence of sociology as a crucial sign that a society had reached a certain level of modernity. The continued work of sociologists, moreover, would promote further modernization by eradicating ideology in favor of rationality.

Things went according to Parsons's plans in the late 1960s. In the years since Parsons's first visit, Soviet sociologists had begun, in Osipov's proud words, to "overcome excessive empiricism" and develop a distinct sociological theory as remote as possible from ideological strictures. The route to this theoretical approach led to Parsons and structural functionalism. While Soviet books and articles still lambasted Parsonian sociologists as apologists for capitalism, "bourgeois idealists," and much else, a new generation of scholars was trying to bring structural functionalism into Soviet sociology.[88] Most important here was A. G. Zdravomyslov, who headed Leningrad's Laboratory of Sociological Studies. Engaged in one of the largest projects of the day, a detailed investigation of industrial relations, he also wanted to put the study of Soviet society on firmer theoretical footing by building connections to the West.[89] Zdravomyslov later credited his conversations with Parsons as "an important stimulus for the further assimilation [*dal'neishego osvoeniia*]" of structural functionalism in the USSR.[90] This theoretical turn in Soviet sociology, like the empirical move a decade earlier, owed more to internal than to external factors. Alexander Vucinich attributed the spread of Parsonian theory among Soviet sociologists to "a growing conservatism" about Soviet society, part of a "relatively new view of Soviet society as a stable system," not a revolutionary one. Soviet scholars used the language and methods of science to establish some intellectual and institutional autonomy from the demands of the party. Such autonomy was, of course, only relative, as evidenced by any number of political upheavals in Soviet scholarship, including, by the early 1970s, in sociology itself.[91] By the early 1970s, party officials attacked some of the structural functionalists for kowtowing to Western theories.

Parsonian structural functionalism came under increasing attack closer to home, too. No purges were involved, but scholarly challenges to Parsons's framework accelerated in the late 1960s.[92] Alvin Gouldner mounted the biggest challenge in a 1970 book sounding an alarm about the "coming crisis of Western sociology." The book leveled an extensive and intensive assault on Talcott Parsons for promoting "academic sociology," with its implicit support for the status quo. Gouldner's final chapter fretted over the arrival of academic sociology in the Soviet Union. Gouldner had hoped that the USSR would be the haven for "critical" or Marxist sociology, which structural functionalism had eradicated in the United States. He noted with disappointment that Soviet industrial development had spurred Westernization there in scholarship as well as in society.

Gouldner, like Parsons, emphasized that the Soviet system required a sociology of the status quo—but was aghast: "the Soviet Union's internal need for the stabilization of its own society" was "conducive to an academicization of Marxism that dulls its critical and revolutionary edge." Soviet sociology may have been critical in the narrow sense—attacking Western scholars—but was hardly the critical sociology that Gouldner desired. The cooperation of American and Soviet sociologists foretold a nightmare convergence along the lines that Marcuse had described: a global "culture dominated by spiritless technicians."[93]

For critics like Marcuse and Gouldner, the emergence of the Soviet Union as an industrial society suggested a bleak future. For Parsons and Inkeles, that same development augured a bright future of convergence along the lines of the American model. With a heightened professional pride, Parsons believed that sociologists like himself did not just replicate but helped to create the scientific mindset that was an essential part of modern industrial societies. Both Parsons and Gouldner exaggerated the role that sociologists played in shaping larger society and especially in shaping Soviet events. It is striking to see how important the USSR was in American debates for, against, or around industrial society. For Barrington Moore, whose view of modernity was full of irony and ambiguity, the Soviet experience played a similarly important role. And yet none of these scholars—Parsons, Gouldner, Marcuse, Inkeles, or Moore—considered themselves to be Soviet specialists.

In the end, the studies of the USSR had the greatest impact in American thought in a field that was, at best, a minor part of Soviet Studies. How did this ironic result come about? The field of sociology emphasized generalizations beyond the individual case. Even though Barrington Moore wrote his first two books about the Soviet Union—and Alex Inkeles his first three—both considered themselves to be students of modern society in general, rather than of one modern society in particular. The generalizing impulse affected all of the social sciences in the postwar decades, but the others had, for their own reasons, maintained a closer connection to their "area." Political scientists faced a predicament similar to that of sociologists, but faced a more difficult challenge. It was easier, after all, to make the case that Soviet society could be studied with the same tools used to understand the industrial West than to make the same claim about Soviet politics.

Interpretations of Soviet society created only a small monographic literature and were of limited use to the U.S. government. Yet they transcended the confines of Soviet Studies and had a much broader impact than any other facet of the field. For much of the postwar period, sociologists focused on the problems of modern societies, both where they came from and how they operated. By the time the RRC had entered its third month of operations, Parsons had asked how studying the Soviet Union might help to address these problems. The answer to his question—the Soviet Union was essential to understanding modern societies—emerged not only in his own work, but in that of others around the center in the 1950s, including Inkeles, Moore, and Marcuse. These studies also had an influence beyond American sociology, into Soviet sociology and into American political science.

CHAPTER 8

SOVIET POLITICS AND THE DYNAMICS OF TOTALITARIANISM

The period between 1947 and 1953 was, by any measure, the heyday of "totalitarianism." The term was some twenty-five years old by then, having been first coined by Benito Mussolini to describe his aspirations for Fascist Party control over Italy. By the 1930s, Mussolini's Italy was lumped with (perhaps overshadowed by) Hitler's Germany and Stalin's USSR as totalitarian states, united by their goal of extinguishing private life beyond state control. The term took on special meanings on the left in the 1940s, as Frankfurt School theorists enumerated totalitarian elements in modern capitalist societies, including but not limited to their native Germany. Upon emigration to the United States, members of the Frankfurt School found that their definition competed with a staunchly anti-Soviet one promoted by the anti-Stalinist Left. The term moved beyond the precincts of the Left and entered everyday political discourse with the enunciation of the Truman Doctrine in March 1947. In asking Congress for aid to Greece, President Harry Truman framed the country not as the birthplace of democracy but as one front in a global struggle. In doing so, he set the terms of U.S. global interests: "totalitarian regimes imposed on free peoples, by direct or indirect aggression, undermine the foundations of international peace and hence the security of the United States." The term *totalitarian* soon came into wide use with reference to the USSR, taking the meaning held by the anti-Stalinist Left into mainstream political debates.[1] Soviet actions in the late 1940s—the domestic *Zhdanovshchina*, the Sovietization of Eastern Europe, and the creation of the People's Republic of China (for which Stalin was widely credited)—all reinforced the notion that the USSR was a totalitarian state. Like fascism, the logic went, it could not be changed from within, it was a risk to global security and U.S. interests, the state dominated (even effaced) society, and it was expansionist.

Stalin's death in 1953 hardly took the term out of circulation. The Soviet Union remained a totalitarian state in policy discussions and political shibboleths. Scholars later would complain about the constant and unsystematic use of the word, suggesting with a tinge of condescension that its ubiquity "in political discourse strongly indicates that it answers to a genuine need."[2] But it was not just politicians who needed the term.

Totalitarianism had an academic (or at least intellectual) career aside from its frequent appearance in public discussions about the USSR. Hannah Arendt's book *The Origins of Totalitarianism* (1951) sought to bring the Frankfurt School critique of totalitarianism—as an aspect of modern society—into American political usage that focused on the USSR. She attributed totalitarianism's rise to the dissolution of the integuments of nineteenth-century society: nation-states, political parties, and hereditary classes. The result was a modern mass society ill equipped to govern itself but equipped with new technologies of power. Under totalitarianism, individuals were completely atomized, bereft of affective ties to each other; the state was not just the dominant but the sole force shaping society. The fact that her historical account fit the Soviet case poorly did not reduce the book's resonance or reach.[3]

In the early 1950s, the idea of a totalitarian USSR was a constant in public discussions, further bolstered by the North Korean invasion of South Korea (again credited to Stalin) and by Arendt's work. Carl Friedrich, a German-born political theorist teaching at Harvard, offered his own definition of totalitarianism, reformulating Arendt's ideas so they might better account for the USSR. Friedrich had earlier contemplated a project along these lines—a comparative analysis of Nazi and Communist political systems—but World War II had interfered.[4] He returned to the topic in 1953 by bringing together an impressive group of scholars and public intellectuals—which convened, ironically, on the very day that American newspapers announced Stalin's death.[5] Friedrich's essay, a touchstone for future scholarship, enumerated five distinctive features of totalitarian societies: an official ideology; a "single mass party of true believers"; monopolies of the means of both violence and mass communication; and a "system of terroristic police control." Like Arendt and the Frankfurt School, Friedrich identified totalitarianism as a syndrome of modernity. Yet, in many other ways, Friedrich's definition marked a departure from Arendt; he focused on systems of control and left aside, at least in this essay, the question of atomization. He admitted the possibility (albeit unlikely) of "evolution" while Arendt saw few ways for a totalitarian society to change.[6]

On these counts and many others, Friedrich faced significant challenges from his distinguished audience. Some scholars questioned the utility of a generic category of totalitarian states. "Each occurrence can be described," commented one, "but no adequate general concept can be defined." Another envisioned totalitarianism at the end of a spectrum rather than in its own distinct category; he proposed the term "partialitarian" to describe, for instance, Eastern European regimes under Soviet rule. The two most important historians of Russia in the United States, Michael Karpovich and Geroid T. Robinson, argued that Friedrich's theory, like Arendt's, did not fit Russian history.[7] George Kennan, settling back into academe after his very brief ambassadorship in Moscow, questioned the utility of a concept that included both Nazism and Stalinism; the two phenomena were "highly disparate things," leading him to "wonder whether there is any generic phenomenon that we can identify...as totalitarianism." Kennan's examples of totalitarianism came from the pens of George Orwell, Franz Kafka, and Arthur Koestler, not the policies of Hitler and Stalin. Perhaps responding to the recent news from Moscow, Kennan also insisted that "totalitarianism is dynamic; it does not stand still"; with Stalin dead, the USSR might "lose some of its totalitarian aspects."[8] Sociologist Alex Inkeles explored totalitarianism as a changing phenomenon in his essay on "the dynamics of totalitarian society"—implying, of course, that totalitarian states had societies, even dynamic ones, and not just atomized masses.[9] Kennan and Inkeles accepted the conference's basic premise (it would have been rude to do otherwise): Hitler's Germany and Stalin's USSR marked the advent of a new form of politics. But little else about totalitarianism seemed settled in the early 1950s.

Friedrich held fast to his notion of totalitarianism after Stalin's death and Khrushchev's rise; indeed, in some ways, his views moved closer to Arendt's. *Totalitarian Dictatorship and Autocracy* (1956), which Friedrich coauthored with his student Zbigniew Brzezinski, deviated little from his earlier article: totalitarianism was a distinctly modern phenomenon that took fundamentally similar forms in interwar Germany, Italy, and the USSR; the five features of totalitarianism remained intact, joined now to a sixth: total control over the economy. In the process of elaborating their position, Friedrich and Brzezinski dismissed the central topics of other political scientists. Totalitarian ideologies were meaningless, merely "trite restatements of certain traditional ideas, arranged in an incoherent way that makes them highly exciting to weak minds." Constitutions and government structures—the focus of Friedrich's prewar project—were "of very little importance." There was no society to speak of; the family constituted the only "oasis in the sea of totalitarian atomization." The book argued that totalitarianism was inevitable after 1917 but awaited the "totalitarian breakthrough" of the late 1920s. Once in place, the totalitarian states could evolve only in the direction of "becom[ing] more total."[10]

Reviewers of the Friedrich-Brzezinski volume, who had the benefit of watching another year of thaw and reading Khrushchev's Secret Speech, seemed skeptical. Alexander Dallin criticized the authors' depiction of totalitarianism as static and historically unique, while Frederick Barghoorn chastised the authors for ignoring "the elements of health, strength, and stability in Soviet society, which to [the authors] seems more a madhouse than a society." Friedrich held firm against these critics and in the face of changing Soviet events. As the thaw spread in the late 1950s, he still insisted upon the "harsh unchanging reality of totalitarianism."[11]

The work of Friedrich's coauthor, Zbigniew Brzezinski, was also received skeptically within the field. Brzezinski's dissertation, published in 1956 as *The Permanent Purge*, complemented *Totalitarian Dictatorship and Autocracy* by defining totalitarianism around the USSR, which he had declared elsewhere to be "the most outstanding example of the totalitarian state."[12] Brzezinski focused on what he saw as the essence of Soviet totalitarianism, the purge. While some observers considered purges to be a paroxysm of irrationality, Brzezinski saw them as a "technique" used "for the achievement of specific political and socio-economic objectives." Denunciations, similarly, were not the result of "the perversity of human nature" but a "calculated effort to realize ambitions of upward mobility." Because purges were functional—serving political and economic needs, facilitating the rotation of elites, and providing individual opportunities for advancement—they would not disappear. Since the 1930s, show trials had been replaced by the "quiet purge." But Brzezinski warned that "to expect…a fundamental mellowing in the political system of the USSR [was] to show a great misunderstanding of totalitarianism and to engage in a dangerous under-estimation of the compelling logic of totalitarian rule." Here, Friedrich and Brzezinski agreed: the totalitarian system was permanent and unchangeable in its fundamentals. Reviewers, again, were unconvinced. One noted that the empirical material—though not the theorizing—in *The Permanent Purge* offered "further refutation if, indeed, that were any longer necessary" of the notion that totalitarian states were static in form and function.[13]

The idea of a static totalitarianism was far from dead, at least in the early 1950s. Friedrich's colleague Merle Fainsod participated in the totalitarianism conference, offering pointed commentary on the permanence of totalitarianism. In those comments and in his early writings on the Soviet Union, Fainsod's caution and resistance to theorizing were visible. These traits had been evident since he arrived at Harvard as a graduate student in the late 1920s. His dissertation topic—international socialism during the World War—led some later colleagues to suggest that Fainsod had been a radical before the war, though Fainsod himself emphasized the need to write "dispassionately" about his subject.[14] His longest prewar engagement with the Soviet Union came in 1932, when he spent much of the year in Moscow searching for Comintern documents on the socialist movement.[15] His sole 1930s publication on the USSR was an article, "The Soviet," in the *Encyclopedia of Social Sciences;* it focused almost exclusively on the formal structure of *sovets* (councils) before noting at the end that "the Soviet state is frankly an organ of class domination." The bulk of Fainsod's writings in the 1940s approvingly examined the New Deal, emphasizing the usefulness of government regulation and showing, as one colleague would put it, that an economic system "would be better off if it had a strong administrative structure."[16] Fainsod's arguments, as well as his nonacademic commitments, put him in the mainstream of northern Democrats in the Depression years. According to an FBI report, Fainsod and his wife were active in the local Citizens Union (which promoted liberal candidates) and an organization supporting the Loyalist cause in the Spanish Civil War.[17] These activities would lead to later troubles.

After the war, Fainsod endured a brief period of purgatory as the Russian Research Center (RRC) began, perhaps due to concerns about his politics and his lack of enthusiasm for behavioral science. For the planning and first year of the RRC's operation, Fainsod served the center only in a "consultative capacity."[18] Soon, he became a mainstay there. He spent the summer of 1949 interviewing Soviet displaced persons (DPs) in the American zone of Germany. In writing up the results for the State Department and for academics, Fainsod focused on "controls and tensions in the Soviet system." He found plenty of both. The Soviet population had become "a seething mass of anxieties, frustrations, and discontents," prevented from "spontaneous uprising" only by the omnipresent secret police. If war should break out, he predicted, "the people who live in Soviet Russia may well turn out to be the most effective atom bomb we have."[19] Yet they would be hard to reach since the power of the Communist Party "permeates every part of Soviet society."[20] This sounded like the totalitarian interpretation that Arendt would later articulate, though Fainsod also identified forces in the USSR that would require the regime to evolve: the "new demands of industrialization and collectivization" would change party composition and perhaps much more.[21] This tone would be more important as he began writing a book on Soviet politics.

Fainsod's *How Russia Is Ruled* (1953) was a field-defining book. In breadth of coverage and depth of detail, it far outstripped anything else in English and soon became a constant presence in classrooms and on professorial bookshelves. It drew on a range of published sources, supplemented by his own DP interviews and those of the Refugee Interview Project (RIP). He praised these "firsthand reports on specific Soviet experiences" as superior to "the grand generalizations which some members of the emigration are prone to develop." Fainsod's depiction of Soviet society had shifted from the "seething mass" in his "Controls and Tensions" article, though he still saw society purely as an object of Soviet politics. While rich in historical perspective, the book had a deterministic quality to it. Russian autocracy "implanted the germinating conception of the monolithic and totalitarian party." Bolshevism, in Fainsod's metaphor, was shaped in utero before 1917; "out of the totalitarian embryo would come totalitarianism full-blown."[22] The totalitarian future was foreordained because it was "implicit in the doctrinal, organizational, and tactical premises" of Bolshevism. From tsar to Stalin was a straight path with no possible detours. Fainsod's use of organic metaphors—seeds and embryos—underscored inevitability; a seed grows into only one possible kind of plant.

After early chapters on the development of totalitarianism, Fainsod turned to a description of its operation. Rather than describe the formal structures of Soviet power, *How Russia Is Ruled* "analyze[d] the physiology, as well as the anatomy of Soviet totalitarianism," revealing "living political processes" at work. Fainsod depicted Stalinist society as beset by conformism, control, and fear. The terror, combined with the long and ubiquitous tentacles of the secret police, made serious opposition to totalitarian rule difficult. He saw many strains in the Soviet system, especially among the peasantry and national minorities, but he followed RIP researchers in suggesting that they did not offer a serious challenge to Soviet power. Fainsod acknowledged some sociological changes under Soviet rule, highlighting especially opportunities for upward mobility—which later became a controversial term in the field—provided by the forced-draft industrialization and the purges of the 1930s. One reviewer agreed that the social transformation of the 1930s had "given millions vested interests in the preservation" of the system.[23] Though the purges of that decade had faded, the specter of the purge remained a crucial part of Soviet totalitarianism. "Behind the totalitarian façade," Fainsod warned, "the instrument of terror can always be found, ready for use when needed, operative, above all, even when not visible by the mere fact that it is known to exist." Totalitarian regimes existed in a "moving equilibrium of alternating phases of repression and relaxation," but their "essential contours remain[ed] unchanged."[24]

At the conference that resulted in *Totalitarianism*, Fainsod acknowledged that some Western observers held "sanguine hopes" that the Soviet Union would undergo a fundamental transformation after Stalin's death. When Kennan, for instance, talked about the possible "erosion" of totalitarianism at Friedrich's conference, Fainsod retorted that "no totalitarian system has been transformed from within." He expressed that position with more drama in the closing words of *How Russia Is Ruled:* "The totalitarian regime does not shed its police-state characteristics; it dies when power is wrenched from its hands."[25]

Fainsod's view of the permanence of totalitarianism was not universally held, with many Soviet experts, for instance, questioning the notion of such societies as static and unchanging. One unusual barometer of the state of the

Sovietological art was an informal exercise undertaken at Harvard to predict the direction of Soviet life after Stalin. In the fall of 1951, RRC director Clyde Kluckhohn proposed a "semi-serious…little game," asking students and faculty to estimate the "probable consequences (immediate and more far-reaching)" of Stalin's death "for the development of Soviet society." The game took place at the behest of Walt Rostow at MIT, who wanted the results for his Soviet Vulnerability Project and would eventually use them in his advice to the White House about how to respond to Stalin's death.[26] Among the thirty-two responses, predictions of some kind of "relaxation" and reform appeared just as often as arguments that the Soviet system would not change. Close to half suggested that the totalitarian aspects of Soviet society would fade after the dictator's death. No one expected "real democracy," but many foresaw the loosening of party control, renewed attention to consumer goods, and a diminution of terror. A handful predicted drastic changes (popular uprising or military coup), but most of the others split between relaxation and continuity.[27] Hardly a scientific study, the informal poll nevertheless encompassed widely divergent scholarly opinions about the USSR even in Stalin's lifetime.

By the time he participated in that game, Barrington Moore Jr. had already started imagining the USSR after Stalin. He had devoted two years, starting in 1950, to an RIP report, "Strengths and Weaknesses of the Soviet System." That report described internal tensions in the Soviet Union and envisioned two possible futures for the Soviet Union after Stalin: a relaxation of political control, especially terror, or a further tightening of control. Moore seemed to consider relaxation more likely, as he argued that the "dominant political criteria must at some points yield" to economic rationality in order for the Soviet Union to survive; the USSR was a modern industrial state that faced a historical imperative to start acting like one.[28] Moore's *Terror and Progress* (1954), based on this U.S. Air Force report, outlined three possible directions for the Soviet future, but gave the most credence to what he called "technocracy—the rule of the technically competent." The rise of "technical and rational criteria of behavior and organization," he argued, would "by definition…imply a heavy reduction of emphasis on the power of the dictator." He expressed optimism that technical rationality might do some of the "work of erosion upon the Soviet totalitarian edifice."[29] Moore planted a seed that would soon be nurtured by political scientists more generally; his book became, after *How Russia Is Ruled*, the most important source for specialists in Soviet politics.[30] One implication of Moore's book that would be important to future scholars was the notion that Stalin's totalitarianism (Moore did not shy away from the term) was functional for a certain stage of Soviet development, but would become dysfunctional later. This turned totalitarianism into a developmental stage, one that would be outgrown as the Soviet state matured.

Fainsod would eventually revise his views about the possibility of mean-ingful change in the Soviet system as he came to terms with new informa-tion: Soviet events (especially Khrushchev's reforms), his own experiences in the Soviet Union in 1956, and his encounter with newly available sources. The changes of the mid-1950s—the emptying of the gulags, the execution of secret police chief Lavrentii Beria, the first signs of openness to the world, Khrushchev's Secret Speech, and his later reforms—would lead Fainsod and many others to rethink their views of the permanence of totalitarianism. Fainsod saw these changes firsthand in the summer of 1956 as part of the inaugural group of recipients of the IUCTG month-long travel grants. His encounters with university students in Moscow provided Fainsod (as he noted in his diary) with "some ground for believing that fundamental criticism is not dead" inside the USSR. These frank conversations with students, which may have sparked his long-running interest in Soviet dissent, indicated that the Soviet Union was indeed changing dramatically.[31] The next year, Fainsod highlighted the possibility of change from below at a conference sponsored by the Congress for Cultural Freedom. He foresaw the rise of a "new middle class" of bureaucrats, engineers, and others favored by the Soviet state. They identi-fied with the regime as careerists, not Communists; as such, they were likely to make increasing demands for rationality and efficiency in the political and economic systems—so much so that they offered "a danger and a challenge to the regime." His conference presentation ended with conspicuous optimism, very much unlike the closing line of *How Russia Is Ruled*: "it is heartening to observe that after nearly 40 years of conditioning the new 'Soviet man,' there are still those who probe limits and dare to overstep bounds. Is it asking too much to believe that the future belongs to them?"[32]

Fainsod's next project looked to the Soviet past, not the future, using a unique source ideally suited for his patient and careful scholarship: the so-called Smolensk Archive. Only a few weeks after the Germans invaded the USSR in June 1941, German intelligence took a haphazard selection of documents from the Smolensk Party Archive back to Germany. American intelligence obtained the records—roughly 500 files totaling some 200,000 pages—during its postwar occupation of Germany, and the materials remained in the hands of the U.S. Army. Army officials organized an initial pass through the German War Documents Collection (of which the Smolensk materials were only a tiny portion) for "current intelligence and operational purposes."[33] Then, the U.S. Air Force's Human Resources Research Institute (the sponsor of Harvard's RIP) got its chance to work with the materials in a rare case of interservice cooperation.[34] Over a dozen government agencies used the German materi-als before making them available for scholarly use.[35] After the documents had been declassified, Fainsod was granted exclusive access through the RAND

Corporation, with support from the CIA; only later did the agency make its microfilms available at the National Archives.[36] Fainsod was lucky that the material had been declassified by then, as the FBI had denied him a security clearance in 1954, based on his 1930s memberships and his signature on two 1940s petitions questioning FBI tactics in investigating Communists on university campuses. In the summer of 1954, the army shipped the entire Smolensk Archive—nine footlockers—to Cambridge.[37]

The book resulting from this material was deeply historical; indeed, the background chapter went all the way back to 1395. It departed substantially from the tenor and conclusions of *How Russia Is Ruled*, undercutting that book's totalitarian framework. While he originally called the book "How Russia Rules Its Regions," that title would hardly have fit the finished work.[38] *Smolensk under Soviet Rule* (1958) instead documented the ways in which regional leaders evaded orders from the center. In a self-critical statement, Fainsod argued that "the central controls which looked so all-inclusive and deeply penetrating on paper did not in fact operate with the thoroughness and dispatch it is so easy to attribute to them." The book devoted as much space to "local counter-pressures" as to central controls. It showed Smolensk as anything but a well-ordered cog in an efficient totalitarian machine: the region fought back against the center, peasants fought against the party, workers against bosses, party against police, and so on. Soviet totalitarianism was "far from perfect," Fainsod concluded: "the totalitarian façade concealed a host of inner contradictions."[39]

Foremost among those contradictions was the rise of a new group with new demands. Fainsod concluded that the 1930s industrialization and purges had created "a formidable combination of vested interests [that] had become involved, one way or another, in the regime's survival." For these groups, "the purge meant rapid advancement at an undreamed-of rate. They marched to power over graves that were still fresh." Their "surging energies from below" were channeled into higher education and the creation of a new elite. Nevertheless, Soviet citizens still held "smoldering grievances and suppressed aspirations," which Fainsod hoped would become "the seedbed of tomorrow's political debates."[40] These conclusions extended the remarks about upward mobility he had made in *How Russia Is Ruled*.

Smolensk undermined the notion of a centralized polity in total control over society. While Fainsod often used the word totalitarian, he never gave it a precise definition. The term usually appeared in the introductory or concluding sections of each chapter, where he emphasized the totalitarian Soviet system. The body of each chapter, on the other hand, documented the internal contradictions and complexities of Soviet rule. Almost like Soviet scholars' ritual bows to Marx and Lenin before turning to empirical material, Fainsod invoked totalitarianism much more than he employed it. He did not make use of Friedrich and Brzezinski's definition of totalitarianism, nor did he use the Smolensk Archive to develop an alternative theory of Soviet power.

The book received an enthusiastic response. Frederick Barghoorn lauded *Smolensk* for "add[ing] to our realization of the weaknesses, failures, poverty, and misery concealed by the totalitarian façade."[41] It also served, another reviewer noted optimistically, to confirm Western scholarship on the USSR; the archives told a story that was "familiar,…[with] no staggering surprises."[42] Indeed, the book was a surprise mostly to those who looked at the work of Fainsod and his colleagues and expected to see the totalitarian interpretation of Soviet politics reigning supreme in the 1950s.

Fainsod's historical-empirical approach offered one challenge to totalitarianism, but more influential was Moore's sociological theorizing. Political scientists of the 1950s were well versed in sociological perspectives that analyzed the Soviet Union as a modern industrial society. The effectiveness of the sociological approach was bolstered by factors both within and beyond Sovietology. The start of the IUCTG travel program in 1956 gave scholars direct encounters with Soviet society. They no longer relied only on speeches and newspaper articles about top-level politics, but could observe Soviet society firsthand. Harvard graduate student Jeremy Azrael, for instance, participated in the exchange in 1958–1959 to study the role of technical expertise in economic decision making—a topic borrowing much from Barrington Moore's ideas. Azrael's guiding star in this work was sociological; he wrote home from Moscow that he expected to return to the United States "with more footnotes to Bauer, Inkeles, and Kluckhohn than to Fainsod"—that is, he would be referring more to RIP sociology than to Fainsod's political science.[43] Though Azrael ultimately concluded that politics, not economics, held primacy in Soviet decision making, he still expressed his doubts about totalitarian arguments.[44]

Other scholars relied heavily on sociological arguments to challenge the notion of totalitarian society. Political scientist Alfred Meyer saw the declining relevance of Soviet ideology as a sign of a profound shift, part of a "broader pattern of changes in the entire social system" that resulted from industrialization and urbanization. The result was "USSR, Incorporated," with Soviet rule approximating that of a corporation in a "company town." Similarly, sociologist Allen Kassof described the USSR as an "administered society." Meyer and Kassof's works were widely discussed, suggesting the resonance of sociological approaches by the early 1960s.[45]

While Soviet experts got their sociology from Moore, most other political scientists got their sociology from a "political development" approach that leaned heavily on Talcott Parsons. Through the 1950s and 1960s, emanating from Princeton's and then Yale's political science departments and organized around the SSRC's influential Committee on Comparative Politics (CCP), political development would shape much of the work in the field. Its universal aspirations—to develop a "general theory" of politics—would shape the study of Soviet politics, too.[46] Political development, a broad term that introduced sociological and psychological theory into the study of politics, emerged as political scientists expanded their purview beyond the North Atlantic to the newly independent nations of Asia and Africa.[47] The approach had significant implications for the study of the Communist world, especially among those political scientists eager to put the study of Soviet politics in conversation with (or, more cynically, in subordination to) generalizable political science.

The CCP vision of political development drew from the behavioralist trend that dominated American social sciences in the 1950s and 1960s. Robert Dahl led the subfield of American Politics away from studies of form and toward studies of process and behavior. Though on the left side of the New Deal in the 1930s, Dahl's determination to examine in depth the actual functioning of politics led to a pluralist approach keenly attuned to the problems of popular input.[48] Dahl aimed to study politics in real life: how interest groups shaped the policy process, what difference elections (and elected officials) made, and what permitted and prevented optimal policy solutions. In a classic article, Dahl argued that the behavioral approach to politics was not just "an emphasis on the term 'science' in the phrase 'political science'"; quoting a famous wartime report on the field, Dahl identified the aims of the behavioral approach as "*stating all the phenomena of government in terms of the observed and observable behavior of men.*"[49] One of his best-known books was *Who Governs?* (1961), a study of municipal governance in Dahl's hometown of New Haven, Connecticut. Dahl concluded that the rhetoric of participatory democracy disguised a system that was run primarily by special interests in league with local officials. Not only that, but Dahl concluded that this was probably best: the complexity of running even a small city was so great that too much citizen input would interfere with policy decisions; good policy was not good politics. Dahl identified the American "democratic creed" as a key source of stability for municipal governments—provided that no one took the creed too literally. He distinguished between democracy as an ideal and polyarchy or pluralism as an actual governing system.[50]

Soviet experts recognized what Dahl was doing in American Politics, and focused even more on what his sometime Yale colleague Gabriel Almond was doing for the rest of the world.[51] Like Dahl, Almond sought to study political behavior. Imbued with admiration for the grand sociological theorizing of Parsons, Almond aimed to develop a theory of politics that would allow comparisons of vastly different political systems. His main instrument was the CCP, which for almost two decades was the leading force in making postwar American political science more cosmopolitan, more theoretical, and ultimately more scientific.[52] Aside from an explicit effort at theorization, Almond and other committee members provided an implicit intellectual structure that underpinned the language, concepts, and topics of their work: a Parsonsian vision of modernization theory. Inhering in the term *political development* was a trajectory that went from traditional to modern. All societies moved along a similar path, shaped by social institutions capable of introducing modern ways of thinking and acting. Factories, bureaucracies, and universities, among others, were signs of modernity as well as instruments of modernization. The CCP efforts to analyze political systems usually mixed case studies from a variety of newly independent nations and modern societies. Since the Soviet Union clearly fell in the latter category, works on the USSR appeared frequently in the CCP's flagship series, Studies in Political Development.

Merle Fainsod's writing in the 1960s illustrated the reception of sociological theories among Soviet experts, as he sought a middle ground between sociological and political understandings of Soviet power. His work on the USSR diminished in scope and significance as Fainsod took on increasing service at Harvard and worked with the U.S. Agency for International Development in South Asia. His articles on development characterized bureaucracy as a "carrier of innovating values," along the lines of political development work in general.[53] The most substantive of his writings on the USSR in those years was a contribution to the CCP volume *Bureaucracy and Political Development* (1963), in which he argued that bureaucracies were "modernizing instruments." He asserted that the Soviet bureaucracy was successful because it created a "technical intelligentsia" imbued with the "values" and "habits" of industrial society. Fainsod nevertheless challenged the generally sunny version of convergence implicit in CCP scholarship. The Soviet experience, Fainsod warned, proved that "democratizing and industrializing tendencies do not necessarily go hand in hand."[54] Accepting the arguments about sociological change, Fainsod still emphasized the political framework: one-party rule. The arguments in this essay soon found their way into a revision of Fainsod's textbook.

The 1963 edition of *How Russia Is Ruled*, completed while Khrushchev was still in power, differed greatly in tone from the original but left much of the descriptive material unchanged. It offered more optimism about the Soviet future, softening the grim tone of the original edition. In order to take into account the changes that "have affected virtually every aspect of Soviet life," Fainsod reworked the conclusion. He credited Khrushchev with developing an "'enlightened' or 'rational' totalitarianism," which contained "welfare concessions" to the population while at the same time "bridling the KGB" to reduce internal tensions. He fit Khrushchev's reforms into a developmental framework, suggesting that Stalin's "supercentralization" might have been useful for rapid industrialization but was "ill suited to the rational management of a highly industrialized society." He singled out the rise of a technical elite as the paramount achievement of the Soviet state. Created to meet the needs of industrialization, this elite offered a direct challenge to party rule along the same lines as those that Moore had predicted a decade earlier. Scientific rationality, Fainsod continued, threatened the "dogmatic constraints of Marxism-Leninism" and required accommodation. But accommodation was not acquiescence; Fainsod predicted that the party would maintain its hold by developing a new ideology that would resonate among the technical elite. Soviet totalitarianism, even if rational or enlightened, was nevertheless totalitarianism; the chances of democratic transformation were small.[55] Fainsod occupied the middle ground between sociology and political science, though he would increasingly emphasize the profound impact of sociological change.

By 1967, Fainsod agreed with Moore that the "industrialization process" was probably "the most important single fact" in the half century of Soviet rule.[56] He stressed the possibility of social transformation in the USSR in a *Problems of Communism* article that year: "As Soviet society has become more professionalized and differentiated, the outlines of an interest-group structure have begun to emerge....The Party itself has become an arena in which these competing interests must be adjusted and reconciled." He predicted that the tendency toward professionalism would increase and that the party "must perforce" cede authority to scientific and technical experts. Elsewhere, he maintained that politics and society were separate realms, and a convergence with the West in social structure did not automatically bring about a convergence of political systems—a caveat Fainsod stressed in his presidential address to the American Political Science Association, given only days after Soviet tanks rolled into Prague in 1968.[57] Fainsod tilted toward the sociological view, but never let it supplant the primacy of the political.

While Fainsod was taken by the CCP approach, Soviet experts H. Gordon Skilling and Robert Tucker began their attack on totalitarianism from a less theoretically robust version of comparative politics. A Canadian, Skilling undertook his graduate education at Oxford, where he was briefly a member of the Communist Party, and then at the University of London's School of Slavonic and East European Studies. Returning to his alma mater, the University of Toronto, Skilling published accounts of Czechoslovakia in academic and non-academic outlets, only a few of them south of the border.[58] He first attacked totalitarianism by terming it a Cold War concept that lacked the "scholarly detachment" that would permit a "deeper understanding of the Soviet system." He then called for comparison; the assumptions of uniqueness embedded in totalitarianism "distort[ed] the understanding of the Soviet system *qua* system of government." Skilling based his conclusions primarily on the Czech case.[59]

While this early article made no reference to Almond's work in political development, Skilling would soon fall under its influence. He later protested that Sovietologists had still "not been much affected by the fresh currents of thought in comparative politics." To back this up, Skilling cited at length Almond's complaint that Sovietologists' totalitarian model led them to "ignore the universal elements in Soviet politics." Skilling accepted Almond's challenge and soon published an influential article that interpreted Soviet politics through the lens of interest groups, an approach he credited both to Almond's efforts at a universal theory and to the writings of Eastern bloc scholars.[60] Skilling identified a "new model" exploring Soviet politics as a "pluralism of elites" and (quoting Dahl) a "polyarchy."[61] Using this last word was a bold step and one hardly in keeping with the ideas of its creator. Dahl preferred the term *polyarchy* to *democracy*, arguing that democracy was an ideal, but had yet to be realized. Polyarchies, as Dahl defined them, were "relatively (but incompletely) democratized regimes…highly inclusive and extensively open to public contestation."[62] This was hardly an appropriate definition of the USSR.

Robert Tucker, too, called for a more fully comparative politics of the USSR, one in conversation with the disciplinary mainstream of political development. A 1961 article looked back skeptically at the prior decade's scholarship on Soviet politics. Previous theories maintained the "underlying assumption…that Soviet politics constitutes a unique subject-matter, a political world that can only be understood in terms of its own queer if not inimitable laws or motivations." At least those seeing the USSR as totalitarian were innocent of such charges; they had compared the Soviet Union to one or two other totalitarianisms. This form of comparison was too static for Tucker, who saw a paradox in works like Arendt's: "theorists of totalitarianism…recognize that a virtual change of regime occurred [from Lenin to Stalin] but their theory does not." Tucker insisted that Stalinism was not simply the inevitable outgrowth of Bolshevism—or, in the words of historian Robert V. Daniels, "the incarnation of Lenin's model of the Party, and little else." Stalinism was a phenomenon that differed from Leninism—and not just in the way that an adult differs from an "embryo."[63]

Tucker aimed at more than just a distinction between Leninism and Stalinism; he hoped to broaden comparative politics by "shed[ding] the blinkers of a Russian specialist" and bringing the study of Soviet politics "into much closer working relations with political science." Tucker devoted the remainder of the article to defining a category of "movement-regimes," which could take into better account historical evolution, allowing movement-regimes to have defined stages. His concept would also provide more cases than totalitarianism's two or three and could include Tunisia, Egypt, Pakistan, Spain, Yugoslavia, and many, many more. Scholars had been too deeply impressed by structural

continuities in the Soviet period, he wrote, to focus on the great differences in
how Bolshevism actually *worked* at different moments. While critical of totalitarianism, Tucker nevertheless remained within the basic assumptions about
how to study Soviet politics.[64] In a sense, he was simply following Fainsod's
shift from the study of anatomy (forms) to physiology (functions).

Frederick Barghoorn, too, was enthusiastic about the possibilities of comparison, and he was especially influenced by the work of his Yale colleagues
Almond and Dahl. As early as 1962, he wanted to organize a conference panel
"devoted to attempting to find the 'interest groups'—if one can be so bold—
which might be regarded as dynamic forces in bringing changes in Soviet society and politics." Barghoorn's ideas about interest groups came through his
contacts with Soviet experts in the U.S. government. Indeed, his comments on
a prepublication draft of Skilling's 1966 article credited government officials
directly: "The main impetus for a more 'pluralistic' approach came from government researchers and policy-makers and was then reflected out to some of
the scholars."[65]

Barghoorn, like Skilling, was eventually swayed as much by political development as by the need to overthrow the totalitarian model. He also served as
a link between scholarship and government work. After writing a dissertation
(for Michael Karpovich) on nineteenth-century intellectual history, Barghoorn
entered the State Department at the lowly rank of associate divisional assistant, soon rising to become press attaché at the Moscow embassy during World
War II. After the war, Barghoorn joined Yale's Political Science Department
and frequently commuted to Washington for government service, consulting
at various times for the State Department, the Psychological Strategy Board,
the air force, the army, RAND, and CIA.[66] Among the most significant of
these projects was an analysis of the materials gathered in Operation Sponge,
based on military intelligence interrogations of DPs who had been Soviet officials. His initial conclusions fed into his view of totalitarianism; Soviet leaders
cared only about maintaining their power over a divided and tension-ridden
society.[67] His early books focused on the operations of Soviet power abroad,
but inspired by Moore's work, he soon sought to track the rise of technical
rationality in the Soviet system. "The pluralistic tendencies set in motion by
industrialization, and by the development of a functional bureaucracy to per-
form the complex tasks of administration have, thus far at least, been held
in check, although there seem to be increased possibilities that this will not
always be true," he wrote in 1956.[68] By the time Barghoorn wrote his textbook
on Soviet politics in the mid-1960s, Moore's influence was even more evident.
He had told one friend that "the Soviet system was being irresistibly drawn
toward empiricism and rationality," writing about technical rationality with
more certainty than Moore himself.[69]

Barghoorn also assimilated many of Almond's ideas. Most important was "political culture," which Almond described in a 1956 article and operationalized in *The Civic Culture*, which he coauthored with Sidney Verba. That book began with the proposition that a political system required "a political culture consistent with it"; democratic institutions meant little without a democratic political culture. What exactly was a political culture? Here, the authors sounded their most Parsonsian: "The political culture of a nation is the particular distribution of patterns of orientation toward political objects among members of the nation."[70] Barghoorn strayed from this definition, even in his essay in the CCP volume *Political Culture and Political Development;* his discussion of the USSR sounded more like Barrington Moore than Gabriel Almond.[71] One of his students termed Barghoorn's use of political science theories "eclectic," but a harsher critic might prefer the term promiscuous.[72] Whatever the word, this tendency to draw inconsistently on theories is evident in Barghoorn's textbook, *Politics in the USSR* (1966), in which each chapter seems to incorporate a different theoretical approach to the USSR: political culture, political development, technical rationality, convergence, and the rise of industrial society, among others. But of all these approaches, technical rationality became the most significant in the 1960s, promoted by CCP scholars and by a growing number of Soviet specialists inspired by Moore.

Zbigniew Brzezinski rebutted this sociological reasoning with increasing vehemence in the 1960s. This was a familiar line of argument for him; he had already criticized Moore's *Terror and Progress* for failing to address the "problem of power"; technical rationality, Brzezinski insisted, simply provided totalitarian rulers with new technologies of control.[73] He attempted to incorporate sociological challenges into the totalitarianism argument without assuming that social change would remake political systems. Watching Khrushchev's reforms in the late 1950s, Brzezinski allowed that the USSR had changed, but he still saw its political structure as stable, rational, and adaptable.[74] He seemed open to the possibility of radical change in the *exercise* of power in the USSR, though not in the *distribution* of power. In a 1961 symposium in *Slavic Review*, Brzezinski identified the Khrushchev reforms as rational responses that met the needs of Soviet rule in the 1950s: Lenin was useful for the consolidation of power, Stalin for rapid industrialization, and Khrushchev for a mature industrial power. He saw the decline of ideological fervor in the USSR and, in an optimistic moment, called it a signal of "the first real step in the direction of the transformation of the system." Yet the "momentous changes" it portended would not in any way "weaken the Party's power." The USSR was just as totalitarian under Khrushchev as it had been under Stalin, but nevertheless had changed. (Here, Brzezinski differed from Robert Tucker, who called the USSR under Khrushchev "less totalitarian" than it had been under Stalin.)[75]

Brzezinski soon enough dispensed with the term totalitarian entirely. Together with Samuel Huntington, he wrote a comparison of political power in the two Cold War antagonists. The book addressed the notion of Soviet-American convergence, an argument implicit in technical rationality arguments. If the logic of modern industrial societies promoted certain social structures (bureaucratic organizations), priorities (economic efficiency), and mentalities (productivity-oriented), then the future would bring the convergence of all modern industrial societies. Huntington and Brzezinski claimed that they set out to write *Political Power: USA/USSR* (1964) in this vein. But the book eventually made the opposite argument: convergence could result only from a "drastic alteration of course." The authors concluded that the "undramatic pattern for the future" would be "the evolution of the two systems" but not their convergence. Perhaps more striking is that the book never used the word "totalitarian" to describe the USSR.[76] It was not that Brzezinski suddenly doubted the ability or desire of Soviet leaders to stay in power, only that he had come to find the term totalitarian distracting for analysis of the Soviet system.

Brzezinski's wariness about the term totalitarian was evident elsewhere as well. In the early 1960s, Brzezinski declined Carl Friedrich's invitation to work on a new edition of *Totalitarian Dictatorship and Autocracy*, so Friedrich plunged ahead on his own. In spite of the cascade of Soviet events under Khrushchev, Friedrich saw little reason to modify his theory. Khrushchev's efforts at de-Stalinization, he argued, "tended to confirm" the totalitarian argument, part of an effort to maintain or augment power. Even in the face of criticisms from all sides in the late 1960s, Friedrich made few fundamental amendments to his notion of totalitarianism as an analytical category. By then, his vision of totalitarianism had long since been overrun and was of little relevance to most political scientists. Since—unlike his one-time coauthor Brzezinski—Friedrich was no Soviet expert, his profile in this field rested on a theory that political scientists considered to be insufficiently theoretical, supported by evidence used tautologically, and in a framework unable to reckon with historical change.[77] Of course, the word totalitarian remained an accepted part of public discussions of the USSR, leading Barghoorn to complain that the word was suitable only for "politicians and journalists," who used the term "imprecisely [and] all too often emotionally"—though it would be hard to imagine that scholarly precision was so important to those who bandied about the term.[78]

Scholars' dissatisfaction with the totalitarianism concept mounted in the 1960s, the result of changes in the USSR and evolving scholarly ideas. Attacks on the term usually had more to do with scholarship than politics. Sociologist Alex Inkeles wrote a farewell address to Sovietologists, complaining that totalitarianism had led them into self-isolation, from which he would escape by

Figure 8.1. Zbigniew Brzezinski in his Columbia office, 1965.

pursuing his "Becoming Modern" project. He expressed this sentiment with typical insight and verve:

> In going to conferences on Soviet affairs, I sometimes have the feeling that the Soviet experts were once put in a kind of sealed chamber, something like a bathysphere, and then put on the bottom of the sea, where we remained permanently locked up in our small world, breathing our special form of rarified atmosphere.

The only escape was to look at broader theories of society, as Inkeles had long done himself. Inkeles argued that the totalitarian model "had a great deal to say" at one point, but changes in the USSR since Stalin's death made it "less relevant." In its stead, Inkeles favored the notion that the USSR was a "mature industrial society" that was "acquiring more and more of the characteristics of the western type of social system."[79] Attuned to the gap between Soviet experts and the disciplines, Inkeles excoriated the totalitarianism approach on two grounds: first, it could not explain the social support for the Soviet system that the interview project had documented. And second, it emphasized Soviet distinctiveness so much that it isolated experts from mainstream social science.

By the mid-1960s, many scholars were already integrating the study of the USSR into political science and applying the political development approach. One place to observe the range of views about Soviet politics was a symposium in *Problems of Communism* that ran intermittently from 1966 to 1969. The spark for this extended exchange was an article by Brzezinski, who was seeking a way to account for Brezhnev, on the one hand, and the increasing scholarly attention to industrial societies, on the other. The Soviet Union, Brzezinski conceded to the sociologists, was "an increasingly modern and industrial society." Yet industrialization, he argued, would not produce liberalization, democratization, or any other kind of political transformation; it would produce instead degradation. Maintaining a "doctrinaire dictatorship" in an industrial society "has already contributed to a reopening of the gap that existed in pre-revolutionary Russia between the political system and the society." The most important way for Soviet leaders to reduce the gap would be to change the nature of senior leadership, giving it a "broader representation of social talent"—he identified scientists, economists, and managers in particular—at the top. But (as he clarified subsequently), Brzezinski did not foresee such a change; short of such radical redistributions of power and privilege, Brzezinski foresaw the "beginning of a sterile bureaucratic phase"—stagnation. And if stagnation led to disintegration, he predicted, what would follow would be an "assertive ideological-nationalist reaction, resting on a coalition of secret police, the military and the heavy industrial-ideological complex."[80] Brzezinski had abandoned the totalitarian model without losing the notion of party control; he had solved the "problem of power" analytically but doubted that Soviet leadership could solve it practically. Brzezinski responded to the sociological challenge to totalitarianism by returning to the principal topic for political scientists: power.

The variety of responses to Brzezinski's article on "Transformation or Degradation" gave a clear sense of how American experts understood Soviet politics in the late 1960s. A total of twenty-one scholars responded to the original piece, including Barghoorn, Robert Conquest, Fainsod, and Friedrich. Brzezinski, in his reply, conveniently mapped out these responses graphically, on a continuum divided into evolutionary and revolutionary change. Two-thirds of the respondents were on the "evolutionary" end of the scale. Four respondents even saw "renovative transformation" as the most likely outcome, with another four seeing that as possible. In other words, a good number of Soviet

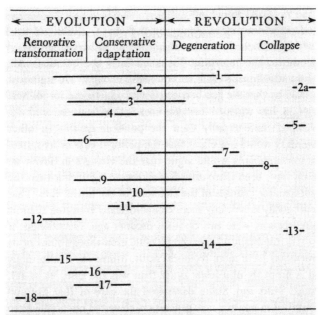

← EVOLUTION →		← REVOLUTION →	
Renovative transformation	Conservative adaptation	Degeneration	Collapse

1—Zbigniew Brzezinski (No. 1, 1966). 2—Michel Tatu (No. 2, 1966). 2a—Michel Garder (whose position is discussed by Mr. Tatu, *idem.*). 3—Frederick C. Barghoorn (No. 3, 1966). 4—Wolfgang Leonhard (No. 4, 1966). 5—Eugene Lyons (No. 4, 1966). 6—Arthur Schlesinger, Jr. (No. 4, 1966). 7—Giorgio Galli (No. 5, 1966). 8—Robert Conquest (No. 5, 1966). 9—Hans J. Morgenthau (No. 5, 1966). 10—Boris Meissner (No. 6, 1966). 11—Robert Strausz-Hupé (No. 6, 1966). 12—Jayantanuja Bandyopadhyaya (No. 1, 1967). 13—Isaac Don Levine (No. 1, 1967). 14—Ernst Halperin (No. 1, 1967). 15—Joseph Clark (No. 1, 1967). 16—Sidney Hook (No. 2, 1967). 17—Merle Fainsod (No. 4, 1967). 18—Arrigo Levi (No. 4, 1967). N.B.: Two contributors to the symposium, Boris Souvarine (No. 2, 1967) and Alexander Bregman (No. 3, 1967), are omitted from the chart since their discussions did not include clear-cut projections for the future.

Figure 8.2. Graphic depiction showing the range of responses to Zbigniew Brzezinski's essay, "The Soviet Political System: Transformation or Degradation," in *Dilemmas of Change in Soviet Politics*, 1969.

experts selected to appear in a State Department–sponsored journal saw the possibility, even the likelihood, that the Soviet regime would lose power without having it "wrenched from their hands," in Fainsod's memorable phrase.[81]

By the time that Brzezinski's chart appeared in 1969, many other non- or antitotalitarian views of Soviet power had wide circulation. Outside of the contributions of U.S.–based political scientists, many historians and overseas scholars from a variety of disciplines were promulgating theories of Soviet power and politics. Australian T. H. Rigby described a Soviet "crypto-politics" derived from a "group model" of Soviet power, with different sectors of the bureaucracy using the party as an arena for articulating interests and accumulating authority. Historian Robert V. Daniels hypothesized along similar lines about a "participatory bureaucracy," which would turn the party into "a forum for the plurality of interests." He also articulated a "circular theory of power" in which "top collective bodies" in the party had a voice in the selection of future leaders.[82] Robert Conquest acknowledged such politics but held out little hope for any significant redistribution of power. The only place of "serious political action" in the USSR was, according to Conquest, at the very top; his subject remained "dynastics," not bureaucracies. He offered a spirited defense of "Kremlinology," the study of the machinations among the top elite, as practiced outside the academy.[83]

A wider range of views could be found within American departments of political science, all at a great distance from Friedrich's works. The notion of totalitarianism as a stage in the evolution of the Soviet Union was increasingly common in the 1960s; Alfred Meyer, a staunch critic of the totalitarian model, for instance, admitted that it applied "for a limited period [of] development, a period of growing pains, of system-building, a period devoted to the 'primitive accumulation' of both the means of production and the authority to rule."[84]

Those arguing in a sociological vein—about the increasing role of technical rationality in Soviet decision making—split into two basic camps. There were monistic views of power: Allen Kassof's "administered society" and Alfred Meyer's "USSR, Incorporated" left little doubt about who was administering or acting as the CEO, respectively. Those who followed Barrington Moore's argument about technical rationality more loyally, though, held a more pluralistic notion of power; rationality was not just a saner form of top-down rule, but would give more responsibility and authority, and eventually more power, to lower levels of the bureaucracy. It is not surprising that this vision of pluralism was especially popular among those scholars inspired by the currents of mainstream political science. Barghoorn and Skilling both worked in the political development framework, and Fainsod drew increasingly upon it.

Skilling, undeterred by criticisms of his interest group approach, convened a conference on that topic in 1967. The resulting book adopted Almond's definition of *interest groups* as duly constituted groups organized to articulate their interests in official settings.[85] Notwithstanding severe criticism from his co-editor, Skilling wrote optimistically about the future of group analyses of Soviet politics. He worked in the same vein as his earlier article, excavating a lineage of interest group analyses of Soviet politics that dated back to Fainsod's book on Smolensk (though admitting that Fainsod himself never used the term interest group) and proclaiming group analysis to be one of the crucial tools for understanding Soviet politics.[86]

Working in a different direction entirely was Robert Tucker, who set aside his call for comparisons in order to focus on Stalin's personality. Tucker's early career had been defined by his Moscow experience. Sent to acquire Soviet publications for OSS during the war, Tucker met and married a Soviet citizen, Evgeniia (Zhenia) Petretsova. They then had a compulsory seven-year honeymoon as Zhenia awaited permission to leave the country with her husband; permission came only after Stalin's death. Later scholars would insinuate that Tucker's focus on Stalin related to the heightened emotions after his and Zhenia's travails in the 1940s. If true, then the personal coincided nicely with the professional; his writings in the 1950s helped to lead a charge against the totalitarian school by focusing attention on Stalin himself. As he noted, understanding de-Stalinization required understanding the "process of Stalinization," which in turn required viewing Stalinism as an evolving phenomenon.[87] Focusing on Stalin as an individual also renewed the possibility of understanding Stalinism historically, as the result of specific events rather than as the inevitable outcome of 1917.

Tucker's 1965 article, "The Dictator and Totalitarianism," was a call to study the psychology of power as the only means of understanding the "dynamics of totalitarianism."[88] In an autobiographical reflection, Tucker wrote that the idea of applying psychology to Stalin came to him while he was walking past the Kremlin one weekend in 1951. He had just been reading the works of Freudian psychologist Karen Horney and was struck by her discussion of the neurotic personality, who feels a disjuncture between self-image and reality. Walking past the gaudy celebrations of Stalin all around the Kremlin, Tucker wondered if they were images of the "idealized self"; Horney, after all, argued that a neurotic would engage in a limitless "search for glory" in an effort to "actualize the idealized self." His work in the 1950s introduced psychological themes into conventional political analyses.[89] Tucker then embarked on a major study of Stalin that would use "Stalin's career as a case-study in dictatorship and personality." The project would show how Stalin "assumed and later reshaped" the role of leader, in the process proving that "the personality of Stalin" was "a motive force in Soviet development."[90] Tucker's biography was framed around Stalin's psychology, especially his lurching from one hero to another before fixing upon Lenin. After Lenin's death in 1924, Stalin sought to be everything that he saw in Lenin: a brilliant thinker, war hero, and powerful leader of a revolution. Hence, he proclaimed a "revolution from above" to match the revolution in 1917; he wrote theoretical tracts on linguistics, political economy, and other topics to match Lenin's writings; and since he had been rejected by the army, he rewrote his own biography to appear as a Civil War hero. Stalin despised

Trotsky for being closer to Lenin than Stalin himself was.[91] The book was well regarded by historians, who were nevertheless befuddled by the psychologizing.[92] Lurking beyond this psychological portrait of a dictator was an argument about history and theory. Insisting that Stalinism bore the imprint of its namesake, Tucker separated the arrival of Bolshevik power from the arrival of totalitarianism.

Tucker's focus on Stalin the individual did not preclude his work along more conventional lines of scholarship. As early as 1956, Tucker identified the growth of middle management as a factor in the USSR after Stalin. Here, too, his focus was psychological as much as political; he described a great discrepancy between managers' "high social-economic status" and their "political impotence."[93] Similarly, his 1961 manifesto for comparative politics revealed his determination to speak to other political scientists as much as to other Soviet experts. In 1965, he tried unsuccessfully to obtain funding for a journal on the comparative study of Communism, which ultimately yielded the Planning Group for the Study of Comparative Communism.[94] This group provided Tucker with a venue for more mainstream political science than did his Stalin psychobiography. He argued initially that comparative Communist studies would build on area studies knowledge to generate broadly applicable models of political behavior, but these hopes soon faded. Later acknowledging that comparative Communist studies had not gotten "beyond the takeoff stage" even after six years, Tucker reversed course, hoping that general theories in political science might once again reinvigorate the study of Communist systems. He cited "political culture" as an approach that could yield fruitful comparisons within Communist studies.[95] He then convened a conference, Political Culture and Comparative Communist Studies, inviting Almond, Barghoorn, and others to debate the applicability of the term in the Communist world. Though the participants had, as the rapporteurs put it, an "overwhelming commitment...to political culture," there was one brief but revealing moment of questioning. One scholar dared to ask whether the term itself needed modification in light of the Eastern European experience. Almond, the impresario of political culture, shut off debate; he exhorted the group to apply rather than challenge the concept. Comparative Communism specialists might learn from theories of political culture but would not help to shape them.[96] The great irony of this exchange is that Almond's influence in the profession was waning at the same time that Soviet specialists were rediscovering his earliest concepts.

Political culture was also visible in the planning group's next book, *Stalinism: Essays in Historical Interpretation* (1977). In what may be his single most important contribution to scholarly discussions of the USSR, Tucker insisted that Stalinism was a unique phase of Soviet history, not the inevitable result of 1917.[97] His criticisms of totalitarianism were in no sense the most radical challenges to the concept. After his initial flirtation with the comparative politics approach, he dove headlong into a more psychological line of argument, focusing more on Stalin than on Stalinism and setting aside analysis of the Soviet *system*.

Tucker was not the only scholar with ambitions to have the study of Soviet politics influence other political scientists. Jerry Hough, a student of Fainsod, immersed himself in mainstream political science to a far greater degree than anyone of his advisor's generation. At the same time, Hough looked skeptically at the sociological argument put forward by Almond and others. When Alex Inkeles presented a draft of his farewell address to Soviet Studies at the RRC, Hough happened to be present. He protested against Inkeles's statements that the totalitarian concept was irrelevant and that the USSR, as a modern industrial society, would necessarily take on the attributes of Western societies. Hough defended the totalitarian model as "a response to a problem"—that is, as an effort to describe the actual workings of Soviet politics. Besides, Hough argued, the industrial society model was a theory of society, not of politics. "Before destroying the totalitarian model," he asked, "is there not a need for another model of the polity to replace it, rather than just [one] from the economic and social sphere?"[98] Much as Daniel Bell and Reinhard Bendix had done in their criticisms of *The Soviet Citizen,* Hough wanted to identify the concrete political implications of social change rather than simply assume that such change would create a new political order.

Hough's first book sought to incorporate sociological arguments without abandoning concern for politics. *The Soviet Prefects* (1969) examined the relationship between technical rationality and political power in the Soviet Union. The topic clearly revealed Hough's immersion in competing approaches to the Soviet Union, which he had imbibed as a Harvard undergraduate while taking classes with Brzezinski, Fainsod, and others. Hough also drew inspiration from Barrington Moore Jr., with whom he took two graduate seminars, praising him for raising "questions about the relationship of industrialization and political development well before this subject became fashionable in political science" and for providing "the most successful model of its time in predicting the major developments in the post-Stalin political system." Hough also credited Fainsod, from whom he learned mostly "by osmosis," for teaching him "about the structure of power in the Soviet Union and about the most fruitful approach to the study of that country." Hough framed his dissertation as, essentially, a battle between Moore's theory of technical rationality and Fainsod's focus on politics; he hoped to test the theory of the "'rationalization' of Soviet society" in an "administrative system that would have driven Max Weber to distraction." Hough wanted to link his study of the Soviet bureaucracy to broader social scientific questions. As he claimed in his dissertation, his work "raises the possibility that…local Party organs have on balance been a 'rational' rather than 'irrational' element in Soviet industrial decision-making."[99]

Since Hough hoped to challenge Weberian notions of bureaucracy, he wanted to look well beyond the Soviet case. In his first job, at the University of Illinois, he immediately sought, as he put it in a grant application, to "develop the kind of background necessary for a comparative approach to Soviet institutions." His first step was to teach the comparative politics survey course, rarely required of Soviet specialists.[100] He also set out to "undertake a detailed research study" on a different country and to learn administrative theory in order to develop a more robust model. A few months later, Hough presented the latest version of his work to generally positive feedback. Fainsod's response addressed the essential tension in Hough's analysis: how to assess the battle between rationality and ideology in the lower echelons of party and state bureaucracies; he cited data from Smolensk to support Hough's argument. The cautious Fainsod also urged Hough to tone down some of his broader claims, writing that he was "somewhat troubled" by Hough's "desire to make a general Hoch Theorie contribution," which could distract from the book's "fresh insights" about Soviet politics and administration.[101]

Hough disavowed his advisor's conceptual modesty. *The Soviet Prefects* was full of broad theory, continuing his efforts to follow in Fainsod's path by accounting for sociological change while remaining attentive to politics. Moore's technical rationality argument implied that industrial decision making would be increasingly disconnected from the party; economic decisions would be made, in a rational society, by economic experts, not party hacks. But Hough noted many "deviations" from the technical rationality model. The Soviets did not establish Weberian bureaucracies, he concluded, because Weber's organizational structures were "based on a narrow concept of rationality that excludes politics." There were political reasons for including local party officials in decision making. They were "indispensable," as he later wrote, for providing local coordination of a myriad of national and regional organs. And they were also supposed to look after local interests and contribute to the "mobilization efforts" of the party at the local level.[102] True to the comment he had made to Inkeles four years earlier, Hough was criticizing political scientists for using sociological theories without being sufficiently attuned to power. Hough also called on his political science colleagues to "abandon language of 'political development' with its inevitable images of lineal development." He proposed a new administrative model, but this was quite narrow in scope and in its details hewed quite closely to the Soviet case. Hough's attempts to rewrite broad theories of politics based on the Soviet case were well received by specialists but garnered little attention from his intended audience: mainstream political scientists.[103]

The difficulty of developing new social science theories more firmly rooted in the Soviet experience—which also plagued Tucker's comparative Communism work—was especially apparent in Hough's next book, *The Soviet Union and Social Science Theory* (1979). The book reflected Hough's energetic efforts to apply the full spectrum of social science tools to the study of the USSR and, perhaps more important, to apply the full range of Soviet expertise to social science theory. He argued that scholars of Soviet politics still assumed fundamental differences between the American and Soviet systems: "Having rejected the totalitarian system with proper righteousness, we [political scientists] still have a deep sense that the differences are so essential that we are not required to rethink our fundamental assumptions about anything." Hough focused on the writings of pluralist political scientists like Dahl. Recent studies of the Soviet Union, Hough declared provocatively, showed that "many phenomena" identified by pluralist political scientists like Dahl "seem to have their counterparts in the Soviet political system during the Brezhnev era." A whole chapter of the book—"The Soviet Experience and the Measurement of Power"—was a direct attack on Dahl's pluralism. Dahl had attacked C. Wright Mills's *Power Elite* (1956) for Mills's inadequate definition of power. Hough turned the tables, showing logical flaws in pluralists' responses and how poorly *they* had defined power.[104]

Hough also provoked readers by turning his own sense that he was an outsider in the field into the claim (in the book's first paragraph) that Sovietologists had lived in a "self-created ghetto," with many of them attracted to the field "out of a conscious or unconscious search for their roots." Hough was certainly right in noting Sovietologists' relative isolation from the mainstreams of their disciplines; Tucker, Skilling, and Inkeles had all made the same point years earlier. But many scholars read a more sinister meaning into Hough's sentence. Some political scientists saw Hough as out of date, wondering who in the late 1970s still read Almond or Dahl.[105] But the real anger about Hough's work would surface later, as he revised his advisor's classic book, *How Russia Is Ruled;* the new version, retitled *How the Soviet Union Is Governed,* came out in 1979, alongside his own *Soviet Union and Social Science Theory.* That book was caught up in different and increasingly heated debates about the proper way to understand the origins and nature of Soviet rule; a variety of approaches were bundled together as "revisionism."

Hough's works in the late 1970s were exemplars of the evolving intellectual orientation of the field over the two preceding decades. When Merle Fainsod and Philip Mosely wrote their analyses of the USSR in the 1950s, they had little interest in connecting to the broader trends of their discipline; their students, however, built more connections to the disciplinary mainstream. It is notable how many of these scholars were trained in major centers of Russian Studies but found themselves teaching at universities that lacked a Russian Studies presence: Frederick Barghoorn (Yale), Jerry Hough (Illinois, Toronto, then Duke), H. Gordon Skilling (Toronto), and Robert Tucker (Princeton). These Soviet experts had offices and intellectual commitments closest to political science departments. At Columbia and Harvard, Sovietologists shared institutions (and hallways) with Russia experts in other departments; whatever this proximity did for deepening their knowledge of Russia, it kept them isolated from the mainstream of their disciplines. Fainsod, unlike Mosely, was shaped by these new approaches to Soviet politics, emphasizing the centrality of sociological changes while remaining skeptical that these would change the fundamentals of Soviet politics.

The steady trend of the field away from doctrinaire totalitarian arguments would be lost amid a new generation's insurgency. By the time this insurgent generation entered the field in the 1960s, there was no single totalitarianism school to oppose. Criticisms of the concept, at least as it was applied to the USSR, dated back to its academic debut in 1953. And Moore's *Terror and Progress* the following year would eventually inspire a reorientation of the field. Many scholars also would draw on the latest work in political science, whether Dahl's pluralism or Almond's political development, to build models of Soviet politics that allowed comparisons to other political systems. Even those scholars who accepted the tenets of totalitarianism typically understood it as only one phase of Soviet development, which was not applicable to the USSR after Stalin. Political outcry over Hough's books in the late 1970s quickly drowned out specialists' yawns that these books were so mainstream as to be outdated. Yet with the word echoing in public discussions of the USSR, the specter of totalitarianism remained.

PART III

CRISIS, CONFLICT, AND COLLAPSE

CHAPTER 9

THE DUAL CRISES OF RUSSIAN STUDIES

Russian Studies scholars undertook diverse and increasingly divergent efforts through the 1960s, energized by new connections to their disciplines, building on the growing exchange programs, and expanding as a national enterprise. Underwriting this burst of enthusiasm was a continuing flow of funds. Money from the National Defense Education Act (NDEA) and the Ford Foundation (plus the State Department and other philanthropies) paid graduate stipends, faculty salaries, administrative support, and the costs of travel to the USSR and around the world. As Indiana historian Robert Byrnes stated near the high tide of funding in 1964, "never since the Renaissance has research been so lavishly financed as it has been in the United States since the second world war." Yet Byrnes also sounded an alarm: "These splendid days are coming to an end as the foundations turn their attention to other interests. If, when that happens, the universities remain unprepared to act, Russian and East European studies will suffer a shattering blow."[1] A few years later, that warning came true.

Fiscal crisis was only part of the story of the stagnation of Soviet Studies in the 1970s and 1980s. Just as important was the internal composition—or perhaps the decomposition—of the field along the lines of both discipline and politics. The crisis of fiscal retrenchment was, perhaps ironically, worsened by the flush years that preceded it. The rapid quantitative expansion pulled different disciplines within Russian Studies in different directions, as each found new inspirations and new audiences beyond their own field. The full meaning of this growing divergence, however, did not become evident until the expansion ended. By the early 1970s, Russian Studies in the United States was undergoing a stagnation that was cultural, political, and institutional and that was exacerbated by a growing sense of fiscal limits. While the Soviet Union did not survive the damage wrought by its stagnation, Soviet Studies did. But it would never be the same.

Different directions emerged not just among the disciplines of Russian Studies but, in some cases, within them. Especially in studies of Soviet politics, the pursuit of "relevance" was a further source of division. The word became a cliché of the 1960s, usually associated with student demands for courses relevant to their own identities and political interests. In Soviet Studies, the word carried a different connotation: being relevant to policy debates. Definitions of relevance narrowed drastically from the 1950s to the 1970s as the marketplace of ideas broadened and the funding base narrowed; more and more scholars came to define policy relevance as the opposite of scholarly disciplines. As a result, experts seeking policy relevance worked on a different track from those seeking scholarly achievements.

There was also the amorphous but all-important impact of "the sixties" in American academic life. Disillusionment with universities seemed one of the few areas of agreement in a society that was increasingly divided; universities faced criticisms from observers on the Left and Right, from students and faculty, and from foundations and government agencies. Scholars in international studies were especially prone to disenchantment. They were discouraged by the Vietnam War, which rapidly dissipated 1950s optimism about American ability to change the world. The failure of other American projects (the Alliance for Progress in Latin America, for instance) further diminished the sense that social science could solve global problems. Vietnam also contributed to a deep distrust of the defense establishment, even on the part of many scholars who had once worked as contractors or consultants in the Pentagon. Connections between scholars and national defense were exposed in ways that called into question not just government support but scholarly ethics. Vietnam contributed to this exposure, as did the public outcry over an army-funded project called Project Camelot, which revealed a group of American social scientists not just studying revolutions in the Third World but (critics charged) countering revolutions. Confidential documents taken from university administrations—some of which touched on Sovietology—during student protests further fanned these flames. Americans' declining confidence in their government had a disproportionate impact in universities, where the controversies were not about a distant and abstract government but about colleagues, students, and advisors who had been working with government agencies.[2]

The combination of fiscal emergency and political crisis buffeted a field that was simultaneously declining and fracturing through the 1970s. Differences in disciplines, politics, and professional aspirations were amplified by the constant competition for increasingly scarce resources. The field lost many of its central institutions. New institutions reflected the tensions between relevance and scholarship and had neither the resources nor the mandates to play the same roles as the institutions they replaced. In the end, Soviet Studies in the 1970s combined the worst of both worlds: Soviet stagnation and American malaise.

As Byrnes noted, the years after Sputnik were a boom time for international studies in American universities, and Sovietology was no exception. The NDEA's Title VI, together with massive infusions from the Ford Foundation, allowed the unprecedented expansion of Soviet Studies programs on dozens of campuses. Public universities like Berkeley, Illinois, Indiana, Michigan, Pittsburgh, Washington, and Wisconsin all built up impressive Russian/Soviet Studies centers, and a handful of private universities—Chicago and Stanford, for instance—joined in as well. Ford spending jumped in the middle of the 1960s, just as lobbying for the federal International Education Act (IEA) succeeded. That bill was signed into law in 1966, promising a further widening of support for international and area programs at American universities, including undergraduate education, graduate training, and research. But the act was never funded; it fell victim to a federal budget crunch exacerbated by spending on the Vietnam War. As IEA raised and then dashed hopes, federal stalwarts like NDEA suffered: Title VI funding for area studies was under a constant threat of elimination in the late 1960s, surviving only through a series of protracted congressional battles and quiet rearguard actions.

Unfulfilled federal promises were only part of the problem. In 1966, after the passage of the IEA but well before its ultimate futility was known, the Ford Foundation announced a major policy change: it would dismantle its International Training and Research Division and curtail spending on international studies in U.S. universities. Ford would reorient its spending toward domestic concerns (a result of growing urban unrest), on the one hand, and toward direct grants to foreign countries, on the other. The end result was that Ford aid for international studies plummeted from a high of $48 million in 1966 to less than $6 million just two years later. In addition to cutting down institutional grants, Ford eliminated its foreign area fellowships, a source of funding for many Soviet Studies graduate students, especially in the social sciences; almost 30% of the fellowships had gone to Soviet Studies applicants.[3] Educators, alarmed by what was happening with IEA and Ford, announced a "crisis of dollars" in international education by 1968. By 1970, after the futility of IEA became clear, Ford increased its grants, but they never approached even half of their previous levels.[4]

The reduction in Ford and NDEA grants was especially painful because they provided over half of the total external support for area studies in American universities. Other federal grants (most prominently, from U.S. Agency for International Development and State) covered another third and other foundations another 5%. Corporate and individual gifts accounted for only 1% of extramural support.[5] This would soon change. Facing the funding challenges in the late 1960s, international studies programs managed to attract private donations. One study tracked a tripling of individual gifts in support of area studies centers and a doubling of corporate support in the 1970s—though this hardly made up for the 40% decline in foundation support.[6]

Reduced foundation support for area studies led to tightened belts at even the wealthiest institutions. At Harvard, the Russian Research Center's executive committee discussed shutting down the center. By 1973, political scientist Adam Ulam, then RRC director, called the center's plight "desperate."[7] For much of the previous decade, the 1974 visiting committee concluded, "the Center has been existing from hand to mouth amidst wandering deliberations and indecision about its future." "It is not self-evident," the committee concluded, "that the Center can and will be continued."[8] Center staff eventually met this challenge, redoubling fundraising efforts and taking on contract research projects. The days of large grants to cover operating expenses—including faculty release time and graduate student fellowships—had ended. It is not hard to detect bitterness about this turn of events. A satire mocking the "Fraud Foundation" dampened the mood at a party celebrating the RRC's twenty-fifth anniversary in 1973. In it, Richard Pipes approached the Ford president, seeking a renewal of a major operating grant. His plea for Russian Studies was met with a hip, incredulous reply: "Man, we support all kinds of studies—black studies, white studies, brown studies, studies in scarlet, rural studies, urban studies—but *Russian Studies?* Don't you think that's a bit—well—passé?"[9]

The RRC soon guaranteed its own future by undertaking an unusual endeavor: a joint fundraising campaign with its closest competitor, Columbia's Russian Institute. Even more striking than two rivals working together was the new target audience. The campaign originally aimed to raise $2.6 million primarily from private sources.[10] As economist and RRC associate director Marshall Goldman told a reporter, "When you are broke you thrash out in all directions." Going after corporate contributions made good sense in the early 1970s, as American-Soviet détente encouraged American businesses to expand into the untapped Soviet market. With puff pieces in the business media, the campaign garnered significant attention for this new approach; *Fortune* titled its article "Why Business Has a Stake in Keeping Sovietology Alive," with a pull quote reading, "Now that trade with the Russians is going strong, expert advice is more needed than ever. But some of our Soviet-watchers are even having trouble raising the money for a subscription to *Pravda*." Not all observers appreciated the joint effort. The official Soviet press welcomed the campaign as proof that the centers' financial troubles were "the fruits of their unseemly activities." Closer to home, Pipes wondered if corporate supporters, interested in trading with the USSR, would put pressure on scholars to avoid "antagonizing the Russians."[11] The campaign was also threatened by international events; as détente waned in Jimmy Carter's administration, the campaign's appeal in the business world faded. Nevertheless, the joint funding drive ensured the continued existence of the RRC; by the early 1980s, over 75% of the center's annual budget came from revenues generated by the campaign.[12] The campaign set up a similarly important endowment for Columbia's RI. The tilt toward individual and corporate donations staved off Sovietology's collapse but did not alter its basic infrastructure.

More important were government sources, and here the landscape changed dramatically in the 1970s. For the first time since the Refugee Interview Project, the Harvard center took on contract research projects for government agencies. The path was not a straight one, as the RRC's executive committee had serious reservations about serving as the institutional sponsor of a U.S. Information Agency contract. Abram Bergson questioned the contract on principle, while Pipes questioned it on the grounds of precedent. "the Center," Pipes stated sweepingly, "has always refrained from involvement in Government supported projects."[13] The RRC declined to sponsor this contract but would soon change its approach to extramural funding as its finances worsened.

The Joint Committee on Slavic Studies also faced elimination after two decades of serving as the field's organizer, representative, sponsor, funding agent, and cheerleader. The committee spent its first decade building up the field's infrastructure, especially periodicals and libraries. The JCSS devoted its second decade to turning the field into a national enterprise and shifting some of its developmental responsibilities to the new American Association for the Advancement of Slavic Studies.[14] By the late 1960s, JCSS had divested itself of most of its original duties: the Slavic Bibliographic and Documentation Center handled library work; the AAASS took over the *Current Digest* and other development tasks; the demise of Ford's Foreign Area Fellowship Program spared it grant-making responsibility. In 1967, the joint committee itself considered "withering away."[15] It proposed creating an ad hoc Committee on the Future Organization of the Slavic Field with representatives from the full alphabet soup of Slavic Studies organs: AAASS, JCSS, and IUCTG.[16] Scholars were well aware that the intellectual tide had turned against the committee's area studies approach. At what would be the final meeting of the JCSS, members bemoaned the power of the disciplines over area programs. The ACLS chair, Frederick Burkhardt, recalled how area studies had first "developed from a sense of national interest." This sentiment had faded, leaving area studies to "justify its existence mainly in disciplinary terms." Other JCSS members agreed, suggesting that the only possible route for a future in area studies would be if scholars could "gear themselves to the current concern with problems generic to the human experience."[17] And if the concerns were "generic," then committees organized geographically seemed superfluous.

With the concurrence of the two sponsoring organizations, SSRC and ACLS, the JCSS disappeared in 1971. In its stead came two other joint committees, one on Eastern Europe and another on Soviet Studies. The restructuring was a boon for the Eastern European field, which enjoyed unprecedented attention and success. After decades of feeling subservient to the Soviet field—and with good reason—the Eastern Europeanists established their own conference series and publication programs, leading to a welter of new scholarship and new enthusiasm in the field. The Ford Foundation expanded its grants in Eastern European studies even as its support for studies of other regions declined. While the field had grown after NDEA in 1958, it took the joint committee that was formed thirteen years later to give the field intellectual coherence and direction.[18]

The story of the Joint Committee on Soviet Studies was a sharp contrast. It dealt only with post-1917 topics and focused exclusively on the social sciences. Humanistic and historical studies of the region were left with no sponsorship whatsoever. The Soviet committee owed its existence more to guilt than to responsibilities or results; sponsors argued that its small grants program would boost morale in the field. But there was a limit to such charity, and the Joint Committee on Soviet Studies was dissolved after only six years.[19] The turn away from humanistic studies of Russia and the Soviet Union was one way in which relevance—even in a scholarly organization—came to be more narrowly defined and more stingily rewarded.

A second organizational change, the demise of the IUCTG, reflected growing tensions in the 1960s. Controversy had been simmering for years, dating back to the first exchange program in 1958, but came to a head a decade later. The issues were in part generational, about both sex and politics, and centered around the organization's chair, Indiana historian Robert F. Byrnes. Young scholars reacted vehemently against IUCTG's policing of student behavior, leading to the recall of a number of students from the USSR. The IUCTG defended its inquiries into personal behavior—particularly the students' social (read: sexual) lives—as a security issue. Embassy staff worried that Soviet authorities were recruiting students by the "sexual entrapment" of married exchangees or by promising to meet a student's dreams—so long as the student dreamed of archival access and the chance to "become better acquainted with Soviet society," as one young scholar was apparently offered.[20] Scholars were also quick to protest about IUCTG procedures that involved the State Department. The debates over name-checks set out in very clear terms, and for the first time, the sharp distinction between government and academic work.

Participants felt that IUCTG programs went overboard with warnings about sex and politics. One early participant recalled that the IUCTG orientation on Soviet life was "grim in the extreme...; our briefers seemed to be preparing us for combat against a web of espionage and sexual seduction." Byrnes apparently told another student that he had warned all American participants "to abstain from all forms of sexual activity not involving persons married to one another." In general, the students felt that the IUCTG treated them like children: not just irresponsible but apparently nonsexual.[21] If embassy and IUCTG officials saw intimate relationships between American and Soviet students as a security risk, most students saw them differently: as an opportunity to understand another culture more deeply, as a natural outcome of having lots of single twenty- and thirty-somethings living in close quarters, and fundamentally as relationships between consenting adults. Students also accused Byrnes, a devout Catholic, of using security issues as a cover for imposing his beliefs on others.

From the very start of the exchange program, IUCTG officials had monitored student behavior. David Munford, the first chief, spent much of his February 1959 visit to the USSR making sure that American students in Moscow and Leningrad were comfortable—but not too comfortable. He asked participants about the conduct of their fellow students, focusing especially on their social contacts with Soviet citizens.[22] When, a few months later, historian Thomas Hegarty announced his engagement to a Soviet woman, Munford was irate. He pressured one of Hegarty's friends to get involved, ultimately leading to what Munford called an awkward "health recall" (his quotation marks). Embassy staff supported Hegarty, though, and the *New York Times* announced the marriage under the headline "Love Recognizes No Iron Curtain."[23]

The replacement of Munford with Byrnes in 1960 may have increased the surveillance. Columbia historian Loren Graham, who led what he called a "rebellion" against Byrnes and IUCTG in 1967–1968, accused the committee of rejecting applicants on the basis of "overt heterosexuality." One married student was sent home for what a fellow student called his "dalliance with a local girl."[24] Many such recalls were the result of information that Byrnes or other IUCTG staff gathered from other students during their month-long winter visits to the USSR. Students worried that their mail, usually sent through embassy channels, was read by diplomats or IUCTG officials.

Byrnes's actions were not always in defense of marriage. He worked vociferously to prevent the marriages of two students who participated in the 1960–1961 exchange. Economist Leonard Kirsch had been flagged during the State Department's name-check, apparently for engaging in left-wing political activities as a student. The State Department pressured IUCTG to withdraw Kirsch from the program, though Byrnes refused to do so after seeing the classified information. Once in Moscow, Kirsch faced difficulty doing his work, perhaps giving him more time to socialize; in any case, he got engaged to Elena Kniazkina. Upon learning of Kirsch's engagement (and about another student's engagement, too), Byrnes and the embassy staff issued stern warnings about "the obvious dangers to themselves, the girls, and the student exchange program." Kirsch followed through on his wedding plans, ultimately moving with Elena to the Boston area; his betrothed classmate wavered under pressure and left the USSR still a bachelor.[25]

The exchangees also faced discipline from Soviet authorities. The first Soviet expulsion of an IUCTG participant took place in June 1960, when political scientist Edwin Morrell was charged with a laundry list of offenses ranging from slander to espionage.[26] Morrell's difficulties came as a great surprise to IUCTG officials, who considered him to be one of their strongest applicants on scholarly as well as on personal grounds. But as his research year ended, he was expelled from the Moscow State University based on his academic advisor's recommendation and unspecified "other facts." Morrell suspected that his 1949 expulsion from Czechoslovakia, where he had done Mormon missionary work, was a factor. Morrell's expulsion had few practical consequences; he left the USSR at about the same time as his fellow exchange students. Nevertheless, the IUCTG and the Moscow embassy vigorously protested against the expulsion; it was a "mystery," Stephen Viederman told the *New York Times*.[27]

Morrell's expulsion was, in fact, less mysterious than Viederman indicated. Byrnes believed that Morrell had been expelled as punishment for his three meetings with CIA agents before leaving for the USSR. Under the guise of discussing future employment possibilities, agents had provided Morrell with a list of "information the Agency wished to obtain from the Soviet Union." There is no evidence that Morrell followed through on any of these CIA requests, but Byrnes considered it no coincidence that the exchangee who had been in "closest contact" with the CIA was the "first and most clearly denounced" by the Soviets. At least one other scholar was prevented from participating in the exchange after he, too, responded to CIA contacts.[28]

Byrnes was especially irate about these problems because he had already reached an agreement that banned CIA contact with students before they left for the USSR. Byrnes told his successor, IREX chief Allen Kassof, that the IUCTG had been gravely concerned by CIA contacts with exchange scholars as early as 1958. That year, an ambitious CIA agent contacted one California historian to invite him to undertake a CIA scavenger hunt while in Moscow, to turn over his correspondence with Soviet scholars, and to provide a report on his experiences after his return. The scholar balked.[29] Senior IUCTG officials quickly sought to stop future contacts with exchange scholars. Thanks to the intervention of Berkeley historian Raymond Sontag, IUCTG made its case to Sontag's friend and former student, CIA director Allen W. Dulles. The director promised that the agency would not contact participants before they left for the USSR. Such predeparture contacts, Byrnes lectured his local CIA representative, would "contaminate the scholar, place his work and even his life in the Soviet Union in jeopardy," and "threaten the continued activity" of the

IUCTG. Another administrator concurred: "since the Russians seem to know that these advance contacts have been made, it would be better, not only for the exchange programs but for the CIA, if the practice were stopped."[30] The agreement specified a ban only on predeparture contacts. The IUCTG accepted, even facilitated, post-trip debriefings by inviting government personnel to the exchange debriefings.[31]

Agreement or no, CIA agents still made predeparture visits to exchange scholars. Historian Allen Wildman was approached in 1960—at least according to a complaint that he wrote to President Eisenhower.[32] CIA agents tried to recruit at least two other scholars, both in California, perhaps because they were farther from headquarters' supervision.[33] Byrnes's blustery protests were not rooted in any wariness about the CIA—he had worked there in the early 1950s, after all—but in his stubborn determination to protect the exchange program.

Espionage accusations would capture national attention in November 1963, when Yale political scientist Frederick Barghoorn was arrested in Moscow. Having recently grown interested in the political development approach, he organized a month-long trip to the USSR to research "citizenship training." Barghoorn was not an exchangee but conducted his research while on a tourist visa.[34] The State Department hypothesized that Soviet officials hoped to exchange the scholar for a Soviet trade official then imprisoned in New Jersey. While noting Barghoorn's long-running ties to State and CIA, State Department reports indicated that he was not working with any government agency, even on a consultant basis, at the time of his trip.[35] Perhaps the clearest indication of the Soviet position came from a laconic entry in the minutes of a late November meeting of the Presidium of the CPSU's Central Committee, a response to President John F. Kennedy's personal appeal for Barghoorn's release: "A mistake was admitted by us [*nami dopushchena oshibka*]."[36] The arrest slowed negotiations on the next academic exchange agreement but had little, if any, lasting impact on scholarly visits to the USSR.

In spite of the concerns about romantic affairs and espionage, the number of forced departures from the USSR was quite small in the early years. The IUCTG sent 145 junior scholars to the USSR in the first five years. Only 2 were recalled (one for questionable "health reasons" indirectly related to IUCTG pressure on Hegarty, another for clipping articles from library copies of decades-old journals). Three more faced expulsion from the USSR: Morrell, Edward Keenan (accused of traveling in closed areas), and George Feifer (likely as retaliation for a newspaper article critical of the USSR). But by the mid-1960s, hasty departures from the USSR became much more common; IUCTG recalled 6 Americans in four years (1963–1967), mostly because of personal conduct. A Columbia literature student was hauled home from Moscow based on student reports of sexual contact outside of marriage—in his case, with another American student. State Department flags, too, were on the rise; 4 of 123 applicants in 1968 were flagged, compared with 5 of almost 1,000 applicants in the ten preceding years.[37] The increasing frequency of flags, recalls, and expulsions all contributed to participants' growing resentment of Byrnes and the IUCTG. The gathering sense that Byrnes was acting unilaterally and inappropriately—even some of his defenders noted his "autocratic" methods—provided ammunition for an attack on IUCTG.[38]

Complaints about IUCTG grew in number and volume over the mid-1960s. Aside from increasing dissatisfaction with name-checks and recalls, scholars also accused Byrnes of favoring his own students in the selection process. These complaints ultimately came to the IUCTG's Committee on the Future. The committee had been formed to consider the future home for the IUCTG administrative office. When IUCTG was formed in 1956, administrative duties were to rotate among member universities, starting at Columbia. Indiana soon followed for a five-year term, with Byrnes as chair. As the program expanded, the IUCTG contemplated becoming a stand-alone organization with a permanent administrative staff; it rejected that possibility in 1964, but the Committee on the Future was convened in 1967 to considered whether the rotations should continue and, if so, where. But soon, the Committee on the Future was at the center of solving what one observer delicately called "the Byrnes problem." Byrnes cooperated with the committee, fully aware that it was unlikely to produce a report favorable to him.[39]

Loren Graham protested to Ivo Lederer, chair of the Committee on the Future, questioning IUCTG policies on name-checks and recalls. He enumerated seven problems with the name-checks, from the fact that they permitted government "influence over the selection procedure" to the way they turned those who examined the confidential records into "security agents." He emphasized the need for academics to keep their procedures wholly free of government interference. This declaration of independence carried over, in some ways, to the question of recall. Graham argued that the recall of "misbehaving" students put the IUCTG in the position of doing the Soviet authorities' business. He excoriated the IUCTG for enforcing policies that were "vestiges of the atmosphere of the nineteen fifties" in terms of both politics and people's private lives.[40]

Graham expressed the sense that young scholars—applicants could be up to forty years old—were still treated like children. The fact that the exchange involved such close work with the U.S. government was, similarly, part of a broader critique of American universities' reliance, financial and logistical, on the federal government. Even scholars who disagreed with some of Graham's critiques shared his anger at Byrnes's "inquisitional methods" and untrustworthiness. Byrnes responded vigorously to the accusations. He portrayed himself as "yield[ing] to none in [his] desire to keep the government removed from the education process"—a statement undoubtedly true regarding CIA inquiries, but not the name-checks.[41]

The tide had already turned against Byrnes. A new Committee on Procedures and Criteria immediately stripped him of the power of unilateral recall and insisted that IUCTG have nothing to do with name-checks.[42] If the State Department wanted to prevent a student from going on the exchange, this committee agreed, it could do so on its own. State Department personnel, including an assistant secretary, responded to this change with an ultimatum: if the IUCTG was not willing to have the name-checks take place, then it would have to forgo any cooperation from the State Department and would have to "get [its] money elsewhere." (The State Department's CU provided roughly $350,000 to IUCTG that year.)[43] The IUCTG committee backed down, continuing the name-checks under slightly different procedures. Flagged cases would no longer be evaluated by a scholar within the field with an appropriate clearance; instead, a "review board of three reputable and suitable persons outside the academic world and the government" would examine the records and make recommendations. While this change addressed some of Graham's concerns—that access to State Department files would "imprison" the reader with personal information about a student or colleague—Graham was not satisfied. The *doktorvater*s who had previously examined files were replaced by what he called a board of "uncles"—but this new procedure would still allow government information to interfere with IUCTG nominations.[44]

The recall procedures were more substantially overhauled. An IUCTG committee limited recalls to academic or urgent health reasons. If State Department officials or Soviet authorities wanted to send someone home, they could do so on their own; as the draft policy put it, the IUCTG should not "do [their] dirty work." These policies left Graham and others unsatisfied, but the Committee on the Future endorsed them.[45] "Maturity and stability" may be relevant in selection and recall, that body concluded, but "political belief and sexual behavior" should have no place in either process.[46] It rejected, too, the notion that IUCTG scholars should be involved in the name-check process and offered a radical break: "selection committees should deal…only with information derived from sources that are customary in the academic community." The committee insisted that the "functions of government…should not be discharged by the community of scholars."[47]

The Committee on the Future then rendered these changes moot while at the same time sidestepping Byrnes. Returning to its original mission, it proposed that a new organization administer the exchanges and seek to expand them. It argued that the rotation of the administrative office among universities was impractical because of the "very considerable burden borne" by the host institution and the "awesome problems" of moving the home base every few years. The Committee on the Future also noted institutional rivalries and "ill-feeling toward the host institution." The committee's recommendation was accepted by the IUCTG's national policy body—"with remarkably little dissent or discussion," as one participant reported.[48]

Ford officials hoped that this new organization, the International Research and Exchange Board, would take on a broader role in the profession, fulfilling the Committee on the Future's aspirations to send more scholars on more programs to more places. It would, in the bureaucratic language of one program officer, "serv[e] as a channel for funding certain *ad hoc* arrangements between this country and abroad; and explor[e] new ways to develop close and significant relationships between individual scholars and research and educational institutions in the United States and abroad." Some Ford officers wanted IREX to be the new home for the vast and vastly successful programs that had been under Ford's International Training and Research Division. While IREX did not become the organization that the Ford Foundation intended, it did effectively help to consolidate various exchange programs; ACLS and IUCTG exchanges were immediately placed under IREX control.[49]

Under founding director Allen Kassof, IREX saw an immediate rise in applications for the flagship junior scholar exchange formerly run by IUCTG. The controversial issues of institutional favoritism and surveillance of behavior disappeared under IREX. And the name-checks, though they still continued, were no longer as controversial. Within two years of its founding, IREX expanded its base of financial support, winning a three-year grant from the National Endowment for the Humanities (NEH). In its early years, IREX was awash in funding. Ford was by far the largest source of support (over $1 million), with the State Department contributing around half that and the NEH providing under $200,000. But the Ford support was short term; as it contemplated a longer commitment, outside consultants (including Marshall Goldman) evaluated the IREX programs in 1972. Their report was enthusiastic, celebrating IREX's success at overcoming the suspicions of being "beholden to one university or clique," which had plagued IUCTG. The institution was so important, they concluded, that "if we do not have IREX, we shall have to invent its identical twin."[50] They called on Ford to make a long-term grant. Some Ford staff did not share their consultants' enthusiasm; they found IREX to be dominated by "bureaucratic self-preservation." State Department officials agreed.[51]

The NEH grant thus came at an opportune time for IREX. Philanthropic sources were declining, none more quickly than the exchange's long-time sponsor. But the NEH grant was also a harbinger of future problems. Ford's Frank

Sutton worried that the increasing reliance on federal funds, even from NEH, might open the exchanges to "short-range political pressures."[52] The symbolic politics of NEH support was significant for another reason, too; it was tacit recognition that the exchanges' principal beneficiaries were humanists; literary scholars and historians together accounted for 75% of the participants while only 15% were social scientists.[53]

There had been a steady decline in the participation of social scientists in the IUCTG exchange over the 1960s, the result of changing disciplinary norms.[54] Natural scientists were few and far between; only nine went in the program's first three years, and that paltry figure included one psychologist and two fisheries specialists. Social scientists turned toward general theories for which local knowledge mattered little. For economists, the obstacles began with the application process, as the Soviets rejected half of the applicants, even those working on the most innocuous topics.[55] The situation worsened over time, and even an ACLS program designed for social scientists attracted few Soviet experts.[56]

The NEH grant was one more sign, among many, that the field of Soviet Studies did not serve the national needs for experts in contemporary Soviet politics and economics. IREX faced increasing criticism as the 1970s wore on. Bertram Wolfe went so far as to worry that American scholars had been "terrorized" during the exchange.[57] In his essay "Can Culture Survive Cultural Agreements?" Byrnes wrote critically of the enterprise he had managed for eight years. He dismissed the research pursued by American exchange participants as frivolous or antiquarian, in large part because Soviet authorities prevented them from working on important questions of contemporary politics and economics. Citing Byrnes, *Commentary* published an article claiming that the exchanges harmed U.S. national interests.[58] Just as the ambitious origins of IUCTG reflected the mood of general expansion through a coordinated network of universities, philanthropies, and government agencies, so too did IREX's problems in the 1970s reflect the new mood and new arrangements: growing skepticism, even hostility, among foundations, universities, and government agencies; tightened belts; and an increasing focus on policy relevance.

The issues facing the field in the 1970s were exacerbated by generational differences. Most of the leading scholars in Soviet Studies, outside of literature at least, had worked for a government agency or worked on a project funded by one. While these projects varied in many specifics, there were few questions raised about the propriety of working with the government. Thousands of pages of archived correspondence from the 1940s and 1950s contain no principled reluctance to work with government, only occasional disappointment when opportunities were denied. The JCSS subcommittee on government-academic relations, founded in 1958, aimed to increase and institutionalize contacts among

Soviet experts in and out of government. The IUCTG case was different—it involved the examination of personal information about scholars—but this, too, had raised few concerns in the past. The IUCTG controversy revealed the ways in which scholars in the late 1960s perceived the government and security issues with new antipathy. IREX staff felt intermittent pressure from scholars over the continuation of the name-checks. When the name-checks ended in 1974, it was not the result of scholarly pressures but a by-product of the debates over government secrecy that roiled Washington in the Watergate years.[59]

IREX also faced increasing pressure to demonstrate policy relevance. Its staff defended the programs by counting the number of scholars working on contemporary topics (as many as 25% in the mid-1970s), compared with almost none in the late 1960s.[60] The point was clear: all parts of Sovietology needed to justify themselves in terms of contemporary relevance; the Politburo mattered more than Pushkin, Brezhnev more than Bulgakov.

Some scholars in the field tried to solve the interconnected problems of relevance and funding by returning to an older model of Sovietological work. University of Washington political scientist Herbert Ellison circulated a "Proposal for a New Approach to Research in Slavic Studies" to the joint committee in 1969. Ellison worried that Soviet Studies "ha[d] lost much of their vitality and sense of purpose." To reverse this, he proposed programs with "a clear research problem focus [and] a specific research output goal." These programs would necessarily bring together scholars from different disciplines, offer research opportunities for graduate students, and address problems of contemporary interest to three prospective audiences: scholars in Soviet Studies, social scientists not focused on the USSR, and Soviet specialists in the U.S. government. Ellison sought to reenergize the field by suggesting work on the scale of the Refugee Interview Project, with the same effort to provide usable research results for government specialists and contributions to theories of society for social scientists.[61] This ambitious program went nowhere; there were no agencies willing to fund such large-scale projects any more. And even if there were, Ellison was searching for something that no longer existed: common ground between general social scientists and area specialists, and between scholars and government agencies.

Columbia's Marshall Shulman offered a diagnosis similar to Ellison's, while also suggesting why Ellison's prescription was unlikely to succeed. Shulman, too, emphasized the need for interdisciplinary work, which had fallen out of favor in the 1960s. In the late 1950s, he argued, the review committee (on which he had served) had called for more attention to social scientific disciplinary approaches. A decade later, he thought that the pendulum had moved too far and needed to come back to area expertise. Like Ellison, Shulman emphasized the importance of using interdisciplinary approaches to "solve current problems." Shulman was not optimistic that his call would be heeded. He noted the field's "dual character," its simultaneous pursuit of knowledge and relevance. In the 1950s, the two pursuits were connected:

> Although the word "defense" had a certain magic…in loosening the legislative purse-strings, it happily ha[d] not been construed in narrow terms, and…made possible academically independent work which at the same time has undoubtedly contributed to a higher level of competence to deal with the international environment.

But this harmonious marriage of policy and profession was on the rocks by the late 1960s; the "climate of the times" had revealed the tensions between pursuing knowledge and relevance, and many in the field felt "an indiscriminate hostility to the government."[62] In spite of the hopes of Ellison and Shulman, Russian Studies could not go back to the future.

New Soviet Studies institutions sought to resolve the tensions between academic and government work. George F. Kennan, one of the central movers behind the institute that would bear his surname, saw the crisis in personal terms. In the early 1970s, Russian Studies lost three of its leading impresarios: Merle Fainsod, Philip Mosely, and Llewellyn Thompson. Each worked in a different sphere—Fainsod as a scholar-cum-advisor, Mosely as a consultant-cum-advisor, and Thompson as a diplomat—but together they defined for Kennan a generation of Russian expertise. Material circumstances were also relevant, especially for those who joined Kennan in contemplating a new organization. An assessment by Princeton historian S. Frederick Starr bemoaned the decline of financial support but looked beyond the familiar litany of financial woes to intellectual ones. The Starr report questioned the relevance of disciplines for undergraduate teaching and policy relevance. It recommended the creation of a new center to attract funds and generate new ideas. It should be located in Washington, D.C., so scholars could take advantage of the Library of Congress, an especially important feature for those who had limited access to major libraries.[63]

Like Ellison and Shulman, Kennan harked back to the 1950s to plan for the 1970s. The full name of his organization—the Kennan Institute for Advanced Russian Studies—echoed an earlier one, R. Gordon Wasson's Committee for the Promotion of Advanced Slavic Cultural Studies, in which he had been active. Kennan envisioned an organization that focused on the humanistic aspects of Russian culture much as Wasson's did. In a genteel act of modesty, Kennan demurred at the suggestion that the new institute carry his name; it would be more appropriate, he thought, to honor his great-uncle, the most important American commentator on Russia in the nineteenth century. Of course, since the diplomat shared his great-uncle's surname, honors would accrue to both Kennans. With the ascension of Russian historian James Billington to the head of the Woodrow Wilson International Center for Scholars, a logical institutional home was soon found; Billington made the creation of a Russian center a condition of his taking the job in 1973. By the end of the following year, the Kennan Institute opened its doors as a component of the Wilson Center.[64]

The Kennan Institute, funded primarily by private donors, soon found itself pulled between scholarship and relevance. From the start, the Kennan Institute founders expressed the tensions between being a "cultural monastery in a highly political city" and filling the "unique role of academic advisor to the policy-makers and politicians in Washington." But even as founding secretary Starr and his graduate advisor-cum-boss Billington celebrated the "broad humanistic study" of Russia, the personnel and activities even in the earliest days suggested competing priorities. The first cohorts of visiting fellows included three historians and five social scientists—but no humanists. The slate of early conferences was even more weighted toward policy; only two of the first nine events were humanistic in orientation, while the second event (on the most recent Communist Party Congress) was cosponsored by the State Department.[65]

National security organs did not content themselves with invitations to Kennan Institute events. In the summer of 1976, senior Pentagon officials at the heart of the national security establishment (the Office of the Secretary of Defense) funded a $150,000 pilot project at the request of Harvard faculty and administrators. The purpose was to determine how the Department of Defense might undertake a "major investment" in Soviet area research. Funding would be generous; as one Pentagon official reported to a Harvard administrator, "money [is] no object" in setting up this center.[66]

Harvard historian Edward Keenan worked with Vladimir Toumanoff, a former State Department official who was helping the RRC to raise government research funds, and political scientist Guido Goldman. The rationale was a familiar one: Keenan and Toumanoff complained that the Soviet Union was "no longer *en vogue*," which left Soviet experts at the mercy of disciplines that cared little for the "'special' features of Soviet Studies." These intellectual trends became all the more important given the collapse of foundation support for area studies. A new organization, the authors hoped, could spend Defense money to rebuild Soviet Studies.[67] Given scholars' general feelings about the Pentagon, Keenan and Toumanoff proposed an "intermediate body," originally to be based at Harvard, to sponsor the work. The RRC committee members insisted that this new entity be "academically respectable" and avoid classified work. While this experimental new program seemed to be focused on topics of contemporary relevance—hardly a surprise for Pentagon funding—Richard Pipes argued for a broader approach more oriented toward scholarship than policy.[68] The proponents of this new program sought support for a what Toumanoff called "common ground," a wide spectrum of social scientific research that would overlap with the interests of government sponsors.[69] When Keenan and Toumanoff began working with academic consultants to shape a research agenda, however, the topics tilted toward policy concerns: the size of the Soviet defense effort, the influence of domestic factors on Soviet foreign policy, and regional development in the USSR. The influx of Soviet émigrés into the United States and Israel—which increased in the early 1970s—also attracted the attention of many of the consultants to this report; most émigrés, the report noted, might become useful "sources of information," while a handful of qualified professionals might be integrated into research projects as scholars.[70] But the émigré plans remained vague while the list of specific research projects and organizational plans was far more specific.

The interim report soon sat at the center of a controversy among within the RRC executive committee, as Pipes questioned Keenan on both substantial and procedural grounds. Based on his recent Washington experiences, Pipes concluded that government officials—and not academic intermediaries—should decide how to spend government funds; he also wanted the RRC role to be more clearly defined. Adam Ulam protested that the field's main need—training for younger scholars—would not be met by the proposal. Pipes further worried that working with the Pentagon might be "political dynamite" and had the possibility of endangering either Soviet Studies writ large or Harvard's RRC. Later issues further demonstrated the scholars' hesitation about working with government agencies. Economist Abram Bergson wanted to be sure that the grants were lucrative enough to cover what he called the "'psychic cost' to a scholar of doing work for the Defense Department."[71] These issues were signs of the times. The minutes reveal far more debate over the founding of this new organization than over programs in the 1950s like the RRC's huge Refugee Interview Project under air force sponsorship or its connections to CIA through MIT's Center for International Studies. Scholars in the early years never doubted their ability to address issues of national security interest, nor their utility to military and security organizations, nor the morality of their involvement.

Keenan, Goldman, and Toumanoff's work led to the creation of the National Council for Soviet and East European Research (NCSEER) in 1978. The organization, led by a board appointed from leading Soviet Studies centers, would address in its initial incarnation three sets of policy concerns: "the size and burden of the Soviet defense effort…, the long-term prospects for the Soviet economy and society…, and Soviet objectives in long-term political-economic-military relations with the United States." Officials from the Office of the Secretary of Defense (OSD) had encouraged the council to think big—at least $1 million per year. That sum was relatively small by defense contracting standards, and funds were eventually routed through the State Department, which was better equipped to handle small grants.[72] The early contracts completed for NCSEER—the nomenclature itself suggests government consulting not scholarly fellowships—were indeed oriented toward political science and economics topics of current policy concern. Ironically, the "consumers" of NCSEER reports had a very different idea of what work was most useful. Andrew Marshall, then as now director of net assessment in OSD, mentioned not the reports that scholars considered to be relevant—he had access to classified reports on these topics already—but the reports on literature, culture, and everyday life in the Soviet Union.[73] As Pipes had suggested, scholars' definitions of policy relevance might not have much use for those actively shaping policy. In spite of Toumanoff's insistence that the council was not a "'laundry' for DOD," the NCSEER functioned very much along those lines, providing scholars with a chance to gain access to clean funding that might otherwise seem "tainted" if it came directly from the Pentagon.[74] The NCSEER recognized the broader problems of Soviet Studies (funding and training) but worked to improve conditions initially in only one sphere: policy-oriented social science.

As NCSEER went from plan to organization, other Sovietologists promoted a different proposal elsewhere in the national security apparatus. Two economists, both with CIA connections, Vladimir Treml (Duke) and Herbert Levine (Penn), proposed that the agency support a research institute to study the USSR.[75] Their proposal cited the usual litany of problems in the field: a decline in resources, an erosion of senior faculty appointments, a decline in graduate student interest, and few jobs for those students who did complete their degrees. Like Keenan and Toumanoff, Treml and Levine mentioned the need to make use of the Soviet émigrés, many of whom were trained social scientists. Interestingly, the scholars' report defined relevance more narrowly than did the CIA. Treml criticized NCSEER for not taking on large-scale and long-term research projects that would "be responsive to the needs of the sponsors."[76] Treml and Levine proposed a "full spectrum" of research projects—but their spectrum was slanted heavily toward policy-oriented social scientists; Soviet domestic and foreign policy and the military topped the list. Ironically, CIA officials criticized the Treml-Levine proposal as "too narrow." The research agenda, CIA officials argued, should cover not just Soviet economics but "party life, society and culture," and other aspects of the Soviet experience. Likewise, the proposed institute should be based in Washington not just for ready access to governmental Soviet experts, but for the chance to "make a dent in our more basic data and archival problems."[77] As with NCSEER, scholars seemed to have a more attenuated definition of policy relevance than did the national security officials themselves.

While Treml and Levine originally questioned NCSEER's plans, they shared a similar view of the state and the stakes of Soviet Studies in the United States. Academic Sovietology provided a continuing stream of new ideas, new sources, and new experts that the national security organs needed for their short-term, problem-oriented work. Some officials seemed to prefer a public campaign to build government support for Soviet Studies at a broader level— an approach that would not just provide research support for current scholars (as NCSEER would do) but would focus especially on training new experts.[78] The agitation took a familiar Washington form: a plea for special consideration advertised as a congressional briefing. The event brought together a wide range of Washington hands, many of whom disagreed sharply with one another about the Soviet Union, to share their common concern that the United States would soon lose a whole generation of Soviet experts (in academic and government work) and would have few ready to replace them. Scholars and government experts alike cited the tightened academic job market as a grave danger for the nation. Among the most important ideas proposed was to catch up with and surpass the Soviet Union in the organization of Cold War expertise. A Washington-based Soviet Studies institute could provide a counterweight to the USSR's Institute of the USA and Canada, founded in the late 1960s; it could also employ a handful of policy-oriented scholars conducting (as the briefing proposed) toward "economics and hard-data social science research." Yet these grand ideas never came to pass, and CIA eventually cast its lot with NCSEER, becoming an official sponsor of that organization in 1981.[79]

Two years later, Title VIII funding guaranteed NCSEER an annual appropriation not subject to the fluctuations of funding that had marred its first years—a "permanent but modest floor," in the words of General William Odom, a Russian Institute Ph.D. then serving as chief of army intelligence. These funds were soon reoriented toward policy-relevant research.[80] Title VIII funds, in the words of one participant, "really saved the field" by "keeping the core organizations"—the Kennan Institute, NCSEER, and a successor joint committee, among others—alive. It did so at a cost, however: administered by the State Department's Bureau of Intelligence and Research, the program "maintains…U.S. expertise in the regions and brings open source, policy-relevant research to the service of the U.S. Government."[81] While institutions sought to define policy relevance broadly, the pressure remained. Relevance came to dominate the field's new programs in the 1970s. While every source of extramural funding—foundation grants, corporate donations, Title VIII and federal contracts—had the potential to reorient the field, contracts from operational agencies (State, Defense, CIA) brought with them, in the words of one observer, heightened "dangers of undue influence, leverage and distortion of scholarly objectivity."[82] Many of these dangers were averted in Title VIII funding. The NCSEER grants were not shaped by government priorities—yet there was a constant need to establish the policy relevance of academic projects.

The desire of government agencies for broad work that fit within scholarly norms was clearly evident in the Soviet Interview Project funded by CIA and the Departments of State and Defense. Like Harvard's Refugee Interview Project some thirty years earlier, the SIP was a large-scale interdisciplinary effort to learn about Soviet society from those who had left it. It also responded to the widely perceived need to make use of the waves of émigrés, primarily Jewish, who had left the Soviet Union in the 1970s. Aside from the proposals oriented toward Washington agencies, the AAASS had established the Committee on Émigré Placement in the mid-1970s and lobbied to use NDEA Title VI funds to allow centers to work with émigrés.[83] Yet these plans were stymied by the so-called Kissinger rule, imposed by the secretary of state in the interests of placating Soviet leaders; that rule banned the use of federal funds to study the new émigré population.[84] The Kissinger rule remained in force longer than its namesake, until 1979—at which point Starr hosted a Kennan Institute meeting to discuss a survey of émigrés proposed by economist James Millar at the University of Illinois. Two members of Andrew Marshall's Pentagon staff were also present. While the funding would come directly from State, Defense, and CIA, Toumanoff agreed to have NCSEER serve as, in Millar's words, a "buffer" between the funders and the project. The SIP had even wider latitude than the Harvard project; Millar indicated that the sponsors wanted the project "not [to] worry about" their interests, but to focus on academic inquiry. Like the Harvard RIP that preceded it, SIP aimed to produce scholarly works, promote young scholars (especially in the neglected field of sociology), and generate a data set that would be of use to other scholars. The central findings were that there was still broad support for some aspects of Soviet life (medical care, state-owned industry), but that the younger and best-educated émigrés— those who had benefited most from the Soviet system—were also the most likely to oppose the regime. The final results of SIP were less dramatic than those of the 1950s project, perhaps because the results of the Harvard project had been assimilated into the field already.[85]

In a preface to an SIP report, RIP alumnus Joseph Berliner suggested that the book would be useful to Mikhail Gorbachev as he set out to reform Soviet institutions. Yet those reforms soon limited the utility of the SIP. By the time the book came out in 1987, Western scholars were conducting the first public opinion surveys in the USSR itself. The reviews of the book were enthusiastic but also acknowledged how quickly times had changed. One political scientist hoped that the project might "forge bridges between the all-too-often-isolated realm of Sovietology and the disciplines of political science, sociology, and economics."[86] Scholars in the 1980s still looked to policy-relevant work to link disparate disciplines.

The pursuit of relevance also was behind a seemingly endless debate in political science about "discipline versus area." One side of this debate worried that Soviet Studies had overinvested in disciplines to the detriment of broader knowledge of the region. It was this sort of expertise that government agencies desired; they wanted detailed knowledge of the language, culture, society, and political system—not cutting-edge academic research. But not just potential employers favored the area model; political scientists like Alfred G. Meyer (Michigan) and Herbert Ellison (Washington) similarly argued that the overall discipline of political science offered little for Soviet experts. Meyer shunned diplomacy in his assessment:

> I have tried for more than two decades of study, to learn methods, approaches, and other theoretical tools from my colleagues in the comparative study of politics; it may well be that I have learned as much from them as any Sovietologist of my generation. The sum total of what has been useful to me, however, has been meager....The discipline of political science obviously has not given many useful tools to the area specialists.

The pursuit of disciplinary expertise, Meyer concluded, had done graduate students a grave disservice; the field "produced many PhD's but few scholars." In the end, "the application of political science models and methods to the study of Soviet and East European politics makes little sense."[87]

The other side of the debate had similarly harsh words. Discipline-oriented political scientists denigrated area studies as unsystematic, insular, and impressionistic. As one partisan put it, the discipline-versus-area debate was one of "rigor versus mortis": disciplinary rigor versus the intellectually lifeless focus on area expertise.[88] John Armstrong worried that Soviet Studies was "derelict in its duty as a branch of knowledge if it failed to relate its problems to broader analytic concerns."[89] Frederic Fleron accused area-oriented scholars of promoting narrow scholarship and even narrower political views; the turn toward discipline, in this argument, would be necessary to "depropagandize academic studies of the Soviet Union."[90] By mixing profession and politics, Fleron's comment foreshadowed later debates that would derive political views from disciplinary perspectives; while he saw discipline as a refuge from anti-Soviet politics, others would interpret a reliance on disciplinary norms as a sign of sympathy for the USSR. The tension between area and discipline took its most anguished form in Sovietology in the late 1960s and early 1970s, as funding rapidly evaporated, institutions changed, and competition accelerated.

The investment in disciplines in the 1960s had hardly been accidental but was a self-conscious effort to prove that Soviet Studies could serve scholarship and policy simultaneously—and instead proved the reverse.

Russian Studies had pioneered the area approach, and in the early days it had earned plaudits for integrated programs of undergraduate teaching, graduate training, and research. Yet other area programs had an easier time resolving the tensions between area and disciplinary forms of expertise. The problems here are evident in the graduate careers of budding Soviet experts, as assembled in a massive analysis of area studies in the early 1970s. Among other things, the results (summarized in table 9.1) showed the great distance between training in Eastern European studies and in other world areas.

Eastern Europe/USSR specialists took almost three times as many language courses as their classmates studying other world regions. One of the principal reasons for this heavy language training was that far fewer graduate students had been to the region they were studying before entering their respective programs. Only one-third of Eastern Europe graduate students had visited the region before graduate school, substantially below the other specializations. Nor did Eastern Europeanists catch up with their colleagues in graduate school. On average, they spent one-third less time in their region than other experts spent in their respective world regions. Another factor shaping course selection was the relative difficulty of learning Russian compared with most area languages. There were two implications of this heavier language burden: Eastern Europe experts took more courses overall, prolonging their graduate careers. And they took half as many courses in their disciplines as other internationally oriented students did. Eastern Europe experts underwent rigorous, multidisciplinary training, much broader than the training of their classmates.[91] But the benefits of building area knowledge—and sharing language and area courses with fellow Russia/Soviet scholars in other disciplines—came at a significant cost: Soviet experts were nowhere near as well steeped in the professional norms of their respective disciplines. And in spite of the additional training, they still lagged significantly behind other

Table 9.1: Graduate Student Coursework in International Studies

Course Type	Course Years of Study by Ph.D. Graduates, 1967–1969	
	Eastern European Studies (incl. USSR)	Other Regional Studies
Language	4.15	1.51
Area	3.20	1.76
Discipline	2.12	5.35
Total	9.47	8.62

Source: Calculated from Richard I. Lambert, *Language and Area Studies Review* (Philadelphia, 1973), 388.

area specialists in terms of language acquisition and residence in the country
of their expertise.

The isolation of Soviet Studies was exacerbated by the rapid expansion of a
sector of the field that was oriented toward narrowly defined policy relevance,
which had even less in common with the mainstream of either area studies or
political science. An increasing number of graduate students earned doctoral
degrees in Soviet politics with a focus on international relations, and they did
so at institutions oriented toward Washington. Political scientists were already
finding themselves isolated from their discipline (by virtue of shortened
coursework and few opportunities to generate theories) and from their area
studies colleagues (by their determination to focus on disciplinary norms). And
now they faced a bifurcation within their own ranks, evidenced by the substantial increase in the number of degrees in Soviet foreign policy. A comparison of Soviet Studies dissertations filed in the early 1960s with those a decade
later demonstrated the change. While international topics were of course not
new, they had expanded dramatically. Indeed, international topics accounted
for over half of the social science degrees in Soviet Studies between 1970 and
1973. The 1960s had brought an expansion in Soviet Studies degrees, and they
brought an explosion of foreign policy topics; indeed, over 60% of the increase
in social science dissertations on Soviet topics in the 1960s is attributable to
foreign policy dissertations alone. The tilt toward international topics was even
more evident later; one scholar counted 121 dissertations on Soviet foreign policy between 1976 and 1987, compared with only 87 on Soviet domestic policy.[92]
Many of these students graduated from programs established in the 1960s
with a clear focus on policy. Not coincidentally, three of the leading programs
were located in Washington: George Washington and Georgetown universities and Johns Hopkins University's School of Advanced International Studies.
The policy orientation was perhaps best exemplified by George Washington
University, which established its Institute for Sino-Soviet Studies in 1961 with
an aim of bringing together scholars and students to shape public discussions
about the Cold War. Many of its staff members were Sovietology stalwarts
who went in and out of government service; indeed, it would not be much of
an exaggeration to say that the Sino-Soviet Institute served as a way station for
intelligence analysts with doctorates.[93] The work on Soviet foreign policy and
on international relations was only tangentially connected to the mainstreams
of either area or discipline; the primary interlocutors were instead midlevel
experts in government agencies and in the para-academic world of policy institutes from RAND to the Washington think tanks.

The distinction between the academic and policy orientations was not absolute but was a dominant presence in studies of Soviet foreign policy. The pioneering generation of American experts on Soviet foreign policy—including

those with government experience—had broad and deep backgrounds. Philip Mosely, Frederick Barghoorn, and Cyril Black had doctorates in history, as did Richard Pipes, who soon would enter the policy world. Pipes's generation also included scholars like Zbigniew Brzezinski (Columbia) and Alexander Dallin (Columbia and then Stanford), who were thoroughly immersed in the field while they still served as consultants to numerous government agencies—and, in Brzezinski's case, as national security advisor. All attended graduate school at Harvard or Columbia, and all were connected to numerous research projects in Russian and Soviet Studies. While their students may have shared the same attitudes and broader training, these students would soon be overwhelmed by those from programs with decidedly narrower orientations. Breadth, of course, does not equate with quality, but it is striking how much this network of policy-oriented programs trained students for different careers and different affiliations. These trends affected not just the study of Soviet foreign policy (which relied on less and less engagement with the USSR) but also the study of Soviet domestic politics. In the dozen years starting in 1976, there were more dissertations on Soviet domestic politics that cited few or no Russian-language sources (23 of 87) than there were dissertations based on research done in the USSR (17).[94]

Generally speaking, the opportunity for crossover between the policy and academic worlds diminished in the 1970s and beyond. There would be, of course, exceptions, like Condoleezza Rice, whose 1981 doctorate from the University of Denver led her to one of the top academic jobs, in Stanford's Political Science Department, and then in George H.W. Bush's White House. By one analysis, the popularity of Soviet foreign policy topics was short-lived, soon to be replaced by security studies more generally. By the late 1970s, Columbia's Robert Legvold reported, "the field of Soviet foreign policy studies [had] lost momentum before it had a chance to flourish."[95] Its demise pulled the policy world one more step away from academic institutions, including both departments and area studies centers.

Those political scientists oriented toward Washington may have had more success than those casting their lots with academe. The Lambert survey suggested a serious disjuncture between aspiration and opportunity for Eastern Europe experts seeking to become full-fledged members of the discipline. For political scientists, the role of Soviet specialists in the field writ large was minimal. One small but simple marker: the first time that a Russia specialist was awarded the Woodrow Wilson Prize for the best book in the field was in 2003, when Mark Beissinger won. Even the best books by political scientists specializing in the USSR—Merle Fainsod, Zbigniew Brzezinski, John Armstrong, and others—had little play outside the ranks of Soviet specialists.[96] For all of their efforts to become disciplinary scholars, Soviet experts had much less disciplinary training than their colleagues, little recognition from the field, and minimal intellectual impact.

Reviewing the report on area studies, Herbert Ellison concluded that the disciplines had come to dominate the field; area studies had simply been "grafted onto" a disciplinary identity. Ellison also admitted, based on more subjective criteria, that area studies had failed to live up to their interdisciplinary promise: political scientists specializing in the USSR, for instance, had failed to influence specialists on other world regions. Gabriel Almond, the impresario of political development, agreed.[97]

The disconnect between discipline and area was especially devastating in the terrible job market of the 1970s. In a field where training was increasingly narrow and isolated and where national needs were determined according to an increasingly narrow definition of relevance, the process of matching production and "consumption" grew increasingly difficult. At the same time, the radical shift of Sovietology's financial fortunes (and those of international studies in general) left a large bulge of students who had benefited from the flush years but then faced slender job prospects.

This increasing narrowness in training and employment gave rise to a personnel crisis in Sovietology that contained within it a seeming contradiction. Government agencies emphasized the growing shortage of Soviet specialists in political science and economics. Meanwhile, academics emphasized the impossibility of the job market of the 1970s: as faculty positions evaporated or were reassigned, there were far too many graduate students competing for the few available jobs. Which was it—shortage or surplus? Where one stood on this question depended on where one sat.

The shortage of academic jobs came about as the expansion of the 1960s led to a peak in doctoral production long after employment retrenchment had set in.[98] Different segments of the market for experts faced different circumstances. Perhaps the most interesting case is Sovietological economics. In an excellent study of the job market, James Millar warned of serious troubles for the 1980s. While his primary concern was the generation of scholars who earned their doctorates between 1969 and 1978, the problem dated back much earlier. The boom in international studies in the 1960s had spread the aspirations for graduate training to an ever-wider group of institutions, producing cohorts that were larger and more varied. The economics profession focused on very different issues in the 1970s than it had earlier, and it had little place left for scholars who specialized in one nation's economy rather than in economic theory and technique. Finally, the age structure of the profession made it likely that the top institutions (which had made the earliest hires in Sovietological economics in the 1950s) were likely to face the first retirements—and therefore would be the first to lose positions in the field, as the retirees would likely be replaced with non-Sovietologists. The field, in other words, was already starting to "die from the top" by the late 1970s.[99] The resulting bulge of Sovietological economists unable to get top academic jobs would have one salutary effect: more trained economists would be ready to pursue non-academic careers, and they might reduce the shortage of experts on the Soviet economy working in government agencies.[100]

Political scientists faced a similar problem: there were more and more graduate students in political science, thanks to the general expansion of the 1960s, but fewer placement opportunities. Especially at elite institutions, Soviet specialists in political science departments were a relatively old group: in the early 1980s, twenty-two of twenty-six (by one count) were full professors. This figure limited the employment opportunities for new Ph.D.'s; since 1975, a 1983 report indicated, only one recent Ph.D. had reached an elite institution. It also indicated that the Soviet field would soon face disproportionately heavy retirements at a time when many of the positions might not be replaced.[101]

For language/literature experts, the situation was more dire, with little of the upside potential of government employment. Though Russian-language programs were entrenched at many institutions, declining language enrollments—a trend dating back to the mid-1960s—had reduced demand. Language programs, with the popularity of the lecture-plus-drill method pioneered in the 1930s, had hired a disproportionate number of part-time and non-tenure-track faculty, and they were especially vulnerable to declining demand.[102] There was no systematic study of historians, but anecdotal evidence and the lack of non-academic employment opportunities suggest that newly minted historians of Russia faced an extremely difficult job market, on a par with that for other historians.

The principal problem for government agencies was the decline of employed Russia experts, who formed a reserve army of expertise. There was little, besides exhortation, that government agencies could do to maintain the level of academic employment in the field. Unable to reverse declines in Soviet Studies employment, the government agencies opted instead to create opportunities for those in the field. The bonanza years, when financial support covered research, training, and infrastructure, were long gone. In the straitened seventies, scholars and government agencies alike discussed the "pipeline" problems but were unable to organize a project large enough to have any impact.

The crisis of the 1970s diminished just about everything about Soviet Studies. In addition to quantitative reduction came a narrowing of what constituted policy relevance. The result of all of these trends was that the only aspect of the field to grow after 1968 was conflict. Soviet Studies in the 1970s was riven by conflicts: between disciplines, between policy and scholarly orientations, and between those with different visions of America's Soviet policy. These debates would take place in the 1970s against a backdrop of fiscal crisis and intellectual stagnation.

CHAPTER 10

RIGHT TURN INTO THE HALLS OF POWER

Amid the straitened circumstances of the late 1960s, many scholars, liberals and conservatives alike, felt increasingly alienated from the universities in which they worked. Conservatives felt a special detachment and distress, related to changes both in academic life and in American-Soviet relations. The rise of disciplinary thinking in the 1960s did not square with their intellectual or political values, and the uprisings at the end of that decade left them estranged from university life and those who inhabited it. Generational change in Soviet Studies coincided with structural changes in the government-academic relationship to create a new kind of interface among the policy, public, and academic spheres, one that was more individual and less institutional. Perhaps most important, conservatives' strong opposition to President Richard Nixon's policy of détente toward the USSR gave them an added reason to get engaged in public affairs.

The founders of Soviet Studies always believed in their importance for U.S. foreign policy. They contributed in many ways: they taught M.A. students (at Columbia's Russian Institute and elsewhere), providing the premier entry ticket for Soviet experts interested in the Foreign Service or intelligence analysis. They worked for RAND Corporation, which funded work on the Soviet economy that became a template for CIA estimates, the Smolensk book, and political studies. They staffed Harvard's Refugee Interview Project, which was meant to provide crucial background for U.S. Air Force strategy. They served as consultants or advisors for dozens of bodies sprinkled throughout the national security establishment and provided testimony to Congress. A small group of Russia experts, most of whom had worked for the government during World War II, became Washington regulars. These scholars saw their government work as completely continuous with their academic work. And they had a point: Margaret Mead and Clyde Kluckhohn served on military boards to set priorities for behavioral science research that was very much like the work others did for the JCSS and other academic bodies. Kluckhohn's final RIP report to the air force shared much with *How the Soviet System Works*. By the same token, Philip Mosely published articles that echoed the advice he was offering to the government agencies that employed him. In addition, Mosely directed traffic along multiple institutional avenues running from academe to the policy world. He represented the War Documentation Project (which produced Merle Fainsod's book on Smolensk) in government circles. He obtained funding and access to government materials for the Research Program on the History of the CPSU, which produced Leonard Schapiro's *The Communist Party of the Soviet Union* (1960) and other works. Another reason that Mosely perceived a direct and essential connection between his work at Columbia (1946–1955 and 1963–1972) and his interventions into public and policy debates was that he was outside any professional disciplinary tradition. By the time he got to Columbia in 1946, Mosely had abandoned his professional career as a historian and turned instead to discussions of contemporary international relations and Soviet affairs. Even in the less disciplinary days of the 1950s, Mosely was little shaped by academic and intellectual trends, turning instead to sophisticated political commentary.

Major sponsors like the Carnegie Corporation and the Ford and Rockefeller foundations valued contributions to public debates about foreign policy. Sovietologists readily obliged. Between 1945 and 1960, Columbia and Harvard scholars alone wrote hundreds of articles in non-academic venues; they appeared in magazines like *Newsweek*, major newspapers like the *New York Times*, and general interest journals like *Foreign Affairs* with remarkable frequency.[1] Collectively, a dozen or so scholars at these two institutions published one article in *Foreign Affairs* each year, one article in a magazine and another in a major newspaper each quarter; in addition, they appeared, on average, as sources or subjects for one major newspaper article each month. Harvard and Columbia had a near-monopoly on the national press, so other scholars, even those at excellent programs like Stanford, Indiana, and Berkeley, were relegated primarily to appearances in local newspapers or mentions in the national press along with groups of others.

These scholars-in-public were soon joined by some of their students. A handful of political scientists and historians, especially, joined some of the government-funded enterprises like the interview project. They also began taking individual consultancies with government agencies and appearing more frequently in non-academic discussions of the USSR and of America's Soviet policy. Alexander Dallin and Marshall Shulman, for instance, had both split their early careers between Harvard and Columbia (Dallin moved to Stanford in 1970); both received degrees in political science, but neither was oriented toward the discipline as it began to adopt a comparative politics framework. Both Dallin and Shulman, in short, began conducting themselves much like

Philip Mosely: they served the profession well, advised graduate students as well as government agencies, and wrote informed political commentary rather than scholarly contributions to the discipline. They were joined in the 1970s by Wellesley economist Marshall Goldman, whose rise as a public commentator on Soviet affairs was not directly connected to his disciplinary work. Finally, there was the special case of Zbigniew Brzezinski. Starting his career at Harvard as a graduate student and junior faculty member, Brzezinski left for Columbia in 1960 and quickly began his meteoric rise in policy and then public work. He declined an offer to leave Columbia for Harvard because (he later recalled) New York was "a better platform for someone with an activist political orienta-tion." Brzezinski frequented the Council on Foreign Relations, where Mosely worked between his Columbia stints, and published often in its journal, *Foreign Affairs*; he also was a regular in the opinion pages of major newspapers and in general interest magazines. After brief service on the State Department's Policy Planning Staff, Brzezinski began working for Hubert Humphrey's presidential campaign.[2] His academic publications petered out, and by the early 1970s he had made the leap into the world of policy and punditry.

Discussions about reducing U.S.–Soviet tensions revealed a growing divi-sion in the ranks of scholars-in-public. Public discussions about ways to improve superpower relations were common in the 1960s, especially after the Cuban missile crisis in 1962. American and Soviet officials negotiated on a series of arms control agreements, efforts generally supported by scholars like Dallin and Shulman. Shulman argued for the U.S. government to take the lead in reducing Cold War tensions as early as 1966, arguing that Western aggressiveness promoted Soviet militancy. After the inauguration of Richard Nixon in 1968, his national security advisor, Henry Kissinger, began promot-ing U.S.–Soviet détente with new energy and effect, seeing it as part of the effort to extract the United States from the deepening quagmire in Vietnam. This intensification of efforts at détente under Nixon soon shaped the policy discussions by Sovietologists; most scholars with public profiles, with the exception of Brzezinski, favored détente in some form. Goldman, when he began writing for a broader audience in the 1970s, was enthusiastic; indeed, his book on détente was subtitled "Doing Business with the Soviets." When Stephen Cohen entered the public fray in the late 1960s and early 1970s, he too came down staunchly in favor of a relaxation of tensions—the lit-eral meaning of détente—which he believed would allow Soviet reformers to defeat Soviet conservatives. Discussions of policy reverberated back into dis-cussions about Soviet Studies itself, as Cohen and Dallin criticized the field for supporting the government's hardline policies. Dallin, for instance, wrote a *Slavic Review* article in 1973 that blasted the field for "biases and blun-ders," which he blamed on Cold War politics.[3] All of these scholars focused on U.S.–Soviet interactions, arguing that American flexibility could induce Soviet domestic reform and reduce its expansionism abroad. Embedded in this argument were many claims that would later come under attack: that the United States was partially responsible for the Cold War; that the Soviet Union would respond to American gestures; and that the Soviet Union itself was capable of change.

The turn toward détente as the basis of America's Soviet policy in the first years of the Nixon presidency was a boon for those scholars oriented toward improving U.S.–Soviet interactions. These Soviet experts devoted their energy to promoting change in the USSR by changing U.S. foreign policy. This goal hardly coincided with that of détente's architect, Kissinger, who was less interested in liberalizing Soviet domestic policy than in using U.S.–Soviet relations as a weapon against China and, ultimately, as a tool for ending the Vietnam War. Ultimate aims aside, the tenor of public discussions of the Soviet Union was generally sympathetic to détente. It was in this context—and against this trend—that academic hardliners entered the public debate.

Richard Pipes, Adam Ulam, and Robert Conquest all rejected what they saw as the soft line on the USSR that came out of academic circles. But their alienation from the field was not just the result of their distress at a new American policy toward the USSR. Their disappointment with the disciplinary turn of Soviet Studies and their disgust with university life amid the protests of the late 1960s were also factors. While each of them began on vastly different intellectual paths, the three converged by the late 1960s, joining the counterrevolution as the disciplinary, student, and policy revolutions accelerated.

Of the three, Pipes was the only one to begin his career as a Russianist. The son of Germanophile Jewish refugees from Poland, Pipes begin his Russian studies in the U.S. Army during World War II at Cornell's ASTP program. There, he met liberal émigrés like Mark Vishniak as well as the radicals who brought the Cornell program so much bad press. From the start of his graduate career at Harvard, Pipes was interested in the dual tracks of scholarship and policy. In a letter to Vishniak, for instance, Pipes revealed an interest in contemporary foreign policy, seeking work in the State Department's Research Section, a descendant of the OSS's wartime Research and Analysis Branch.[4] By 1948, Pipes had fixed on the study of nationalism in Soviet Russia; he envisioned a broad dissertation, moving from Marx through Stalin—a century in all—focusing on the theory of nationalism. The resulting book, *The Formation of the Soviet Union, 1917–1923* (1954), detailed the fate of non-Russian nationalities in the face of growing Soviet power. Through his recounting of the revolutionary Ukrainian Rada, the Georgian Mensheviks, and smaller nationalist movements elsewhere, Pipes detailed conflicts between nationalists and Bolsheviks. The end result was the same in each case: Soviet domination through the use

Figure 10.1. Richard Pipes with students Nina Tumarkin and Daniel Orlovsky, 1971.

or threat of violence. Pipes accused Lenin of using minority nationalism in strictly instrumental terms; it was "something to exploit, and not something to solve." The Soviet Union owed its structure, the façade of national autonomy within a profoundly centralized system, to this nationality policy. The book was a sleeper hit of the early 1950s; it received respectable, even appreciative, reviews and was one of the only books in the RRC monograph series to pay back the $1,000 subvention.[5] Pipes also explored contemporary nationalism, conducting numerous interviews with non-Russian émigrés or exiles from the USSR, most of whom were residing in Europe. These discussions convinced him that the "nationality problem" was even greater in the 1950s than it had been in the Soviet Union's formative years. He called it an "explosive force" within the USSR, where most of the population of the borderlands "detests the present regime" and seeks "separation from everything Russian"—a conclusion based, apparently, on émigré accounts. He soon explored contemporary nationalism at MIT's Center for International Studies, which at that point was still funded exclusively by the CIA. Pipes collected MIT funds to continue his research on non-Russian nationalities in the Soviet Union, which eventually came under the auspices of the Soviet Vulnerability Project.[6]

Through this work, Pipes stressed his distance from these institutions and their reigning ideas. Since his classmate Martin Malia was widely seen as Karpovich's chair apparent, Pipes taught in Harvard's history and literature program. He also challenged the intellectual assumptions of another potential home, the Russian Research Center, writing an article critical of Max Weber, a particular favorite of Talcott Parsons. Beneath Weber's essays on Russia in the early twentieth century, Pipes wrote, was the sociologist's refusal to recognize that Russia marked a "deviation from the general European pattern."[7]

Pipes's work explored one or another aspect of Russia's deviation from Europe. First came histories of Russian conservative thought as a means of emphasizing Russia's distinctiveness. He translated a classic work by nineteenth-century conservative N. M. Karamzin, who had argued that Russia required an absolute ruler to prevent its descent into anarchy; in Pipes's words, Karamzin offered Russia a stark choice between monarchy and democracy, but "preferred to take a chance on excessive power" rather than chaos. Conservatism, Pipes suggested, was the authentic Russian politics, while liberalism and radicalism were imports from the West.[8] The book came at an inflection point in Pipes's career. While he had maintained a base at Harvard—with time off for research trips, a fellowship year in Europe, and a semester visiting at Berkeley—Pipes must have had the feeling of borrowed time. Much to everyone's surprise, not least Pipes's, he was appointed to Harvard's tenured post in Russian history, likely because Malia had published little when the decision was made. Pipes noted in his memoirs that he would have been happy to go to Berkeley after visiting there for a semester, but that job had already gone to Malia in any case.[9]

Even before his tenured appointment at Harvard came through, Pipes began work on a biography of Petr Struve, Gleb's father and one of the most important Russian political figures of the silver age.[10] This research led Pipes to a study of the Russian intelligentsia, the topic of an important 1960 collection that he edited. The book was as much about the history of the intelligentsia as about developments in Soviet culture since Stalin's death. Even historical essays like Pipes's own drew lessons for contemporary life in the USSR and around the world. In his foreword, Pipes noted that understanding how Russian intellectuals navigated the "technical and administrative bureaucracy" in the nineteenth century would be of broad interest because the question emerged "in every modern or 'modernizing' country." Unlike the sociologists who saw the rise of a university-educated population as a force promoting "technical rationality," Pipes identified the essence of this group as a "critical spirit of which 'rationalism' is merely one expression."[11] Like Pipes's writings on nationality, his work on the intelligentsia was historical scholarship with explicit connections to the contemporary scene.

In other writings that came out of his study of Petr Struve, Pipes addressed not contemporary social scientists but historians in the USSR. Pipes introduced his short volume on Social Democracy in St. Petersburg in the 1890s by emphasizing the need to reduce Lenin to "human proportions." Using an array of autobiographical accounts, Pipes described a wide and deep gulf between nascent workers' movements and radical intellectuals. The workers' "innate conservatism," he argued, led them to view radicals' ideas and actions with deep skepticism. Workers sought economic advance and improved conditions. Insofar as they joined with the intellectuals, they did so only in pursuit of these goals. Pipes concluded that the Soviet version of Lenin and the Social Democrats leading the workers into strikes to build class consciousness was wrong in every particular. He also offered a variant of the counterfactual reasoning of which his advisor had been so enamored: if not for 1917, "there is every reason to believe that the Russian labor movement would have become as effective a social and political force as its counterpart in other industrial countries of the world." Following Petr Struve through the radical politics of the late nineteenth century, Pipes envisioned a historical trajectory that was antithetical to the Soviet narrative of heroic radicals bringing class consciousness to the workers, who would, in 1917, lead a popular revolution. In his work on Social Democracy and in an important article on the meaning of populism, Pipes made his challenge clear.[12]

Pipes's visits to the Soviet Union in the early 1960s magnified his strong views about the country. A 1962 article, written for *Encounter* but never published, contained his reflections on one trip. It revealed flares of emotion rarely evident in the genteel Pipes; reading a Soviet source, he wrote (and then crossed out), "evokes a kind of low burning but steady anger." Pipes concluded that the Russia specialist "commits himself emotionally" to his subject because he "must assume some kind of philosophical and moral position to this experiment." Studying other countries, he noted, did not require such explicit emotional commitment nor provoke such anger.[13]

The events of 1968 must have intensified Pipes's low-burning anger. By August of that year, in the wake of the Soviet tank brigades suppressing the experiments of the Prague spring, Pipes told one correspondent that "the greatest difficulty" he faced was "keeping [his] anger about present-day Russians under control." In a comparison that evoked the turmoil of his teenage years, Pipes compared 1968 to 1938, when the Nazis faced little Western challenge to their destruction of Czechoslovakia. He railed against U.S. politics to a French friend the ex-Communist Boris Souvarine: the Johnson administration was "totally isolated from society, especially the thinking element," and was steering the country on a path to "internal and international decline." Nor was he about to become an expatriate in France. "I don't like to visit countries whose politics I don't approve of," he wrote to Souvarine later to explain his long absence from Paris, and he added that French foreign policy was akin to that of "a satellite of the USSR."[14] Expressing anger and alienation in equal measures, Pipes focused initially on national and international affairs, but soon enough he took on domestic, even local, ones as well.

Pipes was especially critical of student activists. In April 1969, a small group took over Harvard's University Hall to protest the institution's numerous connections to the Vietnam War. Pipes seemed revolted but unsurprised by the students' behavior; he attributed their actions to the "dissolution of family and community life" in America, which had created a narcissistic generation of college students seeking "affection, attention [and] moral guidance." The real fault, Pipes later wrote, lay not with the students, who were merely acting their age, but with the faculty members who treated their complaints as legitimate. To Pipes, his colleagues revealed their "self-interest and cowardice" in their dealings with student radicals. In a 1971 afterword to a textbook he had coauthored, he admonished his students' generation for abandoning history in pursuit of contemporary relevance, thereby adopting a "child's view of the world." Refusing to learn from the past, Pipes continued, would drag members of society down to "the status of near-animals." While revolts were nothing new in the history of Western civilization, Pipes noted, those of the 1960s were different; they exhibited an "unalloyed negativism" and a dangerous tendency to "return to the life of perpetual irresponsibility and self-indulgence of the childhood nursery."[15] This attitude toward students may have played a role in the textbook's poor sales.

Adam Ulam, who taught in Harvard's Government Department, had a similar distaste for the student protests, and his path to the alienation of the late 1960s overlapped with Pipes's. Like Pipes, Ulam left Poland on the eve of the Nazi invasion along with his brother Stanislaw, a physicist whom Adam followed throughout the United States until he was sent to Los Alamos. Adam Ulam was also involved in the wartime ASTP, but as an instructor (in

Polish) rather than as a student. After the war, Ulam went to Harvard for graduate work; he studied with Merle Fainsod but ultimately wrote a dissertation on British socialism. Though he was hired as the British Empire specialist at Harvard in 1947, he soon recast himself as a Russianist, noting slyly that he wanted to be teaching "an expanding subject"—the Soviet empire—rather than a contracting one.

Ulam's best-known books came in the 1960s: biographies of Lenin and Stalin and two books on Soviet foreign policy. The books were well constructed, written with a strong narrative and verve; they paid close attention to the personalities at the top of the Soviet leadership. He glibly summarized his approach by claiming that Al Capone, not Lenin, Marx, or Weber, provided the key to understanding the workings of the Politburo.[16] An engaging raconteur, he took great pleasure in conversing with students and other RRC staff about the Soviet Union; for every occasion, he had a quip, usually a comment on someone's individual behavior. He was not so much alienated from his department and discipline as simply remote from them. But Ulam's alienation grew after the University Hall takeover in 1969.

While no fan of the student protestors, Ulam placed the ultimate blame on the faculty, though for different reasons than Pipes did. Through the Cold War and especially in the Kennedy years, he wrote, Harvard had taken on "activities for which it was not really suited, [under] the assumption that it was capable not only of analyzing and instructing but of advising and prescribing." He traced this "governmentalization" of university life to the rise of scholars' participation in shaping foreign policy. Ulam took students at face value when they said they were protesting the university's involvement in national security. The protests, he wrote, were against the professors' beliefs that they held "some special wisdom…which entitle[d] them…to prescribe cures for social ills, solutions for foreign policy dilemmas, and the like."[17] Faculty, not students, had led the fall from academic grace.

Robert Conquest grew alienated from academic Sovietology before Ulam and Pipes and for more directly political reasons. He was an Oxford student in the late 1930s, when many of the most intellectual and interesting students there joined the Communist Party; Conquest was no exception, though his membership was brief. Conquest worked for British military intelligence during World War II. After intensive language training at the School of Slavonic Studies in London, Conquest was posted to Bulgaria, leaving on the eve of its Sovietization in 1948. After the war, he stayed in government, working in the secret Information Research Department, a major front in the propaganda war against the Soviets. In 1952, his Foreign Office career jeopardized by a divorce, Conquest returned to the poetry he had all but abandoned since leaving Oxford. He was supported by the Sidney and Beatrice Webb Fellowship at the London School of Economics—an irony upon which Conquest and his friends feasted. The Webbs had welcomed the Soviet Union as "a new civilization" while Conquest devoted much of his life to attacking the USSR.[18] He fell in with poets Kingsley Amis and Philip Larkin; tongues firmly in cheeks, they called themselves the Movement. Reacting against the politically infused literary ideas of the 1930s, their Movement was anything but *engagé*. Conquest called it "consciously uncommitted to politics"; the commitment was to poetry and to what Larkin called "a fuller and more representative response to life as it appears from day to day." This period of blithe "uncommitment" came to an abrupt end in the fall of 1956, when news of the Soviet crackdown in Budapest vied on the front pages with dispatches from the Middle East about the British-French-Israeli attack on Egyptian control of the Suez Canal. Hungary reminded the poets that Communism was not merely the misguided idealism of Oxford youth, but a dangerous force; Suez demonstrated Britain's precipitous fall from global preeminence. While he would continue to write poetry, Conquest focused increasingly on the Soviet Union, the subject of his continuing government work.[19]

The year 1960 marked Conquest's entry into serious public discussion of the Soviet Union. His book on Soviet nationality policy demonstrated the USSR's centralizing tendencies. To describe the deportation of seven minority nationalities during World War II, Conquest pulled together a range of official sources and personal accounts by survivors who made it to the West. The book, in many ways, set the stage for Conquest's most influential writings on the Soviet Union; he would use the same combination of official documents and personal accounts in describing the purges and would return to Soviet nationality policy in a revised (and more strongly worded) edition and in a book on famine in Ukraine in the early 1930s.[20]

His second book in 1960, *Power and Policy in the USSR*, was a spirited monograph, a defense of "Kremlinology"—that is, the study of personal politics in the highest reaches of the Soviet party and government, as opposed to political science. Conquest focused on "the central group of politicians" in the USSR, not on "large-scale social forces." To study the broader movements without emphasizing the struggle for power at the top, Conquest wrote, was tantamount to learning about horse races by studying only pedigrees and paying no attention to "the actual race." Robert Tucker criticized Conquest for a "reductionism" that left him unwilling to "allow that Soviet politicians may genuinely differ over the merits" of a given policy. Conquest predicted the eventual demise of the Soviet Union: faced with the choice of "evolve or perish," Soviet leaders would be more adept at political maneuvering than at steering change. He remained skeptical about liberalization during Khrushchev's thaw, speaking out more forcefully after Leonid Brezhnev's palace coup. In *Russia after*

Khrushchev (1965), Conquest wrote that a lasting liberalization would require "an evolution of ideology and, with it, institutions"; he saw changes in the former but not the latter. Conquest noted the lack of "conviction" of the Brezhnev Politburo, whose Stalinist tendencies were at best "half-hearted." But even half-hearted Stalinism was a danger; it was still possible (indeed, "not too unlikely") that Soviet leadership would reimpose a strict Stalinist control of society.[21]

While many American academics looked askance at Conquest's Kremlinology, they responded enthusiastically to his 1968 book, *The Great Terror*, a compelling narrative history of the 1930s revolving around Stalin. Conquest's account started with the murder of Stalin's friend and potential competitor Sergei Kirov in 1934 and ended—after 20 million lives were taken—with the German invasion in 1941. The book wove together a wide range of sources, especially contemporary official publications and memoirs of defectors who had been part of the purge as victims, bureaucrats, or officers in the secret police. The result was a remarkable history, documenting the terror of the 1930s but arguing for antecedents back to the start of Soviet rule. The collectivization of agriculture in the first Five-Year Plan (1928–1932) especially shaped the purges; its battles put the question of party loyalty "on [a] war basis." During collectivization, Conquest wrote, Stalin relied on a "new style of terror which was [later] to typify the period of the Great Purge." Conquest began his story about the purges at the top. Stalin was the central force behind the purges; even his closest and most powerful associates were only carrying out Stalin's wishes. Stalin promoted the purges not simply to eliminate his rivals but to make the whole of Russia "silenced and broken"—and also to create a "permanent [and new] economic form" rooted in gulag labor. With the camps, he hinted, Soviet planning "had settled into a new rationality" that could lead to the system's one "solid achievement" of an economic system geared to investment and growth.[22]

The political and economic systems that emerged blood-soaked at the end of the purge survived, Conquest warned, and left "the whole world" living "under Stalin's shadow." Conquest saw the terror as the single event "which affect[ed] the world most directly today," more than anything else in the previous thirty event-laden years. The current Soviet elite was defined by the purge experience; the "principles of rule" that Stalin imposed still held for later generations of Soviet leaders, including Khrushchev, who denounced his predecessor. Even thirty years after the terror's peak, the Soviet Union was "not fully cured, but still suffering from a milder and more chronic form of the affliction." *The Great Terror* received a great deal of attention in both the United Kingdom and the United States. Kennan's *New York Times* review closed with a question of warning that echoed Conquest's own: "Can men who can neither eradicate nor deny nor explain the blood that disfigures their own hands be fit leaders of a great country and a great empire today?" The stain of Stalinism had long outlasted its namesake. Soviet specialists, even those not known as hardliners, admired the book but did not necessarily consider it a work of scholarship.[23]

In the midst of the disciplinary revolution that dominated political science in the 1960s, the student revolutions of 1968–1969, and the Soviet suppression of the Prague spring in 1968 came the final form of alienation that brought Pipes, Ulam, and Conquest into the policy arena: the inauguration of Richard Nixon in January 1969 and, with it, talk of American-Soviet détente. Pipes approached this topic with a direct application of Russian history to present-day Soviet policy. His first major effort came in the form of a paper for the American Historical Association meeting in 1969, later published under the portentous title "Russia's Mission, America's Destiny." It explained the roots of superpower conflict in their respective national histories. The year 1917, Pipes declared, beckoned a Muscovite resurgence: the country "instinctively" envisioned itself as "a nation *sui generis*...part of no state system or international community, the only guardians of true Orthodoxy, once Christian, now Communist." Soviet leaders held nothing but "contempt for that which lies outside one's national boundaries," an attitude rooted in an economic system that grew only through exploitation (of resources, territories, and people). America's "commercial" economy, in contrast, rewarded negotiation rather than exploitation, give-and-take not hand-it-over. George Kennan agreed: "the Russian, if he is going to have anything at all to do with the outside world, wants to subdue, to command." Kennan echoed Pipes in claiming that the notion of "mutually profitable and pleasant international relations" was a "peculiarity of the mercantile, overseas-trading mentality" that made little sense in "those countries whose concepts of international relations arose out of life-and-death encounters with nomadic hordes, or contacts with the universal imperial pretensions of a medieval Byzantium, or both." Though Kennan missed Pipes's presentation, the audience included a less renowned but more influential person: Dorothy Fosdick, a long-time foreign policy aide to Senator Henry "Scoop" Jackson (D-WA). She soon brought Pipes to the attention of her boss and thus helped Pipes enter into the politics of America's Soviet policy.[24]

Fosdick was well positioned to shepherd Pipes into the world of Washington policy debates. She had worked for Senator Jackson almost since his arrival in the Senate in 1952. Raised in a family of prominent liberal internationalists, Fosdick quickly found herself in the policy world in which her family thrived. She joined the State Department during World War II, helping to design the United Nations and other pillars of the postwar international system. In 1948, she joined the department's policy planning staff, headed first by George Kennan and then by Paul Nitze. A liberal who rejected the pacifist and internationalist inclinations of her family, Fosdick was a perfect match for Jackson.[25]

Scoop Jackson was liberal on domestic issues but embraced an assertive U.S. stance in the Cold War. Foreign policy and constituent service fit together nicely in his case; fighting the Soviets required up-to-date weaponry of just the sort that Washington state's largest employer produced; no wonder that Jackson's critics called him the "senator from Boeing." From his seats on key Senate committees related to foreign affairs and national security, and with Fosdick's efforts behind the scenes, Jackson worked to strengthen U.S. defenses.[26] Jackson's visibility rose especially in the late 1960s, a result of both ambition and circumstance. As Nixon and Kissinger pursued détente toward the Soviet Union, Jackson spoke out sharply against it, believing that it would endanger U.S. security. When Kissinger began the Strategic Arms Limitation Talks (SALT), Jackson expanded his attacks on the administration's Soviet policy. He convened hearings in early 1970 as part of the Special Subcommittee on the Strategic Arms Limitation Talks, which he chaired. One of the first invitations went to Pipes.

Pipes used the Senate hearing to establish connections between the Russian past and the Soviet present. Focusing on elite political culture, Pipes described a vast gulf between American and Soviet leadership. Soviet leaders, he wrote, inherited xenophobia from the Russian Orthodox Church and abandoned the Westernizing tendencies of tsarism. As a result, the Soviet *apparat* was "not predisposed by its cultural background to regard itself as part of a broader international community"; it envisioned a "perpetual conflict…in which only one side can emerge victorious." Pipes blamed Russian political culture for Soviet behavior, noting how Soviet ideology "neatly reinforc[ed]…[the leaders'] inherited religiously-inspired outlook." Yet this political culture resonated little with the rest of the population, leaving the Soviet leadership afraid "not of other peoples but of its own." This fear bred insecurity, "which in turn expressed itself, in nations as in individuals, in aggressive behavior." The Soviet leadership also inherited from tsarism an urge to colonize—the very colonization that had led to the creation of the tsarist empire. Pipes drew out the policy implications:

> The implications are not far to seek. A country whose governing apparatus has learned how to deal with foreign peoples from what are essentially colonial practices is not predisposed to think in terms of a stable international community or of balance of power. Its natural instincts are to exert the maximum use of force, and to regard absorption as the only dependable way of settling relations with other states.

What did all of this mean for contemporary American-Soviet relations? Pipes placed great stress on the disjuncture between the Soviet population and its rulers. Citing folklore and proverbs, Pipes insisted that the Russian populace contained little "trace of militarism." But this mattered little in an age when war meant intercontinental missiles, not infantry musters.[27] Pipes's testimony invoked a Russian political culture that dated back deep into the mists of the Russian past.

Among the fans of Pipes's testimony was Robert Conquest, who had already become one of Jackson's informal advisors on Russian affairs. Jackson first learned of Conquest by reading *The Great Terror*. An aide reported that the senator "was profoundly moved by the Conquest book: he recommended it time after time as 'must' reading." Interested in foreign policy, Jackson concluded— as he recounted on the Senate floor—that the "bloody massacres" described by Conquest were not just indications of despotism but were "sources of international instability and turmoil." He soon thereafter put Conquest on the agenda for his annual pilgrimages to London; other British advisors included political scientist Leonard Schapiro and *Survey* editor Leopold Labedz. Conquest praised Pipes's testimony to Fosdick even though it differed greatly from Conquest's own genealogies of the Soviet elite; political alliance seemingly mattered more than common intellectual ground. Conquest shared with Pipes the fear that Western nations, and especially the United States, were not sufficiently energetic in their challenges to Soviet expansion; he credited Jackson as the one "bearing the brunt of the struggle against uninformed waffle" about the Soviet Union.[28] Jackson soon invited Conquest to testify before the Senate subcommittee he chaired.

Conquest's testimony emphasized the radical dissimilarity of American and Soviet policy mechanisms. For too long, Conquest began, Americans acted upon the "unconscious assumption that Communist leaderships are...susceptible to more or less the same pressures and maneuvers" as democratic governments; he implicitly criticized the efforts of academic political scientists to interpret the USSR through the lens of political development. Largely because of the cauldron of the purge, Soviet leaders of the day were "from a tradition which is alien in both aim and method to our own"—and were, even within that tradition, "intellectually third-rate." Jackson was taken by Conquest's commentary, invoking it in later debates.[29]

Ulam, too, tallied the inadequacies of Brezhnev's Soviet *apparat* for Jackson. In a report that the senator had commissioned and in testimony before the Senate Foreign Relations Committee, the Harvard professor offered psychological explanations of the Soviet leaders, arguing that their inferiority complexes and insecurities fundamentally shaped Soviet policy. Like Conquest and Pipes, Ulam also connected Soviet internal repression to the nation's external aggression. Ulam's scars from the domestic battles of the late 1960s were also evident; he exhorted that "the current picture of social unrest and political disunity" in the United States encouraged Soviet assertiveness in the international sphere.[30]

Ulam and Conquest made occasional pilgrimages to Capitol Hill, but only Pipes found a new career in Washington. His opposition to détente found new audiences. Working as a consultant for Jackson, Pipes began to write more frequently about Soviet military affairs. In a Senate committee report, he described Soviet political culture as "inherently military" in orientation. He traced the origins of this back to Lenin, who found "congenial" Carl von Clausewitz's dictum that war was "politics by other means." Pipes warned that the Brezhnev era was especially dangerous. The Soviet leadership knew that they could not count on public support for their policies, and indeed sought to "steel the Soviet population by depriving it of the good things in life to keep it lean, hungry and alert." China was an even greater concern; since the Soviet diplomatic "tricks" that worked on the West had failed in its dealings vis-à-vis China, the USSR "may well throw caution to the wind and rely increasingly on brute force."[31] The Soviet Union had gone from being a general danger, in Pipes's telling, to an immediate and urgent one.

Pipes pressed the case further in later articles. He disparaged Western observers, from fellow Sovietologists to diplomats, for their optimism that the Soviet Union could evolve into a less dangerous force. He attacked Kissinger's détente, arguing that the hope of finding a modus vivendi with the USSR so that both superpowers could better pursue their own interests was one-sided. Echoing Jackson, Pipes argued that détente gave the Soviet Union a green light to pursue a long-term goal: "the slow, patient, piecemeal disintegration of Western Europe" and its "eventual absorption" by the USSR. Pipes was part of a group of scholars (including Conquest and Labedz) who warned of the dangers of détente to U.S. interests. In interviews, articles, and testimony, Pipes stressed the centrality of Russian "historical traditions," the militaristic orientation of Soviet leaders, and their efforts to suppress consumption to keep citizens "pliable in the hands of the state."[32]

Pipes continued his scholarly work amid his frequent commuting to Washington. His major project in the early 1970s was an expansive survey of Russian history, *Russia under the Old Regime* (1974). It brought together a number of arguments he had been making about the Russian origins of Soviet totalitarianism—and expanded on claims he had first made in his intellectual history of conservatism. Pipes argued that Russian society had always been unable to "impose on political authority any kind of effective restraints." The book was, from the preface onward, presentist: "Unlike most historians who seek the roots of twentieth-century totalitarianism in Western ideas, I look for them in Russian institutions." The watchword here was patrimonialism, a term Pipes took from Max Weber. A patrimonial state, like Muscovy, made "no significant distinction between authority and ownership." Muscovite rulers had inherited from the Mongol Golden Horde a vision of the state that was "entirely devoid of any sense of responsibility for public well-being."[33]

Pipes emphasized the historical origins of Soviet totalitarianism by making comparisons, for instance, of social surveillance in Muscovy and the USSR, and of the roles played by merchants' wives in the early nineteenth century and by the wives of Soviet "notables." By the time Pipes got to the middle of the nineteenth century, he was no longer seeking parallels but origins. He traced the lineage of Soviet totalitarianism to the changes in the Russian legal and police systems between 1840 and 1880. To Pipes, the Criminal Code of 1845 bridged ancient Russian despotism and modern totalitarianism: with its enactment, the patrimonial spirit was "at long last…given flesh in neatly composed chapters, articles, and paragraphs." By outlawing criticisms as well as actions against the current regime, and by expanding punishments to include hard labor and branding, the code "was to totalitarianism what the Magna Carta [was] to liberty." The only saving grace in the middle decades of the nineteenth century was that the "machinery of repression was still too primitive" to enforce the laws systematically. The 1870s saw "the legal and institutional bases…for a bureaucratic-police regime with totalitarian overtones," codifying the forms of repression that would define Soviet rule four decades later. While many émigré historians were nostalgic for the supposed liberal and Western tendencies of late nineteenth-century Russia, Pipes saw this period as the birth of modern despotism. He admitted that imperial Russia never became a "full-blown police state," but credited it with being a "forerunner, a rough prototype" of such a thing.[34] While some of Pipes's former classmates considered *Russia under the Old Regime* to be "extreme," Adam Ulam faulted the book's "political predestination of a people." Pipes insisted that Russian despotism was determined by Russian history, not by Slavic genes or Eurasian topography—but saw "very little likelihood" of Russia finding itself in anything other than anarchy or despotism.[35]

In Washington, the fact of Russian despotism mattered more than its origins. Pipes undertook some classified research projects related to Soviet grand strategy. He was expanding his area of expertise beyond issues directly related to the study of Russian political culture and institutions—and at the same time was expanding the reach of his ideas until he was heard as often in briefing rooms as in academic conferences. Pipes's detachment was not a sudden break, though; a conference he had organized to "celebrate" the fiftieth anniversary of 1917 included only a handful of American Soviet experts, who were far outnumbered by European scholars and American public intellectuals like George

Kennan and Hannah Arendt.[36] One of the clearest expressions of his new place in Washington came about in a Top Secret exercise that was the culmination of Senator Jackson's anti-détente work in the 1970s: the so-called Team B exercise in the fall and winter of 1976.

Pipes's work with Team B might seem unlikely, as he had little involvement in one of the central debates to give rise to this experiment in competitive intelligence. The CIA had long organized periodic national intelligence estimates (NIEs) on global topics; these estimates were to reflect the consensus of the "intelligence community," a dozen or so agencies, each with its own special areas of expertise as well as bureaucratic agendas. The ne plus ultra of the NIEs was NIE 11-3/8 on Soviet strategic (nuclear) forces, including discussions of current capabilities, current posture/strategy, and projections of future capabilities. There were significant differences of opinion about how to interpret sketchy and incomplete data in all reports, but none was more contentious than NIE 11-3/8. Bureaucratic politics also played a role; as one joke had it, the State Department thought the Russians were not coming, CIA thought the Russians were coming but would not be able to get here, the Defense Intelligence Agency thought the Russians were coming and indeed were almost here, and air force intelligence thought that the Russians were already here—and working in the State Department.[37] The NIE process acknowledged differences by allowing agencies to express dissenting views in footnotes to the main estimate. The bureaucratic in-fighting over these estimates was hidden from public view by the Top Secret classification, but it nevertheless intersected with a very public debate about the strategic implications of détente—a debate in which Senator Jackson and his aides and allies were leading participants. Pipes was one of many working with Jackson to fight détente. The fight began, oddly enough, with a group supporting President Nixon's policies.

When Nixon and Kissinger began promoting a modest antiballistic missile (ABM) program in 1969, some senators and former diplomats banded together to form the Committee to Maintain a Prudent Defense Policy. Two defense experts led the charge: Dean Acheson, who had been Harry Truman's secretary of state, and Paul Nitze, who had laid the cornerstone for America's Cold War military buildup when working for Acheson. With funds from Nitze's substantial personal assets, the two created a small group to lobby for the ABM, which they saw as a potential bargaining chip in the upcoming arms-control negotiations. Through Albert Wohlstetter, a political scientist at the University of Chicago best known for his work at the air force–created RAND Corporation, the group hired young and ambitious staffers, including Richard Perle and Paul Wolfowitz. Wolfowitz had imbibed Wohlstetter's expansive view of the Soviet threat while in his graduate seminars; Perle's education was less formal, coming on the deck of the Wohlstetters' swimming pool in Hollywood while

Perle was dating Wohlstetter's daughter. Perle and Wolfowitz quickly set to work shoring up congressional support for this limited ABM program, working closely with Pentagon officials. According to Strobe Talbott, the key issue for Perle was not technical specifications but "the quality of the enemy—the essential wickedness, deceitfulness, and aggressiveness of the Soviet Union." After securing funds for the ABM, Perle joined Jackson's Senate staff.[38]

Though Jackson had supported the Nixon administration on ABMs, the relationship quickly deteriorated. Jackson used the SALT subcommittee to promote the skeptical views of Soviet experts like Pipes, Conquest, Schapiro, and Ulam. Jackson and Kissinger came into almost daily conflict over SALT; hostilities ran so deep that Jackson's staff prepared briefing books for the senator's meetings with the national security advisor that were worthy of superpower summits. After SALT passed the Senate in 1972, anti-détente forces mobilized quickly. Wohlstetter effectively brought together the public and classified debates over Soviet defense posture in a 1974 article, "Is There a Strategic Arms Race?" The article was a spirited attack on the national estimates process for the Soviet strategic forces, the NIE 11-3/8 series. Wohlstetter attacked as "myths" the notion that U.S. defense spending provided the impulse for Soviet increases and the criticism that American intelligence had consistently overestimated the Soviet strategic threat. He insisted instead that the Soviet military was simply building up as rapidly as possible, not "racing" against U.S. spending, but only against its own increasingly strained capacities. Official predictions of Soviet missile deployments consistently *under*estimated eventual deployments, Wohlstetter argued, ignoring the rapid expansion of Soviet strategic forces in the mid-1960s. A secret internal report by CIA analysts conceded that Wohlstetter was "essentially correct" in the case of intercontinental ballistic missiles.[39]

Wohlstetter's attack on the CIA came at a difficult time in the agency's history. Nixon and Kissinger had spent the better part of their time in power disparaging, undermining, and marginalizing the intelligence agency; with his famous venom and inverted class consciousness, Nixon associated "those clowns at Langley" with the East Coast elite. But that elite was hardly enthralled with CIA, and establishment scion Vice President Nelson Rockefeller led one of many investigations into CIA activities. In late 1974, investigative journalist Seymour Hersh broke the story about what agency insiders called the "family jewels," 700-plus pages documenting illegal CIA activities at home and abroad: assassinations, coups, and domestic surveillance. Investigative commissions proliferated, each producing lurid details about CIA misdeeds. Even the moderate *Newsweek* called for the agency's abolition.[40] Wohlstetter's punches landed on a weakened target.

While Wohlstetter's arguments over past estimates were part of the run-up to Team B, the exercise itself was an attempt to impose a new set of premises on Soviet military estimates. The President's Foreign Intelligence Advisory Board (PFIAB) attacked the NIE 11-3/8 for 1974 as "seriously misleading" and "deficient," not least because it fed a "sense of complacency unsupported by the facts." The PFIAB activists concluded that the NIEs may have been acceptable in terms of the "most probable" situation but did not explore other possible (if less likely) scenarios.[41] When the PFIAB met with CIA leadership, a handful of PFIAB members—most notably, scientist Edward Teller, Ambassador Clare Boothe Luce, and Washington hand Leo Cherne—went on the attack. They accused the NIEs of a "political 'misassessment' of Soviet intentions" and of failing to consider military capabilities in relation to broader Soviet goals. Teller's criticisms were at once more technical and more sweeping; he worried about Soviet weapons research about which "we do not know or do not understand." Because of this uncertainty, Teller argued, the NIEs should not provide a single best estimate of Soviet aims and capabilities, but a full range of "all alternative hypotheses" not "confuted" by available evidence. What Teller called the "scientific" method would enumerate all of these possibilities but "should not attempt to render judgments about the comparative probability" of each one. He closed with a revealing exhortation, according to notes on the meeting:

> Dr. Teller hoped that the civil defense study could produce some accurate results, but he did not see its accuracy as its greatest value. The greatest value of the study would be if it called high level attention to the subject, which could in turn have the effect of changing US weapon employment [sic] policy and US civil defense planning.[42]

Teller's approach drove the competitive estimate project that took shape in the subsequent months: it would devote as much time to Soviet intentions as to Soviet capabilities; it would seek public attention as well as accuracy; and it would start with the assumption that previous intelligence analyses had woefully understated the Soviet threat. Some CIA officials rightly felt threatened by PFIAB; one worried:

> The real reason (I think) why some members of the Board are pushing for the "competitive estimate" by a group composed of at least some persons outside the Intelligence Community is that they want to be sure that the total package includes all the worst case possibilities that can be thought of.

At the height of the 1976 presidential campaign—while President Gerald Ford was beating back Ronald Reagan's challenge for the nomination from the right—Ford's national security advisor, Brent Scowcroft, secretly approved the competitive process. While PFIAB's initial proposals stressed narrow estimative issues—the inventories and capabilities of Soviet missiles, bombers, and air defense systems—he also approved a vague inquiry into "strategic goals...[and] strategic balance." The proposed competitive estimate soon came to include not just technical evaluations of Soviet weaponry but "conflicting interpretations of the Soviet stance in the world today."[43] There were three Team B's, each covering a topic relating to the Soviet military: missile accuracy, air defense capability, and Soviet strategic objectives. The first two, highly technical and using highly classified data, drew far less attention and controversy than the panel on Soviet strategic objectives, which has generally been referred to as the "Team B."[44] Each of these three was matched against a Team A of CIA analysts.

Richard Pipes quickly emerged as a leading contender for heading up the Team B panel on strategic objectives. The team members, selected by Pipes and approved by CIA, included long-time NIE critic General Daniel Graham, who sparked concerns about his ability to keep a secret. The group's advisory panel, including Paul Nitze, was more illustrious and no less critical of CIA estimates. Paul Wolfowitz, then Senator Jackson's man at the Arms Control and Disarmament Agency, joined the group on the recommendation of Richard Perle. As the final Team B report noted in an oft-quoted phrase, personnel "were deliberately selected from among experienced political and military analysts of Soviet affairs known to take a more somber view of the Soviet strategic threat than that accepted as the intelligence community's consensus."[45]

The strategic objectives panel took as a given that the NIEs were erroneous because they considered "the strategic threat in isolation from political and other considerations." Echoing the complaints of PFIAB members (with whom he consulted), Pipes felt that the NIEs were narrow technical documents that focused on the quantities and capabilities of Soviet weaponry rather than the purposes for which they were built and might be deployed. Pipes set the tone for his panel's work in declaring that the "product of Team B will be a 'lawyer's brief.'" In August 1976, as the panel divided up its responsibilities, Pipes emphasized that the team should focus on specifying the estimates' unstated assumptions, citing the NIEs' implicit statement that "the Soviet military effort is basically defensive and that the Soviets want to spend as little as possible on weapons." His group offered an alternative: the Soviets sought nuclear superiority in order to neutralize the American nuclear threat; given the Soviet conventional military superiority in Europe, it would then have complete freedom of action.[46]

Pipes proudly recounted the first encounter between his Team B panel and the in-house NIE estimators. From the "opening skirmish," the encounter was a "disaster" for the home team; his panel "tore to shreds" the CIA's "troop of young analysts," leaving it "badly mauled." *Competitive* intelligence had become *combative* intelligence. Pipes and others on Team B sought to publicize their results widely, fearing that their report would otherwise be "suppressed" by defeated CIA staffers. They proposed the "unilateral dissemination" of their report to those with appropriate security clearances, but were rebuffed by CIA officials.[47]

By the time Teams A and B presented their final work to PFIAB in December, the outsiders believed that they had prevailed. The meeting must have been more serene than the previous dust-up; Nitze's notes were primarily doodles, culminating in desultory lines with the elusiveness of a haiku: "confrontation/versus nuclear/confrontation/détente/Peace–war."[48] The final Team B report went well beyond such jottings, consisting of a strongly worded attack on the process and the products of NIEs. Of the forty-two pages in the body of the Team B report, only ten offered a reinterpretation of Soviet strategic objectives; the rest criticized the NIE assumptions and estimating process.

The Team B report cataloged what its members saw as numerous errors in specific intelligence estimates, attributing them to a fundamental misunderstanding about "Soviet strategic concepts." The NIEs tended toward "mirror-imaging," trying to interpret Soviet behavior and intentions in American terms. According to the report, Soviet thinking is "Clausewitzian," rooted in a grand strategy that integrated everything from propaganda to nuclear arms. While the Team B report contained little indication of the specific sources from which this argument was derived, it suggested that the key was in the "theoretical pronouncements of Communist leaders" considered in conjunction with "Soviet actions." The conclusion, as Pipes outlined, was that Soviet policies were offensive, in pursuit of "the historic ideal of a worldwide Communist state."[49] Based on growing Soviet military capabilities, and its attendant sense of confidence, the report concluded, the USSR would be able to initiate "*a dramatically more aggressive pursuit of their hegemonial [sic] objectives*, including direct military challenges to Western vital interests."[50] Examining the intelligence on military capabilities based on assessments of Soviet doctrine—derived, it seems, primarily from Soviet leaders' pronouncements—Team B had produced, as it set out to do, a "more somber" analysis of the nuclear threat.

In addition to that alternative scenario, Team B also offered a direct and substantial charge against the whole NIE process. The current process did not take as a starting assumption that the Soviet Union aimed at global hegemony through any means. The argument had a dialectical element to it: since the USSR aimed at world conquest, any efforts to reduce tensions could only, in this argument, be tactics to distract the enemy or to build up resources. Team

B accused CIA of bending to politics: Pipes initially criticized CIA for allow-ing NIE 11-3/8 to be "adversely affected by conditions of domestic politics"—language that was softened in the final report to an "inclination to minimize the Soviet strategic buildup because of its implications for détente."[51] Here, the public attack on détente spurred by Jackson and the classified attack on the CIA neatly merged.

The effect of the Team B conflict on the Soviet strategic NIEs is hard to assess. According to Pipes, the NIE authors were either convinced by the criticisms of the initial battle or were under political pressure to change their tune. In any case, he recounted, the draft NIE underwent a total overhaul, so that "in all essential points [it] agreed with Team B's position."[52] But the 1976 NIE was hardly the first to acknowledge the growing Soviet strategic threat; previous reports had done the same. And, as a new NIE on Soviet strategic objectives noted, the 1976–1977 estimates "continue[d] the trend of the last few years towards a more ominous interpretation of Soviet strategic objec-tives." In reviewing the NIEs from the 1970s, one fact is clear: there was a sharp increase in the number and stridency of dissents from the "consensus" reflected in the official estimates. Even the 1976 NIE reflected the escala-tion of long-standing disagreements within the intelligence community. Of the thirty paragraphs summarizing "Soviet policy for intercontinental forces," for instance, twelve were devoted to dissents, primarily from the chief of air force intelligence, who was occasionally joined by others from military intelli-gence. The tenor, too, was increasingly bellicose: military intelligence officials, for instance, registered dissents that the so-called consensus estimate was "in error," that it "understate[d], as have previous NIEs, the Soviet drive for stra-tegic superiority," and that it did not present "an adequate basis for averting global conflict in the years ahead."[53] Conflicts raged over a variety of issues, from the threats posed by weapons systems to the amount of Soviet defense spending (a controversy that made its way into public debate) to Soviet stra-tegic aims.

Some members of Team B sought to wage this battle against CIA in public. Pipes unsuccessfully sought declassification of the Team B report. Through the fall and winter of 1976, a number of details about Team B's conclusions were leaked to the press.[54] With the approval of a senior CIA official, Pipes provided "general background information" to New York Times reporter David Binder (a former student of Pipes), who published a front-page story on the day after Christmas.[55] Director of Central Intelligence George H. W. Bush expressed deep misgivings about the whole process. In one of the last NSC meetings of the Ford administration, a week before Jimmy Carter's inauguration, Bush complained that he had been "had." Attributing the leaks to a former general (i.e., Graham), he protested that the competitive estimate process had "been caught up in a lot of polemics, some of which I don't understand." On the other hand, Bush reported (contrary to the reports of Team B members), the CIA analysts could not be accused of "knuckling under to Team B."[56]

What was Team B's ultimate legacy? Pipes offered three items. First, Carter's national security advisor, Zbigniew Brzezinski, quietly concluded (according to Pipes) that "Team B had been correct in its assessment." Yet even those, like Brzezinski, who were predisposed to Team B's more somber view of the USSR, made little use of the report. Second, according to Pipes, Team B "contributed to the estimating process at the CIA."[57] Yet there is, at the very least, a significant strain of opinion that the NIE process proved to be impervious to Team B's challenges.[58] Finally, Pipes argued in his memoirs, Team B "deeply influenced" Ronald Reagan.

The somber ideas of Team B and the sunny optimism of Reagan seem an unlikely match. But many, perhaps even most, Team B members and supporters did find their way into the Reagan administration.[59] They were part of a larger stream of those with hardline views of the USSR who joined the Reagan campaign or administration. The most influential conduit was the Committee on the Present Danger (CPD). Nitze, old enough to remember an earlier group with this name in the late 1940s, had helped to lead CPD and many other anti-détente groups. The organizing work took place in the fall of 1976, just as Team B was hard at work, and included most members of Team B's Soviet objectives panel, including Graham, and Wolfowitz. Pipes took an active role in the organization, including writing its opening statement, "What Is the Soviet Union Up To?" (April 1977).[60] The piece opened with a criticism of U.S. foreign policy rooted in "mirror-imaging" and went on to emphasize the radical differences between the two superpowers, basing these differences on history, geography, and political culture; in short, it combined the Team B report with *Russia under the Old Regime*. Though he wrote other briefs for CPD in the late 1970s, Pipes gained widest attention for his *Commentary* article of 1978, "Why the Soviet Union Thinks It Can Fight and Win a Nuclear War," which again built on his previous work. Like "Russia's Mission, America's Destiny," it emphasized the differences between the "middle-class commercial, essentially Protestant" culture of the United States and the "extreme Social-Darwinist view" that permeates Soviet culture, especially its elite political culture. Pipes had originally entitled the piece, perhaps alluding to Wohlstetter's work, "Tango-ing Alone"; arms control, like an Argentinean dance, required two partners. The published title, however, summarized the core argument: the Soviet Union's posture was predicated on an offensive strategy—using missiles for "war fighting," not deterrence. Pipes also criticized the underpinnings of the Carter administration's policy, which ignored Soviet doctrine, a problem that could be cured by "a few evenings spent with a standard manual of Marxism-Leninism," and which did not recognize the fundamental differences between Russian and American society. The latter perhaps could be cured by a few evenings with Pipes's *Russia under the Old Regime*.[61]

These election-year attacks on Carter no doubt brought Pipes to the attention of fellow CPD members like Reagan and his national security advisor, Richard Allen. After serving on a campaign advisory committee for Reagan, Pipes became the Soviet expert on the National Security Council staff. His most important work at NSC came in his second and final year there, 1982: he wrote crucial portions of Reagan's famous Westminster Speech, including the paraphrase of Trotsky predicting that the USSR would end up on the "ash-heap of history." He also spearheaded the administration's effort to formulate a new Soviet policy. His charge from Reagan began from a premise similar to Team B's and familiar from the work of Conquest in the 1960s: Soviet expansionism was the result of the nature of Soviet domestic rule. The final document, approved weeks after Pipes's return to Harvard in January 1983, called for a three-part American approach to the USSR: "external resistance to Soviet imperialism; internal pressure on the USSR...; and negotiations on the basis of strict reciprocity." It took as a given that "Soviet aggressiveness has deep roots in the internal [Soviet] system," so the United States should "seek to redirect [Soviet] energies internally."[62] This document enshrined the ideas that Pipes, Conquest, and Ulam had reported to Senator Jackson a decade earlier.

Pipes had come a long way since first making these claims about the Russian roots of Soviet behavior. In December 1969, he had mentioned them at an academic conference; only a dozen years later, he had incorporated them into official U.S. policy. And he had not neglected his scholarship; in addition to *Russia under the Old Regime*, his two-volume biography of Petr Struve appeared. The book traced Struve as he traversed a wide political spectrum, from young Marxist to European liberal (Kadet) by 1917. He then found himself in increasingly reactionary company among the White Russians after the Bolshevik takeover in 1917. Like Struve, Pipes too had been liberal, voting for Henry Wallace in 1948 and "always vot[ing] Democratic" up until 1972.[63] Pipes's growing dissatisfaction with U.S. foreign policy attracted him to hard-line Democrats like Jackson and soon thereafter to the Republican Party, paralleling neoconservatives like Richard Perle. While Struve soon ended up in exile, Pipes's trajectory took him into the halls of power.

By the 1980s, Pipes worried far more about America's Soviet policy than about its Soviet experts. After leaving the Reagan White House, Pipes wrote *Survival Is Not Enough* (1984), a broadside against arms control, détente, academic Sovietology, and those who thought that the United States could keep the "Stalinist" USSR from its ultimate aim of world conquest by anything other than armaments. His only reason for optimism was that he thought that the Soviet system was approaching a "revolutionary situation," though he expressed firm doubt that any anti-Soviet revolution would occur.[64] Ulam and Conquest offered similarly hardline views about the nature of Soviet rule in the 1980s, as a rapid succession of general secretaries served in the Kremlin. These views had first emerged decades earlier, as Ulam, Conquest, and especially Pipes felt a growing distance from the institutions around them: their students, their colleagues, their universities, and, by the late 1960s, the policies of their government.

CHAPTER 11

LEFT TURN IN THE IVORY TOWER

Into the highly constrained and contentious environment of the late 1960s and early 1970s came a scholarly revolution. This period shared much with the Soviet experience that was so often the subject of these scholars' work. The so-called totalitarian model was, like imperial Russia, weakened internally well before the revolution began; mainstream political scientists like Frederick Barghoorn, Gordon Skilling, and Robert Tucker had already undermined many of its basic tenets. The historiographic upheavals, like the tumult of 1917, had two distinct phases, each with different actors and agents—yet the two revolutions were often conflated. The revolution's leaders envisioned a coherent "revisionist school" yet were in fact a congeries of fractions and factions, much like Bolshevism in 1917. Yet the differences mattered, too. Unlike the Bolsheviks, the scholarly revolutionaries contented themselves with intellectual victories rather than political power, a realm they left to a handful of conservative scholars. And unlike 1917, which pitted political parties against each other, the political divisions of the 1960s and 1970s were not always clear—and were ever more fiercely contested as the battle continued.

The first revolution in studies of the Russian/Soviet past involved interpretations of 1917. Historians like Ronald Grigor Suny and Reginald Zelnik, inspired by Leopold Haimson and armed with sources from their exchange trips to the USSR, had begun rewriting the history of revolutionary Russia. They were joined by political historians like Alexander Rabinowitch and William Rosenberg. Many identified with the Left but saw their historical task in professional terms, trying to distance themselves from the partisan and participant works that had dominated the historiography of 1917. The next wave of revisionism, often conflated with the 1917 group, included scholars writing the history of the 1920s and 1930s. The two groups differed substantially in topics, sources, and origins; while the new scholarship on 1917 made the revolution seem all but inevitable, scholars working on the 1920s emphasized contingency, challenging the claim that Stalinism was the inevitable result of Bolshevism.

The principal impresario trying to overturn this view of Stalinism was political scientist Stephen Cohen. He sought to make the 1920s into a historical epoch unto itself, not merely a brief rest between one phase of revolution beginning in 1917 and another beginning in 1929. Moshe Lewin, working in France in the late 1960s, made a similar claim about the divergent possibilities of the 1920s; Stalinism was not foreordained but only one response to Russia's overweening backwardness. Sheila Fitzpatrick, working in England in the 1960s and in the United States soon thereafter, was the most firmly oriented toward the history profession. All three scholars benefited from the new availability of sources in the 1960s, but in very different ways. Travel to the USSR affected Cohen's attitudes about the country more than it directly aided his research. Lewin made use of sources and scholarship published during Khrushchev's thaw of the late 1950s and early 1960s. Fitzpatrick's views were also shaped by the experience of living in the USSR and by the archival materials she examined. These three scholars differed greatly in terms of backgrounds, aspirations, politics, and intellectual aims, impeding Cohen's efforts to form a revisionist school.

Cohen came to the study of the USSR accidentally and with a strong desire to shape American views of and American policies toward the USSR. He interrupted his undergraduate career at Indiana University (1956–1960) to spend a year at the University of Birmingham, then a hotbed of labor and left-

Figure 11.1. Sheila Fitzpatrick in her Columbia University office, early 1970s.

wing activism—and home to the most active and interesting Soviet Studies program in the United Kingdom. Following a year of courses in Soviet Studies, Cohen signed up for a tour of the USSR, finding himself carrying luggage for a group of elderly Fabian Society members. He concluded that he had visited a "different civilization"; his experiences in the USSR, he later recalled, "eroded gray stereotypes and one-dimensional concepts." Cohen returned to Indiana determined to learn more, leading him to courses with Robert C. Tucker, with whom he began a long friendship. Tucker's ideas in the 1960s—his articles questioning the assumption that Stalinism was incipient in the Soviet system and his questions about alternatives to Stalinism—inspired Cohen to consider the Soviet 1920s as something other than prologue.[1]

Cohen's initial scholarly work on the USSR came while he was still a graduate student at Columbia's Russian Institute in the early 1960s, writing about Old Bolshevik Nikolai Bukharin, Stalin's greatest nemesis aside from Leon Trotsky. A brilliant economist, Bukharin fought against Stalin over Bolshevik policy for most of the 1920s, until losing out decisively in 1929. He was the defendant in a 1936 show trial, and two years later he was shot, apparently with the words "curses to Stalin" on his lips. Cohen's early writings on Bukharin revealed his desire to change American views of Soviet history and also to change American thinking about the contemporary USSR. He argued that Bukharin's ideas, if enacted, would have led Soviet history on a very different path. Armed with Boris Nicolaevsky's personal recollections and Bukharin's theoretical tracts, Cohen saw Bukharin as a paragon of "Leninist Bolshevism"—a "gradualist, reformist Leninism"—which contrasted sharply with Stalinism.[2] At stake was not just the Soviet past but the Soviet future and, perhaps, the soul of socialism.

Cohen announced his goals in his dissertation: to promote a new view of Soviet history and current Soviet politics. There was a chance for a democratic and peaceful socialism after the revolution of 1917, but it was brutally suppressed by Stalin's "revolution from above" in the late 1920s. Challenging what he called the totalitarian view that Stalinism was an inevitable outcome of 1917, Cohen insisted that the future of Bolshevism remained open after Lenin's departure from the political scene in 1923—indeed, all the way until 1929. Through the 1920s, there was no single party line since it was (in one party member's words) "a negotiated federation between groups, groupings, factions, and 'tendencies.'" By the end of the dissertation, Cohen contemplated how the Soviet Union would have been different if only Bukharin had prevailed. Cohen shifted the wistful counterfactual expressed by Michael Karpovich and Alexander Gerschenkron—if not for World War I, then Russia would have become a modern liberal nation— to the late 1920s: if not for Stalin, true socialism might have emerged. Cohen's book *Bukharin and the Bolshevik Revolution* (1973) demonstrated the openness of Bolshevik debate in the 1920s and the centrality of Bukharin to Bolshevik thinking. Bukharin's ideas of the 1920s—allowing debate in the political system, for instance, or strengthening the agricultural sector and thereby rendering Stalin's collectivization unnecessary—were for Cohen "the true prefiguration of the Communist future."[3] And the key figure in that prefiguration was Bukharin, whose ideas represented an alternative path.

Looking well past the 1920s, Cohen saw the whole Soviet era as a battle between Bukharinism and Stalinism. He found glimmers of Bukharin's gradualist vision of industrialization throughout Soviet history, especially in the Khrushchev years. Khrushchev's ouster in 1964 had done little to dampen Cohen's hopes that Bukharin's ideas would someday shape Soviet policy and would allow "socialism with a human face." In his conclusion, Cohen reminded his readers of the relevance of Bukharin for understanding the USSR in the 1970s, setting his book as a framework for understanding contemporary Soviet politics.[4]

Cohen's book generated little of the controversy that marked the work of the 1917 revisionists inspired by Haimson. Frederick Barghoorn and Adam Ulam were enthusiastic, worrying only that Bukharin appeared in too positive a light.[5] Even Leonard Schapiro provided fulsome praise, highlighting the broad implications of Cohen's book while challenging a few of its minor details; Cohen, Schapiro concluded, had "put right some of the sins of the fathers," perhaps including himself. Younger historians like Loren Graham (a reviewer for the publisher) and Peter Juviler waxed enthusiastic about Cohen's work. Graham, in particular, was closely attuned to the politics of the book, praising its ability to rise above the "Cold War hangups" that dominated the field. Only E. H. Carr, long critical of counterfactual history, offered significant dissent, accusing Cohen of promoting "the cult of Bukharin" at the cost of historical accuracy.[6] Carr aside, Cohen's book was well received by scholars from a variety of viewpoints and generations—not necessarily a harbinger of what was to come.

After publishing his Bukharin book in 1973, the focus of Cohen's career shifted. No longer would he publish the major historical research that went into that book; he instead would elaborate on the declarations at the outset and conclusion of the volume. In Sovietological journals, he promoted "the importance of being historical," that is, recognizing Stalin's rise not as a preordained outcome of 1917 but instead as a major upheaval in recent Russian history.[7] He also began writing a critical history of Sovietology, originally entitled "Up from Consensus: A Critique of Historical Soviet Studies"; it eventually appeared in 1985 as "Scholarly Missions." This project further underscored Cohen's explicit desire to overthrow the reigning scholarly interpretations and to promote what he called revisionism in its stead.[8]

Cohen reiterated his findings from *Bukharin and the Bolshevik Revolution* in a variety of academic and general interest outlets. He made the case for Bukharinism as a viable alternative to Stalinism and insisted upon the possibility of something other than Stalinism emerging in the 1920s. He also emphasized the ways in which modern anti-Stalinism in the Soviet Union had created an important if clandestine second life for Bukharin as a symbol of "socialism with a human face." At one conference, he criticized Western scholars for insisting upon a fundamental continuity from Bolshevism to Stalinism; in that view, Stalinism was "the logical, rightful, triumphant, and even inevitable continuation or outcome, of Bolshevism."[9] As Cohen quoted Leon Trotsky, "between Bolshevism and Stalinism [stands] not just a bloody line but a whole river of blood." Cohen's essay was as much historiographic as historical; it devoted as much attention to challenging prior scholarship as it did to rewriting the early history of Bolshevism. The essay downplayed the contemporary implications that weighed so heavily in Cohen's views, though it did mention that the prior scholarship's "continuity thesis" prevented a fuller understanding of "the system's capacity for reform" after Stalin's death in 1953.[10]

Cohen's work outside the academy expanded in the era of détente in the 1970s. He published articles on contemporary Soviet politics in a range of general interest publications, generally tending to the left: *New Republic, Socialism and Democracy,* the *New York Times,* and elsewhere. When writing for wider audiences, he stressed the contemporary implications of Bukharinism. Describing a "pluralist" approach to Soviet politics, Cohen appropriated this term, which was used by Robert Dahl and others, but he gave it a substantially different meaning, perhaps suggesting his growing distance from the disciplinary mainstream.[11] Cohen's sense of pluralism—implying contestations in the highest ranks of Soviet politics—led him to promote détente with the Soviet Union, in the process giving him unlikely comrades like Richard Nixon and Henry Kissinger. As he told a congressional committee in the fall of 1977, "the broadest possible détente" would serve U.S. interests far better than the "bombastic ultimatums" of Senator Henry M. "Scoop" Jackson and the "condescending preaching" of President Jimmy Carter. Only through constructive engagement, he insisted, could the United States discredit the ascendant conservative bloc of the Soviet Politburo; Soviet conservatives benefited from an aggressive U.S. posture. By seeking "fuller relations," the United States could promote the "party reformers" in the senior leadership and marginalize their conservative opponents. He opened his statement with this argument: there had been "significant pressures for political reform inside the Soviet Union" not long ago, and "there is no reason to assume that similar forces do not still exist." Pressed by a skeptical member of Congress, Cohen conceded that he could not name any reformers at the highest level of the Soviet political leadership, and that there were, most likely, none.[12] Cohen faced a difficult challenge in promoting constructive engagement. His argument relied on his encounters with underground rivulets of dissent within the Soviet system, yet these were invisible from afar.[13] Though Cohen himself knew about dissenters within the system, naming them publicly would put them in danger.

Within the academy, Cohen worked to create and lead a revisionist school, recruiting scholars who sought to challenge what he considered to be the reigning totalitarian orthodoxy. He continued to make the case for the existence of Soviet political reformism. His "Friends and Foes of Change," appearing in 1979, clustered the wide "diversity of Soviet opinion" into two broad strands: reformism and conservatism.[14] Citing dissenters' *samizdat* and *tamizdat* (underground works that were "self-published" or published abroad) as well as Western scholarship, he reframed the history of the Soviet Union—from Stalin's rise in the late 1920s through the Brezhnevite "stagnation" that defined his own time—as a battle between these two strands. Conservatives were currently in control but would ultimately yield to the reformers. Why was Cohen so optimistic? First, Soviet history had always alternated between reformism and conservatism and would continue to do so. Second, the Soviet Union faced a variety of problems, many of which were endemic to modern industrial societies, that conservatives would not be able to solve. Only the reformers had the answers to these modern problems. Cohen combined sociological thinking and political optimism to make the case for Soviet reform—and for a reform of American Soviet policy.

Cohen found an ally in Moshe Lewin, a historian who looked far beyond the Politburo battles that shaped Cohen's work. The two shared a commitment to exploring alternatives to Stalinism in the 1920s and a determination to recover such alternatives in present-day Soviet life. Lewin's background was nearly as unusual as his politics; he had been both a *kolkhoznik* (a collective farm worker) in the USSR and a *kibbutznik* in Israel. During his stint on a collective farm, as he fled eastward from his Vilnius home in advance of German troops, Lewin grew interested in becoming a historian of "the great gray mass, the popular classes." After the war, Lewin's "ideological commitment" to Zionism led him to Israel in 1951. Such commitments notwithstanding, Lewin pursued a scholarly career first at Tel Aviv University and then at the Sorbonne. Lewin drew inspiration from his advisor, economic historian Basile Kerblay. Lewin admired Kerblay's ability to move from the highly specific (the construction of the peasant hut, the organization of family life in rural Russia) to the general (the role of agriculture in the national economy, the sociological implications of modernizing a peasant society). Indeed, much of Lewin's own work explored the same interplay of local and national that defined Kerblay's writings.[15]

Lewin's perspective on the Soviet Union was shaped, as he later recalled, by his experiences there but also by his political commitments. Though immersed in Marxism in his youth—"having read volume one of *Capital* at age fifteen, I felt unbeatable"—by the time he reached forty-five, Lewin grew more skeptical; Marxism seemed insufficient to explain the supposedly Marxist USSR. Lewin melded Marxist economics and Weberian sociology to emphasize the political and economic aspects of Russia's backwardness. He rejected the universal trajectory of modernization implicit in both Marx and Weber, showing how Stalinism emerged from the ill-fated efforts at the rapid industrialization of a peasant society. The result was not (as Parsonians expected) the modernization of the peasant, but instead the peasantization of Soviet modernity.[16]

Like Cohen, Lewin focused at first on the 1920s in his dissertation-cum-first book, *Russian Peasants and Soviet Power* (French 1965, English 1968). True to his *kolkhoznik* roots and interest in social history, he studied Russian peasants as much as Soviet power, analyzing the early collectivization in 1928 and 1929. The first half of the book was devoted to the prehistory of collectivization, starting with three chapters outlining the key features of peasant society. The opening sections revealed a certain antipathy for the peasantry; he discussed the peasants' low "cultural level" and cited the fiercely anti-peasant writer Maxim Gorky, in whose views Lewin found "a great deal of truth." The second half of the book turned from the peasants to Soviet power. Relying on the historical scholarship produced by Soviet historians during the thaw, Lewin cataloged the many obstacles to and problems with collectivization. He dealt with the Politburo debates over agricultural policy, covering in close detail the period from Stalin's manipulation of a procurement crisis in early 1928 through the intensification of "class struggle in the villages" in late 1929. Bukharin's attention to peasant interests featured prominently in a chapter ominously entitled "The Last Opposition."[17]

Like Cohen would do later, Lewin let his implicit counterfactual claim peek out at a few moments; he wondered whether the opposition to Stalin could "have managed Russian affairs differently"—or did the "inexorable realities of life in a backward country" preclude an alternative to rapid industrialization? Bukharin's "repugnance" at watching the rise of Stalin's "bureaucratic Leviathan" served as a warning for what would soon follow. Lewin detailed the inexorable turn toward the strategy of a "swift, decisive blow" in the countryside. Collectivization was "purely administrative [as opposed to economic], conceived and executed on a vast scale by the leadership, and appallingly mismanaged at that"; it ultimately gave rise to "Stalinist totalitarian dictatorship." The book ended abruptly with the resumption of collectivization after a brief pause in 1930. Collectivization, which "*played a crucial part in shaping the future of the Soviet Union*," resulted directly from the procurement problems of 1927.[18]

Lewin concluded that Stalin's collectivization policies had run roughshod over Bukharin's policies in 1927 but that the Old Bolshevik nevertheless had an afterlife. Near the end of *Russian Peasants and Soviet Power* is a paragraph attributing post-Stalin reformism across Eastern Europe to Bukharinism: since Stalin's death in 1953, "almost every one of Bukharin's major theories has been revived in the communist world which, without admitting it, is making an enormous effort to implement his program of 1929." One of Lewin's principal aims was to make Stalin's policy of rapid and forced collectivization appear as a choice and not as a foreordained conclusion. To do so (he later noted), Lewin showed Bukharin "in a somewhat sympathetic light"; Lewin argued that Bukharin's agricultural policy held a much greater chance of success than Stalin's, even if Bukharin himself lacked the ability to enact it.[19] Lewin mined an extraordinary range of published sources, primarily official reports, all of which he read widely and closely. He also used some of the few works of Soviet scholarship produced in the short-lived liberalization of the late 1950s and early 1960s, making his book a product of the thaw.

Lewin's next book, too, was a result of the thaw, specifically the publication of Lenin's so-called testament. That long-suppressed document contained evaluations of those angling to succeed him. Lenin had qualified praise for Trotsky and harsh words for Stalin: "excessive self-assurance," an unwillingness to apply appropriate "caution," and rude to boot.[20] Lewin placed this testament at the center of *Lenin's Last Struggle* (1968), which followed Lewin's early work in looking to the 1920s for possible alternatives to Stalinism. His next book, *Political Undercurrents in Soviet Economic Debates* (1974), elaborated upon a minor theme in his dissertation: the legacy of Bukharinism in Soviet politics. The book spelled out, as Cohen's did, how the Politburo disputes of the 1920s mixed political conflicts with economic issues and therefore had a profound impact on the Soviet future. It then fleshed out the Bukharinist inspiration of Communist economic reform programs after Stalin's death.[21]

Lewin's books on collectivization, Lenin, and Bukharinism were closely linked. All three showed how Soviet politics and policies in the 1920s were not preordained but the result of significant internal struggle. All three highlighted the Bukharinist alternative to Stalin and emphasized the long afterlife of Bukharinism after the execution of its namesake. For all of their differences in depth, topic, and heft, they comprised a formidable reinterpretation of early Soviet history, emphasizing political contingency and social circumstances. Yet the reviewers' attention they received was in inverse proportion to the originality of the books. The shortest and least substantial, *Lenin's Last Struggle*, garnered reviews in most of the major Sovietological and disciplinary journals. E. H. Carr praised it as "exemplary," especially admiring Lewin's success at disproving the assumption that "the descent into Stalinism was inherent in the revolution itself."[22] The most empirical and original book, *Russian Peasants,* meanwhile, received only scattered and desultory reviews.[23]

These books were, perhaps, before their time—before the political turmoil in the United States and around the world in the late 1960s, before Stephen Cohen's efforts to create a revisionist school in the early 1970s, and before many other scholars had turned to the serious study of Soviet society. One indication of this delayed reaction is the much-belated reviewing of *Russian Peasants.* The *Slavic Review* and the *Journal of Economic Literature* waited until the mid-1970s before reviewing the book, years after the first edition. It was only in the mid-1970s that references to *Russian Peasants* appeared with any frequency. And the scholars who reviewed Lewin's books in the 1970s did so with deep skepticism. Economists like Gregory Grossman questioned Lewin's (and, by implication, Cohen's) resurrection of a Bukharinist agricultural policy.[24] Carr's review was splenetic; he prefaced his summary of Lewin's major argument about Bukharinism's legacy with "believe it or not" and concluded that the book's central proposition "makes no sense."[25] One factor in this pointed reception may have been Cohen's agitation for revisionism. He and Lewin had offered fulsome praise for each other's books, with Cohen's as much about revisionism as about Bukharin. Rehearsing the conservatism versus reformism labels that he would soon adopt in "Friends and Foes of Change," Cohen spent the first third of his essay discussing revisionism in general before mentioning Lewin's *Political Undercurrents.* Yet another of Cohen's recruits to revisionism had taken scholarship in a direction different from his own—and in a way that contributed fissures to the fractured field of Soviet history in the 1970s.

Sheila Fitzpatrick shared some of Cohen's dissatisfaction with the state of American studies of the USSR, but she sought a different kind of solution. She was, from the first, an outsider in American Sovietology in many dimensions: as an Australian trained in the United Kingdom, as a scholar hoping to specialize in Soviet rather than Russian history, and as a woman in a field that still had very few female graduate students, let alone senior faculty. Fitzpatrick emphasized the professional aims of historians over political agitation and did not see herself as a part of a school of Soviet Studies—a claim rooted perhaps in her outsider status. Her involvement in a revisionist school was not by design; as Fitzpatrick noted in one recollection, it was from Stephen Cohen that she "learned that there were Sovietological revisionists and that [she] was one of them."[26] Even if she had not considered herself a revisionist, though, she set out to revise views of Soviet history.

Such iconoclasm might have come from her father, a widely published Marxist historian of Australia. Brian Fitzpatrick was no Communist and did not see the USSR as "the socialist fatherland," in the words of one admirer. But he nevertheless believed it "well worth supporting." Sheila Fitzpatrick studied music in

university, writing her major paper on the history of Soviet music.[27] Winning
a fellowship to Oxford, she enrolled at St. Antony's College in 1964 to pursue
advanced study in Russian history. Her research there built upon her prior interest in Soviet culture, a topic also of great interest to her advisor, Max Hayward.
Hayward represented a distinctly British model of amateur scholar-diplomat
particularly common at St. Antony's. He had witnessed the *Zhdanovshchina* of
the late 1940s from the British embassy in Moscow and thereafter, in the words
of one friend, devoted his career to serving as a "custodian of Russian literature
in the West," in much the same way as Gleb Struve did in Berkeley.[28] While in
the United Kingdom, Fitzpatrick also came to know both Carr and Schapiro,
whose dislike for each other spilled over from the professional to the personal.
Their animosities aside, Fitzpatrick gravitated to these professional historians,
viewing the work by Hayward and his St. Antony's colleagues as "diplomatic
and literary gossip." Yet she also evinced skepticism for American scholarship
on the Soviet Union, finding it deeply ideological. Even the best works, she
thought, sandwiched good empirical research between "statements of ideological orthodoxy at beginning and end"; other works dispensed even with the valuable empirical material in the middle. She professed less interest in the politics
or guiding interpretations than in the data themselves.[29]

Fitzpatrick's dissertation topic came from her desire to write a historical work about the Soviet period that touched on culture. There were, at the
time, very few works on Soviet history; most accounts of Soviet politics were
written by political scientists while Soviet culture was the province of literature departments. She began with the idea of writing a biography of Anatolii
Lunacharskii, a Bolshevik intellectual and the first People's Commissar of
Enlightenment (i.e., education); Fitzpatrick found "intriguing" this "Bolshevik
who disliked politics [and] wrote plays in his spare time." The fact that he
had left behind such a large published record—drama, criticism, educational
theory, religion, and international relations—made Lunacharskii all the more
tempting as a historical subject. Yet archival sources would be necessary to
narrate Lunacharskii's history—and to fulfill Fitzpatrick's aims of doing a
proper scholarly history of the Soviet period. Visiting Moscow on the British
exchange program, Fitzpatrick faced the usual impediments to research.
Eventually, an archivist at the Central State Archive of the October Revolution
brought Fitzpatrick some protocols from policy meetings at the Commissariat
of Enlightenment. These summaries of the group's weekly meetings provided
the empirical base she needed. Fitzpatrick also immersed herself in the Soviet
intelligentsia, including two warring circles of Lunacharskii family descen-
dants. She also frequented the group of critics connected to *Novyi mir*, including poet Evgenii Evtushenko. Her experience in the Soviet Union was defined
around these intelligentsia contacts and her work in the archives.[30]

Fitzpatrick's *The Commissariat of Enlightenment* (1970) traced the transformation of a revolutionary organization full of "the excitement of a world in flux" into a bureaucratic body with limited responsibilities and even more limited resources—a fall from revolutionary grace that took only four short years. What had begun as an exploration of a leading intellectual had evolved into a "case study in the problems of revolutionary government." In their revolutionary enthusiasm, commissariat officials interpreted their charge broadly, aiming to provide universal general education while also sponsoring scholarly work, cultural events, adult education, and much more. Yet amid revolutionary upheaval and civil war, these aspirations seemed increasingly utopian. By 1921, none of the original goals had been met, and the thrust of policies had moved decisively against these ambitions. At the end of this story of unmet goals, Fitzpatrick found a glimmer of hope; perhaps it was enough, the final sentences noted, that "these policies were formulated" at all amid the chaos of the early Soviet period.[31]

As Fitzpatrick recalled later, she wanted her first book to tell Soviet history as history. She thought this might be controversial in the late 1960s, especially for American scholars, because it meant "studying the society"; she worried that it fit poorly with the American approach that she characterized as "looking at the political system and showing how bad it was."[32] But American scholarly reviewers focused less on the politics of her work and more on its argument, context, and evidence; two younger scholars sympathetic to new scholarly directions—political scientist Gail Lapidus and historian of science Loren Graham—both admired the book's research but bemoaned that the book's detailed analysis of the commissariat's inner workings left "social and political background...thin" and left out a "broader analytical framework." As she completed the book, Fitzpatrick returned to Moscow and then lectured at the University of Birmingham, where she first met Moshe Lewin.[33] Working in the small but fissile group of Sovietologists in the United Kingdom, Fitzpatrick proclaimed not a political agenda but a professional agenda: to write a historical account of a Soviet institution.

Coming to teaching posts in the United States, Fitzpatrick began work on a second volume dealing with Lunacharskii and his Commissariat of Enlightenment. When, in 1975, she joined the Columbia faculty, she was already a familiar figure there. The previous year, she had organized a conference on "the cultural revolution in Russia" under the auspices of Columbia's Russian Institute. The conference took up the subject of an article she had published earlier that year under the same title—a phrase that had struck Fitzpatrick on her first trip to the USSR in 1966. While there, she had followed the turmoil of Mao Zedong's revolution through the prism of the Soviet press. As she followed Lunacharskii's commissariat through the 1920s, she saw parallels with China in the 1960s.[34]

Fitzpatrick defined Russia's cultural revolution, which she dated from 1928 to 1932, in terms that paralleled China's. Its leaders considered it the "proletarian seizure of power on the cultural front" and invoked it to overturn "the fleeing bureaucrat and the wavering intellectual." There were differences, though. The Soviet revolution, unlike the Chinese one, was "somewhere between class war and class war game"; the weapons were "words not bullets," which destroyed careers but not lives. Fitzpatrick dated the arrival of the cultural revolution into "official favour" in 1928; she argued that Soviet officials were responding to rather than generating the upheaval. She characterized the cultural revolution as "a real grass-roots reaction" that was "a spontaneous expression of the attitude of rank-and-file communists." While gesturing toward the bottom-up approach of 1917 revisionists like Suny, Fitzpatrick was always careful with modifiers and delimiters; she also noted the ways that party leaders used dissent from below to serve their own purposes. Though Stalin "had not created" the cultural revolution, he effectively "used" it "as a means of extending political control into the cultural sphere" and, most notably, "discrediting the Party right wing" led by Bukharin.[35] Like the historians of 1917, Fitzpatrick was primarily interested in showing how social forces influenced high politics.

Fitzpatrick's ideas of cultural revolution indicated the capaciousness and the contradictions of a revisionist school. Cohen saw Bukharin as solely a victim of Stalin's treachery where Fitzpatrick instead saw social roots for Bukharin's demise. Bukharin was the ancien régime in a revolutionary period, overthrown by Stalin, yes, but in the name of the dispossessed seeking to eliminate "bourgeois" influence. In spite of this fundamental difference, Cohen remained a supporter of Fitzpatrick, helping her to organize the cultural revolution conference at Columbia in November 1974. That conference soon became a landmark in the field of Soviet history, both for its innovation and for the intense outrage it provoked. Fitzpatrick declared the conference goal to be a simple one: to try to write scholarly, professional histories of Russian society in the Soviet period, especially the tumultuous years of the first Five-Year Plan.[36] The presenters gathered in New York that November were primarily on the younger side, although some sympathetic members of the prior generation served as commentators. Most of the articles in the published volume traced from the late 1920s through the 1930s the tribulations of a single discipline: education, rural economy/sociology, history, law, literature, urban planning. Political scientist Jerry Hough asked to attend the conference as a commentator—and worked quickly to win not just Fitzpatrick's professional loyalty but also her personal attention; they were married within a year of meeting at that conference.[37]

The general pattern of cultural revolution that appeared in most of the essays was similar. Internal disputes in a given discipline accelerated in the mid-1920s; the more radical/proletarian group invoked cultural revolution and called upon external political authority to support its cause. At some point between 1928 and 1931–1932, this radical group established a new orthodoxy, marginalizing the old guard in the process. In each case, then, the cultural revolution began from below—not instigated by the workers but by intellectuals acting in the name of the workers. Moshe Lewin's contribution continued in the vein of his earlier work, situated at the intersection of social and political history; his cultural revolution was about the peasantization of the cities—echoing, many years later, Menshevik complaints about working-class consciousness in World War I era Petrograd. Hough's conclusion did much to stir the pot; he criticized the current scholarship on totalitarianism for failing to account for the cultural revolution and thus misunderstanding the history and politics of Stalinism.[38]

The conference contained a slight but significant revision of what the cultural revolution was. Fitzpatrick changed the end date from 1932 (in her original article) to 1931 in the book, a slight chronological shift that marked a larger intellectual one.[39] In her article, she had dated the end of the cultural revolution to the dissolution of RAPP (Russian Association of Proletarian Writers) in April 1932. Her contribution to the conference volume dated the end to late 1931, with the rehabilitation of bourgeois engineers, attacks on Communist intellectuals, tightening of labor discipline, and a slowdown in promoting workers "from the factory bench."[40] Fitzpatrick's cultural revolution was, suddenly, less cultural (in the sense of arts and scholarship) and more sociological, stressing the promotion of and impediments to upward mobility. Cultural revolution ebbed, and the era that one sociologist famously termed "the great retreat" began.[41] This shift from cultural events to sociological ones is one indication of Fitzpatrick's growing interest in sociological approaches to the USSR, which Hough was then exploring.[42]

After a discouraging response from publishers, *Cultural Revolution in Russia* appeared in 1978. The early reviews of the book were mixed in tone and temper. British economic historian R. W. Davies praised the book, alongside Tucker and Cohen's collection on Stalinism, for marking "the beginning of a new stage in the study of the Soviet Union." Such praise must have especially gratified Fitzpatrick, who later described her motives for organizing the conference as part of her "one-woman crusade to establish the discipline of history in the study of the Soviet past."[43] Yet more indicative of the later response was the item in the *American Historical Review,* which expressed some skepticism about the common trajectory of the essays, but saw the collection as a manifesto "bearing the stamp" of the editor and her husband. As Fitzpatrick later wrote, she felt the controversies surrounding *Cultural Revolution* to be "more for political than intellectual reasons."[44]

Fitzpatrick's next monograph, *Education and Social Mobility* (1979), continued this turn to the sociological. She explained this turn as part of her effort to "remake herself as an American" in scholarly terms and also as the result of her discussions with Hough.[45] The book began as a sequel to her Lunacharskii volume but ultimately moved into quite different territory. While much of the book was an archive-based cultural and institutional history along the lines of *Commissariat of Enlightenment,* other sections became sociological investigations of education in Soviet society. She emphasized class-based "affirmative action" (her words), which provided upward mobility to millions of workers and their children. Even rural dwellers benefited from education, which provided opportunities for "departure from the countryside." (Fitzpatrick also mentioned in this discussion the harsh Soviet policies in rural areas, including collectivization and deportation.) These upwardly mobile workers and peasants—the *vydvizhentsy*—were the intended beneficiaries of the rise of mass education in conjunction with class-based affirmative action. These *vydvizhentsy* became "a loyal elite capable of leading an industrial state." Their leadership, however, differed from that of the Old Bolsheviks, who were predominantly intellectuals like Lenin and Bukharin. Once in power, the *vydvizhentsy* initiated by the mid-1930s a new social conservatism that stood in stark contrast to the excitement of cultural revolution that had preceded it. This great retreat, Fitzpatrick concluded, "was really the secondary consequence" of "the mass promotion of former workers and peasants into the Soviet political elite."[46] Fitzpatrick's argument here grew more similar to Lewin's; they both saw the spread of a lower-class ethos as a central feature, even a cause, of Stalinism.

Reviewers of *Education and Social Mobility* pointed out that the empirical base was both narrower and more problematic than that of *Commissariat of Enlightenment*. More than one reviewer questioned Fitzpatrick's reliance on Soviet statistics, especially to document a trend so closely linked to the regime's mission; categories of worker-born and peasant-born, never simple, were especially problematic given the intensity of Soviet claims and the inherent difficulties of definition.[47] Kendall Bailes, who had just published a book that overlapped substantially with *Education and Social Mobility* in theme and content, challenged Fitzpatrick's claims that the *vydvizhentsy* were a product of Soviet *cultural* policy rather than a side effect of Soviet *economic* policy. Bailes saw such upward mobility as an "inescapable consequence of rapid industrialization," irrespective of Soviet intentions to create a new elite.[48] The differences between Bailes and Fitzpatrick replicated an early discussion of social mobility in the USSR, with Bailes (like Alex Inkeles) emphasizing the imperatives of industrialization and Fitzpatrick (like Merle Fainsod) stressing the political implications.

The final chapter of *Education and Social Mobility,* "The 'New Class,' " was the most sociological. It calculated the number of 1930s *vydvizhentsy* who had risen to leadership positions in the last full year of Stalin's life, 1952. Exactly half of the ministers and deputy ministers were *vydvizhentsy* of the first Five-Year Plan (1928–1932), and *vydvizhentsy* were well represented among Central Committee members, too. These *vydvizhentsy* still dominated in the 1970s, accounting for half of the 1977 Politburo. The impact of this upward mobility went well beyond the cultural retreat of the late 1930s. As they aged, their vision of the Soviet revolution grew increasingly important, eventually crowding out other visions. Fitzpatrick concluded: "For the *vydvizhentsy*, industrialization was a heroic achievement—their own, Stalin's and that of Soviet power—and their promotion, linked with the industrialization drive, was a fulfillment of the promises of the revolution."[49] Her work expanded in terms of chronology and interpretive reach, and increasingly emphasized the sociological impact on Soviet leadership-the result, perhaps of Fitzpatrick's collaboration with Hough.

With this collaboration came growing controversy, as historians greeted Fitzpatrick's work with increasing skepticism and hostility. Particularly jarring was Fitzpatrick's experience at Columbia, where she had been an untenured associate professor. Though a member of the History Department, Fitzpatrick's principal contacts and her office were at the Russian Institute; her fate was, to a large degree, in the hands of the institute's two tenured historians, Leopold Haimson and Marc Raeff. Raeff, a Karpovich student teaching intellectual history, shared his advisor's wariness about the enterprise of Soviet history. The Russian Institute was not a unified place in the late 1970s, leaving untenured faculty in an especially vulnerable spot. Haimson later recalled that he voted in favor of Fitzpatrick's tenure while Raeff voted against, but this split vote among Russianists would be a red flag in a tenure case.[50] Ultimately, she moved to the University of Texas.

Some of the controversy surrounding Fitzpatrick was collateral damage from attacks against Hough. Hough spent his first decade in the field trying to bring the study of Soviet politics into the mainstream of the political science profession and trying to interest his political scientist colleagues in using the USSR as one of their comparative cases rather than as an exception to every political rule. His first book, *The Soviet Prefects* (1969), had been well received, and he soon became one of the leading young scholars of Soviet politics. He was thus an easy choice to revise and update the classic Soviet politics textbook written by his thesis advisor, Merle Fainsod. It was here that the trouble started. The revision of the Fainsod book was a signal moment in the increasing divisions within the field of Soviet Studies and revealed a growing separation of professional political science from policy-oriented work, on the one hand, and historians, on the other.

By all accounts, the decision to invite Hough to update *How Russia Is Ruled* was agreeable to all parties involved: Hough, the Russian Research Center (in whose series the 1953 original and 1963 revision appeared), Harvard University Press, and the Fainsod family (including Merle's wife, Elizabeth, a one-time RRC employee, and daughter Mary, a recent Ph.D. in political science). Hough saw himself as "instinctively a Fainsodian," interested like his advisor in "the structure of power in the Soviet Union."[51] His energy and ambition had given him good standing in the field of Soviet politics and in the field of political science more generally. Yet Hough's ultimate aims might have seemed, from the outset, to be a departure from his advisor's. Fainsod's two books on Soviet politics were as much political history as political science; both were deeply historical accounts with no systematic comparison. Fainsod's interests had expanded in the 1960s as he sought to contribute to the political development approach that dominated his field, but those changes were not fully reflected in his 1963 revision of *How Russia Is Ruled,* and he wrote no other broad analyses of Soviet politics. Hough, in contrast, spent much of the late 1960s and 1970s working on empirical measures of power in the Soviet Union as a route to a new theory of politics—a tendency visible in the articles assembled into *The Soviet Union and Social Science Theory* (1977). Yet this "disciplinization" of Soviet politics had political implications. Adam Ulam, for instance, tempered his praise for Hough's scholarly contributions by questioning the emphasis of his political science scholarship; Hough's efforts to measure empirically Soviet administrative processes, Ulam said, ignored "the underlying premises of the system"—a complaint identical to others levied against sociological works like *The Soviet Citizen.*[52] Hough focused on the process of Soviet power, while Ulam was more interested in its nature.

The conflict over Hough's revision of *How Russia Is Ruled* arose very late in the publication process. When RRC executive committee members received the galleys in August 1978, they were sharply critical of both the style and the content of Hough's revision. Nevertheless, many executive committee members "favor[ed] publication of Hough's book *as his book,*" leaving out Fainsod entirely. But the press refused to drop the name of the original author, a position RRC executive committee member Donald Fanger attributed to its interest in marketing the book. The executive committee quickly discovered that its legal rights were, as director Abram Bergson put it, "minimal." The best that the press would do is put Fainsod as second author and exclude the words *Russia* and *Ruled* from the title. The press was also willing to exclude the book from the RRC series; the RRC executive committee minutes noted that Hough would be informed that the removal from the series was a purely procedural decision and was "in no way a reflection on the scholarly quality of the work," which Richard Pipes, among others, praised in some of its particulars.[53] After difficult negotiations, primarily between RRC and the press, the book appeared. This resolution, however, left a bitterness among most of the parties that still has not healed.

The press proposed the book's new title, *How the Soviet Union Is Governed*, which more accurately reflected its contents and established some lexical distance from Fainsod's original. The new version, after all, focused on techniques of governance rather than on totalitarian rule. Many reviewers fixed on this title change, attributing it to Hough and considering it anathema to Fainsod's ideas. Coincidentally, though, the title echoed one that Fainsod had approved in 1955 for a French edition that never appeared: *Comment l'URSS est gouvernée*.[54] Billed as a "thoroughly revised and expanded" version, Hough's 1979 revision compressed the historical material and added lengthy discussions on policy processes. After explaining the origins of the Soviet system, Fainsod had dispensed with historical analysis, presuming a fundamental continuity over time. Hough, in contrast, dealt with the evolution of the Soviet system. Pipes rightly noted, also, the difference between Fainsod's 1953 conclusion that "the totalitarian regime does not shed its police-state characteristics; it dies when power is wrenched from its hands" and Hough's closing discussion of "within-system evolution."[55] Yet Pipes made no mention of Fainsod's 1963 revision of *How Russia Is Ruled*, which acknowledged dramatic changes to the Soviet system and predicted further changes to come. Fainsod in 1963 emphasized the "rational base" for Khrushchev's policies and identified (much as Barrington Moore Jr. had done a decade earlier) tensions between the "supercentralization" of Stalinism and the "rational management of a highly industrialized society" under Khrushchev. While the chances that the imperatives of industrialization would tear down totalitarian rule did "not appear great," Fainsod had expected the transformation of the system to be ongoing. The closing sentence of the 1963 edition struck a far different tone than that of the original: "Communists and non-Communists disagree fundamentally on many issues, but they share a common interest in the survival of the human race."[56] Pipes may have been comparing the Fainsod of the early 1950s to the Hough of the late 1970s, ignoring the evolution of Fainsod's ideas in the 1960s—after his important visit to the USSR in 1956, his revision of the textbook, and his efforts to connect with the disciplinary mainstream.

In other aspects, there was a significant distance between Fainsod's and Hough's ideas, visible especially in their respective chapters on Stalinism. Hough's chapter on the 1930s, "The Years of Transformation and Petrification," built on his conversations with Fitzpatrick, dwelling on the cultural revolution more than on controls and tensions. Even more controversial was Hough's estimates of the toll of the purges; he rejected Boris Nicolaevsky's estimate of 10.5 million and Robert Conquest's of 3 million. Citing census data and another Soviet source, Hough concluded that a figure in the "low hundreds of thousands," perhaps even in the "tens of thousands," was most likely. This number, so far below other estimates, was sure to provoke controversy—and it did, ensuring that the book received many negative reviews.[57]

Another target of criticism owed its origins to Hough's engagement with broader scholarship in political science. Hough concluded his discussion of local political institutions by noting that a detailed study of Soviet local governance would most likely yield "many of the same conclusions that Robert Dahl did in his study of New Haven."[58] How could anyone equate New Haven, Connecticut, and a Soviet city? critics asked. Did he really consider the USSR to be a democratic society like the United States? Yet this is precisely the opposite of Hough's point. Hough chose New Haven because it was the subject of one of the most important books on U.S. politics, Robert Dahl's *Who Governs?* (1961). Dahl made the point, a foundational one for "pluralist" political scientists, that a handful of interested "influentials" mattered more than the electorate. Hough had already engaged Dahl's argument in a separate article in which he mustered evidence from the Soviet Union to challenge Dahl's definition of power. In *How the Soviet Union Is Governed*, Hough noted that the fate of a Soviet city was not "wholly in the hands of the local leaders or citizenry"—but this fact was not unusual; indeed, such powerlessness was "a universal in modern society."[59] But the intellectual background behind Hough's comparison, indeed behind his whole approach, had little to do with the book's ultimate reception.

Much of the controversy surrounding *How the Soviet Union Is Governed* revolved around issues tangential to the author's politics, as was evident in Richard Pipes's review in *Commentary*. The first was the question of authorship: was Hough entitled to rewrite his advisor's book if he reached quite different conclusions? Pipes also questioned the "moral right" of the publisher to "butcher" Fainsod's book and pointed to the book's removal from the RRC series as an indication of "what the book's original sponsor thought of the matter." The second issue was about U.S. foreign policy. Pipes lambasted the book for its "very unrealistic, sugar-coated view of the Soviet Union" and wondered whether Hough was too soft on the Soviet system. On the other side, Robert Daniels praised Hough for providing an argument for a less confrontational policy toward the USSR.[60] Pipes and Daniels focused as much on the policy implications of Hough's book as on its fundamental claim that the Soviet system of politics was susceptible to "scientific" analysis.

Those more deeply ensconced in political science scholarship took a different tack. Oxford political scientist Archie Brown praised Hough's revision as the most "comprehensive, advanced, and original textbook on the Soviet political system." Another review praised Hough's "relentlessly professional" efforts to apply the techniques of social science to the study of Soviet politics.[61] For the academically inclined, the book was an effort to bring Soviet politics back into political science departments; for those interested in shaping U.S. policy, it was something very different.

The controversy over *How the Soviet Union Is Governed* cast a shadow over political science and historical studies of the Soviet Union in the 1980s. Like the controversies swirling around Fitzpatrick, the issues began with professional concerns but quickly melded with personal and political conflicts.[62] The result was a field that entered the Soviet Union's last decade, the 1980s, sharply divided. Indeed, the controversies in historical and political studies of the USSR came to resemble trench warfare; they were hotly contested conflicts that produced high casualties but yielded little forward progress.

The early 1980s continued in this vein. Fitzpatrick came under attack for her book *The Russian Revolution* (1982). Appearing in an Oxford University Press series designed for the general reader, the book offered a synthetic and synoptic argument about the Russian Revolution that built on many of her earlier writings. Central to the book was an expansion of the parameters of the revolution: it did not end with the Bolshevik takeover but only began there, lasting until the subsiding of the enthusiasms of the first Five-Year Plan in 1932. Perhaps expanding upon Barrington Moore's work, Fitzpatrick focused on three themes that ultimately came to define the revolution: "terror, progress, and upward mobility." Fitzpatrick traced the ebb and flow of revolutionary fervor in the 1920s, emphasizing the role of the *vydvizhentsy,* who challenged the old intelligentsia (within and beyond the Communist Party) and sought to enter a new technical intelligentsia themselves. Bristling at the lack of revolutionary fervor in the New Economic Policy of the 1920s, these radicals were not ready to declare the revolution over until they had created a revolutionary society and had risen into the ruling elite themselves. By 1932, Fitzpatrick argued, the revolution was complete; class-war ideology waned, a new administrative elite took the reins, and Stalin and the secret police each consolidated their roles. Fitzpatrick saw the book as an effort to write a synthetic history of Russia's revolutionary years. She scolded prior historians for being "preoccupied with questions of moral judgment" and insisted that her aim was merely to treat the revolution as "a part of history, not an aspect of contemporary politics." She identified winners and losers but, unlike partisan historians, did not identify with them. Fitzpatrick aimed to explore the social dimensions of the revolution: what did Russians—workers, intellectuals, *apparatchiks*—mean when they talked about class?[63]

Fitzpatrick's book received a chilly reception from most historians. Many criticized her desire to avoid moral judgments, questioning whether it was possible or desirable. Leonard Schapiro, perhaps seeing a little of his nemesis Carr's attitude in Fitzpatrick's discussion, was especially harsh. He attacked Fitzpatrick's arguments, sources, and methods, including her determination to use official descriptions rather than memoir accounts; her "prim summary" of the brutality of early Soviet life; and her determination to focus not on

1917 but on the first fifteen years of Soviet rule. Allen Wildman, a pioneer in social and labor history of 1917, rejected Fitzpatrick's claims that the "chiliastic, truly 'class conscious' workers of 1917" could become the *apparatchiks* of the Bolshevik regime.[64] The *Newsweek* reviewer seemed the most willing to endorse Fitzpatrick's hope that she could "reclaim [the Russian Revolution] for history."[65] Within the ranks of professional historians, politics was very much at work, another sign of the divisions within the field in the early 1980s.

Nowhere were these fissures more visible than in a symposium on Stalinism that appeared in *Russian Review* in 1986, only a year after Mikhail Gorbachev took the helm of a stagnating USSR. The conflict began with a review essay by Fitzpatrick, "New Perspectives on Stalinism." She proclaimed her desire to offer a friendly review and critique of some younger scholars studying Stalinism, part of a movement she identified as "revisionist": J. Arch Getty, Hiroaki Kuromiya, Roberta Manning, Gábor Rittersporn, and Lynne Viola.[66] These scholars hardly constituted a school of thought about Soviet history, but they did share some common traits. All were interested in advancing historical studies of the Soviet Union into the 1930s. All made use of the Smolensk Archive, which had been wallowing in disuse at the National Archives since Fainsod's monograph in 1958. Most of this cohort proclaimed their principal goals in professional rather than political terms, much like Fitzpatrick. Their works were nevertheless often understood as political rather than professional (also like Fitzpatrick). Getty's *Origins of the Great Purges,* relying on the Smolensk materials, stressed the need to rescue the study of the 1930s from "political scientists and émigré journalists" and to put it in historians' hands. His advisor Manning used the same sources for her account of an early purge in the Smolensk region. Viola and Kuromiya, Princeton classmates in the early 1980s, both wrote about the first Five-Year Plan years (1928–1932), Viola about the workers recruited to help collectivize the peasantry, and Kuromiya about the "industrial revolution" under Stalin. Both made use of the Smolensk Archive as well as material they had gathered in the Soviet Union while on IREX grants. Rittersporn, the fifth "young revisionist," relied exclusively on the Smolensk Archive, with a heavier emphasis on the national politics of the purges.[67] While all of these historians wrote, broadly speaking, against the grain of the totalitarian approach, only Manning foregrounded her differences with prior scholars. Political agendas and not just professional ones were occasionally visible. Manning later recalled her desire to shake up American Sovietology; Rittersporn published his first work in radical French and American journals.[68]

In her *Russian Review* article, Fitzpatrick sought to engage this new scholarship, suggesting some concerns and proposing new directions. In positive tones that reflected her own agenda for the study of the USSR, Fitzpatrick saw this new cohort of historians as a group with a strong "desire to assert an identity *as historians*" and with the aim to demonstrate that "Soviet history is a legitimate field." A second characteristic of this group was its effort to distinguish itself from the "older generation of Sovietologists," who could not look beyond "the totalitarian model." While the new cohort shared these traits with Fitzpatrick, they also moved in different directions. Its members were shaped by the profession's trend toward social history—and may have shared, Fitzpatrick speculated, social historians' "instincts [that were] often more radical than that of the historical profession as a whole." She was, however, addressing other social historians about the promises and pitfalls of studying Soviet society. While Fitzpatrick organized her discussion around three different topics, the ensuing debate focused only on the last, "social initiatives and responses"; the other two, social hierarchies and social mobility, would define her future scholarly agenda more than that of the "young revisionists." Fitzpatrick offered a taxonomy of social initiative arranged along a continuum of revolution from above (Stalin's term) to revolution from below (Fitzpatrick's). She noted that most of the social historians had steered away from claims of social initiative for Stalinism, preferring instead to emphasize the "lack of [total] regime control" or policies appealing to "social constituencies." Fitzpatrick concluded the article by expressing her concern that these new social historians—the "young Turks"— had yet to consider Soviet society apart from the Soviet state; as a result, they had not yet written a "real social history" of the 1930s.[69] Unlike social historians of the United States and Western Europe, who had written social histories "with the politics left out" (as the phrase went), political institutions seemed central to the work of social historians of Stalinism.

Fitzpatrick's article became a lightning rod for criticism from all sides. Four respondents to the original article, Stephen Cohen, Germanist Geoff Eley, historian Peter Kenez, and political scientist Alfred G. Meyer, all took her to task. Taken together, the responses revealed both the conceptual problems plaguing the historical study of the Soviet Union and the high emotions and political stakes. Long-time supporter Cohen protested that she did not properly cite Robert Tucker's prior efforts to dethrone notions of totalitarianism, a view he shared with Meyer. Cohen spent more space attacking Fitzpatrick for her treatment of the Great Terror, which he saw as the defining element of the 1930s—"a part of almost everything else" that happened in that decade. Peter Kenez made a similar statement in his response and worried that the revisionists' "outlandish" views left no room for moral judgment. The end result, Kenez feared, was that Stalin would end up "de-demonized," reduced to a minor player in the phenomenon that bears his name.[70]

A round of replies followed, variously emphasizing professional, political, and personal concerns. Most of the young Turk respondents in the second round—including Getty, Manning, and Kuromiya—cited professional concerns over political ones. Getty insisted upon a "strict approach to source criticism, rigorous methodology, and attention to detail"; Manning on the need for hypothesis testing; Kuromiya on historical scholarship as the group's central aim. Their determination to use archival records, to question the generalizations made by memoirists, and to conform to the norms of historical scholarship were central elements of their project. These historians (in the inimitable words of *Russian Review* editor Daniel Field), "cl[u]ng to Clio's gown, and not to Stalin's boots."[71]

The young revisionists shared broad professional goals with Fitzpatrick, but common aims and approaches were quickly lost in a round of recriminations that suggested feelings of personal betrayal. The AAASS sessions on Stalinism became sites of heated conflict, one observer noted wryly, thus "escap[ing] the usual torpor of academic conferences."[72] Some of the young Turks, in their retorts, noted their indebtedness to Fitzpatrick and to Lewin while also identifying interpretive differences. Others took umbrage at Fitzpatrick's comments. William Chase chafed at Fitzpatrick's criticism about a true social history with the politics left out. And Lynne Viola, who by virtue of the alphabet got the last word in the journal, attacked Fitzpatrick's "artificial schools of historiography" and her "simplification"; she also accused Fitzpatrick of a breach of academic ethics for citing an unpublished article without permission. Terms and scholarly trends were often conflated and confused. The term "social history" was in many ways a misnomer; few of the scholars Fitzpatrick cited were interested primarily in people outside political power; they were identifying a broader spectrum of those with political power. It was hardly a surprise that Fitzpatrick's "social historians" were not studying society in isolation; as the replies of the young Turks emphasized, they considered themselves to be political historians or historians of society.[73] By the end of the second fifty-page installment, the "New Perspectives on Stalinism" forum had produced few new perspectives but instead had set many historians, who otherwise had much many areas of agreement, against each other. The debate also had the effect, as political scientists Jerry Hough (recently divorced from Fitzpatrick) and Robert Tucker noted, of sharpening the dividing lines between historians and political scientists.[74] Finally, the debate helped to entrench deeper political divisions in Soviet Studies. Politics and profession had become so intertwined that it was difficult to understand historical arguments apart from political aims—which were usually imputed rather than declared. There was little good faith that the historians writing about the 1930s were actually trying to be good scholars; articles were read for political leanings, not scholarly quality.

The first moves toward "revisionism" had come about with Leopold Haimson's social stability articles in the mid-1960s. In them, he outlined the "dual polarization" in tsarist society, and a generation of historians rewrote the history of 1917 in these terms. As the front line of revisionist battles moved into the Soviet period—first into the 1920s and then into the 1930s—the battles grew increasingly heated. Haimson's dual polarization applied to Soviet specialists as well as to tsarist intellectuals. The field had already made clear its great distance from the world of policy and government—part of a general academic trend of the 1960s, which was accelerated in Soviet Studies by the disputes over Inter-University Committee on Travel Grants (IUCTG) and the exchanges. A generation of Haimsonians tried, in their accounts, to emphasize professional norms over partisanship. But ultimately such partisanship defined the debate as the field moved from histories of 1917 into those of the 1920s and 1930s; political passions remained high, and there could be no retreat into profession. By the mid-1980s, the field was divided along both political and disciplinary lines.

The debate included few voices from the Right. Of those who advised government and believed in totalitarianism, only Robert Conquest, whose *Great Terror* (1968) was subject to attack by the young Turks, contributed to the *Russian Review* forum. His essay brimmed with sarcasm and insults; revisionists had a "strange notion" of historical evidence; in claiming "action from below" (Conquest's term, despite his scare quotes), they were engaging in "fantasy."[75] Richard Pipes, having returned from Washington to Harvard, made no contribution to this debate, even as he was writing his own history of the 1917 revolution. The debate took place strictly within an academic realm.

Whatever light was shed by the *Russian Review* symposium illuminated (to paraphrase Gábor Rittersporn) Western scholarship, not Soviet history.[76] Categories were confused, nerves were frayed, and relationships were damaged. Rather than setting a new agenda for the history of the Soviet Union, the forums helped to draw, and etch in ink (if not blood), the fissures within the field.

CHAPTER 12

PERESTROIKA AND THE COLLAPSE
OF SOVIET STUDIES

The politics of America's Soviet policy loomed large in the early 1980s. With Ronald Reagan in the White House and Richard Pipes on his National Security Council staff, scholars hoping to reduce Cold War tensions vigorously attacked Reagan's Soviet policy. The Soviet Union, meanwhile, was stagnating; Leonid Brezhnev was frail and disoriented in his few public appearances, his condition an apt metaphor for the party he headed. Scholarship in Soviet Studies, too, seemed to be in the doldrums. Economic Sovietology was in a demographic decline, with the founding generation nearing retirement and few junior economists in position to take up their mantle. Humanistic studies of Russia and the Soviet Union were in better shape: literary scholars were closer to the disciplinary mainstream than they had been for decades. Historians used archival access, however partial, to study new topics in new ways—before being dragged into battles over revisionism in the mid-1980s. Political science was growing narrower, with few new sources or new frameworks; one scholar reported that he had switched to the study of Latin America because Soviet politics was "simply boring, wholly lacking ideas or inspiration."[1] It was an inauspicious start to the decade that would see the death of the Soviet Union and the transformation of Russian Studies.

The field had already remade itself in the 1970s, adjusting for its increased scale and decreased funding. The public debate on Soviet affairs was more crowded but also more dispersed. The rise of para-academic institutions devoted to the topic led to a new kind of Soviet expert with fewer connections or commitments to university life and a keener interest in politics. The promotion of "relevance" within the academy gave rise to another segment of scholars whose work overlapped with controversial political issues. The growing political disputes within the field, even where they had no direct link to policy discussions, accounted for further divisions. For all of these reasons, the gap between scholarly and general interest discourses on Soviet affairs had grown substantially since the 1950s. Stanford's Alexander Dallin and Columbia's Marshall Shulman had taken on the mantle of Philip Mosely, producing informed and well-written analyses of contemporary affairs that were more like expert commentary than discipline-oriented scholarship. In the early 1970s, they were joined by Wellesley economist Marshall Goldman and Princeton political scientist Stephen Cohen, both of whom identified more with public debate than with disciplinary discussion. These scholars had come to prominence as policy advocates in the 1970s, favoring détente and closer American-Soviet ties that, they argued, would encourage Soviet reform. It was to challenge this cohort (and détente itself) that conservative academics joined forces with Senator Henry Jackson. The two sides faced off in the Carter administration, where Shulman served as a senior advisor in the State Department while hardliner Zbigniew Brzezinski (whose path to power did not run through Jackson's Senate office) served as national security advisor.[2] Reagan's sweeping electoral victory in 1980 ended talk of détente and brought to power and prominence many of Jackson's protégés, including Pipes. The conservative reorientation gave pro-détente critics a higher profile as opponents of U.S. policy.

Stephen Cohen was ready to take advantage of this opportunity. He had sought to shape America's Soviet policy since the 1960s. In the 1970s, he worked with a group promoting "East-West accord." "There was," he insisted, "no alternative to détente." He also contributed to a document mourning the end of détente, published by the American Committee for East-West Accord.[3] By the early 1980s, his public profile expanded to include the "Sovieticus" column in the *Nation* (widely reprinted) as well as television and radio appearances. Cohen divided his scholarly work and policy advocacy, publishing one book of each in the mid-1980s. The more academic book built on his Bukharin work, connecting the Soviet past and the Soviet present; the other, a collection of his *Nation* columns, connected the Soviet present and U.S. policy. Commentators from Pipes to Ronald Grigor Suny agreed that there were close connections between Cohen's scholarship and his advocacy, and indeed even the academic book closed on a policy note, insisting that "Soviet reformers stand a chance only in conditions of East-West détente."[4]

By the 1980s, some scholars long active in disciplinary debates joined general interest policy discussions. Political scientist Jerry Hough might have been the leading "disciplinarian" in the field of Soviet politics in the 1970s, but thereafter published more broad articles on contemporary events and fewer academic pieces. Spurred by the harsh reception of *The Soviet Union and Social Science Theory* (1977) and *How the Soviet Union Is Governed* (1979), Hough recalled, he turned toward policy: "if the simplest theoretical statement about Russia was going to be treated politically and ideologically in the scholarly world, I should not be wasting my time on little politics, but should participate in big politics where there was an honesty about it being political and ideological, and where it might have an impact."[5] Moving to Duke University, Hough soon headed the Center on East-West Trade, Investment and Communications. He became a fellow at the Brookings Institution and published a book with its press. Erik Hoffmann, another scholar who spent the 1970s oriented toward disciplinary political science, also entered the world of policy debates in the 1980s.[6] Columbia political scientist Seweryn Bialer also became a prominent voice in debates over America's Soviet policy. A sociologist and Communist Party member in his native Poland in the 1940s, Bialer first visited the USSR in 1954; it reminded him, he recalled, of the Nazi regime he had fought against in the Polish underground. After defecting in 1956, he earned a Ph.D. in political science at Columbia and then joined his advisors as a faculty member there. Never oriented toward disciplinary norms, Bialer told one interviewer that to understand the Soviet Union, "one ha[d] to be a journalist"; travel and conversation, not slogging through documents or theorizing, provided Bialer's sources. He was the first Soviet expert to win a MacArthur Foundation genius grant.[7] Bialer's policy views were hard to pin down; he did not take a strong position for or against détente, though he did express interest in continuing the arms-control negotiations unpopular with the Right.

Martin Malia was perhaps the unlikeliest newcomer to public debates. A specialist in nineteenth-century intellectual history, Malia began writing for wider audiences during the Solidarity movement's heyday in Poland (1980–1981) and reported on Soviet events only after 1989. Like his scholarly work, his general interest writings focused on the relationship between ideology and politics. Malia's biography of Alexander Herzen (1961) showed how its protagonist transformed socialism from a German utopian ideal into a factor in Russian political life; though the book ended in 1852, it sought to explain the origins of Soviet Communism.[8] Immersed in French intellectual life during his annual sojourns to France, Malia soon came to understand the USSR through the highly ideological Parisian lens of the late 1940s and early 1950s. Many of his classmates, colleagues, and close friends had been Communists, and even after Khrushchev's Secret Speech in 1956 many remained committed to socialism in terms that (for them) included support for the USSR. These Paris conversations, Malia recalled, convinced him that he was a liberal and not a socialist.[9]

Malia, like Pipes, Ulam, and Conquest, found much about American campus life in the 1960s to be alienating. Malia's estrangement came earlier than Pipes's, in large part because student protests arrived at his university, the University of California at Berkeley, years before they struck Harvard. The year 1964 was an important one for Malia; he began the academic year reaffirming his liberalism—telling his one-time teacher Isaiah Berlin that he would "go into exile" if Republican Barry Goldwater were elected president. After Goldwater lost in a landslide, Malia faced a new problem: Berkeley's free speech movement. Protesting university controls over students' political activity, the movement emerged in the fall of 1964 as a student force that soon found significant faculty support. As the university crisis deepened, Malia wavered and then joined a group of conservative faculty who saw the student protests as threatening the integrity of the university. Malia came to see his role as (in his words) "hold[ing] back the revolution"; he understood Berkeley in the sixties through the revolutionary talk of the Parisian Left in the 1950s and the revolutionary actions of the Bolsheviks in 1917. Deep alienation from university life and, indeed, American society soon set in; for the next few years, Malia still spoke of "exile" to Paris—but to escape the American Left, not the American Right that he had first feared.[10]

If Malia wrote with a French inflection, others wrote from abroad in a more literal sense; Timothy Colton (Toronto) and Archie Brown (Oxford) both contributed to American debates about Soviet affairs. While the public sphere was dominated by political scientists, there were a few historians: Malia, Pipes, and Moshe Lewin, then at the University of Pennsylvania. Not surprisingly, these scholars' views of the Soviet Union of the 1980s were shaped greatly by their historical scholarship; indeed, their public commentary seemed to be direct applications of their interpretations of the Soviet past. This trait did not distinguish them from political scientists, whose interpretations of Soviet politics were staunchly held even amid the dramatic events of the late 1980s.

After years of stagnation, the events of the late 1980s came with dizzying speed and confusion. Mikhail Gorbachev's reforms ebbed and flowed after 1985, as he faced defeats as well as victories. Experts therefore had little trouble referring to Soviet events that supported their arguments and perhaps even less trouble identifying Soviet events that challenged their antagonists' claims. One unfortunate result of this trend was a general difficulty in learning from the Gorbachev era—that is, adapting broader theories in light of the new evidence generated by the daily newspaper headlines.[11] While Gorbachev was able to stir the USSR out of its Brezhnev era stagnation, his policies did little to stir Sovietologists out of theirs.

By the early 1980s, most commentators agreed, the Soviet Union was facing a crisis rooted in the economic slowdown and the steady decline of the government's legitimacy. Softliners and hardliners alike recognized the severity of the economic troubles in the Soviet Union and Soviet citizens' growing alienation. There was also widespread agreement that the Soviet Union had taken a more aggressive international posture, noting especially its invasion of neighboring Afghanistan in 1979 and its strategic arms buildup. The growing sense of crisis, however, led few to predict any dramatic changes in the future. The operative phrase was "muddling through," much as the Soviet Union had done through the stagnation of the 1970s. Discussions of the growing economic crisis in the

Soviet Union were ubiquitous in Western scholarship. One 1980 conference, for instance, brought together thirty academic experts (the vast majority of Sovietological economists in the United States) to discuss the future of the Soviet economy. Their predictions were pessimistic; they saw Soviet economic growth slowing dramatically, with a drastic decline in living standards as defense spending consumed ever-larger portions of the Soviet budget. Yet they had been tracing this trend for over a decade by 1980 and had trouble conceiving of any dramatic change. One participant summed up the mood: while the data revealed severe problems, they did not portend a "crisis scenario."[12] Others less focused on economic models were less circumspect.

Richard Pipes, back at Harvard after two years at the National Security Council, offered his own account of the Soviet crisis in a book oriented toward U.S. foreign policy. *Survival Is Not Enough* (1984) considered the circumstances in the Soviet Union to be dire; the USSR's expansionist international posture required more resources than its faltering economy could provide. Pipes described conditions in the Soviet Union with Leninist language: the crisis amounted to a "revolutionary situation" but lacked the "subjective element," a leader willing to turn a revolutionary situation into a revolution. This subjective element made revolution or Stalinist reversion unlikely—and gradual change the most likely course.[13] The book's title and subtitle ("Soviet Realities and America's Future") addressed Washington, which, Pipes argued, needed a policy that aimed for victory, not just survival. For him, U.S. policy should encourage reform not by slackening its anti-Soviet efforts but by increasing them; reform would result from "failures, instabilities and fears of collapse," not from confidence and comfort.[14] While Pipes's diagnosis of the Soviet problem was similar to those of other scholars, his prescription for U.S. policy was radically different.

Marshall Goldman shared Pipes's sense of the current Soviet situation but differed sharply about possible actions. He offered a scathing account of the Soviet economy, which had become so weak that some future change was inevitable. For many years, Goldman recalled, he had confidently rejected the claim that the Soviet Union was "on the verge of doom, if not collapse"; by 1982, he admitted, the worsening situation led him to change his mind. Furthermore, Goldman warned, revitalizing the economy "could set off uncontrollable political and economic forces." While Goldman did not dwell on policy prescriptions as much as Pipes did, he nevertheless expressed discomfort with the Reagan arms buildup and tough export policy vis-à-vis the USSR. Goldman's *The USSR in Crisis* (1983), perhaps because it was the least hedged statement of the crisis argument, became an excellent way to assess the public debate over the Soviet Union. It became a Rorschach text, with the responses revealing less about Goldman's book and more about reviewers' own hopes for America's Soviet policy. The conservative *National Review,* for instance, cited Goldman's book to lambaste the USSR as incapable of reform. Gregory Grossman, writing in *Fortune,* took Goldman's book as support for restarting arms control negotiations with the USSR.[15] A Brookings economist criticized Goldman for overstating Soviet weakness, suggesting that such claims "could easily lead to ill-conceived Western policies toward the Soviet Union." French hardliner Alain Besançon wrote the nastiest response to Goldman to appear in the American press: he mocked the notion of a Soviet crisis, and he placed little faith in American leaders after Reagan to stand up to the USSR and even less faith in European leaders. He concluded with ominous talk of a Soviet takeover of Western Europe.[16] Debates over America's Soviet policy seemed to drive the analyses of current Soviet conditions rather than the reverse.

For all the talk of crisis and of the necessity of change, the moment always seemed to be in the future and not necessarily the foreseeable future. There was broad agreement about these points across the political spectrum, which were visible in the many reports generated in the early 1980s, either anticipating Leonid Brezhnev's departure or reacting to it. A study group organized by Georgetown's Center for Strategic and International Studies, for instance, concluded that "there is no likelihood that the Soviet Union will become a political democracy or that it will collapse in the foreseeable future." An academically oriented group organized by Erik Hoffmann reached a similar conclusion: "Although the Soviet system changed significantly from Stalin

Figure 12.1. Adam Ulam and Marshall Goldman with Soviet diplomat Genadii Gerasimov at Harvard, 1986. T shirts celebrating the fortieth anniversary of the Russian Research Center are in the backdrop.

to Khrushchev and changed moderately from Khrushchev to Brezhnev, it is unlikely to change much in the 1980s." Scholars suggested a wide range of *possible* outcomes but a narrow band of *likely* outcomes. Bialer, for instance, listed twelve possibilities ranging from neo-Stalinism to revolution before taking the middle ground and concluding that the political elites seemed secure "in the coming decade."[17]

Some scholars saw the demography of the Soviet elite as the most likely spur for change. Pro-détente commentators especially noted the advanced age and poor health of the leading members of the Politburo. Brezhnev's cohort had been *vydvizhentsy* who had risen to prominence under Stalin, but simple arithmetic and biology meant acknowledging that it would not be leading the Soviet Union for much longer. As of 1980, there were only two Politburo members who were significantly younger than sixty-five, one of whom was Mikhail Gorbachev. Scholars like Archie Brown, Stephen Cohen, and Jerry Hough relied on cohort analysis to suggest that this new generation of leaders might bring substantial change. The academic tendency to hedge was very much present: Cohen, for instance, noted that "generational change alone" was not enough to guarantee another era of "reform from above" à la Khrushchev.[18] For Cohen, like for Pipes, the subjective factor mattered.

As new academic voices joined more familiar ones in public discussions, there was a general consensus about Soviet prospects. Its economy was a bloated and rusty industrial behemoth unsuited for the new technologies then reshaping Western economies. Growing economic problems had not halted the Soviets' increasing bellicosity abroad, which was visible in new weapons systems and Third World interventions. There was a growing problem of maintaining the legitimacy of the Soviet regime: the so-called social contract of the Brezhnev era—the state would provide for the citizens and, in exchange, the citizens would not overtly challenge the system—was fraying as state provisions became more and more meager.[19] Still, few expected radical change. Timothy Colton, writing for the establishmentarian Council on Foreign Relations, offered a typical example of projections for the late 1980s. He acknowledged the sclerosis of the system under Brezhnev and credited Iurii Andropov (general secretary for fifteen months in 1982–1984) with changing the mood from "sanctimonious self-congratulation" to the honest recognition of the "backlog of problems." Colton contemplated but rejected the chance of fundamental change in the system; such could take place, he argued, only after a massive ethnic conflict or a defeat in war, neither of which was likely. By the same token, a return to the "primal Stalinism" of the 1930s was equally unlikely. Colton saw only a narrow band of feasible options, from "muddling through" to "moderate reform." Writing during Konstantin Chernenko's brief term as general secretary (thirteen months in 1984–1985), he projected that the aging

Politburo would not turn to the younger members right away. But in any case, Colton did not emphasize that a changing of the generational guard would bring with it any particular impulse for reform or change.[20] Institutions, not individuals, shaped Soviet life at the top; those institutions would not change simply with the arrival of a new leader.

Then came Gorbachev. After Chernenko's death in March 1985, Gorbachev became general secretary of the Communist Party of the Soviet Union (CPSU). Many, like Colton, saw little hope for immediate change.[21] Those commentators most invested in Soviet reform—including Hough, Brown, and Cohen—were optimistic, albeit for different reasons. Brown took the matter personally. Building on the information provided by Gorbachev's university roommate, Zdenek Mlynar, then making his rounds in the West, Brown considered Gorbachev "a man of rare ability and political skills." In the current Soviet political environment, Brown argued, "a new, younger leader with the necessary political will, ideas, and ability can indeed make a difference."[22] Cohen interpreted Gorbachev in terms of an ongoing battle between friends and foes of change, between those promoting Bukharin-style reform and those resisting it. Cohen praised Gorbachev, months before his ascent, as the "best bet for reform in the Kremlin." He warned that Gorbachev merely becoming general secretary would not automatically usher in a new era; he would need to consolidate power over the "foes of change" before embarking on his reforms. To give Gorbachev room to maneuver, Cohen called for an American policy that would reduce Cold War tensions.[23] Pipes criticized Cohen for supposing that the future of the Soviet Union was in American hands; Russia, Pipes insisted, was "no inert matter, devoid of will and interests, capable only of reacting to western initiatives."[24]

Seweryn Bialer shared Cohen's hedged optimism: "the right leader in the right place at the right time can make a very major difference," he wrote after Gorbachev's ascension. Bialer's assessment emerged directly out of his book *The Soviet Paradox* (1986), perhaps the most widely read monograph on the USSR in the mid-1980s. According to Bialer, the USSR was at its strongest and most assertive internationally at the very same time that its domestic situation, weighed down by economic decline, was at its most problematic. He acknowledged the difficulties of reform but argued that Gorbachev might be the right person to succeed and that the mid-1980s was certainly the right time. Gorbachev was a true reformer, Bialer argued, but was as likely to embark on centralization as decentralization, and he was more likely to promote the "reassertion of Soviet power in the world" than to reduce international tensions.[25]

Bialer's final chapter offered a moderate, even bland, prescription for U.S. dealings with the USSR: a "carefully managed policy...with limited, realistic aims." He offered a more direct statement elsewhere: "the best chance for the liberalization of the Soviet Union rests with *our* ability to manage peacefully the conflict with the Soviets." Like Cohen, Bialer made the possibility of Soviet change dependent on U.S. policy—that is, upon the adoption of his preferred policy. At the same time that Bialer promoted "managed rivalry" as the approach most likely to elicit positive change in the USSR, he also criticized those who held the "unrealistic belief" that American policy could influence Soviet international behavior. Pipes had criticized Cohen for arguing that Americans could shape the Soviet future; Bialer criticized Pipes on precisely those grounds, and Bialer himself was hardly immune from the same criticism.[26] This refrain, in other words, was a weapon for criticizing those with different views about U.S. policies, not a sincere acknowledgment of the difficulties of shaping American policy.

Bialer's book, long and detailed but with few citations, appeared about a year after Gorbachev's ascension and quickly became a touchstone for later discussions, much as Goldman's *USSR in Crisis* had three years earlier. Neoconservative Irving Kristol praised the book's assessments of the Soviet paradox as an "antidote" to "the kind of wishful thinking that is now so pervasive in academic circles." He teased Bialer for trying to imagine what Gorbachev really wanted: "it seems doubtful," Kristol corrected, "that anyone achieving absolute power in the Kremlin can afford to have a heart of hearts in the first place." And finally, Kristol roundly condemned Bialer's policy prescription as "the most conventional kind of State Department chatter." For Kristol, *The Soviet Paradox* was useful to the extent that it helped him to criticize others and problematic to the extent that it offered proposals for American policy. Georgetown's Thane Gustafson criticized Bialer for arguing that the paradox required immediate resolution; Soviet leaders could "increase their military strength," he argued, with little disruption in their domestic sphere. Peter Kenez used his review to warn America to maintain "firmness in defense of its vital interests" and skepticism about Gorbachev's claims: "no useful purpose is served by paying back [Soviet] publicists in kind and imitating their rhetorical excesses."[27] Kenez's theme of Potemkin-like reform was a common one among American hardliners well into Gorbachev's rule; those who envisioned an all-powerful USSR did not believe that the widely acknowledged economic crisis would lead to significant political change.

Though Bialer argued that an individual like Gorbachev might really transform the USSR, others argued that the change had more to do with demography than personality. Jerry Hough, for instance, thought that Gorbachev would start changing the direction of the Soviet Union in as little as six months and would seek to open up the economy to the West. Hough had long anticipated a generational transition in the Soviet leadership, and he expected significant changes in Soviet international posture and domestic policy under the first cohort of leaders who remembered Khrushchev's Secret Speech of 1956 but not the purges and show trials of the late 1930s.[28] Hough, like other scholars, was effective at using Gorbachev to prove his theories, but less adept at using Gorbachev to revise those theories or to develop new ones.

The same phenomenon—common descriptions based on radically different assumptions—is all the more visible in those who suggested that Gorbachev's rise did not mark a new era. Marshall Goldman warned, only days after Gorbachev's ascension, that the new general secretary might not bring great changes for the USSR; after all, he was only six years younger than Brezhnev had been when he came to lead the USSR, and that hardly was an era of reform. Gorbachev's arrival, Goldman concluded, "may augur bold moves in domestic and foreign policy. Don't bet on it." Rejecting the argument of generational change in favor of straightforward historical analogy, Goldman implied that there was a broad continuity in Politburo leadership that transcended variables like generation. Pipes took a harder line on this question, using the same argument that he and Robert Conquest had made to Senator Jackson some fifteen years earlier. He insisted, in May 1985, that Gorbachev was selected precisely because "in all respects which matter he resembles the oldsters whose interests he has been appointed to safeguard." While Hough essentialized a generation, Pipes essentialized an institution; the Politburo could produce only leaders who would continue the same policy as the Politburo always had.[29]

Through 1985 and 1986, there was wide disagreement among America's Russia watchers as they applied their prior theories to an uncertain situation. Gorbachev's youth and early rhetoric augured major reform, but actual domestic reforms came more slowly. He wasted little time, though, in reorienting Soviet foreign relations; barely a month after taking the helm of the party, he announced that the latest Soviet missiles would not be deployed to Europe. In his first year, he proposed removing all intermediate-range missiles from Europe. His "new thinking" on international relations led Western observers and diplomats to praise Gorbachev fulsomely, but many skeptics remained. Even his staunchest enthusiasts worried that he would be held back by the entrenched conservative elements in the Politburo. But there, too, there were signs of progress, most notably the removal of Foreign Minister Andrei Gromyko, for decades the Soviets' "Comrade Nyet."

By late 1987, after Gorbachev's highly anticipated November speech denouncing Stalinism, most American commentators agreed that Gorbachev had accrued sufficient power to begin systematic reforms. He had spent the first two years consolidating his position in the Politburo, marginalizing what was left of the Brezhnev generation, and scrambling to improve economic performance through a combination of speed-ups and sobriety. By 1987, the watchwords were not just *perestroika* (restructuring) but also *glasnost'* (openness) and even *demokratizatsiia* (democratization). The changing situation in the USSR led to a shift in American discussions. Two key questions soon emerged. Was Gorbachev really after major reform, or did he just talk a good game? And would major reforms have any chance of success? The issues were exemplified in an article by General William Odom, who had worked for Brzezinski in Carter's White House before serving as director of the National Security Agency under Reagan. Thus far, Odom began, Gorbachev had raised hopes for systemic change but had not yet satisfied these hopes. He identified a paradox in Gorbachev's predicament: change to the system, such as the decentralization of economic decision making, would require strong centralized power. This paradox led Odom to predict that, if Gorbachev was intent on fundamental reform, then "the chances he could control it [were] small, virtually nil."[30] Others who expressed doubts about Soviet reforms confidently used arguments that they had made long prior to Gorbachev's arrival on the scene in 1985. A 1987 symposium in Irving Kristol's neoconservative *National Interest* presented a skeptics' chorus. Robert Conquest suggested that *glasnost'* was strictly for foreign consumption. Underneath the rhetoric of openness and change, he continued, Gorbachev offered little that would change "the essentials of the system." Adam Ulam thought it unlikely that Gorbachev would significantly alter the "foundations of the Soviet edifice," so Americans needed to remain on guard against Soviet international aggression. Briton Peter Reddaway, then director of the Kennan Institute, accepted *glasnost'* at face value but doubted that it could succeed. Most dramatic of all was Alain Besançon, who considered *glasnost'* to be a cover story for Gorbachev's "all-out attack on civil society." If Gorbachev were to succeed, Besançon and coauthor Françoise Thom continued, the Soviet threat would be that much greater—a "revitalized communist power, extremely active abroad, highly aggressive."[31] Skeptics, like optimists, held fervently to their previous views in spite of the dramatic changes in the Soviet Union during Gorbachev's first three years in power.

Even scholars who were convinced that Gorbachev's reform efforts were sincere expressed doubts that he would be able to pull them off. Jerry Hough, for instance, insisted that the question had changed from 1985 to 1987; it no longer centered around whether Gorbachev wanted to change the system—Hough thought yes—but whether he would be able to. He remained optimistic, arguing that Western analysts had "grossly exaggerated" the strength of internal opposition to Gorbachev's reforms, at least within the political apparatus. Hough's language, especially when addressing academic audiences, was provocative. He argued that the dominant scholarly view of the USSR was Trotskyist, which placed the main power in the hands of the *apparat;* he insinuated that the political leadership was too weak to overcome the bureaucrats it ostensibly supervised.[32] Seweryn Bialer, no Trotskyist, had his doubts. He argued in April

1987 that the USSR had entered a "zone of danger"; Gorbachev's changes in the Soviet economy had hurt Soviet workers, who were now deeply opposed to his reforms.[33] Hough, turning again to his cohort analysis, took the opposite tack, arguing that Gorbachev would be able to win over the "Soviet middle class," especially the younger members. All in all, Hough predicted, Gorbachev would be able to "control Soviet social forces" and remain at the helm of the Soviet Union for another dozen years or more.[34] Bialer and Hough both stuck to their interpretive guns as Soviet circumstances changed.

Moshe Lewin, relying on the logic of sociological history, shared some of Hough's optimism. His historical scholarship traced the emergence of a new social structure in the USSR in the 1930s; by the 1980s, he concluded, Soviet society was much more complex than its state and needed a governing structure that could catch up. While he was vague about the specific mechanisms of change, Lewin asserted that Soviet society had "become a powerful 'system maker,' pressuring both political institutions and the economic model to adapt." Gorbachev's reforms, in this telling, were historically necessary and emerged out of the broader social structure rather than out of political maneuvering among the elites. Since, for Lewin, society was generating the reforms, it would hardly be the obstacle that Bialer had predicted. Lewin assimilated Gorbachev's changes into his own world view; they marked the "start of a new age" in the USSR—but a new age that Lewin had ostensibly predicted much earlier.[35] Along the same lines, historian Theodore von Laue would update his 1964 book *Why Lenin? Why Stalin?* which argued that Russian history since Peter the Great was merely the unfolding of historical imperatives of modernization. His latest model, *Why Lenin? Why Stalin? Why Gorbachev?* extended this familiar argument into the 1980s.[36] For Lewin and von Laue, Gorbachev became proof of their viewpoints rather than an impetus to revisit or revise those viewpoints.

Richard Pipes, too, applied long-held beliefs amid changing Soviet circumstances. Like many observers, he wrote about the Soviet crisis as in a crisis before Gorbachev's rise. Even as he recognized Gorbachev's efforts to reform the Soviet system, he spoke out against changing U.S. policy.[37] In policy statements in 1988 and 1989, Pipes wanted to keep the pressure on the USSR. In an article about the "dangers of Détente II," Pipes insisted that "Gorbachev's goal [was] the same as Lenin's, namely global hegemony for the CPSU." Gorbachev was "masterful" at convincing the West to yield, so Pipes stressed the need for redoubled vigilance. Though Americans had "embrace[d] Gorbachev's enticing new line about Soviet 'reforms'"—the scare quotes are Pipes's—the Soviet danger remained as it always had been. The following year, Pipes chaired a task force for the Heritage Foundation that attributed Gorbachev's reforms to "politics rather than policies"; reforms were merely his way of consolidating and maintaining power, not an effort to remake the system. The title of the report revealed the depths of Pipes's skepticism: "Paper Perestroika." *Glasnost'*, in Pipes's telling, was Gorbachev's ploy to mislead the West, and *perestroika* was his effort to maintain a grip on power; if these reforms happened to succeed, then the USSR would pose an even greater danger. Pipes applauded Reagan's hard line, even crediting him with having "created Mikhail Gorbachev," and called for such a hard line to continue for the foreseeable future.[38] Soviet events were entangled with prescriptions for American policy.

As Gorbachev's reforms accelerated in 1987, American observers of all stripes had little trouble fitting them into their prior claims over the nature of the Soviet system. The first steps toward democratization included multicandidate elections and the appointment of nonparty members to responsible positions. Seizing on the breach of security that allowed a West German pilot to land his plane near Red Square, Gorbachev also put the military on the defensive. After 1987, the reforms came at a dizzying pace, with the introduction of *glasnost'* and the abandonment of the impressive censorship structure. So-called cooperatives reintroduced limited private ownership of enterprises in some sectors for the first time in sixty years.

Yet American discussions of the USSR sounded the same refrains. Just days before Gorbachev flew to Washington for his third summit meeting with President Reagan in December 1987, Cohen debated Pipes at Princeton. The discussion began cordially enough. Pipes called on Americans to "keep our cool" and not get overly excited by the reforms; Cohen also abjured direct U.S. support for Gorbachev's reforms but argued that Americans should "view them with hope, compassion and an open mind." The debate rehearsed familiar sentiments: Pipes doubted the possibility of any real change in the Soviet system, while Cohen insisted that the USSR had already transformed itself. Both linked Soviet prospects to American policy: Pipes implicitly credited a hardline posture for forcing change in the Soviet Union while Cohen insisted that such policies would "badly damage and perhaps even doom" chances for Soviet reform. By the end of the discussion, the topic had changed and the mood soured; as the debate shifted to U.S. policy, the exchanges grew testier.[39]

The same was true for discussions of the Soviets' international posture. Zbigniew Brzezinski, for instance, was so unconvinced by Gorbachev's arms control concessions at the Washington summit (December 1987) that his post-summit exhortation—the United States needed a "strategically designed combination of toughness and flexibility" to wring more Soviet concessions—was almost precisely the same as a statement he made well over a year earlier.[40] Brzezinski focused on the continuities in Soviet policy and deemphasized the novelty of Gorbachev's actions. Soviet intentions were shaped by "deep-rooted historical-geographical drives reinforced by…doctrinal perspectives";

they had little to do with "the subjective inclinations of this or that Kremlin leader."[41] Though Brzezinski had long before abandoned the term "totalitarian," he still envisioned a system that could not change. Hough, meanwhile, saw the changes under Gorbachev as the Soviet transformation he had so long anticipated. To better support the reforms, Hough wanted the United States to overhaul its Soviet policy: expand trade links, reach arms control agreements, and reduce American defense spending. Through 1987 and well beyond, Hough observed Soviet events as if they were the natural outcomes of a society that was undergoing rapid transformation; the reforms were not creating a new society so much as "return[ing] Russia toward what is normal."[42] Hough's vision of a normalizing USSR connected closely to his vision of normalizing American-Soviet relations.

As Gorbachev's reforms started running into trouble, skeptics became the dominant voice, repeating the doubts that they had held all along. From 1985 to 1988, things had been going well for those who argued that the Soviet Union was capable of reform. Brown, Cohen, and Hough seemed energized by Soviet events, more confident in their predictions, and at times more dismissive of the skeptics. "Why," asked Cohen pointedly, "do so many American commentators still insist that no significant improvements in the Soviet system are possible?" He listed five explanations, including ethnocentrism ("national conceit") and America's "deep psychological need for an immutably ugly Soviet Union in order to minimize or obscure its own imperfections." Hough invoked psychology, blaming American "insecurities of the transition to superpower status."[43]

As Gorbachev faced increasing difficulties after 1987, so too did optimistic Sovietologists. His economic reforms created enough uncertainty that industrial production plummeted. Shortages of basic goods, even foods like sugar and meat, were rampant; not only were these goods still rationed, but the government had a hard time providing even the low amounts promised through rationing. By the winter of 1989, basic staples rarely made it to the state food stores that were responsible for provisioning most of the country. Well aware that the collapse of the tsarist regime began with a bread riot, Soviet authorities had long provided cheap and plentiful bread. But by 1989, there was less even of that and almost nothing to eat or drink with it; coffee and tea were never seen even in Moscow and St. Petersburg, butter and milk rarely, and meat only *po blatu* (through back channels). Through 1988 and 1989, nationalist troubles magnified. The Baltic republics were the first to protest, but ethnonationalism also exploded in the USSR's west (Ukraine and Belorussia) and south (Central Asia and the Caucasus). In Eastern Europe, events had gone even further, leading to the fall of the Berlin Wall in November 1989 and the phased withdrawal of the Red Army the following year. With the conservative wing of his party already angry, Gorbachev faced new opposition from the Left, leading him to dismiss upstart Boris Yeltsin in 1987. The intellectuals who were his original supporters also began to agitate for greater reforms than Gorbachev was ready to enact.

Meanwhile, the American debate stayed on familiar ground. Marshall Goldman remained consistently skeptical about Gorbachev even during the Soviet leader's greatest successes. By 1990, as the tide turned strongly against Gorbachev amid nationalist uprisings and economic collapse, Goldman celebrated his earlier predictions and blamed Gorbachev for the collapse of the Soviet economy. To Goldman's thinking, Gorbachev was well aware of the economic troubles but reluctant to undertake the radical reforms necessary to change the system. The result was production failure and massive declines in even the most basic of goods. While Goldman admitted that the prospects for a successful transition to a market economy were slim, he nevertheless called on Gorbachev to attempt the radical reforms necessary to make this happen. The result, Goldman predicted, would be mixed: the economy would likely recover, but the reforms would probably cost Gorbachev his job.[44]

As Gorbachev's problems mounted—the rapid dissolution of the Soviet bloc after the Berlin Wall was breached in November 1989, growing protests in the Baltics leading to confrontation and then independence, continued economic woes—Gorbachev's American critics seized the advantage. Seweryn Bialer suggested that his 1986 book had predicted the basic story even if it had underestimated the breadth of the reforms. Pipes, true to his dissertation on Soviet nationality policy in the 1920s, emphasized nationalism with similar confidence. With sweeping language, Pipes insisted that nationalist aspirations in the USSR "will not be satisfied with any arrangement short of independence." He also stressed Russians' rising nationalism, their determination to have a "country in which they are the master race" rather than being part of a federal union with internationalist pretensions. Pipes predicted that Gorbachev, "beset by mounting economic problems as well as social and ethnic unrest,…may well seize dictatorial powers and rule by martial law"; the general secretary would be "more likely" to make a grab for power than to loosen "Russia's grip on its subject peoples."[45] The notion of Russian imperialism and despotism, so central to Pipes's vision of the Russian past, continued to shape his predictions for the future.

In 1989, as Soviet conditions worsened and optimism began to wane, Martin Malia entered the public debates over the Soviet Union. After a number of extended visits in 1988 and 1989 to Moscow, where Malia resumed his habits of his 1960s visits by hanging out with the intelligentsia, he wrote a landmark article, "To the Stalin Mausoleum." Malia insisted on publishing under a pseudonym (originally "N. Perestroikin," eventually changed to "Z") to protect his liberal friends in Russia, whom, he believed, would be in danger for consorting with a politically incorrect foreigner. In "Stalin Mausoleum," Malia offered a polemical triptych: a capsule interpretation of Soviet history, an attack on Sovietology, and a prediction that 1989 had marked "the beginning of communism's terminal crisis."[46] Tellingly, his criticism of Westerners preceded his long historical argument about the "unreality" of the Soviet Union. Malia blamed both politics and profession for what he considered to be the gross miscomprehension of Soviet events. The American Right hoped that Communism "may yet repent of its evil totalitarian ways" and become a market economy, while the Left desperately hoped that the Soviet Union could be reformed enough to "acquire something resembling a human face." The result was the "perestroika pietism of the Gorbophiles" lining up against the "free-market triumphalism of the Gorbophobes." But for Left and Right, Malia argued, views of Gorbachev had more to do with vindicating their own ideas than with anything else. He suggested that Western scholars had not just political biases but also professional disabilities. Their eyes had been clouded by social scientific ideas that emphasized Soviet stability and pluralism; the result was that the "extraordinary, even surreal, Soviet experience [had] been rendered banal to the point of triviality."[47] The outcome was a failure to understand the Soviet system and especially Gorbachev's effort to reform it.

Urgent prose aside, Malia's view of the Soviet Union after Stalin did not differ dramatically from Brzezinski's. Much like Brzezinski arguing that the system could not reform, only degenerate, Malia argued that "*perestroika* is ... not just a reform of a basically sound structure, but the manifestation of a systemic crisis of Sovietism per se." They differed in their reasoning: political scientist Brzezinski emphasized the nature of the Soviet political system while intellectual historian Malia argued that the Soviet Union was the incarnation of an ideology. Since the ideology in question, socialism, was utopian, the system was doomed. Or, in Malia's trenchant phrase, "There is no such thing as socialism, and the Soviet Union built it."[48] The Soviet economy and society (to the extent there actually was a Soviet society) were shaped solely by political objectives— the very political objectives that Soviet leaders publicly declared. The Soviet economy could not accommodate market reforms because it was organized around political, not economic, imperatives; to decouple the economy from political control was tantamount to declaring the bankruptcy of the whole system. In "Stalin Mausoleum" and a handful of essays in the *New York Review of Books*, Malia treated Gorbachev as a leader determined to continue building socialism in spite of the pure impossibility of that goal. He could build a repressive state, but not a socialist one; for Malia, the Soviet party-state shaped all of society around its own political needs and in pursuit of its own chimerical, ideological end point.[49] Giving up on that project would mark the decline of the Soviet Union, not its transformation.

There were other major differences between Malia's and Brzezinski's analyses of the USSR. One simple difference was timing: Brzezinski wrote about degeneration in 1966, while Malia's first writings on *perestroika* as a sign of imminent collapse came almost two dozen years later. When Brzezinski first predicted that the Soviet system could not reform, only degenerate, Malia was fighting the student revolution in Berkeley. By the time Malia turned serious attention toward contemporary Soviet events, the reforms were in trouble. Unlike the Gorbophiles, Malia did not see Gorbachev as a reformer attempting to create a more humane socialism, but as a socialist trying increasingly desperate measures to rescue the Soviet economy. To the extent that he was a reformer, Gorbachev aimed to strengthen the Soviet Union by straightening out its troubled economy. He did not have a package of reforms as much as he lurched, with increasing desperation, from one effort to the next. He first sought *uskorenie* (acceleration) and a crackdown on alcohol to make the economy more productive, and he turned toward broader reconstruction (*perestroika*) only after the *uskorenie* and anti-alcohol campaigns failed. *Glasnost'* was merely the next step in a traditional Soviet reform effort, neither a grand ambition to open Soviet society nor a tactic to deceive the West, but an effort to mobilize public and intelligentsia support against recalcitrant bureaucrats. Gorbachev's reforms, in sum, were a series of increasingly extreme tactical measures rooted in the Soviet "reform" tradition of administrative pressures and purges. Soviet military spending and modernization demonstrated that the system was not changing in its fundamentals. Malia warned that Communist states had surpassed all others not in production or in equality but in "tenacity in holding on to…power." Malia made frequent trips to the USSR through the continuing crisis of the late 1980s, befriending historian Iurii Afanas'ev and other Russian liberals who would become prominent in the 1990s. He took great pleasure in having found a revolution—unlike those of 1917 or 1964—which he could support.[50]

Richard Pipes continued his criticisms of the USSR, on the one hand, and of American observers, on the other. He blamed American experts for believing in Gorbachev's vision of a reformed Soviet Union when no such thing was possible. And he repeated his argument, used against Cohen in the Princeton debate, that there was little if anything that the United States could do to shape Soviet events. At the same time, he continued to sound the tocsin about the Soviet military threat, noting that there was no reason to think that "the Soviet Union is beating swords into plowshares." Pipes's colleague Adam Ulam also predicted that Gorbachev would face the crisis of 1990–1991 by taking a firmer hold on the reins of power.[51]

As scholars originally enthusiastic about Gorbachev observed the growing crisis in the Soviet Union—by 1990–1991, simultaneously national, economic, and political—they continued to rely on their usual explanations and struck out against his critics in the USSR and the West. Both Cohen and Hough, for instance, berated Moscow's liberal intelligentsia, which rallied around Boris Yeltsin after 1990. Cohen, under the headline "Moscow Intellectuals Are Wrong," argued that Gorbachev's reforms were so radical that they "could not have unfolded quickly or smoothly"; Russian intellectuals were too quick to lose faith in Gorbachev, the "great reformer." Hough, too, focused his criticism on the critics, not on Gorbachev. The general secretary, Hough averred, had a "very sophisticated political strategy" that had created "controlled chaos," even if the signs of control eluded many observers. Hough also lambasted his academic colleagues, complaining that they had "too much faith in the judgment of those who were educated and lived in a closed society"—that is, the Moscow intellectuals themselves; by the same token, Western scholars maintained too little faith in "what our [American] social scientists have learned."[52] Other observers who had been prominent in the mid-1980s offered little or no public commentary by the end of the decade: Timothy Colton, for example, devoted himself to a history of Moscow politics while Bialer published little in either academic or general interest outlets.

In August 1991, Gorbachev's crises came home to roost, further energizing his American critics. A group of Politburo and military figures calling themselves the State Emergency Committee locked up Gorbachev in his Crimean dacha and declared themselves in power. Yeltsin, having been disgraced by Gorbachev in 1987 but recently elected to the presidency of the Russian Federation, led the protests against the putschists and helped his long-time adversary return to power—at least for a while. Malia called the coup an "August Revolution" that had finally reversed the October Revolution seventy-four years prior. The putsch was not a coup d'état, as Gorbachev's American supporters called it, but an act of government initiated by senior officials, most of whom had been appointed by Gorbachev himself. Malia argued that Gorbachev had not survived a coup but lost a revolution.[53] Immersed in the milieu of Moscow liberals, who had turned to Yeltsin out of frustration with Gorbachev's insistence on maintaining too much of the Soviet regime, Malia's views were shaped in equal measure by his disputes with American Sovietologists and his ideological interpretation of Soviet history. Events of the fall of 1991 vindicated Malia's argument. Upon returning from his brief captivity, Gorbachev acceded to Yeltsin's demands to restructure the relationship between the USSR and its constituent republics. By December 1991, the Soviet Union disappeared, leaving Gorbachev nothing to rule. And then the fighting really began in the United States.

It was Malia's good fortune that he had refrained from any predictions until Gorbachev's reforms faced continuous crises in late 1989. Coming to commentary so late, Malia spared himself some of the unfulfilled predictions that other observers had made. It was telling, though, that Malia's first predictions about the Soviet future were so closely linked to his condemnations of Sovietology. After the collapse of the USSR, Malia scaled up his attacks on America's Russia experts, criticizing their application of social scientific concepts rooted in the Western experience. He dismissed political scientists and sociologists for adopting "reductionist" analytical tools that saw the USSR as a variant of a modern state rather than as an "ideocratic partocracy." The failure of Sovietology to understand the demise of the USSR, Malia insisted, was "a failure of the social sciences per se."[54]

Malia attacked social historians with special venom, even though they did not use the same concepts nor address contemporary Soviet events as the political scientists did. Pipes offered similar scorn for revisionist social historians, suggesting that their ideas were invalidated by the events of the Gorbachev era. Social historians themselves were all but absent from the major news media during the Gorbachev era. Aside from Cohen, who stood apart from if not opposed to social historians after the 1986 *Russian Review* debate, the only revisionist to write for a broad audience about the Gorbachev era was Moshe Lewin. Others pursued scholarship rather than contributing to the public *perestroika* debates. The attacks on social historians in the 1980s, like those in the 1970s, conflated disciplinary concerns with political ones.

Politics, professional pursuits, and personal conflicts would be increasingly difficult to disentangle in the what-went-wrong debates of the early 1990s. There was one major point of agreement: Western Sovietology had failed in the 1980s because it did not develop a framework to understand what actually was happening. Many observers praised the work of Soviet dissident Andrei Amalrik, *Will the Soviet Union Survive until 1984?* (1970), in order to criticize Western commentators. But Amalrik made a poor example; he indeed had predicted that the USSR would not survive the 1980s, but he had imagined it as the result of a military defeat at the hands of Communist China.[55] While no Western authors shared Amalrik's sense that the system would collapse in the 1980s, there were many who had identified the intersecting crises of legitimacy and production that spurred Gorbachev's reforms. Indeed, the writings of the early 1980s enumerated many of the problems and some possible solutions. Their main limit, in retrospect, was failing to consider the possibility that the Soviet Union would not be able to survive them. Soviet essentialists, those who saw the collapse as intrinsic to the logic of a system that controverted basic principles of society, were of little help here. Malia, for instance, had an easier time explaining why the system would collapse than he did in explaining why it had existed for so long.

Given the overall performance of American Sovietology before Gorbachev—full of gaffes but correct in its broad outlines—it is striking just how fierce the what-went-wrong debate became. Hardliners had led the charge well before the demise of the USSR, publishing criticisms of Western analyses of the Soviet Union for being too easily swayed by social science. Critics like Conquest, Malia, and Pipes were also the quickest to include social historians as their targets. Gorbachev's failings became a weapon with which to attack revisionists in political science and history. In the neoconservative magazine *National Interest,* Conquest defended the term "totalitarianism" against its critics, claiming that it was not a "model" but merely a "description." He also struck out against social historians (among whom he counted Hough) and expected that the late 1980s should have "destroyed revisionist delusions." Pipes, similarly, argued that the events of the 1980s invalidated the work of the social historians of 1917: "the political implications of [the social historians'] argument have been robbed of both relevancy and appeal by the collapse of communism."[56]

Malia's argument was more finely honed than Conquest's, perhaps because he had been making it for longer; in *National Interest,* he repeated some of the criticisms he had made earlier in *Problems of Communism* and, in embryonic form, in his "Z" article of 1990. In his telling, the problem with political science was its insistence on being scientific, on developing and applying general laws that would fit all societies. "The social science perspective necessarily posits that 'society' is essentially the same everywhere," which in turn implied that Soviet society and politics could be interpreted with categories and techniques originally formulated to understand the West.[57] He argued that the best way to move forward was to take a step back, to the "pre–social science innocence" that had existed prior to the 1960s. He also offered a specific link between the social historians and the revisionist political scientists: both resorted to a form of "social reductionism" that led them to believe that the length of Stalin's rule meant that it must have had some social support. Ultimately, his real targets were the scholars who adopted the sociological arguments of Talcott Parsons and Barrington Moore Jr.; they had predicted that the imperatives of modernization—education, urbanization, technical rationality—would undercut stringent political controls. There had been modernization in the USSR, Malia wrote, but it was "rendered sterile" because it was "wholly driven by the political purposes of communism."[58] Malia blamed political science, not politics, for Americans' misunderstanding of the USSR.

Other participants in the *National Interest* symposium also focused on the nature of professional Sovietology rather than on the politics of the scholars. William Odom, for instance, defended political scientists, arguing that their inability to explain the Soviet collapse was the result of "honest errors" more than "political and ideological baggage"—hardly the most flattering defense. He was joined by another political scientist, Peter Rutland, who also defended the profession against accusations of political bias. Indeed, he suggested, the problem may have been the opposite: scholars' efforts to "appear 'non-judgmental'" led them to refrain from bold claims and to hedge even the most modest predictions. The main problem of academic Sovietology, then, was not a failure of politics or ideas, but a "failure of imagination."[59]

Those targeted by the hardliners responded according to two patterns, distinguished primarily by their relationship to the discipline of political science. Authors like Dallin and Cohen, who did not identify closely with their discipline, tended to repeat, indeed intensify, their attacks on American hardliners on political grounds. Dallin criticized those authors—he had in mind especially Pipes and Malia—who believed that the system was "intrinsically unreformable." Though he distinguished between the premises of Pipes's and Malia's arguments—Pipes blamed Russia while Malia blamed Communism—Dallin criticized both. It was foolhardy for them to claim that they knew the system would collapse; the Soviet Union's collapse was "not nearly so inevitable and surely not necessarily so imminent" as they had declared. Just because Gorbachev could not reform the system, Dallin continued, did not mean that the system was inherently unreformable; Dallin clearly believed that it could have been reformed differently, indeed successfully. Elsewhere, he attacked with special venom the view that Russia was inherently despotic, a view he associated especially with Pipes. Dallin noted with alarm the special tendency for hardliners to resort to this sort of historical argument, suggesting the close connections between scholarly arguments and expectations for U.S. policy.[60]

Cohen broadened the attack, blaming not just hardliners in the policy world but academic Sovietologists as well. He lambasted Cold Warriors for their "failed crusade" against Russia—first in a *Nation* cover article (1994) and, eventually, in the title essay of his 2000 book. Cohen accused hardliners, indeed the broader world of politicos and pundits, of fundamentally misunderstanding Russia. His initial targets were George H. W. Bush and Bill Clinton, who actively supported Yeltsin's presidency through rhetoric, diplomacy, and aid. Support for Yeltsin was only the latest episode in the long-running tragedy that Cohen described, yet another example of the American insistence that it could shape Russia according to its own desires. The lesson, Cohen argued, was that the United States needed to support reformers in Russia. Cohen accused U.S. policy makers of following a "missionary" foreign policy, insisting on the right and rectitude of converting Russians to the American way of life.[61] Nor were policy makers, pundits, and journalists the only Americans how shared responsibility for Russia's failures; academics, too, were at fault. In "Russian Studies without Russia" (1999), Cohen depicted Sovietology as deeply and irretrievably tarnished by politics and ideology. The field was also plagued by a broader scholarly tendency toward "conformity" and "orthodoxy," a result of the long shadow cast by McCarthyism. Scholars hedged their language for fear of being called sympathetic to (or, after 1991, nostalgic for) Communism.[62] Cohen wanted to show how Sovietology, beginning in the 1970s, ascended out of the orthodoxy and conformity that had ostensibly defined its first two decades. The language was strong: "external political circumstances" defined the field's structure and content in the 1950s; the Cold War "intruded into academic Sovietology politically and intellectually"; "Cold War zealotry" dominated especially the fields of political science and history, leaving only a handful of "isolated dissenter[s]." By the late 1950s, in Cohen's telling, academic Sovietology was a "highly politicized profession imbued with topical concerns, a crusading spirit, and a know-the-enemy raison d'être." Cohen argued that Cold War politics established the "totalitarianism" school as "the only school of Sovietology, an orthodoxy" from the time of the field's founding in the late 1940s through the arrival of revisionists like Cohen himself in the late 1960s. The totalitarianism school, in this view, focused scholarly attention solely on the top of the political hierarchy to the exclusion of Soviet society and ruled out the possibility of any political, let alone social, change. Only in the late 1960s did other voices come into play, including, of course, Cohen's. This broadening came about for external political reasons, namely, détente, new policies in the USSR, the accumulated experience of the academic exchanges (which immersed scholars in Soviet society), and the rise of young scholars who came of age after Stalin's death.[63] Cohen significantly extended Alexander Dallin's "Bias and Blunders" article of the early 1970s, depicting Sovietology as a field stamped by Cold War politics, political conformism, and government support. His work formed a counterpoint to attacks on the field from the Right by Martin Malia, Richard Pipes, and Robert Conquest: where the Right attacked the field as being in the thrall of political science, Cohen argued that the field was instead ruled by politics.

Discipline-oriented political scientists defended their turf against attacks from the Left and Right. George Breslauer at the University of California, Berkeley, wrote "In Defense of Sovietology," attempting to rebut Cohen's and Malia's attacks on the field. Breslauer described the field, even in the 1950s, as more diverse and open-minded than Cohen's portrayal of the total hegemony of totalitarianism in the 1950s and early 1960s would suggest. Breslauer admitted that Sovietological work, at least that work oriented toward the discipline, was often ahistorical and narrowly cast. Even as Sovietologists rejected Talcott Parsons's loose talk of convergence, they accepted an overall approach heavily indebted to his sociology. They focused on the "static analysis of process" and undertook a "disaggregation" of the system that "did not require prior specification of the essence of the political order." Breslauer acknowledged that the research agenda had focused on "underdocumented micro-processes," often merely to "fill blank spots" while setting aside a description or analysis of the fundamentals of the Soviet political system.[64] In Breslauer's account, the field focused on disagreement and pluralism at low levels of the Soviet political system while ignoring the overall parameters of power in the Soviet Union—much as Malia wrote.

Other discipline-oriented scholars took the offense after being attacked for "committing a social science" (in the inimitable phrase of W. H. Auden). Indeed, some inverted Malia's criticism, arguing that the failure to understand the late 1980s was the result of too little social science, not too much. Frederic Fleron and Erik Hoffmann, both of whom had worked assiduously to bring the study of Soviet politics into the mainstream of American political science, offered a long list of reasons that America's Soviet experts had not immersed themselves in social science theory. These reasons were a mixture of personal and intellectual, amounting to the accusation that American political scientists were unable to look much beyond themselves: they were of middle-class background and therefore elitist; they lived in the American "melting pot" and were ill equipped to understand ethnic politics; they were civilians and therefore had an anti-military bias; and so on. All of these explanations left American Sovietologists unsuited to take the authors' advice about fitting into the discipline—and without insights from the discipline, Sovietologists were unable to understand *perestroika*.[65]

The what-went-wrong debate was in no sense limited to the academy. Officials at the CIA faced a series of congressional and public attacks for having missed the Soviet collapse; they were accused of playing politics and accepting Soviet claims, resulting in one of the worst "strategic blunders" in the Cold War. A report commissioned by the House Permanent Select Committee on Intelligence exonerated CIA from the worst of the attacks, pointing to some of the obstacles to analyzing the Soviet economy. These obstacles were familiar to the economists of the 1940s, too: the difficulties of ruble-dollar comparisons (a variant of the Gerschenkron effect) and the problems inherent in using national income figures to measure social welfare. The committee also identified serious flaws in the presentation of results, especially in years with significant changes, and some problems in data analysis.[66]

But it was in the academy that the what-went-wrong dispute played out most fully, with a great deal of energy expended for relatively little gain. The debate continued, indeed amplified, in the late 1990s. Cohen's "Russian Studies without Russia" provoked a rebuttal from Breslauer's junior colleague M. Steven Fish, "Russian Studies without Studying," a discussion that ended with mutual accusations of libel and defamation.[67] Meanwhile, Pipes and Malia, who shared hardline views about the USSR, attacked each other in the pages of the *New Republic*.[68] For a handful of academics, the conflict between totalitarians and revisionists continued well into the twenty-first century.[69]

The failure to predict or explain Gorbachev was not the result of a fundamental flaw in the structure of Soviet Studies nor in the political or intellectual influences upon it. The failure was instead due to the growing tensions in the field in the 1970s and 1980s, themselves the result of changes within and beyond the academy. At the very moment that its subject faced existential crisis, Soviet experts were unable to explain it. This failure of the 1980s was compounded in the 1990s by the escalation of internal disputes, which worried as much about what went wrong in Sovietology as about what went wrong in the Soviet Union itself.

SOVIET STUDIES AFTER THE SOVIET UNION

Almost two decades into the post-Soviet era, the institutions of Russian Studies are still adjusting. Members of the American Association for the Advancement of Slavic Studies debated its name for years before approving a new one, effective in July 2010.[1] The Kennan Institute for Advanced Russian Studies simply removed the last four words from its name. Many journal and organizational titles, however, were altered to reflect geography or chronology. *Problems of Communism* became *Problems of Post-Communism;* the American Council of Teachers of Russian grew into the American Council for International Education; and *Slavic Review* adopted a subtitle with a geographic reach far broader than its title suggests: "Russian, Eurasian, and East European Studies."[2] The journal is far from the only institution to resuscitate the term "Eurasian," though this time without the claims to cultural uniqueness and spiritual destiny that the émigré Eurasianists like George Vernadsky highlighted. As scholars have observed, the frequent invocations of Eurasia nevertheless carry heavy political baggage.[3]

The biggest change in these institutions has been a substantial increase in collaborations with and programs for scholars from the countries under study. IREX, with a generic name that withstood the Soviet collapse, still sponsors scholarly exchange programs but also has moved into a much wider range of activities, including facilitating American educational and training opportunities for students and scholars from the regions being studied. All of the programs have also expanded opportunities for scholars from the region to work in the United States, either in collaboration with American academics or pursuing their own research. The Kennan Institute, for instance, occasionally has more "regional scholars" (from the former USSR) in residence than Americans. The Kennan Institute, like other institutions supported by Title VIII funding, insists upon "policy relevance," though that term has broadened significantly over time.

Title VIII, first passed in the 1980s, was an effort to establish a new middle ground between service to Mars, national security, and to Minerva, intellectual life. In this way, Title VIII is itself an artifact of the Cold War, not only because it provided for policy-relevant studies about the U.S. antagonist of those days, but also because it supported—and still supports—the study of a single world region.[4] The enterprise of interdisciplinary area studies came into being in the 1940s, seeking to unite scholars irrespective of discipline to address policy problems or to train those who would. Along the way, it was a boon for American studies of the world, providing training grants, travel opportunities, research materials, and jobs. Though the original aims were connected to the national interest, broadly defined, the bonanza years were hardly limited to policy-relevant fields like political science and economics. Studying the region meant knowing its language and culture, spurring bigger and better departments of literature and history. The growth of Slavic humanities was a product, and not a by-product, of the Cold War. The founders and funders of area studies applied a capacious definition of national interest, one that called for serious training and scholarship in the humanities and the social sciences.

As the funds available for area studies shrank in the late 1960s, so too did the definition of national interest. The humanities were excluded from this new definition, and so too was the increasing amount of social science work—especially in political science—oriented toward broader disciplinary concerns. The area studies enterprise was, therefore, already in trouble before the Cold War ended; it faced not just tensions of growth related to the turn toward the disciplines, but also tensions of decline as the meaning of relevance narrowed. Marshall Shulman recalled that, in the 1950s, "the word 'defense' had a certain magic...in loosening the legislative purse-strings," which contributed to the intellectual life of the field. But by the time he was writing in 1970, a "destructive polarization" had gripped the country and put the field at risk.[5] Pulled in different directions by the universal aspirations of postwar American social scientists and divided by the polarization of American campuses, area studies faced severe challenges in the 1960s and 1970s.[6] With the end of the Cold War, area studies faced renewed institutional and intellectual attack. The Social Science Research Council, which had helped to create area studies at midcentury, presided over its dissolution at the twentieth century's end. Its academic programs and training grants were reorganized along thematic lines, with the once-dominant regional committees relegated to an advisory capacity and then approaching extinction.[7]

The decline of the region as a category for funding has helped, or even forced, Russia experts to more fully engage with their respective disciplines. This trend is most noticeable in political science. Mark Beissinger was the first Russia expert to win an American Political Science Association book award, in 2003. Since then, Russia experts have earned more than their share with scholarship oriented toward specialists in other regions or topics. In the Slavic humanities, too, Russia experts have converged with their disciplines, aided especially by the ease of access to Russia and to a revolution in Russian arts and culture. Studies of Russian culture have had a remarkable period of creativity since 1991, aided especially by increased border crossings—both the chance to visit and the influx of a new generation of scholars born in the USSR—and the kaleidoscopic changes of their subject. Literary scholars have joined with anthropologists of (and from) the region to create an especially dynamic and exciting scholarly enterprise.[8] For those focused on the Russian and especially the Soviet past, the collapse of the USSR dramatically improved conditions. What one historian called the "archival gold rush" brought prospectors by the hundreds to long-secret repositories, including the former Central Party Archive, the Foreign Policy Archive, and the Central Committee Archive.[9] Conditions eased in already-accessible archives and in libraries holding materials on Russian and Soviet history; the "special storage" sections in libraries and the "secret portions" of archives disgorged some of their contents to Russian and Western researchers. Post–Cold War Russian Studies continued the dispersion that began in the 1960s as disciplinary identities complemented and then overwhelmed regional ones.

One sign of the growing convergence of Russian Studies with the disciplines has been the increasing focus on a complex of issues centered around nationality (or, in the American context, ethnicity): the history of Russian imperial expansion; national and imperial borderlands; Soviet and post-Soviet nationality policy; the official and unofficial treatment of ethnic minorities in the region; and (especially since 2001) the role of Islam in the region. The quality and prominence of the scholarship on nationality is new, even if the perceived need to focus on the topic is not. From the field's earliest days, before the appearance of Richard Pipes's 1954 book on Bolshevik nationality policy, Sovietologists called for serious investigation of the non-Russian republics of the USSR. Yet these exhortations largely went unheeded; only a shelf of unpublished dissertations and a handful of scholarly monographs dealt with the non-Russian regions in the USSR. The collapse of the USSR and the transformation of ethnically defined Soviet republics into independent nations have invalidated the claims of the Refugee Interview Project (and Soviet officialdom) that nationality would not matter in the Soviet future. In a set of lectures given in 1991, Ronald Grigor Suny, whose first book was on 1917 in Baku, emphasized the importance of nationality policy in the rise, life, and fall of the USSR. This would be the first book in a remarkable renaissance in scholarship on nationality, empire, and borderlands in Russian and Soviet history—and in the Eurasian present. Books on these topics, authored by a cohort of scholars trained since the late 1980s, have won numerous AAASS prizes as well as disciplinary recognition.[10] Though studies of nationality have complicated and extended graduate training, they also have brought scholarship in Russian history, political science, and (for the first time) anthropology in line with broader trends in their respective disciplines. This focus on nationality marks perhaps the greatest break from Cold War writings in Russian and Soviet history, which (hand-wringing about nationality aside) remained centered on Russia itself.

For political scientists, convergence with their discipline entailed the expulsion of policy-oriented work—or, more neutrally, the partition of the scholarly and policy worlds. This separation began in the 1970s as a para-academic world of think tanks, government agencies, and university-based policy centers emerged, which operated apart from academic political science, let alone the rest of the academy.[11] Many scholars celebrate this new division of labor; Mark Beissinger, AAASS president in 2007, observed that punditry "exited the field" after 1991, thus allowing scholars of Russian politics to become more like their political science colleagues. The professionalization of punditry has meant the expansion of this policy sphere and the decline of university-based experts within it.[12]

A policy track within Soviet Studies expanded in the 1970s and 1980s, ultimately shaping both the academic and policy worlds. This change undercut the original purpose of area studies as formulated in the 1940s: to bring together the once-divided roles of social scientist and humanist, graduate advisor and government consultant. Soviet Studies was perhaps the single largest beneficiary of this area studies effort; a vibrant field of study was created, well supported by foundations and federal agencies. Sponsors invested heavily in projects distant from immediate policy concerns, including everything from literature programs to exchanges to libraries and archives. These investments in infrastructure were a key stimulus for the field and allowed it to serve both Mars and Minerva. The relationship could be rocky, as the struggles of Harvard's Refugee Interview Project made all too clear. Yet many scholars commuted smoothly from classroom to briefing room. The relationship between academe and government changed in the 1960s as disciplines exerted a stronger pull, as the events of those years ended the innocence about the coziness between academe and government, and as policy impresarios like Brzezinski made their way to Washington. Those interested in the policy track received ever-narrower training, rarely taking advantage of the institutions that had been so laboriously set up in the 1950s: the library holdings gathered with great difficulty, the exchange programs strenuously maintained, and the language and cultural studies that had been well supported in area studies programs. They focused strictly on policy concerns, receiving less training in cultural context, even language, and they rarely spent significant time in the countries they studied. But the policy credentials provided unprecedented opportunities, producing an ironic result.

Sovietologists have been more prominent in the top rank of U.S. policy making in the two decades since the USSR collapsed than they were in the seven decades it existed. While post-Cold War cabinet meetings hardly became miniature versions of AAASS conventions, a number of Sovietologists—usually on the policy track—accepted senior foreign policy jobs. Indeed, they may have chosen to study the USSR in the first place because of its centrality to Cold War foreign policy. There were a few Soviet experts who made policy during the Cold War: Zbigniew Brzezinski and Marshall Shulman under Jimmy Carter and Richard Pipes under Ronald Reagan. By the late 1980s, an increasing number of policy experts trained in Soviet Studies entered the highest levels of policy making. Jack Matlock, a career Foreign Service officer (M.A., Columbia), replaced Pipes at the National Security Council and then served as ambassador in Moscow in the late 1980s. Condoleezza Rice (Ph.D., University of Denver) left Stanford to join the National Security Council staff for the crucial years 1989–1991. There, she worked closely with Robert Gates (Ph.D., Georgetown), a career CIA officer serving as deputy national security advisor. Gates and Rice, of course, would both serve in George W. Bush's cabinet. But Republicans did not have a lock on using Soviet experts: Madeleine Albright (Ph.D., Columbia, where she studied with Brzezinski) spent decades in both academic and policy positions, including ambassador to the United Nations, before becoming Bill Clinton's secretary of state in 1997. Below cabinet level, there have been many more. Dennis Ross (Ph.D., UCLA), for instance, worked at the Berkeley-Stanford Program, originally a policy-oriented institute, before heading to Washington; he worked for George H. W. Bush's State Department and served as Bill Clinton's special Middle East representative—and then as Barack Obama's staff expert on the region.

Unlike the Cold War era policy makers Brzezinski, Shulman, and Pipes, these post–Cold War figures had a minimal presence in Soviet Studies or in political science. Many of them did their training and initial research on institutions that did not survive the Cold War: Soviet party organs, Warsaw Pact cooperation, union-wide institutions, and the like. Their degrees were primarily credentials for future policy work; they aspired to (and quickly took on) policy dossiers well outside of their original training. The credentials served their new roles well, certifying the policy expert whose expertise was in policy per se, not in any one country or region. As Soviet experts started shaping foreign policy in a world without the USSR, non-experts jumped in to fill the gap; the prominence of economist Jeffrey Sachs shows how much policy expertise had been unshackled from regional knowledge. It was this new sort of policy expert, as much as the collapse of the Soviet Union, that accounted for the decline of the academic Russia expert in public discourse.

As expertise has been construed more broadly, government efforts to support research and training for national security purposes after 9/11 have grown narrower. The challenges that the United States confronted in the middle of the twentieth century should seem familiar in the early twenty-first. The country faced a grave danger, an enemy that threatened hopes for a peaceful and prosperous world. It was a new kind of enemy—not a single nation, but an idea, one whose adherents believed that they could and would convert the whole world to their way of life. Like the recently defeated enemy, this new antagonist sought to expand its power even as it ruled brutally over its subject populations. The United States was poorly equipped to comprehend, let alone respond to, this new global threat. There were few experts in government or universities who spoke the languages and had studied the regions.[13]

As similar as these threats might have been, the responses to the rise of the Soviet threat in the 1940s and to the rise of Islamic fundamentalism in the 2000s could not have been more different. As the preceding pages have demonstrated, Soviet Studies built broadly, deeply, and for the long term in its first decade. The combination of wide interests and deep pockets accounted for the high intellectual caliber of this scholarship as well as its use in policy realms.

Intellectual mobilization after 9/11, in contrast, was relatively narrow and shallow. President Bush introduced a National Security Language Initiative to increase the linguistic capabilities of Americans in Arabic, Chinese, Hindi, Persian, Russian, and Central Asian languages. Secretary of State Condoleezza Rice celebrated it as a twenty-first-century version of Cold War Soviet Studies. But the scope was far smaller, focused primarily on language training.[14]

Narrower still was the Pentagon's much-trumpeted Minerva Research Initiative. Secretary of Defense Robert Gates repeatedly invoked the example of Kremlinology to make the case for Pentagon-funded social science and support for basic research. Leaving aside the nomenclature—Kremlinology was usually practiced by intelligence officers, not scholars—Secretary Gates set himself a difficult task. While government support for Sovietology was broad and gave a great deal of autonomy to scholars, the Minerva initiative was anything but: it specified narrow areas for scholarship, originally envisioned a selection panel of military officials (since abandoned), and insisted on not just policy relevance but contributions to operational concerns at the Department of Defense. The Minerva Research Initiative has generated a small firestorm of controversy among academics wary of Defense funding in general, demonstrating the remarkable distance from the 1950s and 1960s, when such funding sources were unquestioned.[15]

In 1953, during congressional hearings on U.S. Air Force funding for Harvard's Refugee Interview Project, one senator complained that the military got nothing "except just a lot of professor theories and all that stuff." If the military services, he went on, "have not sense enough" to fight the Cold War "without hiring a bunch of college professors…[then] this defense establishment is in one darn bad shape."[16] The senator's comments notwithstanding, these "professor theories" exerted a profound influence in the world of ideas and even in policy circles. They helped scholars to understand modern societies, economies, and political systems as well as medieval history and ancient languages. With financial and logistical support from government agencies, these scholars wielded the most policy influence in the 1950s. Contrary to the claims of later critics, their advice helped to moderate America's Soviet policy in those years.

The history of Soviet Studies offers contradictory lessons about the relationship between national security and intellectual life. The field was an intellectual success when government funds flowed because it attracted an especially wide range of scholars and because its founders conceived of their aims very broadly. Scholars-cum-consultants innocently but fervently believed that the various parts of their job fit together seamlessly. They worked with government officials at the same time that they produced their own scholarship and trained their academic progeny. Seams strained and innocence ended in the 1960s, leading some later scholars to denigrate the field solely on the basis of its ties to government. Amid the dual crises of the late 1960s, pioneers like Shulman hoped to reinvigorate Soviet Studies by returning to the interdisciplinary and applied research that had driven top-notch work in the field's first decade. Yet the successes of Soviet Studies came thanks to unrepeatable historical circumstances: the intellectual mobilization during World War II, the postwar university boom, and the emergence of new sources of funding. These broad forces permitted Soviet Studies to serve both Mars and Minerva, or at least to try. There was no way in 1969, let alone 2009, to go back to the future. There was no way, after the divisions of the 1960s, to recapture the innocence of the postwar years, the notion that government agencies could only support, not distort, intellectual life. Coming from the small and isolated policy-oriented sector of Soviet Studies, secretaries Gates and Rice celebrated themselves in claiming that their new initiatives incorporated the lessons of Soviet Studies. But new enemies, in new times, require new solutions.

ESSAY ON SOURCES

Students of modern American history have a problem that may make other historians envious: a surfeit of published and archival primary sources. Making efficient use of these sources, a large group of historians has produced an explosion of excellent scholarship on post–World War II American intellectual and political life. At the same time, the scholars in Russian Studies have turned increasingly to recounting the history of their field in autobiographical essays and institutional histories. Because my endnotes tend to the laconic, this essay will highlight some of the works of scholarship and recollection that have been most important for writing *Know Your Enemy*. Simply put, these were the materials next to my desk as I wrote.

A great many scholars in modern American history and in the history of science have contributed to a deeper understanding of the institutions and ideas connected to the modern American research university. While the field is too broad to list everything here, a number of works proved to be especially helpful. The origins and operations of modernization theory are brilliantly traced by Nils Gilman in *Mandarins of the Future* (Baltimore, 2003). Howard Brick offers an insightful perspective on postwar social sciences in *Transcending Capitalism* (Ithaca, N.Y., 2006). Ellen Herman takes a compelling and original look at the behavioral sciences within and beyond universities in *The Romance of American Psychology* (Berkeley, 1995). Ron Robin offers a harrowing tour of the "military-intellectual complex" in *The Making of the Cold War Enemy* (Princeton, 2003). Roger Geiger offers an incomparable overview of the state of the universities in *Research and Relevant Knowledge* (Oxford, 1993). Indispensable for the rise and fall of area studies is Robert A. McCaughey, *International Studies and Academic Enterprise* (New York, 1984). While practitioners' histories are often limited by the boundaries of their fields, the essays in *Sociology in America,* ed. Craig Calhoun (Chicago, 2007) transcend those boundaries to offer thoughtful accounts of the field's first American century. Finally, two widely cited and highly critical accounts of academics' relationship to national security are Noam Chomsky, et al., *The Cold War and the University* (New York, 1997); and *Universities and Empire*, ed. Christopher Simpson (New York, 1998).

Other scholarly works important for *Know Your Enemy* do not fit neatly into a single category: Abbott Gleason, *Totalitarianism* (Oxford, 1995); Barry Katz, *Foreign Intelligence* (Cambridge, Mass., 1989); André Liebich, *From the Other Shore* (Cambridge, Mass., 1997); and John W. Kestner, "Through the Looking Glass: American Perceptions of the Soviet Economy, 1941–1964" (Ph.D. diss., University of Wisconsin, Madison, 1999).

Learning about the experiences of Russian Studies scholars was a fascinating opportunity to see an academic world that is not remote in years or in space, and yet operated with some fundamentally different assumptions and ideas. Fortunately, scholars in Russian Studies have been writing careful institutional histories and insightful memoirs for decades already. Such accounts often appear in scholarly journals in the form of published interviews, as *Kritika* has been doing to great effect in the twenty-first century; the pioneer was *Russian History/Histoire Russe,* which published a number of firsthand accounts in the 1990s. Robert F. Byrnes's *Soviet-American Academic Exchanges, 1958–1975* (Bloomington, Ind., 1975) was the first institutional history by a key player in the exchanges. Yale Richmond, who worked on East-West exchanges from various State Department posts, has a similar kind of practitioner's history, *Cultural Exchange and the Cold War* (University Park, Pa., 2003), as well as a memoir, *Practicing Public Diplomacy* (New York, 2008). The best way to learn about the exchange experience is from an evocative set of recollections edited by Cathy Frierson and Samuel H. Baron, *Adventures in Russian Historical Research* (Armonk, N.Y., 2003).

Memoirs have provided a unique opportunity to learn more about some of the most interesting and most controversial scholars in Russian Studies. Particular helpful were Abbott Gleason's *A Liberal Education* (Maynard, Mass., 2009); Loren Graham's *Moscow Stories* (Bloomington, Ind., 2006); and Richard Pipes's *Vixi* (New Haven, Conn., 2003). Though Sheila Fitzpatrick has not written a book-length memoir, she has offered her perspectives on the evolution of the field (and her role in it) in a number of articles and published interviews, including "Revisionism in Retrospect," *Slavic Review* 67:3 (Fall 2008). Full-length biographies of Russian Studies scholars are few, but N. N. Bolkhovitinov, *Russkie uchenye-emigranty* (Moscow, 2005), offers thoughtful assessments of Michael Florinsky, Michael Karpovich, and George Vernadsky. See also Patrick G. Vaughan's "Zbigniew Brzezinski: The Political and Academic Life of a Cold War Visionary" (Ph.D. diss., West Virginia University, 2003).

Finally, there were a few collective assessments of the field that provided useful snapshots of a given moment: *American Research on Russia*, ed. H. H.

Fisher (Bloomington, Ind., 1959); *The State of Soviet Studies*, ed. Walter Laqueur and Leopold Labedz (Cambridge, Mass., 1965); and *Beyond Soviet Studies*, ed. Daniel Orlovsky (Washington, D.C., 1995).

Of course, there is no better way to learn about individuals' experiences in Russian Studies than by listening to them. I was privileged to have the opportunity to speak with a great many scholars and supporters of Russian Studies who were active from the 1940s through the 2000s. These conversations taught me about many of the individuals and institutions, and many of the trends and traumas, that have shaped Russian Studies over the last seventy years. A handful of those communications are cited in the notes; many more are not. I cannot thank everyone individually here, but do want to acknowledge some whose recent deaths have robbed the field of great minds and good men: Joseph Berliner, James Millar, Barrington Moore Jr., William Odom, Marshall Shulman, and Reginald Zelnik.

In regard to the archival collections cited below, I am especially grateful to the following individuals for permission to cite and/or quote from documents to which they control rights: Maria Friedrich (Carl Friedrich Papers), Heidi Dawidoff (Alexander Gerschenkron Papers), George Fischer (for access to his FBI file), Dmitry Gorenberg (AAASS Records), Mary Katzenstein (Merle Fainsod Papers), Alex Inkeles (Refugee Interview Project Reports and Memoranda), Carol Leadenham (Hoover Institution Records), Peter Nitze (Paul Nitze Papers), William Odom (William Odom Papers), Richard Pipes (Richard Pipes Papers), Christine Sleeper (Raymond Sleeper "Admissions File"), Lisabeth Tarlow (Russian Research Center Records), and Judith Vishniac (Barrington Moore Jr. Papers).

ARCHIVAL COLLECTIONS

Oral Histories

Paul H. Buck (1967), Carnegie Corporation of New York Project, Oral History Research Office, Columbia University

John W. Gardner (2000), CCNY Project, Oral History Research Office, Columbia University

Alex Inkeles (1985), Spencer Foundation Project, Oral History Research Office, Columbia University

George Frost Kennan (1972), in Non-Grant Files, Ford Foundation Archives

Martin Malia (2003), Regional Oral History Office, Bancroft Library, University of California, Berkeley

Frederick Osborn (1967), CCNY Project, Oral History Research Office, Columbia University

Nicholas Riasanovsky (1996), Regional Oral History Office, Bancroft Library, University of California, Berkeley

Personal Collections in Archives

Frederick Charles Barghoorn Papers, Yale University Library
Raymond Augustine Bauer Papers, Harvard Business School Archives
Robert F. Byrnes Papers, Indiana University Library
Raymond S. Cline Papers, Library of Congress
Kenneth W. Colegrove Papers, Herbert Hoover Presidential Library
James Conant Papers, Harvard University Archives
Samuel Hazzard Cross Papers, Harvard University Archives
E. E. Day Papers, Kroch Library, Cornell University
William J. Donovan Papers, Army Historical Research Center
Merle Fainsod Papers, Harvard University Archives
Homer Ferguson Papers, Bentley Library, University of Michigan
Lewis Feuer Papers, Brandeis University Library
Raymond Fisher Papers, Bancroft Library, University of California, Berkeley
Carl Joachim Friedrich Papers, Harvard University Archives
Alexander Gerschenkron Papers, Harvard University Archives
Herbert Hoover Post-Presidential Records, Herbert Hoover Presidential Library
Henry M. Jackson Papers, University of Washington Library
Roman Jakobson Papers, MIT Archives
Michael Karpovich Papers, Bakhmeteff Archive, Columbia University
George Frost Kennan Papers, Mudd Library, Princeton University
Clyde Kluckhohn Papers, Harvard University Archives
A. A. Knopf Papers, Harry Ransom Center, University of Texas, Austin
Wassily Leontief Jr. Papers, Harvard University Archives
James Augustine McAlpine Papers, Presbyterian Historical Society
Margaret Mead Papers, Library of Congress
Alfred G. Meyer Memoir, University of Wisconsin, Madison Library
Max F. Millikan Papers, MIT Archives
Barrington Moore Jr. Papers, Harvard University Archives
Philip E. Mosely Papers, Columbia University Library
Philip E. Mosely Papers, University of Illinois Library
Boris I. Nicolaevsky Papers, Hoover Institution Archives
Paul H. Nitze Papers, Library of Congress
Frederick Osborn Papers, American Philosophical Society
Talcott Parsons Papers, Harvard University Archives
Richard E. Pipes Papers, Harvard University Archives
Ithiel de Sola Pool Papers, MIT Archives
Geroid Tanquary Robinson Papers, Columbia University Library
Leonard Schapiro Papers, Hoover Institution Archives
Raymond Sleeper "Admissions File," Harvard University Archives
Boris Souvarine Papers, Houghton Library, Harvard University
Julius A. Stratton Papers, MIT Archives
Gleb Struve Papers, Hoover Institution Archives

Donald Treadgold Papers, University of Washington Library
George Vernadsky Papers, Bakhmeteff Archive, Columbia University
Mark Vishniak Papers, Hoover Institution Archives
Bertram Wolfe Papers, Hoover Institution Archives

Privately Held Collections

Loren Graham Papers
Gregory Grossman Papers (in author's possession)
Yale Richmond Papers

Institutional Archives (Nongovernmental)

American Association for the Advancement of Slavic Studies (AAASS) Records,
    AAASS Office
American Council of Learned Societies (ACLS) Records, Library of Congress
American Historical Association (AHA) Records, Library of Congress
Carnegie Corporation of New York (CCNY) Records, Columbia University Library
Columbia University Central Files (CUCF), Columbia University Archives
Cornell University College of Arts and Sciences Records, Kroch Library, Cornell
    University
Ford Foundation (FF) Records, Ford Foundation Archives (includes Grant Files and
    Non-Grant Files)
Harvard University Dean of the Faculty of Arts and Sciences (FAS) Correspondence,
    Harvard University Archives
Harvard University Dean of the Graduate School of Public Administration, Harvard
    University Archives
Harvard University Russian Research Center (RRC) Records, Harvard University
    Archives (includes records of the Refugee Interview Project, RIP)
Harvard University School for Overseas Administration Records, Harvard University
    Archives
Hoover Institution Records, Hoover Institution Archives
Institute for Social Research (ISR) Records, Bentley Library, University of Michigan
Inter-University Committee for Travel Grants (IUCTG) Records, Columbia University
    Archives
MIT Office of the President Records, MIT Archives
Oklahoma State University President's Papers, Oklahoma State University Library
RAND Corporation Organization Charts, RAND Archives
Revolution and the Development of International Relations (RADIR) Project Records,
    Hoover Institution Archives
Rockefeller Foundation (RF) Records, Rockefeller Archive Center
Russian Review Records, Hoover Institution Archives
Social Science Research Council (SSRC) Records, Rockefeller Archive Center

University of California Office of the President Records, Bancroft Library, University
    of California, Berkeley
University of Colorado Board of Trustees Minutes, University of Colorado Library
University of Illinois Russian and East European Institute (REEI) Records, University
    of Illinois Library

Archival Collections Holding Official U.S. and Russian Materials

Air Force Historical Research Agency (AFHRA)
Declassified Documents Retrieval Service (DDRS)
Digital National Security Archive (DNSA)
Dwight D. Eisenhower Presidential Library
    Special Assistant for National Security Affairs
    White House Confidential Files
    White House NSC Staff Records
FBI Files, obtained via Freedom of Information Act
    Raymond Bauer
    Abram Bergson
    Merle Fainsod
    George Fischer
    Alexander Gerschenkron
    George Vernadsky
Gosudarstvennyi Arkhiv Rossiiskii Federatsii
    fond 8131: Prokurator SSSR
John F. Kennedy Library
    National Security Files
Library of Congress
    Archives of the Library of Congress
National Security Archive, George Washington University Library
    Anne Cahn Collection of CIA Materials, gathered through Freedom of Information
        Act
Rossiiskii gosudarstvennyi arkhiv noveishei istorii (RGANI)
    fond 5: Central Committee
Harry S Truman Presidential Library
    Psychological Strategy Board Records
U.S. National Archives
    Record Group 24: Bureau of Naval Personnel
    Record Group 59: Department of State
        Central Foreign Policy Files (CFPF)
        Decimal File (SDDF)
        Lot File 52–283: Project TROY
        Lot File 58D776: Project TROY
        Lot File 69D162: USSR Country Director
        Lot File 78D441: German War Documents Project

Record Group 160: Army Service Forces
Record Group 263: Central Intelligence Agency
    CREST: CIA Research Tool
Record Group 330: Office of the Secretary of Defense
University of Arkansas Library
    Bureau of Educational and Cultural Affairs (CU) Historical Collection

NOTES

In addition to the abbreviations listed at the front of the book, the following abbreviations appear only in the notes.

ADFL	Association of Departments of Foreign Languages
AER	*American Economic Review*
AFHRA	Air Force Historical Research Agency
AHR	*American Historical Review*
AJS	*American Journal of Sociology*
Annals	*Annals of the American Academy of Political and Social Science*
APSR	*American Political Science Review*
ASEER	*American Slavic and East European Review*
ASR	*American Sociological Review*
CFPF	Central Foreign Policy Files (U.S. State Department)
CUCF	Columbia University Central Files
DDRS	Declassified Document Reference System
DNSA	Digital National Security Archive
FA	*Foreign Affairs*
FRUS	*Foreign Relations of the United States* (U.S. State Department)
ISR	Institute for Social Research (University of Michigan)
JCH	*Journal of Contemporary History*
JFKL	John F. Kennedy Library
JPE	*Journal of Political Economy*
LAT	*Los Angeles Times*
NYHT	*New York Herald-Tribune*
NYT	*New York Times*
PSQ	*Political Science Quarterly*
QJE	*Quarterly Journal of Economics*
RDB	Research and Development Board (U.S. Department of Defense)

REEI   Russian and East European Institute (University of Illinois, Urbana-Champaign)
RG   Record Group
RGANI   Rossiiskii gosudarstvennyi arkhiv noveishei istorii
RR   *Russian Review*
SDDF   State Department Decimal File
SEEJ   *Slavic and East European Journal*
SEER   *Slavonic and East European Review*
SR   *Slavic Review*
SW   Roman Jakobson, *Selected Writings*, 8 vols. (The Hague, 1962–1987)
TLS   *Times Literary Supplement*
USAF   U.S. Air Force
WP   *World Politics*

INTRODUCTION

1. Woodrow Kuhns, preface to *Assessing the Soviet Threat: The Early Cold War Years,* ed. Kuhns (Washington, D.C., 1997), 13. Thomas P. Whitney, *Russia in My Life* (New York, 1962), 26. Albert Parry, *America Learns Russian: A History of the Teaching of the Russian Language in the United States* (Syracuse, N.Y., 1967), 112. Geroid T. Robinson, "Dr. Robinson Cites Vital Need for Understanding of Russians," *NYHT,* 4 November 1945.

2. Although the different terms—Russian Studies, Slavic Studies, Soviet Studies, Sovietology—had different emphases (and connotations), I will shift among them in the book that follows, generally trying to follow contemporary usage without dwelling on the differences.

3. James G. Hershberg, *James B. Conant: Harvard to Hiroshima and the Making of the Nuclear Age* (New York, 1993), 43.

4. Lawrence E. Gelfand, *The Inquiry: American Preparations for Peace, 1917–1919* (New Haven, Conn., 1963), chap. 11. On academics' unrealized efforts to contribute to the U.S. effort in World War I, see Carol S. Gruber, *Mars and Minerva: World War I and the Uses of Higher Learning in America* (Baton Rouge, La., 1975).

5. Kennan to James Russell, 11 October 1950, George F. Kennan Papers (Mudd Library, Princeton University), 139:8.

6. On Russian Studies before World War II, see Stephen Marshall Arum, "Early Stages of Foreign Language and Area Studies in the U.S.: 1915–1941" (Ed.D. diss., Columbia University Teachers College, 1975), 193–206, 499–514; Clarence A. Manning, *History of Slavic Studies in the United States* (Milwaukee, Wis., 1957), chap. 6; Parry, *America Learns Russian,* chap. 6.

7. Peter Buck, "Adjusting to Military Life: The Social Sciences Go to War, 1940–1950," in *Military Enterprise and Technological Change: Perspectives on the American Experience,* ed. Merritt Roe Smith (Cambridge, Mass., 1985). Ellen Herman, *The Romance of American Psychology: Political Culture in an Age of Experts* (Berkeley, 1995),

chap. 5. David H. Price, *Anthropological Intelligence: The Deployment and Neglect of American Anthropology in the Second World War* (Durham, N.C., 2008), chap. 8. Barry Katz, *Foreign Intelligence: Research and Analysis in the Office of Strategic Services, 1942–1945* (Cambridge, Mass., 1989). On the rise of government use of expertise in the 1940s, see Brian Balogh, *Chain Reaction: Expert Debate and Public Participation in American Commercial Nuclear Power, 1945–1975* (Cambridge, 1991).

8. Bundy, "The Battlefields of Power and the Searchlights of the Academy," in *The Dimensions of Diplomacy*, ed. E. A. J. Johnson (Baltimore, 1964), 2.

9. Sigmund Diamond, *Compromised Campus: The Collaboration of Universities with the Intelligence Community, 1945–1955* (Oxford, 1992), chaps. 3–4; David H. Price, *Threatening Anthropology: McCarthyism and the FBI's Surveillance of Activist Anthropologists* (Durham, N.C., 2004); and, more generally, Ellen Schrecker, *No Ivory Tower: McCarthyism and the Universities* (Oxford, 1986). John W. Gardner to Clyde Kluckhohn, 17 October 1947, RRC Correspondence (Harvard University Archives), series UAV 759.10, box 1.

10. The scholarly literature emphasizing intellectual conformism and Cold War imperatives is too large to cite here. See especially Noam Chomsky et al., *The Cold War and the University* (New York, 1997); *Universities and Empire: Money and Politics in the Social Sciences during the Cold War*, ed. Christopher Simpson (New York, 1998); Ron Robin, *The Making of the Cold War Enemy: Culture and Politics in the Military-Intellectual Complex* (Princeton, 2001); and, specifically on Soviet Studies, Charles Thomas O'Connell, "Social Structure and Science: Soviet Studies at Harvard" (Ph.D. diss., UCLA, 1990). For a brief review, see Engerman, "Rethinking the Cold War University," *Journal of Cold War Studies* 5:3 (Summer 2003), 80–95. On the Cold War and various disciplines, see Sonja Amadae, *Rationalizing Capitalist Democracy: The Cold War Origins of Rational Choice Liberalism* (Chicago, 2003); Christopher Simpson, *The Science of Coercion: Communication Research and Psychological Warfare, 1945–1960* (Oxford, 1994); Jesse Lemisch, *On Active Service in War and Peace: Politics and Ideology in the American Historical Profession* (Toronto, 1975); Ido Oren, *Our Enemies and US: America's Rivalries and the Making of Political Science* (Ithaca, N.Y., 2003); and Andrew Abbott and James T. Sparrow, "Hot War, Cold War: Structures of Sociological Action," in *Sociology in America: A History*, ed. Craig Calhoun (Chicago, 2007).

11. Historians of science have been particular attuned to the relationship between sponsorship and scholarship; see, for instance, Chandra Mukerji, *A Fragile Power: Scientists and the State* (Princeton, 1989); *Big Science: The Growth of Large-Scale Research*, ed. Peter Galison and Bruce Hevly (Stanford, 1992); David Kaiser, "The Postwar Suburbanization of American Physics," *American Quarterly* 56:4 (December 2004), 851–888; Hunter Heyck, "Patrons of the Revolution: Ideals and Institutions in Postwar Behavioral Science," *Isis* 97:3 (September 2006), 420–446.

12. From the right, see Ofira Selikar, *Politics, Paradigms, and Intelligence Failures: Why So Few Predicted the Collapse of the Soviet Union* (Armonk, N.Y., 2004); Richard Pipes, "U.S. and Them," *New Republic* 193 (14 October 1985), 32–34; Martin Malia, "From under the Rubble, What?" *Problems of Communism* 41 (1992), 89–106. From the left, see Alexander Dallin, "Bias and Blunders in American Studies on the

USSR," *SR* 32:3 (September 1973), 560–576; Stephen F. Cohen, "Sovietology as a Vocation," in Cohen, *Rethinking the Soviet Experience: Politics and History since 1917* (Oxford, 1985); Stephen White, "Political Science as Ideology: The Study of Soviet Politics," in *WJMM: Political Questions: Essays in Honour of W. J. M. MacKenzie* (Manchester, England, 1974).

13. Paul Samuelson, "Unemployment Ahead," *New Republic* 111 (11 September 1944), 298. Joy Elizabeth Rohde, "'The Social Scientists' War': Expertise in a Cold War Nation" (Ph.D. diss., University of Pennsylvania, 2007).

14. Robert A. McCaughey, *International Studies and Academic Enterprise: A Chapter in the Enclosure of American Learning* (New York, 1984), chap. 7.

15. Elinor G. Barber and Warren Ilchman, *International Studies Review: A Staff Study* (New York, 1979), 6.

16. For views of Russian/Soviet Studies elsewhere, see Richard Sakwa, "The Australasian Contribution to Soviet, East European, and Russian Studies" (University of Melbourne Contemporary European Research Centre, Working Paper no. 1, 2004); Robert Desjardins, *The Soviet Union through French Eyes, 1945–1985* (Houndsmills,England, 1988); Corinna R. Unger, *Ostforschung in Westdeutschland: Die Erforschung des europäischen Ostens und die Deutsche Forschungsgemeinschaft, 1945–1975* (Stuttgart, 2007); I. W. Roberts, *History of the School of Slavonic and East European Studies, 1915–1990* (London, 1991).

17. *Digest of Education Statistics, 1990* (accessed online at http://nces.ed.gov/Programs/digest, February 2009).

18. I have written about this topic elsewhere: Engerman, *Modernization from the Other Shore: American Intellectuals and the Romance of Economic Development* (Cambridge, Mass., 2003), chap. 7; Engerman, "New Society, New Scholarship: Soviet Studies Programmes in Interwar America," *Minerva* 37:1 (Spring 1999), 25–43.

CHAPTER 1

1. Albert Parry, *America Learns Russian* (Syracuse, N.Y., 1967), 84.

2. Robert Schuyler to Robinson, 22 October 1943, Geroid Tanquary Robinson Papers (Columbia University Library), box 50. Simmons, "The Department of Slavic Languages," in *A History of the Faculty of Philosophy, Columbia University* (New York, 1957).

3. Max Solomon Mandell was a Yale instructor and the president of the American Chiropractic Association. Arthur Coleman and Marion Coleman, *Journey into Another World* (Cheshire, Conn., 1974), 1:61. "Dies while Telephoning," *NYT*, 14 September 1929.

4. Jesse J. Dossick, *Doctoral Research on Russia and the Soviet Union* (New York, 1960).

5. Robert F. Byrnes, *Soviet-American Academic Exchanges, 1958–1975* (Bloomington, Ind., 1976), 20.

6. "Dr. Philip E. Mosely, Scholar of Soviet Affairs, Dead at 66," *NYT*, 13 January 1972; Leonard B. Schapiro, "Philip E. Mosely, 1905–1972," in *Communal Families in the*

Balkans, ed. Robert F. Byrnes (South Bend, Ind., 1976). Terentiev was Mosely's ex-wife's name after remarrying; I was unable to learn her born surname.

7. Baron, "Recollections of a Life in Soviet History," *Russian History/Histoire Russe* 17:1 (Spring 1990), 37. Communication with Samuel H. Baron (2003).

8. Mosely to Dear Papa, 8 March 1931; Mosely to Dearest Mother, 5 June and 31 July 1931—all in Philip E. Mosely Papers (University of Illinois Library), box 1. Mosely, "1930–1932: Some Vignettes of Soviet Life," *Survey* 55 (April 1965), 56–57.

9. Marshall D. Shulman, in "Philip E. Mosely Memorial Service" (5 February 1972), REEI Records (University of Illinois Library), box 17.

10. Mosely, "Recent Soviet Trials and Policies" (1938), in Mosely, *Kremlin and World Politics* (New York, 1960), 89–90.

11. Mosely to Simmons, 24 February 1940, RF Records (Rockefeller Archive Center), 1.1/200R/228/2717. Simmons service summary, 1 February 1944, in HUA 300 Biographical File (Harvard University Archives). *Harvard Teachers Union Bulletin,* 1938–1941. Also Simmons, "A Young Man's Problem," *American Scholar* 9:4 (1940), 424–428.

12. Cross to Mosely, 31 May 1939, College of Arts and Sciences Records (Kroch Library, Cornell University), box 13; Simmons to Robert Ogden, 15 June 1939, E. E. Day Papers (Kroch Library, Cornell University), 59:5.

13. Marshall to Fosdick, 31 January 1944, RF 2/1944 785R/278/1901. *RF Annual Report, 1936,* 293.

14. Bloomfield, *Language* (New York, 1933), chap. 28 (quotes on 496, 503, 505).

15. *RF Annual Reports,* 1934–1936.

16. *Bulletin of the ACLS* 31 (June 1940), 33 (October 1941), and 35 (October 1942). Mosely to Vernadsky, 11 October 1939, and Committee Circular, 26 June 1939—both in George Vernadsky Papers (Bakhmeteff Archive, Columbia University), box 6.

17. Wendell Clark Bennett, "The Ethnogeographic Board," *Smithsonian Miscellaneous Collections* 107:1 (14 April 1947), 30. "Report of the March 9th [1941] Conference," Samuel Hazzard Cross Papers (Harvard University Archives), series HUG 4395.10, box 4.

18. Mosely to Stevens, 15 October 1941 (and attached "Proposal for an Intensive Emergency Course in Russian"), RF 1.1/200R/228/2717. Mosely to Marshall, 20 March 1942, RF 1.1/200R/228/2718. *Report of the First Year's Operation of the ILP of the ACLS* (Washington, D.C., 1942), 20–21, annex A.

19. Graves to Stevens, 1 February 1944, in RF 1.1/200R/225/2688. Samuel Waxman, "Foreign Languages and the US Army," *Education* 65 (May 1945), 555.

20. Bloomfield, *Outline Guide for the Practical Study of Foreign Languages* (Baltimore, 1942), 2–4; "Science Comes to Languages," *Fortune* 30 (August 1944), 132–133; Cowan, "American Linguistics in Peace and War," in *First Person Singular II,* ed. Konrad Koerner (Amsterdam, 1991), 73. Harry Kurz, "The Future of Modern Language Teaching," *Modern Language Journal* 27:7 (November 1943), 463.

21. Graves memo, 28 March 1945, ACLS Records (Library of Congress), box D-16.

22. J. A. McAlpine to Capt. Roger Pineau, 11 November 1980, James Augustine McAlpine Papers (Presbyterian Historical Society), 319:51. Commander A. E.

Hindmarsh, "Navy School of Oriental Languages: History, Organization, and Administration" (c. May 1945), University of Colorado Archives. "Report of Survey of Oriental Languages School at University of Colorado" (c. April 1945), President's Papers (Oklahoma State University Library), 1:3. Robert John Matthew, *Language and Area Studies in the Armed Services* (Washington, D.C., 1947), 18n9. Stevens Report, 4 May 1944, RF 1.1/200R/218/2604.

23. Chief of Naval Operations to Chief of Naval Personnel, 6 March 1944, in Bureau of Naval Personnel Records, (U.S. National Archives), RG24, entry 470, box 1204, folder NC155; "Oriental Languages School at C.U. Adds Three More Tongues," *Sunday Morning,* 16 April 1944. Martin E. Malia Oral History (Regional Oral History Office, University of California, Berkeley, 2003), 18.

24. Board of Trustees Minutes, 1944 (University of Colorado Library), 71.

25. University of Colorado Board of Trustees Minutes, 1945 (University of Colorado Library), 211. Hindmarsh to Tucker, 17 December 1943, Bureau of Naval Personnel Records, RG24, entry 470, box 1204, folder NC155. Paul F. Angiolillo, *Armed Forces' Foreign Language Teaching: Critical Evaluation and Implications* (New York, 1947), 145.

26. Posin c.v. (22 March 1941), RF 1.1/200R/228/2717. J. A. Posin, "Russian Studies in American Colleges," *RR* 7:2 (Spring 1948), 63.

27. List of Russian Program Alumni (University of Colorado Archives); Raymond A. Bauer FBI file. Gary May, *Un-American Activities* (Oxford, 1994), 71–72.

28. History of the NSMGA (1944), in Bureau of Naval Personnel Records, RG24, entry 470, box 6; L. Gray Cowan, *A History of the School of International Affairs and Associated Area Institutes, Columbia University* (New York, 1954), chap. 2. Schuyler C. Wallace, "The Naval School of Military Government and Administration," *Annals* 231 (January 1944), 29–33. John D. Millett, "The Department of Public Law and Government," in *A History of the Faculty of Political Science, Columbia University,* ed. R. Gordon Hoxie (New York, 1955), 279–280.

29. Col. Blake R. Van Leer, "A History of the ASTP" (24 May 1944), Army Service Forces Records (U.S. National Archives), RG160, entry 158, box 11. Drill sheets from Cross Papers, series HUG 4305.10, box 2. Board of Trustees Minutes, 1944 (University of Colorado Library), 71.

30. Wellek, "Prospect and Retrospect," *Yale Review* 69:2 (December 1979), 310. Adam Ulam, *Understanding the Cold War* (New Brunswick, N.J., 2003), 71. William N. Fenton, *Reports on Area Studies in American Universities* (Washington, D.C., 1945), parts II–III. Cross to Friedrich, 17 June 1943, School for Overseas Administration Records (Harvard University Archives), series UAV 663.95.1, box 2. Curriculum 71 (27 October 1943), in Army Service Forces Records, RG160, entry 159, box 8. Yale Report attached to Smith to Chilton, 18 August 1944, Army Service Forces Records, RG160, entry 162, box 12, book II (quote on 11).

31. "ASTP Program Issue," *German Quarterly* 17:4 (November 1944); Charles S. Hyneman, "The Wartime Area and Language Courses," *Bulletin of the AAUP [American Association of University Professors]* 31 (August 1945), 434–447; see also two special issues devoted to military language training: *Modern Language Journal* 27:7 (November 1943) and 27:8 (December 1943).

32. Fenton, *Reports on Area Studies;* Alonzo G. Grace, *Educational Lessons from Wartime Training* (Washington, D.C., 1948); Henry C. Herge et al., *Wartime College Training Programs* (Washington, D.C., 1948).

33. Willits to Fosdick, 6 October 1942; Willits memo, 30 September 1942; and Minutes of Officers' Conference (2–4 October 1942), —all in RF 3.1/900/23/173. Willits to Stevens, 26 July 1944, in part quoting [Robert Redfield,] "Social Science Considerations: The Planning of Regional Specialization in Higher Education and Research," 10 March 1944, RF 3.2/900/31/165. Willits to Board, "Plans for the Future Work of the RF" (November 1944), RF 3.1/910/3/18.

34. Stevens, "Proposal for a National Plan of Work on Foreign Languages, Institutions, and Customs," 7 June 1944, RF 1.1/200R/225/2688. Foundation officers circulated the proposal to the secretaries of navy, state, and war; see Stevens to Cordell Hull, 9 June 1944, SDDF (U.S. National Archives), RG59, 800.402/86a, 134, and 7–2744.

35. Graves, "Reflections on the Development of Area Studies in Academic Institutions on the West Coast of the US," 27 September 1944, RF 1.1/200R/225/2689.

36. Graves, "A Memorandum of Regional Studies," 20 April 1943, ACLS Records, box D-17.

37. Willits to Mosely, 25 April 1944, RF 1.1/200R/229/2721.

38. Mosely, "Some Random Notes on the Development of Slavic Studies in the US" (confidential), 28 February 1943, and George E. Taylor to Stevens, 27 February 1943, both in RF 1.1/200R/280/3338.

39. RF, *Conference on Slavic Studies, March 27–28, 1943* (New York, 1943), 3, 10, 18.

40. RF, *Conference on Slavic Studies,* 19, 16.

41. Mortimer Graves and Charles Hyneman, in RF, *Conference on Area and Language Programs in American Universities* (New York, 1944), 35, 4.

42. Ogden to Simmons, 19 February 1942, Cornell College of Arts and Sciences Records, box 13.

43. Simmons, "Study of Russian at the General Education Level" (14 April 1943), Cornell College of Arts and Sciences Records, box 13.

44. Mosely to Stevens, 14 October 1942, and RF Grant RF43035—both in RF 1.1/200R/228/2718.

45. Simmons, "Proposal for a Workshop on Soviet Russia" (n.d.), Cornell College of Arts and Sciences Records, box 13.

46. "Accused Russian Returns to Soviet," *NYT,* 18 January 1950. Kazakevich speech, 24 August 1942, in RF 1.1/200R/228/2725. Day to Howard Preston, 15 July 1944, in Day Papers, 11:19. Kazakevich moved to the USSR in 1949. [Charles de Kiewiet,] "Memo on Instruction and Instructional Procedures in the Army Russian Intensive Language Program," n.d., in Day Papers, 11:14. Pipes, *Vixi: Memoirs of a Non-Belonger* (New Haven, Conn., 2003), 49–50.

47. Col. Herman Beukema, in "Inquiry into Army and Navy Education Program," Hearing before the House Committee on Military Affairs, 19–21 January 1944 (78th Cong., 2nd sess.), 25. Simmons, "Final Report: Intensive Study of Contemporary Russian Civilization" (1943), 19; Stevens meeting report, 20 August 1943, RF 1.1/200R/229/2720. Results of student questionnaire (1943?), in Day Papers, 63:57.

48. Frederick Woltman, "Red Ousted but Cornell Gets Another," *New York World-Telegram*, 27 December 1943. "Dr. Joshua Kunitz Dead at 84," *NYT*, 7 March 1980. "Communists at Cornell," *Time* 43 (10 January 1944), 50. Evelyn Seeley, "Cornell Is Fighting for Its Academic Freedom: Threatened by World-Telegram's Red-Baiting," *PM*, 30 January 1944; Edmund E. Day, "So Cornell's Going Bolshevist!" *Saturday Review* 27 (4 March 1944), 12–13. Simmons, "Russian Studies at Cornell," *New Republic* 110 (15 April 1944), 674–675. Simmons to Day, 26 September 1944, Day Papers, 59:5.

49. Simmons, "Final Report," 17. *USSR: A Concise Handbook*, ed. Simmons (Ithaca, N.Y., 1947); Cross to Simmons, 29 December 1943, in Cross Papers, HUG 4305.10, box 8; Conant to Day, 27 December 1943, RF 1.1/200R/228/2720. Stevens meeting report, 20 August 1943, RF 1.1/200R/229/2720.

50. Grant RF44333, 6 December 1944, RF 1.1/200S/218/2603. "The Far West Looks to the Far East" (1949?), RF 1.1/200S/218/2606.

51. Noyes, "Slavic Languages at the University of California," *ASEER* 3:3 (October 1944), 53–60.

52. Stevens memo, 5–6 May 1943, RF 1.1/205R/19/291. Marshall memo, 8 January 1941, RF 1.1/205R/19/287. "Dr. Alexander S. Kaun," *NYT*, 24 June 1944.

53. Fisher to Robert, 15 November 1977, Raymond H. Fisher Papers (Bancroft Library, University of California, Berkeley). Kennan to Russell, 23 August 1946, George F. Kennan Papers (Mudd Library, Princeton University), 298:11. Willits to Stevens, 16 September 1947, and Sproul to Stevens, 20 October 1947—both in RF 1.2/205R/9/66. Nicholas Riasanovsky Oral History (Regional Oral History Office, Bancroft Library, University of California, Berkeley, 1996), 90. Fahs memo, 11 January 1949, RF 1.2/205R/10/67.

54. Stevens memo, 17 March 1944, RF 1.1/205R/17/255. Fisher had received an honorary doctorate from his alma mater, the University of Vermont, and went by "Dr. Fisher"; see Bickford O'Brien, "Harold Henry Fisher, 1890–1975," *SR* 35:3 (September 1976), 594. Stanford would hire émigré Anatole Mazour in 1945. Compare the July and October drafts of the RF proposal and Tressider to Stevens, 14 October 1944—all in RF 1.1/205R/17/255. Proposal (14 October 1944), RF 1.1/205R/17/255.

55. H. H. Fisher, "Henry Lanz," *ASEER* 5:1–2 (May 1946), 222. Stevens memos, 30–31 January and 1–2 February 1946, both in RF 1.2/205R/8/58.

56. From 1919 until 1938, the institution was called the Hoover War Library; between 1938 and 1947, the Hoover Library on War, Revolution, and Peace; from 1947 to 1956, the Hoover Institute and Library on War, Revolution, and Peace; and since 1956, the Hoover Institution on War, Revolution, and Peace. The text will not focus on these changes.

57. Peter Duignan, *The Hoover Institution on War, Revolution, and Peace* (Stanford, 1989), chap. 1.

58. Fisher, Memo on Study of Foreign Affairs, 6 January 1945, RF 1.2/205R/8/58. Fisher, *America and Russia in the World Community* (Claremont, Calif., 1946), 141, 157.

59. Fellowship list attached to grant report, 20 November 1949, RF 1.2/205R/9/60.

60. Conference on Slavic Acquisitions, 29–30 June 1945, Archives of the Library of Congress, box 1072.

61. Lerner, "The RADIR Project: A Reappraisal" (n.d.), Hoover Institution Records (Hoover Institution Archives), H1/42C. Rotary-Country Studies Report (n.d.), Hoover Institution Records, H1K/248B. Lasswell to Rothwell, 26 October 1948, RADIR Project Records (Hoover Institution Archives), box 2. On funding, see Hoover Institution Financial Report, 4 August 1952, in Meetings of the Hoover Institute Advisory Board, Herbert Hoover Post-Presidential Papers (Herbert Hoover Presidential Library)

62. "Soviet Union in the World Community," in RRC Correspondence (Harvard University Archives), series UAV 759.10, box 4. Rothwell, "International Relations in a World of Revolutionary Change," *WP* 1:2 (January 1949), 272–276.

63. Vucinich, "Soviet Factory," Hoover Institution Records, H1/42C; RADIR Project Records, box 17. "Program Report" (April 1956), in Meetings of the Hoover Institute Advisory Board, Herbert Hoover Post-Presidential Papers.

64. Witold Sworakowski Oral History ("The Dark Years, 1949–55"), quoted in George H. Nash, *Herbert Hoover and Stanford University* (Stanford, 1988), 141. Kenneth Colegrove, "Confidential Report to Frank Mason regarding the Hoover Institution" (28 August 1960), in Hoover Book Correspondence 1960–1961, Kenneth Colegrove Papers (Herbert Hoover Presidential Library).

65. An exception was the University of Washington's small program, which did focus on Asian Russia and the interactions between Russia/USSR and East and Central Asia. Fahs, "Outline of the Humanities" (3 December 1946), RF 3.2/900/31/165. Fahs diary, 18–22 September 1949, RF 1.1/205R/17/258. Fahs memo, 15 September 1947, RF 2/1947 200/366/2480.

66. Horatio Smith, "Preliminary Report of a Committee on Area Studies," 13 July 1943, CUCF-Smith (quotes on 2, 6, 8, 10). Smith to Fackenthal, 10 April 1944, CUCF-Smith.

67. "Report of the Committee on the Proposed Graduate School of Foreign Affairs" (hereafter SIA Proposal), 27 November 1944, and Wallace to Fackenthal, 8 July 1944 (federal)—both in CUCF-Wallace. Draft press release, 19 June 1945, in CUCF-Russian Institute.

68. Marx paper in Robinson Papers, box 17.

69. Robinson, "Trade Unionism and the Control of Industry," *Dial* 67 (12 July 1919), 6, and "Collective Bargaining in Politics," *Dial* 67 (26 July 1919), 50; Robinson, "Russia Re-examined," *Freeman* 1 (21 April 1920), 132–133.

70. Robinson, "The Decentralization of Russian History," *PSQ* 36 (September 1921), 454–455. Robinson, *Rural Russia under the Old Regime* (New York, 1932), 245. Robinson, "The Russian Peasant as Revolutionist," *Freeman* 8 (4 March 1924), 615.

71. John Shelton Curtiss, "Geroid Tanquary Robinson," in *Essays in Russian and Soviet History,* ed. Curtiss (Leiden, 1963), xvi–xviii.

72. Barry M. Katz, *Foreign Intelligence: Research and Analysis in the Office of Strategic Services, 1942–1945* (Cambridge, Mass., 1989), xii. Betty Abrahamsen Dessants, "The American Academic Community and United States–Soviet Union Relations: The Research and Analysis Branch and Its Legacy, 1941–1947" (Ph.D. diss., University of California, Berkeley, 1995), 27n26, 49–50.

73. Katz, *Foreign Intelligence,* chap. 5.

74. Robin W. Winks, *Cloak and Gown* (New York, 1987), 74–75. Robert Hayden Alcorn, *No Bugles for Spies* (New York, 1962), 73–75.

75. Katz, *Foreign Intelligence,* 154.

76. Katz, *Foreign Intelligence,* 145. Stevens to Graves, 10 July 1947, ACLS Records, box D-24; Willits memo, 30 January 1947, RF 1.1/200S/321/3822.

77. SIA Proposal, 7 and appendix, in CUCF-Wallace. Robinson to Austin Evans, 24 May 1944, in Robinson Papers, box 50. Emphasis in original.

78. Robinson, appendix to SIA Proposal, in CUCF-Wallace.

79. Robinson, "A Program of Advanced Training and Research in Russian Studies," 24 April 1947, CUCF-Robinson. Fosdick memo, 27 February 1945, RF 1.1/200S/321/3820.

80. Geroid T. Robinson, "Dr. Robinson Cites Vital Need for Understanding of Russians," *NYHT,* 4 November 1945.

81. Mosely, "Some Personnel Problems in the Field of Slavic Studies" (March 1943), RF 1.1/200R/280/3338; Wallace to Willits, 28 February 1945, CUCF-Wallace.

82. Robinson to Willits, 25 July 1946, RF 2/1946 200/332/2245. Wallace to Fosdick, 27 February 1945, CUCF-Wallace. N. I. Bolkhovitinov, *Russkie uchenyi-emigranty i stanovlenie rusistiki v SShA* (Moscow, 2005), chap. 6.

83. Wallace to Willits, 28 February 1945, CUCF-Wallace; Fosdick memo, 21 March 1946, RF 1.1/200S/321/3821. Edward Mason memo, 8 March 1945, and "Possible Economics Plan," 30 May 1945—both in Robinson Papers, box 50.

84. Wallace to Willits, 17 June 1945, CUCF-Wallace. Wallace to Robinson, 7 November 1945, and Hazard to Robinson, 9 September 1945, both in Robinson Papers, box 50.

85. Kenneth W. Thompson to Willits, 18 February 1954, RF 1.1/200S/322/3826. On the original appointment, see "Plans for Future Work of the RF" (November 1944), RF 3.1/910/3/18.

86. Carolyn Woods Eisenberg, *Drawing the Line* (New York, 1996), 52–53. Richard Johnson memorandum, 17 November 1944, *FRUS 1944,* 2:1057–1058. *From the Morgenthau Diaries,* ed. John Morton Blum (Boston, 1967), 3:338. Mosely, *Kremlin and World Politics,* chaps. 5–6 (quote on 155).

87. Wallace to Pegram, 15 June 1945, CUCF-Wallace.

88. Hazard, *Reflections of a Pioneering Sovietologist* (New York, 1987), 114, 119; Wallace to Fackenthal, 17 February 1945, CUCF-Wallace.

89. Rogers, Mosely Memorial Service, 5 February 1972, REEI (Illinois), box 17.

90. Stevens memo, 15 December 1942, RF 1.1/253R/2/18. Marshall memo, RF 2/1944 785R/278/1901. Simmons to Robinson, 8 October 1945, and Robinson to Bergson, 21 November 1945—both in Robinson Papers, box 50. Robinson to Neal, 29 November 1946, CUCF-Robinson. Simmons to Jakobson, 24 July 1946, Roman Jakobson Papers (MIT Archives), 46:16. Robinson to Vernadsky, 26 July 1946, Vernadsky Papers, box 6. Moscow to SecState, 8 January 1947, SDDF 811.42761 SE/1–847.

91. V. Minaev, "Total'nyi shpionazh v novom izdanii," *Novoe vremia* (10 September 1947), 7.

92. Simmons, "Department of Slavic Languages," 238. Fackenthal to Stevens, 9 April and 4 June 1947, RF 1.2/200R/319/2945. Fahs memo, 5 March 1947, RF 1.2/200R/319/2945.

93. Willits to Stevens, 14 February 1947; Grant RF47047; and Simmons proposal, "Five-Year Program on Teaching Aids and Research Projects in the Field of Slavic Studies" (1947?)—all in RF 1.2/200R/319/2945. Simmons to Fackenthal, 8 April 1947, CUCF-Simmons.

94. Eisenhower to Trustees, 20 September 1948, Jakobson Papers, 2:24; S. Rudi [Steven Rudy], "Iakobson pri makkartizme," in *Roman Iakobson: teksty, dokumenty, issledovaniia,* ed. Genrik [Henryk] Baran and S. I. Gindin (Moscow, 1999).

95. "Columbia Appoints 26 to Its Faculty," *NYT,* 14 September 1943.

96. Buck to Jakobson, 15 January and 11 February 1948, both in Jakobson Papers, 2:29; Jakobson to Simmons, 18 January 1946, 26 July 1948, n.d. [1948], 13 March 1949—all in Jakobson Papers, 46:16. Jakobson to Stender-Peterson, 5 March 1948, Jakobson Papers, 46:27.

97. Eisenhower to Trustees, 20 September 1948, Jakobson Papers, 2:24. Simmons to Robert Harron, 13 September 1948, CUCF-Simmons. Stanislaus A. Blejwas, "The Adam Mickiewicz Chair of Polish Culture: Columbia University and the Cold War (1948–54)," *Polish Review* 36:3 (1991), 324, 328.

98. Robinson, "Russia and the West" [1946?], and "Determining Factors in Soviet Foreign Policy" (12 February 1947)—both in Robinson Papers, 18:1. Robinson memo, 21 March 1946, RF 1.1/200S/321/3821. See also below, pp. 100–101.

99. Simmons to Jacobs, 5 August 1948, CUCF-Simmons. James A. Hagerty, "Hilman Is Elected State Head of ALP [American Labor Party]," *NYT,* 9 April 1944. *The Lamont Case: History of a Congressional Investigation,* ed. Philip Wittenberg (New York, 1957), 24, 30.

100. Minutes, 12 April 1952, RRC Executive Committee Minutes (Harvard University Archives), series UAV 759.5, box 1.

101. Hazard to Robinson, 15 September 1947, Robinson Papers, box 50. Robinson wanted to hire Mandel at OSS; see Abram Bergson FBI File.

102. Robinson to Evans, 11 October 1946, RF 1.1/200S/321/3820. "Report of the [Student] Committee on the Institute," 3 May 1949, Robinson Papers, box 51.

103. Baron, "Recollections," 35–36.

104. Anderson to Fackenthal, 23 May 1947, CUCF-Carnegie; Willits to Jacobs, 5 July 1949, CUCF-Rockefeller Foundation. List from RI Progress Report, 1946–1950, RF 1.1/200S/321/3825; Byrnes, "Harvard, Columbia, and the CIA: My Training in Russian Studies," in Byrnes, *A History of Russian and East European Studies in the US: Selected Essays* (Lanham, Md., 1994). Robinson to Simmons, 22 October 1945, Robinson Papers, box 50.

105. Mosely memo, 13 January 1954, RF 1.1/200S/322/3827, 4. Robinson, "Program of Grants-in-Aid for Graduate Students" (October 1948), and Robinson to Fackenthal, 6 May 1947—both in CUCF-Robinson. Undated Robinson memo [Spring 1950?], Robinson Papers, box 51. Willits to Dean Rusk, 15 October 1953, RF 1.1/200S/322/3826. Robinson letter, 25 April 1948, RF 1.1/200S/321/3822. "Survey of Placement Experience of University Area Centers" (Spring 1953), ACLS Records, box E-87.

106. Robinson to Willits, 28 January 1945, CUCF-Wallace. Fackenthal to Willits, 6 May 1947, CUCF-RF. Robinson, "An Emergency and a Program" [1950?], Robinson Papers, box 51.

107. Gardner memo, 30 March 1948, CCNY Records (Columbia University Library), series III.A, box 164. DeVinney-Thompson correspondence, 9 July 1959, RF 1.1/200S/322/3831.

108. Robinson, "The Ideological Combat," *FA* 27 (July 1949), 525–539. RI Progress Report 1946–1950, RF 1.1/200S/321/3825.

109. RI Progress Report 1946–1950, RF 1.1/200S/321/3825.

110. Geroid T. Robinson, "Russian Institute," *A History of the School of International Affairs and Associated Area Institutes,* ed. L. Gray Cowan (New York, 1954), 64.

111. Gardner memoranda, 2 June and 31 July 1947—both in CCNY Records, series III.A, box 113. Willits memo, January 1947, RF 1.1/200S/321/3822.

112. Grant RF44145; Marshall to Spewack, 24 February 1944; Marshall to Milam, 10 September 1945; Simmons to Marshall, 5 July 1946—all in RF 1.1/200R/198/2374.

113. Simmons to Francis Stevens, 3 October 1947, and Stevens to Simmons, 17 October 1947, both in SDDF 861.42761 SE/10-347. Simmons, "Report on Centers of Slavic Studies in Europe" (September 1947), RF 1.1/200R/198/2374, quotes on 1, 35, 43, 44–45. Moscow to SecState, 4 December 1946, and Stevens memo, "Project for Translation of Russian Periodical Literature in the US," 17 December 1946—both in SDDF 811.20200(D)/12-446.

114. Mosely memo, RF 1.1/200S/322/3827, 13. "Commentaries on the Budget" (1951), ACLS Records, box E-50.

115. Gruliow to JCSS, 16 November 1951, ACLS Records, box H-22. "Report on Soviet Running into Red," *NYT,* 1 April 1952. Webbink to Edgerton, 24 July 1959, ACLS Records, box H-22.

116. Frederick Burkhardt to Cleon Swayzee, 23 December 1963, Donald Treadgold Papers (University of Washington Library), series 1845-2-82–65, box 2. Turner to Treadgold, 21 May 1963, ACLS Records, box H-29.

117. JCSS, 1950–1951 annual report, ACLS Records, box H-31. Luther Evans circular, 9 March 1951, Library of Congress Records, box 1072. Annual meeting, 8 April 1950, SSRC Records (Rockefeller Archive Center), 1/256/1501.

118. "Recent Deaths," *AHR* 81:3 (June 1976), 707–708. From the masthead of *Slavonic Year-Book,* American ser., 1 (1941), n.p.

119. Dimitri von Mohrenschildt, "The Founding of *Russian Review:* A Memoir," *RR* 60:1 (January 2001), 4. Fedotoff White to von Mohrenschildt, 24 February 1941, and Graves to von Mohrenschildt, 14 May 1943, both in *RR* Records (Hoover Institution Archives), 1:2. On Chamberlin, see Norman Naimark, "On the 50th Anniversary: The Origins of the AAASS," *AAASS NewsNet* 38:5 (November 1998), 3.

120. Mosely to Evans, 1 December 1949; Simmons to editorial board, 31 March 1947; Cornelius Krusé to Stevens, 9 January 1947; Simmons to editorial board, 3 January 1948; and Simmons to Marshall, 24 May 1948—all in RF 1.2/200R/279/2652.

121. Grant notification (n.d.) in RF 1.2/200R/279/2653; Simmons to Jakobson, 10 December 1948, Jakobson Papers, 46:16. Simmons, "Editorial Foreword," *ASEER* 7:1 (February 1948), 1–2. Hazard to Vernadsky, 6 January 1951, Vernadsky Papers, box 1.

122. Thomson to Odegaard, 21 March 1949, ACLS Records, box E-67.

123. Fosdick to Willits and Marshall, 6 January 1948, RF 2/1948 200/407/2744. [John Paton] Davies for [Carmel] Offie, 27 May 1948, SDDF 800.43 Eurasian Institute/5–2748. Joseph and Stewart Alsop, "Refugees from Russia Could Tell Us a Lot," *LAT,* 2 November 1948. Kluckhohn to John Davies, 21 July 1948, RRC Correspondence, series UAV 759.10, box 1. Parsons letter, 15 August 1948, RRC Correspondence, series UAV 759.10, box 6. Gardner memo, 6 January 1948, CCNY Records, series III.A, box 164. "Memorandum on Eurasian Research Institute" (7 July 1948), William J. Donovan Papers (Army Historical Research Center), box 73a.

124. Donovan to Clinton [*sic*] J. Barnard, 26 January 1949, Donovan Papers, box 73a. Mosely to Willits, 30 October 1948; "Memorandum on a Eurasian Institute," 19 October 1948, and Mosely comments, 23 October 1948; Willits circular letters, 2–3 March 1948—all in RF 2/1948 200/407/2744. Davis to Offie, 27 May 1948, SDDF 840.42790/5–2748. Quoting Mosely memo, 13 January 1949, RF 2/1949 200/443/2985. Mosely, "Suggested Procedure" (23 October 1948), Donovan Papers, box 73a. Willits to Bennett, 1 August 1946, RF 2/1945 200/332/2245.

125. Chester I. Bernard to Donovan, Donovan Papers, box 73a.

126. Kluckhohn to Kennan, 24 April 1951, Merle Fainsod Papers (Harvard University Archives), series HUG(FP) 4382.8, box 2. Charles T. O'Connell, "The Munich Institute on the USSR: Origin and Social Composition," Carl Beck Papers, no. 808, 1990.

127. Gardner memo, 30 July 1951, CCNY Records, series III.A, box 113. Mosely to Robert Franklin, 2 March 1953, CUCF-Philip Mosely. George Uri Fischer, *Insatiable: A Story of My Nine Lives* (Philadelphia, 2000), 172. Black, "Foreword," to Black, ed., *Rewriting Russian History,* 2nd ed. (New York, 1962), ix–x.

128. See, for instance, the reviews of Fedor Belov, *The History of a Soviet Collective Farm,* by Alexander Vucinich (*ASEER* 15:4 [December 1956], 550–551) and Alexander Gerschenkron (*AHR* 61:3 [April 1956], 656–657). *Rewriting Russian History: The Soviet Secret Police,* ed. Simon Wolin and Robert M. Slusser (New York, 1957); and *Soviet Education,* ed. George Louis Kline (New York, 1957).

129. George F. Kennan Oral History (1972–1973), Non-Grant Files, FF Archives, 22.

130. Willits-Evans memo, 27 February 1945, RF 1.1/200S/321/3820. Wallace to Willits, 11 October 1950, RF 1.1/200S/321/3825.

131. Mosely to Nicolaevsky, 8 September 1950, Boris I. Nicolaevsky Papers (Hoover Institution Archives), 493:19, and later correspondence in 493:20. Robinson, "Russian Institute," 63; Columbia University Harriman Institute, *The Russian Institute/Harriman Institute of Columbia University: 50 Years, 1946–1996* (New York, 1996), 83.

132. Cleon Swayzee (FF) discussions with JCSS, 9–10 October 1953, ACLS Records, box E-87.

133. This complaint about nationalities had been levied since the very first years of academic Soviet studies; Charles B. Fahs, "Area Studies: A Reexamination," 22 September 1948, RF 3.2/900/31/165.

134. Wittenberg, *Lamont Case,* 30, 42. Willits to Stevens, 22 April 1954, and Mosely to Willits, 10 March 1954—both in RF 1.1/200S/322/3828.

135. Mosely, DD Form 48, 7 August 1964, in Mosely Papers (Illinois), box 12. Over the years, these included CIA, RAND, the Arms Control and Disarmament Agency, the U.S. Information Agency, the Atomic Energy Commission, and others.

136. RI circular, 22 April 1954, RF 1.1/200S/321/3825.

CHAPTER 2

1. Samuel Stouffer et al., *Studies in Social Psychology in World War II,* 4 vols. (Princeton, 1949–1950). Ellen Herman, *The Romance of American Psychology: Political Culture in an Age of Experts* (Berkeley, 1995), 66–74.

2. Uta Gerhardt, *Talcott Parsons: An Intellectual Biography* (Cambridge, 2002), chap. 3. Peter Buck, "Adjusting to Military Life: The Social Sciences Go to War, 1941–1950," in *Military Enterprise and Technological Change: Perspectives on the American Experience,* ed. Merritt Roe Smith (Cambridge, Mass., 1985).

3. Kluckhohn's pride in his work does not account for other factors leading to the Japanese surrender—most especially the atomic destruction of Hiroshima and Nagasaki. There is a particular irony here in Kluckhohn's comment, below, about the role of atomic physics during the war. Kluckhohn, *Mirror for Man: The Relationship of Anthropology to Modern Life* (New York, 1949), 176–177.

4. Alex Leighton, *Human Relations in a Changing World: Observations on the Use of the Social Sciences* (New York, 1949), 43–44 and passim.

5. Mead, "The Study of National Character," in *The Policy Sciences: Recent Developments in Scope and Method,* ed. Daniel Lerner and Harold D. Lasswell (Stanford, 1951), 85. Parsons was joined by five coauthors, though according to one biographer he drafted the letter: "Atomic Power: A Communication," *Washington Post,* 19 August 1945; Gerhardt, *Talcott Parsons,* 150–151. Kluckhohn, *Mirror for Man,* 288.

6. Saul Padover to Daniel Lerner, 11 January 1952, RADIR Project (Hoover Institution Archives), box 15.

7. This work, like many other writings, uses "behavioralism" as shorthand for "behavioral sciences"; as behavioralists make clear, their work bears no relation to the "behaviorism" of B. F. Skinner.

8. Parsons, "Some Problems Confronting Sociology as a Profession," *ASR* 24:4 (August 1959), 553; emphasis in original. Howard Brick, *Transcending Capitalism: Visions of a New Society in Modern American Thought* (Ithaca, N.Y., 2006), chap. 4.

9. Nils Gilman, *Mandarins of the Future: Modernization Theory in Cold War America* (Baltimore, 2003), chap. 3. Jamie Nace Cohen-Cole, "Thinking about Thinking in Cold War America" (Ph.D. diss., Princeton University, 2003), 154–160.

10. Frederick Osborn Oral History (CCNY Project, Oral History Research Office, Columbia University, 1967), 64. "Red Psychology Is Too Much for a Psychologist," *NYHT,* 18 August 1948.

11. Larry Gerber, "The Baruch Plan and the Origins of the Cold War," *Diplomatic History* 6 (Autumn 1982), 69–95. David Holloway, *Stalin and the Bomb* (New Haven, Conn., 1994), 161–166.

12. Donald Young to Osborn, 6 November 1945, Frederick Osborn Papers (American Philosophical Society).

13. Gardner notes, 3 June and 7–9 July 1947—both in CCNY Records (Columbia University Library), series III.A, box 42. An internal history concludes that the notes are "most revealing as to the ease with which the Corporation moves around Washington"; see Memorandum for Counsel: Harvard RRC, CCNY Records, series III.A, box 164.

14. [John Gardner,] "Russian Studies" (15 July 1947), in RRC Correspondence (Harvard University Archives), series UAV 759.10, box 1. Gardner to Kluckhohn, 28 July 1947, CCNY Records, series III.A, box 164. Henry Shattuck to James Conant, 25 January 1950, James Conant Presidential Records (Harvard University Archives), UA.I 5.168, box 382. John W. Gardner Oral History (CCNY Project, 2000), 9–11, 52–53. Paul H. Buck Oral History (CCNY Project, 1967), 53–54.

15. Kluckhohn to Buck, 3 November 1947, Dean of Faculty of Arts and Sciences (FAS) Correspondence (Harvard University Archives), UA.III 5.55.26. Parsons, "The Department and Laboratory of Social Relations: The First Decade" (1956), Harvard University Archives, HUF 801.4156.2, 61.

16. Jamie Cohen-Cole, "The Creative American: Cold War Social Science and the Cure for American Conformity," *Isis* (forthcoming). RRC Report, 1950–1951, RRC Correspondence, series UAV 759.10, box 11. Parsons, "Clyde Kluckhohn and the Integration of the Social Sciences," in *Culture and Life: Essays in Memory of Clyde Kluckhohn,* ed. Walter W. Taylor, John L. Fischer and Evon Z. Vogt (Carbondale, Ill., 1973), 35.

17. Gorer, "Some Aspects of Russian Psychology" (9 January 1948), and Inkeles comments (13 February 1948), both in RRC Seminars, series UAV 759.8, box 1. Gorer and John Rickman, *The People of Great Russia: A Psychological Study* (London, 1949).

18. Kluckhohn to Gardner, 23 July 1947, RRC Correspondence, series UAV 759.10, box 1. Gardner notes, 7–9 July 1947; Charles Dollard, notes on conversation with Osborn, 30 September 1947—both in CCNY Records, series III.A, box 164.

19. Donald C. McKay to Kluckhohn, 18 November 1947, RRC Correspondence, series UAV 759.10, box 2.

20. Kluckhohn to Paul H. Buck, 13 June 1949, RRC Correspondence, series UAV 759.10, box 3. David W. Bailey to Buck, 24 June 1949, in Records of the Dean of FAS, UA.III 5.55.26.

21. Basic information on Troy is from Allan A. Needell, "'Truth Is Our Weapon': Project TROY, Political Warfare, and Government-Academic Relations in the National Security State," *Diplomatic History* 17:3 (Summer 1993), 399–420.

22. Paul H. Buck to John Burchard, 21 October 1950, and Burchard to Buck, 5 February 1951—both in Dean-FAS Correspondence, series UA.III 5.55.26.

23. Brophy to James Webb, 30 January 1951, State Department Records (U.S. National Archives), lot 52–283, 1:2. Donald L. M. Blackmer, *The MIT Center for International Studies: The Founding Years, 1951–1969* (Cambridge, Mass., 2002), 8–10. Allan A. Needell, *Science, Cold War, and the American State: Lloyd V. Berkner and the Balance of Professional Ideals* (Amsterdam, 2000), 163–164.

24. *Project TROY: Report to the Secretary of State,* 4 vols. (15 February 1951), in State Department Records, lot 52–283, 1:1.

25. HR 66/1, "Need for a Defector Policy from a Research and Development Standpoint" (6 February 1951), OSD Records (U.S. National Archives), RG330, entry 31, 246:27.

26. W. Park Armstrong Jr. to Mr. Barrett, 27 March 1951, and "B" [Lloyd Berkner?] to Mr. Trueheart, 23 April 1951—both in State Department Records, lot 58D776, box 1097V.

27. NSC 86/1, "United States Policy on Soviet and Satellite Defectors" (3 April 1951), DDRS, document CK3100062072. William A. Curtin to Psychological Strategy Board, 9 October 1951, Psychological Strategy Board Records, Staff Office Member Files (Harry S Truman Presidential Library), box 1, classification 000.1. Donald MacArthur, "DOD Behavioral and Social Science Programs," in Ithiel de Sola Pool Papers (MIT Archives), box 71. Gregory Mitrovich, *Undermining the Kremlin: America's Strategy to Subvert the Soviet Bloc, 1947–1956* (Ithaca, N.Y., 2000), 78–80.

28. Jerome Bruner, *In Search of Mind: Essays in Autobiography* (New York, 1983), 210–211.

29. Blackmer, *MIT Center,* 18–20.

30. Marshall to Killian, 29 August 1951, Records of the Office of the President (MIT), 48:16. Rostow, "Development: The Political Economy of the Marshallian Long Period," in *Pioneers in Development,* ed. Gerald M. Meier and Dudley Seers (Oxford, 1984), 241n23. Blackmer, *MIT Center,* 20.

31. The summary for 1953–1954 reports on purchase orders for a dozen RRC affiliates working at MIT that year; see William R. Jones to Verna G. Johnson, 24 November 1953, Dean-FAS Correspondence, series UA.III 5.55.26. RRC Executive Committee Minutes, 30 April 1952, RRC Executive Committee Minutes (Harvard University Archives), series UAV 759.5, box 1.

32. Buck marginalia on Kluckhohn to Buck, 25 April 1952, Dean-FAS Correspondence, series UA.III 5.55.26. J. R. Killian Jr. to K. A. Stratton and J. E. Burchard, 12 January 1951, Records of the Office of the President (MIT), 220:7.

33. "People Involved in the Work of the Center" (20 May 1952), Records of Chancellor Julius A. Stratton (MIT Institute Archives), box 4.

34. MIT CENIS, "The Vulnerability of the Soviet Union and Its European Satellites to Political Warfare" (1952), White House Confidential Files (Dwight D. Eisenhower Presidential Library), subject files, box 62, ii–iv, viii (hereafter CENIS, "Vulnerability").

35. CENIS, "Vulnerability," 2–10.

36. "Some Informal Speculations about Possible Consequences of Stalin's Death" (February 1952), in RRC Research Papers (Harvard University Archives), series UAV 759.275, box 9. See chapter 8 for a brief summary.

37. W. W. Rostow, "The Dynamics of Soviet Society," 1:1, appendix to *TROY: Report.*

38. Rostow, "Dynamics of Soviet Society," 1:83, 1:147. CENIS, "Vulnerability," part II-A, 42. W. W. Rostow, *The Dynamics of Soviet Society* (New York, 1953), 169–170, 198.

39. For the response to Stalin's death, see Rostow, *Europe after Stalin: Eisenhower's Three Decisions of March 11, 1953* (Austin, Tex., 1982).

40. Fainsod, Kluckhohn, and Stratton to Millikan, 20 February 1953, in Clyde Kluckhohn Papers (Harvard University Archives), series HUG 4490.7, box RAND/RDB/RRC. Kluckhohn to Ralph Collins, 8 July 1953, RRC Correspondence, box 22.

41. Mosely to Millikan, 11 September 1952, Records of the Office of the President (MIT), 220:7.

42. Rostow to Daniels, 19 June 1952, in Merle Fainsod Papers (Harvard University Archives), series HUG 4382.8, box 1.

43. Interim Report, 9 March 1948, RRC Correspondence, series UAV 759.10, box 1. Charles Dollard notes on conversation with Kluckhohn, 22 March 1948; Devereaux Josephs notes on conversation with Alger Hiss, 24 March 1948—both in CCNY Records, series III.A, box 164.

44. E. V. Kodin, *Garvardskii proekt* (Moscow, 2003), chap. 5. These figures do not include Red Army personnel in the eastern zone.

45. "An Analysis of Soviet Society," part I (1949), in ISR Records (Bentley Library, University of Michigan), box 5. The Survey Research Center was incorporated into the ISR well after this report was completed.

46. Rensis Likert to John F. Stearns, 16 June 1948, and Burton R. Fischer to Boris Nicolaevsky, 12 August 1948—both in ISR Records, box 41. "An Analysis of Soviet Society," ISR Records, box 5.

47. Angus Campbell to Burton F. Fischer, 17 August 1948, ISR Records, box 41.

48. Interim Report, 9 March 1948, RRC Correspondence, series UAV 759.10, box 1. Minutes of 6 February and 13 February 1948, RRC Seminars (Harvard University Archives), series UAV 759.8, box 1. Minutes of Air Research Unit meeting, 5 June 1948, Archives of the Library of Congress, box 1014.

49. Christopher Simpson, *Blowback: America's Recruitment of Nazis and Its Effects on the Cold War* (New York, 1988), 115–116; Gerhardt, *Talcott Parsons,* 178–180.

50. Dzh. Iu. U. Fisher [George Fischer], "Dve strasti," in *V poiskakh istiny: puti i sud'by vtoroi emigratsii,* ed. V. S. Karpov et al. (Moscow, 1997), 201. On army work, see FBI form 1 (21 August 1951), in Fischer FBI File.

51. Fischer, *Insatiable: A Story of My Nine Lives* (Philadelphia, 2000), 158; Fischer, "Soviet Émigrés in the U.S. Zone of Germany" (25 July 1948), RRC Reports, series UAV 759.275, box 4. Fischer to Inkeles and Kluckhohn, 12 April 1950, RRC Correspondence, series UAV 759.10, box 8. Fischer, "Soviet Refugees in Germany and the Harvard Interview Project" (3 November 1950), RRC Seminars, series UAV 759.8, box 1.

52. Fischer to Kluckhohn, 13 August 1950, in RIP Correspondence, series UAV759.175, box 3. Karpov et al., *V poiskakh istiny,* documents 1.2.1–1.2.5; and Charles T. O'Connell, "The Munich Institute for the Study of the USSR: Origin and Social Composition," Carl Beck Papers in Russian and East European Studies, no. 808, 1990.

53. See Paul Friedrich's 1949 letters in RRC Correspondence, series UAV 759.10, box 8. Fainsod, "Controls and Tensions in the Soviet System," APSR 44:2 (June 1950), 266. Kluckhohn to Bowers, 20 January 1950, RIP Correspondence, series UAV759.175, box 2. The policy was adopted after World War II; see Morton Keller and Phyllis Keller, *Making Harvard Modern: The Rise of America's University* (Oxford, 2001), 208.

54. Michael Sherry, *The Rise of American Air Power: The Creation of Armageddon* (New Haven, Conn., 1987), chap. 7. Martin J. Collins, *Cold War Laboratory: RAND, the Air Force, and the American State, 1945–50* (Washington, D.C., 2002), chap. 1. Raymond V. Bowers, "The Military Establishment," in *The Uses of Sociology,* ed. Paul F. Lazarsfeld et al. (New York, 1967), 236. Air University Regulations 80–1 (27 July 1949) and 80–9 (20 February 1951), AFHRA, microfilm A2573, frames 1794–1796, 1805.

55. On his Harvard career, see Sleeper, Admissions File (Harvard University Archives), UAV 161.201.13, box 152.

56. For firsthand descriptions of Project Control's aspirations and operations, see Lt. Col. Raymond S. Sleeper, "Air Power, the Cold War, and Peace," *Air University Quarterly Review* 5:1 (Winter 1951–1952), 17–18; and "An Outline of Project Control," 21 September 1953, Fainsod Papers, series HUG 4382.5, box 1. For overviews, see Tami Davis Biddle, "Handling the Soviet Threat: 'Project Control' and the Debate on American Strategy in the Early Cold War Years," *Journal of Strategic Studies* 12:3 (1989), 273–302.

57. Sleeper interview, 3 June 1986, cited in Charles Thomas O'Connell, "Social Structure and Science: Soviet Studies at Harvard" (Ph.D. diss., UCLA, 1990), 351–353.

58. *Fellows of the Social Science Research Council, 1925–51* (New York, 1951), 42. Bowers c.v. (15 June 1968), Biographical Files (University of Arizona Archives).

59. Kluckhohn-Sleeper letters, 17 March and 29 May 1950—both in RRC Correspondence, series UAV 759.10, box 10. George W. Croker, "Some Principles Regarding the Utilization of Social Science Research within the Military," in Stanford University Institute for Communication Research, *Case Studies in Bringing Behavioral Science into Use,* vol. 1 of *Studies in the Utilization of Behavioral Science* (Stanford, 1961), 122–123. Sleeper to Kluckhohn, 25 October 1948, RRC Correspondence, series UAV 759.10, box 6 (quote).

60. Bowers, "Military Establishment," 238–240. Croker, "Some Principles," 123–125.

61. Alex Inkeles Oral History (Spencer Foundation Project, Oral History Research Office, Columbia University, 1985), 32–33. Inkeles, *Social Change in Soviet Russia* (Cambridge, Mass., 1968), vii–ix. Jenna Malamud Smith, *My Father Is a Book: A Memoir of Bernard Malamud* (Boston, 2006), 112–114. Inkeles's Cornell advisor, Leonard Cottrell, was a frequent consultant to the USAF; see Bowers, "Military Establishment," 241, 249.

62. Conant to Buck, 19 March 1951, and Kluckhohn to Buck, 9 January 1951, both in Conant Presidential Records, series UA I.168, box 410.

63. Inkeles Oral History (Spencer), 33.

64. Kluckhohn, foreword to Alex Inkeles, *Public Opinion in Soviet Russia: A Study in Mass Persuasion* (Cambridge, Mass., 1950), vii.

65. Inkeles, "The Soviet Union as a Psychological Warfare Target" (n.d.), in RIP Project Reports (Harvard University Archives), series UAV 759.175.70, box 2.

66. Minutes of Research Seminar, 5 March 1948, RRC Seminar Notes, series UAV 759.8, box 1. Parsons, "Notes for Panel Discussion on the Objectives of Area Study," 28 November 1947, in Records of the Dean of the Graduate School of Public Administration (Harvard University Archives), series UAV 715.17, box P-R.

67. "History of the HRRI, July–December 1952," AFHRA, microfilm K2679:47–49. Kluckhohn to Bowers, 3 February 1950, attached to Kluckhohn to Buck, 29 March 1950, Dean-FAS Correspondence, series UA.III 5.55.26.

68. Kluckhohn to Buck, 9 May 1950, Dean-FAS Correspondence, series UA.III 5.55.26. Raymond Bauer to Clyde Kluckhohn, 22 October 1952, in Raymond Augustine Bauer Papers (Harvard Business School Library), 8:34. "History of the HRRI, July–December 1953," AFHRA, microfilm K2898:1859–1861. Kluckhohn to Col. George Croker, 14 February 1954, RRC Correspondence, series UAV 759.10, box 23.

69. Kluckhohn to Bowers, 2 May 1950, RRC Correspondence, series UAV 759.10, box 7. Communication with Alex Inkeles (2003).

70. Collated from the information in RIP Correspondence (Harvard University Archives), series UAV 759.175, box 6. On the ASU, see Robert Cohen, *When the Old Left Was Young: Student Radicals and America's First Mass Student Movement, 1929–1941* (Oxford, 1993), chaps. 6–7. Robert C. Tyler, "The American Veterans Committee: Out of a Hot War and into the Cold," *American Quarterly* 18 (Fall 1966): 419–436. Though neither the ASU nor the AVC appeared on the attorney general's list of subversive organizations, they (along with other groups, like Americans for Democratic Action) did appear on many state lists; see Eleanor Bontecou, *The Federal Loyalty-Security Program* (Ithaca, N.Y., 1953), appendix VI.

71. The HUAC investigation focused on his wartime friendship with William Remington. FBI form 1, 14 April 1954, in Raymond A. Bauer FBI file. On OLS, see FBI form 1, n.d., in Bauer FBI File. Helen W. Parsons note, n.d., RRC Correspondence, series UAV 759.10, box 7; "Student at Harvard Called by Committee," *NYT,* 12 May 1950. Bauer's self-criticism is in letter to Kluckhohn [Spring–Summer 1950?], RIP Correspondence, series UAV 759.175, box 1.

72. Kluckhohn, "Analysis Plan," 17 April 1951; Bauer, "Notes on Analysis Plan," n.d.—both in RIP Correspondence, series UAV 759.175, box 2.

73. Bauer Circular Memorandum, 27 August 1951, Bauer Papers, 8:34.

74. Inkeles letter, 21 June 1950, RIP Minutes of Planning Meetings (Harvard University Archives), series UAV 759.175.8.

75. One briefing highlighted the "training of Russian-language research personnel"; see "RRC Briefing of the Directorate of Intelligence," 15 December 1952, RRC Correspondence, series UAV 759.10, box 18. For comparison, see David Kaiser, "Cold War Requisitions, Scientific Manpower, and the Production of American Physicists after World War II," *Historical Studies in the Physical and Biological Sciences* 33 (2002): 131–159.

76. Kluckhohn to Sleeper, 29 May 1950, RIP Correspondence, series UAV 759.175, box 8. Minutes of Planning Meeting, 18 July 1950, in RIP Minutes, series UAV 759.175.8. The Bureau of Applied Social Research project was classified as "intelligence methods research" in "History of the HRRI, July–December 1952," AFHRA, microfilm K2679, 39.

77. "Analysis Plan," in Kluckhohn to Bowers, 21 August 1951, RIP Workbook (Harvard University Archives), series UAV 759.175.95, vol. 2.

78. Anna Marta Holian, "Between National Socialism and Soviet Communism: The Politics of Self-Representation among Displaced Persons in Munich, 1945–1951" (Ph.D. diss., University of Chicago, 2005).

79. Harvard's pilot studies also identified the problem of bias; see Fainsod, "Controls and Tensions," 267n3.

80. The groups were the Anti-Bolshevik Bloc of Nations and the Union of Struggle for the Liberation of the Peoples of Russia; see W. M. Pinkerton, "Attacks by Nationality Groups," 5 November 1953, RRC Correspondence, series UAV 759.10, box 24.

81. Communication with Frederick Wyle (2005). Kluckhohn to Bowers, 21 August 1951. "Analysis Plan," RIP Workbook, series UAV 759.175.95, vol. 2. Bauer, Research Memo 1 (2 June 1950), RIP Workbook, series UAV 759.175.95, vol. 1.

82. Communication with Frederick Wyle (2003). The project faced criticisms from newspapers by and for Soviet DPs in Germany; see, for instance, "'Ekspeditsiia' garvardskogo universiteta," *Russkaia Mysl,'* 5 May 1951; "Provokatsionnoe 'liubopy-tstvo': Po povodu ankety, budto-by, Garvardkskogo universiteta dlia ukraintsev," *Ukrainski Visti,* 17 May 1951; John Kelso, "Harvard Quiz in Germany Favored Reds, Says Savant," *Boston Post,* 10 January 1953.

83. Fischer letter to Cambridge staff, 15 July 1950, RIP Correspondence, series UAV 759.175, box 3.

84. Alice H. Bauer, "Guide for Interviewing Soviet Escapees" (August 1953), in RIP Project Reports, series UAV 759.175.75, box 1. Alex Inkeles and Raymond A. Bauer, *The Soviet Citizen: Daily Life in a Totalitarian Society* (Cambridge, Mass., 1959), 13. On language skills, the personnel security questionnaires list three interviewers from Russia and indicate two others of Russian descent. Gloria Donen Sosin, *Red Letter Year* (White Plains, N.Y., 2004), 135.

85. Inkeles to Maj. Robert Work, 8 May 1950, and Kluckhohn to Sleeper, 9 May 1950—both in RIP Correspondence, series UAV759.175, box 8. List of air force requirements (n.d.), in RIP Correspondence, series UAV759.175, box 1.

86. Inkeles to Sleeper, 20 July 1950, and Bauer notes on conversation with Sleeper, 11 August 1950—both in RIP Correspondence, series UAV 759.175, box 8. Minutes, 18 July 1950, RIP Minutes, series UAV 759.175.8.

87. Bauer to Kluckhohn, 22 October 1952, Bauer Papers, 8:34.

88. Scrivner and Rep. Harold Ostertag (R-NY) in *Congressional Record,* vol. 99, part 6 (1 July 1953), 7834–7835. Verna Johnson to Paul Buck, 7 July 1953, Dean-FAS Correspondence, series UA.III 5.55.26. Scrivner in "Department of the Air Force Appropriations for 1954," Hearings before the Subcommittee of the Committee on Appropriations, U.S. House of Representatives, 83rd Cong., 1st sess. (15 May 1953), 70–71.

89. Ferguson in *Congressional Record,* vol. 99, part 7 (22 July 1953), 9467. "The American Forum of the Air," 19 July 1953, Homer Ferguson Papers (Bentley Historical Library, University of Michigan), 13:6.

90. R. W. Pratt to Edward Reynolds, 7 July 1953, Dean-FAS Correspondence, series UA.III 5.55.26.

91. Ellen Schrecker, *No Ivory Tower: McCarthyism and the Universities* (Oxford, 1986), chap. 7.

92. John Kelso, "Harvard Study of Russia Called 'Insane'—Costs U.S. $450,000," *Boston Post,* 28 September 1953. Michael Maccoby, "Ferguson Blasts Center for University Policies," *Harvard Crimson,* 29 September 1953.

93. "Names Asked on Red Study at Harvard," *Boston Post,* 6 October 1953. "Investment at Harvard," *Boston Traveler,* 1 October 1953; the *Boston Herald* editorials "The Weapon of Knowledge" ran from 15 October through 17 October 1953. Kluckhohn to Trevor Gardner (Office of the Secretary of the Air Force), 30 October 1953, RRC Correspondence, series UAV 759.10, box 23. David L. Halberstam, "Research Center Studies Soviet Social System," *Harvard Crimson,* 5 October 1953.

94. Gene M. Lyons, *The Uneasy Partnership: Social Science and the Federal Government in the Twentieth Century* (New York, 1969), 143–145. Draft memorandum, "Organization of the HRRI," n.d., AFHRA, microfilm A2573: 1893.

95. Bruce Hevly, "Reflections on Big Science and Big History," in *Big Science: The Growth of Large-Scale Research,* ed. Peter Galison and Hevly (Stanford, 1992).

96. RRC Report for President's Review Committee (January 1952), Fainsod Papers, series HUG 4382.8, box 4. Elizabeth Fainsod to Bauer, 27 January 1953, Bauer Papers, 8:34.

97. Paul Hencke, "What Russia Will Do Next," *Nation's Business* 43:3 (March 1955), 27–28.

98. Inkeles and Bauer, *Soviet Citizen,* 5. Bauer, Inkeles, and Kluckhohn, *How the Soviet System Works: Cultural, Psychological, and Social Themes* (Cambridge, Mass., 1956), 10.

99. As Berliner notes, David J. Dallin had called attention to "His Majesty, Blat," in an earlier work; see Dallin, *The New Soviet Empire* (New Haven, Conn., 1951), chap. 11. Berliner was the first to use the word *tolkach* in an American scholarly journal; sixteen of twenty-two subsequent uses made reference to his work.

100. Paul R. Gregory, *Restructuring the Soviet Economic Bureaucracy* (Cambridge, 1990), 173n8.

101. Berliner recalled three decades later that the RIP showed how "in most respects Soviet society reflected the characteristics of a class society of the Western industrial kind"; Berliner, foreword to *Politics, Work, and Daily Life in the USSR: A Survey of Former Soviet Citizens,* ed. James R. Millar (Cambridge, 1987), x.

102. For citations, see Bauer et al., *How the Soviet System Works,* appendix.

103. Moore, "The Strengths and Weaknesses of the Soviet System" (HRRI Technical Report, no. 2, 1952). Moore, *Terror and Progress: Some Sources of Change and Stability in the Soviet Dictatorship* (Cambridge, Mass., 1954).

104. George Fischer, *Soviet Opposition to Stalin: A Case Study in World War II* (Cambridge, Mass., 1952). Alexander Dallin, *German Rule in Russia, 1941–1945: A Study of Occupation Policies* (Cambridge, Mass., 1957).

105. As measured in pages of final reports and using the project's own categories; see Bauer et al., *How the Soviet System Works,* 252–256.

106. Clyde Kluckhohn, Raymond A. Bauer, and Alex Inkeles, "Strategic Psychological and Sociological Strengths and Vulnerabilities of the Soviet Social System," Final

Report to the Air Force, October 1954, in RIP Reports, series UAV 759.175.75, box 5 (hereafter Air Force Report), quotes on 14–16.

107. Kluckhohn et al., Air Force Report, chaps. III-B-2, III-B-3.

108. Bauer et al., *How the Soviet System Works,* 239, 243 (emphasis added).

109. Inkeles and Bauer, *Soviet Citizen,* 353.

110. Kluckhohn et al., Air Force Report, chapter III-C-7; quotes on 327, 330.

111. Arthur Melton to Marshall D. Shulman, 14 December 1955; Myron Barlow to Shulman, 6 December 1955—both in RRC Correspondence, series UAV 759.10, box 31. Kluckhohn et al., Air Force Report, 402.

112. See the Harvard Project on the Soviet Social System, at http://hcl.harvard.edu/collections/hpsss/index.html (accessed December 2007).

113. Langer oversaw all of the area research and training programs, leaving the associate director (political scientist Marshall Shulman) with a great deal of latitude in running the Russian center.

114. "Allocation to Disciplines" [Summer 1954?], RRC Correspondence, series UAV 759.10, box 22. John Gardner notes on conversation with Milton Graham, 19 November 1954; William Marvel notes on conversations with Frank Keppel, John Fairbank, and Milton Graham, November 1954, and on visit to RRC, February 1955—all in CCNY Records, series III.A, box 164.

115. Shulman remarks, 30 January 1958, RRC Correspondence, series UAV 759.10, box 42.

116. Hunter Heyck, "The Russian Research Center and the Postwar Social Sciences" (paper presented at the Davis Center, Harvard University, December 2008).

117. Clifford Geertz, *After the Fact: Two Countries, Four Decades, One Anthropologist* (Cambridge, Mass., 1995), 102. Donald McCloskey, "Alexander Gerschenkron," *American Scholar* 62 (Spring 1992), 243.

118. Report of the Visiting Committee of the Russian Research Center, 6 June 1952, Conant Presidential Records, series UA.I 5.168, box 443. Replies to Berliner memorandum, 26 June 1953, RRC Correspondence, series UAV 759.10, box 24.

119. Replies to Shulman memorandum, 25 May 1960, RRC Correspondence, series UAV 759.10, box 51.

CHAPTER 3

1. Cyril E. Black and John M. Thompson, "Graduate Study of Russia," in *American Teaching about Russia,* ed. Black and Thompson (Bloomington, Ind., 1959), 63.

2. Data derived from Jesse J. Dossick, *Doctoral Research on Russia and the Soviet Union* (New York, 1960).

3. Five scholars had both Columbia and Harvard connections, while three had neither. Ralph T. Fisher Jr., "The American Association for the Advancement of Slavic Studies: From Its Origins to 1969" (August 1970), 10–11, 153n14, AAASS Records (hereafter cited as AAASS History).

4. On Dartmouth, see CCNY Records (Columbia University Archives), series III.A, 130:1; on Bryn Mawr, see CCNY Records, series III.A, 66:10.

5. Robert A. McCaughey, *International Studies and Academic Enterprise: A Chapter in the Enclosure of American Learning* (New York, 1984), 153–154. FF, *Annual Reports,* 1952–1955.

6. Weisblat to Swayzee and Munford, 20 October 1955, FF Records (Ford Foundation Archives), Non-Grant Files, series SK036141, box 28.

7. "Informal Conference to Review the Soviet and East European Fellowship Program" (3 December 1955), FF Records, Non-Grant Files, series SK036141, box 28. David L. Szanton, "Shaping the Course of Area Studies," *SSRC Items* 45:2–3 (June–September 1991), 26.

8. Docket Excerpt, 26 May 1955, FF Records, Grant Files, 55–105. Sunderland and Weisblat to Howard and Swayzee, 29 November 1955, FF Records, Non-Grant Files, series SK036141, box 28. JCSS Subcommittee on Grants, Progress Report, 15 October 1958, FF Records, Grant Files, 57–213.

9. Fisher, AAASS History, 11, 153n15. The others were Princeton historian Cyril Black (Columbia senior fellow), Indiana historian Robert Byrnes (ditto), historian Henry Roberts (faculty), librarian Melvin Ruggles (graduate student), Harvard political scientist Marshall Shulman (graduate student), and John M. Thompson (graduate student). All but Thompson also had ties to Harvard. The eighth member, University of Washington historian Donald Treadgold, had been a Harvard graduate student.

10. JCSS Minutes, 4 May 1957, SSRC Records (Rockefeller Archive Center), 1/1/24/256/1502. The meeting minutes cite only "one visitor to the United States." Robert Byrnes, a participant at that meeting, later mentioned a similar sentiment, as expressed "two decades ago" by Aron; see Byrnes, "The Academic Labor Market: Where Do We Go from Here?" *SR* 36:2 (June 1977), 290.

11. "Graduate Training in Russian Studies: Summary of a Discussion at a Meeting of the Joint Committee and Guests" (6–7 December 1957), in ACLS Records (Library of Congress), box H-28 (hereafter Graduate Training Summary).

12. Harold H. Fisher, "Growing Pains of Slavic and East European Area Training," *ASEER* 17:3 (October 1958), 349.

13. John M. Thompson, "The State of Russian Studies outside the East: Impressions of Visits to a Dozen Universities, September 1957," SSRC Records, 1/1/24/256/1502. Report title notwithstanding, Thompson visited eleven universities: Berkeley, Chicago, Indiana, Michigan, Minnesota, Notre Dame, Stanford, Syracuse, UCLA, Washington, and Wayne State.

14. JCSS Minutes, 4 May 1957, SSRC Records, 1/1/24/256/1502.

15. *American Research on Russia,* ed. Harold H. Fisher (Bloomington, Ind., 1959).

16. Cleon O. Swayzee to John M. Thompson, 18 February 1959, FF Records, Non-Grant Files, series SK035670, box 38.

17. Cyril E. Black et al., "An Appraisal of Russian Studies in the United States," *ASEER* 18:3 (October 1959), 433.

18. Citations in Engerman, "American Knowledge and Global Power," *Diplomatic History* 31:4 (September 2007), 607–610.

19. Graduate Training Summary, 6. J. Thomas Shaw, "AATSEEL: The First Fifty Years," *SEEJ* 35 (1991), 147.

20. JCSS Minutes, 4 May 1957, SSRC Records, 1/1/24/256/1502. Black et al., "Appraisal of Russian Studies," 422.

21. JCSS Minutes, 9–10 October 1959, SSRC Records, 1/1/24/256/1502.

22. Graduate Training Summary, 8.

23. Black et al., "Appraisal of Russian Studies," 431–432.

24. JCSS Minutes, 4 May 1957, SSRC Records, 1/1/24/256/1502.

25. "The Organizational Problem in Slavic Studies" (16 May 1958), SSRC Records, 1/1/24/255/1500.

26. JCSS Minutes, 4 May 1957, SSRC Records, 1/1/24/256/1502.

27. Fisher, AAASS History, 12.

28. Shulman, "Organization and Publications in the Field of Soviet Studies" (20 March 1958), in Donald Treadgold Papers (University of Washington Library), collection 1845–2, box 2.

29. Black et al., "Appraisal of Russian Studies," 439. In the early twenty-first century, there were representatives of six disciplinary organizations: language, history, political science, sociology, geography, and anthropology. Economics and literature associations no longer have such an agreement with the AAASS, though both were part of the original board. Fisher, AAASS History, 105–114, and AAASS Web site www.aaass.org (accessed 29 February 2008).

30. John Newbold Hazard, *Reflections of a Pioneering Sovietologist* (New York, 1987), 116.

31. Fisher, AAASS History, 11, 153n16.

32. JCSS Minutes, 18–19 March 1960, SSRC Records, 1/1/24/256/1502.

33. Fisher, AAASS History, 15–16.

34. Fisher, AAASS History, 21, 24, 32.

35. "*Slavic Review:* Report of the Managing Editor, January 1–October 1, 1962," AAASS Records, box 2.

36. "List of Payments by Donors to AAASS," 27 July 1962, AAASS Records, box 2. Fisher, AAASS History, 93–94, 76, 90.

37. Donald W. Treadgold to Gordon B. Turner, 4 May 1964, Treadgold Papers, collection 1845–2-82–56, box 4.

38. JCSS Minutes, 2–3 December 1966, ACLS Records, box H-21.

39. McCaughey, *International Studies and Academic Enterprise,* chap. 7.

40. Theodora E. Carlson, *Guide to the National Defense Education Act of 1958* (Office of Education, circular no. 553, 1959), 3.

41. Donald N. Bigelow and Lyman H. Legters, "National Defense Education Act Language and Area Centers: A Report on the First Five Years," *Office of Education Bulletin,* no. 41 (1964), 119.

42. Derived from FF, *Annual Reports,* 1961–1966.

43. U.S. Department of State, External Research Staff, *Language and Area Studies Centers in American Universities* (Washington, D.C., 1964).

44. P. M. Raup, "The Development of Organized Support for International Studies at the University of California Berkeley" (December 1962), Grossman Papers.

45. John M. H. Lindbeck, *Understanding China: An Assessment of American Scholarly Resources* (New York, 1971), 79.

46. Bigelow and Legters, "NDEA Language and Area Centers," 14.

47. Stephen Arum, "Early Stages of Foreign Language and Area Studies in the United States, 1915–1941" (Ed.D. diss., Columbia University Teachers College, 1975), 568.

48. University of California, Berkeley, *Asiatic and Slavic Studies on the Berkeley Campus, 1896–1947* (Berkeley, 1947), 8–9. Jason Morton, "Fifty Years of Slavic Studies at Berkeley: The Prelude to 1957," University of California, Berkeley *ISEEES [Institute of Slavic, East European, and Eurasian Studies] Newsletter* 25:1 (Spring 2008), 5–9.

49. Bigelow and Legters, "NDEA Language and Area Centers," 114; Raup, "Development of Organized Support," 3.

50. Lynn Lubamersky, "History of the Russian and East European Institute" (1993), in Indiana University Archives.

51. Michigan information available from Center for Russian and East European Studies Web site, http://www.ii.umich.edu/crees/aboutus/mission (accessed March 2008).

52. Ralph Fisher, "Swimming with the Current," *Russian History/Histoire Russe* 21:2 (Summer 1994), 157–163.

53. Based on *Area Studies Programs at American Universities* (Washington, D.C., 1956); *Area Studies Programs at American Universities* (Washington, D.C., 1959); *Language and Area Studies Programs at American Universities* (Washington, D.C., 1964); Bigelow and Legters, "NDEA Language and Area Centers," appendix E.

54. The data from 1950–1960 are based on Dossick, *Doctoral Research;* later data are calculated from Jesse J. Dossick's annual reports, which appeared in the December issues of *Slavic Review* under the title "Doctoral Dissertations on Russia, the Soviet Union, and Eastern Europe Accepted by American, Canadian and British Universities." This calculation excludes Eastern Europe but includes the handful of Canadian and British doctorates.

55. See previous note for sources. "Early 1960s" is 1960–1963, "early 1970s" is 1970–1973.

56. J. A. Posin, "Russian Studies in American Colleges," *RR* 7:2 (Spring 1948), 63–64. O. A. Maslenikov, "Slavic Studies in America, 1939–1946," *SEER* 25 (1947), 530. Arthur P. Coleman, *A Report on the Status of Russian and Other East European Languages in the Educational Institutions of the United States* (New York, 1948). Untitled article, *AATSEEL[American Association of Teachers of Slavic and East European Languages] Bulletin* 9:1 (15 September 1951), 1. Dmitri von Mohrenschildt, "Russian Studies in the United States," *AATSEEL Bulletin* 10:3 (15 March 1953), 46–47. Benjamin Fine, "Study of Russian Falls Off in U.S.," *NYT,* 28 November 1954. Fine estimated 5,000 students of Russian in the fall of 1954.

57. Modern Language Association, *Report of Surveys and Studies in the Teaching of Modern Foreign Languages, 1959–61* (New York, 1961); Richard I. Brod, "Foreign Language Enrollments in US Colleges, Fall 1970," *ADFL Bulletin* 3:2 (December 1971); Brod, "Foreign Language Enrollments in US Colleges, Fall 1974," *Modern Language Journal* 60:4 (April 1976).

58. "Earned Degrees in Foreign Languages," *ADFL Bulletin* 1:1 (September 1969), 20–23.

59. Byrnes to Gordon Turner, 18 May 1961, and Turner to Donald W. Treadgold, 13 December 1962—both in ACLS Records, box H-29.

60. Dallin, "On Relations between Government and Universities in Regard to Studies of Communism" (draft/limited use), 10 January 1962, attached to Treadgold to Gordon Turner, 4 May 1964, in Treadgold Papers, collection 1845-2-82–56, box 4.

61. Treadgold to Dallin, 27 November 1962, and Turner to Treadgold, 13 December 1962—both in ACLS Records, box H-29.

62. "Notes on Meeting of Soviet Specialists from U.S. Government and JCSS," 24 October 1963, ACLS Records, box H-29. The government representatives were Matthew Gallagher, Raymond Garthoff, and Helmut Sonnenfeldt.

63. Willits memo of conversation with Philip E. Mosely, 29–30 November 1943, RF Records (Rockefeller Archive Center), 1.1/200R/229/2720. Roger F. Evans memo of conversation with George E. Taylor, 9 February 1945, in RF Records, 2/1945 785/311/2108. John Gardner memorandum of conversation with Ernest J. Simmons, CCNY Records, series III.A, box 113.

64. "Minutes of the Meeting to Discuss the Exchange of Persons with the USSR," 27 February 1946, in State Department Records (U.S. National Archives), RG59, lot 69D162, 10:1651. George C. Herring Jr., *Aid to Russia, 1941–1946: Strategy, Diplomacy, and the Origins of the Cold War* (New York, 1973), chap. 8.

65. Francis B. Stevens to Mr. Mitchell, 22 December 1947, in State Department Records, lot 69D162, 10:1651.

66. Robert F. Byrnes, *Soviet-American Academic Exchanges, 1958–1975* (Bloomington, Ind., 1976), 34–37.

67. NSC 5607, "Statement of Policy on East-West Exchanges," 29 June 1956, DDRS, document CK3100069191.

68. Lacy, "US-USSR Exchange Policy" (1 July 1957), in Office of the Special Assistant for National Security Affairs (Dwight D. Eisenhower Presidential Library), Operations Control Board series, subject subseries, box 2. Congress amended McCarran-Walter to loosen the fingerprinting requirements in October 1957; Walter L. Hixson, *Parting the Curtain: Propaganda, Culture, and the Cold War, 1945–1961* (New York, 1997), 152.

69. For a summary of programs as of 1959, see "Report on the East-West Exchange Program" (early 1960?), in Department of State, CU Historical Collection (University of Arkansas Library), 320:26.

70. David C. Munford to Cleon O. Swayzee, 5 August 1955, FF Records, Non-Grant Files, series SK035944, box 39.

71. Jacob D. Beam to Secretary of State, 11 July 1956; "Memorandum on Student and Professor Exchanges with the Soviet Union," 25 July 1956; memorandum of conversation with Harvard's Marshall D. Shulman, 10 January 1956; and Livingston T. Merchant to Jacob Beam and Francis Stevens, 29 December 1955—all in State Department Records, lot 69D162, box 8.

72. David C. Munford to Don K. Price, Shepard Stone, and Cleon O. Swayzee, 27 November 1956, in FF Records, Non-Grant Files, series SK035944, box 39.

73. Agenda for JCSS Annual Meeting, 13 November 1955, SSRC Records, 1/1/24/256/1501.

74. Munford to Swayzee, 5 August 1955, and John B. Howard to Don K. Price, 28 September 1955—both in FF Records, Non-Grant Files, series SK035944, box 39.

75. Communication with Allen Kassof (2009). Byrnes, *Soviet-American Academic Exchanges,* 39.

76. William Marvel, memorandum of conversation with Schuyler Wallace, 20 February 1956, CCNY Records, series III.A, 514:6.

77. Summary of IUCTG recipients in Philip E. Mosely Papers (Columbia University Library), box 9. See RRC Executive Committee Minutes (Harvard University Archives), series UAV 759.5, box 1. Byrnes, *Soviet-American Academic Exchanges,* 40.

78. Communication with Stephen Viederman (2003).

79. Byrnes, *Soviet-American Academic Exchanges,* 43.

80. Inter-University Educational Conference (November 1957), in Robert F. Byrnes Papers (Indiana University Library), box 22.

81. Baron, "Russian People Passive about Communism," *Des Moines Tribune,* 30 September 1959. Riasanovsky, "My Historical Research in the Soviet Union," and Baron, "A Tale of Two Inquiries," both in *Adventures in Russian Historical Research: Reminiscences of American Scholars from the Cold War to the Present,* ed. Baron and Cathy A. Frierson (Armonk, N.Y., 2003). Communication with Marshall D. Shulman (2004). Inter-University Educational Conference (November 1957), Byrnes Papers, box 22. Fainsod, "Russian Diary" (1956), in Merle Fainsod Papers (Harvard University Archives), series HUG 4382.8, box 4. IUCTG, "Study and Research in the Soviet Union, 1960–61" (July 1961), 83, 85, 90, 96, in Mosely Papers (Columbia), box 10. Communication with John M. Thompson (2004). Other senior scholars who traveled on the IUCTG program included Frederick Barghoorn, John Hazard, and Roman Jakobson.

82. Yale Richmond, *Cultural Exchange and the Cold War: Raising the Iron Curtain* (University Park, Pa., 2003), chap. 3. Frederick T. Merrill, memorandum of conversation with David Munford and Stephen Viederman, 29 May 1959, SDDF 511.613/5–2959. Herbert Kupferberg, *The Raised Curtain: Report of the Twentieth Century Fund Task Force on Soviet-American Scholarly and Cultural Exchange* (New York, 1977), 67–69. IUCTG circular in Mosely Papers (Columbia), box 11.

83. Dwight D. Eisenhower, *Waging Peace, 1956–1961: The White House Years* (Garden City, N.Y., 1965), 411. Allen W. Dulles to Gordon Gray, 2 July 1959, and "Soviet-American Student Exchange" (July 1959?)—both in Office of the Special Assistant for National Security Affairs (Dwight D. Eisenhower Presidential Library), NSC Briefing Notes series, box 7.

84. FF, *Annual Report, 1959.* "Report of the Visit of the Harvard Delegation to the University of Leningrad and Other Academic and Research Institutions in the Soviet Union, January 31–February 13, 1959," Fainsod Papers, series HUG 4382.8, box 4. Allen G. Kassof, "Academic Exchanges with the USSR," 16 June 1976, Yale Richmond Papers. Byrnes, *Soviet-American Academic Exchanges,* 62–63. "E. B." to Cleon Swayzee, 21 May 1963, FF Records, Non-Grant Files, series SK035944, box 39. Faculty Committee on Exchanges, 30 November 1959, RRC Correspondence (Harvard University Archives), series UAV 759.10, box 40.

85. *ACLS Annual Report, 1959–60,* 4. A. N. Nesmeianov to Burkhardt, 17 March 1961, RGANI, 5/35/159/120–124.

86. Robert J. Martens, memorandum of conversation with Frederick Burkhardt, 29 February 1960, SDDF 511.613/2–2960. S. Romanovskii to Central Committee, CPSU, 22 February 1961, RGANI 5/35/159/50–57.

87. Robert J. Martens, memorandum of conversation with Frederick Burkhardt, 18 November 1959, SDDF 511.613/11–1859. William Marvel memorandum, 11 September 1961, CCNY Records, series III.A, 404A:10.

88. Topics included the historian V. O. Kliuchevskii (Robert Byrnes) and old believers in the seventeenth and eighteenth centuries (Michael Cherniavsky). Robert J. Martens, memorandum of conversation with Frederick Burkhardt, 26 June 1962, SDDF 511.613/6–2662.

89. E. Willis Brooks to IUCTG Committee on the Future, 2 January 1968, Loren Graham Papers. See also Byrnes, *Inter-University Committee Report to the Ford Foundation, 1965–1969* (Bloomington, Ind., 1970), 13–14.

90. "CU Grants for IUCTG and IREX Programs," 24 September 1975, in CU Historical Collection, 332:29. Byrnes, *Soviet-American Academic Exchanges*, 125–133. Byrnes, in U.S. Senate, Committee on Foreign Relations, *Perceptions: Relations between the United States and the Soviet Union* (Washington, D.C., 1979), 426.

91. Munford to Merrill, 27 March 1958, CU Historical Collection, 228:7.

92. Byrnes, *Soviet-American Academic Exchanges*, 102–105.

93. Communication with Patricia Albjerg Graham (2004). Communication with Stephen Viederman (2003).

94. Byrnes, *Soviet-American Academic Exchanges*, 102, 105. IUCTG reference forms (1960 and 1963), REEI Records (University of Illinois Library), box 4. Data from Willis Brooks to IUCTG Committee on the Future, 2 January 1968, Loren Graham Papers. Almost all of the information on name-checks comes from IUCTG personnel or records, though the little information from other sources seems to confirm the IUCTG internal account.

95. Byrnes to Trani (1974), in Byrnes Papers, box 6. Byrnes, "Harvard, Columbia, and the CIA: My Training in Russian Studies" (1988), in Byrnes, A *History of Russian and East European Studies in the United States: Selected Essays* (Lanham, Md., 1994), 248–249, 254–255. Communication with Nick Cullather (2003). Byrnes to Ivo Lederer, 27 October 1967, Loren Graham Papers; "Meeting on Candidate for Study in the Soviet Union," 22 June 1960, SDDF 511.613/6–2260.

96. IUCTG circular (November 1957), Mosely Papers (Columbia), box 9. IUCTG circular (1960), Mosely Papers (Columbia), box 11. "Policies and Procedures of the IUCTG" (1968), in Central Files (Columbia University Archives), subject subseries, folder IUCTG.

97. FAFP, *Directory: Foreign Area Fellows, 1952–1963* (New York, 1964). FAFP, *Directory: Foreign Area Fellows, 1952–1972* (New York, 1973). Data include the Ford fellows who received their awards through ACLS/SSRC joint committees after 1962.

98. Fisher, AAASS History, 61.

99. Data from various Dossick reports entitled "Doctoral Dissertations on Russia, the Soviet Union, and Eastern Europe Accepted by American, Canadian and British

Universities," which appeared in the December issues of *Slavic Review* in 1964 and
1970–1972.

100. Cited in his obituary: "Dr. Henry L. Roberts Is Dead: Taught History at Dartmouth,"
NYT, 18 October 1972. Given Roberts's high standards, it should be noted that he
accepted a higher percentage of submissions to *Slavic Review* when he served as
editor than did his predecessor (and successor), Donald Treadgold; "*Slavic Review:*
Report of the Managing Editor, January 1–October 1, 1962," AAASS Records, box
1. "Report of the Managing Editor of *Slavic Review*" (11 January 1968), AAASS
Records, box 2.

101. Roberts, "From the Editor," *SR* 24:3 (September 1965), n.p.

102. Walter Z. Laqueur, "In Search of Russia" (1964), in *The State of Soviet Studies,* ed.
Laqueur and Leopold Labedz (Cambridge, Mass., 1965), 10–11.

103. Elinor G. Barber and Warren Ilchman, *International Studies Review: A Staff Study*
(New York, 1979), 6.

CHAPTER 4

1. Gerschenkron, "American Research on the Soviet Economy" (1964), in Gerschenkron,
Continuity in History and Other Essays (Cambridge, Mass., 1968), 525.

2. Abram Bergson, "Russia Turns to Economic Competition," *Challenge* 6:5 (February
1958), 50–54; and Gregory Grossman, "Soviet Economy and World Power," in
American Assembly, *International Stability and Progress: United States Interests and
Instruments* (New York, 1957).

3. Bergson, "Reliability and Usability of Soviet Statistics: A Summary Appraisal,"
American Statistician 7:3 (June–July 1953), 13.

4. Bergson to Wassily Leontief Jr., 31 March 1947, Wassily Leontief Jr. Papers
(Harvard University Archives), series HUG 4517.5.

5. John W. Kestner, "Through the Looking Glass: American Perceptions of the Soviet
Economy, 1941–1964" (Ph.D. diss., University of Wisconsin, Madison, 1999), 38–45.
Barry M. Katz, *Foreign Intelligence: Research and Analysis in the Office of Strategic
Services, 1942–1945* (Cambridge, Mass., 1989), 141–142. Thomas P. Whitney, *Russia
in My Life* (New York, 1962), chaps. 2–3. Mark Perlman, "Political Purpose and the
National Accounts," in *The Politics of Numbers,* ed. William Alonso and Paul Starr
(New York, 1987), 142–145.

6. R&A 1004, "Russian National Income and Defense Expenditures" (8 September
1943), in *OSS/State Department Intelligence and Research Reports,* ed. Paul Kesaris
(Washington, D.C., 1977), part VI, reel II, doc. 9, pp. 9–10, 1 (hereafter *OSS
Reports*).

7. Kestner, "Through the Looking Glass," 50–51, 54; Bradley F. Smith, *The Shadow
Warriors: OSS and the Origins of the CIA* (New York, 1983), 381. R&A 1899, "Russian
War Damage and Possible Reparation Claims, Part I: General Statements"
(8 March 1944), *OSS Reports*, VI/II/24, pp. 1–2.

8. R&A 2060, "Russian Reconstruction and Postwar Foreign Trade Development"
(8 September 1944), *OSS Reports,* VI/III/11, pp. 9, iv, vii.

9. Kennan, "Russia: Seven Years Later" (1944), in Kennan, *Memoirs, 1925–1950* (Boston, 1967), 510, 509. R&A 2060, "Russian Reconstruction," iv. Kestner, "Through the Looking Glass," 80–82.

10. R&A 2669, "The Capabilities and Intentions of the USSR in the Postwar Period" (3 January 1945), *OSS Reports,* VI/IV/5, pp. 2a–4, 25, 26, 31–32, 36–37, 49, 50.

11. Betty Abrahamsen Dessants, "The American Academic Community and United States–Soviet Union Relations: The Research and Analysis Branch and Its Legacy" (Ph.D. diss., University of California, Berkeley, 1995), 137–145, 164–169. Charles Bohlen and Geroid Robinson, "The Bohlen-Robinson Report: The Capabilities and Intentions of the Soviet Union as Affected by American Policy" (1945), *Diplomatic History* 1:4 (October 1977), 389–399. Melvyn P. Leffler, "The American Conception of National Security and the Beginnings of the Cold War, 1945–1948," *AHR* 89:2 (April 1984), 356–358. Kestner, "Through the Looking Glass," 74–79.

12. Bergson, "Recollections and Reflections of a Comparativist," in *Eminent Economists: Their Life Philosophies,* ed. Michael Szenberg (Cambridge, 1992), 61. Abram Burk, "A Reformulation of Certain Aspects of Welfare Economics," *QJE* 52:2 (February 1938), 310–334. Marshall Goldman, Paul Samuelson, and Martin Weitzman, "Abram Bergson Memorial Minute," *Comparative Economic Studies* 47:2 (June 2005), 493. E. J. Mishan, "Welfare Economics," in *International Encyclopedia of the Social Sciences,* ed. David Sills (New York, 1968), 16:504–512.

13. Bergson, "Recollections and Reflections," 62. Communication (unchecked) with Abram Bergson (1999).

14. Solomon Fabricant, review of *Structure of Soviet Wages* by Abram Bergson, *Review of Economics and Statistics* 27:1 (February 1945), 34–35. Wiles, "Are Adjusted Rubles Rational?" *Soviet Studies* 7:2 (October 1955), 144–145.

15. James Millar, "Bergson's Structure of Soviet Wages," *Comparative Economic Studies* 47:2 (June 2005), 289–295. Bergson, *The Structure of Soviet Wages: A Study in Socialist Economics* (Cambridge, Mass., 1944), 208, 216–217, x.

16. R&A 2060, "Russian Reconstruction," appendix A.

17. A. C. Pigou quoted in John W. Kendrick, "The Historical Development of National-Income Accounts," *History of Political Economy* 2 (Fall 1970), 305.

18. See the symposium on Irving Fisher, "The Best Form of the Index Number," *Quarterly Publications of the American Statistical Association* 17 (March 1921), 533–551.

19. R&A 2060, "Russian Reconstruction," appendix A.

20. "Conference of Social Scientists (September 1947)," RAND Report R-106 (June 1948), 31, 231, 261–262.

21. On OSS, see SAC-Washington to J. Edgar Hoover, 13 July 1946, in Alexander Gerschenkron FBI File, 77–30528–3.

22. Harry Schwartz, "A Critique of 'Appraisals of Russian Economic Statistics,'" *Review of Economics and Statistics* 30:1 (February 1948), 38.

23. Gerschenkron, "The Soviet Indices of Industrial Production," *Review of Economics and Statistics* 29 (November 1947), 217. Clark, "Russian Income and Production Statistics," *Review of Economics and Statistics* 29:4 (November 1947), 215–217. Clark,

Critique of Russian Statistics (London, 1939), 46. Jasny, "Soviet Statistics," *Review of Economics and Statistics* 32:1 (February 1950), 95, 98–99, 93.

24. Bergson, "Reliability and Usability," 15–16. Bergson, *Soviet National Income and Product in 1937* (New York, 1953), 7–10n10.

25. Gerschenkron to Joseph A. Kershaw, 2 November 1949, Gerschenkron Papers, series HUG(FP) 45.10, box 11; Gerschenkron to Charles Hitch, 9 January 1950, Gerschenkron Papers, series HUG(FP) 45.10, box 8. USSR, Council of People's Commissariats, *Gosudarstvennyi plan razvitiia narodnogo khoziaitsva SSSR na 1941 god (Prilozheniia k postanovlenniu SNK SSSR i TsK VKP(b), no. 127 ot 17 ianvar'ia 1941 g.)* (Baltimore, 1951). Lynn Turgeon, "On the Reliability of Soviet Statistics," *Review of Economics and Statistics* 34:1 (February 1952), 75–76.

26. R. W. Davies, "The Making of Economic Policy," in *Behind the Façade of Stalin's Command Economy,*, ed. Paul R. Gregory (Stanford, 2001), 63.

27. Bergson, "How Reliable Are Soviet Statistics?" *New Republic* 120 (16 May 1949), 10. Gregory Grossman, *Soviet Statistics of Physical Output of Industrial Commodities: Their Compilation and Quality* (Princeton, 1960), chap. 10.

28. Gerschenkron, "Reliability of Soviet Industrial and National Income Statistics," *American Statistician* 7:2 (April–May 1953), 18.

29. Berliner, "Aspects of the Informal Social Organization of Russian Industry," Technical Research Report, no. 5 (Maxwell Air Force Base, Ala., 1952), 132–134.

30. Bergson, "A Problem in Soviet Statistics," *Review of Economics and Statistics* 29:4 (November 1947), 234–235.

31. Hans Speier, "Summary of Political and Economic Area Studies," RAND Report D-5866 (24 December 1958), 10–13. Joseph A. Kershaw to Gerschenkron, 12 September 1952, Gerschenkron Papers, series HUG(FP) 45.10, box 11. Leontief, *The Structure of the American Economy, 1919–1929: An Empirical Application of Equilibrium Analysis* (Cambridge, Mass., 1941); Leonard Silk, *The Economists* (New York, 1976), 163.

32. Norman M. Kaplan et al., "A Tentative Input-Output Table for the USSR, 1941 Plan Year," RAND Research Memorandum RM-924 (1952). RAND Organization Chart for 1949 (RAND Corporation Archives).

33. Gerschenkron, "Soviet Indices," 221. Charles Hitch to Gerschenkron, 18 November 1948, Gerschenkron Papers, series HUG(FP) 45.10, box 8. Gerschenkron, "A Dollar Index of Soviet Machinery Output, 1927–28 to 1937," RAND Research Report R-197 (April 1951).

34. Gerschenkron, "Dollar Index." Ira O. Scott Jr., "The Gerschenkron Hypothesis of Index Number Bias," *Review of Economics and Statistics* 34:4 (November 1952), 386–387. Nicholas Dawidoff, *The Fly Swatter: How My Grandfather Made His Way in the World* (New York, 2002), 161.

35. Clark, *Critique,* 46; and Paul Studenski and Julius Wyler, "National Income Estimates of Soviet Russia: Their Distinguishing Characteristics and Problems," *AER* 37:2 (May 1947), 610.

36. Gerschenkron to Hitch, 9 January 1950 (no. 1), Gerschenkron Papers, series HUG(FP) 45.10, box 8.

37. Gerschenkron, preface to Donald R. Hodgman, *Soviet Industrial Production, 1928–1951* (Cambridge, Mass., 1954), x.

38. In the 1960s, Gerschenkron trained leading scholars in European economic history but not in the Soviet field.

39. Joseph S. Berliner, *Factory and Manager in the USSR* (Cambridge, Mass., 1957).

40. Donald R. Hodgman, *Commercial Bank Loan and Investment Policy* (Champaign, Ill., 1963).

41. Erlich, *The Soviet Industrialization Debates, 1924–1928* (Cambridge, Mass., 1960). Padma Desai, "Alexander Erlich: Biographical Sketch," in *Marxism, Central Planning and the Soviet Experience: Economic Essays in Honor of Alexander Erlich*, ed. Desai (Cambridge, Mass., 1983).

42. Campbell, "The Growth of Soviet Output," *SR* 21:3 (September 1962), 522, 523. Warren Eason, review of *Real National Income of Soviet Russia* by Abram Bergson, *Annals* 347 (May 1963), 192–193. Goldman, "Abram Bergson: A Mentor," *Comparative Economic Studies* 47:2 (June 2005), 500. Jeffrey Sachs, in "Testimonials," *Comparative Economic Studies* 47:2 (June 2005), 496.

43. Bergson, *Soviet National Income*, chap. 3. Bergson, *Structure*, 11.

44. Paul R. Gregory, "The Political Economy of Stalinism: A Bergson Retrospective," *Comparative Economic Systems* 47:2 (June 2005), 415–416. Bergson, "Socialist Economics" (1948), in Abram Bergson, *Essays in Normative Economics* (Cambridge, Mass., 1966), 234. Bergson, *Soviet National Income*, 50–51 (emphasis in original).

45. Bergson, *Soviet National Income*, 87, 95, 98.

46. Jasny, "On the Wrong Track," *Journal of Political Economy* 55:3 (August 1947), 352–353. Jasny, *To Live Long Enough: The Memoirs of Naum Jasny, Scientific Analyst*, ed. Betty A. Laird and Roy D. Laird (Lawrence, Kans., 1976), 108; Jasny to Clide [*sic*] Kluckhohn, 20 January 1948, and Leontief to Kluckhohn, 30 December 1947—both in RRC Correspondence (Harvard University Archives), series UAV 759.10, box 2. Alec Nove, review of *A Dollar Index of Soviet Machinery Output* by Alexander Gerschenkron, *Economic Journal* 63:249 (March 1953), 163–166. Clark, "The Soviet Crisis," in Congress of Cultural Freedom, *The Soviet Economy: A Discussion* (London, 1956), 14. Jasny, "Correspondence," *Soviet Studies* 8:3 (June 1957), 333. Correspondence among Jasny, Merle Fainsod, and Charles E. Odegaard (December 1951), SSRC Records (Rockefeller Archive Center), 2/1/81/496/6108. JCSS report, n.d. (1951?), ACLS Records (Library of Congress), box E-50.

47. Grossman, "National Income," in *Soviet Economic Growth: Conditions and Perspectives*, ed. Abram Bergson (Evanston, Ill., 1953).

48. P. J. D. Wiles, review of *Soviet Economic Growth* edited by Abram Bergson, *Annals* 291 (January 1954), 194. Jasny to SSRC, 3 December 1951, SSRC Records, 2/1/81/496/6108.

49. Maurice C. Ernest, "Economic Intelligence in CIA" (1984), in *Inside CIA's Private World: Declassified Articles from the Agency's Internal Journal, 1955–1992*, ed. H. Bradford Westerfield (New Haven, Conn., 1995), 307. Ludwell Lee Montague,

General Walter Bedell Smith as Director of Central Intelligence, October 1950–February 1953 (University Park, Pa., 1992), 150, 152–153.

50. Noel E. Firth and James H. Noren, *Soviet Defense Spending: A History of CIA Estimates, 1950–1990* (College Station, Tex., 1998), 13; Ernst, "Economic Intelligence," 307; Montague, *General Walter Bedell Smith,* 152.

51. James Noren, "CIA's Analysis of the Soviet Economy," in *Watching the Bear: Essays on CIA's Analysis of the Soviet Union,* ed. Gerald K. Haines and Robert E. Leggett (2003, accessed online at www.cia.gov, March 2007).

52. Millikan, "The Nature and Methods of Economic Intelligence" (1951), *Studies in Intelligence* 1:1 (Spring 1956), 1, accessed at www.foia.cia.gov (June 2008).

53. Millikan, "Nature and Methods," 15–18; Firth and Noren, *Soviet Defense Spending,* 13–20.

54. Robert R. Bowie and Richard H. Immerman, *Waging Peace: How Eisenhower Shaped an Enduring Cold War Strategy* (Oxford, 1998), 98, 79, 99, and chap. 8 on Solarium. H. W. Brands, "The Age of Vulnerability: Eisenhower and the National Security State," *AHR* 94:4 (October 1989), 969.

55. "Solarium Project," 8 May 1953, in White House–NSC Staff Records (Dwight D. Eisenhower Presidential Library), Executive Secretary series, Subject subseries, box 15.

56. NIE 65 (9 June 1953), "Soviet Bloc Capabilities through 1957," DNSA document SE00146, 7–8.

57. SE-46 (3 July 1953), "Probable Long-Term Development of the Soviet Bloc and Western Power Positions," DDRS document CK3100275122, 1–2.

58. This paragraph is based on a detailed comparison of the Solarium task forces prepared by J. C. Campbell for Robert Cutler; dated 11 August 1953, it appears in White House Office, NSC Staff Records, Executive Secretary series, subject subseries, box 15. Large portions of the Solarium reports appeared in *FRUS, 1952–54,* 2:417, 415–416.

59. Bowie and Immerman, *Waging Peace,* 142, chap. 4. NSC 162/2, "A Report to the National Security Council on Basic National Security Policy" (30 October 1953), DDRS document CK3100391157, 14.

60. Townsend Hoopes, *The Devil and John Foster Dulles* (Boston, 1975), 286 (emphasis in original). Eisenhower to Dulles (1955), quoted in Kestner, "Through the Looking Glass," 250.

61. Kestner, "Through the Looking Glass," 228. Cutler to Rusk, RF Records (Rockefeller Archive Center), 1.2/200S/538/4600.

62. Mosely, memorandum of conversation with Arthur F. Burns, 15 September 1953, and Solomon Fabricant to Joseph H. Willits, 8 September 1953, both in RF Records, 1.2/200S/538/4600.

63. Vibha Kapuria-Foreman and Mark Perlman, "An Economic Historian's Economist: Remembering Simon Kuznets," *Economic Journal* 105:433 (November 1995), 1535. Kestner, "Through the Looking Glass," 229–230; Mosely, memorandum of conversation with Burns, 15 September 1953, and Cutler to Burns, 29 September 1953, both in RF Records, 1.2/200S/538/4600.

64. NBER, "Proposal for a Study of the Performance of the Russian Soviet Economy" (September 1953), RF Records, 1.2/200S/538/4600.

65. Milton Friedman and Rose D. Friedman, *Two Lucky People: Memoirs* (Chicago, 1998), 338, 419. G. Warren Nutter, *The Extent of Enterprise Monopoly in the United States, 1899–1939: A Quantitative Study of Some Aspects of Monopoly* (Chicago, 1951). RAND Organization Chart for 1949 (RAND Corporation Archives).

66. Nutter, *The Growth of Industrial Production in the Soviet Union* (Princeton, 1962), xxvi. Paul Craig Roberts, "Foreword," in Nutter, *Political Economy and Freedom: A Collection of Essays*, ed. Jane Couch Nutter (Indianapolis, Ind., 1984), x. Chalmers R. Roberts, "The Men around the Big Men," *Washington Post*, 10 November 1963.

67. Nutter, "Some Observations on Soviet Industrial Growth," *AER* 47:2 (May 1957), 619–624. Marion W. Boggs to NSC Planning Board, 30 January 1957, White House Office, NSC Staff Records, NSC Registry series, box 17.

68. Nutter, "On Measuring Economic Growth," *JPE* 65:1 (February 1947), 51–63; exchange between Nutter and Bergson student Herbert Levine in *JPE* 66:4 (August 1958), 357–363 (caterpillar on 362). Nutter, "The True Story of Russia's Weakness," *U.S. News and World Report* 42 (1 March 1957), 47, 119.

69. Richard F. Kaufman, "CIA Economic Intelligence on the USSR, 1949–1960," *Post-Soviet Affairs* 11:3 (1995), 286–288.

70. RR-53, "Long-Run Soviet Economic Growth" (13 December 1954), in *CIA's Analysis of the Soviet Union, 1947–1991*, ed. Gerald K. Haines and Robert E. Leggett (Langley, Va., 2000), 174–176.

71. Kaufman, "CIA Economic Intelligence," 287.

72. Cline, *Secrets, Spies, and Scholars: Blueprint of the Essential CIA* (Washington, D.C., 1976), 146–147.

73. Allen Dulles, "Russia's Growing Threat Could be a Weakness," *U.S. News and World Report* 40 (11 May 1956), 124–125. Dulles, "The Challenge of Soviet Industrial Growth," in Princeton University Conference, *The Challenge of Soviet Industrial Growth: Papers Delivered at a Meeting of the Princeton University Conference, December 11–12, 1956* (Princeton, 1957), 62–75.

74. Allen Dulles statement, "Comparisons of the United States and Soviet Economies," Joint Economic Committee Hearings, 86th Cong., 1st sess. (13 November 1959), 4, 6; Morris Bornstein, "Comparisons of Soviet and United States National Product," in *Comparisons of the United States and Soviet Economies: Papers Submitted by Panelists Appearing before the Subcommittee on Economic Statistics* (86th Cong., 1st sess., 1959), 390–391.

75. "Gaps, Lags, and Politics," *Wall Street Journal*, 3 May 1962; "Do You Believe What You Read?" *LAT*, 11 May 1962.

76. Bergson, *Soviet National Income*, 65.

77. Nutter, review of *Economic Trends in the Soviet Union* edited by Abram Bergson and Simon Kuznets, *Annals* 351 (January 1964), 207–208. Nutter, *Growth of Industrial Production*, 267–269.

78. Holland Hunter, review of *Growth of Industrial Production in the Soviet Union* by G. Warren Nutter, *Journal of Business* 36:2 (April 1963), 250–251. Gerschenkron, "Dollar Index," 57.

79. Kuznets, "A Comparative Appraisal," in *Economic Trends in the Soviet Union,* ed. Bergson and Kuznets (Cambridge, Mass., 1963), 334, 337, 370.

80. Jasny, *To Live Long Enough,* 111, 120. Donald R. Hodgman, review of *Soviet Industrialization* by Noam Jasny, *SR* 22:2 (June 1963), 356–358. Alexander Erlich, review of *Soviet Industrialization* by Noam Jasny, *AER* 52:4 (September 1962), 846–848. Norman M. Kaplan, "Arithmancy, Theomancy, and the Soviet Economy," *JPE* 61:2 (April 1953), 93–116.

81. Jasny, *Soviet Industrialization, 1928–1952* (Chicago, 1961), 444. He did make some adjustments to 1926/1927 prices, which are best explained in Jasny, *The Soviet Price System* (Stanford, 1951).

82. Jasny, *Soviet Industrialization,* 22. Zaleski, review of *Soviet Industrialization* by Noam Jasny, *JPE* 70:4 (August 1962), 416–417.

83. Judith G. Thornton, "The Index Number Problem in the Measurement of Soviet National Income," *Journal of Economic History* 22:3 (September 1962), 388.

84. Grossman, "Economics," in *American Research on Russia,* ed. Harold H. Fisher (Bloomington, Ind., 1959), 48–49. Abraham C. Becker, "Intelligence Fiasco or Reasoned Accounting? CIA Estimates of Soviet GNP," *Post-Soviet Affairs* 10:4 (1994), 296. James R. Millar et al., "An Evaluation of the CIA's Analysis of Soviet Economic Performance, 1970–90," *Comparative Economic Studies* 35:3 (Summer 1993), 36. Robert W. Campbell, "Research on the Soviet Economy: Achievements and Prospects," in *Study of the Soviet Economy: Direction and Impact of Soviet Growth,* ed. Nicolas Spulber (Bloomington, Ind., 1961), 129–133.

85. Gerschenkron, "American Research," 533–534. James Millar, "Where Are the Young Specialists on the Soviet Economy and What Are They Doing?" *Journal of Comparative Economics* 4 (1980), 317–329.

86. Robert Solow, "How Did Economics Get That Way and What Way Did It Get?" in *American Academic Culture in Transformation: Fifty Years, Four Disciplines,* ed. Thomas Bender and Carl E. Schorske (Princeton, 1998).

87. C. D. Goodwin, "Area and International Studies: Economics," in *International Encyclopedia of Social and Behavioral Sciences,* ed. Neil J. Smelser and Paul B. Baltes (Oxford, 2001), 685.

88. See, for instance, Vladimir G. Treml, *Censorship, Access, and Influence: Western Sovietology in the Soviet Union* (Berkeley, 1999). V. Kudrov, "Pravda o nas znal Bergson," *Izvestiia,* 5 November 2003; V. M. Kudrov, *Soviet Economic Performance in Retrospect: A Critical Re-Examination* (n.p., 1998).

89. Robert F. Byrnes, *Inter-University Committee Report to the Ford Foundation, 1965–69* (Bloomington, Ind., 1970), 11. For an economist's sense of the lack of attention to economic issues in Russian/Soviet history, see, for instance, R. W. Davies, "Introduction: From Tsarism to NEP," in *From Tsarism to the New Economic*

Policy: Continuity and Change in the Economy of the USSR, ed. Davies (Ithaca, N.Y., 1991), 24–25.

90. *The Soviet Economy: Toward the Year 2000,* ed. Bergson and Levine (London, 1983). Photograph, provided by James Millar, in author's possession.

CHAPTER 5

1. J. Thomas Shaw, "AATSEEL: The First Fifty Years," *SEEJ* 35 (1991), 147. Most of the subjects of this chapter taught Russian topics in departments of Slavic language and literature; I use the term "Slavicist" to refer to them here.

2. Nabokov, *Pnin* (Garden City, N.Y., 1957), 10–11.

3. Roman Jakobson to Nathan Pusey, 8 February 1960, Roman Jakobson Papers (MIT Archives), 2:29.

4. See the "discussion" among Ivan Rudnytsky, Arthur Adams, Omeljan Pritsak, and John Reshetar in *SR* 22:2 (June 1963). For an exception, see George Stephen Nestor Lukyj, *Literary Politics in the Soviet Ukraine, 1917–1934* (New York, 1956).

5. Uil'iam Todd III [William Todd III], "Konteksty literaturnoi kritiki: amerikanskie uchenye i russkaia literatura," *Novoe literaturnoe obozrenie* 12 (1995), 153–155.

6. Simmons, *An Outline of Modern Russian Literature (1880–1940)* (Ithaca, N.Y., 1943), 73–74.

7. Simmons, "Introduction: Soviet Literature and Controls," in *Through the Glass of Soviet Literature: Views of Russian Society,* ed. Simmons (New York, 1953), 26.

8. *Continuity and Change in Russian and Soviet Thought,* ed. Simmons (Cambridge, Mass., 1955).

9. The essays are by Leon Stilman and Robert M. Hankin.

10. Simmons quoted in "Part V Review," in Simmons, *Continuity and Change,* 452.

11. Jesse Dossick, *Doctoral Research on Russia and the Soviet Union* (New York, 1960).

12. RI program description, 29 April 1946, in CUCF (Columbia University Archives), Subject: Russian Institute (RI).

13. William Edgerton was an exception, writing his dissertation on the nineteenth-century novelist N. S. Leskov.

14. Brown, *Soviet Attitudes towards American Writing* (Princeton, 1962), 271.

15. Friedberg, *Russian Classics in Soviet Jackets* (New York, 1962), 19, 156–157, 174, 165.

16. Brown, *The Proletarian Episode in Russian Literature, 1928–1932* (New York, 1953), 70, 86.

17. Mathewson, *The Positive Hero in Russian Literature* (New York, 1958), 1–3.

18. Edward J. Brown, "The First Twenty Years," in *Russianness: Studies on a Nation's Identity,* ed. Robert L. Belknap (Ann Arbor, Mich., 1990), 229.

19. Mathewson, *Positive Hero,* 23, 319, 323.

20. Simmons, *Russian Fiction and Soviet Ideology: Introduction to Fedin, Leonov, and Sholokhov* (New York, 1958), 3, 6.

21. Struve, quoting himself in *Soviet Russian Literature, 1917–1950* (Norman, Okla., 1951), x–xi.

22. K. Iu. Lappo-Danilevskii, "Gleb Struve—istorik literatury," in Struve, *Russkaia literatura v izgnanii,* 3rd ed. (Paris, 1996), 9–11.

23. His salary was originally paid by the Rockefeller Foundation; Regents Committee on Finance Report, 28 June 1946, Office of the President Records (Bancroft Library, University of California, Berkeley), series 4, 27:8.

24. Ivan Bunin, *The Well of Days,* trans. Gleb Struve and Hamish Miles (London, 1933). N. A. Mishnayev, *A Heroic Legend...,* trans. Gleb Struve and Bernard Pares (London, 1935); Struve, *Russkii evropeets: materialy dlia biografii i kharakterstiki kniazia P. B. Kozlovskogo* (San Francisco, Calif., 1950); Orwell, *Skotskii khutor,* trans. M. Kriger and G. Struve (Frankfurt, 1950).

25. Marc Raeff, *Russia Abroad: A Cultural History of the Russian Emigration, 1917–1939* (Oxford, 1990).

26. Struve, *Soviet Russian Literature,* x, 253–255, 242, 187, 38, 246–249, 192.

27. Struve, *Soviet Russian Literature,* 56. Struve, *Geschichte der Sowjetliteratur* (Munich, 1957), 394. Milovan Djilas, *The New Class: An Analysis of the Communist System* (New York, 1957).

28. Maguire book review, *Soviet Studies* 24:4 (April 1973), 624–626. Communication with Robert Hughes (2006). Boris Filippov, "...Vechnost' predolet,'" *Novoe russkoe slovo,* 16 June 1985, 4.

29. Struve, *Soviet Russian Literature,* 26–27, 311–312.

30. M. Karpovich, book review, *Novyi zhurnal* 46 (1957), 251–254. Struve, "The Double Life of Russian Literature," *Books Abroad* 28:4 (Autumn 1954), 403. Struve, *Russkaia literatura v izgnanii: opyt istoricheskogo obzora zarubezhnoi literatury* (New York, 1956), 5, 394, 6, 397, 290, 7. In the section that follows, the terms emigration, Russia Abroad, and Russians in exile are used interchangeably, even though in some contexts and quarters, the differences among the terms were significant and hotly contested.

31. Struve, "The Chekhov Publishing House," *Books Abroad* 27:3 (Summer 1953), 262–263.

32. Struve, "The Transition from Russian to Soviet Literature," in *Literature and Revolution in Soviet Russia, 1917–1962,* ed. Max Haywward (Oxford, 1963), 23.

33. Karpovich, "The Chekhov Publishing House," *RR* 16:1 (January 1957), 53–58. Struve, "Chekhov Publishing House." George Kennan Oral History (1972–1973), Non-Grant Files (Ford Foundation Archives).

34. See Howland Sargeant to Nancy Hanks, 19 May 1955, referring to George Kennan letter to Sargeant, 7 December 1954, in White House Central File (Dwight D. Eisenhower Presidential Library), Confidential File, subject series, box 14.

35. Oleg A. Maslenikov, "Publications of the Chekhov Publishing House," *ASEER* 13:2 (April 1954), 252–254. Struve, "Western Writing on Soviet Literature," in *The State of Soviet Studies,* ed. Walter Z. Laqueur and Leopold Labedz (Cambridge, Mass., 1965), 105. A new and apparently unrelated Chekhov Publishing House came into being in the late 1960s; see Edward Bailey Hodgman, "Détente and the Dissidents: Human Rights in US–Soviet Relations, 1968–1980" (Ph.D. diss., University of Rochester, 2003), 222–224.

36. The books were Gumilev, *Otravlennaia tunika i drugie neizdannye proizvedeniia*, ed. Struve (New York, 1952); Mandel'shtam, *Sobranie sochenii*, ed. Struve and B. A. Filippov (New York, 1955).
37. Nicholas V. Riasanovsky, "Gleb Petrovich Struve, 1898–1985," *SR* 44:3 (Autumn 1985), 611–612.
38. Struve, "Iu. G. Oksman (1895–1970)," *Russkaia Mysl'* 2812 (15 October 1970), 8.
39. Martin Malia Oral History (Regional Oral History Office, Bancroft Library, University of California, Berkeley, 2004), 119–121. Communication with Jack Matlock (2007). John McSweeny to Department of State, 18 June 1963, State Department CFPF, RG59 (U.S. National Archives), EDX USSR.
40. Malia Oral History, 120–122. Malia to Struve, 30 March 1962, Gleb Struve Papers (Hoover Institution Archives), 32:14.
41. Adam B. Ulam, *Understanding the Cold War: A Historian's Personal Reflections*, 2nd ed. (New Brunswick, N.J., 2002), 168; Malia Oral History, 121–123.
42. Malia to Struve, 31 December 1962, Struve Papers, 32:14.
43. Kathryn Feuer, along with her husband, philosopher Lewis Feuer, and teenage daughter, Robin, spent a semester in Moscow while Lewis Feuer was on the ACLS exchange. Lewis Feuer, "Cultural Scholarly Exchange in the Soviet Union in 1963 and How the KGB Tried to Terrorize American Scholars and Suppress Truths" (n.d.), in Lewis Feuer Papers (Brandeis University Library), 38:28.
44. Malia to Struve, 12 October 1962, Struve Papers, 32:14. "Rekviuum" was first published in a stand-alone edition in Munich by Tovarishchestvo zarubezhnykh pisatelei before appearing in Akhmatova, *Sochineniia*, ed. Struve (Washington, D.C., 1965). Igor' Losievskii, *Anna vseia Rosi: zhizneopisanie Anny Akhmatovoi* (Kharkov, 1996), 171.
45. Lewis Feuer, "Cultural Scholarly Exchange." Kathryn Feuer to Struve, 10 June and 1 August 1963, both in Struve Papers, 28:1.
46. N. N. [Oksman], "'Stalinisty' sredi sovetskikh pisatelei i uchenykh," *Russkaia Mysl*,' 3 August 1963.
47. Gosudarstvennyi arkhiv Rossiiskoi Federatsii, fond 8131 (Prokurator SSSR), opis' 31, delo 95946. Stephen V. Bittner, *The Many Lives of Khrushchev's Thaw: Experience and Memory in Moscow's Arbat* (Ithaca, N.Y., 2008), 188–189.
48. Struve, "Russian Literature," in *World Literature since 1945*, ed. Ivar Ivask and Gero von Wilpert (New York, 1973), 582, 590. Struve, "Soviet Literature in Perspective," in *Soviet Literature in the Sixties: An International Symposium*, ed. Max Hayward and Edward L. Crowley (New York, 1964), 130.
49. V. Setchkarev, book review, *RR* 44:4 (October 1985), 411. O. Raevskaia-Kh'iuz, "Pamiati G. P. Struve," *Vestnik russkkogo khristianskogo dvizheniia* 145 (1985), 198–201. "The Early Years of Slavic Studies at the University of California-Berkeley" (17 February 2005, audiotape in author's possession).
50. Steven C. Caton, "Contributions of Roman Jakobson," *Annual Review of Anthropology* 16 (1987), 223–260; Linda R. Waugh and Monique Monville-Burston, "Introduction: The Life, Work, and Influence of Roman Jakobson," in Jakobson, *On Language*, ed. Waugh and Monville-Burston (Cambridge, Mass., 1990), 41–44.

51. Quoted in Israel Shenker, "Jakobson: Great in Any Language," *NYT,* 11 October 1971.
52. Jakobson's correspondence with Simmons and Harvard provost Paul Buck are in Jakobson Papers, 2:2 and 43:1. Karpovich to Buck, 26 December 1948, Michael Karpovich Papers (Bakhmeteff Archive, Columbia University), series I, box 1.
53. Michael Flier, curator, *One Hundred Years of Slavic Studies at Harvard* (Cambridge, Mass., 1996).
54. Lawrence E. Feinberg, "Slavic Linguistics in the U.S., 1945–1995," in *Beiträge zur Geschichte der Slawistik in den Nichtslavischen Ländern,* ed. Giovanna Brogi Bercoff et al. (Vienna, 2005), 472–473.
55. Frances J. Whitfield, "Linguistics," in *American Research on Russia,* ed. H. H. Fisher (Bloomington, Ind., 1959), 141–142.
56. Caton, "Contributions of Roman Jakobson," 237; Hugh McLean, "A Linguist among Poets," in *Roman Jakobson: What He Taught Us,* ed. Morris Halle (Columbus, Ohio, 1983), 18.
57. Jakobson, *My Futurist Years,* ed. Bengt Jangfeldt, trans. Stephen Rudy (New York, 1992). Jakobson and Krystyna Pomorska, *Dialogues* (Cambridge, Mass., 1983), 2, 10–11. Jakobson, "Towards the History of the Moscow Linguistics Circle" (1979), in Jakobson, *Selected Writings,* ed. Stephen Rudy, *et al.* 8 vols. (New York, The Hague, Berlin, 1962–1987), 7:279–282. The eight volumes of *Selected Writings* had a variety of different editors, including Stephen Rudy and many others; for simplicity's sake, the volumes will be referred to below simply as *SW* followed by volume and page.
58. Jakobson, *My Futurist Years,* 30. A. A. Markov, "Primer statisticheskogo issledovaniia nad tekstom 'Evgeniia Onegina' illiustriruiushchii sviaz' ispitanii v tsep," *Izvestiia Imperatorskoi Akademii Nauk,* 6th ser., 7:3 (15 February 1913), 153–162.
59. Vladimir Markov, *Russian Futurism: A History* (Berkeley, 1968).
60. Jakobson, "On Realism in Art" (1921) and "Futurism" (1919), both in *Language in Literature,* ed. Krystyna Pomorska and Stephen Rudy (Cambridge, Mass., 1987), 29.
61. Krystyna Pomorska, *Russian Formalist Theory and Its Poetic Ambience* (The Hague, 1968), 42.
62. Jakobson, "Linguistics and Poetics" (1960), in Pomorska and Rudy, *Language in Literature,* 66–69, 87.
63. Jakobson, "Retrospect," *SW* 1:631.
64. Viktor Shklovskii, *Knight's Move* (1923), quoted in Wellek, *A History of Modern Criticism, 1750–1950,* 8 vols. (New Haven, Conn., 1955–1992), 7:320.
65. Jakobson, "Noveishaia russkaia poeziia. Nabrosok pervyi: Podstupy k Khlebnikovu" (1921), *SW* 5: 305–306.
66. Jakobson, "Linguistics and Poetics," 64.
67. Jakobson and Tynianov, "Problems in the Study of Language and Literature" (1928), in Pomorska and Rudy, *Language in Literature,* 47–49. Jurii Streidter, *Literary Structure, Evolution, and Value: Russian Formalism and Czech Structuralism Reconsidered* (Cambridge, Mass., 1989), chap. 2; Victor Erlich, *Russian Formalism: History, Doctrine* (The Hague, 1954), chap. 9.
68. Jakobson, "The Statue in Pushkin's Poetic Mythology" (1937), in Pomorska and Rudy, *Language in Literature,* 320.

69. Caton, "Contributions of Roman Jakobson," 247.

70. "Implications of Language Universals for Linguistics" (1961), in Jakobson, *On Language*. Morris Halle, "On the Origins of Distinctive Features," in Halle, *Roman Jakobson: What He Taught Us*, 77–78. Waugh and Monville-Burston, "Life, Work, and Influence of Roman Jakobson," 11.

71. McLean, "Linguist among Poets," 17–18. Caton, "Contributions of Roman Jakobson," 237. Horace Lunt, "Slavic Historical Linguistics," in Halle, *Roman Jakobson: What He Taught Us*, 52. Jakobson, "Beitrag zur allgemeinen Kasuslehre: Gesamtbedeutung der russischen Kasus" (1936), *SW* 2:23–71.

72. See the contents of *SW*, vol. 4, but cf. Edward L. Keenan, *Josef Dobrovský and the Origins of the Igor' Tale* (Cambridge, Mass., 2003), 15–19.

73. Wellek, "American Literary Scholarship," in Wellek, *Concepts of Criticism*, ed. Stephen G. Nichols Jr. (New Haven, Conn., 1963), 303–304; Wellek, "My Early Life," in *Contemporary Authors: Autobiographical Series*, ed. Mark Zardzony (Detroit, Mich., 1988), 7:217.

74. Wellek, "Literary History," in *Literary Scholarship: Its Aims and Methods*, ed. Norman Foerster et al. (Chapel Hill, N.C., 1941), 97, 130.

75. Brooks, "Poem as Organism" (1941) and "Literary Criticism" (1962), quoted in Gerald Graff, *Professing Literature: An Institutional History* (Chicago, 1987), 188, 190.

76. Wellek, "The Revolt against Positivism" and "Concepts of Form and Structure"— both in Wellek, *Concepts of Criticism*, 275, 65.

77. Wellek, "Modern Czech Criticism and Literary Scholarship," in Wellek, *Essays in Czech Literature* (The Hague: Mouton, 1963).

78. Wellek, "Retrospect and Prospect," *Yale Review* 69:2 (December 1979), 310.

79. *Columbia Dictionary of Modern European Literature*, ed. Horatio Smith (New York, 1949). Wellek, *Czech Literature at the Crossroads of Europe* (Toronto, 1963).

80. He also chaired JCSS's Subcommittee on Translation and Reproduction. JCSS reports in SSRC Records (Rockefeller Archive Center), 1/1/256/1501. Gordon B. Turner, "The Joint Committee on Slavic Studies, 1948–1971: A Summary View," *ACLS Newsletter* 23:2 (Spring 1972), 9. On Wasson's group, see Jakobson Papers, 5:84–85; and the report in Philip E. Mosely Papers (University of Illinois Library), box 4.

81. Wellek and Austin Warren, *The Theory of Literature* (New York, 1949), parts II–IV.

82. Lawrence Gaylord Jones, "Roman Jakobson and the Postwar Slavists," in *Roman Jakobson: Echoes of His Scholarship*, ed. Daniel Armstrong and C. H. van Schoonveld (Lisse, Netherlands, 1997), 197.

83. Hugh McLean, "Jakobson's Metaphor/Metonymy Polarity: A Retrospective Glance," in *Roman Jakobson: Teksty, dokumenty, issledovaniia*, ed. G. Baran [Heinrich Baran] (Moscow, 1999), 727–729.

84. Wellek, "The Crisis of Comparative Literature" (1959), in Wellek, *Concepts of Criticism*, 283, 287. Wellek and Warren, *Theory of Literature*, 291.

85. Wellek, "Crisis of Comparative Literature," 295.

86. On Rozanov, see Wellek, *History of Modern Criticism*, 7:254–256, 302–305, 258–259.

87. Jonathan Culler, "Wellek's *Modern Criticism*," *Journal of the History of Ideas* 49:2 (April–June 1988), 348. Wellek, "Reply to Bernard Weinberg's Review of My *History*

of *Modern Criticism*," *Journal of the History of Ideas* 30:2 (April–June 1969), 281–282;
Wellek, "Reflections on My *History*" (1977), in Wellek, *The Attack on Literature and
Other Essays* (Chapel Hill, N.C., 1982), 145.

88. Robert W. Simmons Jr., review of *A History of Modern Criticism* by René Wellek,
vols. 3–4, *SEEJ* 11:2 (Summer 1967), 222–224. Bernard Weinberg, review of *A History
of Modern Criticism* by René Wellek, *Journal of the History of Ideas* 30:1 (January–
March 1969), 133.

89. On Yale's aspirations, see Mosely memorandum, 31 January 1948, SSRC Records,
2/1/495/6110.

90. David A. Hollinger, "The Canon and Its Keepers: Modernism and Mid-Twentieth-
Century American Intellectuals," in Hollinger, *In the American Province: Studies in
the History and Historiography of Ideas* (Bloomington, Ind., 1985).

91. These propositions are taken from two of the classic essays on modernist literature:
Irving Howe, "The Culture of Modernism," in Howe, *Decline of the New* (New
York, 1970); Lionel Trilling, "On the Teaching of Modern Literature" (1961), in
Trilling, *Beyond Culture: Essays in Learning and Literature* (New York, 1965).

92. Trilling, "On the Teaching of Modern Literature," 22–23.

93. Irving Howe, introduction to Dostoevsky's *Notes from the Underground,* in *Classics of
Modern Fiction,* ed. Howe (New York, 1968), 3–12; also cited in Edward Alexander,
Irving Howe: Socialist, Critic, Jew (Bloomington, Ind., 1998), 35–37.

94. Trilling, "On the Teaching of Modern Literature," 23; Howe, introduction to
Tolstoy's *Death of Ivan Ilyich,* in Howe, *Classics of Modern Fiction,* 113–121.

95. R. P. Blackmur, *Eleven Essays in the European Novel* (New York, 1964), vi. The
compound noun "Tolstoevsky" appears frequently in Slavicist venues; it was, for
instance, the nickname of a course offered by Harvard's Renato Poggioli. See the
obituary of Poggioli in *SEEJ* 9:1 (Spring 1965), 117–119.

96. For instance, Trilling thanks Rufus Mathewson for translating an Isaac Babel
speech; Trilling, "Isaac Babel" (1955), in Trilling, *Beyond Culture,* 105n.

97. Frank, *Dostoevsky: The Seeds of Revolt, 1821–1849* (Princeton, 1976), preface.
Frank, "Nihilism and *Notes from the Underground,*" *Sewanee Review* 69:1 (Winter
1961), 1.

98. George Noyes, "Slavic Languages at the University of California," *SEER* 3:3
(October 1944), 56.

99. Wellek, "A Sketch of the History of Dostoevskii Criticism," in *Dostoevsky:
A Collection of Critical Essays,* ed. Wellek (Englewood Cliffs, N.J., 1962), 7.

100. A. N. Nikoliukin, *Vzaimosviazi literatur Rossii i SShA: Turgenev, Tolstoi, Dostoevskii
i Amerika* (Moscow, 1987), 238.

101. Engerman, *Modernization from the Other Shore: American Intellectuals and the
Romance of Russian Development* (Cambridge, Mass., 2003), chaps. 6–8 and
passim.

102. Trilling, "Isaac Babel," 103.

103. Edmund Wilson, "In Honor of Pushkin" (1937), in Wilson, *The Triple Thinkers:
Twelve Essays on Literary Subjects,* 2nd ed. (Oxford, 1948), 31–33.

104. Wellek, "A Sketch," 13–14.

105. Edward J. Brown, "Literature," in Fisher, *American Research on Russia*, 123–138; and Struve, "Western Writing."

106. Book review citations: J. T. Shaw, *SEEJ* 3:2 (Summer 1959), 177–179; Johannes Holthusen, *SEEJ* 9:3 (Autumn 1965), 315–320; Herbert Bowman, *SEEJ* 15:1 (Spring 1971), 66–68; Horace Lunt, *SEEJ* 18:3 (Autumn 1974), 331–334; Herbert Bowman, *SEEJ* 20:3 (Autumn 1976), 334–336.

107. Wellek, *History of Modern Criticism*, 7:354. Wellek, review of *Dostoyevski in Russian Literary Criticism* by Vladimir Seduro, *ASEER* 17:3 (October 1958), 370–372. Frederic Jameson, *The Prison-House of Language: A Critical Account of Structuralism and Russian Formalism* (Princeton, 1972), 85; Sean Homer, *Frederic Jameson: Marxism, Hermeneutics, Postmodernism* (Cambridge, 1998), 27.

108. See, for instance, Tzvetan Todorov, "Présentation," in *Théorie de la littérature: Textes des formalistes russes réunis*, ed. and trans. Todorov (Paris, 1966). Barry Scherr, "Formalism, Structuralism, Semiotics, Poetics," *SEEJ* 31 (1987), 134–135.

109. Wellek, "The New Criticism: Pro and Contra" (1978), in Wellek, *Attack on Literature*, 100; Catherine Gallagher, "The History of Literary Criticism," in *Academic Culture in Transformation: Fifty Years, Four Disciplines*, ed. Thomas Bender and Carl E. Schorske (Princeton, 1997), 163–167. Peter Steiner, "Slavic Literary Studies Yesterday and Tomorrow," *Profession* 87 (January 1987), 6–7. Wellek, *History of Modern Criticism*, 7:357–358.

110. Brown, "Literature," in Fisher, *American Research on Russia*, 131–133.

CHAPTER 6

1. Anatole Mazour was at Stanford, and Columbia was home to Michael Florinsky and Vladimir Simkhovitch, but after the war it was dominated by Geroid Tanquary Robinson. For a fuller list of scholars, see George Vernadsky, "Teaching and Writing Russian History in America," *Russian Orthodox Journal* 33 (August 1959), 11, 26.

2. A. Kerenskii, "M. M. Karpovich," *Novyi zhurnal*, no. 58 (1959), 5; Mosely, "Professor Michael Karpovich," in *Russian Thought and Politics*, ed. Hugh McLean, Martin E. Malia, and George Fischer (Cambridge, Mass., 1957), 2.

3. More influential were M. M. Bogoslovskii and D. M. Petrushevskii; Mosely, "Professor Michael Karpovich," 3.

4. S. Tkhorzhevskii, "V. O. Kliuchevskii, kak sotsiolog i politicheskii mystitel,'" *Dela i dni* 2 (1921), 154–155.

5. Karpovich, "Klyuchevsky and Recent Trends in Russian Historiography," *SEER* 21 (March 1943), 33.

6. Quoted in Terence Emmons, "Kliuchevskii's Pupils," *California Slavic Studies* 14 (1991), 72–73.

7. Morton White, *Social Thought in America: The Revolt against Formalism* (Boston, 1957), chap. 4. Wladimir Berelowitch, "History in Russia Comes of Age," *Kritika* 9:1 (Winter 2008), 124.

8. Kliuchevskii, "Kurs russkoi istorii" (1904), in *Sochineniia*, 8 vols. (Moscow, 1956), 1:25–26. Karpovich, "Klyuchevsky," 39.

9. Kliuchevskii quoted (without citation) in George Vernadsky, *Russian Historiography: A History,* ed. Sergei Pushkarev (Belmont, Mass., 1978), 139. Mosely, "Professor Michael Karpovich," 3.

10. See Mosely, "Michael Karpovich, 1888–1959," *RR* 19:1 (January 1960), 56–60; and the articles in Karpovich's own *Novyi zhurnal* 58 (1959) and 59 (1960).

11. "Boris A. Bakhmeteff, 1880–1951," *RR* 10:4 (October 1951), 311–312.

12. Pipes interview (1995), in Andrew Snekvik, "Historiographic Trends in Russian History after World War II in America: Karpovich, Berlin, and the Harvard Group" (B.A. thesis, Stanford University, 1995), 62; Martin Malia Oral History (Regional Oral History Office, Bancroft Library, University of California, Berkeley), 32.

13. Roman Gul', "M. M. Karpovich: chelovek i redaktor," *Novyi zhurnal* 58 (1959), 25. Kerenskii, "M. M. Karpovich," 5. Alla Zeide, "Creating 'a Space of Freedom': Mikhail Mikhailovich Karpovich and Russian Historiography in America," *Ab Imperio* 2007#1, 246–247.

14. Karpovich, *Imperial Russia, 1801–1917* (New York, 1932), 8, 14. Witt Bowden, Michael Karpovich, and Abbott Payson Usher, *An Economic History of Europe since 1750* (New York, 1937), 289, 301. Karpovich, *A Lesson on Russian History* (The Hague, 1962), 8–10. Martin E. Malia, "Michael Karpovich, 1888–1959," *RR* 19:1 (January 1960), 60.

15. Karpovich, "The Historical Background of Soviet Thought Control," in *The Soviet Union: Background, Ideology, Reality,* ed. Waldemar Gurian (Notre Dame, Ind., 1951), 16–17. Malia, "Michael Karpovich," 63–64, 67. Karpovich in Bowden et al., *Economic History,* 694–696; Karpovich, *Imperial Russia,* 74, 85, 94.

16. Alexander Dallin interview (1995), quoted in Snekvik, "Historiographic Trends," 50.

17. Karpovich, "How Revolution Came to Russia" (1947), "The State in Russian History" (1952), and "Contemporary Russia in Relation to Her Historical Background" (1950)—all in Karpovich Papers, series II, box 14.

18. Karpovich to Vernadskii, 27 April 1948, George Vernadsky Papers (Bakhmeteff Archive, Columbia University), box 4. Karpovich to Kluckhohn, 4 March 1948, RRC Correspondence (Harvard University Archives), series UAV759.10, box 2.

19. By one count, 60% of Harvard students wrote on intellectual history compared with 40% nationally; Snekvik, "Historiographic Trends," 45. John S. Curtiss, "History," in *American Research on Russia,* ed. Harold H. Fisher (Bloomington, Ind., 1959), 26.

20. N. N. Bolkhovitinov, *Russkie uchenye-emigranty (G. V. Vernadskii, M. M. Karpovich, M. T. Florinskii) i stanovlenie rusistiki v SShA* (Moscow, 2005), 88, 91; Pipes, *Vixi: Memoirs of a Non-Belonger* (New Haven, Conn., 2003), 90. Hans Rogger interview (1995), in Snekvik, "Historiographic Trends," 78.

21. Leonard Krieger, "European History in America," in *History: The Development of Historical Studies in the United States,* ed. John Higham (Englewood Cliffs, N.J., 1965), 302. Peter Novick, *That Noble Dream: The "Objectivity Question" and the American Historical Profession* (Cambridge, 1989), 380, 382.

22. Nicholas Riasanovsky interview (1995), in Snekvik, "Historiographic Trends," 69.

23. Robert F. Byrnes, *Awakening American Education to the World: Archibald Cary Coolidge, 1866–1928* (Notre Dame, Ind., 1982), chap. 7.

392 NOTES TO PAGES 157-161

24. Sergius Yakobson, "The Library of Congress: Russian Program and Activities," *American Review on the Soviet Union* 7:4 (August 1946), 51–66. Edvard Kasinets [Edward Kasinec], "K 100-letnemu iubileiu Slaviano-baltiiskogo otdela N'iu-Iorkskoi publichnoi biblioteku," in *Most cherez okean*, comp. Elena Kogan (Moscow, 2005). *The Library of the Hoover Institution on War, Revolution, and Peace*, ed. Peter Duignan (Stanford, 1985). Richard Stites, "Soviet Studies in Helsinki," *AAASS Newsletter* 31:1 (January 1991), 7; communication with James Billington (2005).

25. Malia Oral History, 34–35. Pipes, *Vixi*, 67–70. George Fischer, *Insatiable: A Story of My Nine Lives* (Philadelphia, 2000), 150.

26. Michael Ignatieff, *Isaiah Berlin: A Life* (New York, 1998), 209–210. Berlin, "The Hedgehog and the Fox" (1951), in Berlin, *Russian Thinkers*, ed. Henry Hardy and Aileen Kelly (New York, 1994), 24.

27. Ramin Jahanbegloo, *Conversations with Isaiah Berlin* (London, 1992), 189.

28. Berlin, "Political Ideas in the Twentieth Century," *FA* 28:3 (April 1950), 384.

29. Walicki, "Berlin and the Russian Intelligentsia," in *The One and the Many: Reading Isaiah Berlin*, ed. George Crowder and Henry Hardy (Amherst, N.Y., 2007), 50–51, 55. Herzen, *From the Other Shore* (New York, 1956), 36–37.

30. Berlin to Lillian Schapiro (1941), in Berlin, *Flourishing: Letters, 1928–1946*, ed. Henry Hardy (London, 2004), 378. Edward Acton, "Eugene Lampert: Distinguished Scholar of Russian History," *Guardian*, 9 October 2004. Malia Oral History, 34.

31. Berlin, introduction to Alexander Herzen, *My Past and Thoughts*, trans. Constance Garnett (Berkeley, 1995), xlii. Ignatieff, *Isaiah Berlin*, 242.

32. Nicholas Dawidoff, "Shura and Shaya: An Afternoon with Sir Isaiah Berlin," *American Scholar* 67:2 (Spring 1998), 102.

33. Nicholas Dawidoff, *The Fly Swatter: How My Grandfather Made His Way in the World* (New York, 2002).

34. Gerschenkron, "Economic Backwardness in Historical Perspective" (1952), in Gerschenkron, *Economic Backwardness in Historical Perspective* (Cambridge, Mass., 1962), 8; Gerschenkron, "Russian Agrarian Policies and Industrialization, 1861–1914" (1965), in Gerschenkron, *Continuity in History and Other Essays* (Cambridge, Mass., 1968), 152.

35. Gerschenkron, "Reflections on Economic Aspects of Revolutions" (1964), in Gerschenkron, *Continuity in History*, 273; Gerschenkron, "Problems and Patterns of Economic Development, 1861–1958" (1960), in Gerschenkron, *Economic Backwardness*, 141–142.

36. Nicholas Riasanovsky Oral History (Regional Oral History Office, Bancroft Library, University of California, Berkeley), 32.

37. Charles J. Halperin, "George Vernadsky, Eurasianism, the Mongols, and Russia," *SR* 41:3 (Autumn 1982), 482.

38. Nicholas V. Riasanovsky, "The Emergence of Eurasianism," *California Slavic Studies* 4 (1967), 39–72. Halperin, "George Vernadsky," 481–482. P. N. Malevskii-Malevich (1928), quoted in Ilya Vinkovetsky, "Classical Eurasianism and Its Legacy," *Canadian-American Slavic Studies* 34:2 (Summer 2000), 135n47.

39. Vernadsky, "Teaching and Writing Russian History," 11. Vernadsky ultimately completed five of his six volumes; Karpovich never finished any of his.

40. Vernadsky, *Ancient Russia* (New Haven, Conn., 1943), 6. Vernadsky, *Kievan Russia* (New Haven, Conn., 1948), 1–4, 12.

41. Vernadsky, *The Mongols and Russia* (New Haven, Conn., 1953), v, 337. Marx Szeftel, review of *The Mongols in Russia* by George Vernadsky, *RR* 14:1 (January 1955), 65–67.

42. See, for instance, Valentine Alexandrovich Riasanovsky, *Fundamental Principles of Mongol Law* (Bloomington, Ind., 1965).

43. Vernadsky, *A History of Russia,* 3rd rev. ed. (New Haven, Conn., 1951), 5, 7, 94, 90, 239, 240, 388, 392–393, chap. 19. Vernadsky, *Political and Diplomatic History of Russia* (Boston, 1936), 4–6.

44. For instance, "Peace Views of Russia Are Defended," *New Haven Evening Register,* 13 May 1946. Telegram to Communications Section, 9 January 1945, and Summary File, Case 100–10481 (14 May 1946), both in George Vernadsky FBI File.

45. The offer was from the University of London; see Charles J. Halperin, "Russia and the Steppe: George Vernadsky and Eurasianism," *Forschungen zur osteuropäischen Geschichte* 36 (1985), 78.

46. Pipes, book review, *Kritika* 7:2 (Spring 2006), 386. Minutes of the Committee on International and Regional Studies (Harvard), 17 July 1947, Carl Friedrich Papers (Harvard University Archives), series HUG 17.6, box 9. Riasanovsky to Vernadsky, 23 May 1969, Vernadsky Papers, box 57.

47. G. N. Kozliakov, "'Eto tol'ko personifikatsiia ne nashego ponimaniia istoricheskogo protsessa…': Georgii Vladimirovich Vernadskii (1887–1973) i ego 'Ocherki po russkoi istoriografii,'" in Vernadskii, *Rosskaia istoriografiia* (Moscow, 1998), 19.

48. Berlin, introduction to *Russian Intellectual History: An Anthology,* ed. Marc Raeff (New York, 1966), 6.

49. The dissertations were written, respectively, by Stanley Zyzniewski, Joseph L. Sullivan, Kenneth Whiting, Joseph S. Sebes, and Donald R. MacDonald.

50. Nicholas V. Riasanovsky, *Russia and the West in the Teachings of the Slavophiles: A Study of Romantic Ideology* (Cambridge, Mass., 1952), 203, 178.

51. Riasanovsky, *A Parting of the Ways: Government and the Educated Public in Russia, 1801–1855* (Oxford, 1976).

52. Raeff, *The Origins of the Russian Intelligentsia: The Eighteenth-Century Nobility* (New York, 1966). Raeff, *The Well-Ordered Police State: Social and Institutional Change through Law in the Germanies and Russia, 1600–1800* (New Haven, Conn., 1983). Raeff, preface to *Political Ideas and Institutions in Imperial Russia* (Boulder, Colo., 1994), 1. Gregory L. Freeze, "Marc Raeff, 1923–2008," *SR* 68:1 (Spring 2009), 226–227.

53. Malia, *Alexander Herzen and the Birth of Russian Socialism* (Cambridge, Mass., 1961). Malia Oral History, 38. Berlin nevertheless considered Malia's book to be a "masterpiece"; Berlin to Andrzej Walicki, 13 March 1962, in Walicki, "Isaiah Berlin as I Knew Him," *Dialogue and Universalism* 15:9–10 (September–October 2005), 53.

54. James H. Billington, *Mikhailovsky and Russian Populism* (Oxford, 1958). Samuel H. Baron, *Plekhanov: The Father of Russian Marxism* (Stanford, 1963).

55. Pipes, *The Formation of the Soviet Union: Communism and Nationalism, 1917–1923* (Cambridge, Mass., 1954). Pipes, *Vixi,* 61–62.

56. Robert V. Daniels, *The Conscience of the Revolution: Communist Opposition in Soviet Russia* (Cambridge, Mass., 1960), 398.

57. Lewis H. Siegelbaum, "Robert V. Daniels and the Long Durée of Soviet History," *RR* 54:3 (July 1995), 330–331.

58. Daniels, "Is Sovietology Dead, Too?" *New Leader* 74:10 (9–23 September 1991), 8. Communication with Robert V. Daniels (2003).

59. Peter Reddaway, "Leonard Bertram Schapiro, 1908–1983," *Proceedings of the British Academy* 70 (1984), 515–542; T. H. Rigby, "Leonard Schapiro as Student of Soviet Politics," in *Authority, Power and Policy in the USSR: Essays Dedicated to Leonard Schapiro,* ed. Rigby, Archie Brown, and Peter Reddaway (New York, 1980). Ignatieff, *Isaiah Berlin,* 25, 28.

60. Schapiro to Goodwin, 25 April 1954, Leonard Schapiro Papers (Hoover Institution Archives), 15:1. Schapiro, *The Future of Russia* (London, 1955). Jonathan Haslam, *The Vices of Integrity: E. H. Carr, 1892–1982* (London, 1999), 157–165.

61. Schapiro, *The Origin of the Communist Autocracy: Political Opposition in the Soviet State: The First Phase, 1917–1922* (New York, 1955), 355, 361.

62. Schapiro, "My Fifty Years of Social Science," *Government and Opposition* 15:3–4 (July–October 1980), 486–489. Schapiro, *Origin,* viii.

63. Alfred G. Meyer Memoir (University of Wisconsin, Madison, Archives), chap. 14. Grant applications for 1956 evaluated in Geroid Tanquary Robinson Papers (Columbia University Library), box 54. This section will follow the project's nomenclature, specifically the use of "CPSU" though that name was adopted only in 1952.

64. Mosely to Robert Amory Jr., 7 October 1958, Philip Mosely Papers (University of Illinois Library), box 39.

65. Gerhart Niemeyer, review of *The Communist Party of the Soviet Union* by Leonard Schapiro, *RR* 20:1 (January 1961), 65–68. Donald W. Treadgold, *Lenin and His Rivals: The Struggle for Russia's Future, 1898–1906* (New York, 1955).

66. William Henry Chamberlin, *The Russian Revolution, 1917–1921,* 2 vols. (New York, 1935). Engerman, "William Henry Chamberlin and Russia's Revolt against Civilization," *Russian History/Histoire Russe* 26:1 (Spring 1999), 45–64.

67. Lewis S. Feuer, "Bertram David Wolfe, 1896–1977," *RR* 36:4 (October 1977), 533–535.

68. Daniel Singer, "Armed with a Pen," in *Isaac Deutscher: The Man and His Work,* ed. David Horowitz (London, 1971), 33–34.

69. Deutscher, *Stalin: A Political Biography* (Oxford, 1949). Deutscher, *Russia: What Next?* (Oxford, 1953), esp. chap. 10.

70. List of visiting scholars through 1952–1954, RRC Correspondence, series UAV759.10, box 18; Stephen Viederman circular, 3 April 1961, IUCTG Records (Columbia University Archives), 1:1.

71. Deutscher, "Mr. E. H. Carr as Historian of the Bolshevik Regime," *Soviet Studies* 6:4 (April 1955), 339–340.

72. Carr, *A History of Soviet Russia,* appeared between 1950 and 1978: *The Bolshevik Revolution, 1917–1923* (3 vols.), *The Interregnum, 1924* (1 vol.), *Socialism in One*

Country, 1924–1926 (3 vols.), and *Foundations of a Planned Economy, 1926–1929* (2 vols., one with R. W. Davies). Two of the volumes were too large to appear as a single book and were bound as two books.

73. Haslam, *Vices of Integrity*, 196, 202, 157–165. Ignatieff, *Isaiah Berlin*, 235.

74. Philip Mosely to Leon Epstein, 10 August 1961, Mosely Papers (Illinois), box 5.

75. On Columbia and Yale job offers, see Hazard to Robinson, 9 September 1945, and Wallace to Robinson, 7 November 1945, both in Robinson Papers, box 50. Haslam, *Vices of Integrity*, 141, 176–177.

76. Haimson interview (1995), in Snekvik, "Historiographic Trends," 54. Leopol'd Khaimson [Haimson], "O vremeni i o sebe," *Otechestvennaia istoriia*, (2005 #6), 187.

77. Haimson to Kluckhohn, 8 April 1948, RRC Correspondence, series UAV 759.10, box 2. Haimson, "Russian 'Visual' Thinking," in *The Study of Culture at a Distance*, ed. Margaret Mead and Rhode Métraux (Chicago, 1953), 271. A full list of Mead project papers, by Haimson and others, appears in Margaret Mead Papers, box G-86.

78. Haimson, *The Russian Marxists and the Origins of Bolshevism* (Cambridge, Mass., 1955), 209–210. Anna Krylova, "Beyond the Spontaneity-Consciousness Paradigm: 'Class Instinct' as a Promising Category in Pursuing Historical Analysis," *SR* 62:1 (Spring 2003), 3–6. Haimson project proposal (1953–1954), RRC Correspondence, series UAV 759.10, box 23.

79. John Curtiss, review of *The Russian Marxists and the Origins of Bolshevism* by Leopold Haimson, *RR* 15:4 (October 1956), 281–283; Samuel H. Baron, review of *The Russian Marxists and the Origins of Bolshevism* by Leopold Haimson, *AHR* 61:4 (July 1956), 968–969.

80. André Liebich, *From the Other Shore: Russian Social Democracy after 1921* (Cambridge, Mass., 1997), 322–324. L. O. Dan to N. V. Vol'skii, 28 May 1959, in *Iz Arkhiva L. O. Dan*, ed. Boris Sapir (Amsterdam, 1987), 154. *The Mensheviks from the Revolution of 1917 to the Second World War*, ed. Leopold H. Haimson (Chicago, 1974).

81. Haimson, "The Problem of Social Stability in Urban Russia, 1905–1917," *SR* 23:4 (December 1964) and 24:1 (March 1965) (hereafter cited as 1:page number and 2:page number). Quotes from Haimson, "Problem of Social Stability," 1:629, 1: 634–635, 2:12.

82. Haimson, "Problem of Social Stability," 2:16–17.

83. Arthur P. Mendel, "Peasant and Worker on the Eve of the First World War," *SR* 24:1 (March 1965), 23–33. Haimson, "Reply," *SR* 24:1 (March 1965), 52. "Interview with Leopold Haimson," *Kritika* 8:1 (Winter 2007), 6.

84. Diane Koenker, "*Slavic Review*'s Greatest Hits," *AAASS NewsNet* 44:5 (October 2004), 19–21.

85. Moscow Embassy to Secretary of State, 28 June 1963, State Department CU Historical Collection (University of Arkansas Library), 229:1. Moscow Embassy to Secretary of State, 23 July 1963, State Department CFPF, RG59 (U.S. National Archives), EDX US-USSR.

86. Cohen project proposal to IUCTG for 1963–1964 in REEI Records (University of Illinois Library), box 4. IUCTG list of applicants for 1964–1965 from E. Willis Brooks (in author's possession).

87. Ralph Fisher notes on IUCTG meeting, 16 February 1964, REEI Records (Illinois), box 4.

88. Stites, "Exploration and Adventure in the Two Capitals," 61–62, and Engelstein, "Prisoner of the *Zeitgeist*," 117—both in *Adventures in Russian Historical Research: Reminiscences of American Scholars from the Cold War to the Present*, ed. Samuel H. Baron and Cathy A. Frierson (Armonk, N.Y., 2003).

89. IUCTG, "Study and Research in the Soviet Union, 1960–61" (July 1961), 68, in Philip Mosely Papers (Columbia University Library), box 10. "Background Paper: Graduate Student Exchange" (22 January 1962), CU Historical Collection, 229:23.

90. Frank Siscoe and Leslie Brady, memorandum of conversation with Deputy Minister of Higher Education Prokofiev and others, 4 April 1961, SDDF, RG59 (U.S. National Archives), 511.613/4–461.

91. Keenan, "Muscovite Political Folkways," *RR* 45:2 (April 1986), 115–181.

92. Zelnik to Mosely, 8 November 1961, Mosely Papers (Illinois), box 7. Zelnik, IUCTG application, 1961, in Mosely Papers (Columbia), box 10.

93. Laura Engelstein, "Before Class: Reginald Zelnik as Labor Historian," in Reginald E. Zelnik, *Perils of Pankratova: Some Stories from the Annals of Soviet Historiography*, ed. Glennys Young (Seattle, 2005), 90–92. Zelnik, *Labor and Society in Tsarist Russia: The Factory Workers of St. Petersburg, 1855–1870* (Stanford, 1971), 2–3.

94. Haimson, "Observations on Some Current Issues in Russian Labor History and on the Contribution of Reginald Zelnik to Their Articulation and Exploration," *Russian History/Histoire Russe* 23:1–4 (1990), 3. Zelnik, "Before Class: The Fostering of a Worker Revolutionary, Construction of His Memoir," *Russian History/Histoire Russe* 20:1–4 (1993), 61–80.

95. Zelnik, *Labor and Society*, 384–385. Emmons, review of *Labor and Society in Tsarist Russia* by Reginald Zelnik, *RR* 31:2 (July 1972), 297–298.

96. Pipes, review of *Labor and Society in Tsarist Russia* by Reginald Zelnik, *APSR* 68:1 (March 1974), 333–334.

97. Zelnik, *Labor and Society*, 1. Haimson, "Observations," 8–9. Engelstein, "Before Class," 92.

98. Zelnik, "On the Side of Angels: The Berkeley Faculty and the FSM," in *Free Speech Movement: Reflections on Berkeley in the 1960s*, ed. Robert Cohen and Zelnik (Berkeley, 2002). Franz Schurmann, Peter Dale Scott, and Zelnik, *The Politics of Escalation in Vietnam* (Boston, 1966). David A. Hollinger, "Profession and Politics: Reginald Zelnik as Campus Leader," in Zelnik, *Perils of Pankratova*, 109–113.

99. Communication with William G. Rosenberg (2009). Rosenberg, "Russian Liberals and the Bolshevik Coup," *Journal of Modern History* 40:3 (September 1968), 328, 335. Rosenberg, "Les Liberaux Russes et le changement de pouvoir en mars 1917," *Cahiers du monde russe et soviétique* 9:1 (March 1968), 46–57.

100. Rosenberg, *Liberals in the Russian Revolution: The Constitutional Democratic Party, 1917–1921* (Princeton, 1974), 465.

101. Communication with William Rosenberg (2009). See reviews of William Rosenberg, *Liberals in the Russian Revolution:* Leonard Schapiro, *Soviet Studies*

28:4 (October 1976), 629–630; Rex Wade, *AHR* 81:2 (April 1976), 428–429; Daniel Mulholland, *RR* 34:2 (April 1975), 212–213.

102. Alexander Rabinowitch, "Founder and Father," *Bulletin of the Atomic Scientists* 61:1 (January–February 2005), 30–33.

103. Mosely, "Boris Nicolaevsky: The American Years," in *Revolution and Politics in Russia: Essays in Memory of B. I. Nicolaevsky,* ed. Alexander Rabinowitch and Janet Rabinowitch (Bloomington, Ind., 1972), 33. Leopold H. Haimson, *The Making of Three Russian Revolutionaries: Voices from the Menshevik Past* (Cambridge, 1987), chap. 2.

104. Rabinowitch, "Discussion," on *Slavic Review* Web site, www.slavicreview.uiuc.edu (accessed February 2009).

105. Rabinowitch, *Prelude to Revolution: The Petrograd Bolsheviks and the July 1917 Uprising* (Bloomington, Ind., 1968), ix. Communication with Alexander Rabinowitch (2009).

106. Rabinowitch, *Prelude to Revolution,* 234, 229, 6. Theodore von Laue, review of *Revolution and Politics in Russia,* edited by Alexander Rabinowitch and Janet Rabinowitch, *AHR* 74:1 (October 1968), 234–235.

107. Rabinowitch, *The Bolsheviks Come to Power: The Revolution of 1917 in Petrograd* (New York, 1975), 311, 313, xvii.

108. By "on your side," Suny clarified, he did not mean that he was pro-Soviet but that he was interested in reducing American-Soviet tensions. Communication with Ronald Grigor Suny (2004). Suny, "Confessions," in *Intellectuals and the Articulation of the Nation,* ed. Suny and Michael D. Kennedy (Ann Arbor, Mich., 1999), 53–54.

109. Suny, "Fifteen Years après le Déluge: What's Left of Marx?" *AAASS NewsNet* 47:1 (January 2007), 1. Suny, "Confessions," 54. Suny, "Old Left, New Left, and the U.S.S.R.," *Activist* (Oberlin, Ohio) 9:2 (Spring 1969), 7. Suny, "Review Essay: The Kolkos' View of the Cold War," *Activist* 14:2 (Spring 1974), 35.

110. Ronald Grigor Suny, *The Baku Commune, 1917–1918: Class and Nationality in the Russian Revolution* (Princeton, 1972), 11, 350.

111. Suny, *Baku Commune,* 233, 344, 352.

112. Suny, "Toward a Social History of the October Revolution," *AHR* 88:1 (February 1983), 51. Rabinowitch, "The October Revolution Revisited," *Social Education* 45:4 (April 1981), 246.

113. Lewis H. Seigelbaum, "The Late Romance of the Worker in Western Historiography," *International Review of Social History* 51 (2006), 466.

114. Jonathan D. Smele, "The Study Group on the Russian Revolution: The First Thirty Years," *Revolutionary Russia* 18:2 (December 2005), 201–203, 214.

115. Byrnes, "Can Culture Survive Cultural Agreements?" in *Détente,* ed. G. R. Urban (New York, 1976), 81–82. Pipes, *Vixi,* 128.

116. *Petr Andreevich Zaionchkovskii: sbornik statei i vospominanii k stoletiiu istorika,* ed. L. G. Zakharova, S. V. Mironenko, and T. Emmons (Moscow, 2008); and *P. A. Zaionchkovskii, 1904–1983 gg.: Stat'i i vospominaniia o nem,* ed. G. V. Kosheleva (Moscow, 1998).

117. Emmons, "P. A. Zaionchkovskii: Nauchnyi rukovoditel' inostrannykh stazherov," in Kosheleva, *P. A. Zaionchkovskii,* 117. Malia, "The Historiographical Legacy of Terence Emmons," *Russian History/Histoire Russe* 32:2 (Summer 2005), 134–135.

118. Ronald Grigor Suny's formulation is in "Rehabilitating Tsarism: The Imperial Russian State and Its Historians," *Comparative Studies in Society and History* 31:1 (January 1989), 169–171.

119. Terence Emmons quoted in G. M. Hamburg, "From Social Science to Literary Narrative: Terence Emmons and the Writing of Imperial Russian History, 1958–2004," *Russian History/Histoire Russe* 32:2 (Summer 2005), 143.

120. The sixteen included one scholar each from Germany and Japan; the others were all North American; Zakharova et al., *Petr Andreevich Zaionchkovskii*, 865–874. Emmons, "P. A. Zaionchkovskii," 117–121.

121. B. N. Komissarov, "As otechestvennoi amerikanistiki," in *Russkoe okritie Ameriki: sbornik statei, posviashchennyi 70-letiiu Akademika N. N. Bolkhovitinova*, ed. A. O. Chubar'ian (Moscow, 2003), 7–33.

122. Stephen Viederman to IUCTG Executive Committee, 18 July 1961, IUCTG Records (Columbia University Archives), 1:2.

123. Edward L. Keenan, "The Exchange and the Study of Russian History," in IREX, *Historical Continuity and Change* (Washington, D.C., 1980), 23, 25.

CHAPTER 7

1. Arthur S. Barron, "Social Relations," in *American Research on Russia*, ed. H. H. Fisher (Bloomington, Ind., 1959), 77. Jesse J. Dossick, *Doctoral Research on Russia and the Soviet Union, 1960–1975* (New York, 1976).

2. Kluckhohn, "Notes on Discussion of Social Relations Research in Connection with the Russian Research Center," 3 June 1948, RRC Correspondence (Harvard University Archives), series UAV 759.10, box 1.

3. Howard Brick, *Transcending Capitalism: Visions of a New Society in Modern American Thought* (Ithaca, N.Y., 2006), chap. 4.

4. Francesca M. Cancian, "Varieties of Functionalism," in *International Encyclopedia of the Social Sciences*, ed. David L. Sills (New York, 1968), 6:29.

5. Notes on RRC Seminar, 5 March 1948, RRC Seminar Minutes (Harvard University Archives), series UAV 759.8, box 1.

6. Parsons, *The Social System* (Glencoe, Ill., 1951), 187–188, 193, 526–533.

7. Parsons, *The Structure of Social Action: A Study in Social Theory with Special Reference to a Group of Recent European Writers* (New York, 1937), 488–495. Parsons, "The Professions and Social Structure" (1939), in Parsons, *Essays in Social Theory*, rev. ed. (Glencoe, Ill., 1956).

8. Parsons, "Social Sciences and Modern Industrial Society" [1955?], in Talcott Parsons Papers (Harvard University Archives), series HUG(FP) 42.41, box 6. The archival materials offer no explanation of this paper's original purpose nor the reason it remained unpublished.

9. Raymond A. Bauer, Alex Inkeles, and Clyde Kluckhohn, *How the Soviet System Works: Cultural, Psychological and Social Themes* (Cambridge, Mass., 1956), 230, 218, chap. 8.

10. Bauer et al., *How the Soviet System Works*, 27, chaps. 12–13, 19.

11. George Fennessey to Mark Carroll, 3 December 1964, RRC Correspondence, series UAV 759.10, box 68.

12. Raymond A. Bauer, *Nine Soviet Portraits* (Cambridge, Mass., 1955), xv, 173.

13. "Social Change in Soviet Russia" (1954) and "The Challenge of a Stable Russia" (1958)—both in Inkeles, *Social Change in Soviet Russia* (Cambridge, Mass., 1968).

14. Berliner, *Factory and Manager in the USSR* (Cambridge, Mass., 1957); Field, *Doctor and Patient in Soviet Russia* (Cambridge, Mass., 1957); H. Kent Geiger, *The Family in Soviet Russia* (Cambridge, Mass., 1968).

15. Inkeles and Bauer, *The Soviet Citizen: Daily Life in a Totalitarian Society* (Cambridge, Mass., 1959), 3–4, 284, 279, 383.

16. Inkeles and Bauer, *Soviet Citizen,* 391–392, 379.

17. U.S. Senate, Committee on Foreign Relations, *Review of Foreign Policy, 1958,* part I (Washington, D.C., 1958), 173–213.

18. Bauer, "Social Psychology of Political Loyalty in Liberal and Totalitarian Societies" (American Association for the Advancement of Science, 1953), in RIP Reports (Harvard University Archives), series UAV 759.175.75, box 1.

19. Robert A. Dahl, "The Behavioral Approach in Political Science: Epitaph for a Monument to a Successful Protest," *APSR* 55:4 (December 1961). The PTA example is from Dahl, *Who Governs? Democracy and Power in an American City* (New Haven, Conn., 1961), chap. 11.

20. Deutscher, *Russia: What Next?* (Oxford, 1953); Deutscher, *Russia in Transition and Other Essays* (New York, 1957).

21. Inkeles and Bauer, *Soviet Citizen,* 391.

22. See the reviews of *Soviet Citizen* by scholars in the field: Robert Tucker, *SEEJ* 4:3 (Autumn 1960), 281; John Reshetar (RIP interviewer), *APSR* 54:3 (September 1960), 736–737; Leonard Schapiro, *British Journal of Sociology* 11:3 (September 1960), 290–291.

23. Bell, "Ten Theories in Search of Reality: The Prediction of Soviet Behavior in the Social Sciences," *WP* 10:3 (April 1958), 350–351.

24. Bendix, review of *The Soviet Citizen* by Alex Inkeles and Raymond Bauer, *Public Opinion Quarterly* 24:2 (Summer 1960), 373–377.

25. Committee on Regional Studies Annual Report, 10 June 1958, RRC Correspondence, series UAV 759.10, box 40.

26. Inkeles and Peter H. Rossi, "National Comparisons of Occupational Prestige," *AJS* 61 (January 1956), 338–339.

27. Inkeles, "Industrial Man: The Relation of Status to Experience, Perception, and Value," *AJS* 66:1 (July 1960), 2, 31. "Industrial man" was a common phrase in 1950s social science, meaning either industrialists (as Lloyd Warner used it in his ethnography of business life) or human beings in industrial societies (as Inkeles and Clark Kerr used it).

28. Inkeles and David H. Smith, *Becoming Modern: Individual Changes in Six Developing Countries* (Cambridge, Mass., 1974), 9. Joseph R. Gusfield, review of *Becoming Modern* by Alex Inkeles and David Smith, *AJS* 82:2 (September 1976), 443–448; Inkeles, "Understanding and Misunderstanding Individual Modernity," *Journal of Cross-Cultural Psychology* 8:2 (1977), 135–176.

29. Inkeles, *One World Emerging? Convergence and Divergence in Industrial Societies* (Boulder, Colo., 1998).

30. "L. C. Ledyard Willed $2,000,000 to Library," *NYT,* 4 February 1932; "Miss Muriel Morris a Bride," *NYT,* 21 December 1910; "Society: At Home and Abroad," *NYT,* 17 December 1911. Security forms in RIP Correspondence (Harvard University Archives), series UAV 759.175, unnumbered box, folder "Personnel Security Questionnaires." Moore, "Grandfather: Lewis Cass Ledyard, 1851–1932" (2000?), in Barrington Moore Jr. Papers (Harvard University Archives), accession 17296.

31. Moore, "Social Stratification: A Study in Cultural Sociology" (Ph.D. diss., Yale University, 1941). Moore, "The Wasp at Sea: Didactic Tales" (2000), in Moore Papers, accession 17296. Communication (unchecked) with Barrington Moore Jr. (2004).

32. Moore, "A Comparative Analysis of Class Struggle," *ASR* 10:1 (February 1945), 31–37. Moore, "The Communist Party of the USA: An Analysis of a Social Movement," *APSR* 39:1 (February 1945), 31–41; Moore, "Some Readjustments in Communist Theory: A Note on the Relation between Ideas and Social Change," *Journal of the History of Ideas* 6:4 (October 1945), 468–482.

33. John W. Gardner to Clyde Kluckhohn, 17 October 1947, RRC Correspondence, series UAV 759.10, box 1. Kluckhohn and Parsons to Paul H. Buck, 1 June 1948, Parsons Papers, series HUG(FP), 42.8.4, box 18. Executive Committee Minutes, 7 November 1950, RRC Executive Committee Minutes (Harvard University Archives), series UAV 759.5, box 1. George Ross et al., "Barrington Moore's *Social Origins* and Beyond: Historical Social Analysis since the 1960s," in *Democracy, Revolution, and History,* ed. Theda Skocpol et al. (Ithaca, N.Y., 1998), 2.

34. Moore, *Soviet Politics: The Dilemma of Power: The Role of Ideas in Social Change* (Cambridge, Mass., 1950), 9, 214, 158, 81.

35. Minutes of seminar meeting, 15 April 1948, RRC Seminars, UAV 759.8, box 1.

36. Moore, *Soviet Politics,* 405–406, 410.

37. See the reviews of *Soviet Politics* by Barrington Moore: Niebuhr, *Nation* 171 (23 September 1950), 270–271; Wolfe, *Saturday Review of Literature* 34 (3 February 1951).

38. Moore to Kluckhohn, 9 May 1949, RRC Correspondence, series UAV 759.10, box 5. Moore, "Soviet-American Relations: Contradictions and Prospects" (APSA, 1950), in RRC Correspondence, series UAV 759.10, box 13.

39. Moore, "Limitations and Possibilities of the Project Interview Data" (1951), RRC Correspondence, series UAV 759.10, box 13. Moore to Herman Sander, 12 December 1955, and Marshall Shulman, notes of conversation (December 1955?), both in RRC Correspondence, series UAV 759.10, box 31.

40. Moore to Inkeles and Kluckhohn, 5 June 1950, RRC Correspondence, series UAV 759.10, box 9. Moore, "Some Sources of Strength and Weakness in Soviet Society" (American Sociological Association presentation, 1951), in RRC Research Papers (Harvard University Archives), series UAV 759.275, box 8.

41. Moore, "Strengths and Weaknesses of the Soviet System" (July 1952), in RRC Refugee Interview Project Reports and Memoranda (Harvard University Archives), series UAV 759.175.75, box 5, pp. 1, 5, 64–67.

42. Moore, *Terror and Progress: USSR: Some Sources of Stability and Change in the Soviet Dictatorship* (Cambridge, Mass., 1954), 178, 224, 185, 224, 191, 189, 225–226, 231.

43. Moore, *Terror and Progress,* 288. Moore, "The Outlook," *Annals* 303 (January 1956), 9–10.

44. See reviews of *Terror and Progress* by Barrington Moore: Warren B. Walsh, "What Next in Russia?" *NYT,* 11 April 1954; Julian Towster, *APSR* 48:4 (December 1954), 1159–1160; Nicholas Timasheff, *Review of Politics* 17:4 (October 1955), 562–564.

45. Moore, *Terror and Progress,* xii.

46. David Gleicher to Marshall Shulman, 24 February 1955, RRC Correspondence, series UAV 759.10, box 29.

47. Moore, "Reflections on the Meaning of Soviet Experience for Industrial Society" (9 November 1955), RRC Research Papers, series UAV 759.275, box 8, quotes on 1–2, 9–11, 8. Seminar discussion, 9 November 1955, transcribed in RRC Research Papers, series UAV 759.275, box 14.

48. Tim B. Müller, "Die gelehrten Krieger und die Rockefeller-Revolution: Intellektuelle zwischen Geheimdeinst, Neuer Linken, und dem Entwurf einer neuen Ideen Geschichte," *Geschichte und Gesellschaft* 33:2 (2007), 206–214.

49. Marcuse to Max Horkheimer, 30 March 1949, in *Collected Papers of Herbert Marcuse,* ed. Douglas Kellner (London, 1999–2007), 1:2, 63–264. Marcuse, "Study of Soviet Philosophy," attached to Kluckhohn to Bundy, 18 March 1954, Dean-FAS Correspondence (Harvard University Archives), series UA.III 5.55.26. Marcuse, "Some Social Implications of Modern Technology" (1941) and "Thirty-three Theses" (1947)—both in Marcuse, *Collected Papers,* 1:39–66, 215–228. Marcuse, "Recent Literature on Communism," *WP* 6:4 (July 1954), 517, 519. Marcuse, "Dialectic and Logic," in *Continuity and Change in Russian and Soviet Thought,* ed. Ernest J. Simmons (Cambridge, Mass., 1955), 356.

50. Marcuse, *One-Dimensional Man: Studies in the Ideology of Advanced Industrial Society* (Boston, 1964), 17, xv.

51. Moore to McGeorge Bundy, 27 December 1953, Dean-FAS Correspondence, series UA.III 5.55.26. Moore to Marshall D. Shulman, 24 February 1955, RRC Correspondence, series UAV 759.10, box 29.

52. That work eventually appeared as Moore, "Totalitarian Elements in Pre-Industrial Societies," in Moore, *Political Power and Social Theory: Six Studies* (Cambridge, Mass., 1958).

53. Moore, "Dictatorship and Industrialism" (1953? 1954?), RRC Research Papers, series UAV 759.275, box 8.

54. Donald L. M. Blackmer, *The MIT Center for International Studies: The Founding Years, 1951–1969* (Cambridge, Mass., 2002), chap. 3. Moore to Shulman, 21 December 1955, RRC Correspondence, series UAV 759.10, box 34. Moore, *The Western Impact upon the Structure of Authority in Indian Society* (Cambridge, Mass., 1955), 2:2, 4:5.

55. Moore, "Work Done to Date by Barrington Moore, Jr., on Dictatorship and Industrialism" (12 December 1956), RRC Correspondence, series UAV 759.10, box 38.

56. Moore was hardly the first to see the American Civil War as a revolutionary moment. Moore cited Charles Beard and Mary Beard, but not W. E. B. DuBois, who made a similar argument.

57. Cyril E. Black, *The Dynamics of Modernization: A Study in Comparative History* (New York, 1966), 172–174.

58. Moore, *Social Origins of Dictatorship and Democracy: Lord and Peasant in the Making of the Modern World* (Boston, 1966), xv–xx, 430–432, 447, 313, 506.

59. Moore, *Social Origins*, 11–12, 482, 457, 431. Communication with Victoria Bonnell (2003). Phrasing borrowed from Thorstein Veblen's description of anti-Bolshevism and the Versailles Treaty.

60. Jonathan Wiener, "Review of Reviews: Barrington Moore's *Social Origins of Dictatorship and Democracy*," *History and Theory* 15:2 (1976), 146–175. Michael Kennedy and Miguel A. Centeno, "Internationalism and Global Transformations in American Sociology," in *Sociology in America: A History*, ed. Craig Calhoun (Chicago, 2007), 703. Citation data derived from ISI Web of Knowledge (www.isiwebofknowledge.com, accessed 29 November 2007).

61. Gerschenkron to Black, 13 December 1955, Alexander Gerschenkron Papers (Harvard University Archives), series HUG(FP) 45.10, box 2.

62. Parsons, "Some Principal Characteristics of Industrial Societies," in *The Transformation of Russian Society: Aspects of Social Change since 1861*, ed. Cyril Black (Cambridge, Mass., 1960), 13, 14–16, 22–23. Parsons, *Social System*, chap. 2.

63. Parsons, "Communism and the West: The Sociology of the Conflict" (late 1950s?), Parsons Papers, series HUG(FP) 42.41, box 6. Parsons, "Polarization and the Problem of International Order," *Berkeley Journal of Sociology* 6 (1961), 131–132.

64. Parsons, "Some Principal Characteristics," 19–20. Parsons, "Communism and the West."

65. Ethan Pollock, *Stalin and the Soviet Science Wars* (Princeton, 2006).

66. Leopold Labedz, "Soviet Attitudes towards Sociology," *Soviet Survey*, no. 10 (1956), 6–15. P. N. Fedoseev, "IV mezhdunarodnyi sotsiologicheskii kongress," in Fedoseev, *IV Mezhdunarodnyi sotsiologicheskii kongress* (Moscow, 1960), 11.

67. Dmitri N. Shalin, "The Development of Soviet Sociology, 1956–1976," *Annual Review of Sociology* 4 (1978), 171, 177–178. Leopold Labedz, "Sociology as a Vocation," *Survey* 48 (July 1963), 57–65. "Postanovlenie komissii TsK KPSS po voprosam ideologii, kul'tury, i mezhdunarodnykh partiinykh sviazei o sozdanii Sovetskoi sotsiologicheskoi assotsiatsiiu" (11 February 1958), in *Sotsiologiia i vlast'*, ed. L. N. Moskvichev (Moscow, 1997–2001), 1:44.

68. Ilya Zemtsov, *IKSI: ocherk istorii razvitiia sovetskoi sotsiologii* (Jerusalem, 1976), 5–6.

69. "Peredovaia," *Voprosy filosofii*, 1956#1, 9, 11.

70. A. Zdravomyslov, "Sotsiologiia: otkrytiia i vozmozhnosti," *Sovetskaia Rossiia* (21 March 1964).

71. Ia. C. Kapeliush and A. I. Prigozhin, "Sobranie sovetskoi sotsiologicheskoi assotsi-atsii," *Voprosy filosofii*, 1966#6, 157.

72. E. V. Beliaev et al., "Vsesoiuznyi simpozium sotsiologov," *Voprosy filosofii*, 1966#2, 156–165; A. M. Rumiantsev, T. Timofeev, and Ia. Shcheinin, "Dlia progressa nauki i truda," *Izvestiia*, 12 May 1966. "Sessiia sotsiologov," *Pravda*, 23 November 1967.

73. Osipov, "Predislovie," in *Sotsiologiia v SSSR,* ed. Osipov (Moscow, 1966), 1:7–9. Alex Simirenko, "Sociology," in *Social Thought in the Soviet Union,* ed. Simirenko (Chicago, 1969), 394, 397.

74. Vladimir Kantorovich, "Rodstvennaia nam nauka," *Literaturnaia gazeta* (5–12 May 1966).

75. "Pis'mo Akademika A. M. Rumiantsev i doktora filosofskii nauk G. V. Osipov sekretar' TsK KPSS P. N. Demichevu o razvitie konkretnykh sotsiologicheskikh issledovanii v SSSR" (13 April 1967) and "Ob organizatsii Instituta konkretnykh social'nykh issledovanii Akademii Nauk SSSR" (22 May 1968)—both in Moskvichev, *Sotsiologiia i vlast',* 1:93–97 and 142.

76. Robert K. Merton and Henry W. Rieken, "Notes on Sociology in the USSR," *Symposia Studies Series* 10 (March 1962), 10–12.

77. George Fischer, *Science and Politics: The New Sociology in the Soviet Union* (Ithaca, N.Y., 1964).

78. Daniel Bell, "The 'End of Ideology' in the USSR?" in *Marxist Ideology in the Contemporary World: Its Appeals and Paradoxes,* ed. Milorad Drachkovich (Stanford, 1966).

79. Parsons diary, 9 May 1964, and Parsons, "Report of Cultural Exchange Visit to the Soviet Union, May 5–22, 1964"—both in Parsons Papers, series HUG(FP) 15.4, box 19.

80. Parsons, "Social Sciences"; Fischer, *Science and Politics,* 19. Parsons, "An American Impression of Sociology in the Soviet Union," *ASR* 30:1 (February 1965), 123.

81. Untitled handwritten notes, opening with "General idea: Close parallel of Communism to Calvinism," in Parsons Papers, series HUG(FP) 15.4, box 19.

82. Parsons originally intended a single volume, but ultimately divided the project into two, the other being *Societies: Evolutionary and Comparative Perspectives* (Englewood Cliffs, N.J., 1966). The split is discussed in correspondence among Inkeles (the series editor), Parsons, and Prentice-Hall staff (1964–1965) in Parsons Papers, series HUG(FP) 15.4, box 9.

83. Parsons, *The System of Modern Societies* (Englewood Cliffs, N.J., 1971), 54, 67, 74, 106, 123–128.

84. Parsons to Helen Parsons, 11 October 1967, Parsons Papers, series HUG(FP) 15.10, box 3.

85. Parsons to Joseph Slater, 27 October 1967, Parsons Papers, series HUG(FP), 15.60, box 3.

86. Matthew Evangelista, *Unarmed Forces: The Transnational Movement to End the Cold War* (Ithaca, N.Y., 1999), 210–211. Parsons to Carl Kaysen, 22 November 1967, Parsons Papers, series HUG(FP) 15.60, box 3.

87. Parsons to L. E. Thompson, 18 January 1968, and Parsons to Rostow, 16 January 1968, both in Parsons Papers, series HUG(FP) 15.60, box 3.

88. G. V. Osipov and M. N. Rutkevich, "Sociology in the USSR, 1965–1975," *Current Sociology* 26:2 (1978), 3. M. S. Bakhitov, "Problema prichinnosti v sotsiologii i kritika funktsionalizma," *Voprosy filosofii,* 1963#9, 78–88.

89. A. G. Zdravomyslov and V. A. Iadov, *Chelovek i ego rabota* (Moscow, 1967). Zdravomyslov and Iadov, "O programmirovanie konkretnogo sotsial'ogo issledovaniia," *Voprosy filosofii,* 1963#8, 74–83.

90. Zdravomyslov, "Ot sotsial'nogo deistviia k sisteme sovremennykh obshchestv: Pamiati Talkotta Parsonsa (1902–1979)," in Zdravomyslov, *Sotsiologiia rosiiskogo krizisa* (Moscow, 1999), 255. Zdravomyslov, "Bez osmysleniia togo, chto sdelal my, sotsiologii net," in *Rossiiskaia sotsiologiia shestidesiatykh godov: v vospominaniiakh i dokumentakh,* ed. G. S. Batygin (St. Petersburg, 1999).

91. Alexander Vucinich, "Marx and Parsons in Soviet Sociology," *RR* 33 (January 1974), 12–13. "Zapiska Nauchnogo Soveta po problemam zarubezhnykh ideolog-icheskikh techenii pro Sektsii obshchestvennykh nyk Prezidiuma AN SSSP o sessii Nauchnogo Soveta" (11 February 1969), in Moskvichev, *Sotsiologiia i vlast'*, 2:74–77. Zemtsov, *IKSI*, 54–56.

92. Immanuel Wallerstein, "The Culture of Sociology in Disarray: The Impact of 1968 on U.S. Sociologists," in Calhoun, *Sociology in America.*

93. Alvin W. Gouldner, *The Coming Crisis of Western Sociology* (New York, 1970), 11, 452, 466–467, 473–474.

CHAPTER 8

1. Abbott Gleason, *Totalitarianism: An Inner History of the Cold War* (Oxford, 1995), chap. 2.

2. Robert C. Tucker, "Towards a Comparative Politics of Movement-Regimes," *APSR* 55:2 (June 1961), 283.

3. Arendt, *The Origins of Totalitarianism* (New York, 1951); Gleason, *Totalitarianism,* chap. 3; Margaret Canovan, *Hannah Arendt: A Reinterpretation of Her Political Thought* (Cambridge, 1992), chap. 2.

4. Friedrich and Brzezinski, *Totalitarian Dictatorship and Autocracy* (Cambridge, Mass., 1956), vii; grant application, "Russian Constitutional and Administrative History in Modern Times and Its Relation to the Constitutional Development of the Rest of Europe" (1937–1938), in Carl Joachim Friedrich Papers (Harvard University Archives), series HUG(FP) 17.10.

5. Invitees in Friedrich Papers, series HUG(FP) 17.12, box 33.

6. Friedrich, "The Unique Character of Totalitarian Society," in *Totalitarianism: Proceedings of a Conference Held at the American Academy of Arts and Sciences, March 1953,* ed. Friedrich (Cambridge, Mass., 1954), 52–53, 55–57.

7. George Denicke, Andrew Gyorgy, Karpovich, and Robinson in the "Discussion" in Friedrich, *Totalitarianism,* 75, 381, 80–82.

8. Kennan, "Totalitarianism and Freedom," in Friedrich, *Totalitarianism,* 19, 29, 82–83.

9. Inkeles, "The Totalitarian Mystique: Some Impressions of the Dynamics of Totalitarian Society," in Friedrich, *Totalitarianism,* 88.

10. Friedrich and Brzezinski, *Totalitarian Dictatorship and Autocracy,* 3, 7, 9–10, 81, 18, 246–247, 295–299, 300.

11. See the reviews of *Totalitarian Dictatorship and Autocracy:* Dallin, *RR* 17:2 (April 1958), 143–144 and Barghoorn, *PSQ* 72:4 (December 1957), 613–614. Friedrich talk, "Continuity and Change in Soviet Communism" (1–5 November 1959), in Friedrich Papers, series 17.60, box 4.

12. Brzezinski, introduction to *Political Controls in the Soviet Army* (New York, 1954), 1, 6, 84. Brzezinski, "Russo-Soviet Nationalism" (M.A. thesis, McGill University, 1950), 140–146.

13. Brzezinski, *The Permanent Purge: Politics in Soviet Totalitarianism* (Cambridge, Mass., 1956), 8, 37, 89, 145, 165, 173. John Stearns Gillespie, review of *The Permanent Purge* by Zbigniew Brzezinski, *Journal of Politics* 19:2 (May 1957), 293–295.

14. Adam Ulam, *Understanding the Cold War: A Historian's Personal Reflections* (New Brunswick, N.J., 2004), 107. Fainsod, "The Origins of the Third International, 1914–1919" (Ph.D. diss., Harvard University, 1932), 2.

15. Marquis W. Childs, "International Socialism and the World War," *St. Louis Post-Dispatch*, 6 October 1935. Washington Office memo, 1 November 1963, in Fainsod FBI file.

16. Fainsod, "The Soviet," in *Encyclopedia of Social Sciences*, ed. E. R. A. Seligman (New York, 1937), 14:269–273. Fainsod, "Regulation and Efficiency," *Yale Law Journal* 49:7 (May 1940), 1209–1211. Fainsod and Lincoln Gordon, *Government and the American Economy* (New York, 1941). Joseph Berliner to Wang Xi, 25 October 1983, RRC Correspondence (Harvard University Archives), series UAV 759.95.1, box 18.

17. Boston Office memo, 31 October 1963, Fainsod FBI file. These accusations, which Fainsod never had an opportunity to explain, correct, or rebut, came at a time of intense scrutiny of political pasts by an organization whose reputation rested on overestimating political threats.

18. "Interim Report of the Russian Research Center" (early 1948?), RRC Correspondence (Harvard University Archives), series UAV 759.10, box 1.

19. Fainsod, "Controls and Tensions in the Soviet System," Department of State External Relations, ser. 3, no. 2 (18 December 1949), 2, 20. Margaret Mead, "Notes on Trip to Harvard" (13–14 February 1950), Margaret Mead Papers (Library of Congress), box G-87. The paper would eventually become an annex to the Project Troy report and also appeared in *APSR* 44:2 (June 1950), 266–282.

20. Fainsod, "The Postwar Role of the Communist Party," *Annals* 263 (May 1949), 20.

21. Fainsod, "Postwar Role," 21–22; Fainsod, "Recent Developments in Soviet Public Administration," *Journal of Politics* 11:4 (November 1949), 712–714.

22. Fainsod, *How Russia Is Ruled* (Cambridge, Mass., 1953), 12, 47, 489, 31, 59.

23. See the reviews of *How Russia Is Ruled*: Harry Schwartz, "Rewards and Terror," *NYT*, 11 October 1953. Warren Walsh, *RR* 13:3 (July 1954), 214–216.

24. Fainsod, *How Russia Is Ruled*, 354–355, 500.

25. Fainsod-Kennan "Discussion," in Friedrich, *Totalitarianism*, 31–32. Kennan apparently struck the term *erosion* from the published version of his paper, likely in favor of "impaled and destroyed" (25). Fainsod, *How Russia Is Ruled*, ix, 105, 247, 312, 418, 476, 494, 499–500.

26. Kluckhohn to Walter [*sic*] Rostow, 11 February 1952, RRC Correspondence, series UAV 759.10, box 17. Rostow, *Europe after Stalin: Eisenhower's Decisions of March 11, 1953* (Austin, Tex., 1982).

27. "Some Informal Speculation about Possible Consequences of Stalin's Death" (February 1952), RRC Research Papers (Harvard University Archives), series UAV 759.275, box 9.

28. Moore, "Strengths and Weaknesses of the Soviet System" (July 1952), RRC RIP Project Reports and Memoranda (Harvard University Archives), series UAV 759.175.75, box 5.

29. Moore, *Terror and Progress: USSR: Some Sources of Change and Stability in the Soviet Dictatorship* (Cambridge, Mass., 1954), 231.

30. George W. Breslauer, "In Defense of Sovietology," *Post-Soviet Affairs* 8:3 (1992), 205–207.

31. "Russian Diary, 1956," Fainsod Papers, series HUG 4382.8, box 4. On Fainsod's long-standing interest in dissent, the source is communication with Mary Fainsod Katzenstein (2008).

32. Fainsod, "Changes in the Structure of Soviet Power" (June 1957), in Fainsod Papers, series HUG 4382.8, box 3. On the discussion of his paper, see Isabel de Madariaga, "The Science of Kremlinology," *Commentary* 24:3 (September 1957), 263–264.

33. Patricia K. Grimsted, "The Odyssey of the Smolensk Archive" (Carl Beck Papers in Russian and East European Studies, no. 1201, 1995). [RDB,] Program Guidance in Human Resources, 25 January 1950, in Records of OSD (U.S. National Archives), RG330, entry 341, box 241. "German War Documents Project," 5 February 1953, State Department Records, RG59, lot 78D441, box 1.

34. F. O. Carroll to Walworth Barbour, 16 May 1952, State Department Records, RG59, SDDF 110.21/5–1652. Operations Control Board Minutes, 10 February 1954, re: "Special (Mosely) Project," in White House Office–NSC Staff Records (Dwight D. Eisenhower Presidential Library), Operations Control Board Secretariat series, box 11.

35. Christian Herter to Stowe, 30 September 1957, State Department Records, RG59, lot 78D441, box 1. A steering committee came under the auspices of the American Historical Association; see AHA Statement, 10 August 1956, AHA Records (Library of Congress), box 474; Lynn Case to Shepard Stone, 4 May 1957, AHA Records, box 490.

36. Hans Speier, "Summary of Political and Economic Studies," RAND Report D-5866 (1958), 9. Los Angeles Office memo, 30 October 1963, Fainsod FBI File. Dagmar Horna Perman, "Microfilming of German Records at the National Archives," *American Archivist* 22:4 (October 1959), 442.

37. Boston Office memo, 30 October 1963, Fainsod FBI File. Maj. Gen. John A. Klein to Fainsod, 29 June 1954, and Fainsod to Hans Speier, 21 October 1957—both in Merle Fainsod Papers (Harvard University Archives), series HUG 4382.5, box R-RAND. Speier to Fainsod, 21 November 1957, Fainsod Papers, HUG 4382.5, box Si–Sy.

38. For original title, see Joseph M. Goldsen to Fainsod, 12 November 1957, in Fainsod Papers, series HUG 4382.5, box Si–Sy.

39. Fainsod, *Smolensk under Soviet Rule* (Cambridge, Mass., 1958), 85, 449–450, 454.

40. Fainsod, *Smolensk under Soviet Rule,* 453, 363, 451–452, 429, 454.

41. Barghoorn review of *Smolensk under Soviet Rule* by Merle Fainsod, *RR* 18:3 (July 1959), 238–239.

42. Henry L. Roberts, "Documents of Discontent," *NYT Book Review*, 5 October 1958.

43. Azrael to Marshall Shulman, 17 March and 7 December 1958—both in RRC Correspondence, series UAV 759.10, box 43.

44. Azrael's dissertation, "Political Profiles of the Soviet Technical Intelligentsia and Managerial Elite" (Ph.D. diss., Harvard University, 1961), contained numerous references to RIP sources, more than his book *Managerial Power and Soviet Politics* (Cambridge, Mass., 1966).

45. Meyer, "USSR, Incorporated," *SR* 20:3 (October 1961), 369–376. Kassof, "The Administered Society: Totalitarianism without Terror," *WP* 16:4 (July 1964), 558–575.

46. Almond, "Propensities and Opportunities," in Almond, *Political Development: Essays in Heuristic Theory* (Boston, 1970), 13, 25. Almond, "A Developmental Approach to Political Systems," *WP* 17:2 (January 1965), 183–214.

47. Almond, "Comparative Political Systems," *Journal of Politics* 18:3 (August 1956), 391–393. Almond, "A Functional Approach to Comparative Politics," in *The Politics of Developing Areas*, ed. Almond and James S. Coleman (Princeton, 1960), 3–5.

48. David M. Ricci, *The Tragedy of Political Science: Politics, Scholarship and Democracy* (New Haven, Conn., 1984), chap. 5.

49. Dahl, "The Behavioral Approach in Political Science: Epitaph for a Monument to a Successful Protest," *APSR* 55:4 (December 1961), 763–772, quoting David Truman (emphasis in original).

50. Robert A. Dahl, *Who Governs? Democracy and Power in an American City* (New Haven, Conn., 1961).

51. Almond was at Yale 1946–1950 and 1959–1963.

52. Nils Gilman, *Mandarins of the Future: Modernization Theory in Cold War America* (Baltimore, 2003), chap. 4; CCP, *A Report on the Activities of the Committee, 1954–1970* (New York, 1971).

53. C. A. H. Thompson to Fainsod, 7 July 1964, in Fainsod Papers, series HUG 4382.5, box 8 and related materials in box 1. Fainsod, "The Structure of Development Administration," in *Development Administration: Concepts and Problems*, ed. Irving Swerdlow (Syracuse, N.Y., 1963).

54. Fainsod, "Bureaucracy and Modernization: The Russian and Soviet Case," in *Bureaucracy and Political Development*, ed. Joseph La Palombara (Princeton, 1963), 233, 255–256, 234.

55. Fainsod, *How Russia Is Ruled*, 2nd edition (Cambridge, Mass., 1963), 580–582, 462, 583, 596, 592.

56. Minutes, 1 May 1967, RRC Executive Committee Records, series UAV 759.5, box 2.

57. Fainsod, "Roads to the Future" (1967), in *Dilemmas of Change in Soviet Politics*, ed. Zbigniew Brzezinski (New York, 1969), 131, 133–135, 130. Fainsod, "Some Reflections on Soviet-American Relations," *APSR* 62:4 (December 1968), 1096.

58. John N. Hazard, "Foreword," in *Pluralism in the Soviet Union: Essays in Honour of H. Gordon Skilling*, ed. Susan Gross Solomon (New York, 1982); and Skilling, *The Education of a Canadian: My Life as a Scholar and Activist* (Montreal, 2001).

59. Skilling, "Soviet and Communist Politics: A Comparative Approach," *Journal of Politics* 22:2 (May 1960), 305, 312–313.

60. He was especially indebted to Czech Michael Lakatoš. Skilling is paraphrasing Almond's comments, given orally at the Conference on Soviet and Communist Studies of APSA in September 1964. Skilling, "Interest Groups and Communist Politics," *WP* 18:3 (April 1966), 438, 449.

61. Skilling, "Soviet and American Politics: The Dialectic of Opposites," *Canadian Journal of Economics and Political Science* 31:2 (May 1965), 273–274.

62. Dahl, *Polyarchy: Participation and Opposition* (New Haven, Conn., 1971), 8. Dahl, "Introduction," in *Regimes and Oppositions,* ed. Dahl (New Haven, Conn., 1973), 18.

63. Tucker, "Towards a Comparative Politics," 281, 282. Daniels, "The Secretariat and the Local Organizations in the Russian Communist Party, 1921–1923," *ASEER* 16:1 (February 1957), 49.

64. Tucker, "Towards a Comparative Politics," 281, 289.

65. Barghoorn identified Sidney Ploss at the State Department and Robert Conquest in Britain. Barghoorn to Shulman, 13 December 1962, Frederick Barghoorn Papers (Yale University Library), 2:3. Barghoorn to Skilling, 10 August 1965, Barghoorn Papers, 3:16.

66. Biographical details from 1957 c.v., in Barghoorn Papers, 2:1; Thomas F. Remington, "Fathers and Sons: The Dialectics of Soviet Studies," in *Politics and the Soviet System: Essays in Honour of Frederick C. Barghoorn,* ed. Remington (London, 1989).

67. HICOG [High Commissioner for Germany]-Frankfurt to State Department, 1 May 1950, State Department Records, RG59, SDDF 761.00/5–150.

68. Barghoorn, *Soviet Russian Nationalism* (Oxford, 1956), vii–viii, 266.

69. Barghoorn to Cyril Black, 25 January 1965, Barghoorn Papers, 2:7.

70. Almond and Sidney Verba, *The Civic Culture: Political Attitudes and Democracy in Five Nations* (Boston, 1965 [1963]), 3, 13.

71. Barghoorn, "Soviet Russia: Orthodoxy and Adaptiveness," in *Political Culture and Political Development,* ed. Lucien W. Pye and Sidney Verba (Princeton, 1965), 470–471, 508, 509.

72. "Eclectic" from communication with Thomas F. Remington (2007).

73. Brzezinski, "Totalitarianism and Rationality," *APSR* 50:3 (September 1956), 751–763.

74. Brzezinski, *The Soviet Bloc: Unity and Conflict* (Cambridge, Mass., 1960).

75. Tucker, "The Question of Totalitarianism," *SR* 20:3 (October 1961), 380; Brzezinski reply, *SR* 20:3 (October 1961), 385.

76. Brzezinski and Huntington, *Political Power: USA/USSR: Similarities and Contrasts, Convergence or Evolution* (New York, 1964), xi, 436. Skilling, "Interest Groups and Communist Politics," 441n31.

77. Robert Burrowes, "Totalitarianism: The Revised Standard Version," *WP* 21:2 (January 1969), 281–294.

78. Barghoorn, *Politics in the USSR: A Country Study* (Boston, 1972), 11.

79. Inkeles, "Models and Issues in the Analysis of Soviet Society," *Survey* 60 (July 1966), 3–17.

80. Friedrich, "Foreword to the Revised Edition," in Friedrich and Brzezinski, *Totalitarian Dictatorship and Autocracy* (Cambridge, Mass., 1965), vii–viii. Friedrich, "The Evolving Theory and Practice of Totalitarian Regimes," in Friedrich et al., *Totalitarianism in Perspective: Three Views* (New York, 1969), 153. Brzezinski, "The Soviet Political System: Transformation or Degradation?" (1966) and "Concluding Reflections" (1968)—both in Brzezinski, *Dilemmas of Change*, 30, 31–33, 162, 153–154.

81. Chart by Edward McGowan in Brzezinski, *Dilemmas of Change*, 157.

82. Rigby, "Crypto-Politics," *Survey* 50 (January 1964), 183–194. Daniels, "Soviet Politics since Khrushchev," in *The Soviet Union under Brezhnev and Kosygin: The Transition Years*, ed. John W. Strong (New York, 1971), 22–23.

83. Conquest, *Power and Policy in the USSR: The Struggle for Stalin's Succession, 1945–1960* (New York, 1967), 14–16, 393.

84. Meyer, "The Comparative Study of Communist Systems," *SR* 26:1 (March 1967), 5.

85. Skilling, "Groups in Soviet Politics: Some Hypotheses," in *Interest Groups in Soviet Politics*, ed. Skilling and Franklyn F. Griffiths (Princeton, 1971), 19; Almond, "Functional Approach," 33–37.

86. Skilling, "Group Conflict in Soviet Politics: Some Conclusions," in Skilling and Griffiths, *Interest Groups in Soviet Politics*.

87. Tucker, "The Politics of De-Stalinization" (1957), in Tucker, *The Soviet Political Mind: Studies in Stalinism and Post-Stalin Change* (New York, 1963), 36–37. Tucker, "The Metamorphosis of the Stalin Myth," RAND Research Memorandum RM-1223 (1954).

88. Tucker, "The Dictator and Totalitarianism" (1965), in Tucker, *The Soviet Political Mind: Stalinism and Post-Stalin Change* (New York, 1971), 46.

89. Karen Horney, *Neurosis and Human Growth: The Struggle toward Self-Realization* (New York, 1950), 38–39. Tucker, "A Stalin Biographer's Memoir," in *Introspection in Biography: The Biographer's Quest for Self-Awareness*, ed. Samuel H. Baron and Carl Pletsch (Hillsdale, N.J., 1985). Tucker, *Philosophy and Myth in Karl Marx* (Cambridge, 1961). Tucker, "The Psychological Factor in Soviet Foreign Policy," RAND Research Memorandum RM-1881 (1957).

90. Tucker project description (1967), in Barghoorn Papers, box 3.

91. Tucker, *Stalin as Revolutionary, 1879–1929: A Study in History and Personality* (New York, 1973), 79–82, 161.

92. See the reviews of *Stalin as Revolutionary*: Lewin, *Journal of Modern History* 47:2 (June 1975), 364–372; Slusser, *AHR* 79:3 (June 1974), 820–822.

93. Tucker, "Forces for Change in Soviet Society" (1956), RAND Research Memorandum RM-1636.

94. Minutes of JCSS meeting, spring 1966, in SSRC Records (Rockefeller Archive Center), 1/1/24/256/1503.

95. Tucker, "On the Comparative Study of Communism," *WP* 19:2 (January 1967), 242–257. Tucker, "Communism and Political Culture," *Newsletter of the Planning Group on Comparative Communism* 4:3 (May 1971), 3–11.

96. Alexander Eckstein challenged Almond; see "Report of the Conference on Political Culture and Comparative Communist Studies," *Newsletter of the Planning Group on Comparative Communism* 5:3 (May 1972), 2–4.

97. Tucker, "Stalin and the Revolution from Above" and "Some Questions on the Scholarly Agenda," both in *Stalinism: Essays in Historical Interpretation,* ed. Tucker (New York, 1977).

98. Seminar discussion on Inkeles, "Competing Perspectives on Soviet Society" (3 November 1965), RRC Research Papers, series UAV 759.275, box 16.

99. Communication with Jerry Hough (2004). Hough, *The Soviet Prefects: The Local Party Organs in Industrial Decision-Making* (Cambridge, Mass., 1969), vii. Project proposal, spring 1959, RRC Correspondence, series UAV 759.10, box 44. Jerry Fincher Hough, "The Role of the Local Party Organs in Soviet Industrial Decision-Making" (Ph.D. diss., Harvard University, 1961), 4.

100. Hough, "The Technical Elite vs. the Party: A First-Hand Report" (1959), RRC Research Papers, UAV 759.275, box 6. Hough fellowship application (spring 1965) and Philip Monypenny letter, 8 February 1965—both in RRC Correspondence, series UAV 759.10, box 67.

101. Hough, *Soviet Prefects,* ix. Seminar discussion on Hough, "Local Party Organs as Prefects: Some Implications" (15 February 1966), RRC Research Papers, series UAV 759.275, box 16. Fainsod to Hough, 20 June 1967, and Fainsod to Abram Bergson, 11 March 1966—both in RRC Correspondence, series UAV 759.10, box 79.

102. Hough, *The Soviet Union and Social Science Theory* (Cambridge, Mass., 1979), 3–4.

103. Hough, *Soviet Prefects,* 281, 97, 288, 113, 317, 300–303. Erik P. Hoffmann, "Social Science and Soviet Administrative Behavior," *WP* 24:3 (April 1972), 445–446.

104. Hough, *Soviet Union and Social Science Theory,* xiv, 9, 13. Dahl, "The Concept of Power," *Behavioral Science* 2 (July 1957), 201–215.

105. Hough, *Soviet Union and Social Science Theory,* 1. See the reviews of *The Soviet Union and Social Science Theory:* Mary McAuley, *Soviet Studies* 31:2 (April 1979), 286. John A. Armstrong, *APSR* 73:2 (June 1979), 636–637.

CHAPTER 9

1. Byrnes, "USA: Work at the Universities," in *The State of Soviet Studies,* ed. Walter Z. Laqueur and Leopold Labedz (Cambridge, Mass., 1965), 29.

2. On Camelot, see Joy Elizabeth Rohde, "'The Social Scientists' War': Expertise in a Cold War Nation" (Ph.D. diss., University of Pennsylvania, 2007). Africa Research Group, *How Harvard Rules: Being a Total Critique of Harvard University, Including New Liberated Documents, Government Research, and the Educational Process Exposed, Strike Posters and a Free Power Chart* (Cambridge, Mass., 1969). Jerry L. Avorn, *Up against the Ivy Wall: A History of the Columbia Crisis* (New York, 1968). James N. Rosenau, *International Studies and the Social Sciences: Problems, Priorities and Prospects in the United States* (Beverly Hills, Calif., 1973), 16–20.

3. Derived from FF, *Annual Reports,* 1961–1966; Philip E. Mosely, "International Affairs," in *U.S. Philanthropic Foundations: Their History, Structure and Management,* ed. Warren Weaver (New York, 1967), 401–402.

4. Francis X. Sutton, *Funding for International Education* (New York, 1975), 4–8.

5. Irwin T. Sanders, *A Crisis of Dollars: The Funding Threat to International Affairs in U.S. Higher Education* (New York, 1968), table 4.

6. Edwin A. Deagle Jr., *A Survey of United States Institutions Engaged in International Relations Research and Related Activities* (New York, 1981), table 12.

7. Minutes, 13 November 1973, RRC Executive Committee Minutes (Harvard University Archives), series UAV 759.5, box 3.

8. RRC Visiting Committee Report, 30 May 1974, RRC Correspondence (Harvard University Archives), series UAV 759.10, box 95.

9. Undated document (by Abbott Gleason), "Anniversary Party, 1973," in RRC Correspondence, series UAV 759.10, box 87.

10. "Soviet Studies," [Ford Foundation] *Letter,* 1 February 1976; Theodore Shabad, "Columbia and Harvard Ask Funds to Save Centers for Soviet Study," *NYT,* 24 November 1976.

11. Herbert E. Meyer, "Why Business Has a Stake in Keeping Sovietology Alive," *Fortune* 96 (September 1975), 156–162. Neil Ulman, "When the State Department Wants to Find Out More about Russia, It Often Heads to Harvard," *Wall Street Journal,* 1 March 1977. "TASS Sees Last Gasp in Fund Drive for Russian Studies Centers in U.S.," *NYT,* 25 November 1976.

12. RRC Annual Report, 15 October 1982, RRC Correspondence, series UAV 759.95.1, box 13.

13. Minutes, 16 March 1970, RRC Executive Committee Minutes, series UAV 759.5, box 3.

14. In 1967, the JCSS changed its name to the Joint Committee on Slavic and East European Studies; the text will stick with the original abbreviation to avoid confusion with successor committees. Gordon B. Turner, "The Joint Committee on Slavic Studies, 1948–1971: A Summary View," *ACLS Newsletter* 23:2 (Spring 1972), 6–26.

15. Draft Minutes of JCSS, 15–16 December 1967, AAASS Records (AAASS, Cambridge, Mass.), box 1. The quotation is from Robert Byrnes.

16. Warren W. Eason to Leon Twarog, 24 March 1968, and John M. Thompson to Edward J. Brown, 4 January 1968—both in AAASS Records, box 1.

17. JCSS Minutes, 19 February 1971, SSRC Records (Rockefeller Archive Center), 1/1/24/256/1504.

18. Cyril E. Black to Francis X. Sutton, 3 May 1968, in author's possession. Rudolf L. Tökés, "East European Studies in the United States: The State of the Arts [*sic*] and Future Research Strategies," *East European Quarterly* 8:3 (Fall 1974), 337–352.

19. FF Request, no. ID-1836 (29 October 1973), Grossman Papers. Elbridge Sibley, *The Social Science Research Council: The First Fifty Years* (New York, 1974), 136–137.

20. "Restrictions, Surveillance, and Harassment of American Exchange Students in the USSR," attached to Moscow Embassy to State Department, 9 March 1959, SDDF 511.613/3–959. Belgrade Embassy to State Department, 29 March 1961, SDDF 511.613/3–2961.

21. Stites, "IREX Tremendae: Thirty Years of Research in Russia" (1998), in author's possession. Letter to Loren Graham, 18 November 1967, Loren Graham Papers.

22. David Mark to State Department, 30 March 1959; Moscow Embassy to State Department, 9 March and 19 January 1959—all in SDDF 511.613.

23. Munford to Byrnes, 3 July 1959, Byrnes Papers, box 22. Moscow Embassy to State Department, 26 May 1959, and State Department to Moscow Embassy, 28 May 1959—both in SDDF 511.613/5–2859. Harrison E. Salisbury, "Love Recognizes No Iron Curtain," *NYT*, 9 June 1959. The diplomatic dispatches and *NYT* article mention Luisa Ivanovna Hegarty, a daughter of Uruguayan parents, but do not give her surname prior to marriage.

24. Loren Graham to Ivo Lederer, 21 September 1967, Graham Papers. Communication with Terence Emmons (2007).

25. "Meeting on Candidate for Study in the Soviet Union," 22 June 1960; Moscow Embassy to State Department, 28 April 1961; State Department to Moscow Embassy, 2 May 1961; Moscow Embassy to State Department, 9 May and 13 June 1961—all in SDDF 511.613. Graham, *Moscow Stories* (Bloomington, Ind., 2006), 217, 44–53.

26. Recounted in A. Vasil'chikov and G. Smolin, "Eshche odna stranitsa v dos'e 'skandal TsRU,'" *Pravda*, 1 March 1967.

27. Seymour Topping, "Soviet Backs Contact with West Despite Ouster of U.S. Student," *NYT*, 6 August 1960.

28. Byrnes to Sam Simpson, 15 December 1960; William B. Edgerton to Herman B. Wells, 28 June 1963; Letter to Edgerton, 29 April 1963—all in Byrnes Papers, box 23.

29. Letter to Raymond Sontag, 5 April 1958, Byrnes Papers, box 23.

30. Byrnes to Simpson, 15 December 1960, Byrnes Papers, box 23. Gordon B. Turner to Robert F. Byrnes, 23 January 1961, ACLS Records (Library of Congress), box H-29.

31. Byrnes to Kassof, 4 August 1969, Byrnes Papers, box 23. William Edgerton, "Adventures of an Innocent American Professor with the CIA and the KGB," *Russian History/Histoire Russe* 24:3 (Fall 1997), 327.

32. [Name deleted] to Eisenhower, White House Central Files (Dwight D. Eisenhower Presidential Library), Confidential File, subject subseries, box 14. Wildman's name was blacked out in the sanitized version of the letter, but the folder heading is "Wildman letter" and the information in the letter corresponds to Wildman's biography.

33. Byrnes to Simpson, 12 October 1961, and O'Brien to Byrnes, 10 June 1966, both in Byrnes Papers, box 23.

34. Frederick C. Barghoorn to Intourist, 23 September 1963, in Frederick C. Barghoorn Papers (Yale University Library), 2:3. "Reconstructed Itinerary for Professor Barghoorn" and State Department to Moscow Embassy, 13 November 1963—both in National Security Files (JFKL), box 190.

35. Malcolm Toon to Department of State, 3 December 1963, State Department, CFPF Records, EDX US-USSR. George C. Denny Jr. to Dean Rusk, "Soviet Motives in

Barghoorn Arrest Obscure," 12 November 1963, DDRS document CK3100453321. David Klein to McGeorge Bundy, 15 November 1963, National Security Files (JFKL), box 190.

36. Minutes of Presidium meeting, 26 November 1963, in *Prezidium TsK KPSS, 1954–64,* ed. A. A. Fursenko (Moscow, 2004), 1:779. The Presidium reached this decision shortly after Kennedy's assassination.

37. E. Willis Brooks to IUCTG Committee on the Future, 2 January 1968, Graham Papers.

38. George Feifer, "Sasha's Creed: 'Russia Right or Wrong,'" *NYT Magazine,* 28 April 1963. Stephen Viederman to IUCTG Executive Committee, 18 July 1961, IUCTG Records (Columbia), 1:2. Letter to Loren Graham, 18 November 1967, Graham Papers. Students' backgrounds from communication with Loren Graham (2004). Communication with Thomas Hegarty (2007).

39. Byrnes, *Soviet-American Academic Exchanges, 1958–1975* (Bloomington, Ind., 1975), 93. Agenda for National Advisory Committee, 16 February 1964, REEI Records (University of Illinois Library), box 4. Communication with Allen Kassof (2004).

40. Graham to Lederer, 21 September 1967, Graham Papers.

41. Marshall Shulman to Ivo Lederer, Robert Byrnes, and Leon Lipson, 25 October 1967; Byrnes to Lederer, 27 October 1967; Marshall Shulman et al. to "Dear Friend and Colleague," 21 November 1967; George Gibian to Ivo Lederer, 27 November 1967; and Letter to Graham, 5 April 1968—all in Graham Papers.

42. Leon Lipson, "Chairman's Report on Selection Procedures" (February 1968), Graham Papers. "Some Interim Criteria and Procedures on Selection and Recall" (17 November 1967), Graham Papers.

43. IUCTG Committee on Procedures and Criteria Meeting, 27 December 1967, Graham Papers. "CU Grants for IUCTG and IREX Programs," 24 September 1975, in CU Historical Collection (University of Arkansas), 332:29. Yale Richmond, *Practicing Public Diplomacy: A Cold War Odyssey* (New York, 2008), 144–145.

44. "Resolution of the Subcommittee on Procedures of IUCTG Committee on the Future, 13 January 1968," Graham Papers.

45. Draft policy on "Recall Criteria and Procedures" (January 1968); dissenting recommendations of 23 March 1968; Graham's Minority Report of 2 April 1968—all in Graham Papers.

46. IUCTG Committee on the Future, "On Scholarly Exchanges and Relations with the Soviet Union and Eastern Europe in 1970–1980" (Bloomington, Ind., 1968), 38 (hereafter IUCTG Committee on the Future Report).

47. IUCTG Committee on the Future Report, 39.

48. Minutes of IUCTG Annual Policy Meeting, 19–20 April 1968, in IUCTG Records (Columbia), 1:2. IUCTG Committee on the Future Report, 32, 27. Marshall D. Shulman to Grayson L. Kirk, 22 April 1968, Graham Papers.

49. David E. Bell to McGeorge Bundy, 26 July 1968, in FF Grant Files, 68–801. Allen Kassof announcement, July 1968, CU Historical Collection, 218:23.

50. Yale Richmond to Mr. Chapman, 11 June 1976, Yale Richmond Papers (in author's possession). Marshall I. Goldman and Norman Holmes Pearson, "A Survey of the

International Research and Exchange Board (1968–1972)," 43, 48, summary 3. David
E. Bell to McGeorge Bundy, 26 July 1968, FF Records, Grant Files, 68–801B.

51. Sutton, "Remarks for the October 19 [2000] Kennan Center Conference"
(in author's possession). Korbonski to Felice D. Gaer, 15 January 1977, FF Records,
Grant Files, 68–801. Moscow Embassy to State Department (March 1976?), CU
Historical Collection, 332:28.

52. Francis X. Sutton to Felice D. Gaer, 17 January 1979, Richmond Papers.

53. "Policies and Procedures of the Inter-University Committee" (1968), Central Files
(Columbia University Archives), subject subseries, folder IUCTG.

54. Byrnes, introduction to *Inter-University Committee Report to the Ford Foundation,
1965–69* (Bloomington, Ind., 1970), 11.

55. Byrnes, *Soviet-American Academic Exchanges*, 39.

56. ACLS *Annual Reports, 1970–1971* through *1973–1974*. Moscow Embassy to State
Department, 27 January 1969, CFPF, EDX US-USSR.

57. Bertram Wolfe to Allen Kassof, 10 June 1976, Bertram Wolfe Papers (Hoover
Institution Archives), box 94.

58. Byrnes, "Can Culture Survive Cultural Agreements?" in *Détente*, ed. G. R. Urban
(New York, 1976). Theodore Draper, "Appeasement and Détente," *Commentary* 61:2
(February 1976); letters in subsequent issues.

59. Communication with Yale Richmond (2004).

60. "IREX Exchange of Graduate Students and Young Faculty…: Participants Doing
Research in the Humanities and Social Sciences on Topics of Contemporary
Concern" (13 January 1978), enclosed in Daniel C. Matuszewski to Yale Richmond,
13 January 1978, in Richmond Papers.

61. "Proposal for a New Approach to Research in Slavic Studies," attached to Herbert
J. Ellison to Gordon B. Turner, 31 October 1969, SSRC Records, 1/1/24/256/1504.

62. Marshall D. Shulman, "The Future of Soviet Studies in the United States," *SR* 29:3
(September 1970), 582–588.

63. Communication with James Billington (2005). Blair Ruble, *The Kennan Institute:
Thirty Year Report* (Washington, D.C., 2004), 9. S. Frederick Starr with Bruce
Boisture, *Russian and Soviet Studies in the United States: A Review* (Columbus,
Ohio, 1972), 19, 50.

64. Communication with James Billington (2007).

65. Billington (1975) and Starr (1972), both quoted in Courtney Brown Jenkins, "The
House That George Built: The Kennan Institute for Advanced Russian Studies in
Washington, D.C., 1974–89" (senior thesis, Brown University, 2007), 33, 25. Ruble,
Kennan Institute: Thirty Year Report, 41–47, 132–134. A similar ratio holds, too, for
the first occasional papers; of twenty-nine appearing before 1978, seven were in
history or the humanities; see Ruble, *Kennan Institute: Thirty Year Report*, 240.

66. On contracts, see Toumanoff to Keenan, 11 May 1976; RRC Executive Committee
Minutes, 17 May 1976—both in RRC Executive Committee Minutes, series UAV
759.5, box 3.

67. Edward Keenan and Vladimir Toumanoff, First Interim Report for Department
[*sic*] of Net Assessment, Contract 001–76–C–0347, enclosed in M. C. Barstow to

Andrew Marshall, 15 October 1976, in RRC Executive Committee, series UAV 759.5, box 3 (hereafter First Interim Report).

68. RRC Executive Committee, 27 September 1976, RRC Executive Committee Minutes, series UAV 759.5, box 3.

69. Communication with Vladimir Toumanoff (2008).

70. Keenan and Toumanoff, First Interim Report.

71. RRC Executive Committee, 28 February and 19 April 1977 and 11 May 1976—all in RRC Executive Committee Minutes, series UAV 759.5, box 3.

72. Keenan memorandum, 6 May 1977, RRC Executive Committee, series UAV 759.5, box 3. RRC Executive Committee, 13 July 1977, RRC Executive Committee Minutes, series UAV 759.5, box 3. Draft contract, 19 May 1977, attached to Keenan memorandum, 20 May 1977, Grossman Papers. Communication with Andrew Marshall (2005).

73. From bibliography in Vladimir Toumanoff Virtual Library, at www.nceeer.org (accessed March 2008). Communication with Andrew Marshall (2005).

74. For "laundry," see RRC Executive Committee, 19 April 1977, RRC Executive Committee Minutes, series UAV 759.5, box 3. For "tainted," see Keenan and Toumanoff, First Interim Report.

75. Vladimir G. Treml, Herbert S. Levine, and M. Mark Earle Jr., "A Draft Proposal for the Creation of an Institute for the Study of the Soviet Union," attached to NIO/E [National Intelligence Office/Europe] memorandum, 12 January 1977, CIA Research Tool (CREST) computers (U.S. National Archives), document CIA-RDP83M00171R000500230001–7; and a draft dated 29 November 1977, Grossman Papers.

76. Vladimir Treml to M. Mark Earle, 5 November 1976, Grossman Papers.

77. Director of Performance Evaluation and Improvement, ICS [unknown internal CIA abbreviation], to National Intelligence Officer for Economics, 17 January 1977, CREST document CIA-RDP83M00171R000500230001–7.

78. Memorandum from Assistant to the National Intelligence Officer for Political Economy, 4 January 1978, CREST document CIA-RDP81B00401R002400200071–9.

79. Gerald Sullivan, "U.S. Research on the USSR and Eastern Europe: A Critical Resource for Security and Commercial Policy" (August 1977), Grossman Papers. Toumanoff to Abram Bergson, 11 September 1981, RRC Correspondence, series UAV 759.95.1, box 14.

80. Odom quoted in "United States–Soviet Research Studies," hearing before the U.S. Senate Committee on Foreign Relations, Subcommittee on European Affairs (97th Congress, 2nd session, 22 September 1982), 23.

81. Communication with Blair Ruble (2008). Title VIII Grant Program description at http://www.state.gov/s/inr/grants (accessed January 2009).

82. Felice D. Gaer, "Russian and Soviet Studies in the United States: The University Scene" (1980?), Grossman Papers.

83. Letter to Victor Erlich, 14 March 1975, AAASS Records, box 1.

84. James R. Millar, "History, Method and the Problem of Bias," in *Politics, Work, and Daily Life in the USSR: A Survey of Former Citizens,* ed. Millar (Cambridge, 1987), 3–9, 28.

85. Joseph S. Berliner, foreword to Millar, *Politics, Work, and Daily Life,* viii.
86. Carol Nechemias, review of *Politics, Work, and Daily Life* edited by James Millar, *APSR* 83:2 (June 1989), 664–666.
87. Meyer, "Comparative Politics and Its Discontent: The Study of the USSR and Eastern Europe," in *Political Science and Area Studies: Rivals or Partners?* ed. Lucien W. Pye (Bloomington, Ind., 1975), 103–104, 101, 109.
88. Richard D. Lambert, *Language and Area Studies Review* (Philadelphia, 1973), 138 (hereafter *LASR*).
89. John A. Armstrong, "Comments on Professor Dallin's 'Bias and Blunders in American Studies on the USSR,'" *SR* 32:3 (September 1973), 586.
90. Frederic J. Fleron Jr. to Gordon B. Turner, 16 September 1970, SSRC Records, 1/1/24/256/1504.
91. Lambert, *LASR,* 336, 53, 187, 56.
92. Data derived from Jesse J. Dossick's annual reports appearing in the December issues of *Slavic Review.* This calculation excludes Eastern Europe topics but includes the handful of Canadian and British doctorates—comparing doctorates filed 1960–1963 versus 1970–1973. Peter Rutland, "Sovietology: From Stagnation to *Perestroika?* A Decade of Doctoral Research in Soviet Politics" (Kennan Institute Occasional Paper, no. 241, 1990), 4.
93. Examples include John Hardt, Raymond Garthoff, and Carl Linden.
94. Rutland, "Sovietology," 4–5.
95. Elisabeth Bumiller, *Condoleezza Rice: An American Life* (New York, 2007), chaps. 3–4. Robert Legvold, "The Study of Soviet Foreign Policy: The State of the Field and the Role of IREX," in *Foreign Area Research in the National Interest: American and Soviet Perspectives,* ed. Walter D. Conner (Washington, 1982), 24.
96. From list of winners on the APSA Web site, www.apsanet.org (accessed March 2008).
97. Ellison, "The Challenge of the Lambert Report," *AAASS Newsletter* 11:4 (Winter 1971), 2. Almond and Laura Roselle, "Model Fitting in Communist Studies," in *Politics and the Soviet System: Essays in Honour of Frederick C. Barghoorn,* ed. Thomas F. Remington (London, 1989).
98. Robert F. Byrnes, "The Academic Job Market: Where Do We Go from Here?" *SR* 36:2 (June 1977), 286–291.
99. Elinor G. Barber and Warren Ilchman, *International Studies Review: A Staff Study* (New York, 1979), 35. James Millar, "Where Are the Young Specialists on the Soviet Economy, and What Are They Doing?" *Journal of Comparative Economics* 4 (1980), 317–329. By 1988, economists made up only 6% of the AAASS membership; Dorothy Atkinson, "Soviet and East European Studies in the United States," *SR* 47:3 (Autumn 1988), 404–405.
100. Walter D. Connor, "Soviet and East European Studies in the National Interest: Academia, Government, and Public," in *Foreign Area Research in the National Interest: American and Soviet Perspectives* (IREX Occasional Paper, no. 1:8, 1982), 13.

101. Jonathan R. Adelman, "A Profile of the Field of Soviet Politics; or, Who Will Study Stalin's Successors?" *PS* 16:1 (Winter 1983), 38–44.

102. Alex M. Shane, "The Slavic Workforce in the United States and Canada: Survey and Commentary," *SEEJ* 22:3 (Autumn 1978), 416–423.

CHAPTER 10

1. Calculated from searches in *Reader's Guide to Periodical Literature* (Minneapolis, 1901–), ProQuest Historical Newspapers (http://www.proquest.com/en-US/catalogs/databases/detail/pq-hist-news.shtml), and Hein On-Line Resources (http://heinonline.org). http://www.jstor.org.resources.library.brandeis.edu/ for JSTOR.

2. Brzezinski, cited in Patrick G. Vaughan, "Zbigniew Brzezinski: The Political and Academic Life of a Cold War Visionary" (Ph.D. diss., West Virginia University, 2003), 58, chap 2. According to Brzezinski, he was the most-published author in *Foreign Affairs* between 1960 and 2000; communication with Zbigniew Brzezinski (2004).

3. Shulman, *Beyond the Cold War* (New Haven, Conn., 1966). Dallin, "Russia as a Frustrated Superpower," *Washington Post*, 5 November 1967. Dallin, "Bias and Blunders in American Studies on the USSR," *SR* 32:2 (September 1973), 560–576. Marshall I. Goldman, *Détente and Dollars: Doing Business with the Soviets* (New York, 1975).

4. Pipes to Vishniak, 13 February 1946, Mark Vishniak Papers (Hoover Institution Archives), box 6.

5. Pipes to Karpovich, 10 June 1948, Michael Karpovich Papers (Bakhmeteff Archive, Columbia University), series I, box 2. Pipes memorandum (1948) in RRC Correspondence (Harvard University Archives), series UAV 759.10, box 10. Pipes, "The Genesis of Soviet National Policy" (Ph.D. diss., Harvard University, 1950). Pipes, *The Formation of the Soviet Union, 1917–1923: Communism and Nationalism* (Cambridge, Mass., 1954), 41, 49, 296. Pipes, *Vixi: Memoirs of a Non-Belonger* (New Haven, Conn., 2003), 73. For a typical review, see John Shelton Curtiss, review of *The Formation of the Soviet Union* by Richard Pipes, *ASEER* 14:3 (October 1955), 409–410. Helen W. Parsons to Abram Bergson, 20 July 1965, RRC Correspondence, series UAV 759.10, box 69.

6. Pipes, *Vixi*, 74. Pipes to Kluckhohn, 26 July 1951, RRC Correspondence, series UAV 759.10, box 13. Max Millikan to Kluckhohn, 18 June 1952, and Kluckhohn to Millikan, 24 April 1952—both in RRC Correspondence, series UAV 759.10, box 16. Millikan to Philip Mosely, 8 July 1952, Max Millikan Papers (MIT Archives), box 13. RRC Report to Dean Bundy, 14 October 1954, RRC Correspondence, series UAV 759.10, box 27. Gregory Mitrovich, *Undermining the Kremlin: America's Strategy to Subvert the Soviet Bloc, 1947–1956* (Ithaca, N.Y., 2000), 17–21.

7. Pipes, "Max Weber and Russia" (1955), in Pipes, *Russia Observed: Collected Essays on Russian and Soviet History* (Boulder, Colo., 1989), 173.

8. Marshall Shulman to Walter Stoessel, 6 October 1955, CCNY Records (Columbia University), 514:6. N. M. Karamzin, *Memoir on Ancient and Modern Russia:*

A Translation and Analysis, ed. Pipes (Cambridge, Mass., 1959). Pipes, "Karamzin's Conception of the Monarchy" (1957), in Pipes, *Russia Observed*, 54.

9. Pipes, *Vixi*, 90–91, 81. Martin Malia Oral History (Regional Oral History Office, Bancroft Library, University of California, Berkeley, 2005), 88–89. Riasanovsky to Karpovich, 26 April 1957, Karpovich Papers, series I, box 6.

10. Pipes to Struve, 17 July 1956, Gleb Struve Papers (Hoover Institution Archives), 34:4.

11. Pipes, foreword and "The Historical Evolution of the Russian Intelligentsia," both in *The Russian Intelligentsia*, ed. Pipes (New York, 1961 [1960]), [ii–iii], 57, 61.

12. Pipes, *Social Democracy and the St. Petersburg Labor Movement, 1885–1897* (Cambridge, Mass., 1963), xi, viii, 14, 119. Pipes, "*Narodnichestvo*: A Semantic Inquiry," *SR* 23:3 (September 1964), 441–458.

13. Pipes, *Vixi*, 89–90, 97, 98–99. Unpublished (and untitled) article for *Encounter* on his 1962 trip to USSR, in Richard E. Pipes Papers (Harvard University Archives), series HUG(FP) 98.45, 2:26.

14. Pipes to Mosely, 30 August 1968, in Mosely Papers, box 6. Pipes to Souvarine, 20 March 1968, in Boris Souvarine Papers (Houghton Library, Harvard University), folder 1022/5. Pipes to Souvarine, 8 February 1972, Souvarine Papers, folder 1022/6.

15. Pipes quoted in Israel Shenker, "Harvard Faculty Members Divided on Student Protests and Their Meaning," *NYT*, 25 April 1969. Pipes, *Vixi*, 107–111. Pipes, "Afterword," in J. H. Hexter and Richard Pipes, *Europe since 1500* (New York, 1971), 1110–1113. According to Pipes, the book's 1971 edition was a repackaging, not a revision, of the 1968 edition; Pipes, *Vixi*, 109, 104–106.

16. Ulam, *The New Face of Soviet Totalitarianism* (Cambridge, Mass., 1963). Ulam, *Understanding the Cold War: A Historian's Personal Reflections*, 2nd ed. (New Brunswick, N.J., 2002), 71, 114, 132.

17. Ulam, *The Fall of the American University* (New York, 1972), 75, 95, vii.

18. Andrew Brown, "Scourge and Poet," *Guardian*, 15 February 2003; George Walden, "History on His Side," *Telegraph*, 11 June 2005; Jim Hoagland, "Portrait of a Man Reading," *Washington Post*, 10 August 1969. Conquest, *Power and Policy in the USSR: The Struggle for Stalin's Succession, 1945–1960* (New York, 1967 [1960]), x, 3.

19. Conquest, "Introduction," in *New Lines*, ed. Conquest (London, 1956). Larkin letter to Conquest, quoted in Andrew Motion, *Philip Larkin: A Writer's Life* (New York, 1993), 265–266. Blake Morrison, *The Movement: English Poetry and Fiction of the 1950s* (Oxford, 1980), 91, 249–250. Amis, "Why Lucky Jim Turned Right" (1967), in Amis, *What Became of Jane Austen?* (London, 1970), 201. Amis suggested that Conquest stayed in government well after 1956; Amis, *Memoirs* (London, 1991), 146.

20. Conquest, *The Soviet Deportation of Nations* (London, 1960), xii.

21. Conquest, "In Defense of Kremlinology" (1962), in Conquest, *Tyrants and Typewriters: Communiqués from the Struggle for Truth* (Lexington, Mass., 1989), 161. Conquest, *Power and Policy*, 5–7. Tucker, review of *Power and Policy* by Robert Conquest, *RR* 21:2 (April 1962), 185–187. Conquest, *Common Sense about Russia* (New York, 1960), 175. Conquest, *Russia after Khrushchev* (New York, 1965), 260–264.

22. Conquest, *The Great Terror: Stalin's Purge of the 1930s* (New York, 1968), 535, 482, 565–571, 3, 26–27, 494–495. The text here adopts Conquest's singular

usage—purge—when explicating his views. Conquest relied heavily on *The Secret History of Stalin's Crimes* (New York, 1953), by Alexander Orlov, a former senior bureaucrat in the Soviet secret police who defected to the West in 1937.

23. Conquest, *Great Terror*, xi, 519–522. Kennan, "The Purges Unpurged," *NYT Book Review*, 27 October 1968. See the reviews of *The Great Terror*: Alec Nove, *Soviet Studies* 20:4 (April 1969), 536, 541; Alexander Rabinowitch, *Annals* 383 (May 1969), 178–179. Treadgold, *AHR* 74:5 (June 1969), 1670–1671.

24. Pipes, "Russia's Mission, America's Destiny: The Premises of US and Soviet Foreign Policy" (1970), in Pipes, *U.S.–Soviet Relations in the Era of Détente* (Boulder, Colo., 1981), 5, 6, 13, 16–17. Kennan to Pipes, 2 March 1970, George F. Kennan Papers (Mudd Library, Princeton University), 267:11. Pipes, *Vixi*, 130.

25. Martin Walker, "Dorothy Fosdick: Strategist of the Cold War," *Guardian*, 24 February 1997.

26. Robert G. Kaufman, *Henry M. Jackson: A Life in Politics* (Seattle, Wash., 2000), chap. 4.

27. The testimony, on 18 March 1970, was widely reprinted under different titles, including the colloquial and apt "Why the Russians Act like Russians." The version cited here is "A Historian's Reflections: Russian Foreign Policy," *Vital Speeches of the Day* 36:23 (15 September 1970), 729–732.

28. Jackson, "Internationally Recognized Human Rights" (11 February 1977), in *Henry M. Jackson and World Affairs: Selected Speeches, 1953–1983*, ed. Dorothy Fosdick (Seattle, Wash., 1990), 201. Similar wording appears in the recollection of Jackson's aide Charles Horner, who may well have drafted Jackson's speech: Horner, "Human Rights and the Jackson Amendment," in *Staying the Course: Henry M. Jackson and National Security*, ed. Dorothy Fosdick (Seattle, Wash., 1987), 115. Kaufman, *Henry M. Jackson*, 259–260. Conquest to Fosdick, 7 February 1972, and Conquest to Jackson, 23 July 1969, both in Henry M. Jackson Papers (University of Washington Archives), series 3560-06, 73:15.

29. Hearings on International Negotiation, U.S. Senate, Committee on Government Operations, Subcommittee on National Security and International Relations (91st Cong., 1st sess., 15 December 1969), 2–4. Jackson opening statement for Schapiro testimony, 16 April 1970, in Jackson Papers, series 3560-06, 83:31.

30. Ulam testimony to U.S. Senate Committee on Foreign Relations (93rd Cong, 2nd sess., 20 August 1974. Ulam, "Communist Doctrine and Soviet Diplomacy: Some Observations," memorandum prepared at the request of the U.S. Senate, Committee on Government Operations, Subcommittee on National Security and International Operations (Pursuant to S. Res. 24, 91st Cong.) (Washington, 1970).

31. Pipes, "Some Operational Principles of Soviet Foreign Policy" (1972), in Pipes, *U.S.–Soviet Relations*, 25, 31.

32. "America, Russia, and Europe in the Light of the Nixon Doctrine" (1973), in Pipes, *U.S.–Soviet Relations*, 52–53, 57. "Détente: An Evaluation," *Survey* 20:2–3 (Spring–Summer 1974), 1, 3, 27. Pipes, "Détente and Reciprocity," in *Détente*, ed. George R. Urban (London, 1976), 175–176, 180, 196.

33. Pipes, *Russia under the Old Regime* (New York, 1974), xxi, 78, 74.

34. Pipes, *Russia under the Old Regime*, 110, caption to image 34 (n.p.), 294, 293, 295, 298, 305, 313.

35. See the reviews of *Russia under the Old Regime*: Treadgold, *SR* 34:4 (December 1975), 812–814. Riasanovsky, *RR* 35:1 (January 1976), 103–104. Ulam, "Russia under the Old Regime," *NYT*, 13 July 1975; Dorothy Atkinson, *AHR* 81:2 (April 1976), 423–424. Pipes, "Response to Wladslaw G. Krasnow," *RR* 38:2 (April 1979), 192, 196.

36. Pipes, *Vixi*, 131, 106. Pipes, *U.S.–Soviet Relations*, 47. *Revolutionary Russia*, ed. Pipes (Cambridge, Mass., 1968).

37. Anne Hessing Cahn, *Killing Détente: The Right Attacks the CIA* (University Park, Pa., 1998), 89–90.

38. Strobe Talbott, *The Master of the Game: Paul Nitze and the Nuclear Peace* (New York, 1989), 111–114. Paul Nitze's handwritten notes (May 1969?) in Paul H. Nitze Papers (Library of Congress), 74:11. Ann Roll to OSD Security Office, 10 July 1969, in Nitze Papers, 74:9; Perle to Nitze, 17 June 1969, in Nitze Papers, 74:10. Kaufman, *Henry M. Jackson*, 210–214.

39. Perle to Jackson, 14 March 1974, Jackson Papers, series 3560-28, 1:10. Wohlstetter, "Is There a Strategic Arms Race?" *Foreign Policy* 15 (Summer 1974), 10, 13. John Prados, *The Soviet Estimate: U.S. Intelligence and Russian Military Threat* (New York, 1982), 192–199. "Wohlstetter, Soviet Strategic Forces, and National Intelligence Estimates" (1974?), Anne Cahn Collection (National Security Archive).

40. Hersh, "Huge CIA Operation Report[ed] in US against Anti-War Forces, Other Dissidents in the Nixon Years," *NYT*, 22 December 1974. A. J. Langguth, "Abolish the CIA!" *Newsweek* 85 (7 April 1975), 11.

41. George Anderson to Ford, 8 August 1975, cited in Cahn, *Killing Détente*, 115. "An Alternative NIE," 18 June 1975, and Fritz W. Ermath to Director of Strategic Research, 5 February 1976, both in Cahn Collection.

42. All quotations are from "Briefing to PFIAB on the Track Record Study" (28 April 1976), attachment A to Henson DeBruler, Memorandum for the Record, 28 April 1976, in Cahn Collection.

43. George A. Carver Jr. to E. Henry Knoche, Admiral Daniel Murphy, and Edward Proctor, 5 May 1976; Richard T. Boverie to Brent Scowcroft, 21 June 1976; Howard Stoertz Jr. to Robert W. Galvin, 23 December 1975—all in Cahn Collection.

44. For the sake of economy, the text below follows the general use of "Team B" to refer to the Soviet strategic objectives panel.

45. E. H. Knoche to Bush, 30 August 1976, and John A. Paisley to Knoche, 11 August 1976, both in Cahn Collection. For a full list, see "Intelligence Community Experiment in Competitive Analysis: Soviet Strategic Objectives, an Alternative View," U.S. National Archives, RG 263 (CIA), entry 23, box 1(hereafter Team B Report), 3. Jack Davis, "The Challenge of Managing Uncertainty: Paul Wolfowitz on Intelligence-Policy Relations," *Studies in Intelligence* 39:5 (1996), 36; Cahn, *Killing Détente*, 150.

46. Donald Suda notes on meetings of 9, 18, and 25 August 1976, all in Cahn Collection.

47. Pipes, "Team B: The Reality behind the Myth," *Commentary* 82:4 (October 1986), 32–34. Cahn, *Killing Détente*, 158. Richard Lehman, Memorandum for the Record,

5 November 1976, and Paisley to Lehman, 17 November 1976, both in Cahn Collection.

48. Pipes, "Team B." Nitze notes in Nitze Papers, 163:8.

49. Team B Report, 1, 2, 41, 42. Pipes drafted this section; see Donald Suda, notes on meeting, 26 August 1976, Cahn Collection.

50. Team B Report, 47; emphasis in original.

51. Pipes's draft recommendations (14 October 1976), in Nitze Papers, 163:8. Team B Report, 4.

52. Pipes, "Team B," 34. The drafts of NIE 11-3/8-76, which would be necessary to corroborate this claim, have not been declassified.

53. Prados, *Soviet Estimate*, 248–257. NIE 11-4-77, "Soviet Strategic Objectives" (12 January 1977), iii, DNSA document SE00503. NIE 11-3/8-76, "Soviet Forces for Intercontinental Conflict through the Mid-1980s" (21 December 1976), 1:16–24, DNSA document SE00502.

54. "Washington Whispers," *U.S. News and World Report* 81 (15 November 1976), 5; William Beecher, "Special Unit Analyzing U.S. Spy Data," *Boston Globe*, 20 October 1976. On Pipes, see Donald Suda, Memorandum for the Record, 7 December 1976, in Cahn Collection.

55. Binder, "New C.I.A. Estimate Finds Soviet Seeks Superiority in Arms," *NYT*, 26 December 1976; Pipes, *Vixi*, 138. Pipes, Memorandum for the Record, 22 December 1976, Cahn Collection.

56. NSC Minutes, 13 January 1977, available at www.fordlibrarymuseum.gov (accessed January 2007).

57. Pipes, "Team B," 39. Communication with Zbigniew Brzezinski (2004). Pipes, *Vixi*, 140. Robert C. Reich, "Re-examining the Team A–Team B Exercise," *International Journal of Intelligence and Counterintelligence* 3:3 (Fall 1988), 387–403.

58. See, for instance, the partisan report by a Senate group: "The National Intelligence Estimates A-B Team Episode Concerning Soviet Strategic Capability and Objectives," U.S. Congress, Senate, Report of the Senate Select Committee on Intelligence, Subcommittee on Collection, Production and Quality(Washington, 1978). Raymond L. Garthoff, "Estimating Soviet Military Intentions and Capabilities," in *Watching the Bear: Essays on the CIA's Analysis of the Soviet Union*, ed. Gerald K. Haines and Robert E. Leggett (Washington, D.C., 2001) (accessed online at http://www.cia.gov/library/. Matthew Evangelista, "Second-Guessing the Experts: Citizens' Group Criticism of the CIA's Estimates of Soviet Military Policy," *International History Review* 19:3 (August 1997), 583–589.

59. Pipes, *Vixi*, 140. *Alerting America*, ed. Charles Tyroler II (Washington, D.C., 1984), ix–xi.

60. Détente Assessment Committee press release, 7 April 1976, and Eugene V. Rostow to Dean Rusk and others, 19 March 1976—both in Raymond S. Cline Papers (Library of Congress), box 16. Nitze with Ann M. Smith and Steven L. Reardon, *From Hiroshima to Glasnost: At the Center of Decision* (New York, 1989), 350. Max M. Kampelman, introduction to Tyroler, *Alerting America*, xv. Pipes, *Vixi*, 141.

61. "What Is the Soviet Union Up To?" (4 April 1977), in Tyroler, *Alerting America*, 10–15. Pipes, "Why the Soviet Union Thinks It Can Fight and Win a Nuclear War," in Pipes, *U.S.–Soviet Relations*, 147–148. Original title in draft of article in Nitze Papers, 36:5. Pipes, "Soviet Global Strategy" (1980), in Pipes, *U.S.–Soviet Relations*, 172, 192; Pipes, "Militarism and the Soviet State" (1980), in Pipes, *U.S.–Soviet Relations*, 200–204.

62. Charles Tyroler II to Nitze, 19 September 1980, Nitze Papers, 144:2. Communication with Uri Ra'anan (2006). Pipes, letter to the editor, *Journal of Cold War Studies* 5:3 (Summer 2003), 161. National Security Study Directive 11-82, 21 August 1982, DNSA document PR01655. National Security Decision Directive 75 (17 January 1983), DNSA document PR01485. The "redirect" phrase is from a draft (16 December 1982), published in Norman A. Bailey, *The Strategic Plan That Won the Cold War: NSDD 75*, 2nd ed. (McLean, Va., 2000), 73.

63. Pipes, *Vixi*, 127n69.

64. Pipes, *Survival Is Not Enough: Soviet Realities and America's Future* (New York, 1984), 200.

CHAPTER 11

1. Communication with Stephen F. Cohen (2004). Robert C. Tucker, "The Dictator and Totalitarianism," *WP* 17:4 (July 1965), 564. Cohen, "Scholarly Missions: Sovietology as a Vocation," in Cohen, *Rethinking the Soviet Experience: Politics and History since 1917* (Oxford, 1985), 29–33.

2. Nicolaevsky, *Power and the Soviet Elite: "The Letter of an Old Bolshevik" and Other Essays*, ed. Janet Zagoria (New York, 1965). Cohen-Nicolaevsky correspondence of August 1965 in Boris I. Nicolaevsky Papers (Hoover Institution Archives), 476:34. Cohen, "The Real Bolshevist," *New York Review of Books* 9 (21 December 1967).

3. Stephen Frand Cohen, "Bukharin and Russian Bolshevism, 1888–1927" (Ph.D. diss., Columbia University, 1969), 3, 12, 622. Cohen, *Bukharin and the Bolshevik Revolution, 1888–1938* (New York, 1973), 386.

4. Cohen, *Bukharin*, xvii, 304–305, 381, 384–386, xvi.

5. Barghoorn, "Untangling the Party Lines," *Washington Post Book World*, 17 February 1974. Ulam, review of *Bukharin and the Bolshevik Revolution* by Stephen Cohen, *AHR* 80:2 (April 1975), 440–442.

6. Schapiro, "Bukharin's Way," *New York Review of Books* 21:1 (7 February 1974). Graham, review of *Bukharin and the Bolshevik Revolution* by Stephen Cohen, *RR* 33:3 (July 1974), 324–326; Juviler, review of *Bukharin and the Bolshevik Revolution* by Stephen Cohen, *PSQ* 89:4 (Winter 1974–1975), 892–894. Graham to Angus Cameron, 2 July 1969, A. A. Knopf Papers (Harry Ransome Center, University of Texas, Austin), 756:5. Carr, "The Legend of Bukharin," *TLS*, 20 September 1974, 329–330.

7. Cohen, "Stalin's Revolution Reconsidered," *SR* 32:2 (June 1973), 264–270; Cohen, "Politics and the Past: The Importance of Being Historical," *Soviet Studies* 29:1 (January 1977), 137–145.

8. Cohen, "Politics and the Past," 138n3.

9. Cohen, "Bolshevism and Stalinism," in *Stalinism: Essays in Historical Interpretation*, ed. Robert C. Tucker (New York, 1977), 4.

10. Cohen, "Bolshevism and Stalinism," 5–6. The quotation from Leon Trotsky, "Stalinism and Bolshevism" (1937), is a fuller version than the one in Cohen's text.

11. William E. Odom, "Bolshevik Politics and the Dustbin of History," *Studies in Comparative Communism* 9:1–2 (Spring–Summer 1976), 196.

12. Cohen, "Common and Uncommon Sense about the Soviet Union and American Policy," testimony in U.S. Congress, House of Representatives, Committee on International Relations, Subcommittee on Europe and the Middle East, *The Soviet Union: Internal Dynamics of Foreign Policy, Present and Future* (95th Cong., 1st sess., 27 September–26 October 1977), 199–200, 211, 197, 202.

13. On Cohen's work in Moscow, see Valerii Pisigin, "V poiskakh russkoi al'ternativy," in *Stiven Koen i Sovetskii Soiuz/Rossiia*, ed. Gennadii Bordiugov and Leonid Dobrokhotov (Moscow, 2008), 24–26.

14. Cohen, "Friends and Foes of Change: Reformism and Conservatism in the Soviet Union," *SR* 38:2 (June 1979), 187–202, and his response to commentaries in the same issue of the journal, Cohen, "What Is Fundamental," 220–223.

15. Paul Bushkovitch, "Moshe Lewin" (from 1982 interview), in Middle Atlantic Radical Historians' Association, *Visions of History* (New York, 1984), 285, 286. Lewin, "Basile Kerblay and His Scholarship: Selected Probes," *Cahiers du monde russe* 45:3–4 (July–December 2004), 379–384.

16. Bushkovitch, "Moshe Lewin," 290–291.

17. Lewin, *Russian Peasants and Soviet Power* (New York, 1975 [1968]), 21–22.

18. Lewin, *Russian Peasants*, 146, 15, 335, 482, 509, 244 (italics in original).

19. Lewin, *Russian Peasants*, 12, 335.

20. Lewin, *Lenin's Last Struggle* (New York, 1968), 80.

21. Lewin, *Political Undercurrents in Soviet Economic Debates: From Bukharin to the Modern Reformers* (Princeton, 1974).

22. [Carr,] "The Death of Vladimir Ilyich," *TLS*, 18 December 1969, 1453. Sidney Monas, *Soviet Studies* 22:3 (January 1971), 448–450; Stanley L. Page, *AHR* 74:5 (June 1969), 1668–1669; Carr, *English Historical Review* 85:335 (April 1970), 442.

23. See the reviews of *Russian Peasants and Soviet Power:* Jerzy F. Karcz, *Journal of Economic Literature* 7:3 (September 1969), 821–823. [Ivarch McDonald,] "Costs of Collectivization," *TLS*, 10 October 1968, 1156. Allan B. Ballard, *Problems of Communism* 17:2 (March–April 1968), 67–68.

24. Herbert J. Ellison, review of *Russian Peasants and Soviet Power* by Moshe Lewin *SR* 31:2 (June 1972), 429–431; Nicolas Spulber, review of *Russian Peasants and Soviet Power* by Moshe Lewin, *AHR* 81:3 (June 1976), 637. Gregory Grossman, *Journal of Economic Literature* 14:3 (September 1976), 913–915. Steven Rosefielde, "Moshe Lewin's Interpretation of the Industrialization Debates, 1921–1929, and the Postwar Literature on Economic Reform," *RR* 34:4 (October 1975), 489–497.

25. Cohen, "Politics and the Past." Carr, "The Legacy of Stalin," *TLS*, 23 January 1976, 89.

26. Fitzpatrick, *The Cultural Front: Power and Culture in Revolutionary Russia* (Ithaca, N.Y., 1992), xii.

27. Don Watson, *Brian Fitzpatrick: A Radical Life* (Sydney, Australia, 1979), xvii–xviii. Sheila Fitzpatrick, "My Father's Daughter," in *Against the Grain: Brian Fitzpatrick and Manning Clark in Australian History,* ed. Sheila Fitzpatrick and Stuart Mcintyre (Melbourne, Australia, 2007). Fitzpatrick, *Cultural Front,* xi. "Interview with Sheila Fitzpatrick," *Kritika* 8:3 (Fall 2007), 480–481.

28. Vera S. Dunham, "Max Hayward, 1924–1979," *SR* 38:3 (September 1979), 548–549 (quoting Patricia Blake).

29. "Interview with Sheila Fitzpatrick," 481.

30. Sheila Fitzpatrick, "A Student in Moscow, 1966," *Wilson Quarterly* 6:3 (Summer 1982), 134–135, 137–140. "Interview with Sheila Fitzpatrick," 481–482.

31. Fitzpatrick, *The Commissariat of Enlightenment: Soviet Organization of Education and the Arts under Lunacharsky, 1917–1921* (Cambridge, 1970), xi, xv–xvi, 288–290.

32. Tim Dymond, "Social and Subjective: Soviet History after the Cold War: An Interview with Sheila Fitzpatrick," *Limina* 8 (2002), 43.

33. See reviews of *Commissariat of Enlightenment:* Loren Graham, *PSQ* 88:1 (March 1973), 137–138; Gail Lapidus, *APSR* 67:2 (June 1973), 658–659. Communication with Sheila Fitzpatrick (2004).

34. Fitzpatrick, *Cultural Front,* xii.

35. Fitzpatrick, "Cultural Revolution in Russia, 1928–1932," *JCH* 9:1 (January 1974), 37, 50–51, 35–36, 49, 51–52, 36.

36. Fitzpatrick, "Cultural Revolution Revisited," *RR* 58:2 (April 1999), 202–203, 205.

37. *Cultural Revolution in Russia, 1928–1931,* ed. Sheila Fitzpatrick (Bloomington, Ind., 1978), v–vii. David Joravsky's article on psychology demurred from the "cultural revolution" framework. Hough recollections (2008) on Sheila Fitzpatrick in author's possession. Communication with Sheila Fitzpatrick (2004).

38. Lewin, "Society, State, and Ideology during the First Five-Year Plan," in Fitzpatrick, *Cultural Revolution,* 49, 55. Lewin uses the English term "ruralization" but provides the Russian word *okrest'ianivanie,* with the root *krest'ian,* or peasant. Hough, "The Cultural Revolution and Western Understanding of the Soviet Union," in Fitzpatrick, *Cultural Revolution,* 246–247.

39. Michael David-Fox offers a thoughtful retrospective on the concept in "What Is Cultural Revolution?" *RR* 58:2 (April 1999), 181–201.

40. Compare Fitzpatrick, "Cultural Revolution," *JCH,* 37, to Fitzpatrick, "Cultural Revolution as Class War," in Fitzpatrick, *Cultural Revolution,* 34–35.

41. Nicholas S. Timasheff, *The Great Retreat: The Growth and Retreat of Communism in Russia* (New York, 1946).

42. Jerry Hough, "Political Participation," in Hough, *The Soviet Union and Social Science Theory* (Cambridge, Mass., 1977). It was not Hough but Fitzpatrick who made the only direct reference to the "Brezhnev generation" in *Cultural Revolution;* see Fitzpatrick, "Cultural Revolution as Class War," 39–40.

43. Fitzpatrick, "Cultural Revolution Revisited," 205. R. W. Davies, review of *Cultural Revolution in Russia* edited by Sheila Fitzpatrick, *Soviet Studies* 31:2 (April 1979), 300–303.

44. James C. McClelland, review of *Cultural Revolution in Russia* edited by Sheila Fitzpatrick, *AHR* 84:2 (April 1979), 507–508. Fitzpatrick, "Cultural Revolution Revisited," 203.

45. Fitzpatrick, *Cultural Front,* xii. Communication with Sheila Fitzpatrick (2004).

46. Fitzpatrick, *Education and Social Mobility in the Soviet Union, 1921–1934* (Cambridge, 1979), 14, 158, 253.

47. See reviews of *Education and Social Mobility:* Wayne Vucinich, *Annals* 455 (May 1981), 188–189; Robert C. Williams, *SR* 39:3 (September 1980), 500–501.

48. Bailes review of *Education and Social Mobility* by Sheila Fitzpatrick,, *RR* 39:4 (October 1980), 504–506. James McClelland makes a similar point in his review of Bailes's book *Technology and Society under Lenin and Stalin: Origins of the Soviet Technical Intelligentsia, 1917–1941* (Princeton, 1978); McClelland, "What Made Stalinism Work?" *History of Education Quarterly* 24:3 (Autumn 1984), 450.

49. Fitzpatrick, *Education and Social Mobility,* 244–249, 254.

50. Leopol'd Khaimson [Leopold Haimson], "O vremeni i o sebe," *Otechestvennaia istoriia,* 2005#6, 194–195.

51. Communication with Jerry Hough (2008). Hough, *The Soviet Prefects: The Local Party Organs in Industrial Decision-Making* (Cambridge, Mass., 1969).

52. RRC Executive Committee Meeting, 8 August 1978, RRC Executive Committee Minutes (Harvard University Archives), series UAV 759.5, box 3.

53. RRC Executive Committee minutes, 8 August 1978; Bergson, in memo of conversation with Pipes, 15 August 1978; Keenan, in minutes, 8 August 1978; Bergson and Fanger, in memo of conversation, 15 August 1978; press view in minutes, 18 August 1978; Bergson-Pipes conversation, 15 August 1978; Pipes, in minutes, 8 August 1978—all in RRC Executive Committee, series UAV 759.5, box 3.

54. Fainsod to A. Lejard, 25 March 1955, and related correspondence, Boris Souvarine Papers (Houghton Library, Harvard University), folders 2202–2204. The French *gouvernée* encompasses a range of meanings, including both "ruled" and "governed."

55. Jerry F. Hough and Merle Fainsod, *How the Soviet Union Is Governed* (Cambridge, Mass., 1979), 570. Bergson-Pipes conversation, 15 August 1978, RRC Executive Committee, UAV 759.5, box 3.

56. Fainsod, *How Russia Is Ruled* (Cambridge, Mass., 1953), 500. Fainsod, *How Russia Is Ruled,* 2nd edition (Cambridge, Mass., 1963), 462, 583, 591–592, 601.

57. Hough and Fainsod, *How the Soviet Union Is Governed,* 176–177.

58. Hough and Fainsod, *How the Soviet Union Is Governed,* 512–513, 655nn65–66.

59. Dahl, *Who Governs? Democracy and Power in an American City* (New Haven, Conn., 1961). Hough, "Political Participation," 121–123. Hough and Fainsod, *How the Soviet Union Is Governed,* 513.

60. Pipes, "Revisionist Revision," *Commentary* 68:4 (October 1979), 87–88. Robert C. Daniels, review of *How the Soviet Union Is Governed* by Jerry Hough and Merle Fainsod, *New Republic* 181 (25 August 1979), 31–33.

61. Archie Brown, "The Soviet Union," *TLS,* 25 January 1980. See also academic reviews of *How the Soviet Union Is Governed:* Robert J. Osborn, *RR* 38:4 (October 1979), 466–468. William Zimmerman, *SR* 39:3 (September 1980), 482–486; John

C. Campbell, *FA* 57:4 (Summer 1979); Holland Hunter, *Annals* 453 (January 1981), 279–280.

62. Fitzpatrick, "Cultural Revolution Revisited," 205.

63. Fitzpatrick, *The Russian Revolution* (Oxford, 1982), 8, 153–154, 4–5, 9, 6. This question would eventually lead Fitzpatrick to write "Ascribing Class: The Construction of Social Identity in Soviet Russia," *Journal of Modern History* 65:4 (December 1993), 745–770.

64. Diane Koenker, review of *The Russian Revolution* by Sheila Fitzpatrick, *Journal of Modern History* 58:4 (December 1986), 1000–1001. Schapiro, "Upward Mobility and Its Price," *TLS*, 18 March 1983. Wildman, review of *The Russian Revolution* by Sheila Fitzpatrick, *SR* 43:2 (Summer 1984), 309–311.

65. Anders Jaroslaw, review of *The Russian Revolution* by Sheila Fitzpatrick, *Newsweek*, 16 May 1983.

66. Fitzpatrick, "New Perspectives on Stalinism," *RR* 45:4 (October 1986), 357–358. Fitzpatrick, "Afterword: Revisionism Revisited," *RR* 45:4 (October 1986), 409.

67. Getty, *The Origins of the Great Purges: The Soviet Communist Party Revisited, 1933–1938* (Cambridge, 1985), vii. Roberta T. Manning, "Government in the Soviet Countryside in the Stalinist Thirties: The Case of Belyi Raion in 1937" (Carl Beck Papers in Russian and East European Studies, no. 301, 1984). Lynne Viola, *Best Sons of the Fatherland: Workers in the Vanguard of Soviet Collectivization* (Oxford, 1987); Hiroaki Kuromiya, *Stalin's Industrial Revolution: Politics and Workers, 1928–1932* (Cambridge, 1988). Rittersporn, "The State against Itself: Socialist Tensions and Policy Conflict in the USSR, 1936–1938," *Telos* 41 (1979), 87–104.

68. Roberta Thompson Manning, "Adventures in the Smolensk Archives: Confessions of an American Sovietologist," in *Vozrashchenie "Smolenskogo Arkhiva"* (Moscow, 2005).

69. Fitzpatrick, "Revisionism in Retrospect: A Personal View," *SR* 67:3 (Fall 2008), 690. Fitzpatrick, "New Perspectives," 357–358, 368, 371, 373. Fitzpatrick, "Revisionism Revisited," 409.

70. Cohen, "Stalin's Terror as Social History," *RR* 45:4 (October 1986), 376–377, 384. Eley, "History with the Politics Left Out-Again?" *RR* 45:4 (October 1986), 385–394. Meyer, "Coming to Terms with the Past … and One's Older Colleagues," *RR* 45:4 (October 1986), 406–407. Kenez, "Stalinism as Humdrum Politics," *RR* 45:4 (October 1986), 399–400, 396.

71. Getty, "State, Society, and Superstition," *RR* 46:4 (October 1987), 393–394; Manning, "State and Society in Stalinist Russia," *RR* 46:4 (October 1987), 410–411; Kuromiya, "Stalinism and Historical Research," *RR* 46:4 (October 1987), 406. [Daniel Field,] "From the Editor," *RR* 46:4 (October 1987), 375.

72. Jane Burbank, "Controversies over Stalinism: Searching for Soviet Society," *Politics and Society* 19:3 (1991), 325.

73. Viola, "In Search of Young Revisionists," *RR* 46:4 (October 1987), 430–431. Chase, "Social History and Revisionism of the Stalinist Era," *RR* 46:4 (October 1987), 382.

74. Hough, "The 'Dark Forces,' the Totalitarian Model, and Soviet History," *RR* 46:4 (October 1987), 397; Tucker, "The Stalin Period as a Historical Problem," *RR* 46:4 (October 1987), 424.

75. Conquest, "Revisionizing Stalin's Russia," *RR* 46:4 (October 1987), 386–390.

76. Rittersporn, "History, Commemoration and Hectoring Rhetoric," *RR* 46:4 (October 1987), 422.

CHAPTER 12

1. Robert Wesson, "Decadent Scholarship," *NYT,* 25 October 1982.

2. Odd Arne Westad, "The Fall of Détente and the Turning Tides of History," in *The Fall of Détente: Soviet-American Relations during the Carter Years,* ed. Westad (Oslo, 1997), 10–11.

3. Cohen, "Soviet Domestic and Foreign Policy," in *Common Sense in U.S.–Soviet Relations,* ed. Carl Marcy (Washington, D.C., 1978), 19.

4. Cohen, *Rethinking the Soviet Experience: Politics and History since 1917* (Oxford, 1985), 157. Cohen, *Sovieticus: American Perceptions and Soviet Realities* (New York, 1985). Richard Pipes, "U.S. and Them," *New Republic* 193 (14 October 1985), 32–34. Suny, "The Evil Empire Revisited," *Michigan Quarterly Review* 28 (Fall 1989), 591, 598.

5. Communication with Jerry Hough (2008).

6. See, for instance, Hoffmann, "Social Science and Soviet Administrative Behavior," *WP* 24:3 (April 1972), 444–471.

7. Mark A. Uhlig, "A Refugee, Then a Defector," *NYT,* 27 July 1986. Bialer, *Stalin's Successors: Leaders, Stability, and Change in the Soviet Union* (Cambridge, 1980), 305. He is still the only American Russia/Soviet expert to have won the fellowship.

8. Martin Malia, *Alexander Herzen and the Birth of Russian Socialism* (Cambridge, Mass., 1961). Martin Malia Oral History (Regional Oral History Office, Bancroft Library, University of California, Berkeley, 2003), 39.

9. Malia Oral History, 106–112. François Furet, *The Passing of an Illusion: The Idea of Communism in the Twentieth Century,* trans. Deborah Furet (Chicago, 1999), 415–421.

10. Berlin to Andrzej Walicki, 7 September 1964 and 22 October 1969, both in Walicki, "Isaiah Berlin as I Knew Him," *Dialogue and Universalism* 15:9–10 (September–October 2005), 70, 76. Malia Oral History, 168–171, 130, 185.

11. For the sake of variation, this chapter will use terms like "the late 1980s," "the Gorbachev era," and "*perestroika*" as synonyms, though of course the era lasted until 1991, there were other players besides Gorbachev, and *perestroika* was only part of his reform effort.

12. Daniel L. Bond and Herbert S. Levine, "An Overview," in *The Soviet Economy: Toward the Year 2000,* ed. Abram Bergson and Levine (London, 1985), 21.

13. Pipes, *Survival Is Not Enough: Soviet Realities and America's Future* (New York, 1986 [1984]), 200.

14. Pipes, "Can the Soviet Union Reform?" *FA* 63 (Fall 1984), 53–54, 56.

15. Marshall I. Goldman, *The USSR in Crisis: The Failure of an Economic System* (New York, 1983), xii, 182, 123–124. Goldman, "Academic Infallibility: Who Dares to Check?" *Harvard International Review* 27:3 (Fall 2005), online at www.harvardir.

org/articles/1422 (accessed May 2008). Goldman, "Why an Embargo Might Backfire," *NYT,* 21 August 1983. See reviews of *USSR in Crisis:* Chilton Williamson, *National Review* 35 (22 July 1983), 889. Gregory Grossman, *Fortune* 107 (27 June 1983), 145–147.

16. Edward A. Hewett, "Tinkering with the Soviet Economy," *NYT Book Review,* 10 July 1983. Besançon, "The 'Crisis' in the Soviet Union," *Atlanta Daily World,* 14 July 1983.

17. Robert F. Byrnes, preface to *After Brezhnev: Sources of Soviet Conduct in the 1980s,* ed. Byrnes (Bloomington, Ind., 1983), xvii. Erik P. Hoffmann, "Soviet Politics in the 1980s," in *The Soviet Union in the 1980s,* ed. Hoffmann (New York, 1984), 227. Bialer, *Stalin's Successors,* 283–285.

18. Hough, *The Soviet Leadership in Transition* (Washington, D.C., 1980). Cohen, "Mikhail Gorbachev: Best Bet for Reform in the Kremlin," *LAT,* 11 November 1984.

19. Variants of the social contract thesis, promulgated by George Breslauer, Gail Warshofsky Lapidus, Walter Conner, Seweryn Bialer, and others, were common in the early 1980s. See a summary and citations in Linda J. Cook, *The Soviet Social Contract and Why It Failed: Welfare Policy and Workers' Politics from Brezhnev to Yeltsin* (Cambridge, Mass., 1993), chap. 1.

20. Colton, *The Dilemma of Reform in the Soviet Union* (New York, 1984), 36, 62, 65–66, 41.

21. See the updates in Colton, *Dilemma of Reform in the Soviet Union,* 2nd edition (New York, 1986).

22. Brown, "Can Gorbachev Make a Difference?" *Détente* 3 (May 1985), 7. Brown, "Gorbachev: New Man in the Kremlin," *Problems of Communism* 34:3 (May–June 1985), 6.

23. Cohen, "The Friends and Foes of Change: Reformism and Conservatism in the Soviet Union," *SR* 38:2 (June 1979), 187–202. Cohen, "Mikhail Gorbachev: Best Bet for Reform in the Kremlin," *LAT,* 11 November 1984.

24. Pipes, "U.S. and Them," 34.

25. Bialer, "The Rise of a Red Star," *Washington Post,* 17 March 1985. Bialer, "Will Russia Dare Clean Up Its Economic Mess?" *Washington Post,* 21 April 1985. Bialer, *The Soviet Paradox: External Expansion, Internal Decline* (New York, 1986), 124–125, 171, 148, 125, 376.

26. Bialer, "Soviet-American Conflict: From the Past to the Future," in Center for National Policy, *U.S.–Soviet Relations: Perspectives for the Future* (Washington, D.C., 1984), 21. Bialer, *Soviet Paradox,* 353–354.

27. See reviews of *The Soviet Paradox:* Kristol, "What Every Soviet Leader Wants," *Fortune* 114 (1 September 1986), 119–120. Gustafson, *New Republic* 195 (25 August 1986), 29–32. Kenez, *New Leader* 69 (7–21 April 1986), 18–19.

28. Hough, "Give Him Six Months," *NYT,* 21 March 1985. Hough, *Soviet Leadership in Transition,* esp. chap. 3.

29. Goldman, "Will Gorbachev Be Brezhnev II?" *NYT,* 12 March 1985. Pipes, "Afterword, May 1985," in Pipes, *Survival Is Not Enough,* 283. On essentialist views,

see Alexander Dallin, "Causes of the Collapse of the USSR," *Post-Soviet Affairs* 8:4 (1992), 279–302.

30. William Odom, "How Far Can Soviet Reform Go?" *Problems of Communism* 35:6 (November–December 1987), 18–33.

31. "What's Happening in Moscow?" *National Interest* 8 (Summer 1987), 4 (Conquest), 11–12 (Ulam), 26 (Reddaway), 27–28 (Besançon and Françoise Thom).

32. Hough, "Gorbachev Isn't Khrushchev," *Washington Post,* 22 February 1987. Hough, "The Gorbachev Reform: A Maximal Case," *Soviet Economy* 2:4 (October–December 1996), 304.

33. Bialer, "Gorbachev's Move," in *Gorbachev: The Debate,* ed. Ferenc Fehér and Andrew Arato (Atlantic Highlands, N.J., 1989), 60.

34. Hough, "Gorbachev Consolidating Power," *Problems of Communism* 36:4 (July–August 1978), 43, 40.

35. Moshe Lewin, *The Gorbachev Phenomenon: A Historical Interpretation* (Berkeley, 1991), 145–146, 153.

36. Von Laue, *Why Lenin? Why Stalin? A Reappraisal of the Russian Revolution, 1900–1930* (Philadelphia, 1964). Von Laue, *Why Lenin? Why Stalin? Why Gorbachev? The Rise and Fall of the Soviet System* (New York, 1993).

37. Pipes, "Where's the Glasnost?" *Wall Street Journal,* 1 December 1987.

38. [Pipes, chair, Task Force on the Dangers of Détente II,] *Gorbachev's Challenge: Détente II* (Washington, D.C., 1988), 4, 82, ii. Pipes, task force chair, "U.S.–Soviet Relations," in *Mandate for Leadership,* vol. 3: *Policy Strategies for the 1990s,* ed. Charles L. Heatherly and Burton Yale Pines (Washington, D.C., 1989); Pipes, "Paper Perestroika: Gorbachev and American Strategy," [Heritage Foundation] *Policy Review* 47 (Winter 1989), 15.

39. "Perestroika," *Princeton Alumni Weekly,* 9 December 1987, 21–27.

40. Brzezinski, "Summit Score: Reagan 3, Gorbachev 1," *Wall Street Journal,* 15 December 1987. Brzezinski, *Game Plan: A Geostrategic Framework for the Conduct of the U.S.–Soviet Conflict* (Boston, 1986), 245–247.

41. Brzezinski, *Game Plan,* 99.

42. Hough, *Russia and the West: Gorbachev and the Politics of Reform* (New York, 1988), 8, chap. 10.

43. Cohen, "Sovieticus," *Nation* 244 (13 June 1987), 789. Hough, *Russia and the West,* 243, 245.

44. Goldman, "Gorbachev the Economist," *FA* 69:2 (Spring 1990), 44.

45. Bialer, "Gorbachev's Program of Change: Sources, Significance, Prospects," *PSQ* 103:3 (Autumn 1988), 417. Pipes, "Russia's Shuddering Empire," *New Republic* 201 (6 November 1989), 55.

46. Malia Oral History, 192–193. "Z" [Malia], "To the Stalin Mausoleum," *Daedalus* 119:1 (1990), 333. A version appeared as "The Soviets' Terminal Crisis," *NYT,* 4 January 1990.

47. [Malia], "Stalin Mausoleum," 296, 298.

48. [Malia], "Stalin Mausoleum," 298. Malia, *The Soviet Tragedy: A History of Socialism in Russia, 1917–1991* (New York, 1994), 496.

49. Malia, "A Manifesto for Soviet Democracy," *New York Review of Books*, 29 March 1990; Malia, "A New Russian Revolution?" *New York Review of Books*, 18 July 1991.
50. [Malia], "Stalin Mausoleum," 322–325, 337, 340. Malia Oral History, 194. Malia, "The Soviet Union Has Ceased to Exist," *NYT*, 31 August 1990.
51. Pipes, "What Is to Be Done?" *National Review* 41:10 (2 June 1989), 42. Pipes, "The Soviet Union Adrift," *FA* 70:1 (1990), 86, 73. Ulam, "The Fatal Shore," *New Republic* 204 (4 February 1991), 24.
52. Cohen, "Moscow Intellectuals Are Wrong," *NYT*, 11 March 1991. Hough, "Gorbachev's Politics," *FA* 68:5 (Winter 1989–1990), 38, 27, 35. Hough, "Understanding Gorbachev: The Importance of Politics," *Soviet Economy* 7:2 (April–June 1991), 107–108.
53. Malia, "The August Revolution," *New York Review of Books*, 26 September 1991.
54. Malia, "From under the Rubble, What?" *Problems of Communism* 41:1–2 (January–April 1992), 93, 105. Malia, "A Fatal Logic," *National Interest* 31 (Spring 1993), 84–85.
55. Amalrik, *Will the Soviet Union Survive until 1984?* (New York, 1970).
56. Conquest, "Academe and the Soviet Myth," *National Interest* 31 (Spring 1993), 95, 94, 96. Pipes, "1917 and the Revisionists," *National Interest* 31 (Spring 1993), 12.
57. Malia, "A Fatal Logic," 84.
58. Malia, "From under the Rubble," 105, 101, 104.
59. Odom, "The Pluralist Mirage," *National Interest* 31 (Spring 1993), 100, 104–105. Rutland, "Sovietology: Notes for a Post-Mortem," *National Interest* 31 (Spring 1993), 112, 121.
60. Dallin, "Causes of the Collapse of the USSR," 673–674, 687, 689. Dallin, "The Uses and Abuses of Russian History," in *Post-Communist Studies and Political Science: Methodology and Empirical Theory in Sovietology*, ed. Frederic J. Fleron Jr. and Erik P. Hoffmann (Boulder, Colo., 1993), 131–132.
61. Cohen, "America's Failed Crusade in Russia," *Nation* 258 (28 February 1994), 261–263. Cohen, *Failed Crusade: America and the Tragedy of Post-Communist Russia* (New York, 2001 [2000]).
62. Cohen, "Russian Studies without Russia," *Post-Soviet Affairs* 15:1 (January–March 1999), 39, 53; Cohen, *Failed Crusade*, 21, 26, 23, 67.
63. Cohen, "Scholarly Missions: Sovietology as a Vocation," in Cohen, *Rethinking the Soviet Experience*, 11, 9, 15, 4, 22, 24, 25, 28, 170n105.
64. Breslauer, "In Defense of Sovietology," *Post-Soviet Affairs* 8:3 (July–September 1992), 230, 220.
65. Fleron and Hoffmann, "Sovietology and Perestroika: Methodology and Lessons from the Past," *Harriman Institute Forum* 5:1 (September 1991), 5, 6–8, 2.
66. Willard C. Mathias, *America's Strategic Blunders: Intelligence Analysis and National Security Policy, 1936–1991* (University Park, Pa., 2001), chaps. 8, 15. James Millar et al., "An Evaluation of the CIA's Analysis of Soviet Economic Performance, 1970–1990," *Comparative Economic Studies* 35:2 (Summer 1993), 33–57.
67. Cohen, "Russian Studies without Russia"; Fish, "Russian Studies without Studying," *Post-Soviet Affairs* 17:4 (October–December 2001), 332–373. Cohen, "Comment on Fish," *Post-Soviet Affairs* 17:4 (October–December 2001), 375; Fish, "Reply to Cohen," *Post-Soviet Affairs* 17:4 (October–December 2001), 377.

68. Pipes, "East Is East," *New Republic* 220 (26 April–3 May 1999), 100–108. Malia, "Communist Destiny," and Pipes, "Reply," *New Republic* 220 (7 June 1999), 4–5.

69. Alice Gomstyn, "Where the Cold War Still Rages," *Chronicle of Higher Education* 50 (6 February 2004), A12–14.

EPILOGUE

1. Katherine Verdery, "What's in a Name and Should We Change Ours?" *AAASS NewsNet* 46:2 (March 2006), 1–4. As of July 2010, the organization will become the Association for Slavic, East European, and Eurasian Studies.

2. Robert Huber is planning a series of essays on the history of the major Russian Studies organizations of the 1990s; so far, only one has appeared: Huber, *A History of the American Councils for International Education* (Carl Beck Papers in Russian and East European Studies, no. 1703, 2004).

3. Mark von Hagen, "Empires, Borderlands, and Diasporas: Eurasianism as Anti-Paradigm for the Post-Soviet Era," *AHR* 109:2 (April 2004), 445–468; Stephen Kotkin, "Mongol Commonwealth? Exchange and Governance across the Post-Mongol Space," *Kritika* 8:3 (Summer 2007), 487–531.

4. For a twenty-first-century call for Russian Studies as essential to the national interest, see Stephen E. Hanson and Blair A. Ruble, "Rebuilding Russian Studies," *Problems of Post-Communism* 52:3 (May–June 2005), 49–57.

5. Marshall D. Shulman, "The Future of Soviet Studies in the United States," *SR* 29:3 (September 1970), 582–588.

6. Pio D. Uliassi, "Government-Sponsored Research on International and Foreign Affairs," in *The Use and Abuse of Social Science: Behavioral Science and National Policy-Making,* ed. Irving Louis Horowitz (New Brunswick, N.J., 1971).

7. For a heated attack on this change from the Russian Studies perspective, see Robert T. Huber, Blair A. Ruble, and Peter J. Stavrakis, "Post-Cold War 'International' Scholarship: A Brave New World or a Triumph of Form over Substance?" *SSRC Items* 49:1 (March 1995), 30–35.

8. For one of many excellent overviews and agendas, see Julie A. Buckler, "What Comes after Post-Soviet in Russian Studies?" *PMLA* 124:1 (January 2009).

9. Mark von Hagen, "The Archival Gold Rush and Historical Agendas in the Post-Soviet Era," *SR* 52:1 (Spring 1993), 96–100.

10. Suny, *The Revenge of the Past: Nationalism, Revolution, and the Collapse of the Soviet Union* (Stanford, 1993). The recent literature on nationality, empire, and border-lands is too large to cite here.

11. James Allen Smith, *The Idea Brokers: Think Tanks and the Rise of the New Policy Elite* (New York, 1991).

12. Beissinger, "Political Science and the Future of Russian/Post-Soviet Studies" (paper presented at Davis Center, Harvard University, December 2008).

13. Francis Fukuyama blames the rise of the disciplines for this circumstance—Fukuyama, "How Academia Failed the Nation," *SAISphere* 2004 (http://www.sais-jhu.edu/pressroom/publications/saisphere/2004/fukuyama.htm, accessed April 2009).

14. Thanks to a new federal role for education, the new initiative did devote more energy than did the JCSS Review Committee (1957–1958) to encourage language study in primary and secondary schools. See http://www.ed.gov/about/inits/ed/competitiveness/nsli/index.html (accessed February 2009).

15. An SSRC symposium includes a number of mostly skeptical views of Minerva: http://www.ssrc.org/essays/minerva (accessed January 2009).

16. Senator John McClellan (D-AR) quoted in John Kelso, "Harvard Study of Russia Called 'Insane': Costs U.S. $450,000," *Boston Post*, 28 September 1953.

ACKNOWLEDGMENTS

It is both a great pleasure and a great relief to write these acknowledgments—a pleasure to thank, in print, the many people who have helped this book to get finished and get better. And a relief that the project, which felt so unmanageable for so long, is at last completed.

Since the relationship of funding and scholarship is a central theme of *Know Your Enemy,* it seems only fair to start by acknowledging the significant financial assistance that was indispensable to it. Research leaves supported by the Radcliffe Institute for Advanced Study and the National Endowment for the Humanities were most important in providing time to research and write; thanks to my departmental colleagues and to Dean Adam Jaffe at Brandeis for accommodating these leaves and making it possible for me to take full advantage of these fellowships. Research grants from the Gilder-Lehrman Institute, the Kennan Institute, the Rockefeller Archive Center, and—most important—Brandeis's Norman and Mazer Funds for Faculty Research supported a good portion of the archival work in New York, Washington, and elsewhere. I will let readers draw their own conclusions about how these funding sources shaped or distorted the book.

The chance to participate in a number of conference presentations and special projects offered camaraderie and criticism on sections of the book. Thanks to David Hollinger and Richard Cándida Smith for organizing a recorded oral history of Martin Malia, and of course to Malia for subjecting himself, under less than ideal circumstances, to lengthy interviews. Tim Colton, Terry Martin, and Lis Tarlow provided an office in which I could work and got me involved in the planning for the sixtieth anniversary of the Davis Center at Harvard, which provided a great opportunity to learn other perspectives on the past, present, and future of Soviet studies. Early presentations at Yale and UCLA helped me to realize the scope and direction of the project, while later ones at the Smithsonian Institution, Harvard (the Russian history workshop as well as the international history seminar), and MIT allowed me to hone my arguments. I'm especially grateful to the Russian historians at the University of Michigan, who gave me important suggestions at a crucial moment, all in the pleasant confines of Ron Suny's living room. A writing group that Meg Jacobs and I began as I started this book provided both criticism and support on various chapters; while the membership has shifted slightly, stalwarts Chris Capozzola, Dan and Helen Horowitz, Meg Jacobs, and Bruce Schulman were there from hopeful start to harried finish.

I am very grateful to those who read portions of the manuscript. A handful slogged through a substantially longer version and offered keen and cogent criticisms that improved the book immeasurably. Tom Gleason and Howard Brick offered everything from small corrections to big questions in the comments that they provided to the publisher. I owe a special debt of gratitude to my colleague Gregory Freeze; even while serving as full-time graduate dean and part-time professor, he managed to read the whole manuscript and offered numerous helpful suggestions. Thanks to Johanna Bockman, Stanley Engerman, Cynthia Hooper, Blair Ruble, and Michael Willrich for their feedback on specific chapters. The book would have been better had I been able to take account of all the suggestions I received.

I benefited from the hard work of a number of research assistants, mostly on brief assignment both in the Boston area and elsewhere; thanks to Yoni Appelbaum, Kate Donovan, Tom Jorsch, Margot Kaminski, Jeremy Kuzmarov, Winglam Kwan, Rob McGreevey, Jennifer Miller, Sara Rhodin, Vasilii Schedrin, Susan Sypko, Will Walker, and Matthew Whitman. A number of archivists were so helpful that they functioned as unpaid researchers: Alan Divack (Ford Foundation Archives), Sally Kuisel (National Archives), Tom Rosenbaum (Rockefeller Archive Center), and Jocelyn Wilk (Columbia University Archives); I'm also grateful to the crew at the Harvard University Archives, especially Kyle DeCicco-Carey, Tim Driscoll, Michelle Gachette, Robin McElheny, and Barbara Meloni.

I am very pleased to be one of Sydelle Kramer's authors; her feedback and advice helped to shape the book, after which she guided me smoothly through to signing a contract. Luckily for me, the contract meant working with Oxford University Press—or, more specifically, with Susan Ferber, a phenomenon and a force to be reckoned with. Susan offered important advice on a few early chapters and then page-by-page commentary on the full manuscript. Along the way, she answered dozens of queries large and small, shepherding the book through Oxford and its author through writing it with equal skill and aplomb. She is so quick to reply to e-mails that her out-of-office message (apologizing for a delay in responding) comes at the same time as her actual reply—a fact made all the scarier by the sheer number of authors whom she treats similarly. Susan is a treasure for our profession.

Along the way, a number of people have helped in ways that don't easily fit into a single description. Tom Gleason encouraged me in the project even before I began it, offering his usual combination of support, criticism, and good humor. Blair Ruble, from his perch at the Kennan Institute, has provided moral as well as financial support over my career. Susan Solomon reached out—and spoke out—whenever we were at conferences together to help me write a better book. Brandeis colleagues Caren Irr, Jane Kamensky, Rick Parmentier, and Michael Willrich have proven stalwarts in smooth as well as rough waters.

Ethan Pollock has been a good critic, a great supporter, and an even better friend through the ups and downs of this project. From frequent pep talks to a marathon reading of the penultimate draft, Ethan has improved the book in countless ways but, more important, has been a constant source of friendship and advice for what I might call "our" third book.

Last and most important, my family. My parents, Stan and Judy Engerman, have supported not just my career but much more. It's a special treat that they now get to spend so much time near us as well as my brothers, Mark and Jeff, and their families. My wife, Stephanie Wratten, has helped the book in many ways, but she has helped me in so many more. Having read (and joked about) my share of acknowledgments, I am all too aware of the difficulty of expressing gratitude for the unusual combination of love and logistics that sustains authors like me. I hope that this awkward description serves as some small portion of my thanks and my love. Thanking our children will be easier. Nina, who marvels at the fact that I've been working on this project since before she was born, will be thrilled to see her name in print—even if she thinks the book is boring. Simon, judging by his current behavior, will simply judge the book by its cover—more specifically, by the taste of the cover as he takes a bite. They have done little to make the book better, but everything to bring new kinds of joy into our lives. I dedicate this book to them.

LIST OF ILLUSTRATION CREDITS

1.1 Geroid Robinson receiving Medal of Freedom, 1947 (With permission of the University Archives, Columbia University in the City of New York)

1.2 Geroid Robinson lecturing at the Russian Institute, 1947 (Rockefeller Archive Center)

1.3 Philip Mosely and Fred Stolling, 1953 (With permission of the University Archives, Columbia University in the City of New York)

2.1 Alex Inkeles lecturing at Harvard, early 1950s (Harvard Yearbook Publications)

2.2 Air Force employee Herman Sanders with Refugee Interview Project papers, 1955 (Jay Leviton-Atlanta)

4.1 Herblock cartoon, 1964 (The Herb Block Foundation)

8.1 Zbigniew Brzezinski in his Columbia office, 1965 (With permission of the University Archives, Columbia University in the City of New York)

8.2 Graphic depiction of responses to Brzezinski article, 1969 (With permission of Zbigniew Brzezinski)

10.1 Richard Pipes with students Nina Tumarkin and Daniel Orlovsky, 1971 (Schlesinger Library, Radcliffe Institute, Harvard University)

11.1 Sheila Fitzpatrick in her Columbia University office, mid-1970s (With permission of Sheila Fitzpatrick)

12.1 Adam Ulam and Marshall Goldman with Soviet diplomat Genadii Gerasimov, 1986 (Harvard University Archives, UAV 605.295.8, box 3)

INDEX

Friedrich, Paul, 54
"Friends and Foes of Change" (Cohen),
	291
Fulbright, J. William, 185
The Future of Russia (Schapiro), 165

Galbraith, John Kenneth, 46
Gardner, John, 36, 45, 46, 55
Gates, Robert, 337, 338
Geiger, Kent, 65
Geneva Conference (1955), 86
Georgetown University, Center for
	Strategic and International Studies,
	314
Gerasimov, Genadii, 314*f*
German Rule in Russia (Dallin), 66
German documents. *See* War
	Documentation Project
Gerschenkron, Alexander, 29, 70, 93, 126,
	159–60, 288
	graduate training of, 109
	influence of, 109, 160
	reputation of, 159
	on Soviet economy, 105–6, 108–9
"Gerschenkron effect," 108–9, 125
Getty, J. Arch, 305–7
glasnost', 318–19, 325
	Besançon and Thom on, 319
	Conquest on, 319
	Pipes on, 321
Goldman, Guido, 250–51
Goldman, Marshall, 238, 263, 310,
	313–14, 314*f*
	Besançon on, 314
	on Gorbachev, 318, 323
	Grossman on, 314
	The National Review on, 314
Goldwater, Barry, 311
Gorbachev, Mikhail, 6, 128, 305, 315
	anti-alcohol campaign of, 325
	arms control concessions of, 321–22
	Bialer on, 316–17, 319–20
	Brown, A., on, 316
	Brzezinski on, 321–22
	Cohen on, 316
	Conquest on, 319
	coup attempt against, 326

denouncing Stalinism, 318–19
	Goldman, Marshall, on, 318, 323
	Hough on, 317–19
	Kenez on, 317
	Lewin on, 320
	Malia on, 324
	"new thinking" on international
		relations by, 318
	Odom on, 319
	Pipes on, 320–21
	reforms of, 312, 321, 322, 325
	Ulam on, 319
Gorer, Geoffrey, 47, 60
Gorky, Maxim, 137, 292
Gouldner, Alvin, 203–4
Graham, Daniel, 280
Graham, Loren, 241, 244, 296
Graves, Mortimer, 20
The Great Terror (Conquest), 271, 274
"Green Books." *See* Joint Economic
	Committee
Gromyko, Andrei, 318
Grossman, Gregory, 78, 109, 110, 125
	on Goldman, M., 314
	on Lewin, 294
	on Soviet economy, 113
"The Growing Prosperity of the Soviet
	Union" (Soviet pamphlet), 106–7
Gruliow, Leo, 38
Gumilev, Nikolai, 139
Gustafson, Thane, 317
Gutman, Herbert, 177

Haimson, Leopold, 78, 162, 168–71
	criticism of, 170
	dual polarization thesis of, 307–8
	on Fitzpatrick, S., 300
	influence of, 170
	on Menshevism, 169
	on revisionism, 307–8
	on social stability, 169
Harper, Samuel, 13
Harris, Chauncy, 85
Harvard Crimson, 64
Harvard Refugee Interview Project
	(RIP), 51, 64*f*, 56–69, 181, 338–39
	as "big science," 64

Hughes, H. Stuart, 4
Hughes, Robert, 138
Humanities Fund, 155, 161
Humphrey, Hubert, 185
Hungary, 270
Huntington, Samuel, 222

IEA. *See* International Education Act
"In Defense of Sovietology" (Breslauer), 330–31
Indiana University, 51, 78, 81–82
industrial society, 5–6
  Marcuse on, 194
  Moore on, 194
  Parsons on, 196–97
Inkeles, Alex, 16, 28, 48, 56f, 50, 56–57, 93, 180, 182–87
  Bell on, 186, 229
  Bendix on, 186–87, 229
  receiving tenure, 55, 187
  on Soviet life, 66
  on Stalin's death, 183–84
  on totalitarianism, 208, 222
the Inquiry, 2
In Stalin's Time (Dunham), 131
Institute for the Study of the History and Culture of the USSR, 54
Institute of Pacific Relations (IPR), 2, 22
  summer language instruction, 15
Intelligentsia, Russian and Soviet
  Cohen on, 326
  Fitzpatrick, S., on, 304
  Hough on, 326
  Pipes on, 266–67
International Congress of Slavists, 151
International Education Act (IEA), 237
International Journal of Slavic Linguistics and Poetics, 142
International Research and Exchange Board (IREX), 179, 246–48, 305, 333
Inter-University Committee on Travel Grants (IUCTG), 139, 171, 213, 215, 239
  academic disciplines of grantees of, 91, 127, 247
  complaints against, 240–46, 308

Committee on Procedures and Criteria, 245
  and Ford Foundation, 87, 91
  founding and early years, 87–91
  historians receiving grants from, 167, 170–72, 175, 178, 179
  policing of student behavior, 240–43
  recalls and expulsions from, 242–45
  senior scholar program, 90
  and Soviet Ministry of Higher Education, 88
  and State Department, 90–91, 243–44, 248
IPR. *See* Institute of Pacific Relations
Inter-University Project on the History of the Menshevik Movement, 169
IREX. *See* International Research and Exchange Board
Islamic fundamentalism, 338
"Is There a Strategic Arms Race?" (Wohlstetter), 278
IUCTG. *See* Inter-University Committee on Travel Grants
Izvestiia, 38

Jackson, Henry "Scoop," 272–75, 290, 310
  hostilities with Kissinger, 278
Jakobson, Roman, 32, 129, 142–46
Jameson, Frederic, 151–52
Japanese in United States, internment of, 17
Jasny, Naum
  attacking Bergson, 112, 124
  Kaplan's criticism of, 124
  on Soviet economy, 105, 113, 121–22, 122t, 125
JCSS. *See* Joint Committee on Slavic Studies
Jelavich, Charles, 23, 73, 81
job market 1970s, 259
Joint Committee on Slavic Studies (JCSS), 38, 132, 147, 239–40, 261
  and American Association for the Advancement of Slavic Studies, 77–79
  and *American Slavic and East European Review*, 38

NBER. *See* National Bureau of
Economic Research
NCSEER. *See* National Council for
Soviet and East European Research
NDEA. *See* National Defense Education
Act
NEH. *See* National Endowment for the
Humanities
Nevskii cotton mill strike, 173
New Criticism, 130, 146, 157
The New Masses, 21
"New Perspectives on Stalinism"
(Fitzpatrick, S.), 305–7
Newsweek, 262
New York Public Library, 157
New York Times, 98, 262
Nicholas II (Tsar), 156
Nicolaevsky, Boris, 52, 174, 288, 302
Niebuhr, Reinhold, 190
NIEs. *See* National Intelligence
Estimates
Nimitz, Nancy, 109
Nitze, Paul, 272, 277, 280
Nixon, Richard, 263, 290
détente policy of, 6, 261, 263–64
promoting ABM program, 277
Not by Bread Alone (Dudintsev), 138
Notes from the Underground (Dostoevsky),
149
Nove, Alec, 112
Novyi mir, 295
Novyi zhurnal, 155
Noyes, George, 22
NSC 86/1 (1951), 49
NSC 162/2 (1953), 116–17
NSC 5607 (1956), 86
NSMGA. *See* Naval School of Military
Government and Administration
Nutter, G. Warren, 118
on Soviet economy, 120–24, 122*t*

Obama, Barack, 337
Odom, William, 253
on Gorbachev, 319
on Russian Studies, 328
Office of Research and Reports (ORR). *See
under* Central Intelligence Agency

Office of Strategic Services (OSS), 3, 26,
76
achievements of, 29
measuring Soviet economy, 97, 99–100
model of cooperative research, 41
Office of the Secretary of Defense
(OSD). *See* Department of Defense
Office of War Information, 3, 44
Oksman, Iu G., 140–41
OLS. *See* Oriental Languages School
(U.S. Navy)
"On a Generation That Squandered Its
Poets" (Jakobson), 145
One-Dimensional Man (Marcuse), 194
One World Emerging (Inkeles), 187
Operation Solarium, 4, 115–16
Operation Sponge, 220
Oppenheimer, J. Robert, 41
Oriental Languages School (OLS, U.S.
Navy), 16–17, 23, 59
The Origin of the Communist Autocracy
(Schapiro), 165–66
The Origins of the Great Purges (Getty),
305
The Origins of Totalitarianism (Arendt),
207
Orlovsky, Daniel, 178, 265*f*
ORR. *See under* Central Intelligence
Agency
Osborn, Frederick, 45
OSD. *See* Department of Defense
Osipov, G. V., 199
OSS. *See* Office of Strategic Services
Ostarbeiteren, 53

Pankratova, A. M., 32
"Paper Perestroika" (Pipes), 321
Pares, Bernard, 20–21
Pareto, Vilfredo, 102
Parsons, Helen, 47
Parsons, Talcott, 44–46, 53, 55, 180–81, 204
on Communism, 198
criticisms of, 203
cultural exchange and, 199–200, 202
on evolution of modern societies,
200–201
general theory of action, 45